TIPPOO SULTAUN

A TALE OF THE MYSORE WAR

TIPPOO SULTAUN.

P. 397.

TIPPOO SULTAUN
A TALE OF THE MYSORE WAR

MEADOWS TAYLOR

GYAN

Published by

Gyan Publishing House
5, Ansari Road
Daryaganj, New Delhi-110002
Phone: 011-47034999, 9811692060
E-mail: books@gyanbooks.com

Distribution Network
gyanbooks.com
India, USA, Canada, UK, Australia, France

ISBN : 978-81-212-4117-5 (PB)
First Published, 1880

2nd Impression 2020

Printed at: Gyan Press, Delhi.

Tippoo Sultaun
Author: Meadows Taylor

TIPPOO SULTAUN;

A TALE OF THE MYSORE WAR.

BY THE LATE

COLONEL MEADOWS TAYLOR.

SECOND EDITION.

LONDON:

C. KEGAN PAUL & CO., 1 PATERNOSTER SQUARE.

1880.

TO

WILLIAM NEWNHAM, ESQ.,

MY BEST AND EARLIEST FRIEND IN INDIA,

THIS VOLUME

IS WITH GRATEFUL ESTEEM

DEDICATED.

TIPPOO SULTAUN.

CHAPTER I.

TOWARDS the close of a day of intense heat, about the middle of the month of June, 1788, a party consisting of many persons might be seen straggling over the plain which extends southwards from the Fort of Adoni, and which almost entirely consists of the black alluvial deposit familiarly known in India under the name of 'cotton soil.'

The leader was a man perhaps about fifty years of age; he rode a powerful Dekhan horse of great spirit, but whose usual fiery comportment was tamed by the severe exertion he had undergone, from the miry roads through which he had travelled the greater part of the day. Indeed he began to show evident symptoms of weariness, and extricated himself from every succeeding muddy hollow—and they were very frequent—with less power. His handsome housings too were soiled with dirt; and the figure of his rider, which merits some description, was splashed from head to foot.

It has been already stated that he was a man of advanced age. His face, which was wrapped up, as well as his head, in thick folds of muslin, in order to protect them from the scorching heat of the sun, showed a dark complexion much pitted with the smallpox; but his eyes were very large, and of that intense black which is but rarely seen even among the natives of India, and which appeared to flash with a sudden light when any stumble of his gallant horse provoked an impatient jerk of the bridle, and a volley of curses upon the mud and the road, if such it could be called. His dress was of cloth-of-gold,—a suit which had been once magnificent, but which, soiled and tarnished as it was, he had chosen perhaps to wear as a mark of his rank, and thus to ensure respect from the people of the country, which might have been denied to money alone. It was open at the breast, and under the shirt of muslin worn within the alkhaluk, or upper garment, a broad rough chest could be seen,—a fair earnest of the power of him we describe.

A handsome shawl was girded around his waist, and his somewhat loose trousers were thrust into a pair of yellow leather boots, which appeared to be of Persian workmanship. Over his shoulder was a gold belt which supported a sword; but this in reality was confined to the waist by the shawl we have mentioned, and appeared more for ornament than use. A bright steel axe with a steel handle hung at his saddle-bow on the right hand; and the butt-end of a pistol, much enriched with chased silver, peeped forth on the left, among the fringe of the velvet covering of the soft saddle upon which he rode. A richly ornamented shield was bound to his back by a soft leather strap passing over his chest; and the shield itself, which hung low, rested between his back and the cantle of the saddle, and partly served as a support.

In truth, soiled and bespattered as he was, Abdool Rhyman Khan was a striking figure in those broad plains, and in his own person appeared a sufficient protection to those who followed him. But he was not the only armed person of the party. Six or seven horsemen immediately followed him,—his own retainers; not mounted so well nor dressed so expensively as the Khan himself, but still men of gallant bearing; and the party, could they have kept together, would have presented a very martial and imposing appearance.

At some distance behind the horsemen was a palankeen, apparently heavily laden; for the bearers, though there were as many as sixteen, changed very frequently, and could but ill struggle through the muddy road into which at every step they sunk deeply; nor did the cheering exclamations of those who were not under the poles of the palankeen appear to have much effect in quickening the pace of those who carried it; and it was very evident that they were nearly exhausted, and not fit to travel much further.

In the rear of all was a string of five camels, which required the constant attention of the drivers to prevent their slipping and falling under their burdens; and with these were a number of persons, some on foot carrying loads, and a few mounted on ponies, who were the servants of the Khan, and were urging on the beasts, and those laden with the cooking utensils, as rapidly as it was possible to proceed in the now fast-closing darkness.

Behind all were two led horses of much beauty, whose attendant grooms conducted them through the firmest parts of the road.

'Alla! Alla!' cried one of those mounted on a stout pony,—he was in fact the cook of the Khan,—'that I, Zoolficar, should ever have been seduced to leave the noble city of Hyderabad, and to travel this unsainted road at such a time of year! Ai Moula Ali,' he continued, invoking his patron saint, 'deliver us speedily from this darkness! grant that no rain may fall upon this already impassable road! I should never survive a night in this jungle. What say you, Daood Khan—are we ever to reach the munzil?* are we ever to be released from this jehanum, where we are enduring torment before our time? Speak, O respectable man! thou saidst thou knew'st the country.'

'So I do, O coward! What is the use of filling our ears with these fretful complaints? Hath not the munificence of the Khan provided thee with a stout beast, which, with the blessing of the Prophet, will carry thee quickly to thy journey's end? Was it not the Khan's pleasure to pass Adoni, where we might have rested comfortably for the night? and are we who eat his salt to grumble at what he does, when we saw that the Khanum† Sahib (may her name be honoured!) was willing to travel on? Peace, then! for it is hard to attend to thy prating and pick one's way among these cursed thorns.'

'Well, I am silent,' replied the other; 'but my mind misgives me that we never reach the munzil, and shall be obliged to put up in one of these wretched villages, where the kafir inhabitants never kill meat; and we shall have to eat dry bread or perhaps dry rice, which is worse, after this fatigue.'

'Ah, thou art no soldier, Zoolfoo,' cried another fellow who was walking beside him, 'or thou wouldst not talk thus. How wouldst thou like to have nothing for two days, and then perhaps a stale crust or a handful of cold rice, and be glad to thank the Provider of good for that,—how wouldst thou?'

'No more, I pray thee, good Nasur!' cried the cook, visions of starvation apparently overpowering him,—'no more, I beseech thee! Methinks thy words have already had a bad effect on the lower part of my stomach, and that it begins to reproach me for a lack of its usual sustenance. I tell thee, man, I can put to myself no idea of starvation at all. I was never able to keep the Rumzan (for which I pray to be pardoned), and am obliged to pay heavily every year for some one to keep it for me,—may grace abound to him! I pray Alla and the Prophet, that the Khan may strike off somewhere in search of a roof for the night.'

* Stage. † Feminine of Khan; as Begum, feminine of Beg.

The Khan had stopped: the increasing darkness, or rather gloom,—for there was still somewhat of daylight remaining, and the sun had not long set,—the muttering of thunder, and the more and more vivid flashes of lightning proceeding from an intensely black and heavy cloud which occupied the whole of the horizon before him, were enough to cause anxiety as to his proceeding further or not.

A hard or tolerably firm road would have relieved this, but the track upon which they journeyed became almost worse as he proceeded; and the man he had sent on some little distance in advance, to observe the best passage for the horses, appeared to be guiding his with increased difficulty.

'I was an ass, and the son of an ass, to leave Adoni,' muttered the Khan; 'but it is of no use to regret this now:—what had better be done is the question. My poor Motee,' he continued, addressing his horse, 'thou too art worn out, and none of thy old fire left in thee. How, my son, wouldst thou carry me yet further?' and he patted his neck.

The noble beast appeared to understand him, for he replied to the caress by a low whinny, which he followed up by a loud neigh, and looked, as he neighed, far and wide over the plain.

'Ay, thou see'st nothing, Motee; true it is, there is no village in sight: yet surely one cannot be far off, where if they will admit us, we may get food and shelter. What thinkest thou, Ibrahim,' he continued, addressing one of his retainers, 'are we near any habitation?'

'Peer O Moorshid,' replied the man, 'I know not; I never travelled this road before, except once many years ago, and then I was with the army; we did not think much of the road then.'

'True, friend,' answered the Khan, 'but now we have need to think. By the soul of Mohamed, the cloud beyond us threatens much, and I fear for the Khanum; she is ill used to such travelling as this; but she is a soldier's wife now, and I must teach her to bear rough work.'

'The Palkee will be with us presently, and I doubt not the bearers well know the country, Khodawund,' said another of the horsemen.

'True, I had not thought of them; perhaps when it arrives, it would be advisable to stop a little to take breath, and then again set forward.'

A few moments brought the bearers and their burden to where the Khan stood; and a few hurried questions were put to them by him as to the distance to the next village, the road, and the accommodation they were likely to find for so large a party.

'Huzrut!' said the Naik of the bearers, 'you have but little choice; we did not think the road would have been so bad as this, or we would never have left the town or allowed you to proceed; but here we are, and we must help to extricate you from the difficulty into which we have brought you. To return is impossible; there is no village at which you could rest, as you know. Before us are two; one not far off, over yonder rising ground—my lord can even see the trees,—and another beyond that, about a coss and a half; to which, if the lady can bear the journey, we will take her, as there is a good bazaar and every accommodation. My lord will reward us with a sheep if we carry her safely?'

'Surely, surely,' said the Khan, 'ye shall have two; and we will travel a short stage to-morrow, as ye must be tired. So what say you, my soul?' he cried to the inmate of the palankeen; 'you have the choice of a comfortable supper and a dry lodging, or no supper and perhaps no roof over your head; you see what it is to follow the fortunes of a soldier.'

'Let no thought of me trouble you,' replied a low and sweet voice from the palankeen; 'let the bearers and yourself decide, I am content anywhere.'

'How say you then, Gopal?'

'Let us smoke a pipe all round, and we will carry you to the large village,' replied the Naik.

''Tis well,—do not be long about it; I doubt not we shall be all the better for a short rest.'

Fire was quickly kindled; every one dismounted from his beast, and all collected into groups. Tobacco was soon found, the hookas lighted, and the gurgling sound of half-a-dozen of them arose among the party.

A smoke of tobacco in this manner gives almost new life to a native of India. The trouble of the journey or the work is for awhile forgotten; and after a fresh girding up of the loins and invocation of the Prophet or their patron goddess (as the parties may be Hindoo or Mohamedan), the undertaking is resumed with fresh spirit. After a short pause, the whole party was again in motion.

No one had, however, observed the extremely threatening appearance of the sky. The cloud, which had been still, now began to rise gently;—a few small clouds were seen as it were to break away from the mass and scurry along the face of the heavens, apparently close to their heads, and far below the larger ones which hung heavily above them. These were followed very quickly by others: the lightning increased in vividness at every flash; and what was at first confined to the cloud which has been mentioned, now spread itself gradually all over the heavens! behind—above—around—became one blaze of light, as it were at a signal given by a rocket thrown up from behind the cloud before them. In spite of appearances, however, they hurried on.

'It will be a wild night,' observed the Khan, replacing and binding tighter the muslin about his head and face.

As he spoke he pointed to the horizon, where was seen a dull reddish cloud. To an unpractised eye it looked like one of the dusky evening clouds; but on closer and more attentive observation, it was clearly seen to rise, and at the same time to be extending right and left very rapidly.

'I beg to represent,' said Daood Khan, who had come from behind, 'that there is a group of trees yonder not far from the road, and, if my memory serves me well, there should be an old hut in it; will my lord go thither?'

'It is well spoken, Daood,' said his master, 'lead on.'

There was no wind—not a breath—but all was quite still; not even a cricket or grasshopper chirped among the grass: it seemed as though nature could scarcely breathe, so intense was the closeness.

'Alla! Alla! I shall choke if there is no wind,' said the fat cook, fanning himself with the end of a handkerchief.

'You will have enough presently,' said Nasur.

'Inshalla!' exclaimed one of the camel drivers, 'the Toofans* of the Carnatic are celebrated.'

'Alas!' sighed the cook, and wished himself anywhere but in the Carnatic.

At last a low moaning was heard,—a distant sound, as if of rushing water. The rack above them redoubled its pace, and went fearfully fast: every instant increased the blackness on each side and behind. They could no longer see any separate clouds above, but one dense brown black ropy mass, hurrying onward, impelled by the mighty wind. Soon nothing was visible but a bright line all round the horizon, except in front, where the wall of red dust, which proved that the previous rains had not extended far beyond where they were, every moment grew higher and higher, and came nearer and nearer.

They increased their speed to gain the trees, which were discernible a quarter of a mile before them. 'Once there,' said the Khan, 'we can make some shelter for ourselves with the walls of the tents passed round the trees.'

* Storms.

No one replied to him; each was thinking of the storm, and what would happen when it came. The horses even felt the oppression, and snorted violently at intervals, as though they wished to throw it off.

At last, a few leaves flew up in the air: and some lapwings, which had been nestling under the stones by the wayside, rose and made a long flight to leeward with loud screamings, as though to avoid the wind.

One little whirlwind succeeded to another; small quantities of leaves and dry grass were everywhere seen flying along near the ground over the plain. The body of dust approached nearer, and seemed to swallow up everything in it. They anxiously watched its progress, in the hope that it would lessen in fury ere it approached them, for they could see the trees through the gloom against the bright line of the horizon, apparently at a great distance, disappearing one by one.

Meanwhile the roaring increased; the roar of the wind and that of the thunder were fearfully mingled together. Amidst this there arose a shrill scream from the palankeen; the fair inmate had no longer been able to bear the evident approach of the tempest.

The Khan was at her side in a moment. 'Cheer thee, my rose!' he cried; 'a little further and we shall reach a friendly grove of trees. The road is harder now, so exert yourselves,' he continued to the bearers; 'five rupees, if you reach the trees ere the wind is upon us!'

The men redoubled their pace, but in vain; they still wanted half the quarter of the mile when the storm burst. With one fearful flash of lightning, so as almost to blind them, and to cause the whole to stagger backward, a blast met them, which if they had withstood they had been more than men. The palankeen rocked to and fro, tottered under their failing support, and fell at last heavily to the ground. There was no mischief done, but it was impossible to proceed further; they must abide the storm where they stood in the open plain.

And now it came in pitiless earnest. As if the whole power of the winds of heaven had been collected and poured forth bodily upon one spot, and that where they stood,—so did it appear to them; while the dust, increasing in volume every instant, was so choking, that no one dared to open his mouth to speak a word. The horses and camels instinctively turned their backs to the wind, and stood motionless; and the men at last, forcing the camels to sit down, crouched behind them to obtain some kind of shelter from the raging storm.

Thus they remained for some time; at last a drop of rain fell —another, and another. They could not see it coming amidst the dust, and it was upon them ere they were aware of it: they were drenched in an instant. Now, indeed, began a strife of elements. The thunder roared without ceasing one moment: there was no thunder for any particular flash—it was a continued flare, a continued roar. The wind, the rain, and the thunder made a fearful din, and even the stout heart of the Khan sunk within him. 'It cannot last,' he said;—but it did. The country appeared at last like a lake shown irregularly by the blue flare of the lightning.

Two hours, or nearly so, did they endure all this: the tempest moderated at length, and they proceeded. It was now quite dark.

'Where is Ibrahim?' asked one suddenly.

'Ay, where is he?' said another. Several shouted his name; but there was no reply.

'Ibrahim!' cried the Khan, 'what of him? He must be gone to the trees; go, one of ye, and call him if he be there.'

The man diverged from the road, and was soon lost in the darkness; but in a short time an exclamation of surprise or of terror, they could not say which, came clearly towards them. The Khan stopped. In another instant the man had rejoined them.

'Alla! Alla!' cried he, gasping for breath, 'come and see!'

'See what?' shouted the Khan.

'Ibrahim!' was his only reply, and they followed him rapidly.

They could hardly distinguish what it was that the man pointed out; but what appeared like a heap at first in the darkness, soon resolved itself into the form of a man and horse. The Khan dismounted and approached; he called to him by name, but there was no answer. He felt the body—it was quite dead; horse and man had fallen beneath the stroke of the lightning.

'We can do nothing now,' said the Khan. 'Alas! that so good a man, and one who has so often fought beside me, should have thus fallen! Praise be to Alla, what an escape we have had!'

'It was his destiny,' said another,—'who could have averted it?'

And they rode on, but slowly, for the road was undistinguishable from the ground on each side, except where a hedge of thorns had been placed to fence in some field. Here those who were on foot fared very badly, for the thorns which had fallen, or had been broken off from branches, had mixed with the mud, and sorely hurt their naked feet. The rain continued to pour in torrents; and the incessant flare of the lightning, which revealed the track every now and then, seemed to sweep the ground before them, nearly blinding both horse and man: it showed at times for an instant the struggles both were making in the now deeper mire.

They reached the smaller village at last; there were only three or four miserable houses, and in the state they were, there was but little inducement to remain in want of food and shelter till the morning; so taking with them, much against his inclination, one of the villagers as a guide whom they could understand, as he was a Mohamedan, and some rags soaked with oil tied on the end of a stick to serve as a torch, they once more set forward.

They had now scarcely three miles to travel, but these seemed interminable. The rude torch could not withstand the deluge of rain which poured upon it, and after a struggle for life it went out. There remained only the light of the lightning. The guide, however, was of use; now threatened, now encouraged by the Khan, he showed where the firmest footing was to be obtained, and piloted the little cavalcade through the almost sea of mud and water, in a manner which showed them that they would have fared but ill without his aid.

At last, O welcome sight! a light was seen to glimmer for awhile amidst the gloom; it disappeared, twinkled again, appeared to flit at a little distance, and was seen no more.

'What was that, Rahdarec?'* asked the Khan; 'one would think it was some wild spirit's lamp abroad on this unblessed night.'

'It is the village, noble sir,' said the man simply; 'we have no evil spirits here.'

'Ul-humd-ul-illa! we are near our home then; it cannot be far now.'

'Not a cannon-shot; we have a small river to cross, and then we reach the village.'

'A river!'

'Yes, noble Khan, a small one; there is no water to signify.'

But the Khan's mind misgave him. 'It must be full,' he said to himself, 'after this rain; how can it be otherwise? Every hollow we have passed has become a roaring stream; but we shall see. Ya, Moula Ali!' he exclaimed aloud, 'I vow a gift to all the priests of thy shrine, if thou wilt protect me and mine through this night.'

* Guide.

They had not gone much further before the dull sound of the river was heard but too plainly, even above the wind and the thunder, which now roared only at intervals. One and all were fairly terrified; and that there should be such an end to their really manful struggles through the tempest disheartened them: but no one spoke till they arrived at the brink, where through the gloom could be seen a muddy torrent rushing along with fearful rapidity.

'It is not deep,' said the guide; 'it is fordable.'

'Dog of a kafir!' cried the Khan, 'thou hast deceived us, to get us away from thy miserable village. By Alla! thou deservest to be put to death for this inhospitality.'

'My life is in your hands, O Khan!' returned the man; 'behold, to prove my words, I will venture in if any one will accompany me; alone it is useless to attempt it. Will no one go with me?'

But one and all hesitated; the gloom, the uncertainty, and the dread of death alike prevailed.

'Cowards!' exclaimed the Khan, 'dare ye not do for him whose salt you eat that which this poor fellow is ready to undertake because I only reproached him with inhospitality? Cowards and faithless! ye are worse than women.'

'I am no woman or coward,' said Daood Khan doggedly. 'Come,' he added to the guide, 'as thou art ready to go, give me thy hand and step in, in the name of the Most Merciful!'

'Bismilla! Daood, thou hast a stout heart—I will remember thee for this. Step on in the name of Alla and the twelve Imaums! Halloo when thou art on the other side.'

They entered the water carefully, holding tightly each other's hand, and each planting his foot firmly ere he ventured to withdraw the other. The torrent was frightfully rapid, and it required all the power of two very strong men to bear up against it; but at length the shallow water was gained, and a joyful shout from the other side told to the Khan and his expectant party that the passage had been made in safety.

'Now make haste and get a torch, and bring some people with you,' shouted the Khan; 'meanwhile we will make preparations for crossing.'

Not much time elapsed before a few persons were seen approaching the river's bank from the village, bearing several torches, which in despite of the wind and the rain, being all fed with oil, blazed brightly, and cast their light far and wide.

The Khan had been endeavouring to persuade his wife to trust herself to his horse, instead of to the palankeen, in crossing the river; and after some representation of its superior safety, he had succeeded. She was standing by him, closely veiled, when the torches appeared on the other side.

What she saw, however, of the stream, as revealed fully by the light, caused an instant change in her resolution: she was terrified by the waters; and indeed they were very awful to look on, as the muddy, boiling mass hurried past, appearing, as was the case, to increase in volume every moment.

'There is no time to lose,' shouted the villagers, observing there was irresolution among the party; 'the water is rising fast—it will soon be impassable.'

'The horse, the horse, my soul!' cried the Khan in despair; 'the bearers will never carry you through that torrent.'

'I dare not, I should faint in the midst; even now my heart is sick within me, and my eyes fail me as I look on the waters,' replied the lady.

'Khodawund!' said the Naik of the bearers, 'trust her to us; on our lives, she reaches the other side safely.'

'Be it so then, Gopal; I trust thee and thy party; only land her safely, and thou shalt be well rewarded.'

The lady again entered the palankeen; both doors were opened in case of danger. The stoutest of the bearers were selected, and the Naik put himself at the head. 'Jey, Bhowanee!' cried one and all, and they entered the raging waters.

'Shabash! Shabash! Wah-wah! Wah-wah!' resounded from the villagers, and from the Khan's attendants, as the gallant fellows bore up stoutly against the torrent. Oil was poured upon the torches, and the river blazed under the light. The Khan was close behind on his gallant horse, which, snorting and uneasy, was very difficult to guide. There was not a heart on either bank that did not beat with almost fearful anxiety, for the water appeared to reach the palankeen, and it required the exertions of all the men to keep it and those who carried it steady.

'Kuburdar! kuburdar!* a little to the right!—now to the left!—well done! well done!' were the cries which animated and cheered them; and the passage was accomplished all but a few yards, when the water suddenly deepened—the leading bearers sank almost up to their chests. Trials were made on either side, but the water was deeper than where they stood; the eddy had scooped out the hollow since Daood had crossed.

'Have a care, my sons!' cried the Naik, whose clear voice was heard far above the din. 'Raise the palankeen on your shoulders. Gently! first you in front—now those behind!

* Take care! take care!

Shabash! now let every man look to his footing, and Jey Kalee!'

They advanced as they shouted the invocation; but careful as they were, who could see beneath those muddy waters? There was a stone—a large one—on which the leading bearer placed his foot. It was steady when he first tried it; but as he withdrew the other, it rolled over beneath his weight and what he bore: he tottered, stumbled, made a desperate effort to recover himself, but in vain: he fell headlong into the current.

The palankeen could not be supported, and but one wild piercing shriek was heard from the wife of the Khan as it plunged into the water.

'Ya, Alla! Alla!' cried the Khan in his agony—for he had seen all—'she is lost to me for ever!' And throwing himself from his horse, encumbered as he was, he would have been drowned, but for one of the bearers, who supported him to the brink, and, assisted by the rest who immediately recovered the palankeen, bore him rapidly to the village.

CHAPTER II.

THE confusion which ensued is indescribable. The few persons on the bank of the river rushed hither and thither without any definite object; and screams from some women, who had followed the men from the village out of curiosity, rent the air, and added to the wildness of the scene.

On a sudden an exclamation broke from a youth who stood not far off; and before they could turn to see what had occasioned it, he had darted from the spot, and precipitated himself into the waters.

Cries of 'He will be lost! he will be lost!' flew from mouth to mouth; and a dozen turbans were unwound and thrown to him from the brink, as he still struggled with the current, supporting the slight and inanimate form of her who was supposed to have been swept down the stream at first.

Without waiting for a moment to answer the numberless queries which were showered upon him by the spectators, or to ascertain whether the senseless form he bore had life in it or not, he hastily covered the features from view; and, declining the assistance of some old crones who thronged around him, he pressed through them and hurried with the utmost rapidity to his home.

Those who partly carried and partly supported the Khan himself conducted him to the chowrie or public apartment for travellers; and seating him upon such carpets and pillows as could most readily be found, they proceeded to divest him of his wet garments, arms, and boots, with an officious zeal, which, in spite of the protestations of his servant Daood, all persisted in exerting. The Khan suffered all patiently, apparently with almost unconsciousness, only at times uttering low moans and interjections, which showed his thoughts to be absorbed in the fate of her he deemed lost for ever. Gradually, however, the kind attentions of his servant, whose sobs could not be repressed as he bent over him in his attempts to remove his inner vest, which the others had hesitated to touch, recalled his wandering senses; and, staring wildly about him, he demanded to know where he was. Instantly, however, a fresh recollection of the scene which had passed flashed into his mind, and all the words he could find utterance for were an incoherent demand of Daood if the Khanum had been found.

'Alas, Peer O Moorshid!' was the reply, 'your slave saw nothing; he assisted my lord here and—'

'Was she not instantly rescued? What were all of ye doing that she ever passed from your sight?' exclaimed the Khan. 'Holy Alla! give her back to me or I shall go mad,' he continued, starting up and rushing from the spot into the air, followed by his attendant and a few of the others who lingered about.

Distractedly the Khan hurried to the river-side, and in the misery of despair began to search for the body of his wife. He ran from place to place, shouting her name; he looked everywhere for any trace of her remains, while his faithful attendant in vain besought him to withdraw from the spot, for that further search was unavailing. His words were unheeded: all the Khan saw, through the almost inky darkness, was the faint glimmer of the wild waters hurrying past him; and the only sounds he heard were their dull and sullen roar, above which arose the shouts of his servants on the other side, and at intervals a shrill neigh from one of the horses. Two or three persons only remained about the river-side, and these seemed unacquainted with what had occurred; all who had seen it had dispersed when the young man bore off the insensible girl he had rescued. After some time of fruitless search the Khan silently relinquished it, and sadly and slowly turned towards the village.

Meanwhile the young man we have mentioned carried the

lady with the utmost speed he was able to his own home, a respectable house situated on the other side of the village from where the Khan was: without ceremony he entered the zenana, still bearing her in his arms, to the astonishment of an elderly dame, his mother, and several other women, servants and others who happened to be there, and to whom the news of the disaster was being brought piecemeal, as first one and then another hurried in with parts of the story.

'Holy Prophet! what hast thou brought, Kasim Ali?' cried his mother;—'a woman! By your soul say how is this,—where didst thou get her?—wet, too!'

''Tis the Khan's wife, and she is dead!' cried many at once.

'I care not what she is,' cried the young man; 'by the blessing of Alla I saw her and brought her out of the water; she is still warm, and perhaps not dead; see what ye can do speedily to recover her. She is as beautiful as a Peri, and——but no matter, ye can do nothing while I am here, so I leave you.'

Whatever Kasim's thoughts might have been, he had sense enough not to give them utterance; and, leaving the fair creature to their care, he again hurried forth, to see whether he could render further assistance to the unfortunate travellers.

Left among the women of the house, the Khan's wife became an object of the deepest interest to these really kind people. Her wet clothes were removed; cloths were heated and applied to her body; she was rubbed and kneaded all over; the wet was wrung from her hair; and after awhile they had the satisfaction of hearing a gentle sigh escape her,—another and another at intervals.

'Holy Alla!' cried one of the women at last, 'she has opened her eyes.'

The light was apparently too much for them, for she shut them again and relapsed into stupor; but the respiration continued, and the alarm that she had died ceased to exist. Gradually, very gradually, she regained consciousness; and ere many hours had elapsed she was in a deep sleep, freed from all anxiety regarding her lord, whom on her first recovery she had presumed was lost.

The Khan and Daood had scarcely again reached the chowrie, when a large body of men with torches, shouting joyfully, approached it. Daood's heart leaped to his mouth. 'She cannot have been saved!' he cried, as he advanced to meet them.

'Ul-humd-ul-illa!' cried a dozen voices, 'she has, and is in the Patél's* house.'

Without any ceremony they broke in upon the unfortunate

* The chief or magistrate of a village.

Khan, who sat, or rather lay, absorbed in his grief. Alone, the memory of his wife had come vividly over him; and when he raised his head, on their intrusion, his wet cheek very plainly told that his manly sorrow had found vent.

'Ul-humd-ul-illa!' cried Daood, panting for breath.

'Ul-humd-ul-illa!' echoed Kasim.

'Do not mock me, I pray you,' said the Khan sadly, 'for grief is devouring my heart, and I am sad even to tears. And yet your faces have joy in them,—speak! she cannot live! that would be too much to hope. Speak, and tell truth!'

'Weep not, noble Khan,' said Kasim; 'she lives, by the blessing of Alla,—she is safe in my own mother's apartments; and such rude care as we can give her, or such accommodation as our poor house affords, she shall have.'

The Khan started to his feet. 'Thou dost not mock me then, youth? Ya Alla! I did not deserve this! Who saved her? By the soul of the Prophet, any recompense in the power of Abdool Rhyman, even to half his wealth, shall be his who rescued her!'

'He stands before thee, O Khan!' cried Daood, who had recovered his speech; 'it was that brave fellow who rushed into the water and rescued her, even while my lord was being carried hither.'

In an instant rank and power were forgotten, and the Khan, impelled by his emotion, ere Kasim could prevent him, had folded him in a sincere and grateful embrace. Nay, he would have fallen at his feet, but the young Kasim, disengaging himself, prevented it and drew back.

'Not so, protector of the poor!' he cried; 'your slave has but done what any man would do in a like case. Kasim Ali Patél would have disgraced himself had he turned from that helpless being as she lay in such peril on the bank.'

The Khan was struck with admiration of the young man, who with excited looks and proud yet tempered bearing drew himself up as he uttered the last words; and indeed the young Patél was a noble figure to look on.

He had not attempted to change his clothes since his rescue of the lady, but had thrown off his upper garment; he was therefore naked to the waist, and his body was only partially covered by the dark blanket he had cast over his shoulders. His tall and muscular frame was fully developed; and the broad chest, long and full arms, and narrow waist, showed the power which existed to be called into exertion when opportunity required. Nor was his countenance less worthy of remark. Although he had hardly attained manhood, yet the down on his upper lip and chin, which was darkening fast, proved that perhaps twenty years had passed over him, and added not a little to his manly appearance. His dark expressive eyes, which glistened proudly as the Khan regarded him, a high aquiline nose, large nostrils expanding from the excitement he had been in, exquisitely white and regular teeth, and, added to all, a fair skin—far fairer than the generality of his countrymen could boast,—showed that he was perhaps of gentle blood, which indeed his courteous manner would have inclined most observers to determine.

'Thou art a noble fellow, youth!' cried the Khan, 'and I would again meet thee as a brother; embrace me therefore, for by the soul of my father I could love thee as one. But tell me, —you saved her?—how?—and is she safe in your house?'

A few words explained all: the eddy in its force had cast the lady upon a bank below, almost immediately after her immersion, and fortunately with her head above the water. Had she not been terrified by the shock so as to lose her consciousness, she would have been able to drag herself upon the dry land, though she could not have got to shore, as part of the river flowed round the bank on which she had been cast. Thus she had continued in very imminent danger until rescued; for any wave or slight rise of the water must have carried her down the stream; and who in that darkness and confusion would ever again have seen her?

Gradually therefore the Khan was brought to comprehend the whole matter; and, as it ought, his thankfulness towards the young Kasim increased at every explanation. It is not to be supposed, however, that he was the less anxious about her who had been saved; he had been with some difficulty restrained from at once proceeding to the Patēl's house, and desisted only when Daood and his companion declared that such a proceeding would be attended with risk to the lady. She too had been assured that he was safe, they said; and in this comforting certainty, overcome by fatigue and excitement, she had fallen asleep.

'But that is no reason why my lord should not come to my poor abode,' said Kasim; 'this open room is ill-suited to so damp a night, and my lord has been wet.'

'I need but little pressing,' he replied, and rose to accompany him.

Arrived at the house, which, though only a large cabin, was yet of superior extent and comfort of appearance to the rest in the village, the Khan found that every preparation the inmates had in their power had been made for him. A carpet was spread, and upon it was laid a comfortable cotton mattress; this was covered with a clean fine sheet, and some very luxurious pillows placed against the wall invited him to repose.

Fatigue rapidly asserted its mastery over even the Khan's iron frame. He had been assured by Kasim's mother that his lady slept sweetly, and, an ample repast concluded, he attempted for a time to converse with the young Patél, but without much success.

The young man took in truth but little interest in the replies. The Khan himself was abstracted; sleep gradually overpowered him, and he sunk down upon the bedding in total unconsciousness after a short time.

After seeing him covered, so as to prevent the cold and damp coming to him, the young Patél left him to the care of Daood, and withdrew. His own bedding was in an inner room of the house, near to the apartments of the women, and his mother heard him gently pass to it, and joined him ere he had lain down.

'My blessings on thee, my brave boy!' cried the old lady, melting into tears at the mingled thoughts of what might have been her son's danger, and his gallant conduct; 'my blessing and the blessing of Allah on thee for this! thou art thy father's son indeed, and would that he were alive to have greeted thee as I do!'

'It is of no use regretting the dead now, mother: what I did I am glad of,—and yet I could not have done otherwise; though I thought of thee, mother, when I cast myself into the raging waters: thou wouldst have mourned if Allah had not rescued me and her. But tell me,' he continued, to avert the old lady's exclamations at the very thought of his death, 'tell me, by your soul,—say, who is she? she is fair as a Peri, fair as a Houri of the blessed Paradise; tell me if thou knowest whether she is his wife, or—or—'

'His daughter, thou wouldst say, my son.'

'Ay, why not?'

'I understand thy thoughts, but they must pass away from thee. She is no daughter of his. She hath but newly used the missee;* she must be his wife. Hast thou not asked the servants?'

'I have not, mother; but art thou sure of this?'

'I am.'

'Then a bright vision has faded from my eyes,' said Kasim despondingly: 'the brightest vision I have yet seen in my young life. It seemed to be the will of Allah that she should be mine;

* A powder which women apply to their teeth only after marriage.

for she had been lost to the world and to him, only that I saved her!'

'Forbid such thoughts,' said his mother quietly, for she knew the fiery yet gentle spirit of the young man, and how easily she might offend where she only intended kindness. 'She can be nothing to thee, Kasim.'

'Her fate is with mine, mother: from the moment I was impelled to rescue her from the waters, I felt that my life was connected with hers. I knew not, as she lay on the sand-bank, that she was beautiful or young; and I could not have hesitated, had there been a thousand devils in my path, or the raging waters of the Toombuddra.'

'Alas! my son,' she replied, 'these are but the fantasies of a young spirit. It was thy generous nature, believe me, which impelled thee to rescue her, not thy destiny.'

But the young man only sighed; and after awhile, finding that her words had but little power to remove the feelings which the events of the night had excited, she blessed him and retired to her repose.

Left to himself, Kasim in vain tried to court sleep to his eyelids. Do what he would, think of what he would, lie how he would,—the scene of the Khan's advance across the flood,—the waters hurrying by,—the rough eddies caused by the resistance to it made by the bearers, upon which the light of the torches rested and flashed,—their excited cries, which rung in his ears,—their every step which seemed before his eyes,—till the last, when all fell,—and then that one wild shriek! Again the despairing shout of the Khan, and the eager assistance rendered to him when he cast himself into the river,—the hurried search for the body, and the exertions of the bearers to raise the palankeen in hopes that it might be in it,—their despair when it was not,—the renewed search, for some moments unsuccessful,—then the glimpse of her lying on the bank, and his own efforts,—all were vivid, so vivid that he seemed to enact over again the part he had performed, and again to bear the lifeless yet warm and beautiful body to his home with desperate speed.

'I saw she was beautiful, O how beautiful!' he said; 'I felt how exquisite her form. I saw her youthful countenance,—hardly fifteen can she be,—and she the bride of that old man! Monstrous! But it is my destiny: who can overcome that? Prince and noble, the beggar and the proud, all have their destiny; this will be mine, and I must follow it. Ya Alla, that it may be a kind one!'

He lay long musing thus: at last there was a noise as though of talking in his mother's apartment. He heard a strange voice—it must be the lady's: he arose, crept gently to the door of the room, and listened. He was right: her pure, girl-like and silvery tones came upon his ears like music; he drank in every word with eagerness,—he hardly breathed, lest he should lose a sound.

He heard her tell her little history; how she had been sought in marriage by many, since he to whom she was betrothed in childhood had died: how her parents had refused her to many, until the Khan, whose family were neighbours, and who had returned from Mysore a man of wealth and rank, hearing of her beauty, had sought her in marriage. Then she related how grandly it had been celebrated; how much money he had spent; what processions there had been through the noble city of Hyderabad; what rich clothes and jewels he had given her; and how he was now taking her with him to his new country, where he was a soldier of rank, and served the great Tippoo. All this she described very vividly; and with the lightheartedness and vivacity of girlhood; but at the end of all she sighed.

'For all the rank and pomp, she is unhappy,' thought Kasim.

Then he heard his mother say, 'But thou sighest, Khanum, and yet hast all that ever thy most sanguine fancy could have wished for.'

'Ay, mother,' was the reply, 'I sigh sometimes. I have left my home, my mother, sisters, father, and many friends, and I go whither I know no one,—no, not one. I have new friends to make, new thoughts to entertain, new countries to see; and can you wonder that I should sigh for the past, or indeed for the future?'

'Alla bless thee!' said the old lady; and Kasim heard that she had blessed her, and had taken the evil from her by passing her hands over her head, and cracking the joints of her fingers against her own temples.

'Thou wilt be happy,' continued his mother; 'thou art light-hearted for thine own peace,—thou art very, very beautiful, and thy lord will love thee: thou wilt have (may Alla grant many to thee!) children, of beauty like unto thine own; and therefore do not sigh, but think thou hast a bright destiny, which indeed is evident. Thy lord is young and loves thee,—that I am assured of, for I have spoken with him.'

'With him, mother?'

'Ay, with him; he came a little while ago to the screen to ask after thee, and spoke tenderly: young, wealthy, and a soldier too, ah! thou art fortunate, my daughter.'

'But he is not young, mother,' she said artlessly. Kasim was sure there was regret in the tone.

'Why then, well,' said the old lady, 'thou wilt look up to him with reverence, and as every woman should do to her lord. But enough now; thou hast eaten, so now sleep again. May Alla give thee sweet rest and a fortunate waking!'

Kasim heard no more, though he listened. His mother busied herself in arranging her carpet, and then all was still. He thought for awhile, and his spirit was not easy within him: he arose, passed through the outer chamber, where the Khan still slept, and his servants around him, and opening the door very gently passed on into the open air.

CHAPTER III.

It was now midnight, and the storm had passed away. In the bright heavens, studded with stars, through which the glorious moon glided, almost obliterating them by her lustre, there existed no sign of the tempest by which it had so lately been overcast. The violent wind had completely lulled, if indeed we except the gentlest breath, which was hardly enough to stir lazily here and there the leaves of an enormous Peepul-tree that occupied an open space in front of the Patél's house, and which also appeared sleeping in the soft light; while on every wet leaf the rays of the moon rested, causing them to glisten like silver against the sky. The tree cast a still shadow beyond, partly underneath which the servants of the Khan and the bearers of the palankeen all lay confusedly,—so many inanimate forms, wrapped in their white sheets, and reposing upon such straw or other material as they had been able to collect, to protect them from the damp ground.

In the broad light, the camels of the Khan were sitting in a circle around a heap of fodder, into which every now and then they thrust their noses, selecting such morsels as they chose from the heap; while the tiny bell which hung around the neck of each tinkled gently, scarcely disturbing the stillness which reigned around. Beyond, the moonlight rested upon the white dome and minarets of the small village mosque, which appeared above the roofs of the houses; and the Hindoo temple also caught a share of her beams, revealing its curious pyramidical form at some distance, among a small grove of acacia trees. Far away in the east the cloud which had passed over still showed itself,—its top glistening brightly against the deep blue of the sky: while from it issued frequent flickerings of lightning, which played about it for an instant and disappeared; and a low and very distinct muttering of thunder succeeded, showing that the tempest was still proceeding on its threatening yet fertilising course. The cloud and the distance all seemed in one, for the light of the moon did not appear to illuminate much beyond Kasim's immediate vicinity.

He stood for a moment, and gazed around, and into the sky at the glorious orb. She looked so mild, so peaceful, riding in silence; whilst all around was so mellowed and softened by the blessed light, that, in spite of his habitual indifference to such scenes—an indifference common to all his countrymen—he could not help feeling that his heart was softened too.

The natives of India are perhaps heedless of natural beauties, but if there be any to which they are not indifferent, it is those of the glorious moonlights which are seen in the East, so unlike those of any other country. There, at almost every season, but particularly in the warmest, it is impossible for nature to supply anything more worthy of exquisite enjoyment than the moonlight nights; there is something so soft, so dreamy, in the bright but silvery light, so refreshing, from the intense glare of the sun during the day,—so inviting to quiet contemplation, or to the enjoyment of society, with whomsoever it may chance to be,—that it is no wonder if the majority of Asiatics, both Mahomedans and Hindoos, should love it beyond the day, or appreciate more keenly the beauties it reveals. There, too, moonlight in those seasons has no drawbacks, no dangers; there are no dews to harm, nor cold to chill; and if there be a time when one can enjoy warmth without oppression, light without glare, and both in moderation, it is at the time of full moon in most months of the year in India.

After regarding with some feelings of envy perhaps the sleeping groups, Kasim sauntered leisurely towards the river's bank, his limbs mechanically obeying the action of his thoughts. The stream was still swollen and muddy, but it had subsided greatly, and the bank upon which the lady had been thrown was now no longer an island. Kasim walked there. 'It was here,' he said, 'that she lay: another moment, perhaps, and she would have been swept away into eternity! I should have felt for the Khan, but I should have been more at rest in my heart than I am now.'

Kasim Ali, or Meer Kasim Ali, as he was also called, for he

was a Syud, was the only son of the Patél of ——; indeed the only child, for his sisters had died while they were very young. His father was of an old and highly respectable family of long descent, which had won renown under the Mahomedan sovereigns of Bejapoor in their wars with the infidels of the Carnatic, and had been rewarded for their services by the hereditary Patélship or chief magistracy, and possession of one or two villages, with a certain percentage upon the collections of the district in which they were situated. They had also been presented with some grants of land to a considerable extent, and the family had been of importance and wealth far superior to what it was at the period of our history. The troublous times between the end of the Bejapoor dynasty and the subsequent struggles of the Mahratta powers, the Nizam, and Hyder Ali, for the districts in which their possessions lay, had alienated many of them, and caused them to pass into other and stronger hands.

The family however was still respectable, and held a good rank among those of the surrounding country. Syud Noor-ud-deen, the father of Kasim, was much respected, and had at one time served under the banner of Nizam Ali in his wars against the Mahratta powers, and had been instrumental in guarding the south-western frontiers of his kingdom against their incursions.

But his death, which had occurred some years before the time of which we were speaking, had still more reduced the consequence of the family; and his widow and only son could not be expected to retain that influence which had resulted partly from the station and partly from the unexceptionable conduct of the old Patél.

Still there were many who looked forward to the rapid rise of the young man, and to the hope that he would in those stirring times speedily retrieve the fortunes of the house. On the one hand were the Mahrattas, restless, greedy of conquest; among whom a man who had any address, and could collect a few horsemen together, was one day an adventurer whom no one knew,—another, a leader and commander of five hundred horse. On the other was the Nizam, whose armies, ill-paid and ill-conducted, were generally worsted in all engagements; but who still struggled on against his enemies, and in whose service titles were readily to be won, sometimes, but rarely, accompanied by more substantial benefits. Again, in the south, the magnificent power of Hyder Ali had sprung out of the ancient and dilapidated kingdom of Mysore, and bid fair, under his successor Tippoo, to equal or to surpass the others.

As Kasim Ali grew to manhood, his noble appearance, his great strength, skill in all martial exercises and accomplishments, his respectable acquirements as a Persian scholar, and his known bravery,—for he had distinguished himself greatly in several encounters with the marauders and thieves of the district,—had caused a good deal of speculation among the families of the country as to whose side he would espouse of the three Powers we have mentioned.

Nor was he in any haste to quit his village: naturally of a quiet, contemplative turn of mind, fond of reading and study, he had gradually filled his imagination with romantic tales, which, while they assisted to develop his susceptible temperament, also induced a superstitious reliance upon destiny, in which he even exceeded the prevailing belief of his sect.

His mother, who read his feelings, had repeatedly besought him to allow her to negotiate for the hand of many of the daughters of families of his own rank in the neighbourhood, and even extended her inquiries to those of the many partly decayed noble families of Adoni; but no one that she could hear of, however beautiful by description or high by birth or lineage, had any charms in the eyes of the young Kasim, who always declared he chose to remain free and unshackled, to make his choice wherever his destiny should, as he said, guide him.

It is not wonderful, then, that upon one thus mentally constituted, and whose imagination waited as it were an exciting cause, the events of the night should have had effects such as have been noted:—but we have digressed.

'Ay,' thought Kasim, 'her beauty is wondrous,—even as I saw it here by the light of the torches, as I wrung the wet from her long silky hair, and when, lifeless as she appeared, I laid her down by my mother,—it was very wondrous. What then to see her eyes open—her lips move—to hear her speak—to see her breathe, to see her move! and what to sit with her, beneath the light of a moon like this, and to know that she could only live for and love but one! to lie beside her on some shady terrace—to hear no sound but her voice—to drink in her words like the waters of the blessed well of Paradise—to worship her on the very knees of my heart! This,' cried the enthusiast, 'this would be Heaven before its time,—this, one of the seventy Houris, whom the Prophet (may his name be honoured!) has promised to the lot of every true believer who doeth his law. But I have no hope—none! What if the Khan be old, he is yet her lord, her lawful lord; and shall the son of Noor-ud-deen, that light of the faith and brave among the brave, shall he disgrace his name by treachery to him upon whom he hath exercised hospitality? No, by Alla, no,' cried the young man aloud,

'I will not; better that I should perish than hold such thoughts; but, Alla help me! I am weak indeed.'

And thus arguing with himself, exerting the better principle, which ever had been strong within him, Kasim returned to the house, entered it as gently as he had quitted it, and unknown to any one reached his chamber; there, soothed by his ramble in the calm air and the tone of his later reflections, he sank at last into slumber.

But his dreams were disturbed, as often follows exciting causes; and visions, now happy now perplexing, of the fair inmate of his house flitted across his mind while he slept; they were indefinite shadows perhaps, but he did not wake so calmly in the morning as he had gone to rest; and his heart was neither so light, nor his spirit so free of care, as before. Nevertheless he repeated the morning prayer with fervour, and commended himself to the blessed Alla, to work out his destiny as best he pleased.

It was late ere the Khan rose, for fatigue had oppressed him, and he had slept heavily. It was reported to his anxious inquiries that the lady had arisen, bathed, and was well; nor could the Khan's impatience to behold once more one who was really dear to him be longer delayed. The apartment where his wife rested was made private, and in a few moments he was in her presence.

How thankful was he to see her well—nay with hardly a trace of any suffering upon her! Her eyes were as bright, her smile as sunny and beautiful, as they had ever been. Her hair, which she had washed in the bath, and which was not yet dry, hung over her shoulders and back in luxuriant masses; and if its quantity, and the manner in which it was disposed accidentally about her face, caused her fair skin to seem paler than usual, it only heightened the interest her appearance excited.

'Alla bless thee!' said the Khan, much moved, as he seated himself by her,—for she had risen upon his entrance,—'Alla bless thee! it is more to Abdool Rhyman to see thee thus, than to have the empire of Hind at his feet. And thou art well?'

'Well indeed, my lord,—thanks to him who protected me in the tempest,' she said, looking up devoutly; 'and thanks to her who, since I was brought hither, has not ceased to tend me as a daughter.'

'Ay, fairest,' said her lord, 'what do we not owe to the inmates of this house, and indeed to all this village? without their aid we had been lost.'

'I have an indistinct remembrance of some danger,' said the lady; 'I think I recollect the palankeen entering the waters, and their frightful appearance, and that I shut my eyes; and I think too,' she added after a pause, and passing her hand across her eyes, 'that it seemed to slip, and I shrieked; and then I knew nothing of what followed, till I awoke all wet, and the women were rubbing me and taking my clothes off. And then I remember waking again, and speaking to the kind lady who had so watched me; and I think I asked her how I had been brought here; but she made light of it, would not let me speak much, and so I went to sleep again, for I was weary. They said too thou wert well;—yet,' she continued after a pause, 'something tells me that all was not right, that there was danger. But my memory is very confused—very.'

'No wonder, my pearl, my rose!' cried the Khan; 'and how I bless that good lady for keeping the truth from thee! as thou wert then, the remembrance of it might have been fatal. And so thou dost not know that thou wert nearly lost to me for ever,—that I had seen thee plunged beneath that roaring flood, and little hoped ever to have been greeted by that sweet smile again?'

'Alas, no!' said the lady shuddering; 'and was I indeed in such peril? who then saved me?—it was thou surely, my noble lord! and I have been hitherto unmindful of it,' she cried, bowing her head to his feet? 'how insensible must thou not have thought me!'

'Not so, beloved, not so,' was the eager reply of the Khan as he raised her up; 'I had not that happiness. I cast myself, it is true, into the waters after thee when the bearers fell, but it was useless. I should have been lost, encumbered as I was with my arms, only for the bearers who saved me. No, even as Alla sends visitations of evil, so does he most frequently in his wisdom find a path of extrication from them; there was a youth—a noble fellow, a very Roostum, and by Alla a Mejnoon in countenance,—who saw the accident. His quick eye saw thy lifeless form cast up by the boiling water, and he rescued thee at the peril of his own life,—a valuable one too, fairest, for he is the son of a widow, the only son, and the head of the family,—in a word the son of her who has tended thee so gently—'

'Holy Prophet!' exclaimed the lady, 'was I in this peril, and so rescued? At the peril of his own life too,—and he a widow's son, thou saidst? What if he had been lost?' And she fell to musing silently.

Gradually however (for the Khan did not hazard a reply) her bosom heaved: a tear welled over one of her eyelids, and fell upon her hand unnoticed,—another, and another. The Khan let them have their course. 'They will soothe her better than my words,' he thought, and thought truly.

After awhile she spoke again; it was abruptly, and showed her thoughts had been with her deliverer.

'Thou wilt reward him, noble Khan,' she said; 'mine is but a poor life, 'tis true, but of some worth in thy sight, I know,—and of much in that of those I have left behind. My mother! it would have been a sore blow to thee to have heard of thy rose's death so soon after parting.'

'Reward him, Ameena!' cried the Khan, 'ay, with half my wealth, would he take it; but he is of proud blood and a long ancestry, though he is but a Patél, and such an offer would be an insult. Think—thou art quick-witted, and speak thy thought freely.'

'He would not take money?' thou saidst.

'No, no,—I dare not offer it.'

'Jewels perhaps, for his mother,—he may have all mine; thou knowest there are some of value.'

'He would set no value upon them; to him they are of no use, for he is not married.'

'Not married! and so beautiful!' she said, musing aloud.

'Nor to his mother,' continued the Khan, who had not heard her exclamation,—'she is an old woman. No, jewels would not do, though they are better than money.'

'Horses, arms,—they might gratify him, if he is a soldier.'

'Ay, that is better, for he is a soldier from head to heel. But of what use would they be to him without service in which to exercise them? Here there are no enemies but plunderers now and then; but—I have it now,' he continued joyfully after a pause,—'service! ay, that is his best reward,—to that I can help him. By the Prophet, I was a fool not to have thought of this sooner. He will be a rare addition to Tippoo's Pagha. I am much mistaken, too, in a few months, if he have an opportunity (and, by the blessing of the Prophet, it is seldom wanting against either the English or Hindoo Kafirs), if he do not win himself not only renown, but a command perhaps like my own. Tippoo Sultaun is no respecter of persons.'

'Ay, my noble lord, such an offer would be worthy of thy generosity and his acceptance,' was the lady's reply: 'and he could easily follow us to the city.'

'And why not accompany us? I for one should be glad of his society, for he is a scholar as well as a soldier, and that is more than I am. Besides one of my men fell last night, and his place is vacant.'

'Fell! was drowned?' she exclaimed.

'No, my pearl, his hour was come; he fell by the hand of Alla, struck by lightning.'

'Ay, it was very fearful,' she said shuddering, 'I remember that;—who fell, didst thou say?'

'Ibrahim.'

'Alas! it was he that twice saved thy life.'

'It was; but this was his destiny, thou knowest: it had been written, and who could have averted it? What sayest thou, shall I offer the Patél the place.'

'Not Ibrahim's, since thou askest me,' she said; 'as he is of gentle blood, ask him to accompany thee; or say, "Come to Abdool Rhyman at Seringapatam, the leader of a thousand horse,"—which thou wilt. Say thou wilt give him service in thine own risala, and hear his determination.'

'Well spoken, my rose!' said the blunt soldier; 'verily I owe him the price of thy glorious beauty and thy love, both of which were lost to me, but for him, for ever. So Alla keep thee! I will not disturb thee again till evening, and advise thee to rest thyself from all thy many fatigues and alarms—Alla Hafiz!'

'A very Roostum! a Mejnoon in countenance,' thought the fair creature, as, shutting her eyes, she threw herself back against the pillows; 'a noble fellow, my lord called him, and a scholar, —how many perfections! A widow's son,—very dear to her he must be,—she will not part with him.'

Again there was another train of thought. 'He must have seen my face,—holy Prophet! I was not able to conceal that; he carried me too in his arms, and I was insensible; what if my dress was disordered?' and she blushed unconsciously, and drew it instinctively around her. 'And he must have seen me too in the broad light when he entered this room: what could he have thought of me? they say I am beautiful.' And a look she unthinkingly cast upon a small mirror, which, set in a ring, she wore upon her thumb, appeared to confirm the thought, for a gentle smile passed over her countenance for an instant. 'What could he have thought of me?' she added. But her speculations as to his thoughts by some unaccountable means to her appeared to disturb her own; and, after much unsatisfactory reasoning, she fell into a half dose, a dreamy state, when the scenes of the night before—the storm—the danger—the waters—and her own rescue, flitted before her fancy; and perhaps it is not strange, that in them a figure which she believed to be a likeness of the young Patél occupied a prominent and not a disagreeable situation.

CHAPTER IV.

It was now evening: the gentle breeze which came over the simosa-grove loaded the air with the rich perfume of the blossoms. Cattle, returning from the distant pastures, lowed as they approached the village; and a noisy herd of goats, driven by a few half-naked boys, kept up an incessant bleating. Far in the west the sun had set in brilliancy; and a few light and exquisitely tinted clouds floated away towards the rocky range of the Adoni fortress, whose rugged outlines could be seen sharply defined against the sky. There were many beauties there, but they only remained to the living.

The grave of the Khan's retainer had been filled in, and the long narrow mound raised on the top: one by one, those who had attended the funeral turned away and retired; but the Khan and Kasim, anxious to pay the last marks of respect to the deceased, stayed till all had been smoothed down, and the place swept. Garlands of flowers were strewn upon the grave,—they left the dead to its corruption, and returned home.

But among soldiers, especially Asiatics,—whose belief in fatality, while it leads them to be often reckless of life, yet when a stroke of sorrow comes teaches them resignation—death makes perhaps but little impression, unless any one near or dear is stricken down. The Khan and his host, having partaken of the hearty meal supplied by the Patél, and most exquisitely cooked by the stout functionary we have before alluded to, and having each been supplied with that soother of many mortal ills a good hooka, had already almost forgotten the ceremony they had assisted in, and were well disposed to become excellent friends, and to detail to each other passages in their lives, which they would for ever have remained ignorant of but for the fortuitous circumstances in which they had been placed.

And it was after a recital of his own deeds, which, however modestly given, could not fail of having impressed Kasim with a high sense of his gallant conduct, that the Khan said, 'My brother, I was an adventurer, as you might be; young and active, hairbrained perhaps, and ready for any exciting employment, with only my arms and an indifferent horse, I entered the service of Hyder Ali. You see me now the commander of a thousand horse, having won a reputation at the sword's point second to none in his gallant army. Why shouldst thou not have the same fate,—thou who hast personal attractions, greater power, and scholarship to aid thee—all of infinite value to an adventurer? What sayest thou then, wilt thou serve him whom I serve,—Tippoo, the lion of war, the upholder of the Faith? Speak, O Patél, for I love thee, and can help thee in this matter.'

'My lord draws a bright picture to dazzle mine understanding,' he answered; 'I have dreamed of such things, of attaining to giddy eminences even of rank and power; but they are no more, I well know, than the false visions of youth, the brighter and more alluring as they are the more deceptive and unattainable.'

'By my beard, by your salt, I say no!' cried the Khan; 'I have said nothing but what is a matter of every-day occurrence in the army. What was Hyder's origin?—lower, infinitely lower than thine own. Thy ancestry was noble,—his can be traced back a few generations, beginning with a Punjabee Fakeer, and descending (not much improved i' faith) to his father Hyder, whose mother was only the daughter of a cloth-weaver of Allund, somewhere by Koolburgah. It is destiny, young man, destiny which will guide thee—which, on thy high and broad forehead, shines as brightly as if thy future history were already written there in letters of gold."

'My lord's words are enticing, very enticing,' said the youth, 'and ever have I felt that the inactive life I am leading was a shame on me in these times; but I like not the service of the Nizam, and the Mahrattas are infidels; I would not shame my faith by consorting with them.'

'Bravely spoken! hadst thou come to Tippoo Sultaun mounted and armed as thou shouldst be,—even alone and unbefriended as I did to his father,—he would have enrolled thee upon handsome pay at once in his own Pagha.* With me, thou wilt have the benefit of a friend; and I swear to thee upon this my beard, and thy salt,' cried the Khan generously, 'I will be a friend and a brother to thee, even as thou hast been one to me, and her who is as dear to me as my own life's blood. I owe this to thee for her life,—for the risk of thine own, when we were nothing to thee, by Alla, but as the dust of the earth,—I owe it for thine hospitality; I desire thee for a companion and a friend; and, above all, my spirit is vexed to see one like thee hiding here in his village, and marring his own destiny by sloth and inaction. Dost thou think that service will come to seek thee, if thou dost not seek it?'

The young man felt the spirit-stirring address of the rough but

* Household troops.

kind soldier deeply, but he still hesitated: the Khan tried to guess his thoughts.

'Dost thou think,' he said, 'that I have sweet words at my command wherewith to entice thee? Ay, that is my mistake, and I have spoken too freely to one who has never yet known contradiction nor received advice.'

'Not so, not so, noble Khan, almost my father!' cried Kasim; 'I beseech thee not to think me thus haughty or impatient. By your beard, I am not—I thought but of my mother—of the suddenness of this—of my own—'

'Poverty, perhaps,' said the Khan; 'do not be ashamed to own it. Thou wouldst go to service as a cavalier, as thou art, gallantly armed and mounted,—is it not so?'

'It is: I would not serve on foot, nor have I money to buy a horse such as I would ride into battle.'

'Right! thou art right, by the Prophet, but let not this trouble thee. We spoke of thee this morning: we dare not offer thee money—nay, be not impatient—we dare not offer thee jewels, else both were thine. We could offer thee honourable service; and, if thou wilt accept it, as my brother thou art entitled to look to me thine elder, thou knowest, for such matters as thou needest. With me are two horses, the best of the Dekhan blood, beside mine own Motee: him thou canst not have: but either of the others, or both, are thine; and if they do not suit thee, there are others at the city where thou shalt be free to choose. See, I have conquered all thy scruples.'

The young man was much affected, and the Khan's kindness fairly brought the tears to his eyes. 'Such service as I can do thee, O generous being,' he exclaimed, 'I vow here under mine own roof and by the head of my mother,—I will follow thee to the death. Such honourable service as I would alone have ever accepted is in my power, and I accept it with gratitude to thee and thine, whom the Prophet shield with his choicest care!'

'It were well that your arrangements were quickly concluded, for I cannot wait beyond to-morrow,' said the Khan.

'It will be ample for my slender preparations,' replied the youth. 'I will break this to my mother now.'

'You do right, Meer Sahib; I honour thee for thy consideration; and I too will to the Khanum: she will be glad to hear that her deliverer and her lord are now friends and brothers in service.'

Kasim sought his mother; she was with her guest as he passed the door of the inner chamber; so he desired a girl who was without to inform his mother he desired to speak with her in his own apartment.

There was not much to tell her, and yet he knew that it would grieve the old lady. 'But I cannot continue thus,' he thought aloud; 'the fortunes of our house have fallen, and the Khan's words bear conviction with them. I can retrieve them,—I may perhaps retrieve them, I should rather say; and, after all, she will rejoice to hear of me, and the fortune and rank I shall, by the blessing of Alla, speedly win; and then—' but here his thoughts became quite inexpressible, even to himself; for there rushed suddenly before his imagination such a tide of processions, soldiery, elephants, wars, camps, as almost bewildered him; while here and there a figure mingled with all, which, had he been closely questioned, he must have admitted was that of the fair Ameena. But his mother interrupted what we will say he was striving to put from him, by entering and standing before him.

'Thou didst send for me, my son,' she said; 'what news hast thou to tell? Was the Khan pleased with the Zeafut?* was the meat well cooked? By the Prophet, he hath a glorious cook; what dishes he sent into the Khanum, of which we have been partaking! By thine eyes, I have not tasted such since—since—'

But while the old lady was trying to remember when she had last eaten of such savoury messes as she spoke of, her son gently interrupted her, and said gravely, as he rose and seated her in his own place, 'Mother, I have much to tell thee, so collect thy thoughts and listen.'

She was attentive in a moment, and eagerly looked for what he should say,—with not a little apprehension perhaps, for there was sadness, nay even a quivering, perceptible in the tone with which he spoke.

Her grief was uncontrollable at first:—yet he gradually unfolded all his hopes—his previous determination to enter service when he could with honour—his desires for an active life—and his great chances of speedy advancement under the patronage of his friend;—and he laid them before his mother with a natural eloquence, under which her first sudden shock of grief fast yielded. Kasim saw his opportunity, and continued,—

'So much as thou lovest me, mother, wilt thou not have pride when I write to thee that I command men, that I have fought with the infidel English, that I have been rewarded, that I am honoured? Wilt thou not feel, and then say,—"If I had prevented him, there would have been none of this." And doth it

* Entertainment.

not behove every believer now to draw his sword in defence of the faith? Look around:—the English are masters of Bengal and Oude; they hold Mahamed Ali of the Carnatic and him of Oude in a base thraldom; they thirst for conquest, and are as brave as they are cunning;—the Mahrattas have taken Hindostan and the Dekhan, and are every day making encroachments upon Nizam Ali's power, which totters upon an insecure foundation;—and do not the eyes of every true believer turn to Tippoo, a man who has raised himself to be a monarch? I say, mother, I believe it to be my destiny to follow his fortunes: I have long thought so, and have eagerly watched the time when I should be able to join him. It has come, and dost thou love thy son so little, as to stand in the way of fame, honour, wealth, everything that is dear to me as a man, and as thy son?'

The old lady could not reply: but she arose and cast herself upon the manly breast of her son, and though she sobbed bitterly and long, yet at last she told him in accents broken by her emotion she was convinced that he was acting wisely, and that her prayers night and day would be for his welfare.

And her mind once being reconciled to the thought of parting with him, she made every preparation with alacrity. Such few garments as were necessary, and were the best among his not over-abundant stock, were put aside and looked over; and one or two showy handkerchiefs and scarfs which she possessed, with deep gold borders to them, were added to his wardrobe. 'I shall not want them,' she said; 'I am old, and ought not to think of finery.'

Nor did Kasim neglect his own affairs; having made the communication to his mother, he at once sought the Kurnum, or accountant of the village, and disclosed his intentions to that worthy functionary. Though somewhat surprised at his sudden decision, he did not wonder at its being made; and, as he was a rich man, he liberally tendered a loan of money to enable Kasim to live respectably, until such time as he should receive pay from his new master. He despatched a messenger for his uncle, his mother's brother, who arrived at night; and early the next morning he had concluded every arrangement for the management of his little property and the care of his mother.

These matters being arranged to his satisfaction, Kasim sought the Khan with a light heart and sincere pleasure upon his countenance. He found him busied inspecting his horses, and greeted him heartily.

'Well,' asked the Khan, 'how fared you with the lady your mother after you left me?'

'Well, excellently well,' was the reply; 'she made some opposition at first, but was reasonable in the end.'

'Good! then I have no blame on my head,' he said laughing; 'but tell me, when shalt thou be prepared?'

'Now, Khan Sahib, even now am I ready; speak the word, and I attend you at once.'

'Why then delay, Kasim? Bismilla! let us go at once; the Khanum is well, and if thy good mother can but give us a plain kicheree* we will set off soon; the day is cloudy and there will be no heat.'

'I will go bid her prepare it: and when I have put on some travelling garment better than this, Khan Sahib, and got out my arms, as soon as thou wilt we may be in our saddles. I am already impatient to see the road.'

The meal was soon despatched by master and servant—the camels loaded—the horses saddled. No one saw the farewell Kasim took of his mother; but it was observed that his cheek was wet when he came out of his house accoutred and armed,—a noble figure indeed, and one which drew forth an exclamation of surprise and gratification from the Khan.

CHAPTER V.

And in truth, accoutred as he was, and dressed in better clothes than he had hitherto worn, Meer Kasim Ali was one on whom the eye of man could not rest for a moment without admiration, nor that of a woman without love. He wore a dark purple silk vest, bordered round the throat and openings at the chest with broad gold lace and handsome gold pointed buttons; a crimson waistband with a deep gold border was around his loins, in which were stuck several daggers of various forms and very beautifully chased silver handles; and on his shoulder was a broad gold belt or baldric, somewhat tarnished it is true, but still handsome. This supported a long sword, with a half basket-hilt inlaid with gold and lined with crimson velvet; the scabbard was of the same, ornamented and protected at the end by a deep and richly chased ferule. At his back was a shield much covered with gilding and brass bosses.

* Rice and pulse boiled together.

'By Alla and the twelve Imaums!' cried the Khan, 'thou art worthy to look on, and a jewel of price in the eye of an old soldier. But there are the steeds,—take thy choice; the chesnut is called Yacoot;* he is hot, but a gallant beast, and perfect in his paces. The other I call Hyder, after him who was my first master; he is steadier perhaps, and not so active: say which wilt thou have?'

'I think, with your permission, Khan Sahib, I will mount Yacoot;' and so saying, he approached him and bounded into the saddle.

'Alla, what a seat!' cried the Khan in an ecstasy of admiration, after Kasim had mounted, and the horse had made several wonderful bounds: 'he does not move,—no, not a hair's-breadth! even I should have been disturbed by that. Inshalla! he is a good horseman. Enough, Meer Sahib,' he cried, 'enough now; Yacoot is a young beast and a fiery devil, but I think after all he will suit thee better than the other.'

'I think Yacoot and I shall be very good friends when we know each other better,' said Kasim; 'but see, the Khanum waits, and the bearers are ready. Put the palankeen close up to the door that it may be more convenient,' he added to them.

They obeyed; and in a few moments a figure enveloped from head to foot, but whose tinkling anklets were delicious music in the ears of Kasim, emerged from the threshold of the house, and instantly entered the palankeen. Another followed, and busied herself for a few moments in arranging the interior of the vehicle. This was Kasim's mother, whose heart, almost too full for utterance, had much difficulty in mustering words sufficient to bid her lovely guest farewell.

'May Alla keep you!' said the old lady, blinded by her tears; 'you are young, and proud and beautiful, but you will sometimes think perhaps of the old Patélne. Remember all I have told you of my son; and that as the Khan is a father to him, so you are his mother:—ye have now the care of him, not I. May Alla keep thee! for my old eyes can hardly hope to see thee again;' and she blessed her.

'Willingly, mother,' she replied; 'all that constant solicitude for his welfare can effect, I will do; and while I have life I will remember thee, thy care and kindness. Alla Hafiz! do you too remember Ameena.'

The old lady had no reply to give; she shut the door of the palankeen with trembling hands—and the bearers, understanding

* Ruby.

the signal, advanced, raised it to their shoulders, and bore it rapidly forward.

'Come,' cried the Khan, who had mounted; 'delay not, Kasim.'

'Not a moment—a few last words with my mother, and I follow thee.'

She was standing at the door; he rode up to her and stooped down from the horse gently. 'Thy blessing, mother, again,' he said—'thy last blessing on thy son.'

She gave it; and hastily searching for a rupee, she drew a handkerchief from her bosom, and folding it in it, tied it around his arm. 'My blessing, the blessing of the holy Alla and of the Imaum Zamin be upon thee, my son! May thy footsteps lead thee into happiness—may thy destiny be great! May I again see my son ere I die, that mine eyes may greet him as a warrior, and one that has won fame!'

'I thank thee, mother; but saidst thou aught to her of me?'

'I told her much of thee and of thy temper from thy youth up: it appeared to interest her, and she hath promised to befriend thee.'

'Enough, dear mother! remember my last words—to have the trees I planted looked to and carefully tended, and the tomb protected. Inshalla! I will return to see them grown up, and again be reminded of the spot where I saved her life.'

And so saying, and not trusting himself to speak to many who would have crowded around him for a last word, the young man turned his horse, and, striking his heels sharply into its flank, the noble animal bounding forward bore him away after his future companions, followed by the blessings and dim and streaming eyes of most who were assembled around the door of his mother's home.

The old lady heeded not that her veil had dropped from her face; there was but one object which occupied her vision of the many that were before her eyes, and that was the martial figure of her son as it rapidly disappeared before her. She lost sight of him as he passed the gate of the village; again she saw him beyond. There was a slight ascent, up which the party, now united, were rapidly advancing: he reached them. She saw him exchange greeting with the Khan, as he checked his bounding steed, fall in by his side, apparently in familiar converse, and for a short time more the whole were brightly before her, as a gleam of sunlight shone forth, glancing brightly from their spear-heads and the bosses on their shields, and upon the gay colours of their dresses. A bright omen she thought it was of the future. But they had now attained the summit. Kasim and the Khan disappeared gradually behind it; then the attendants—the palankeen—the servants—the camels, one by one were lost to her gaze. Suddenly the place was void; she shook the blinding stream from her eyes, and looked again—but there was no one there; her son and his companions had passed away, she thought for ever. Then only, she perceived that she was unveiled, and hastily retreating into her now lonely and cheerless abode, for the while gave herself up to that violent grief which she had been ill able to repress as he left her.

'Ay, now thou lookest like a gentleman, as thou art in very truth,' said the Khan, after they had ridden some miles. 'What sayest thou, Meer Sahib, hast thou been instructed in the use of the arms thou wearest? Canst thou do thy qusrut*—use a mugdoor†—play with a sword and shield? and what sort of a marksman art thou?'

'As a marksman, Khan, I have pretty good practice at the deer which roam our plains and devastate our corn-fields; as to the rest, thou knowest I am but a village youth.'

'Modestly spoken, Meer Sahib. Now take Dilawur Ali's matchlock, and kill me one of those deer yonder;' and he pointed to a herd which was quietly browsing at some distance: 'we will put it on a camel, and it will be a supper for us.'

'I will try, Khan Sahib,' returned Kasim joyfully and eagerly; 'only stay here, and dismount if you will, lest they should see you; and if I can get within shot, thou shalt have the deer.'

'Give him thy gun then,' said the Khan to his retainer; 'is it properly charged?'

The palankeen was put down, and all waited the issue with much interest and anxiety.'

The Khan went to the palankeen. 'Look out, my rose,' he said; 'I have dared the Patél to shoot a deer, and he is gone to do it. Look, see how he creeps onward, like a cat or a panther.'

The lady looked out. It was very exciting to her to see the motions of the young man; and, if it may be believed, she actually put up a mental prayer for his success. 'Ya Alla, give him a steady hand!' she said inwardly, and looked the more.

'He will be near them soon,' said the Khan, shading his eyes with his hands; 'there is a nulla yonder which will afford him cover; canst thou see? Mashalla! this is better than shooting one oneself.'

'They have seen him!' cried the lady, as one of the deer which had been lying down got up and gazed warily about. They will be off ere he can get within shot.'

* Gymnastic exercises.

† A heavy club.

'Not so, by your eyes!' cried the Khan; 'he has crouched down. See! raise thyself a little higher; look at him crawling.'

Kasim's progress was slow, and had he been alone he would have given up the pursuit; but he knew the Khan was observing him, perhaps Ameena. It was enough,—he crept stealthily on.

'He will never get near them,' said the fat cook. 'Who is he —a village Patél—that he should shoot? Ay, now, at my city we have the real shooting; there, over the plains of Surroo Nuggur, thousands of antelopes are bounding with no one to molest them, except Nizam Ali, who goes out with the nobles and shoots a hundred sometimes in a day. I was once there, and killed—'

'With thy knife, O Zoolfoo, and roasted it afterwards I suppose,' said Nasur: 'don't tell us lies; thou knowest thou never hadst a gun in thy hand since thou wast born.'

'That is another lie,' retorted Zoolfoo. 'By the beard of Moula Ali, if I was yonder I would have fired long ago: we shall have no venison for supper I see plainly enough. See how he is crawling on the ground as a frog would,—can't he walk upright like a man?'

'He knows well enough what he is doing, you father of owls,' was the reply. 'Inshalla! we shall all eat venison to-night, and thou wilt have to cook us kabobs and curries.'

'Venison and méthee-ke-bajee make a good curry,' mused the cook; 'and kabobs are also good, dried in the sun and seasoned.'

'Look! he is going to shoot,' cried the Khan; 'which will it be? I wager thee a new dooputta* he does not kill.'

'Kubool! I agree,' said the lady; he will kill by the blessing of Alla,—I feel sure he will.'

But Kasim's gun went down.

'He is too far off yet,' she said: and he was. He saw a mound at a little distance from him, and tried to reach it, crawling on as before.

But the deer saw him. He observed their alarm, and lay motionless. They all got up and looked:—he did not move. The buck trotted forward a few paces, saw what it was, and ere the young man could get his gun to his shoulder as he lay, he had turned.

'I told you so,' cried the Khan; 'they are off, and I have won.'

'There is yet a chance,' said Ameena anxiously.

* Scarf.

'I said he would not kill,' said the cook; 'we shall have no venison.'

They were all wrong. Kasim saw there was no chance unless he rose and fired; so he rose instantly. The deer regarded him for an instant, turned as with one motion, and fled bounding away.

'There is yet a chance,' cried Ameena again, as she saw the gun pointed. 'Holy Alla! he has won my wager!' she added, clapping her hands.

He had, and won it well. As the herd bounded on, he waited till the buck was clear of the rest. He fired; and springing high into the air it rolled forward on the ground; and while it yet struggled, Kasim had drawn his knife across the throat, pronouncing the formula.

'Shookr Alla!' cried the cook, 'it is Hulal* at any rate.'

'Shabash!' exclaimed the Khan, 'he has done it:—he is as good as his word,—he is a rare marksman. So thou hast won thy wager, Pearee,'† he added. 'Well, I vow to thee a Benares dooputta: thou shalt have one in memory of the event.'

She would not, however, have forgotten it without.

'Go, some of ye,' continued the Khan, 'and take the lightest laden of the camels, for the Syud is beckoning to us: bring the game hither speedily.'

The deer was soon brought, and laid near the palankeen, where the Khan stood. The bright eye was already glazed and suffused with blood.

'Ay, now thou canst see it,' he said to the lady, who, closely veiled, yet had apertures for her eyes through which she could observe distinctly. 'Is it not a noble beast?—fat, too, by the Prophet! It was a good shot at that distance.'

'It was partly accident, Khan Sahib,' replied Kasim.

'Not so, by your beard, not so, Patél; it was no chance. I should be very sorry to stand for thee to shoot at even further than it was.'

'I should be very sorry to shoot at my lord, or any one but an enemy,' he returned, 'seeing that I rarely miss my mark whether on foot or on horseback.'

'I believe thee,' returned the Khan; 'but where is that lazy cook?' he cried, after he had mounted.

'Hazir!'‡ cried Zoolfoo, urging on his pony from behind as fast as he could, for it shied at everything it saw. 'Your slave is

* Lawful to be eaten. † Beloved. ‡ Present.

coming,' he shouted, as the Khan grew impatient. And at last, joining his hands together, he was in his presence.

'Kya Hookum?' he asked, 'what orders has my lord for his slave?'

'See that there is a good curry this evening; and if thou canst get méthee, put it in;—dost thou hear?'

'My lord and the Meer Sahib shall say they have never eaten such,' said the functionary joyfully! 'Inshalla! it will be one fit for the Huzoor himself.'

He fell back. 'I thought,' he said, 'how it would be,—venison and méthee; yes, I had thought as much: my lord has a good taste.' And the idea of méthee and venison comforted him for the rest of the day's journey.

And now the party rode on merrily, though not fast. The Khan became more and more pleased with his new friend every hour that they rode together. Kasim's stores of learning were not extensive; but so far as he possessed knowledge of books he unfolded it to the Khan. He recited pieces of Hafiz,—passages from the Shah Namah, of which he had read selections. He repeated tales from the Ikhlak-i-Hindee, from the Bostan, and ghuzuls* from the earlier Oordoo poets; until the Khan, who had never thought of these accomplishments himself, and who knew none who possessed them, was fairly astonished.

But after a few hours' ride they were near the village they were to rest at. 'If thou knowest any one in it,' said the Khan, 'we shall be able to get a good place for the night.'

'I knew the Patél well, Khan Sahib; he was my father's friend. I will gallop on, and secure such a place as may be fitting for you and the Khanum to rest in.'

When they arrived, they found the Patél with Kasim Ali ready to receive them at the door of a neat but small mosque which was in the village. A few tent walls were placed across the open part, to screen them from the weather and the public gaze,—then carpets spread; and soon some were resting themselves, while others wandered into the bazaars or were employed in various offices for the Khan. Particularly the cook, who, after sending for a village butcher to skin and cut up the deer, selected some prime parts of the meat, which he proceeded to dress after the following fashion, and which we cordially recommend to all uninitiated.

The meat was cut into small pieces, and each piece covered with the ingredients for seasoning the dish, which had been ground with water to the consistence of paste. Then some

* Songs.

butter and onions were put into a pan, and the onions fried till they were brown. Into this was placed the meat, some salt, and sour curds or butter-milk: then it was suffered to simmer gently, while Zoolfoo every now and then stirred it with great assiduity. When it was partly done, the vegetables were added; and in a short time most savoury steams succeeded, saluting the hungry noses of a few lean and half-starved village dogs; these, attracted by the savour, prowled about with watering chops in the vicinity of the fireplace, much cursed by the cook, and frequently pelted with stones as they ventured a little nearer. Many kites were wheeling and screaming overhead, and a good many crows sat upon the nearest stones,—upon the wall and other slight elevations,—apparently, by their constant chattering and croakings, speculating upon their probable share.

'May your mothers and sisters be destroyed!' cried the cook, at length fairly perplexed between the dogs, the kites, and the crows, each of which watched the slightest inattention in order to attempt to carry off anything they could see: 'may they be destroyed and dishonoured! Ya Alla!' he continued in exclamation, as he saw a dog coolly seize hold of and run away with part of the leg of the deer, 'Ya Alla! that is Jumal Khan's portion;—drop it, you base-born!—drop it, you son of a vile mother!' and he flung a stone after the delinquent, which had happily effect on his hinder portion, and made him limp off on three legs, howling, and without his booty. 'Ha! I hit you, did I? that will teach you to steal!' and he picked up the meat.

'But, holy Prophet, I am ruined!' he again exclaimed. And indeed it was provoking enough to see several kites in succession making stoops at the little board upon which he had been cutting up the meat for the kabob; at every stoop carrying off large pieces, which, holding in their talons, they fairly ate as they sailed over him, screaming apparently in exultation.

'Holy Prophet! that I should have eaten such dirt at the hands of these animals. Ho! Meer Sahib!' he continued to Kasim who approached, 'wilt thou keep watch here while I cook the dinner? for if thou dost not there will be none left; one brute had carried off this leg which I have just rescued, and while I was about that, the kites ate up the kabob.'

The Syud could not help laughing at the worthy functionary's distress.

'Well, as there is no one near, Zoolfoo, I will sit here;' and he seated himself upon a log of wood not far from him. 'Now we will see if any of these sons of unchaste mothers will come near thee: thou deservest this for what thou art doing for us there, which smelleth well.'

'It is a dish for a prince, Meer Sahib,' said the cook, giving the contents of the pot an affectionate stir. 'I say it is a dish for the Huzoor, and such an one as I have often cooked for his zenana.'

'Then thou wast in the kitchen of Nizam Ali?'

'Even so, Meer Sahib; there is plenty to eat, but little pay; so I left the Huzoor to follow the fortunes of the Khan,—may his prosperity increase!'

'Ay, he is a noble fellow, Zoolfoo, and a generous one;—see what he hath done for me already.'

'Thou didst enough for him,' said the cook drily. 'Knowest thou that the Khanum is a bride, and that she is only fourteen or fifteen, and as beautiful as the moon at the full?'

'Is she?' said Kasim carelessly.

'Is she!' retorted the cook; 'I saw her three months ago, for she was a neighbour of mine. I have known her for years, but that she does not know.'

'Indeed! that is very extraordinary,' said Kasim absently.

'Not at all,' replied the cook; 'my sister was servant in their house for some years,—nay, is there still. She told me all about this marriage; it was very splendid.'

'Indeed!' said Kasim again.

'Ay, truly; and the maiden was very loth to be married to one so old. But she was of age to be married, and her parents did not like to refuse when such a man as Abdool Rhyman offered for her—Khan they call him, but he was only the son of a soldier of the Huzoor's—quite a poor man. They said—indeed Nasur told me—that he has two other wives at Seringapatam, but he has no child.'

'That is very odd,' said Kasim.

'Very,' returned the cook. But their conversation was suddenly interrupted by one of the men, who approached, and relieved Kasim of his watch.

CHAPTER VI.

THEY rested in the town of Bellary the next day; and as there was an alarm of parties of Mahratta horse being abroad, though they could hear of no one having suffered from them, the Khan on account of the baggage he had with him, determined on travelling the eastern road by Nundidroog; from thence he could reach the city, either by Bangalore, or the western road, as best suited him. But no enemy appeared, though several alarms were given by the people.

At one place, however, after some days' travel, they heard that a party of horse had passed the day before; and at the stage after, they kept a watch all night,—with some need in fact, for a marauding party of great strength were undoubtedly in their vicinity, as was plainly to be seen by the conflagration of a small village at some coss distant, which could easily be distinguished from the town wherein they rested for the night.

'This looks like danger,' said the Khan, as from the tower in the middle of the village he and Kasim looked forth over the wide plain;—'the rascals yonder are at their old work. Strange that there are none of our horse hereabouts to check them, and indeed I marvel that the rogues dare venture so far into Tippoo's country.'

'If it were day we could see their number,' replied Kasim; 'as it is, we must take heart,—Inshalla! our destiny is not so bad as to cause us to eat dirt at the hands of those thieves.'

'If I were alone, Kasim, I tell thee I would now put myself at the head of ye all, and we would reconnoitre that village; perhaps it may only have been a chance fire after all.'

But soon after, one or two persons mounted on ponies arrived, bringing the news that their village had been attacked in the evening; and that, after the robbers had taken all they could, they had set fire to several houses and gone off in a southerly direction—it was supposed towards Gootee.

'Our very road!' said the Khan; 'but let us not fear: we had better travel on slowly, for it is probable that they have hastened on, and long ere this are beyond the pass. In that case there is but little fear of our overtaking them.'

'I will stand by you and the Khanum to the death,' said Kasim, 'and that thou well knowest. They said there were not more than fifty fellows, and I dare say their fears exaggerated them one-half at least. But if I might suggest anything, I would bring to your consideration the propriety of hiring a few young fellows from this village; they will be able to protect the baggage, and at least assist us should there be any danger.'

'A good thought, Kasim; see thou to it when the dawn breaks—nay now, if thou canst find any. I will remain here and watch.'

Kasim descended the tower, and at the foot found some of the very men he wanted; they were half-naked figures, sitting around the fire they had kindled; their heavy matchlocks leaned against the wall, and their waists were girded round with powder-horns, small pouches filled with balls, and other matters necessary for their use. There were two or three armed with swords and shields, and the whole group had a wild and picturesque appearance, as the fire, upon which they had thrown some straw at the young man's approach, blazed up, illuminating the foot of the tower and the house near it, and causing the shadows of the men to dance about in distorted figures. Two or three were sitting upon their hams, between whom a coarse hooka went its round, and was every now and then replenished; whilst the rest stood warming themselves over the blaze, or lounged about at no great distance.

'Salaam Aliekoom!' said Kasim, as he approached them; 'say which among you is the chief?'

'Aliekoom salaam!' returned one, advancing. 'I am the Naik of these worthy men. Say what you want; command us—we are your servants. What see ye from the tower?'

'Nothing but the blazing village,' said Kasim.

'The fellows have not left a roof-tree standing, they say,' rejoined the Naik; 'but the place was not defended, for the young men were all absent; and it is supposed the Mahrattas had news of this before they attacked it—they are arrant cowards.'

'You have found them so, then?'

'We have; we have twice beaten them off during the last few days, and killed one or two of them.'

'Mashalla! thou art a sharp fellow; what do they call thee?'

'Nursingha is my name; I am the nephew of the Patél.'

'Good! Then what sayest thou, Nursingha, to accompanying our party for a few days, until we are well past the hills, or indeed to Balapoor; thou shalt have a rupee a-day and thy food, and six of thy men half, if thou wilt.'

'What say you, brothers?' cried Nursingha to the rest; 'what say you to the stranger's offer? They seem men of substance, and they are the Government servants—we can hardly refuse.'

'What are we to do?' asked one.

'Fight, if there is necessity,' said Kasim; 'canst thou do that?'

'There is not a better shot in the Carnatic that Lingoo yonder,' said the Naik.

'He may shoot well and not fight well,' returned Kasim.

'I never feared Moosulman or Mahratta yet!' said Lingoo.

'Crowed like a good cock!' cried Kasim; 'but thou art on thine own dunghill.'

'I have fought with Hyder Ali many a time; and he who has done that may call himself a soldier,' retorted Lingoo.

'Well, so much the better; but say, what will ye do? here are ten or twelve; half that number is enough to protect the village, especially as the Mahrattas are gone on; will ye come?'

'Pay us half our due here first,' said the man, 'and we are ready—six of us. Have I said well, brethren?'

'Ay, that is it,' cried several. 'How know we that the gentlemen would not take us on, and send us back empty-handed, as the last did?'

'By Alla, that was shameful!' cried Kasim; 'fear not, ye shall have half your money.'

'Kasim, O Kasim Ali!' cried a voice from the top of the tower, interrupting him,—it was the Khan's, and he spoke hurriedly,—'Kasim, come up quickly!'

'Holy Prophet, what can it be?' said Kasim, turning to the tower, followed by several of the men. They were soon at the summit.

'What see you yonder?' asked the Khan, pointing to a light which was apparently not very far off.

'It is only a watchfire in the fields of the next village,' said the Naik. But as he spoke there broke forth a blaze of brilliant light, which at once shot up to the heavens, illuminating a few clouds that were floating gently along, apparently near the earth.

'That is no watchfire,' cried Kasim, as it increased in volume every moment; 'it is either a house which has accidentally caught fire, or the Mahrattas are there. Watch, all of ye; if there are horsemen, the light will soon show them.'

'There again!' exclaimed several at once, as a bright flame burst out from another corner of the village, and was followed by others, in various directions. 'It must be the Mahrattas and yet none are seen!'

'They are among the houses,' said the Khan; 'they will not come out till they are obliged.'

He was right; for while all were watching anxiously the progress of the flames, which they could see spreading from house to house, there rushed forth in a tumultous manner from the opposite side a body of perhaps twenty horsemen, whose long spears, the points of which every instant flashed through the gloom, proved them to be the Mahratta party.

'Base sons of dogs!' cried the Khan; 'cowards, and sons of impure mothers!—to attack defenceless people in that way!—to burn their houses over their heads at night! Oh for a score of my own risala,—ay, for as many more as we are now, and those rogues should pay dearly for this!'

'Who will follow Kasim Ali?' cried the young man. 'By the soul of the Prophet, we are no thieves, and our hearts are strong. I say one of us is a match for two of those cowards: who will follow me?'

'I!'—'and I!'—'and I!' cried several; and turned to follow the young man, who had his foot on the steps ready to descend.

'Stop, I command you!' cried the Khan; 'this is no time to risk anything: look yonder,—you thought there were but twenty; if there is one, there are more than fifty.'

They looked again, and beheld a fearful sight. The now blazing village was upon a gentle slope, hardly a mile from them; the light caused the gloom of night to appear absolute darkness. In the midst of this there was one glowing spot, upon which every eye rested in intense anxiety. Around the ill-fated village was an open space, upon which bright ground were the dark figures of the Mahratta horsemen in constant motion; while the black forms of persons on foot—evidently the miserable inhabitants, in vain striving to escape—became, as they severally appeared, objects of fearful interest. Now many would rush from among the houses, pursued by the horsemen; several would disappear in the gloom, and they supposed had escaped; whilst others but too plainly fell, either by the spear-thrusts or under the sword-cuts of the horsemen. They could even see the flash of the sword when the weapon descended; and sometimes a faint shriek, which was heard at an interval of time after a thrust or blow had been seen, plainly proved that it had been successful.

'By Alla, this is hard to bear!' exclaimed Kasim; 'to see those poor creatures butchered in cold blood, and yet have no means of striking a blow in their defence!'

'It would be impossible for us to do any good,' said the Khan; 'suppose they were to come on here after they had finished yonder. I see nothing to prevent them.'

'Inshalla! Khan, they will come; but what thinkest thou, Nursingha?'

'They owe us a grudge, and may make the attempt. Nay, it is more than probable, for they are stronger than ever, and they cannot reckon on your being here.'

'We had as well be fully prepared,' said the Khan; 'have ye any jinjalls?'*

'The Patél has two,' said the man.

'Run then and bring them here,—also what powder ye can find;

* Heavy wall-pieces on swivels.

bring the Patél himself too, and alarm the village. Kasim,' he continued, 'wait thou here; there is an apartment in the tower,—thither I will bring the Khanum, and what valuables we have with us. I do not fear danger, but we had better be prepared.'

In a short time the Khan returned, conducting his wife; she was veiled from head to foot, and Kasim heard them distinctly speaking as they were coming up the stairs.

'Not there, not there!' said the lady; 'alone, and in that dark place, I should give way to fears; let me ascend, I pray thee,—I am a soldier's daughter, and can bear to look on what men and soldiers can do.'

'No, no, my life, my soul!' returned the Khan, 'it is not fit for thee; if they should fire upon us, there will be danger; besides there are many men,—thou wouldst not like it; remember too I am near thee, and once the village is alarmed thou wilt have many companions.'

'I am not afraid,' she said; 'I had rather be with men than women at such a time.'

'Well, well, Ameena, rest thou here now at all events; should there be need thou canst join us hereafter.'

The Khan a moment afterwards was on the top of the tower.

'Seest thou aught more, Kasim?' he asked.

'Nothing,—the village continues to burn, and the men are there; but either the people have escaped, or they are dead, for none come out now.'

'Sound the alarm!' cried the Khan to some men below, who, bearing a large tambourine drum and a brass horn, had assembled ready for the signal. 'If the horsemen hear it, it will tell them we are on the alert.'

The deep tone of the drum and the shrill and wild quivering notes of the horn soon aroused the villagers from their sleep, and numbers were seen flying to the tower for refuge, believing the Mahrattas were truly upon the skirts of the village. The Patél was among the rest, accompanied by his family. He was soon upon the tower, and was roughly saluted by the Khan.

'Thou art a worthy man for a Patél!' cried he; 'but for me, thy village might have shared the fate of that one yonder. Look, base-born! shouldest thou like to see it burning as that is? Why wert thou not here to watch, O unfortunate?'

'I—I did not know—' stammered the Patél.

'Not know! well at any rate thou knowest now; but as thou art here, do something for thyself, in Alla's name. Where is thy gun, thy sword?'

'I can only use a gun, noble sir; and that perhaps to some

purpose. Run, Paproo,' he said to a man near him; 'bring my gun hither. Now we are awake, the Khan shall see, if there is occasion, that we can fight as well as sleep.

'I had as well go down,' said Kasim, 'and prepare the men below: the women and children can get into the tower; those whom it will not contain must remain at the foot in these houses. It will be hard if any harm reaches them there.'

In a short time all was arranged: the women and children, whose cries had been distracting, were in places of safety, and as quiet as the neighbourhood of the Mahratta horse, the sudden alarm, and the natural discordance of their own language (the Canarese) would allow them; and on the summit of the tower about twenty men, for whom there was ample room, were posted, all well armed with matchlocks. The two jinjalls were loaded, a good many men were stationed around the foot of the tower, and all were ready to give whatever should come a very warm reception.

The fire of the village burned lower and lower, and at last became only a dull red glow, with occasionally a burst of sparks. While they speculated upon the route of the horsemen, who had disappeared, a few of the wretched inhabitants of the village which had been destroyed came running to the foot of the tower.

'Defend yourselves! defend yourselves!' they cried with loud voices; 'the Mahrattas are upon you—they will be here immediately!'

'Admit one of them,' said the Khan; 'let us question him.'

The man said he had passed the horsemen, who were trying to get across a small rivulet, the bed of which was deep mud; they had not been able to find the ford, and were searching for it; but they knew of the village, were elated with success, and determined to attack it.

'They shall have something for their trouble then,' said the Khan; 'they know not that Abdool Rhyman Khan is here, and they will buy a lesson: let them come, in the name of the Most Merciful!'

'Away, some of ye!' cried the Patél to those below; 'watch at the outskirts! and, hark ye, they will come by the north side, —there is an old house there, close to the gate,—when they are near, fire the thatch; as it burns, we shall be able to see and mark them.'

'I thank thee for that,' said Kasim; 'now let all be as silent as possible. Listen for every sound,—we shall hear their horses' feet.'

There was not a word spoken. Even the women were still,

and the children; now and then only the wail of an infant would be heard from below. All looked with straining eyes towards the north side, and the best marksmen were placed there under the direction of Kasim.

'Thou art pretty sure of one,' said the Khan to him; 'I wish I could shoot as well as thou.'

'A steady hand and aim, Khan Sahib;—do not hurry; if not the man, at least thou canst hit the horse. Inshalla! we shall have some sport.'

'I had better take one of the jinjalls; the Feringhees (may they be accursed!) have sorely plagued us often by firing a cannon full of balls at us; so give me a few, I pray. I will ram them down into the piece, and it will be less liable to miss than a single bullet.'

'Mashalla! a wise thought,' said Kasim, handing him some balls; and a scattered fire of praises ran from mouth to mouth at the Khan's ingenuity: 'we shall now see whether we are to eat dirt or not.'

They were now all silent for awhile.

'Hark!' said Kasim at length; 'what is that?'

They all listened more attentively; the village dogs—first one, then all—barked and howled fearfully.

'They come!' cried the Khan; 'I have been too long with bodies of horse not to know the tramp.'

'Now every man look to his aim!' cried Kasim cheerfully; 'half of ye only fire. And you below, fire if you see them.'

Almost as he spoke, they saw the light; at first they were uncertain whether the spies had fired the old house or not—it burned so gently; but by degrees the flame crept along the outside and round the edges; then it disappeared under the thatch, and again blazed up a little. The noise increased, though they could see no one in the gloom, but they could hear very distinctly.

'If one of those owls would but pull away a little of the old roof, it would blaze up,' said the Patél. 'By Crishna, look! they have even guessed my thoughts. Look, noble Khan!'

They saw one of the scouts advance from under the cover of some of the houses, and pull violently at one of the projecting rude rafters; and instantly the flame appear beneath.

'Another pull, good fellow, and thou hast earned five rupees!' cried the Khan in an ecstasy, as he held the butt of the wall-piece; 'another pull, and we shall have a blaze like day.'

It seemed as if the fellow had heard the Khan's exclamation, for he tugged in very desperation; they heard the roof crack;

at last it fell in; and the sudden blaze, illuminating all around vividly, fell on the wild yet picturesque group which was rapidly advancing over the open space before the village.

CHAPTER VII.

The Mahratta horsemen did not perceive the snare which had been laid for them: they concluded that the fire was accidental (and opportune, since it showed them the way to their plunder), and on they came at a fast gallop,—fifty perhaps: wild figures they would have been deemed at any time,—how much more so when, brandishing their long spears, and with loud shouts, they dashed forward! The light shone broad on their muffled faces and on the gay red housings of their saddles, and glanced from their spear-points and other weapons.

'Hurree Bōl!' cried the leader to his men, turning round on his saddle, waving his sword, which all could see was dim with blood.

'Hurree! Hurree Bōl!' arose the cry from fifty hoarse voices, which mingled with the quick trampling of the horses.

'Now!' cried the Khan.

'Wait one instant, for the sake of Alla!—let them come up,' exclaimed Kasim.

They were close to the burning hut, when Kasim, whose matchlock had been steadily aimed, resting upon the parapet, fired. The leader reeled back in his saddle, waved his sword wildly in the air, and fell.

'Bismilla-ir-ruhman-ir— !' shouted the Khan; the rest of the invocation being lost in the loud report of the cannon. With it were the flashes and reports of a dozen other matchlocks; and as the smoke cleared away, they could plainly see four of the men on the ground struggling, and two or three others apparently badly hit supporting themselves in their saddles.

'Give me another gun, another gun!' cried Kasim; 'there is no time to load. Another gun, I say! Will no one hand me one?' he continued, vainly endeavouring to load his own quickly.

'Do you not hear?' exclaimed a female voice near him; and as he turned to look, he saw a figure snatch one from a villager, and hand it to him: as she did so, her veil dropped—it was Ameena!

'Come on, ye base born!' cried the Khan, who was pointing the remaining jinjall at the group, which, staggered by their loss, had halted for a moment. 'Come on, ye sons of dogs,—come on ye kafirs and idol-worshippers,—come and taste of death from the hands of true believers! Ha! do ye hesitate? then ye shall have it again, by Alla!' and he fired. 'Look you, Meer Sahib,' he cried in exultation; 'two are down—another! by the Prophet, well shot!'

'Here is another gun, Meer Sahib,' said the same sweet voice; and the lady handed him one.

'What, thou here, my pearl! Shabash! thou shouldst have shot too if thou couldst hit. So, thou wouldst not remain below; no wonder, with those screaming women: and thou art welcome here too, if thou darest to look on, and see those murdering villains go down like sparrows. Another, by Alla! See, the dog fairly rolls over and over! Why do ye not come, O valiant eaters of dirt? By your souls, come on,—we have more for ye!'

'They have had enough, I think, Khan,' said Kasim; 'they are drawing off.'

And they were indeed. The plundering band, unprovided with matchlocks, could make little impression on a village so well defended, and hastily turned about their horses; those who had remained below were informed of this by the Patél, who had descended; and, led by him, quickly advanced to the edge of the village, from whence they could fire without exposing themselves.

'Who will strike a blow with Kasim Patél?' cried the youth, who was not now to be controlled. 'Come, who will?—there are the horses saddled below.'

In vain was it that the Khan held him for an instant, and he heard the voice of gentle entreaty from the lady: he hurried down the steps, followed by several of the Khan's men, and throwing themselves on their horses they dashed after the fugitives.

They soon cleared the village, and what followed was intensely watched by the Khan and Ameena.

'Holy Alla, protect the youth!' ejaculated the lady.

'Ameen!' cried the Khan; 'look! he is upon them now, and Dilawur-Ali, Moedeen, and Fazel after him. See—one goes down beneath that cut!' for they saw the sword of Kasim flash in the light. 'He is by another; the fellow cuts at him. Well parried, by the Prophet! now give it him! A curse on the darkness,' he continued after a pause, as, shading his eyes with his hand, he endeavoured to pierce the thick gloom. 'Canst thou see, Ameena?'

'No, my lord. I lost him as you did—Alla be his shield!'

'To be sure he is: what could those cowards do against such an arm and such a heart? I tell thee, girl, we had eaten dirt but for him.'

Ameena sighed; she remembered the excited cries of the young man and his flashing eyes, as she handed him the gun. 'He is a brave youth,' she said.

A few scattered shots here and there, which were further and further removed every moment, showed that the marauders were retreating, and soon the men began to return one by one; in a few minutes they saw Kasim Ali and his companions approaching quietly, which assured them there was no more danger, and that the party had retired beyond the limits of safe pursuit.

'Come down and meet them, fairest,' said the Khan; 'they who have fought so well for us deserve a warm welcome.'

As Kasim and his companions rode up, they were greeted with hearty congratulations on their success, and all crowded round him so thickly, that he had much ado to force his way to where the Khan stood. But he reached him after some little elbowing and good-humoured remonstrance; and just at that moment, a torch which had been lighted was raised above the heads of the crowd; it disclosed his figure, apparently covered with blood.

'Holy Alla, he is wounded!' exclaimed the lady; 'he will bleed to death!' and she moved as though she would have advanced.

'Tut, tut, foolish one!' cried the Khan, holding her back; 'it ought to be gladness to thee to see the blood of thine enemies and mine. Thou art not hurt, Kasim?'

'A trifle, I believe, Khan—a slight wound on my chest from one of the rascals, which hath bled somewhat and stained my clothes; but he paid dearly for the blood he drew.'

'I'll warrant he did; and as for thy wound, we must see to it. I have some skill in such matters, and perhaps the Khanum will be able to find an old sheet or something to tie it up. So sit down here; and do thou, Ameena, search for some rags. Well, so thou canst give an account of some of them, Kasim?'

'Of two, Khan Sahib; one fellow I cut down as we started—he is living, I think—the other fought better.'

'And is dead for his pains; well, I do not begrudge thee this cut, it will do thee no harm. See, here is the Khanum with the rags—never mind her, this is no time for ceremony with such as thou. Ho! Daood, Zoolficar, some water here! and do you, Kasim, take off that vest, we shall soon see what has happened. A trifle, a trifle, after all. Alla be praised!' he continued, when the garment was removed, and the broad and muscular chest of the young man exposed to view; 'a few days will heal it up.'

But Ameena thought otherwise; she had heard of wounds, but this was the first she had seen; and a gash which, though not deep, extended half across the chest of the young man, was in her eyes a more serious matter than her lord appeared to think. She felt very faint and sick as she looked upon it, but rallied on perceiving that Kasim considered it a trifle, as indeed it was, and readily assisted to bind it up.

She was very near him, and it was exquisite pleasure to feel her gentle touch upon his shoulder, as she assisted to hold the bandages which the Khan passed round his chest; he fancied too that once her glance met his, and he could not help trying to catch it again: he succeeded at last, through the veil. Her lustrous dark eyes flashed very brightly; he could not see their expression, but it was certain to him that they had sought his own, and met them.

'We want still another handkerchief, or something, to tie over all,' said the Khan when he had finished; 'hast thou one, Ameena?'

'I have—here it is,' she replied; ungirding one from around her waist. 'The Meer Sahib is welcome to it.'

'I owe a thousand obligations,' returned Kasim; 'if I were your brother you could not have done more for me: how unworthy am I to receive such attention—I who am but your servant!'

'Do not say so,' cried both at once; 'thou art far more than this to us.'

'Ah!' thought Kasim, 'I am but a moth playing around a lamp, tempted by bright and dazzling light, and hardly as yet warned. I am a fool to think on her; but can I ever forget her face as she stood yonder and cheered me by her presence?—the second time I have seen it, but perhaps not the last.' The Khan roused him from his reverie.

'Lie down,' he said; 'there will be the less flow of blood.'

Kasim obeyed readily; for the same fair hands that had helped to bind his wound had also spread a soft mattress for him, and placed a pillow for his head. Perhaps the loss of blood had affected him a little, for in a few moments he felt drowsy and gradually fell asleep; and Ameena sate watching him at a little distance, for the Khan had gone to see what had been done with the bodies of those who had fallen.

But, as is often the case after violent excitement, his sleep, though at first heavy and profound, did not long continue thus.

Perhaps too the wound pained him, for he was restless, and moved impatiently from side to side.

The Khan was long absent, and Ameena still kept her watch; she might have withdrawn, yet there was something so exciting and novel to her in her position—it was a source of such quiet delight to her to watch the features of him who had saved her life, and now had been wounded in her defence,—and she was so thickly veiled that he could not see her even were he awake—that she remained.

Rapidly her mind brought before her the events of the last few days. Her own young life in the world had hardly begun, and yet more dangers had been present to her than she had ever pictured to herself, rife as her imagination had been upon the subject when she left her home. She had been already rescued from death, now perhaps from violence; and he who had been the sole instrument of her protection in the one case, and who had fought under her own eyes in the second, lay before her. She had hardly heard him speak, yet she thought she could remember every word he had spoken; and then came vividly to her remembrance the glance, the earnest hurried glance, which told her would have dwelt longer had it dared. And as she remembered this, her heart fluttered under sensations very new and almost painful to her; she could not define them,—but involuntarily she drew nearer to the sleeping youth and watched the more.

She saw his brow contracted as if with pain; and, as he every now and then stirred and the light fell on his features, she could observe his lips move as though he spoke, but she could not catch a word. For a few minutes it was thus, but at last he spoke interruptedly; it was of war, of the fight he had lately been engaged in; and she could distinguish a few words, defiance to the marauders, encouragement to the men around. Then there was another pause, and he slept peacefully, even as a child. 'May he rest safely, O Alla!' she said.

But again he dreamed; sounds escaped him,—low mutterings which were undistinguishable; she bent her ear even closer;—she could not hear aught for awhile that she understood, but at length there was one word which made her very soul bound within her, and caused in the moment a feeling of choking and oppression in her throat almost unbearable,—'Ameena!' it was repeated twice distinctly, yet very softly.

'Holy Alla! he knows my name!' she said mentally; 'he thinks of me—I am present to his sleeping fancies amidst war and turmoil which still pursue him. How could he have heard my name?'

But the voice of the Khan was heard at some little distance, and interrupted her chain of questions. 'He must not find me here,' she thought, rising hastily, and gently stealing from the spot into the place which had been screened off for her occupation. Indeed for the last few moments hidden thoughts had suddenly sprung forth, and she could hardly await unconcernedly, beside the sleeping youth, him who now sought her.

The Khan passed Kasim. 'He sleeps well,' he said to Daood, who was with him; 'hath any one watched by him?'

'No one, Khodawund: the men were all with my lord.'

'That was ill; one of ye should have remained; where is that idle cook? he hath no need of rest; let him sit up here, if he can keep his eyes open; and do ye all take what sleep ye can, for we shall start, Inshalla! ere noon to-morrow.'

'You are to remain with Kasim Sahib,' said Daood to the cook, rousing him, 'and not to stir till morning breaks, or he awakes—dost thou hear?'

'I do, good Daood; but methinks thou mightest sit with me too, seeing that it is near morning. By thy beard, I do not like being alone.'

'O coward! thou art not alone; see, thou hast the hero of the night lying beside thee—one who has slain some men since he last ate; whereas thou hast not even slain a fowl. I tell thee there is no danger: yonder is my bedding—I shall not be far off if thou wantest me.'

Soon all was silent around, even the village dogs had ceased to bark; the clamour of women and of crying frightened children had subsided; and, except the watchfires in several parts, which threw up their strong red glare against the sky, around which most of the villagers were assembled in groups, nothing indicated that any conflict or alarm had taken place. Scattered about, the Khan's attendants and servants lay wrapped in their sheets in deep sleep. The horses even, apparently secure of rest, had lain down, and all was still, except one of the horses which had been captured, which every now and then sent up a shrill neigh that sounded far and near in the stillness of the night. But above, on the tower, the Patél and several of his best men still kept watch.

Kasim slept still restlessly, and often sighed and muttered in his sleep. 'His thoughts are with the battle,' thought Zoolficar; 'they say it was a brave sight to see the Mahrattas go down one by one before his aim: he shot them as he would deer in the jungle—may their mothers be polluted! Alla! Alla! guide us safely now; this is the third alarm we have had in this accursed country—but hark! What was that he said?—Ameena! again

Ameena!—the Khanum—why should he dream of her? Poor youth, he would have been a fitter mate for her than that man of camps and battles. But it may not be of her he dreams—perhaps he has some one he loves of the same name. Ay, it is very likely; so dream on, Meer Sahib, may thy slumbers be lighter!'

But they were not; after little more than an hour's restless slumber, he awoke, and found the worthy functionary by his side.

'How! thou here, Zoolfoo! art thou not sleepy?'

'It was my lord's order that I should watch you, noble sir, and I only obey it. Methinks you have rested but indifferently, for your sleep has been disturbed, and you have been speaking.'

'Ah well, I have but few secrets,' he said gaily, 'so I fear not for the words; and in truth this cut is rather painful, and too tightly bandaged. See if thou canst find a barber, Zoolfoo; I will have these straps undone.'

'If my lord will trust me,' replied Zoolfoo, 'I will ease his pain. Ere I was a cook I was a barber; and Hyderabad is not an indifferent place to learn how to dress wounds. Mashalla! our young men are rare hands at street brawls.'

'Well, do thy best—at this hour it will be hard to find any one.'

Zoolfoo was as good as his word. In a short time the bandages were arranged more easily, as the bleeding had stopped in a great measure, and Kasim found himself refreshed by the change. A hooka too was not to be despised, and this Zoolfoo soon brought from among his stores.

Gradually Kasim lead him to talk of his city, of his home, of his family; he earnestly wished to know more particulars of the Khanum, of her early life, and her ill-assorted marriage. Zoolfoo mentioned his sister.

'Ay, her who thou saidst was servant in the Khanum's family.'

'The same: she was the Khanum's nurse for awhile, and she is very fond of her.'

'Why did she not bring her then?'

'She wished to come, but the Khan said she would be a trouble on the road, and he left her behind; but—'

'Perhaps the Khanum did not wish it?'

'Not wish it? Sir, she was grieved to part with her, for she had tended her from her birth, and loved her as her own daughter.'

'Then you have often heard of her?'

'I have, a thousand times. My sister was her own attendant, and never quitted her till the hour of her departure.'

'Know you then how she came to marry the Khan? You said once before that he was of no family.'

'I will tell you,' said the cook. 'Her father is a Munsubdar,* of Nizam Ali's court nominally he has good pay, and one or two villages to support his rank; but he was expensive in his youth, for he was a gay man, and perhaps not over scrupulous. Gradually the difficulties of the Government caused all the salaries of the officers to fall into arrears. Then came with that a train of distresses; the elephant was sold, some jewels pledged,—then some horses went, and their servants were discharged. There were heavy mortgages made upon the villages, and other difficulties occurred; the interest accumulated, and the creditors grew very clamorous; some more jewels were sold, and they were quieted for awhile; but lately they were in distress, I heard,—indeed my sister told me her pay and that of other servants had been reduced, and that the family denied themselves many luxuries to which they had been accustomed. This daughter, Ameena, was marriageable, and her great beauty was known; they had many offers for her, but they looked high; they thought the Huzoor † himself might ask for her, and that the fortunes of the house might rise; and while this was going on, the Khan Sahib, who had his emissaries abroad to look out for a beautiful wife, heard of her. He offered himself immediately; his low birth was not thought of, for he had great wealth and bestowed it liberally, and finally the marriage took place with much pomp. The poor child was dazzled; and you see her here, Meer Sahib, exposed to all the vicissitudes of travelling in unsettled times,—one day drowned,—another, attacked by those villainous Mahrattas,—whom your worship has freed us of,—when, rose as she is, she never ought to have left the zenankhana of a youthful and valiant lord.'

Kasim sighed involuntarily. 'It was a base thing,' he said, 'to sell one so fair and young.'

'It was, Meer Sahib,—you have rightly called it a sale; for the Khan had to pay off a heavy mortgage upon two of the villages, which has restored the family to affluence: however the thing is done now, and there is no helping it. I pity the poor Khanum, however, for she has to face two old wives, who will not thank the Khan for bringing one so young and beautiful to his house.'

'You should keep a watch over her yourself, Zoolfoo.'

'I will, so may Alla give me power!' he said earnestly; 'she does not know me as yet, but I will soon contrive to let her know, and thus I may be able to serve her at a pinch.'

'And, remember, I am ever ready to aid you,' said the young

* A nobleman who holds an office in a native court. † Prince.

man; 'I have saved her life once, and, by the blessing of Alla, no harm shall come to so fair a creature while I have power to help her.'

Just then the morning, which had been long in breaking, showed pretty plainly; and Kasim arose, and performing his ablutions, cried with a loud voice the Azan, or call to prayers. This too aroused the Khan, and joined by several others, they repeated, as indeed was their wont, their prayers together.

'I am as stout as ever, Khan Sahib, I thank you,' answered Kasim in reply to the many inquiries of the former; 'the wound pained me a trifle, and your good Zoolficar, who is very expert, loosened the bandages for me; since then it has been quite easy. But how say you—march or halt, which shall it be?'

'Let us take counsel of the Patél, he seems a decent fellow,' returned the Khan, 'and abide by his advice,—he knows the country.'

He was summoned, and the result of the consultation was advice to them to depart immediately. 'I am disinterested, noble sirs,' he said; 'for if otherwise, my own fears would prompt me to make you stay by me; but after your conduct last night I put myself and my village out of consideration.'

'And the men, Meer Sahib?'

'I had half engaged them yesterday, when the alarm was given; how say you, Patél, can we have them?'

'Surely, surely! half of those I have shall accompany you; for I fear no further molestation.'

They were summoned, and at once expressed their readiness to go; after this, the preparations were soon completed, a hasty meal of kicheree* was cooked and eaten, and, girding up their loins carefully—seeing that their arms were properly loaded—making every preparation for defence, if necessary,—the party assembled to start.

Nine of the Mahrattas had fallen in the attack; of these, two lived, desperately wounded; five horses had been secured, two had been killed, and the remainder had been carried off by the horsemen.

The horses the Khan appropriated to his own use, and generously gave what plunder was found upon them and on the bodies to be divided among the sufferers of the village they had seen burned, directing the Patél to account for the sum. He had in vain attempted to press it upon Kasim.

Now, therefore, our travellers are once more upon the wide plains, moving warily and close together: altogether they are

* Rice and pulse boiled together.

twelve good horsemen, and, with the six or seven villagers, armed with long matchlocks, and the grooms mounted on the ponies which the servants had ridden, present a very formidable appearance; while the dry gravelly road allows them to push forward at a good pace without interruption.

The road from Bellary to the Mysore country appears flat, but in reality is not so; the land rises in long and gentle undulations some thousand feet in the course of about one hundred miles,—that is, from the town of Bellary to where it enters a rugged pass between some mountains, one side of which is formed by the rough and stony back of the fort of Pencondah. As the traveller advances from Bellary, he sees these undulations, each of many miles perhaps in length; and when arrived at the top of one, expecting to descend, he finds another spread out before him, perhaps of equal length, the summit of which he must reach in like manner. The difference this causes in the climate is most remarkable; a few days' travel produces an entire revolution; and from the steaming heat of the Carnatic, at Bellary and above it, the traveller as he proceeds southward breathes a purer, cooler, and more genial atmosphere.

The heat which had existed where we began our narrative, and which rendered travelling irksome, had now given place to coolness, which even at near midday made them glad to wrap shawls or other warm garments around them; and thus, while it invigorated man and beast, enabled them to push on rapidly without fatigue.

They had travelled for two days without alarm, and were within an easy distance of the entrance of the pass, when, on arriving at the top of one of the summits we have mentioned, they saw with some alarm a body of horse before them, scattered, and apparently on the same track as themselves.

'It is the Mahrattas!' cried the Khan.

'True,' said Kasim; 'but I fear them not now—we are too strong; see, the rogues turn!'

'They do,' said the Khan; 'but never fear, let us spread out a little on each side; they think us some small party, whom they can plunder with impunity.' The little manœuvre was done, and had an instant effect. The Mahratta horsemen, who were coming down about a mile distant at the gallop, suddenly halted, held a hurried consultation for awhile, and then struck off to the right, down a road which lead to the westward, and, having gone a good distance, quite out of shot, again halted.

'They are wary fellows,' said Kasim, 'and have profited by our former lesson; but as we pass them we will fire a shot or two: that will teach them their distance, or I am mistaken.'

It was done, and had the desired effect: the horsemen moved further away, though they travelled in a parallel line. Shots were, however, discharged from time to time; and the whole party, including the lady, were amused at their consternation, as they scattered at every discharge.

Gradually, as they neared the pass, the Mahrattas dropped behind; and after they had entered the rocky valley, the first turn shut them from their view altogether.

'Now we are properly on our own ground,' said the Khan, 'and soon we shall see one of the frontier posts; there we shall be secure from all alarms, and from thence to the city there is no fear.'

As he said, after a short travel further, they approached a strong village, well garrisoned; and here, after their many perils and escapes, they rested safely for three days ere they pursued their journey; indeed Kasim's wound needed rest.

The information the Khan gave was acted upon, and a party of horse scoured the country in every direction, but without success; the marauders had made their escape, and were no more seen.

CHAPTER VIII.

LEAVING for the present the Khan and his companions to pursue their way to Seringapatam, we claim the usual privilege of writers to transport our readers where, and as suddenly, as we please, and

> 'To take up our wings and be off to the west.'

To the perfect understanding of the events connected with this veritable history, therefore, we feel ourselves obliged to retrograde a few years, and to leave the glowing climate of the East for a while, to breathe in idea the colder yet more congenial air of England.

It was on the evening, then, of a wet and sleety day of December 1785, that a large and merry family group sat around a cheerful fire in the comfortable drawing-room of the rectory of Alston, in ——shire. It consisted of the rector, his lady, and two sons, one of whom, Edward, had returned from college for the vacation, and who was a youth of perhaps eighteen years of age; his brother Charles was somewhat younger, of that awkward period of life, between school and college, which is not often productive of much gratification to the possessor, and which all desire to see changed,—fond mothers, perhaps, again to childhood,—fathers, to manhood,—and sisters, to anything more agreeable and ornamental than the awkwardness and *mauvaise honte* peculiarly attendant upon that epoch in life.

There were three girls, one between Edward and Charles, and another some years younger; a third, as yet a child. Anywhere, any individual of the family would have been very remarkable for good looks; but here, when all were assembled together, they were a sight round that cheerful blazing fire which caused the eye of the mother to glisten with something like a tear of pleasure as she looked around the circle, and the heart of the father to swell with proud satisfaction.

Mr. Compton, the rector, the second son of a baronet of the county, had early been destined to the Church. In addition to a very handsome private fortune bequeathed to him by his father, the rich living of Alston had been secured to him while he was at college, and he had succeeded to it as soon as he was of age to be ordained. He had married early in life the sister of an old friend and college chum, also a baronet of a neighbouring county, and the union had proved one of continued happiness. With an ample fortune, gentle and refined tastes and pursuits,—an excellent musician, a tolerable painter, a good classic, and with literary abilities above an ordinary standard,—Mr. Compton had resources within himself which ensured him a placid and equable enjoyment of life. A sincere and pious man, his ministry was a blessing to his numerous parishioners; and his society, where so much intelligence and accomplishment prevailed, was eagerly sought for by all the families of the county neighbourhood.

With no remarkable strength of character, Mrs. Compton was yet an admirable woman; she was possessed of but few accomplishments, but then those were not the days when youth was crammed with knowledge; she had, however, a fair share for a lady of that period. Perhaps her talent for music had partly attracted the notice, and helped, with her amiable disposition and great personal charms, to win the admiration, and eventually to secure the affections of her husband. In her career as a mother she had been kind and loving, even beyond a mother's usual fondness; and if at times her excess of affection had overpowered the sense of her duty in checking the foibles of her children, yet she had so gentle and admirable a monitor at her side, one whose advice and example she esteemed the most precious blessings vouchsafed to her, that she had been enabled not only to bring up her children in perfect obedience to her, and in strict moral and religious principles, but in that complete harmony of intercourse among themselves, the result of judicious training and pure example.

In truth so completely united a family, though perhaps not of rare occurrence, is not so often to be seen as might be desirable to society; and the young Comptons were noted through the neighbourhood for their extreme good-breeding, and for the devoted affection they bore one another.

Happy indeed as we know the family to have been,—as it must needs have been from its constitution,—it had suffered already one stroke of sorrow, which, mingling as it ever will in all the affairs of life, and with those who apparently are farthest removed from its influence, had come in a shape and at a time but little expected by any.

Their eldest son, Herbert, was a high-spirited yet fine-tempered youth. He was destined by his father for the Church, in the offices of which he himself felt such satisfaction, that no employ ment or pursuit in life, he thought, could equal the gratification afforded by them. Herbert, however, had from the first shown an unconquerable repugnance to the sacred calling. It had been proposed to him on his leaving school, preparatory to his entering on his college course; and though he had gone through one or two terms at Oxford with credit, yet he continued to implore his father so strongly not to persist in destining him to this profession that at last Mr. Compton yielded, and the plan was abandoned.

Nor was Mrs. Compton suprised to hear a declaration made with much fear and hesitation, that a military life of all others was that in which he felt assured he should succeed best, as it was most consonant to his high spirit and daring character.

Much entreaty was used—kind, gentle, loving entreaty—by both his parents, especially his mother, to whom it was an agonising thought that her first-born, her boy of whom she was so proud, should embrace a profession which would expose him to other that the ordinary dangers of life. All was however of no avail; and at the age of eighteen, or thereabouts, his father, whose family influence was great, was enabled to purchase for him a commission in a regiment of the line.

There was at that time no immediate cause to suppose that the regiment would be called out on active service; and as that to which he had been appointed was after a short time quartered in their own neighbourhood, they had the gratification of seeing Herbert happy, fond of his corps and his duties, beloved by his brother officers, and studying all the details of science connected with his new profession; and indeed his noble appearance in his uniform, and his now gay cheerful disposition—so different from what his deportment had been while in uncertainty about himself and his future career—in a great degree reconciled his parents to the change in their plans for his life.

Promotion, if the means were at hand, was no difficult matter to obtain in those days; and Mr. Compton, by the advice of a relative, a general officer who had assisted him in obtaining the commission in the first instance, had purchased Herbert on as far as a company, and was waiting for a favourable opportunity for exchanging him into a cavalry regiment. But while the negotiations for purchase were proceeding, sudden orders arrived for the regiment to proceed on foreign service,—to India in fact, where the increased possessions of the East India Company required additional protection.

This news was a thunderbolt to the family, coming as it did so unexpectedly. It might have been foreseen and thought of; but it had not, for Herbert was with them, and that was enough; and any idea of his leaving them, if distantly contemplated, had never been allowed to dwell in their hearts. It was in vain that Mrs. Compton besought Herbert, in the agony of her maternal affection, to resign, to exchange, to ask for leave of absence, to carry into effect the negotiations which had been pending.

The young man loved his mother with an intensity of affection, but he saw also to yield to its dictates in this instance would be to forfeit his honour and the obligations of his duty. Mr. Compton forbore to urge him at all; his fine feelings at once told him that the young man was right; and though it was a sore trial to part with one so dear, to relinquish him to the chances of hard service in so distant and then unknown a land, yet he did not murmur; and in many a secret prayer in his closet, and daily in his family worship, commended him, as a father's affection only can prompt prayer for a child, to the protection of that merciful Providence which had as yet bestowed on him and his unnumbered blessings.

But there was yet another on whom this unlooked-for blow fell even more heavily than on those we had mentioned. Amy Hayward, the only daughter of a gentleman of fortune, whose estate joined the fields and extensive lawns and grounds which formed the glebe of the rectory, had from the earliest times she could remember been the companion and playmate of all the Comptons. Her two brothers had shared the intimacy with her, and whenever the boys were at their respective homes, there was a daily intercourse kept up between them,—daily meetings, rambles in Beechwood Park, fishing in the brawling trout-stream which ran through it, nutting in its noble woods, and a thousand other joyous amusements peculiar to a happy country childhood.

We say country childhood, for we feel that there is the widest difference between that and a childhood spent in a town. With the former there is a store of remembrances of gentle pleasures, of those natural delights which are so inseparable to boyhood or girlhood,—when the first gushes of the deep-seated springs of feeling are expanded among the beauties of natural scenes, in themselves peaceful, and speaking quiet to the heart, ever too prone to excitement when full vent is given to joyous spirits;—where every occupation is fraught with delights, which, if the faintest remembrance remains in after life, are treasured up as the purest perhaps of all the pleasurable impressions the heart has ever known.

How different is the town boy! he is a man before his time; and in that one word how much meaning is there! How much less innocence—how many cares! his amusements lack the ease of hilarity and freedom; he sees the dull monotonous streets teeming with spectacles of vice or misery,—the endless form of busy man ever before him, instead of bright skies, the green recesses of the woods, the fresh balmy air, the thousand exquisite creations of nature, ever appealing to his best sympathies. A city can teach him little that can remain to benefit his understanding, or invigorate its keenest and most delicious enjoyment, a complete appreciation of nature in all her forms; but, on the contrary, it may induce a callousness, which too often grows upon him in after life, and causes those simple pleasures to be despised or unnoticed, in which, after all, perhaps, are contained the germs of the purest enjoyment.

Amy was a few years younger than Herbert; beautiful as a child, that beauty had grown up with her, and appeared to increase. But her features were not regular, nor could she properly be called handsome; and yet if large, lustrous, loving eyes, a fair and bright complexion, and long and light brown curling hair, with a small figure, in which roundness, activity, and extreme grace were combined, can be called beauty, she possessed it eminently. Her face too, which was ever varying in expression and lighted up with intelligence, was a fair index to her mind,—full of affection and keen perception of beauty. If Herbert had not the latter quality so enthusiastically as she had, he at least had sufficient with cultivation to make him a tolerable draughtsman; and Beechwood Park contained so many natural charms, that, as they grew up, there was scarcely a point of blue and distant landscape, rocky brawling stream, or quiet glade, which they had not sketched in company.

We have said they had been inseparable from childhood—ay, from the earliest times; though the young Comptons and Haywards joined in all their pastimes, yet Herbert had ever a quiet stroll with Amy. Her garden, her greenhouse, her rabbits, her fowls, her gold and silver fish—all were of as much interest to him for her sake as to herself. And so it had continued: childish cares and pastimes had given place to more matured amusements and pursuits, and the intercourse of the elders of the families continued to be so harmonious, that no interruption had ever occurred to their constant society.

If Herbert or Amy had been questioned on the subject, they could hardly have said that as yet they loved; but it would be unnatural to suppose that, knowing and appreciating each other as they did, they should not have loved, and that ardently. The fire had been kindled long ago, and slumbered only for a passing breath of excitement to fan it into a bright and enduring flame.

It was, then, on the day which followed a night of intense anguish to all—that on which no longer any opposition had been made to Herbert's departure, and they were beginning to bear to talk of it with some calmness, that Mr. Compton said to his lady, as they sat after breakfast, 'You had better write this sad news to the Haywards, my love; they have always felt such an interest in Herbert's welfare, that they ought to hear this from ourselves, before it is carried there by the servants, and perhaps broken abruptly to them.'

'I will be the bearer of the news myself,' said Herbert, starting up; 'no one ought to tell it but me; and it would distress you, dear mother, to write it; besides, I promised to go over to Amy, either yesterday or to-day, to sketch with her, as she wants to see the new style I have learned.'

'Thank you, my kind darling,' she replied; 'you have indeed saved me the necessity of inflicting a pang on them, and one on myself too. And you must screw up your courage to the sticking-place when you mention it to Amy,' she added almost gaily, with some emphasis on the name; 'poor child, she will grieve to hear it indeed!'

'Yes, she will be sorry, very sorry, I know,' said Herbert; 'but it can't be helped now, and I must put as good a face as I can upon the matter to them all. I will be as gay as I can,' he said, taking up his hat and opening the door, 'and will not be long away.'

Poor fellow! the last words were tremulous enough for a gay captain to utter, and his mother and father thought so too.

'It will be unexpected to them,' he said after a painful pause.

'Very indeed, dearest,' was the only reply she could make, for her tears were flowing silently and fast.

CHAPTER IX.

For the convenience of the families, a gravel walk had been made through the rectory fields to the little river which divided them from the park. Across this Mr. Hayward had thrown a very elegant rustic bridge, the joint design of Amy and Herbert, to replace a rude yet picturesque one formed of planks with side-rails, which had existed previously.

Over this, Herbert rapidly passed onwards into the park; and avoiding the walk, which had been carried by a considerable detour through some beautiful glades, struck at once across the sward, in a direct line for the house.

At any other time, the extreme beauty of the day, and of the park under its influence, would not have failed to attract the attention of the young man, and to have caused him to stop more than once to admire for the hundredth time some noble avenues of beech and oak—some picturesquely-grouped herd of deer or flock of sheep, or some exquisite effect of light and shade as the soft floating clouds transiently caused it. He would perhaps have sauntered gently; but now he hurried on, wrapt in his own reflections, and they were not of the most agreeable or intelligible kind. The flocks of sheep as he passed, fled startled at his quick approach, while the deer raised themselves from their recumbent postures and gazed wonderingly at him, whom they almost knew.

'By Heaven!' he exclaimed, as he reached the hall-door and rang for admittance, 'I hardly know what I am come about, or what to say. But it must be done,—so I will let things take their chance. I can invent no plan of proceeding which will spare them pain or myself either. No,—better leave it to the force of circumstances.'

'Is any one at home, Edward?' he said to the footman who answered the bell.

'Yes, sir, Master and Miss Amy are in the study.'

'Thank you;' and he passed on with a beating heart.

'Well, noble captain, what news?' 'Ah, I am so glad you are come, Herbert, I want you *so* much,' were the greetings of the father and daughter, in their hearty, unformal, and affectionate manner. 'Mamma tried to persuade me to go out with her to pay a visit to the Somervilles,' continued Amy, 'but I would not, for I felt somehow or other that you would come, and, as I said, I want you. You have been such a truant of late, that I was really beginning to be half angry with you. So ponder well on the escape you have made of my wrath by this opportune appearance.'

Herbert said something about his duties, only half intelligible to himself.

'Yes,' continued the light-hearted girl, 'those duties are horrid things; ever since you have been a soldier, we have seen nothing of you at all, and I am very much disposed to be very angry with your colonel and all your regiment for not giving you perpetual leave of absence. I declare I have no companion now, for you know the boys are both at college. He is very naughty not to come oftener,—is he not, papa?'

'Perhaps Herbert is right, my love, in not humouring so giddy a girl as yourself. But here he is now, so make the most of him, for there may be another week or fortnight of duty which he has come to tell you of.'

How near he had guessed the truth,—unconsciously—only so far short of its sad reality!

Herbert winced. 'I am sure if I had but known that I was wanted, I would have come,' he said hesitatingly; 'but the truth is, I have been occupied both at home and at the barracks for the last few days by some business which I could not leave.'

'Well, your being here proves that to be all over, and so you are not to think of going away to-day,' said Amy. 'I want you to help me with a drawing I am doing for Lady Somerville; and as she is a great connoisseur, it must be as good as our united heads and fingers can make it; and before we sit down to that, I wish you to run down to the river with me, and sketch a group of rocks, hazel-bushes, and reeds, which I want for the foreground of my picture. Now, no excuses, Herbert, though you look as if you were going to begin some,—I will not hear them. Wait here with papa, till I put on my bonnet and get my sketch-book.

'Now, don't let him go, I pray you, papa,' she continued, looking back from the door she had just opened, 'for I shall not be five minutes away.'

'You hear your doom, Herbert,' said Mr. Hayward gaily; 'so

come, sit down, tell me all about your regiment, and how this exchange of yours prospers. A dashing young fellow like you ought to be in the cavalry, and I hope to hear of your soon exchanging the scarlet for the blue.'

'That is all off, I am sorry to say, sir,' replied Herbert.

'Off! what do you mean? Surely your father told me that he had lodged the money for the exchange, and that the matter had only to pass through the forms of the War Office.'

'So he had; but an event has happened which has put an end to all our hopes upon the subject.'

'What, is the man dead?'

'No, sir, he is well enough, but—' and Herbert hesitated.

'But what, Herbert? If there is anything that I can do,—you know there can be no ceremony between us.'

'No, no, sir, I well know that; and—'

'Why what is the matter with the boy?' cried Mr. Hayward, observing that Herbert seemed to be struggling with some strong emotion; 'has anything happened?'

'You may as well know it at once,' replied Herbert, mastering his feelings. 'I am come on purpose to tell it to you, lest you should hear it in some out-of-the-way manner. My regiment is ordered abroad, and I am to go, of course.'

'Well, I am glad to hear it,' said Mr. Hayward; 'you will have a pleasant continental frolic, and see something of the world;—and sorry too, since we shall lose you for a time.'

'But our destination is not the continent, but India,' said Herbert sadly.

'Good God! you don't mean that,' exclaimed Mr. Hayward, rising. 'Pardon me, my dear boy, that I should have spoken lightly on a subject which is so distressing. India! that indeed is a sad word: can nothing be done to prevent this? cannot you exchange? cannot—'

'I would not if I were able, dear sir,' said Herbert. 'I feel this to be my duty; I could not in any honour leave the regiment at such a time, without a suspicion of the basest motives being attached to my character.'

'Tut, tut, Herbert! the thing is done every day, so let not that distress or prevent you.'

Herbert shook his head.

'I say it is, I could tell you a dozen instances.'

'Perhaps you might, where the only enemy was the climate; but our possessions in the East are menaced, and the service will be active. I learned this when the news came to the regiment; and as none of the officers have attempted an exchange, except one or two whose characters are not high, I feel that I cannot.'

'And you are right, Herbert,' said Mr. Hayward, after a pause, 'you are right. God help your parents! your poor mother—this will be a sad blow to her!' and he paused, as a tear glistened in his eyes.

'It was at first, certainly, sir; but they are already more composed, and are beginning to bear to talk of it.'

'And how soon are you to go? The Government will give you some time, surely, for preparation.'

'Very little, I am sorry to say. We march for Dover on Monday, and sail, we hear, in ten days or a fortnight.'

'Monday! Bless me, and to-day is Thursday; this is the worse news of all. Poor Amy, what will she say?'

'Yes, sir,' said Herbert, 'I want your advice, whether to mention it to her myself or not. I cannot refuse to accompany her now; indeed, you saw she would take no denial. I will do exactly as you please.'

'Why, it is an unpleasant matter to any of us to think or speak of, and I really do not know what to say. But as you are the person concerned, and can give her every information yourself,' continued Mr. Hayward, after a pause, 'perhaps you had better talk it over with her. Break it as gently as you can, however, for it would be useless to deny to you that she will be very sorry to hear it.'

'Come, Herbert!' cried Amy, opening the door; 'I have been longer away than I thought. Come, here are books and paper, and my stool for you to carry; so make haste.'

'You will be discreet with her, Herbert,' said Mr. Hayward gently, giving his hand.

Herbert could only press it in acknowledgment. In a moment afterwards they were gone.

Mr. Hayward turned to the window involuntarily, to watch them as they descended the gentle slope of the lawn. There was a vague thought in his mind that they had better not have gone; but as he could find no reason for the idea, he dismissed it. He was a benevolent, simple-hearted man; he had had neither the necessity nor the inclination to study character, and could not at once estimate the effect such a communication as his daughter was about to receive would have upon her; nor did it at once strike him that the long and intimate association she had held with Herbert could have produced any tenderer feeling than she had ever expressed or appeared to entertain. Her mother, had she been there, might have judged differently; but, as Mr. Hayward soliloquised, as their retreating figures were lost to his view behind a low shrubbery, 'Matters must take their own course now; it is too late to recall them.'

Onwards they went; leaving the broad walk which led by the side of the lawn and shrubberies, they at once struck across the park, down one of the noble glades of beech-trees from whence the place took its name. The day was bright and warm—one of those blessed days of June, when all nature seems to put forward her choicest productions for the gratification and admiration of man—when cowslip and daisy, buttercup and wild anemone, with a thousand other flowers of lowly pretensions yet of exquisite beauty, have opened their bright blossoms to the sunlight, and are wooing it in silent thankfulness.

The verdant carpet beneath them was full of these, glowing in their freshest bloom; the sheep and lambs, dotted here and there upon every slope, lazily cropped the short, soft herbage; and the tinkling of their bells and the faint bleating of the lambs, now distant, now near, mingled with the hum of the many bees which busily drew their loads of sweets, roaming from flower to flower. Butterflies of many hues, their gorgeous wings glaring in the bright light, fluttered swiftly along, coquetting as it were with the flowers, and enjoying in their full vigour the sunny brightness of their short lives.

There was no wind, and yet a freshness in the air which tempered the heat of the sun; the beech-trees, with their shining leaves, appeared sleeping in the sunlight, and as if resting, during the short period there might be allowed them, from their almost ceaseless waving. Far around them the park stretched away into broad glades, some ended by woods, others presenting peeps of blue and dim distance; while through all there was a vapour floating, sufficient only to take off the harshness from every outline, whether of tree or distance, and to blend the whole harmoniously into that soft dreamy appearance, so exquisite and so soothing to behold.

'How lovely the park is to-day, Herbert!' said Amy, 'is it not? Every step we take seems to present a new picture which ought to be drawn. Look now at that group of sheep and deer almost intermixed; the deer have chosen the fern which is partly under that magnificent beech, the sheep are all among them, and their young lambs enjoying their merry gambols; the light is falling in that beautiful chequered manner which I strive in vain to represent; and yet how great are the masses, how perfect the unstudied composition, how exquisite the colour! The brightest and warmest green, spangled with flowers, is before us; this is broken by the shadows: beyond the tree there is a delicious grey, melting imperceptibly into the most tender blue. Is it not a picture now, Herbert?'

'A lovely one indeed, Amy; a study worthy of Berghem or Cuyp. What exquisite perceptions of nature must they have had! their pictures, and those of many of the same class, how simple! and yet painted with the most consummate art and nicest finish. Scarcely a flower escapes them, yet there is not one too many represented, nor one in any way interfering with the harmony of their colouring. I often long for such power; for we only can appreciate their skill and genius, by our own awkward attempts to imitate them. Indeed, when I look on the works of any of these great masters, my own appear so contemptible in my eyes, that I am tempted to forswear the gentle craft altogether.'

'Indeed, you are to do no such thing, Herbert, but help me to sketch, and to blunder on through many a drawing yet, I have no idea of being put out of conceit of my own performances, for which I have a high respect, I assure you. But come, if we stay loitering by every old beech-tree and group of sheep or deer, I shall get no sketch done in time for you to copy on my drawing, and shall be obliged perhaps to listen to some terrible excuses of duty or business. So come, we have yet a good way to walk.'

Beguiling the way, little more than a quarter of a mile, by gentle converse upon familiar, yet to them interesting subjects, they reached the busy, murmuring river,—now stealing quietly under a bank,—now chafed in its passage over a few stones,—here eddying past a rock and covered with white foam,—there widening out into a little pool, partly natural, partly artificial, the glassy surface of which was broken into circles by the rapid rising of the trout, which eagerly leaped after the flies that sported upon it.

There was a small pathway beside the stream which had been the work of all the boys some years ago; in some places it wound through thickets of alder and hazel, which met above it, forming a green alcove impervious to the sun; again, under some mossy bank or wide-spreading ash, where a rustic seat had been erected. Further as it advanced, it led round a projecting bank to a little open báy surrounded by rocks, one of which jutted out boldly into the stream that brawled noisily past it; and the open space, once a level spot of greensward, had been laid out irregularly in a little garden, which now bloomed with many sweet and beautiful flowers, of kinds despised perhaps nowadays, but not the less lovely for all that. Tall hollyhocks there were, and roses;

and honeysuckles had been trained up against the rocks, with jessamine, clematis, and other creepers, which poured forth their fragrance on the air.

Many a time had the little circles of Beechwood and Alston united here, and many a joyous pic-nic and dance had occupied hours which could never be forgotten by any.

It was a lovely spot indeed; the rocky bank around the little circle was, as we have said, covered with creepers; festoons of ivy hung from above, and over all nodded some ash or other forest-trees, mingled with underwood and fern. On the opposite side of the river, worn away by the water which had run past it for countless years, the bank was high and steep, covered with ivy and drooping fern; all sorts of little peering wild flowers lurked among its recesses, with mosses whose colours glistened like emerald and gold; above it grew two or three noble ashes and beeches, whose feathery foliage descended in minute and graceful sprays down to the bank, and waved with every breath of wind.

A tiny summer-house, or hermitage as they had called it, made of pine-logs and thatched with heath, stood in the corner formed by the projection round which they were passing; and thither they directed their steps, for it commanded a view of the whole of the little amphitheatre, the rock, the river, and the bank beyond. Though there was a kind of garden, yet there was nothing artificial in its appearance; the few flowers looked almost like the spontaneous growth of the spot, and did not interfere with the perfectly wild yet beautiful character of the scene, which otherwise was as nature in one of her bountiful moods had fashioned and left it,—a nook wherein man might worship her the more devoutly. The whole glowed under the bright beams of the noonday sun, and there was not a breath of wind to disturb the complete serenity and dreamy effect of the place.

'Now sit down here, Herbert,' said Amy, 'and begin yonder by that ivy. You are to draw me all the jutting rock, the water eddying round it, the reeds here by the brink, and give me a bit of distance beyond; and I do not think,' she added with enthusiasm, 'that the world could show a lovelier spot to-day than our little hermitage. I only wish I could grasp it all, and put it upon my paper as I see it: do not you often feel so?'

'Indeed I do, Amy, and am vexed at my own clumsy attempts to imitate nature; but I will do my best for you to-day. I may not soon again have such an opportunity.

'You mean there will not be such another delicious day, Herbert; but I do not despair now of the weather.'

Herbert was silent; he had thought his remark might have led to the subject he did not know how to break. He looked at his companion, and he felt how hard it would be to leave one so beautiful, nay, so loved as she was. He had never spoken to her of love; but now the hour approached when he was to leave her, and there were feelings within him struggling for expression which he could ill restrain; his thoughts oppressed him, and though he continued to sketch he was silent.

'You are very dull and absent to-day, Herbert,' she said at length, as she continued looking over his shoulder; 'but you are drawing that foliage and the old rock very nicely, so I must not scold you;' and again she continued to converse. She tried many topics, she spoke eloquently and feelingly of her boundless love of nature, she told him what she had been reading, asked him a thousand questions about his duties, his regiment, his companions,—all of which he answered mechanically; for his heart was too busy for him to heed the replies his tongue gave.

'Upon my word, I do not know what to make of you to-day, Herbert,' she cried, laughing, as he had given some absurd reply to one of her questions or sallies which was not in any way relative to it. 'You draw most meritoriously, and better than ever I saw you before, but my words fall on heedless ears; for I am sure you have neither heard nor understood a word of what I have been saying this hour past. Now make haste,—a few touches will finish that, and you can add figures afterwards if you like. I am sure you are unwell. If you are so, I insist on your giving up the drawing.'

'I shall never again have such an opportunity, dear Amy,' he said; 'not at least for a long time, so I had better do all I can now.' There was much sadness in his tone.

'What do you mean by that? this is the second time I have heard you say it,' she replied anxiously; 'you surely cannot be going to leave us again; the regiment has only been here two months, and—tell me, I beseech you, Herbert,' she continued as he looked up from the drawing, and distress was very visible upon his countenance; 'tell me what you have to say. Why do you look so sad?'

'Because, dear Amy, I have news which will pain you,—that is, I think it will,—for we have ever been so linked together: you have guessed the truth,—I am indeed to leave,—and that so soon that my own brain is confused by the sudden orders we have received.'

She turned as pale as death, and her lips quivered; all the misery and danger she had ever heard of foreign service rushed at once overwhelmingly into her thoughts. She tried to speak, but could not.

'It must be told sooner or later,' he thought, laying down the sketch and drawing towards her; he continued, though with much difficulty in preserving his composure,—

'The regiment is ordered upon service, Amy, and after many thoughts I find I have no alternative but to accompany it. We march for Dover in a few days; the transports, we hear, will meet us there; and after we have embarked, the convoy fleet for India will join us at Portsmouth or Plymouth.'

'For India!' were the only words the poor girl could utter, as she sunk helpless and fainting upon the seat.

CHAPTER X.

'Amy, dear Amy!' cried the young man, agonised by her bitter sobs, which ceased not, though he had raised her up, and supporting her hardly-sensible form strove to console her, but in vain. 'Amy, speak to me! one word, only one word, and you will be better: call me by my name—anything—only do not look so utterly wretched, nor sob so bitterly. God knows I have enough to bear in leaving you so suddenly, but this misery is worst of all. Dear Amy, look up! say that you will try to conquer this, and I shall have the less to reproach myself with for having told you of so much.' But she spoke not; she could not utter one word for the choking sensation in her throat. She passed her hand over it often, tried in vain to swallow, and gasped in the attempt.

'Good God, you are ill!' exclaimed Herbert hurriedly; what can be done? what can I get? My own Amy!—dearest, dearest!—do not look so.' But his entreaties were of no avail against her overpowering grief; she had struggled with the hysterical feeling till she could no longer oppose it, and yielded to its influence.

Distracted, Herbert knew not what to do. Aid there was none nearer than the house, and he could not leave her—he dared not. He raised her gently, and bore her like a child to the river's brink. He unloosed her bonnet, and sprinkled water on her face; it revived her; and after some time and difficulty he succeeded in making her drink a little from his closed hands.

She recovered gradually, but lay sobbing still bitterly upon the grass, weakened and exhausted by the violence of her emotions. Herbert continued to hang over her in the greatest anxiety, and to implore her to speak in the tenderest epithets. He had not discovered how dear she was to him till he had heard his fate; and he had tried to argue himself out of the belief, but without avail. His high sense of honour then came to his aid, and he thought that it would be wrong to declare such feelings to her when he might never return; and fervently as he loved her, he could have spared her the bitterness of that lingering hope which is so akin to despair.

But in those moments he had forgotten all; thoughts of the past and for the future, all centred in intense affection for the helpless being before him, whose artless mind had not attempted any disguise of her devoted love for her companion of so many years.

At last she recovered sufficiently to raise herself up; and this, the first sign of consciousness she had given, was rapture to Herbert. He bent down to her, and attempted to lift her to her feet. She was passive in his hands, even as a weak child; and partly supporting, partly carrying her, he led her to the hermitage. There he seated her on the rustic bench, and kneeling down beside her, while one arm was passed round her,—for she could not have sat alone without support,—he poured forth with the impetuosity and tenderness of his disposition his vows of love, and his entreaties for some token that he had not angered her by his abruptness.

'But one word, my Amy! but one word, dearest!—one word, that in those far distant lands I may feed on it in my heart, while your beautiful face is present to my imagination. Dearest, we have loved each other with more than children's love from infancy; we have never expressed it, but now the trial has come, and you will not be the one to deny yours at such a time. O Amy, speak to me one word to assure me that I may call you mine for ever!'

Much more he said, and more passionately, but her hand was not withdrawn from his, nor did she remove herself from him. A tear at last forced its way from her closed eyelids, for she dared not to open them. Soon others followed; they fell hot and fast upon his hand for a little while; and at length, as she strove to speak, but could not, she was no longer able to control her emotion, and she fell upon his neck and wept aloud.

The young man strained her to his heart, and as he wiped the fast-falling tears from her eyes, he poured such consolation as he could find words to utter into her perturbed heart. She did not question his love,—she had no doubt of that; but there was one all-engrossing thought—his absence—beneath which even her light and joyous spirit quailed; and while it caused her to shiver in very apprehension of perils which her thoughts could not define, she clung the closer to him, and strove to shut out the evils with which her mental visions were overcast.

The trying test of coming absence, of dangers to be braved, hardships to be endured, had at once broken down all barriers of formality, and opened to them the state of each other's affections in that perfect confidence, that pure reliance,—the gentle growth of years, it is true,—but which had at once expanded without a check, and would endure for ever.

Who can tell the exquisite pleasure of such a first embrace? Pure love, such as theirs, had little of the dross of passion in it. The knowledge that years must elapse ere they could meet again, the silent dread that it might never be, put a thought of possession far from them; and in the perfect purity and ecstasy of feeling of those moments,—in the indulgence of thoughts, new, yet so inexpressibly sweet to them,—it is no wonder in that sequestered and lovely spot, that hours should have passed, and time should have been unheeded; nor was it until the lengthened shadows warned them of the decline of the day, that they could speak of parting, or of the object of their visit.

The sketch had lain on the ground unheeded. Amy took it up. 'It will be to me the silent witness of what has this day happened,' she said, 'and the dearest treasure I possess, Herbert, when you are gone from me. Now one little favour I beg, that you will sketch in ourselves,—me, as I lay fainting on the bank yonder, and you as you bent over me; for I think it was there and then I first heard you say you loved me, Herbert. To me it will be a comfort and a solace till you return, and then we will come here together, and you shall see that not a shrub or flower has been altered. Four years you said, dearest! they will soon pass, and I confess I have hope beyond what I thought I should ever have possessed. Four years! methinks in anticipation they are already gone, and we sit here,—you a bronzed soldier with a thousand tales for me to hear, and I will sit at your feet and listen, your unchanged and unchangeable Amy.'

Herbert regarded her with intense admiration, for her sadness had passed away; and though tears trembled in her bright eyes with every word she spoke, there was a joyous tone in her voice and in her expression; and his spirit caught that hope from hers which, under other circumstances, would have been denied him.

'Willingly, most willingly, dearest,' he said, taking the drawing from her; and in a few moments he had sketched in the figures;—she, raising herself up, had recovered consciousness, and he, bending anxiously over her, had implored her to speak to him. There was such force and tenderness in the attitudes that it told the simple story at a glance.

'It is too plain, Herbert,' she said half reproachfully; 'I shall not dare to show any one your boldest and by far most beautiful sketch; nay, you are even making a likeness of me, which is too bad; but I need not fear, for no one shall ever see it but myself. My last look shall be of it at night, and with that my last thought shall be with you. Now that is enough; I will not have another touch, lest you spoil it; give it me, let me carry it home, and miser-like lock it up from every one but myself.'

'You may have it if you will, dearest, but I must beg it for to-night at least. I will make a small sketch from it, and will bring it over early to-morrow.'

'It is only upon your promise not to keep it longer than to-morrow morning that you may have it, Herbert. I am nearly inclined to make you stay at Beechwood to copy it, lest anything should befall it; but I am not selfish enough to detain you from those who love you as dearly as I do.'

Slowly they retraced their steps through every bowery path and open glade; the blossoms of the lime and horse-chestnut filled the air with luscious sweetness, and their broad shadows were flung wide over the richly-coloured sward. They wandered on, hardly heeding the luxuriant beauty of the landscape, with their arms twined round each other, while they spoke in those gentle, murmuring tones, which, though low, were yet distinct, and of which every word was striven to be remembered for years afterwards.

'My father must know all,' said Amy, as they approached the house; 'we have nothing to fear from him, and therefore nothing to conceal; but I dare not speak, Herbert, so—'

'I do not flinch from the trial, dearest,' was his reply. 'If you can bear it, I would rather you were present, but—'

'No, no, no! I could not bear it, Herbert,' replied the blushing girl; 'and I had better not be present, I know, for we should both lose courage. No, you must tell all to papa; and leave me to my own solitude for a while, for indeed I require it. And now here we are at home; I need not say—for you know papa as well as I do—conceal nothing, for we have nothing to conceal.'

She ran lightly on through the hall, and up the broad staircase. Herbert followed her beautiful figure till he could see it no longer; then listened till he heard the door of her chamber close after her. 'She has gone to pray for herself and me,' he thought, and thought truly. The study-door was before him; his heart beat very fast, and his hand almost trembled as he placed it upon the handle; but his resolution was made in an instant, and he passed in.

Mr. Hayward laid down the book he had been reading, and took the spectacles from his nose as Herbert entered. 'You are a pretty pair of truants,' he said cheerfully; 'an hour or two indeed! why 'tis just six o'clock! and where is Amy?'

'She is gone to her room, sir, for a short time; she said she would not be long absent.'

'And what have you been about? Come, let me see. You know I am a great admirer of your spirited sketches, Herbert; so hand me your day's work, which ought to be an elaborate affair, considering the time you have been about it.' And he replaced his spectacles.

Herbert blushed crimson; he felt his face glowing painfully; he had forgotten the roll of paper, which he had kept in his hand, and he could not deny that it was the sketch Mr. Hayward wished to see. He hesitated a little, grew somewhat indecisive in his speech: and, as the old gentlemen was beginning to suspect the truth, Herbert had told all, and stood before him glowing with manly emotion and proud feelings of rectitude. There was nothing to conceal, Amy had said, so he concealed nothing. He told him how he had intended not to have spoken to her; but how, overcome by the anguish of seeing her so prostrated by grief, he had revealed to her all his feelings, even at the risk of her displeasure. 'Amy loves me, sir,' he continued proudly; 'nor does she seek to deny it. We have too long shared each other's thoughts for any reserve to exist between us; and to you we fearlessly commit ourselves, in frank confession of our fault, if we have committed any.'

Mr. Hayward only mused for a moment; he loved Herbert too well, and had known him too long, to hesitate. 'May God bless you both, my dear boy!' he cried, rising from his chair, and extending his arms to embrace the young man. 'May God bless you! If there had not been this dreadful absence to contemplate, I should have counted this one of the happiest moments of my life; as it is, I am thankful that Amy is loved by such an one as you, Herbert; but where is she? I can remain no longer without seeing you together.' He rang the bell.

'Tell Miss Hayward that I want her here as soon as possible,' said the old gentleman to the servant.

A few minutes only elapsed, during which neither spoke. At

last her light footstep was heard on the stairs; descending slowly it passed over the hall so lightly that even Herbert's ear could hardly detect it; he fancied it hesitated at the door, and he flew to open it; and the smile of joy, of triumph, which met her hurried glance, served in some measure to assure her; her father stood with open arms, and lips quivering with emotion. 'God bless you! God bless you!' was all he could utter, as she rushed into them, and sobbing, hid her burning face in his bosom; nor did she venture to withdraw it for long, nor he to disturb her; the gush of joy which welled from his heart, as he strained her to it, was too pure to relinquish easily.

'If I have been wrong, dear father, forgive me!' was all she was able to utter, after a silence of some moments.

'Nay, I have nothing to forgive, my sweet pet,' he said: 'I had looked for this happiness only as a consummation of my dearest wishes, and it is now as unexpected as grateful. But I will keep you no longer, Herbert,' he said to him, 'nor must Amy either, for there are others who have stronger claims upon you than we have, and I dare not detain you from them. I wish however, and Amy will second the wish I know, that you would come over to-morrow as early as you can, and give us a quiet day and evening together; it will be as much a source of gratification to you to dwell on when you are away, as it will be to us; so say, will you come?'

At any time the invitation would have been welcome, but now the imploring looks of the fair girl were arguments which could not be resisted.

'I will be with you as early as I can,' Herbert replied, 'as soon as I can complete a task I have here, and I will not leave you till night; so for the present farewell, and I beg you to procure me the forgiveness, and I will add the blessing, of her whom I hope to call a second mother.'

'You need have no doubts,' said Mr. Hayward; 'you have nothing to apprehend, but, on the contrary, I can assure you that this subject will be one of great delight to her; so once more, God bless you!'

Amy followed him to the hall-door, apparently to shut it after him, but she passed out with him, after a moment's coquetting with the handle. 'You will not fail, dear Herbert? I could not bear disappointment now,' she said to him, her eyes filling and sparkling like violets with dew-drops hanging in them.

'Nor for worlds would I give you one moment's pain, dearest; fear not, I shall be with you soon after noon to-morrow. Good-bye, and God bless you!'

Perhaps it was that they had approached very nigh each other as they spoke, and he could not resist the tempting opportunity, or perhaps,—but it is of no use to speculate,—certain it is that he drew her to him gently, and imprinted one fervent kiss on her lips. She did not chide him, but felt the more cheerful afterwards that she had received it.

Herbert hurried home, and instantly sought his parents; he told them all, nor concealed from them one thought by which he had been actuated, nor one struggle against his love which he had failed to overcome. They were both much affected, for indeed it was a solemn thing to contemplate the plighting of their son's faith with Amy, on the eve of such a separation. Yet they were gratified; and in their prayers that night, and ever afterwards, they commended the beloved pair to the guardianship and protection of Him whom they worshipped in spirit and in truth.

CHAPTER XI.

THE morrow came—a bright and joyous day, on which the spirit of beauty and of love revelled in every natural creation, and was abroad over the whole earth,—a day of dreamy, voluptuous repose, when one feels only fitted to hold silent converse with nature in intense admiration of the glorious perfection of her works.

The sun was almost overpoweringly bright, and the world abroad rejoiced in his beams. Man everywhere should have rejoiced too; yet there were some hearts which his effulgence could not illumine, which his cheering influence could not enliven. The breakfast-table at the rectory was a silent one, where heretofore all had been joyous and cheerful; for it was useless to struggle against the grief which pervaded the whole family. Mr. Compton and Herbert strove the most manfully and with best success to cheer the rest and themselves, but Mrs. Compton dared not look at any one; and she sat silently, with quivering lips, and eyes filled with tears, of which she was unconscious, except as those drops, starting from the pure fountain of a mother's love, ran down upon her cheek, and were hastily brushed away. Her eyes were now fixed upon vacancy, and again wandered to her son, and were withdrawn only when it became agony to repress the emotion she felt.

Who can fathom the depth of a mother's love for such a son, one on whom she had doated, even to weakness, from his birth? We dare not attempt to depict it, nor can it be expressed; but it has been felt by millions, and will continue to be so while the tenderest and holiest feelings of love are continued as blessings to us.

Herbert fulfilled his appointment faithfully; ere he had passed the little bridge many paces, the maiden met him, for she had long sat and watched for him; and they strolled on, away through the most sequestered glades of the park, resting at whiles on hillocks of thyme and mossy banks, which courted occupation as they wandered by. Time flew lightly, and in that perfect bliss which can be only known once,—so pure are the sensations, that the heart does not hope to feel them again; and which, if once enjoyed, remain indelibly impressed upon it for ever.

They wandered on; they had no thought for anything around them, no eyes to behold beauties, except in the luxury of their own thoughts. Their minds were like stringed instruments in perfect unison,—each touch by the one was responded to by the other with harmony. They spoke of the future with confidence, with that pure hope only known to the young who have never felt the agony of hope deferred. There was no cloud now over their bright future. Four years! to look back on it was nothing; they could remember the occurrences of four years ago as though they were yesterday, and those to come they thought would pass as fast.

He spoke to her of the gorgeous East, of the temples, the palaces, the almost fairy-land he was to see, and they pictured to themselves a land so bright and fair that they longed to roam over it in company. He promised her letters,—not cold formal ones written at a sitting, but daily records of hi thoughts, and minute descriptions of the varied scenes he should pass through. He promised sketches too, by every opportunity, of everything about him,—of his tent, his room, even of his table where he should sit and hold conversations with her in writing, as well as of the scenery and magnificent remains of the country.

And in this exquisite converse all care for the time had passed away from them; for though the feeling of parting did often float through their minds, yet it would have been hard had it been allowed to damp the buoyancy of two such naturally cheerful hearts as theirs; and they entered the drawing-room of Beechwood together, glowing with such pleasure, and with such joyous expressions upon their faces, that Mrs. Hayward, who had been long waiting for them, and had expected a far different scene, was affected with joy instead of sorrow; and though the result was much the same, yet her equanimity was soon restored, and the hearty blessing and greeting she gave the pair, as they advanced to receive it, gratified her benevolent and loving heart.

Herbert stayed with them till the night was far spent; there was perfect confidence and perfect love among the party; and if these are seldom vouchsafed together in life's pilgrimage, they make the period of that intercourse so marked in its purity of character that it is the better appreciated and the longer remembered.

But sadness came at length,—the dreaded day of departure drew nigh;—the Sabbath, Herbert's last day with his parents, was held sacred by both families; and as they now had a common interest in him who was about to leave, they passed it together at the rectory. There is little pleasure in dwelling upon a scene so sad,—in depicting the sorrow of those who were assembled. Mr. and Mrs. Hayward did the utmost their kind hearts could suggest to comfort their friends, and in some measure succeeded; but the time passed heavily, the conversation, however it was directed, only tended to the same point,—but that was too painful a one to be discussed freely, and was only alluded to with difficulty. Mrs. Compton tried in vain to sit out the evening in the drawing-room, and at length was obliged to retire to her own chamber, where she was followed and tended by her friend and Amy with true affection.

Poor Amy! she had a hard part to bear. To conceal her own miserable feelings, in order that she might not be an additional weight upon the already oppressed spirits of others, was a task she was barely equal to; yet she strove well to master her grief, and to all appearance hers was the only light heart of the party. Herbert had promised to accompany her home through the park, so that she would be spared the misery of bidding him farewell before others, even though they might be her own parents, and this also consoled her.

In their evening worship, Mr. Compton took occasion to allude to Herbert's departure; his prayer was beautiful and simple, and in fervent supplication he earnestly commended him to the Almighty's care and protection. The bitter sobs of Mrs. Compton could throughout be heard above his own tremulous voice, but he persevered manfully, and all of that assembly arose more calm and more reconciled to what was now inevitable.

Mr. Hayward's carriage was soon afterwards at the door; it was announced in the drawing-room, and he and Mrs. Hayward arose to depart. They were both deeply affected; as may well be imagined Herbert was so too, and spoke with difficulty; but they blessed him, and gave him their fervent wishes for success, and a safe return within the time he had appointed, as warmly as if he had been one of their own children.

'I have only one last favour to beg, dear Mrs. Hayward,' he said, as he handed her into the carriage, 'that you will allow Amy to walk home under my escort; I shall feel very thankful, if you will consent.'

'I will not refuse you, Herbert,' she said: 'be gentle to her, for she loves you very deeply; never disappoint her in writing, for I am well convinced your letters will be her life while you are away. I will endeavour to make every allowance for the delay which needs must occur in the transmission of letters from such a distance; but still you must be punctual and regular. Remember, these are my last and only commands upon you; take Amy with you now, but do not keep her out late, for the dews are heavy and may hurt you both. Now God bless you!'

'My letters shall be my best answers to your commands,' said Herbert; 'believe me, I shall not miss a single opportunity of sending many to you all, for you will never be absent from my thoughts. The time will soon pass, and I hope and trust we shall all again be reunited in this dear spot—till then good-bye! good-bye!'

'Mrs. Hayward says I may escort Amy home through the park, sir,' said Herbert to Mr. Hayward, who was following; 'we shall hardly lose our way in this beautiful moonlight, and I hope you have no objection?'

'Not if you promise you will not be late, Herbert; but I leave her to your own discretion; I have not the heart to part you to-night; so farewell, my brave boy! I trust we shall see you back soon a colonel at least. You will not forget to write punctually, as well for our sake as for Amy's.'

'I have already promised Mrs. Hayward that,' said Herbert, 'and most faithfully will I fulfil it.'

'Then I will say no more, but again farewell, and God bless you!'

He wrung Herbert's hand warmly, and with cordial sincerity, and stepping into the carriage, it drove rapidly away.

'Now, dearest,' said Herbert, 'at least we can have a few moments which we can call our own—moments to be the food of years; when every word, however trivial, that one has uttered, will be to the other the most precious in the stock of our hearts' remembrances. Come, let us stroll gently on.'

She took his arm, and they wandered onwards towards the park. The moon was nigh the full, and her bright orb shed a mellow light on all around. A few fleecy clouds floated near her in the deep blue heaven, but not enough to dim her lustre, and her beams illuminated while they softened every object in the well-known pathway.

The perfect silence which reigned around them, only broken at intervals by the faint tinkling of the sheep bells here and there, or the feeble bleat of a lamb, was soothing to them; and the wide glades of the park, seen dimly in the distance, appeared to melt away into air, more like the momentary visions of dreams than the realities they had been accustomed to for years. They had much to say to each other; for they were young, ardent, confiding—loving with the intenseness of a first and sincere attachment, the gentle growth of years; yet theirs was not the language of passion, but those sobered, chastened, and now sorrowful feelings, which were the result at once of their long attachment and their dread of parting; and they lingered on, nor knew how swiftly time was flying, and that their sad farewell must be spoken at last. They walked up to the house several times, and thought to leave each other; but always some new word was spoken, some train of thought aroused, which carried them away again, forgetful of their promises not to delay.

Nor could Amy's buoyant heart support her to the last as it had done through the day,—indeed through the last few days; bitter were her sobs as she clung to the manly form of him she loved,—bitter and more violent, as the clock of the out-offices struck an hour—she did not, could not count it,—which seemed to be a last warning to her to leave him; she almost longed to do so, and yet had not the power; nor could Herbert bring himself to utter the wish for her to go.

They stood before the hall-door, irresolute, as the clock struck; and gently, in as soothing words as he could frame his thoughts to utterance, he reminded her of his promise to her mother and of her strict injunctions. 'It was only from my promise that we have enjoyed these exquisite moments,' he said, 'and I would not vex her, Amy.' But still they lingered; she was helpless as a child, her tears fell very fast, and convulsive sobs shook her sadly. Herbert supported her with one arm, while he wiped away her tears, and kissed the beautiful face which, upturned to his, had lost its cheerful expression, and now wore one of such mental anguish as had never before visited it, that he almost reproached himself for having caused it. It required all his self-possession to restrain a violent outbreak of passionate emotion; for his heart was full even to bursting, and could he have shed tears, he thought it would have relieved him, but they were denied him. They could speak but little; all he could utter were words of consolation, which, repeated again and again almost unintelligibly, fell on heedless ears, for the misery of her mind repelled them. But it could not last; sooner or later he must leave her, and he felt that every moment was causing her additional pain, while no immediate alleviation could follow.

He drew her gently towards the door; she understood his meaning, and acquiesced, by making no resistance; they ascended the steps together; the door had been left unfastened on purpose to receive her, and he felt this delicate mark of kindness in her parents deeply; it seemed even to comfort Amy that she should be able to reach her chamber unobserved.

'Go and pray for me, as you pray for yourself, dearest! it will soothe you more than my words or feeble consolations,' he said, as opening the door he led her within it; 'soon I will join my prayers to yours, and ascending together to Him who is alone able to grant them, they will bring us that peace which indeed passes understanding. Go! may He who looks down from yonder bright and glorious heaven upon us, bless you for ever, my angel, and keep you in safety!'

He could not add more, nor did she dare to reply, though some indistinct murmurs escaped her; he clasped her to his heart in one ardent embrace; kissed her forehead—her eyes—her lips in passionate fervour; and then disengaging her from him,—for she did not, could not oppose it,—he led her softly within the hall; and not daring to hazard a second glance upon her, he gently closed the door, and with an almost bursting heart rushed from the house.

He did not go far thus. Nature, who will not be denied vent for such bitter feelings as his were, and which had been so long and so ill repressed, demanded relief; and overcome by emotion, his temples throbbing as though they would burst, with a choking sensation in his throat, which caused him to breathe with difficulty, he threw himself upon a rustic seat by the side of the walk. For awhile the agony he suffered was almost insupportable, but afterwards a passionate burst of tears, which he could not check or repress, came to his relief. He leaned his head upon his hand and sobbed bitterly for many minutes; but he arose at last, in some degree soothed by the effort nature had made to relieve the sorrow which had well-nigh overpowered him.

Herbert left his home the next morning amidst the unrestrained and bitter grief of all. All his mother's previous resolutions failed her; for a while she refused to be comforted; dread, that he was going from her for ever, oppressed her with a weight which she could not throw off by the most strenuous mental exertions. Mr. Compton strove to console her, and Herbert was as cheerful as he could be under the circumstances. But it was all of no use; deep affection would find its vent, and no wonder, when all had been so knit together in the ties of love as that family.

But after breakfast, which they had vainly tried to eat, and the viands which had been provided remained untasted upon the table, the carriage was announced. To each of his brothers and his younger sisters Herbert bade a tender farewell, promising them all sorts of presents and drawings from eastern climates; but who shall paint his last moments with his dear and honoured mother? It would be profanation of such feelings to attempt their delineation—they can be felt only, never described. Mute with sorrow, Mrs. Compton could not speak to him, as he folded her in a last embrace; and as he tore himself away from her, and hurried to the carriage, she tottered to the window, and supporting herself by the side panel, with eyes dim with weeping and now almost blinded by her tears, she watched him as long as sight of him was spared her. She saw him throw himself into the carriage —his father attending him to it—the door shut—the orders given to proceed; but ere the postilion could urge his horses forward, she had sunk senseless upon the ground.

The regiment marched that day towards Dover, where his father joined Herbert in a few days. Here they were detained only as long as was sufficient to provide the requisite necessaries to the regiment for a hot climate, and the duties of furnishing these to his men kept Herbert continually employed. He had some idea at one time of returning home, even for a day or two, but the remembrance of the pangs which both his mother and Amy had suffered was too fresh in his mind to allow of his indulging in so selfish and indeed a useless gratification. He had his father with him, whose presence was not only a solace, but who prevented, as much as was in his power, Herbert's giving way to the grief which at times he could not repress, and which endured in despite of him.

At length the day arrived for the embarkation, and a gallant but painful sight it was to see so many brave fellows leaving their native land, their homes, their parents, children, and other perhaps dearer ties—prepared to shed their blood in their country's cause—to brave the perils of an unknown land and dangerous climate for her sake. Yet, as the regiment moved towards the pier from the barracks in open column, headed by their band, playing the most lively marches, to which the firm and measured tread of the men formed a noble accompaniment, there could not be seen a sorrowful face among the whole; for their colours were unfurled, and floated proudly to the breeze; and as each man's eye rested upon those emblems of their national honour which he had sworn to guard, it glistened with that undefinable sensation of glowing pride which soldiers only know, and feel most deeply on an occasion like this.

The regiment was attended by all the other officers of the garrison, and the inhabitants of the town, and was loudly cheered as they passed along. The boats waited beside the pier: each division was marched in an orderly manner into its respective boats, and at a signal given the oars were dipped at once, and the whole mimic fleet stretched at their utmost speed towards the ships, which lay at some distance from the shore.

Three hearty English cheers followed them, led regularly by an officer of distinction, who stood upon a capstan for the purpose; while the band of his corps, which was stationed upon the pier, played the slow march of the departing regiment with admirable expression. The three cheers were as heartily returned from the boats, and the gallant corps sped quickly on to their vessels.

Mr. Compton accompanied his son on board, and stayed as long as it was possible. The anchors of the fleet were a-peak, their topsails loosed, when they arrived on board; and when the men were somewhat settled, and order restored, the signal was made for sailing; soon the anchors were at the cat-heads, the topsails sheeted home, and the vast fabrics began their march over the deep, to be continued through storm or calm to the end. But as sail after sail was set, the vessels began to move the faster, until it was no longer possible to retain the boat which was towing astern, in which he was to return; he was aware that every indulgence had been shown him in having been allowed to remain so long, and he could make no opposition to its being ordered alongside.

'May He who alone is able to protect you, Herbert,' he said, as he wrung his hand, 'keep you in health! You go, I am well aware, to many dangers, but I leave you in confident hope that we may meet again; and my most fervent supplications shall ever be for you. Be careful of yourself; you are strong, active, temperate,—blessings which you cannot prize too highly. And now embrace me, my dear boy—I dare speak no more.'

He left the deck: Herbert watched him down the side safely into the boat; the rope was cast off, and in another instant it was dancing in the wake of the vessel astern; the boatmen set their sail, and soon the tiny bark was dancing merrily along over the waters. Herbert gazed till it became a speck, and then disappeared; but Mr. Compton saw the tall vessels, which had spread every sail to court a gentle and favourable wind, longer, and he watched the last faint glitter of their white canvas with straining eyes and an aching heart, till he could see them no longer upon the blue horizon.

. . . .

We must now return to a point in our narrative from which we have very widely digressed, in order to put our readers in possession of what we have detailed of the history of Herbert Compton; and we will return to the happy party which was assembled round the cheerful fire at Alston Rectory.

Besides the family, Amy was there; and, since the events we have detailed, she was often at Alston for days together: she was bright and joyous as ever, indeed much improved in personal appearance. Little more than a year had elapsed since Herbert had left them, but the letters he had written had been so regularly received, that the miserable apprehensions which all had indulged on his departure were completely dispelled; they knew that he was happy, and enjoyed excellent health, that he had formed pleasant friendships, and liked the country, which he described with eloquence. Still, as he had gone on service soon after his arrival, they were anxious, and looked eagerly for news.

'Come, let us have a glee, girls,' said Mr. Compton, after a game of forfeits had been played with all its pleasant, noisy fun, which seems now to have abandoned us; 'come, we must have some music. Get you to the harpsichord, Amy, and I will help out my own bass with my violoncello.'

'What shall we sing, sir?' answered Amy, gaily, going at once to the instrument; 'here are all kinds,—comic, lively, and grave. Ah! I have hit at once upon Herbert's favourite,—"When winds breathe soft."'

'Very good; you could not have anything better; and we all know that your heart will be in your song;—but, let us see.'

The parts were soon arranged; Amy led the glee, the delicious harmony of which appeared to float in the air above their heads, so perfectly was it sung by voices, excellent in themselves, and attuned by constant practice. Others followed; for as they had begun with glees, so they agreed to continue.

At last, after a pause, Mr. Compton, patting her cheek, said,—

'Well, you have sung so well, Amy, that I think I shall have a letter for my pet to-night.'

'A letter!—for me? Ah, sir, from whom? not from Herbert?'

'Indeed I hope so, my darling,' added Mrs. Compton; 'you know we were disappointed by the last packet, and Mr. Compton heard yesterday from his London agent, saying that a Bombay vessel had arrived with letters, and that he would forward ours the next day.'

'I am so happy! dear, dear Mrs. Compton,' cried the joyful girl, throwing her arms around her, and kissing her; 'I feel so very happy! And when will the letters come?'

'I expect the boy every moment with the bag,' she replied; 'he should have been here before this; but perhaps the post is late at —— to-day, on account of the weather.'

'Then we shall have a delighful evening, indeed,' said Amy; 'shall we not, boys and girls? Herbert's letters to all of you shall be read first, and then I will read just such scraps of mine as I please. You know how I love to tyrannise over you, and tempt you with a great deal that you must not see.'

'Well, here is the bag!' cried Edward, taking it from the servant, who just then entered. 'Now we shall see!' and he opened it. 'What! only one?—that is a disappointment! It is for you, father.'

'Ah, from my agents I see; perhaps the letters have not been delivered; but we shall hear all about it.' They crowded round him, but poor Amy's heart sunk within her; she almost sickened lest there should be no news of Herbert.

'Dear Sir,' read Mr. Compton, 'we are sorry to inform you that there were no letters for you or for Miss Hayward, per *Ocean* from Bombay, and we are sorry to add that the general news is not so favourable as we could wish—'

'Look to Amy! look to Amy!' cried Mrs. Compton, suddenly and anxiously.

It was indeed necessary,—for she had fainted. It was long ere she recovered; she had naturally a powerful mind, but it had been suddenly, perhaps unadvisedly, excited; and when such disappointment ensued, she had not been able to bear up against it, the more so as this was the second she had experienced within a short time, and there was no doubt from the previous public information, that severe fighting had been apprehended, in which Herbert's regiment must take a part.

In vain was it that Mr. and Mrs. Hayward tried to console her, —they had felt the disappointment as keenly as Amy; for the time, therefore, all were sad, and the evening which had begun so cheerfully, was concluded in painful and almost silent apprehension; nor did the accounts which appeared in the newspapers some days afterwards convey to them any alleviation of their fears.

CHAPTER XII.

It is now necessary to revisit Abdool Rhyman Khan and his party, whom we left at a small village in the pass leading behind Pencondah, and in their company to travel awhile through those districts which lay between them and the city whither they were bound.

There were no dangers now in their path, no attacks from the Mahrattas to be apprehended, nor was there the irksome heat which oppressed and wearied them before. A few showers had already fallen, the earth had put on its verdant covering, and travelling was now a pleasure more than a fatigue. The Khan had intended proceeding by easy stages, but the news he had heard of rumours of fresh wars, of the personal activity of Tippoo among the army, which was always the forerunner of some campaign, made him more than usually solicitous to press forward.

So on the fifth day they were at Balapoor; and leaving the lady to the care of the servants to rest for awhile, the Khan, accompanied by Kasim, rode forward to the town and fort of Nundidgroog, where he knew some of his own men were stationed.

'Do you see that pile of rocks yonder?' said the Khan to Kasim, as they rode along.

'I do; why do you ask?'

'Because,' he replied, 'that is a place well worth seeing, and one which was a rare favourite of Hyder Ali's—may his memory be honoured!'

'Why? Had he a summer-house there?'

'Yes, there is a sort of a house there, to be sure,' returned the Khan laughing; 'but not one of pleasure, I should think. Many a poor wretch has been in it, who would have given the wealth of the world, had he possessed it, to have got out again.'

'It is a prison then?'

'It is, and one from which but few return alive.'

'How so? You do not mean to say that they are murdered?'

'I mean to tell you plainly, that you had better not get into it; few of our people have ever been sent there, for it is reserved for the kafir English—may their tribe be accursed!—and a few of them are now and then thrown from the top, to terrify the rest into submission to the Sultaun's will, and to become a feast for the kites and crows. Look! I suppose some of them have been cast over lately, for there are vultures wheeling in the air overhead, and making stoops as if they would alight.'

Kasim shuddered; he thought it a base death for any one to die, to be thrown from thence—to reach the bottom haply alive!—and to be left to struggle there maimed and helpless—to linger till death came, accelerated perhaps by the jackals or vultures.

'Have you ever seen this, Khan?' asked Kasim.

'Never, but I know those who have: the office of executioner is no enviable one to a soldier; and he who has this post, though as arrant a coward as can well be in the field, yet can stand by and see brave men hurled over these rocks; for, to do them justice, the English are brave as lions and their courage cannot be quelled: we learned that at Perambaukum, to our cost.'

'Ay, I have heard of that. Report states it to have been a good battle.'

'Mashalla! you may say so; and, blessed be Alla! the arms of the true believers were victorious over the infidels; yet they fought well, and, though a handful of men, defied our utmost attacks and continued charges.'

'Then you were there, Ali Khan?'

'Yes. I was then in the Pagha—the Royal Guard; and I was desired by Hyder (peace be on his name!) to protect Tippoo Sahib, who led the charges. He fought like a tiger as he is, and many of the infidels tasted of death at his hand; but one of them, as we charged and overthrew their last square, made a thrust with his bayonet at the young prince, which—praise to Mahomed!—I parried; and in return, caused him to taste of death. The young man never forgot that deed, and some others I was fortunate enough to perform before him, and I am what I am.'

'Then, like those of his rank, he does not forget benefits?'

'Never; he is faithful to those he loves, but a bitter foe to those who provoke him. Above all, the English are his detestation; he sees their restless love of intrigue and power; he knows how they have sown dissensions in Bengal, and wrested many fair provinces from the sway of the true believers; he fears their abilities and knowledge of the arts of war; and though he has some French in his service, yet he can see plainly enough that they have not the powers of the others either to contrive or to execute. Above all, he fears the prophecy about him by a holy man whom he consulted, which no doubt you have heard.'

'No, indeed, I have not.'

'Not heard that? Ajaib! it is very strange; but how could you, after all. Know then, that as he sat one day in one of the innermost apartments of the palace in the garden of the Deria Doulut—where no one could by any possibility have access to him, and where he was engaged in study—there was heard a voice conversing with him, and his was gradually raised till it became furious, as, Inshalla! it often does to the terror of his enemies.'

'Taajoob!' exclaimed Kasim, 'who was it?'

'Willa alum! (God knows),' replied the Khan. 'But listen: it is said the Mushaek*—for so he appeared to be—cried to him with a loud voice, and bade him beware of the English Feringhees, for they were plotting against him; and that though the day was far distant, yet danger threatened him from them which could not be avoided. Then some say that the being (may Alla forgive me if he hears it!) upbraided the Sultaun with many errors of faith, and with being given to idolatry in private, and with doing magic, to the hurt of his own soul; and it was this which made him so angry.'

'And who was it after all?'

'Alla knows!' said the Khan mysteriously; 'Alla knows! Some people say it was a Fakeer named Shah Yoonoos, who had wandered in unknown to anybody, and had reached the Sultaun's chamber; but others say it was one of the spirits of the air (over whom it is known he has power) who had taken that form to visit him by day. But Alla only knows the truth, after all. Certain it is, however, that he does perform rites which I, as a humble and pious Mahomedan, would object to.'

'Did no one try to seize the intruder?'

'Many, so it is said; but he passed forth from among them all, and has not been seen since.'

'Most extraordinary, certainly! I marvel not now, Khan, that he should be so suspicious of the English. I for one long to have a blow with them, and to see how they fight.'

'Inshalla! the opportunity will not be long wanting; you will have it ere you have been long with us. But among our people here we shall learn something, for they have always the quickest information from the capital.'

Shortly afterwards they rode into the outer court of the Temple

* Holy man.

of Nundi, at the town under the fort of Nundidroog, and the scene which presented itself to the eyes of Kasim was as novel as it was interesting.

The court was a large square, contained in a sort of piazza formed by a colonnade of huge square blocks of granite placed in three rows, about twelve feet asunder, each piece probably sixteen feet in height; across these at the top, to form a roof, were transverse pieces of equal length. The spaces between the pillars thus placed, formed excellent stalls for horses, and the enormous area was thus converted into one huge stable,—where of old the Brahmin priests had wandered, dispensing charitable aid to the wretched, or instructing those who thirsted for knowledge.

In the centre were a few gay tents, and many camels were sitting and standing around them; several elephants too were busied with huge piles of leafy branches before them, selecting the tenderest morsels, and brushing away flies with others. Around were groups of men,—some lying under a rude screen, formed of three spears tied together, with a cloth thrown over them; others lounging and swaggering about, gaily dressed, and armed to the teeth; many were gathered into knots, and, either sitting upon spread carpets or standing together, were occupied in smoking, or listening to some itinerant musicians or story-tellers. In various parts were little booths, where coarse confectionery was sold; and many a portly-bellied group of money-changers, with their keen and shrewd eyes, were sitting on the ground, naked to the waist, with heaps of courees and pice* spread before them. There were women selling fruit out of baskets and sacks, others hawking about sour curds; with a thousand other busy, bustling occupations going on with vigour, for which the presence of the cavalry found full employment.

Before them, and above the piazzas, appeared the richly ornamented and curious high pyramidical roofs of the temples, and their massive and decorated gateway; and above all frowned the bare rock of the fort,—a naked mass of about eight hundred feet perpendicular, arising from a rugged and woody slope of an equal height. The walls around the summit, which were built upon the very giddy verge, were bristling with cannon, and the numbers of men about showed that it possessed many defenders.

All these objects, assisted by the bright colours of the costumes, the caparisons of the horses, camels, and elephants, some of which were already equipped for travel, formed a picture which, glowing under the slanting beams of an afternoon

* Copper coin.

sun, caused the young man's heart to bound with delight as they entered the large square and rode onwards among the motley crowd.

'What think you of my fine fellows, Kasim?' said the Khan, as they passed various groups of stout, soldier-like men. 'Inshalla! they are worth looking at.'

'Ul-humd-ul-illa! they most truly are,' replied the young man, who was, to say the truth, somewhat bewildered by the excitement of the scene. 'And do you really command all these, O Khan?'

'Most of them, I daresay, are my youths, Kasim; but I have no doubt some of the garrison of the fort are here also, and it would be difficult to distinguish them. But these are not all; Mashalla! and praise to the Sultaun's bounty, we have as many more at least—nay, three times as many—at the city. But there is surely more activity than usual going on, and this looks marvellously like the preparations for a march; so let us press on to the tent yonder, for there shall we find Hubeeb Oolla Khan, or Shekh Jaffur Sahib, my Jemadars, who will answer my queries. I marvel none of my rogues have yet found me out.'

'Why, they can hardly see your face, Khan,' said Kasim; 'and I daresay they little expect you to drop, as it were, from the clouds thus suddenly among them.'

'Perhaps not; but here we are at the tent: dismount, and let us enter together.'

As he spoke, the Khan alighted, and unfolding the muslin scarf which had been tied about his face, he was instantly recognised by a number of the men who were lounging about in front of it, and who now crowded round him with congratulations.

'The Khan Sahib is come!' shouted several to their companions.

'My lord's footsteps are welcome!' cried those who were nearest. 'Inshalla! victory waits upon them.'

'It is a fortunate hour that has brought him,' cried another, who pressed forward, and bowed before him. 'What are my lord's wishes? let him order his slave Dilawur Ali to perform them.'

'Ha! art thou there, friend?' said the Khan. 'Well, since thou wishest for employment, go on, and tell the Jemadar Sahib that I am here. Which of the officers is with you?'

'Jaffur Sahib, Khodawund! he will have rare news for my lord;' and he departed.

'This looks like a march,' said the Khan to another: 'say, is it so?'

'It is, protector of the poor! but we know but little of the true cause as yet, though many rumours are afloat; the most prevalent is—'

But here he was interrupted by the Jemadar himself, who had hurried from his tent, and now advanced towards them. The two leaders embraced cordially.

'Ul-humd-ul-illa! you are welcome, Khan Sahib,' said Jaffur; 'but do not remain here: come, I pray you, to your servant's tent, and rest after your journey.'

He went in, and was soon seated upon the soft cushions of the Jemadar's musnud. Kasim followed, but, uncertain how to act, he continued standing, until he was desired by the Khan to be seated near him. This, together with the Khan's marked attention to the young man, appeared rather to disconcert the Jemadar, who regarded the new comer with some suspicion, and Kasim could not help imagining with some dislike. I shall have an enemy in this man, thought Kasim for an instant; but again, he reflected that he had nothing to fear, and soon ceased to regard the furtive looks of the Jemadar, which were cast upon him from time to time, as the Khan appealed to him in support of his opinions or remarks during the conversation, which naturally turned upon the movements of the corps of cavalry he commanded.

It was true that the corps was about to move: all the outposts, except a few of those immediately upon the Mahratta frontier, had been called in, and had joined within the past day or two; and the morrow had been fixed for the departure of the whole from Nundidroog towards the capital. For the reason of this many rumours were in circulation: the Jemadar said that a sudden rupture with the English was one; that there was only to be a muster of the cavalry was another; and after that was finished the Sultaun intended to go a-hunting into the forest bordering upon Coorg. But there was a third, which had been confirmed by news that day received from the city, that some very angry messages had passed between the Rajah of Travancore and the Sultaun, and that both had ordered musters of their forces. This the Jemadar thought the most likely of all, as he knew there had been negotiations pending between the Sultaun and the Rajah relative to some forts which had been taken possession of in a manner that did not appear warrantable by the latter.

For the present, the Khan and Kasim were the guests of the Jemadar; and having partaken of refreshment, they set out to procure a resting place for the night, or one where they should be able to have their tents pitched.

As they went forth, many were the hearty greetings which saluted the Khan; every veteran especially, whose bronzed and furrowed face showed that the scorching heats of summer had for many a year passed over him in constant and active employment; and many a man, whose deeply-scarred face or breast gave a sure proof of often tried courage, met him with that hearty familiarity, and yet scrupulous deference, which, while it yielded nothing to the man, yet showed submission to authority and high respect for rank. All were unanimous in rejoicing that the Khan had returned, in such terms as, while it gratified Kasim to think he had become the friend and companion of one so honoured and beloved, caused him also to suspect that the Jemadar Jaffur Sahib was not much liked among them.

Nor indeed was he. Sprung from the lowest rank of the people, he possessed ferocity of character, which had early attracted the notice of the Sultaun, and he had risen rapidly to the station he held. He had also been a ready instrument in his hand to effect any cruelty he willed; and if war was to be carried into any district where Mahomedanism had not advanced, and forcible conversions of the inhabitants were to be made, or if any of the unoffending people were to be hung because they would not become converts, Jaffur Sahib was generally selected, as well from his address as a soldier, as from his unscrupulous character, from among the others of the same stamp who abounded about the person of the Sultaun. He was born at Arcot, and inherited all the narrow prejudice and extreme bigotry peculiar to his townsmen, and hated all English with a malignity, in which perhaps he was only excelled through all that host by the Sultaun himself.

The presence of Kasim, in such intimate association with his commander, immediately became a source of vexation to him; and as suddenly as he had seen him, he had conceived a violent aversion to him. He saw generous courage, honesty, and faithfulness written upon the brow of the young man; and as none of these found any place in his own heart, so did he at once dislike the fancied possessor of them; for he knew the Khan's generous nature, and how easily all the authority he had by incessant intrigues possessed himself of, might be reduced in a moment by one who, after becoming acquainted with the details of the service, could not fail of observing that many abuses existed under his fostering care. The Khan had not mentioned Kasim to him, nor could he divine in what capacity he attended upon his person, and he burned with curiosity to discover. When the Khan was gone, therefore, he addressed himself to his chief

Sontaburdar, or bearer of a silver club, whose name was Madar Sahib, a man who had followed his fortunes, and often shared whatever spoil was wrung from the unfortunate whom they could get into their power. There was something too in his retainer's face which seemed to expect the question; and at the slight turn of his master towards him, who had been musing 'with the finger of deliberation placed between the teeth of vexation,' he folded his hands and bent himself to listen. They were alone, for every one else had followed the Khan when he went out.

'The curses of the Shietan upon the old fool,' he said; 'could not he have kept away for a day longer? I tell thee, Madar, this appearance of his is not only a thousand rupees out of my pocket, but the loss to me of all the honour, credit, and influence which a short campaign would have given. I say a curse on him.'

'Ameen!' said his servant; 'my lord's star is unfortunate to-day; but, Inshalla! it will brighten.'

'And then that smooth-faced boy that he has brought with him,' he continued, not heeding the other's remark, 'I'll warrant, his prime favourite. Knowest thou aught of him?'

'Nothing, Khodawund; but I can inquire.'

'Do so,—see what hath brought them together. Perhaps he is the brother of this new wife he has married—the old dotard! if so, we may soon expect to get our leave to depart, Madar, for the old Khan will use his utmost influence to secure a good place near himself for his pet.'

'Alla forbid! my lord has no cause to think so as yet; but I go, and will soon bring the information.'

While this colloquy was going on, the Khan and Kasim had gone forward to seek for a place of temporary refuge; and after examining many parts of the broken cloisters, all of which afforded but indifferent shelter, Dilawur Ali, who had been looking about, suddenly returned.

'I have found a place, O Khan,' he cried; 'come and see; it is clean, and if we had any kanats,* we could make it comfortable enough for a night's lodging.'

They followed him onwards to the end of the large square; and entering through a small doorway, found themselves in a square court, in the centre of which was a cistern of water, which could be approached by easy steps for the convenience of bathers. There was a deep cloister all round, supported upon carved pillars of wood, which afforded ample accommodation for the Khan's party. It was the upper part of the outside, however,

* Tent-walls.

which attracted their attention and admiration; and indeed the exquisite design and ornaments of the screen would merit a description at our hands, if anything so intricate could be described so as to give any idea of the building, but it consisted of a regular number of highly ornamented niches in the most florid Hindoo style, each niche containing some many-armed image of Hindoo veneration, male or female, in grotesque attitudes. The whole was of pure white stucco, and contrasted brightly with the dark green of some noble tamarind-trees which nodded over it, their light feathery sprays mingling with the innumerable angles and pinnacles of the architecture. Above these rose the tall summits of the temples, and again the naked grey mass of the huge granite rock frowned over all, appearing to overhang the scene.

'Ay, this will do right well,' cried the Khan; 'we have not been in such comfortable quarters for many days. The camels will soon be here, and then a place can be screened off and made private. Often as I have been at the fort, I never discovered this quiet spot before: truly the kafir who built it had wisdom; and for once (may the Prophet pardon me!) I honour one of the accursed race. What sayest thou, Kasim?'

'I doubt not that forgiveness will be easily granted for an offence so slight, Khan Sahib. I confess that I for one have many friends among the unbelievers; and, though I hate their idolatry, yet I cannot help loving their gentle dispositions, and admiring their genius, which after all is the gift of Alla to them as much as to us.'

'You must not give vent to such opinions as those, Kasim,' replied the Khan; 'must he, Dilawur Ali? for at the city there is nought breathed but destruction of the infidels of all denominations; and if thou wouldst not make enemies, thou must chime in with the prevailing humour, or keep thy thoughts to thyself.'

'Good advice, noble Khan,' said Dilawur Ali; 'there are quick ears enough to hear, and ready tongues enough to convey to the Sultaun (may his prosperity increase!) whatever malice or spite may dictate to bad hearts; and we need not go very far from this place to find many. Thou must pardon this freedom of speech,' he continued to the young man; 'but I am an old soldier, and the Khan Sahib can tell you that I have fought beside him, and I have often known a young man ruined by in discretions of which he was not aware.'

'I thank you much for your speech,' said Kasim, 'and desire your friendship. Inshalla! we shall know each other well ere long.'

'Inshalla!' replied the other; 'when the Khan Sahib is settled here for the night safely, if you will come to my tent, I will give you such information regarding this our service,—for I presume you have joined it,—as may be of use to you hereafter.'

'Ay, go to him, Kasim,' said the Khan; 'Dilawur Ali is a Syud, a worthy man, and religious too,—in all respects fit for thy company. From him thou wilt learn many things which I could not tell thee, and which will not be lost upon thee.'

As they spoke, the palankeen of the Khan was seen approaching,—the bearers with some difficulty threading their way through the crowd. Kasim ran to meet it, and conduct it to the spot where the Khan was; and for the first time for many days, nay since the attack upon the village, he caught a glimpse of the fair inmate; for the doors were slightly open as it approached; and though, as a good Mussulman ought to do, he would have turned away his head from any other, yet he could not resist the opportunity of looking through the crevice; and he thought that, if perchance her eye should rest on his, a moment's glance would satisfy him, and would assure him that he was not forgotten.

The bearers were about to make a wrong turn as they came up, and Kasim called loudly to them. Ameena heard his voice; and the temptation to steal a passing glance at him (who we must own had been more in her thoughts than her lord might have liked could he have seen them) caused her to withdraw from her face the end of her garment with which she had covered it for an instant, that she might see the better; she would not have done so perhaps, could she have guessed that he was looking for her. But as it happened, some obstruction in the way of the bearers obliged them to stop so close to him, that the palankeen brushed his person, and they could have spoken, so near were they. Their eyes met once more; his in admiration which he could not conceal, hers in confusion which impelled her instantly to cover her face, but not before she had seen that the scarf she had given him to bind up his wound still occupied a prominent place upon his breast. 'He has not thrown it away,' she said to herself. She little knew how he valued it.

Her palankeen was carried on through the door into the place we have described. The others had departed, and she was alone with her lord, who, bidding her his usual hearty and kind welcome, opened the doors wide, and displayed to her the view which had surprised and delighted the others previously; and she broke out into a burst of girlish admiration at a sight she so little expected when her palankeen entered the gloomy doorway.

CHAPTER XIII.

MADAR waited for a while, until he saw that the Khan's servants had arrived; when, taking his silver stick of office with him, he sought their little separate encampment, which, busy as it had seemed elsewhere, was now swallowed up in the mass that occupied the space around them. He lurked about the busy and tired men for some time, not hazarding a remark to any one, lest he should meet with a sharp repulse, which indeed was to be expected; seeing that after a long march, men who must provide and cook their dinners, have much more to do than to hold conversations with prying inquirers.

At last, seeing Daood, the Khan's attendant, busy preparing his master's hooka, he advanced towards him, and seated himself upon his hams close to him.

'Salaam Aliekoom, brother!' said he.

'Salaam!' was the only reply Daood chose to give.

'Mashalla! the Khan has returned in good health.'

'Shookr Khoda! he has.'

'Inshalla! he will long continue so.'

'Inshalla!'

'And so he has married a young wife! Well, the Khan is a powerful man,—a youth, yet.'

'Inshalla, brother!' and Daood continued his employment most assiduously, humming a popular tune.

'The brother of the Khanum is a fine-looking youth—may his prosperity increase!'

Daood looked at the speaker with no amicable eyes. 'Who, in the name of the Sheitan, art thou, O unlucky man? How darest thou, even in thy speech, to allude to the Khanum, and what mean these questions? Go! stay not here, or it may be that some of our folks may lay a stick over thee; and haply myself, if thou stayest much longer. Go, I tell thee; or thou mayst chance to eat dirt.'

Madar saw plainly enough there was little to be gained by conversation with Daood, so he left him; and after a while tried a groom who was busy with one of the Khan's horses.

With him he was more successful, and soon he learned the history of the young man and the events which had occurred during their march from Hyderabad. Stored with these, he was preparing to depart, when he was roughly accosted by Kasim and Dilawur Ali, who had observed him in conversation with the groom; for Dilawur Ali well knew the character of the man to be of the worst kind, and that the inquiries he was making were to gratify the curiosity of his master, or perhaps to serve worse purposes.

Dilawur Ali was an officer who commanded a Duffa or division of the corps, and a man of some authority; so he cared little, now that his commander had arrived, either for the man or his master. For he was secure in the Khan's favour, and well knew that the Jemadar dared not complain to him, even should his servant receive ill usage, or at anyrate hard words. So he cried out lustily, 'Ho! Madar Sahib, what seekest thou among the newly-arrived servants of the Khan? By the soul of the Prophet, thine appearance is like a bird of ill-omen,—like the first vulture to a dying sheep. What has he been asking of thee?' he said to the groom; 'speak, and fear not.'

'May I be your sacrifice,' replied the man; 'he did but ask about the Patél Sahib yonder,' for so Kasim continued to be called among them.

'And what wouldst thou know about me, O base-born!' cried Kasim; 'what am I to thee or to thy master?'

'Nothing, nothing, noble sir; only my master (may his prosperity increase!) bid me ask, in order that he might know something of one whose appearance is so like that of a youth brave in war; and he saw too that your worship had been wounded, and naturally wished to know whether the Khan Sahib (may his name be exalted!) had been in any danger on the way down, which may Alla avert!'

'Thy words are smooth for once,' said Dilawur Ali, 'and well calculated to disarm suspicion; but I know thee well, Madar Sahib, and thy master too, and I warn thee of both, Kasim. In the present case there may be no harm meant, and perhaps it is unjust to accuse or to suspect thee; but thou hadst as well take the hint, for, Inshalla! we are neither fathers of owls or of jackasses, and can see and hear as far as other people: dost thou understand?'

'I will tell thee more plainly, Madar Sahib,' said the young Patél,—whose blood was fired by the thought that any one should be so soon prying into his affairs in the camp,—'that if ever I catch thee about this encampment of ours, or tampering with any of my lord the Khan's servants, I will break every bone in thy skin: dost thou hear?'

'My lord!' began the fellow.

'Nay, no more,' continued Kasim, 'or I may be tempted to give way to wrath; begone, in the name of the devils on whose errand thou camest. I like thee not, by Alla! thy face is like an executioner's,—a fellow who would give a brave man a cup of poison, or stab him from behind with a knife, and boast he had done some valiant deed.'

Some others who were standing by caught the words of the young man, and laughed loudly at the truth he had so unwittingly told; and their taunts, added to the previous ones he had been obliged to hear, caused Madar to slink off as fast as possible, followed by the jeers and abuse of those who had joined in the laugh against him.

'He is off like a maimed cur!' cried one. 'You have eaten dirt!' cried another. 'Alla give thee a good digestion of it, and appetite for more the next time thou comest!'

'Let us seize him and cut off his beard and mustachios! such an impotent coward and prying rascal is not worthy to wear the emblems of manhood—let him be shaven like an eunuch!' cried a masculine virago, the wife of a camel-driver, setting her arms a-kimbo, who thought it a fair opportunity to join in. 'Return, O Madar Sahib, that I may spit on thy beard!'

Madar did not apparently choose to accept this polite invitation, for he thought it possible that the first threat might be attempted, and the shout of laughter which followed the latter part of the speech caused him to quicken his pace considerably; and only once looking behind him, to throw a glance of hate towards those by whom he had been menaced, he pursued his way, and was soon lost in the crowd.

'There goes a spiteful heart,' said Kasim; 'didst thou see the look he cast behind him?'

'Ay, brother,' replied Dilawur Ali; 'thou hast said truly, he has a spiteful heart, and I could tell thee many a tale of his iniquity; but I am half sorry that we did not speak him fair.'

'I am not: I would rather have an open enemy than one under the garb of civility or friendship.'

'The scoundrel will tell all he has heard, and as much more as he can invent, to the Jemadar yonder.'

'And what of that?' said Kasim; 'what have I to fear?'

'This is no place to speak of him,' said his friend; 'come to my tent, I will tell thee much of him.'

And truly the account the worthy Syud gave of the Jemadar was not calculated in any way to allay fear, if any had existed in Kasim's heart: for it was one of deceit, of villany often successful, of constant intrigue, and of cruel revenge; but the young man's fearless spirit only made light of these, which might have disquieted a more experienced person; and he asked gaily,

'But what makest thee think that he bears me any enmity? we have as yet hardly seen each other.'

'I know it from his vile face, Kasim. While the Khan often spoke to thee kindly in his presence, his eyes wandered to thee with a bad expression, and they no sooner left thee than he and that Sontaburdar of his exchanged furtive glances. I was watching them, for I saw at once he would be jealous of thee.'

'He may do his worst,' said Kasim, 'I care not.' But in spite of this expression, his heart was not quite so free of care about what had happened as it had been before he had heard Dilawur Ali's stories.

Madar returned, burning with spiteful and revengeful feelings, and with much excitement visible in his countenance, he rushed into his master's presence and flung his turban on the ground, while he gnashed his teeth in rage.

'What news hast thou, Madar? What has been done to thee? speak, good man. What has happened?'

'Judge if I have not cause to be revenged, Khodawund: I am less than a dog; and may my grave be unblessed if I do not avenge the insults I have suffered both for myself and you, O my lord!'

'Why, what has happened?'

'I tell you, you have been reviled by that son of perdition Dilawur Ali, and the boy whom that old fool the Khan has brought with him. Hear, Jemadar Sahib, what they said; they said they would—Inshalla!' and Madar twisted up his mustachios fiercely as he spoke, 'defile your beard, and throw dirt on it; they called you a coward and less than man. They said they did not value you a broken couree; and they threatened to beat me, to break every bone in my skin; and set up a vile woman, one without shame, with an uncovered face, to abuse me in vile terms, to call me an eunuch, and to threaten to shave my beard and mustachios; and this before a thousand others, loochas and shodas * like themselves. But I will be revenged. Ya Alla! ya Hoosein! ya Hyder!' he cried, as he took up his turban which he had thrown down in his passion, and began to tie it awry upon his head. 'I will be revenged!'

'They said this?—Ah, Kumbukht!'—cried the Jemadar, who had heard out his servant's tale with some difficulty,—'they said it,—and thou hadst ears to hear it? Alla! Alla! am I a sheep or a cow to bear this?—I who am, Inshalla! a tiger, an eater of men's hearts,—before whom men's livers turn to water,—that I should be obliged to devour such abomination!

* Dissolute vagabonds.

What ho! Furashes! any one without there! go, bring Dilawur Ali, Duffadar, and— But no,' he said mentally, checking the torrent of passion; 'it cannot be so. I have no authority now to punish, and they would defy me; the Khan would take fire in a moment if he heard I had been inquiring into the station of this proud youth,—whom, Inshalla! I will yet humble.'

'Go,' he continued to the servants, who had suddenly entered the tent; 'when I want you I will call again; at present I would be alone with Madar.'

'And so thou heardest all this abuse of me, and ate dirt thyself, and had not the heart to say a word or strike a blow in return! I could spit on thee, coward!'

'May I be your sacrifice, Khodawund, I was helpless; what could I have done in that crowd? had I only returned a word, the woman whom they set up would have poured filthy abuse on me.'

'They shall rue the day that they uttered the words thou hast repeated: Madar, they shall wish their tongues had never said them, and that their hearts had eaten them, ere they had birth: Ul-humd-ul-illa! I have yet power, and can crush that butterfly, whose gay bearing is only for a season,—but not yet—not yet.'

'And who is this proud fool?' he continued after a pause to Madar, who had been drinking in every word of his master's soliloquy with greedy ears, and rejoicing in the hope of speedy revenge. 'Who saidst thou he is?'

'A Patél, noble sir,—a miserable Patél of a village, Alla knows where,—a man whose mother, Inshalla! is vile.'

'I care not for his mother,—who is he? and how comes he with the Khan? Tell me, or I will beat thee with my shoe!'

'My lord,—Khodawund!—be not angry, but listen: he is the Patél of a village where the Khan and his young wife were nearly drowned; he saved the lady, and he fought afterwards against some Mahrattas when they attacked the village where the Khan was resting for the night, and was wounded in his defence.'

'And this is all, Madar?'

'It is, protector of the poor! it is all; they say the Patél is a Roostum—a hero—a man who killed fourteen Mahrattas with his own hand, who—'

'Bah!' cried Jaffur impatiently, 'and thou art a fool to believe them;' and he fell to musing. 'He must have seen her face,' he said at length aloud.

'He must,' echoed his attendant; 'they say he carried her in his arms from the river.'

'Khoob! and what said they of her beauty?'

'That she is as fair as the full moon in the night of Shub-i-Barăt.'

'Khoob! and he has seen her again, I doubt not, since then.'

'Willa alum!' said Madar, raising his thumbs to his ears. 'How should your slave know? but it is likely,—people cannot conceal their faces when they are travelling.'

'No, nor, Inshalla! wish to do so! but we shall see,—take care that you mention not abroad what occurred this evening,—they will forget it.'

'But my lord will not!'

'I never forget an insult till I have had its exchange, and that thou well knowest, Madar. Begone! make it known without that I may now be visited. We will consider of this matter.'

But we must return to the Khan, whose active furashes had encircled several of the pillars of the cloisters with high tent walls, swept out the inclosures thus made, spread the carpets, and converted what was before open arches and naked walls and floors into a comfortable apartment, perfectly secure from observation. Ameena took possession of it, and was soon joined by her lord, who, in truth, was in nowise sorry after the fatigues of the day to enjoy first a good dinner, and afterwards the luxury of a soft cotton mattress, and to have his limbs gently kneaded by the tiny hands of his fair wife, while she amused him with a fairy tale, or one of those stories of intrigue and love which are so common among the Easterns.

The cool air of the Mysore country had apparently invigorated her, and the languor which the heat and the fatigue of constant travelling had caused in the Carnatic had entirely disappeared, and given place to her usual lively and joyous expression. She had thrown a deep orange-coloured shawl, with a very richly-worked border, around her, to protect her from the night breeze that blew chilly over the tent walls, which did not reach to the roof of the building they were in, and it fell in heavy folds around her, appearing to make her light figure almost more slender from the contrast. She was inexpressively lovely, as she now bent playfully over the Khan, employed in her novel vocation, and again desisting, began afresh some other story wherewith to beguile the time till the hour of repose arrived.

'Alla bless thee, Ameena!' said the Khan, after one of her lively sallies, when her face had brightened, and her eyes sparkled at some point of her tale,—'Alla bless thee! thou art truly lovely to-night: the Prophet (may his name be honoured!) could have seen no brighter Houris in Paradise (when the will of Alla called him there) than thou art.'

'I am my lord's slave' said the lady, 'and to please him is my sole endeavour day and night. Happy is my heart when it tells me I have succeeded—how much more when I am honoured with such a remark from thine own lips, O my lord! And as to my beauty'—and here she threw a glance into the little mirror she wore upon her thumb,—'my lord surely flatters me; he must have seen far fairer faces than mine.'

'Never, never, by the Prophet!' cried the Khan, with energy; 'never, I swear by thine own eyes, never. I have but one regret, Ameena, and that cannot be mended or altered now.'

Ameena's heart suddenly failed her, for Kasim came to her remembrance, and she thought for an instant that he might suspect.

'Regret! what dost thou regret?' she asked hesitatingly. 'Anything that thy poor slave hath done? anything—'

'Nothing, fairest, on thy part; it was for myself.'

Her heart was suddenly relieved of a load. 'For thyself?' she said gaily; 'what dost thou regret, Khan Sahib?'

'That I am not twenty years younger, for thy sake, Ameena,' he said with much feeling. 'Methinks now, to see these grey hairs and this grey beard,' and he touched them as he spoke, 'so near thy soft and waving tresses, I seem more like a father to thee than a husband: and yet thou art mine, Ameena. I would thou wert older, fair one!'

'And if I were, I should not be so fair,' she said artlessly.

'I care not, so that we had grown old together; at least I should have seen thy beauty, and the remembrance of it would have been with me.'

Ameena sighed; her thoughts wandered to Kasim's noble figure and youthful yet expressive countenance; in spite of herself and almost unconsciously she drew her hand across her eyes, as if to shut something ideal from her sight.

The Khan heard her sigh; he would rather not have heard it, though his own remark he knew had provoked it. 'I have said the truth, Ameena, and thou wouldst rather I were a younger man,' he said, looking at her intently. 'But what matter? these idle words do but pain thee. It is our destiny, sweet one, and we must work it out together.'

'Ay, it is our destiny,' she said.

'The will of Alla!' continued the Khan, looking up devoutly, 'which hath joined two beings together so unsuited in age, but not in temper I think, Ameena. Thou art not as others, wilful and perverse—heavy burdens—hard to carry—and from which there is no deliverance; but a sweet and lovely flower, which a monarch might wear in his heart and be proud of. So thou truly art to Rhyman Khan, and ever wilt be, even though enemies should come between us.'

'Enemies! my lord,' she said with surprise in her tone; 'I never had an enemy, even in my own home: and I am here with thee in a strange land, where I know no one who could be mine enemy!'

'May Alla put them far from thee, fairest!' he replied affectionately; 'and yet sometimes I fear that thou mayst have to encounter enmity.'

'I have heard it said by my honoured father, Khan, that as the blessed Prophet had many enemies, and as the martyrs Hassan and Hoosein came to their sad deaths by them, it is the lot of all to have some one inimical; but he meant men, whose occupations and cares call them into the world,—not women, like me, who, knowing no one but my servants, cannot make enemies of them if I am kind.'

'But I mean those who would be jealous of thy beauty, and seek thus to injure thee,—from these I alone fear,' replied her husband.

'I fear not, Khan,' she said, simply and confidently, 'neither for thee nor myself. I cannot think that thou couldst ever give thy Ameena cause for jealousy, or any one else cause of jealousy of her. Alla help me! I should die if such could be—'

'Nay, there thou shalt be safe,' he said, interrupting her; 'for never, never shalt thou have cause to say of Rhyman Khan that he was false to thee. I am a soldier, and one whose honour has known neither stain nor spot; and yet—'

He had stopped suddenly and appeared to think; and, while he thought, suddenly an idea flashed into her mind,—could she have already a rival? She could not bear it to rest there for an instant, ere she threw it off in words.

'Speak, O Khan!' she cried; 'thou hast none but me who claims thy love? thou hast not belied thyself to one who has here none to protect her?—no father—no mother—none but thee! Oh, my lord!—*thou* canst not have deceived the child who trusted thee and never asked of thee aught?' She was very excited.

'I have not deceived thee, Ameena; but I have not told thee all my history,—I have not told thee as yet what sooner or later thou must know. I have not told thee how that for years I pined for the love of woman, such pure child-like love as thine, and found nought after a short intercourse but bitter words and a constant seeking after wealth which I had not to bestow,—how I have had to bear constant upbraiding from those out of whose families I chose them, because I would not spend my substance upon wasteful parents,—upon sons whose very existence was a disgrace to them. Hadst thou known this, Ameena, thou wouldst not marvel that I sought one like thee in a distant land,—one who, removed from every tie, and with no one to sow dissension between us, should learn to love and trust Rhyman Khan as, Inshalla! he ought to be loved and trusted.'

She knew not how to reply; on the one hand the concealment of other ties which the Khan had kept secret so long and now revealed so unexpectedly, and the undefined dread of the hate of rivals, smote her to the very heart; on the other, her attention was powerfully arrested by the bold truthfulness of his disclosure; she was affected by the picture of desolation he had drawn of his own state, and his disappointments, and she was soothed to think that all he had sought for years was centred in her. She was silent,—she could not speak under such conflicting thoughts.

'Thou hast not told me all,' she said at length; 'thou hast not said how many—' she could not finish the sentence.

'There are two, dearest Ameena,—two, on each of whom I fixed hopes which have been broken in many ways. I have never had a child to bless me; and where love should have been, and mildness like thine to compensate for such a disappointment, rancour has come and ill-temper, and with them despair to me, —hopelessness of that quiet peace which my mind seeks when war and its perils and excitements are past. When disappointment came with the first, I thought a second might perchance be more to me than she had been: alas! I soon was undeceived, and bitterly too, Ameena. But, after all, who can say there are no flowers to be pulled in the rugged pathways of their lives? Had this not happened, I should never have known thee, my rose, —never have seen that look of pity which thy beauteous eyes wear now! It is from these I fear thou wilt have to bear some jealousies, some enmity; and canst thou brave somewhat for the love of Rhyman Khan? Continue to be to me as thou art now, and my wealth, my power, nay my life-blood itself, are thine, as freely as thou carest to use them. Now thou knowest all, and a heavy weight is gone from my heart, which had long abode there. Speak,—art thou content?'

'I would I had known this earlier,' she said sadly, after a while; 'but as it is, I am thankful to hear it even now. My lord knows well that I am but a child, and no match for the intrigues of those who are more versed in the world's wisdom. I feel that it has saddened and sobered me; and where I had hoped in my bright fancy to roam as I listed in the garden of thy love, unchecked and unheeded by any one but thyself, I must cover myself with the veil of discretion and deliberation, and take heed to my steps lest I fall into the snares which jealousy will not fail to place for me.'

'Alla forbid!' cried the Khan fervently; 'thou hast no cause to fear them.'

'I know not,' she replied; 'but I can scarcely hope that there may be friendship between me and those whom you describe; there may be a show for a while, but the end will be bitterness.'

And the poor girl wept; for she had suddenly been disturbed upon her height of security, or at all events of unmolested occupation, and even in a few minutes she could not help expecting some rude collision which would perhaps cast her down headlong. And her own peaceful home—its freedom from care, its loving affection, its harmless pleasures—rose so vividly to her mind, that she could not help for the time regretting bitterly that she had left it, to endure such a prospect as appeared to open before her. Nor did the Khan disturb, except by a caress or a well-timed word of cheerful hope, the thoughts which he knew must be passing in her heart, but to which he could not respond in a manner to make her forget them on the instant; they must have their vent, he thought, and thought wisely. She lay down and wept, till sleep gradually asserted its mastery over her wearied form and rudely-excited thoughts.

'She shall never come to harm, so help me Alla and his holy prophet!' said the Khan mentally, as he bent over her and gently drew some covering upon her without disturbing her; 'she shall never know harm or evil, as long as the arm or power of Rhyman Khan can shield her! She still sobs,' he said, as every now and then a sob broke softly from her, like to that from a child who has cried itself to sleep, and her bosom heaved under the oppression. 'I would to Alla I had not caused her this pain! and yet it was inevitable. Their jealousy and malice will be great I know, and their power is great, but, Inshalla! there will be no fear of their machinations, and I will soon teach her to despise them; they too will cease to use them when they see them of no avail and unheeded.'

CHAPTER XIV.

THE day after, the Khan's Risala halted at Bangalore, from whence it was ordered to escort some treasure, military stores, and many English prisoners to the capital.

The Khan having now taken the command, he was enabled to employ Kasim in many useful offices, both as a scribe and in the execution of his orders; and he was delighted to find in him one whom he could trust, and whose advice was often of use in matters that perplexed his own uninventive mind. And although he held no situation as yet in the Government service, nor was enrolled in the regiment, yet he gradually became looked up to, even during the few days he had been with it, by the subordinate officers, who naturally wished to curry favour with one so much in association with their chief; accordingly Kasim was courted by almost all—feasted and made much of. Some, indeed, regarded him with jealousy, at the head of whom was the person we have already named, Jaffur Sahib; and as their opinions became known to one another, they gradually formed a party, which, though its numbers were small, made up for that deficiency in bitter dislike.

The most prominent of these, besides Jaffur Sahib himself, was Naser-oo-deen, the chief accountant and secretary of the regiment,—one of those corrupt and wily scoundrels so often to be found in the persons of those who have been educated in the daily observance of schemes and fraud: for his father had filled a high situation as moonshee or secretary near the person of Hyder Ali; and it is impossible for any one to fill a similar place in any native court, without having daily opportunities of improvement in the arts of intrigue, falsehood, and corruption. He was also a constant associate of Jaffur Sahib; and in many a plan for cheating the Government by false musters of men, and extra charges for grain and forage, they had been nearly associated,—indeed, had divided the spoil between them.

Naser-oo-deen had also been the agent for the supply of forage and other necessaries to a large number of the Khan's horses which were in the Risala; and as he seldom looked after these accounts himself, there had been a very handsome profit to be gained from them by the subordinates. It was probable that upon the first ground, therefore—that is, so far as the regiment was concerned—Kasim and the Moonshee would never have come in contact with each other; but they were not long in doing so when the private interests of the Khan were in question.

For want of occupation Kasim had solicited some employment from the Khan, who had desired him to look after his own horses, and to examine the accounts the Moonshee should furnish of their expenditure; and for this office Kasim was well fitted, not only from his knowledge of writing, but from his experience as a Patél of the prices of grain and forage. The accounts had used to be daily submitted to the Khan, and during his absence they had accumulated to a large amount. Occupied in other duties and affairs, the Khan could not afford time to hear them read, and gave them over for examination to his young friend, who, in the careful scrutiny he made of them, and his readiness in comprehending their intricate nature, convinced the Moonshee that he had to deal with a person of no ordinary exactitude and ability.

Kasim, in his inspection of the documents, had much occasion to suspect that the rates and quantities charged were far greater than the truth; but he did not dare at first to make any accusation against a man of the Moonshee's apparent probity and respectability. He had seen enough, however, to put him on his guard for the future, and there was soon ample reason to confirm his suspicions that all was not as fair as the accounts showed. While they were at Bangalore he made a daily memorandum of the prices of grain in the several bazaars, and inquiries also of the men who rode the Khan's horses in the regiment, and of the grooms also, as to the quantities used; and on comparing them with the memorandums furnished to him by the Moonshee, the deceit was too flagrant to pass unnoticed. Accordingly he sought that worthy, and, without any accusation, ventured to point out some inaccuracies, as he supposed they must be, in the accounts, as compared with the market rates. These the Moonshee tried to support with all the effrontery he was able to muster for some time; but Kasim was steady, and in the end triumphed. It was, however, an offence which rankled deeply in the Moonshee's mind, and in an evening converse with his friend the Jemadar, he alluded to the matter in no very amiable humour.

'Things have come to a pretty pass since the Khan has brought that boy with him!' said he indignantly to the Jemadar when they were alone.

'How? has he interfered with you, as he appears to wish to do with everyone else?'

'To be sure he has—it seems he can read; and the old fool,

without thinking about it, gave him all my accounts of the Pagha to look over, instead of signing and passing them at once.'

'And he discovered—'

'No, nothing in them, Alla be praised! so that there is a good round sum to divide between us; but he evidently suspected the rates of grain, which, believe me, Jemadar, you put too high.'

'Not a whit, not a whit, since we have got the money.'

'But I say it was, for it led the young prying fellow to ask the prices of grain in the bazaars, and of forage too; and, as it seems he is a Patél, he knows more about the matter than we do ourselves; so, when I gave him the accounts to-day, he showed me a memorandum of every day's nerrikh,* and began comparing it as simply as possible with the account and showing the difference. By the Prophet! I could have struck him for his pretence of ingenuousness, and his seeming unconsciousness that he was detecting me. I tried to bully him, Jemadar Sahib, and said I had eaten the Khan's salt longer than he had, and was not to be suspected by a boy; but it would not do; he told me not to be angry, that he might be mistaken, and that he would show the accounts to the Khan if I liked; but this you know would not have answered my purpose, for the old fellow would have fired up in a moment.'

'And what did you do? you surely did not alter them?'

'Why, what else could I do, Jemadar? I at last pretended to see the mistake and make fresh accounts.'

'In other words, O cowardly fool! you ate dirt; you allowed him to obtain a mastery over you which you will never regain. You call yourself a Moonshee!—a man of letters! Shame on you, I say, to allow yourself to be dictated to by a boy! Had I a beard like yours, I would cut it off for very shame.'

'But, Jemadar—' he interposed.

'I tell thee I can hear nothing; I know this will not end here—the fellow's prying should have been stopped at once; and his suspicions will never rest, believe me, till he has found out the whole; and at any rate we shall lose money.'

'We shall, certainly.'

'How much?'

'Two hundred rupees, I dare say.'

'Alla! Alla! so much! and the worst is that our trade is stopped.'

'I fear so; how can it be otherwise, as he observes the rates?'

'Could you get him to take the accounts himself, Moonshee Sahib, we might find him out ourselves overcharging in a few

* Rate of prices

days, and so they would fall back to us, and he would be ruined.'

'Alla knows!' sighed the Moonshee; 'at any rate it is worth trying; I will see to it. I am only afraid your turn will come next.'

'I'll tell you what, Naser, the thought is not to be borne. What! lose my monthly gains, without which this service is nothing to me!—Inshalla! no. If there is a Kasim Ali Patél, there is at least a Shekh Jaffur Jemadar. I tell thee, man, I was not born to eat dirt at his hands, but he at mine; and if I cannot see into the depths of futurity like the Sultaun (may his name be honoured!), yet I can see far enough to behold this boy's disgrace at my hands. Dost thou hear—at my hands? thou shouldst know by this time that I rarely fail of my purpose.'

'May Alla grant it!' said the Moonshee piously.

'I tell thee,' he continued, 'I hated him from the first, because I found he would stand between me and the Khan. He abused me in hearing of all the camp; those words have gone forth among the men, and as I look in their faces I fancy that the remembrance of them comes into their heart, and that they exult over me. I tell thee this is not to be borne, and I will have an exchange for it, or I will see why; dost thou understand?'

'I do.'

'And thou must aid me.'

'Surely—with my pen, with my advice, my—'

'Bah! thy advice—who asked for it? who wants that of a fool who could not defend his own papers? when I have occasion for thee in this matter I will tell thee, and see that thou doest it; and—'

'My lord is not angry with his poor servant?' said the Moonshee cringingly.

'I have good cause to be so, but must eat my vexation for the present. Go! you have your dismissal.' He mused for a while after the Moonshee had left him, and then called to Madar, who waited without.

'Have you discovered anything more about the Khan's wife, Madar?' he asked.

'Nothing, my lord, except that she is very beautiful.'

'That you said before: nothing between her and the Patél?'

'Nothing, except that he had seen her.'

'That too you told me: does he see her now?'

'Willa Alum!'* was the reply.

'It would be as well for us if he did.'

* God knows.

'Shall your slave try to effect it?'

'I have been thinking of it, Madar; you might contrive something. I tell thee I hate that boy more and more; it is only this moment that I have heard from Naser-oo-deen Moonshee that his accounts have been suspected by him.'

'Does the Khan know of it?'

'No, not as yet; but there is no security for us, and there is no saying what may happen, for this boy holds a sword over us.'

'I understand,—my lord will trust me; and depend on it that, sooner or later, I find a way of helping him to revenge these insults.'

It was thus to screen their own iniquity, of which they were conscious, that these schemes were being undertaken against the peace of two individuals who had never harmed any of the plotters; and in the course of our history we shall follow them to their conclusions.

The consciousness of his own evil practices and corruption, as regarded the public service, made the Jemadar jealous of any one who should usurp the place he had held with the Khan; not because the Khan liked him, but because, being indolent by nature, and unacquainted with the details of the private economy of his Risalas, the Khan was glad enough to find that any one would undertake that for him, which he could not bring his mind to take any interest in, or indeed to understand. And if Kasim had succeeded in detecting the Moonshee, what might not *he* have to fear, whose peculations were even of a more daring nature, and extended to the men, the horses, and the establishment of the corps! The Jemadar brooded over these thoughts incessantly; and his avaricious and miserly spirit could as ill brook the idea of pecuniary loss, as his proud and revengeful heart the prospect of disgrace, and the insult he had been told by his emissary that he had already received.

After a few days' halt at Bangalore, for the purpose of preparing carriages for the removal of the English prisoners to the capital, and the collection of some of the revenue of the district, which was also to be escorted thither, the morning arrived on which they were to set out, and each corps was drawn up in front of the Mysore gate of the fortress; while the Khan, attended by Kasim and some others, rode into it in order to receive the prisoners, and the Khan his last orders from the Governor.

While he was employed in his audience, Kasim rode hither and thither, observing with delight the impregnable strength of the fortress,—the cannon, the arms and appearance of the disciplined garrison, and the few French soldiers and officers who were lounging about. He had never before seen a European; and their appearance, their tight-fighting and ungraceful dress, inspired him with no very exalted idea of their prowess.

'Can these be the men,' he thought, 'to whom the Sultaun trusts, instead of to the brave hearts and sturdy arms of the men of Islam? but so I am told, and I am to see more at the capital. Well, it is strange that they should have the talents for such contrivances in war, as never enter into our hearts: our only defence is a strong arm and a good sword and shield; and if we had not to fight against the English kafirs, we should not require these French, who after all are only infidels too. But here come the prisoners, I suppose,' he added, as a few soldiers, horse and foot, with drawn swords, advanced from behind an adjacent wall; 'the brave kafirs, as all call them, and hate them because they are so brave; I confess I do not, and only because they are the Sultaun's enemies, and infidels into the bargain.'

His curiosity was raised to the highest pitch to see these unhappy men, who, in defiance of the treaty of 1784, were kept in the fortresses of the country without a hope of deliverance, and cut off from any chance of communication with their countrymen on the coast. Among the few with whom Kasim had associated, 'the English' were the continued subject of conversation; their religion, their manners, and their persons were ridiculed and held up to scorn by all, but their bravery none could deny; and that man held himself far exalted above his fellows who had entered into personal combat with or slain one of them. Many were the tales then in circulation,—some exaggerations of reality, others stern scenes of hard fighting,—which even figurative language failed to exalt above their due estimation.

In company with the Khan, with Dilawur Ali and with others, Kasim had heard many of these relations; and indeed, whenever he listened in the camp, either to itinerant story-tellers, or to those gathered around a watchfire, the English were alike the theme of execration for their religion and their falsehood, or on rare occasions praised for their devoted bravery. No wonder then was it that he watched for their coming with very eager anxiety: figuring to himself what they might be, he thought to have seen them a martial-looking people, and that in their persons he should realise his own ideas of what a warrior ought to be,—tall and finely formed, haughty in appearance, with an eye of fire and an arm of iron.

One by one the prisoners came before him, and some of them heavily chained, others free; but all men on whose faces the rigour of captivity had set its seal. Melancholy and pale, many of them wasted by sickness, and by mental and bodily sufferings, they were shadows of what they had been; their clothes hung in rags about them, and, though not dirty, they were of a colour which proved that they themselves had washed them from time to time; a few of them had worn-out uniform coats upon them, whose stained and discoloured appearance fitted well with the wretched condition of their wearers. Their step was slow and weak, and those who wore fetters with difficulty moved at all; none of them spoke, but many of them gazed around upon the walls, and looked up into the bright heavens, and smiled, as though they were glad that motion and air were once more allowed to refresh their cramped and emaciated limbs and weary spirits.

In spite of his previous determination to hate them with the same spirit as that of his companions, Kasim felt he could not; there would, in spite of his efforts to repress it, arise a feeling of pity, that men whom he doubted not were as brave as the race was represented to be, should exhibit so sorrowful an appearance,—one which told a forcible tale of unalleviated misery. Following those on foot were several in small doolies, whose emaciated and ghastly looks told of their sickness and unfitness for removal.

He had expected a feeling of triumph to arise in his heart as he should behold the infidel English captives; but there was something so touching in the appearance of the melancholy procession, that he felt none; he could much rather have wept as he looked on it, than joined in any expression of ill-will towards the prisoners.

As they advanced, a few boys who were near hooted the captives, and abused them in obscene language. This they did not appear to deign to notice; at last one boy, more bold than the rest, took up a stone, and accompanying it with a savage oath, flung it against the prisoner nearest to him, and, having struck him, was greeted with a loud shout of joy by his companions.

Almost ere he was aware of his own intention, and impelled by the wanton insult upon one so helpless, Kasim violently urged his horse across the open space up to the boy—who, having been successful in his first fling, had picked up another stone with a similar intention—and struck him severely several times with the whip he had in his hand. Screaming with pain, the boy ran off to a distance; and his associates, terrified at the punishment their companion had received, dispersed at once.

Kasim could not resist speaking to the prisoner on whose

behalf he had acted; and riding up to him, he hoped, not knowing whether he should be understood, that he was not hurt, adding, that he had punished the young miscreant who had thrown the stone.

The voice was one of kindness, and it was long since one like it had sounded in the young Englishman's ears.

'I am not hurt,' he said, in good Hindostanee; 'and if I had been, an act of kindness such as yours would have amply repaid me for receiving it. Gallant soldier! you, it would seem, have not been taught as your countrymen to hate the English. Do not, however, speak to me: an act of courtesy to one of us may chance to bring disgrace upon you, and I would not have you receive that return for your kindness. May God protect you!'

They passed on, and Kasim remained in the same spot, gazing after him; his tall figure and proud air, his pale but handsome face and deeply-expressive blue eyes,—such as Kasim had never seen before,—his fluent speech and manly tone,—above all, his last words, 'May God protect you!' affected him powerfully.

'God protect you!' he repeated; 'he believes then in Alla; how can he be an infidel? He said, "Alla Hafiz!" and he spoke like a Mussulman; why should he be hated? I will see him again. By Alla! such a man is worth knowing, and I may be able to befriend him; surely he is a man of rank.'

But here his surmises were put an end to by Dilawur Ali, who, riding up to him, bade him accompany him, for the Khan was ready to proceed.

'Then you saw the kafirs,—may their end be perdition!' said the rough soldier.

'I did, brother,' returned Kasim; 'miserable enough they look, and as if they could hardly move; how are they to travel?'

'There are covered carts for some, Meer Sahib, for they cannot bear the sun,—doolies for others who are weak; and one or two, who are officers I hear, are to be allowed an elephant,—but we shall see.' And they rode rapidly through the gate of the fort.

'I thought he was an officer,' exclaimed Kasim; 'I thought he was more than one of the lower rank;' as the Englishman with whom he had spoken was desired to mount an elephant which bore a handsome umbara.*

'Why? what know you of him?'

'Nothing; but I spoke a few words to him, and it struck me he was a man of breeding and rank.'

'You had better beware, Kasim,' said his companion; 'acts

* A kind of howdah.

may be misinterpreted, and men like you never want enemies to assist others in thinking ill of them.'

'Thank you for your advice,' said Kasim; 'but I have done or said nothing that I am ashamed of.' Kasim afterwards mentioned what he had done to the Khan, who could not help praising the young soldier's action.

'By the Prophet, well done!' he cried, as Kasim related the incident; 'I am glad the young Haram-zada was soundly whipped; he will know how to throw stones another time. I have fought against the Feringhees, and hate them; and yet, in such a case, I think I should have acted as thou didst, Kasim. Hast thou spoken to the Feringhee since?'

'No: Dilawur Ali seemed to think I had done wrong even in addressing him at all; but I should like much to speak with him; they say he is a Sirdar of rank.'

'I hear he has accepted the Sultaun's offer of pardon, and that he will serve in the army; so at least the Governor of the fort hoped; but we shall see. I doubt it, for the Feringhees are very obstinate, and Tippoo has gained over none as yet by fair means.'

'Then there are some in the army?'

'A few only who have been honoured with the rite of Islam; but they are of the lowest grade, and he does not trust them. Go you then, when we have pitched the camp, and ask this Feringhee whether he will serve with us under the banner of the lion of the Faith.'

CHAPTER XV.

KASIM hardly need be desired to do this; he longed to have some amicable conversation with one who had already excited such interest in his heart, and, as soon as possible after his few duties were discharged, he went to the tents which had been pitched for the English, and sought out his acquaintance. They met with pleasure; on Kasim's part, with the result of the interest he had felt,—on the other's with joy that among so many enemies there was one from whom he had received kindness, and who now again sought him.

'I little thought to have seen you again,' said the officer (for so in truth he was), 'and this visit is a proof to me that we are not enemies.'

'No, certainly,' said Kasim; 'I have no enmity towards you.'

'Perhaps then you can inform me and my poor comrades why we are being removed to the capital; to us it is inexplicable.'

'You are to enter the service of the Sultaun, we hear,' replied Kasim; and from the flush of indignation which rose in the other's pallid face, he could see how that idea was spurned by him.

'Never!' he cried, 'never! and the Sultaun knows this full well; months, nay years ago, he offered the alternative between this and death, and we spurned it with contempt. He will try us again, and receive the same answer; and then, perhaps, he may relieve us by death from this imprisonment, which is worse.'

'Then it has been severe?'

'What! are you in the Sultaun's service, and know not of our condition?'

'I am not in his service,' said Kasim; 'chance threw me into the society of the officer with whom I travel to the city. I may enter it there, which my friend wishes me to do, if it can be effected advantageously.'

'Do not enter it, I beseech you,' cried the Englishman with sudden enthusiasm; 'with so tender and gallant a heart, thou couldst not serve one who is a tiger in nature, one whose glory it is to be savage and merciless as his namesake. Rather fly from hence; bear these letters from me to Madras,—they will ensure thee reward—service—anything thou choosest to ask; take them, and the blessing of Heaven go with thee! thou wilt have succoured the unfortunate, and given news of their existence to many who have long ago mourned us as dead.'

'Feringhee!' said Kasim earnestly, 'thy gallant bearing has won my regard, and my friendly feeling will ever be towards thee; but I abhor thy race, and long for the time when I shall strike a blow against them in fair and open field. I enter the service of the Sultaun at the city, whither we go; and this is answer enough to thy request; ask me not, therefore, to do what I should be ashamed of a week hence. I will speak to my commander about thy letters, and doubt not that they will be forwarded.'

'The only gleam of hope which has broken on me for years has again faded from my sight,' said the young officer with deep melancholy. 'I well know that no letters will be forwarded from me. If thy master, or he who will be so, has denied my existence, and broken his solemn treaties in my detention, and that of the other poor fellows who are with me, thinkest thou he will allow me to write word that I am here?'

'And is it so?' said Kasim; 'I believe thee; thine enemies even say that the English never lie. If it be possible to forward thy letters, I will do it, and ask thee for them; and now farewell! If Kasim Ali Patél can ever help thee, ask for him when thou art in trouble or danger; if he is near thee, he will do his utmost in thy behalf;' so saying Kasim left him, and returned to the Khan.

'I thought it would be as thou hast related,' said he to Kasim, as the latter detailed the conversation; 'such a man is neither to be bribed nor threatened. Even their bitterest enemies must say of these unbelievers that they are faithful to death. May Alla help him! for I fear the Sultaun's displeasure at this, his last rejection of rank and service, may be fatal to him and to the rest; men's determinations, however, do not hold out always with the fear of death before their eyes—but we shall see. Whatever is written in his destiny he must accomplish.'

'Ameen!' said Kasim: 'I pray it may be favourable, for I honour him though he is a kafir.'

On the fifth day afterwards they approached the city. Kasim, with delight that his journey was ended, and that he should enter on his service without delay; the Khan, with mingled feelings of joy at returning to his master and his old companions in arms, and of vexation at the thoughts of his two wives, and the reception Ameena was sure to meet with from them. This, in truth, was a source of the most lively uneasiness to him, for he could not but see that, say what he would to comfort her, the spirit of Ameena had considerably drooped since the night at Nundidroog, when he told her of their existence. Still he hoped the best; and he said to himself, 'If they cannot agree, I shall only have to get a separate house, and live away from them.'

'Behold the city!' cried many an one of those who led the force, as, on reaching the brow of a slight eminence, the broad valley of the river Cavery burst upon them; in the centre of which, though still some miles distant, appeared Seringapatam, amidst groves of trees, and surrounded by richly-cultivated lands, watered by the river. Not much of the fort, or the buildings within it, could be seen; but the tall minarets of a large mosque, two enormous Hindoo pagodas and some other smaller ones, and the white-terraced roofs of the palaces, appeared above the trees; and as they approached nearer, the walls and defences of the fort could be distinguished from the ground upon which it was built.

Passing several redoubts which commanded the road, they reached the river, and fording its uneven and rocky channel with some difficulty, they continued on towards the fort itself, whose long lines of rampart, high walls, bastions, and cavaliers, from which cannon peeped in every direction, filled Kasim with astonishment and delight.

As they rode onwards through the bazaar of the outer town, they saw at the end of the street a cavalcade approaching, evidently that of a person of rank. A number of spearmen preceded it, running very fast, and shouting the titles of a person who was advancing at a canter, followed by a brilliant group, clad in gorgeous apparel, cloth-of-gold, and the finest muslins, and many in chain-armour, which glittered brightly in the sun.

Ere Kasim could ask who it was, the cortége was near the head of his corps, which drew off to one side to allow it to pass. As the company advanced, the Khan dashed his heels into the flanks of his charger, and flew to meet it: Kasim saw him halt suddenly, and present the hilt of his sword to one who, from his appearance and the humility of the Khan's attitude, he felt assured could be no other than the Sultaun.

Just then one of those bulls which the belief of the Hindoos teaches them are incarnations of divinity, and which roam at large in every bazaar, happened to cross the road lazily before the royal party. The attendant spearmen strove to drive it on; but not accustomed to being interfered with so rudely, it resisted their shouts and blows with the butt-end of their spears, and menaced them with its horns. There ensued some little noise, and Kasim, who was watching the Sultaun, saw him observe it.

'A spear, a spear!' he heard him cry; and as one of the attendants handed him one, he exclaimed to his suite, 'Now, friends, for a hunt! Yonder fellow menaces us, by the Prophet! Who will strike a blow for Islam, and help me to destroy this pet of the idolators?—may their mothers be defiled! Follow me!' And so saying, he urged his noble horse onwards.

The bull seeing himself pursued, turned for an instant with the intention of flight, but it was too late; as it turned the spear of the Sultaun was buried in its side, and it staggered on, the blood pouring in torrents from the gaping wound, while it bellowed with pain. One or two of the attendants followed his example; and the Sultaun continued to plunge his weapon into the unresisting animal as fast as he could draw it out, until at last it fell, groaning heavily, having only run a few yards.

'Shabash, shabash! (Well done, well done!) who could have done that but the Sultaun? Inshalla! he is the victorious—he is the slayer of man and beast!—he is the brave in war, and the skilful in hunting!' cried all the attendants and courtiers. But there were many others near, who vented their hate in silent yet bitter curses—Brahmins, to whom the slaughter of the sacred animal was impiety not to be surpassed.

'Ha!' cried the Sultaun, looking upon the group, one of whom had disgust plainly marked upon his countenance; 'ha! thou dost not like this. By the soul of Mahomed we will make thee like it! Seize me that fellow, Furashes!' he cried fiercely, 'and smear his face with the bull's blood; that will teach him to look with an evil eye on his monarch's amusements.'

The order was obeyed literally; and, ere the man knew what was said, he was seized by a number of the powerful attendants; his face was smeared with the warm blood, and some of it forced into his mouth.

'Enough!' cried the Sultaun, leaning back in his saddle as he watched the scene, and laughing immoderately, pointed to the really ludicrous but disgusting appearance of the Brahmin, who, covered with blood and dirt, was vainly striving to sputter forth the abomination which had been forced into his mouth, and to wipe the blood from his face. 'Enough! bring him before us. Now make a lane in front, and give me a spear. Away with thee!' he cried to the Brahmin, 'I will give thee a fair start; but if I overtake thee before yonder turning, thou art a dead man, by Alla!'

The man turned at once, and fled with the utmost speed that terror could lend him; the Sultaun waited a while, then shouted his favourite cry of 'Alla yar!' and, followed by his attendants, darted at full speed after the fugitive. The Brahmin, however, escaped down the narrow turning, and the brilliant party rode on, laughing heartily at their amusement.

Kasim watched all he saw with disgust; for, though a Mohamedan, and a sincere one, he had never heard of a sacred bull being destroyed; and there was something so wanton and cruel in the act of its destruction, that it involuntarily brought to his memory the words of the young Englishman, and his character of the Sultaun. But he had not time for much reflection, for the corps was once more in motion, and he became absorbed in admiration and wonder at all he saw—the extent and wealth of the bazaars—the crowds of people—the numbers of soldiers of gallant bearing—the elephants moving to and fro—and beyond all the fort, the interior of which he now longed to see; but the Khan turned off to the left, having passed the town, and after riding a short distance they entered the camp without the walls, and halted within its precincts.

Leaving Kasim with his tents, which had arrived, and were

being pitched for the accommodation of Ameena, the Khan, accompanied only by his servant Daood, rode into the fort, to his own house, in order to break the news of his marriage to his wives, and to prepare them for their new associate. 'There is sure to be a storm,' he said, 'and it may as well burst upon me at once.'

Alighting therefore at the door, where he was welcomed affectionately by his servants, the news quickly spread through the house that the Khan was come. He only delayed while he washed his feet and face, to cleanse them from the dust of the road, as well as to refresh himself a little ere he passed on into the zenana.

The two ladies, who had expected his arrival, and who had employed a person abroad to inform them of it, were sitting on a musnud smoking at one end of the room, with their backs to the door. As he entered, the gurgling of their hookas became doubly loud; a few slave girls were standing about the apartment, who made low salaams as he approached them; but the ladies neither rose nor took the slightest notice of him.

The Khan was surprised at seeing them together, as when he had left them they were bitter enemies, and he stopped suddenly in his approach. It was evident at once to him that they had heard of his marriage, and made common cause against him; he was justly enraged at this, and at the want of respect, nay insult, with which they now received him.

'Kummoo-bee! Hoormut-bee!' he cried; 'women! do ye not see me? Where is your respect? How dare ye sit as I approach? Am I a man, or am I less than a dog, that ye take no more notice of me than if I were a stone? Speak, ye ill conditioned!'

'Ill-conditioned!' cried Kummoo-bee, who, though the youngest wife, was the worst-tempered, and who led the reply; 'ill-conditioned! Alla, Alla! a man who has no shame—a man who is perjured—a man who is less than a man—a poor, pitiful, unblest coward! Yes,' she exclaimed, her voice rising with her passion as she proceeded, 'a namurd! a fellow who has not the spirit of a flea, to dare to come into the presence of women who, Inshalla! are daughters of men of family! to dare to approach us, and tell us that he has come, and brought with him a vile woman—an unchaste—'

'Hold!' cried the Khan, roused to fury as the words fell on his ear, advancing and seizing a slipper which was on the ground; 'dare to say that again, and I will beat thee!'

'Yes, beat us, beat us!' cried both breathlessly at once

'beat us, and our cup of shame will be full. Beat us, and you will do a valiant deed, and one that your new mistress will approve of,' cried Hoormut.

'Alla, Alla! an old man, one with white hairs, to bring a new mistress to his wives' house! Shame, shame!' vociferated Kummoo.

'I tell thee, woman, she is my wife!' roared the Khan. 'Ye will receive her as such this evening; and cool your tempers in the meanwhile, or by Alla and the apostle, I swear that I will send ye both to your relations, and they may keep ye or not, as they please, for I will not; so bethink ye what ye do; this is my house, and, Inshalla! I will be its master;' and so saying, and not waiting to hear any reply, he left the apartment.

CHAPTER XVI.

It was early in the fifth month after Herbert Compton had seen the shores of his native land grow dim in his aching sight, that the bold western coast of the peninsula of India met the earnest and watchful gaze of all who were assembled upon the deck of the noble vessel which bore them over the blue and sparkling sea.

All that day, before a fresh and lively breeze, the ship had careered onwards to her haven, dashing from her bows the white and hissing foam, which spread itself around her, and mingled in her wake; while, startled from their gambols in the deep, many a shoal of sprightly flying-fish, rising from under the very bows, would take a long flight to leeward, and disappear within the limpid breast of their mother ocean.

Above, the sky was blue, and without a cloud to dim its brightness; and that pureness gave to the sea an intensity of colour which is unknown save where those cloudless skies exist. The fresh wind had curled the sea into graceful waves, which threw their white crests upwards to the sky as they broke, in seeming playfulness, or rejoicing in their gladness. Away through the glassy depths darted the gaudy dolphin and merry porpesse, now chasing each other with many an eager bound, now in a shoal together leaping far above the crystal billows, or appearing to reach the summits of the lucid waves, and, as they broke, sinking down to rest for an instant among their sparkling foam, only to renew the sport in endless variety upon others.

Scattered around them was the fleet, some vessels near, others far distant; some nearly buried under the load of canvas which was stretched to court the wind—others, under a less quantity, gracefully surmounting every wave, and at times showing their brightly coppered sides amongst the white foam in which they were encircled. They were like living beings, urging their way over the bright ocean; for at that distance no human form could be distinctly descried upon their decks, and their rapid progress seemed to be an act of their own gigantic power.

'Land! land on the lee bow!' was the joyful cry heard towards noon from the main-topgallant cross-trees. 'Land!' was re-echoed by all on deck, and each turned to congratulate his fellow-voyagers upon the happy news. Even as they looked, a wreath of white smoke burst from the side of the leading frigate, and mingled with the blue wave; while, with the report which followed, the joyful and long-looked-for signal of land flew to the mast-head, and was repeated by the fleet far and near.

Now every gaze was turned from the deck, and men looked with straining eyes to pierce the haze of the horizon, as if the land lay still above it; and soon there appeared a darker blue outline of rugged form visible; for a while, to an unpractised eye, it was only that of a mist or distant cloud; but it became gradually firmer and more decided, and ere an hour had elapsed, there was no doubt that it was the land of their destination—the land in which many were to die—many to suffer privation and hardship, in war, in captivity, in weary sickness—from which few were destined to return, except with ruined health, bronzed features, and altered tempers from those which in youth and ardent hope they now bore with them.

Few, however, had thoughts of the future; the day was bright and joyful, and, as they neared the shore, it appeared to smile a welcome upon them. The naked precipices of the Ghats reared themselves out of the dark and endless forests which the brilliant sun and soft warm atmosphere softened with tender tints; and as many a one longed to roam far away among those recesses, little thought they how there lurked the demon of deadly fever, who would have smitten them with death had they ventured to intrude upon his solitary domain—solitary, except to the wild elephant, the bison, the bear, and the serpent, which roamed unmolested everywhere, and shared it with him.

As they neared the coast, many a white sail of picturesque form could be seen gliding along it; others, issuing from little harbours and creeks, whose shores were clothed with groves of tall palm-trees, which all had heard of, but none as yet had seen.

As the fleet was descried from the shore, little boats shot out, spreading their wide sails, and as they neared the ships, became objects of intense interest. They would now first see a native of that noble land—a Hindoo, one who worshipped idols, whose faith and manners had been undisturbed for ages; while in the West had spread new faiths, new systems, where everything was daily advancing in civilisation. Fearlessly did the tiny boat advance upon the ship, giving a signal for a rope; and as it was thrown, one of its dark-skinned crew leaped into the chains, and was on deck in a instant—an object of wonder and admiration to those who for the first time beheld him. Tall and finely formed, his figure was a model of symmetry, his eyes large and lustrous, his features regular and amiable in expression, his body naked, except a white cloth around his loins, and a small cap upon his head, quilted in curious patterns.

He had brought fish, he said, to those who, from having made a few voyages, had picked up some few words of his native tongue; and had a few plantains, some eggs and butter, vegetables of the country, and sour curds—all delicious luxuries to those who had long been confined to the usual shipboard fare with dry biscuit. Soon his stock was disposed of, and descending the side, the rope was cast off, and once more his little barque danced over the sparkling waves towards the shore.

They were yet far from Bombay; and as evening approached, the signal-gun and requisite flags warned the fleet to take in sail and stand out to some distance from the shore.

The sun went down in glory. As he descended, a few light clouds formed about him, and the wind dropped to a gentle whispering breeze, but just enough to fill the sails, and the fleet glided onwards in quietness.

As the sun sank, the heavens became one mass of gold, almost too brilliant to look upon! and the clouds, tinged with reddish tints, could only be distinguished by the dazzling colours of their edges. At last it disappeared into a sea of waving, restless, molten gold; and as the waters gradually and lingeringly gave up their brightness, and the beams of light faded from the sails of the ships, the heavens became a mass of most gorgeous colours—crimson, and gold, and purple, fading into dim greenish yellows and tender violet tints on each side; which, as the mind strove to remember them for ever, and the eye to fix them there, but appeared for a while, then faded away, and were no more seen.

Gradually but swiftly night clothed all objects in gloom, and the horizon and sky appeared to blend into one; except in the west, where, so long as light remained, its restless and ever-varying form showed against the last lingering light of day. For a while all watched the beauty of the heavens, spangled with brightly-gleaming stars, and fanned by a gentle and cool wind, which, blowing from the shore, brought with it, they fancied, perfumes of flowers such as those with which they could imagine nature in her profusion had decked the land of which they had had a transient, yet exquisite glimpse. Then, one by one, they dropped the cheerful converse into which they had fallen in groups, and, as the night advanced, sank into gentle slumbers, rocked by the easy motion of their vessel,—to dream of the glories which the coming morrow pictured to their excited imaginations; or of a home, humble perhaps, but endeared by a thousand remembrances of love, of parental affection, of wandering in cool and shady places, beside streams whose murmurings sounded gently in their ears.

Herbert's were thus. A feverish vision of palaces amidst gardens, where the graceful palm-tree and acacia waved over fountains which played unceasingly, and threw up a soft and almost noiseless spray into the air, and where he wandered amidst forms clad in such oriental garbs as his fancy supplied, gorgeous and dazzling with gold and gems—gradually faded from him, and was succeeded by one of peaceful delight.

He seemed to wander once more with Amy, amidst the green and mossy glades of Beechwood: again the well-known path beside the stream was threaded,—his arm was around her, and the familiar converse they had held sounded in his ears,—reply and question, even as they had uttered them together. He had drawn her closer and closer to him as they proceeded, and, as he strained her to his heart in one long and ardent embrace, he thought the murmur of the stream was louder, and he awoke:—it was only the ceaseless splash of the waters against the vessel's side, which came audibly to him through his open port-hole, and which at once dispelled the illusion.

But he composed himself again, to endeavour to recall the fleeting vision, to hear again the words of ideal converse, to hold in thrilling embrace the loved form which only then had been present with him. Vain and futile effort! and strange power of dreams, which enables us often to hold communings with those beloved—though thousands of miles intervene. How strongly does the mind in such moments supply the thoughts and words of two, amid scenes sometimes familiar, more often ideal, and yet palpable in sleep, but dissipated by waking fancy, and often leaving no traces of their existence upon the memory but a confused phantasy, which imagination strives to embody in vain!

Herbert lay restless for a while, and failing of his purpose, he roused himself, looked out over the waters which glistened faintly under the rays of a waning moon; and feeling the air to be fresh, as though it were near the dawn, he arose, dressed himself, and went on deck, in order to watch for the first break of morning over the land they were approaching.

The scattered ships had approached each other during the night, and stood on under easy sail; dreamy they looked,—even as giant spectres walking over the deep. There were some from whose white sails the moon's faint light was reflected, and which glistened under her beams. Others, dark and deeply in shadow, showing no token of the busy life which existed within, or the watchful care which guided them onwards.

Gradually a faint gleam shot up into the eastern sky, a paler colour than the deep blue which had previously existed; it increased, and the lustre of the stars was dimmed. Soon, as all gazed to welcome it, a blush of pink succeeded; and as the day sprang into existence, the frigate's signal-gun boomed over the quiet sea. The joyous day grew into being rapidly; hues of golden, of crimson, flashed upwards, and spread themselves over the sky, revealing by degrees the long and broken line of mountains, which, in parts obscured by the mists floating upon them, and again clear and sharp against the brilliant sky, continued as far as the eye could reach from north to south. Light mists covered the coast and the foot of the mountains, and concealed both from their longing gaze; but as the sun arose in dazzling brilliancy, and the red blush of his morning beams rested upon the ships, the sea, the mountain peaks and naked precipices, the clouds seemed gradually to rise from their slumber, until, broken by his power, they floated upwards slowly, as if nature were purposely lifting her veil from the scene and revealing her beauties by degrees.

They were soon at the entrance of the harbour of Bombay. The islands which guard it rose like fairy creations from the breast of the ocean, wooded and smiling under the light of the sun. Away to the right were the noble range of Ghats,—their peaked and broken summits presenting forms strange to eyes used only to the green and swelling eminences of verdant England; the grounds below them were covered with everlasting forests, and the shore lined by groves of palms, from among which peeped many a white temple with conical roof, or mosque with slender minarets. Before them stretched out the magnificent harbour, studded with bold and lofty islands, among which the mysterious Elephanta and gloomy Carinjah reared their giant forms and wooded sides, bounded by the town and fort of Bombay, which arose from the water's edge, and whose white and terraced houses and noble fortifications gleamed brightly in the sunlight.

Many a tall ship lay there, resting from her travel over the deep, and craft of every description shot here and there over the waters. An Arab dhow, with her high and pointed stern, the pavilion upon it gaily painted—her decks crowded with men clad in the loose robes and heavy turbans of Arabia, and her huge square sail set to catch the breeze—sailed near them. Many gaily-painted Pattamars, with their lateen sails as white as snow, mingled with the fleet; while others of smaller size could be seen stretching across the harbour from the Mahratta continent, bearing their daily supplies of market produce for the populous town.

It was a scene of novel yet exquisite beauty; and, lighted up by the powerful beams of an eastern sun, could not fail of making a lasting impression upon those who, after their weary voyage, saw their eastern home burst upon them in such splendour; nor was there one of all the numerous host contained in those vessels who could look upon it without feelings of mingled emotion.

From the General who commanded,—who, remembering the brilliant career which others had run, hoped in the coming wars to win fame and wealth,—to the lowest private, whose imagination revelled in fancied scenes of excitement far removed from his ordinary dull routine of duty, or of dissipation, which the cold climate of England could not afford,—all were excited far beyond their usual wont; and exclamations of surprise, of wonder, or of gratification, as things new or beautiful or strange passed under their observation, arose from the various groups upon the deck.

Herbert Compton had left England without contracting a particular friendship for any of his brother officers; his close connection and constant intercourse with his own family, and latterly his attachment, had prevented this; but he had not the less observed a cheerful and friendly intercourse with all. He was pained, however, to see how, during the voyage, and the constant and unrestricted intercourse of which the space of a vessel was naturally productive, many of them showed tempers and dispositions which debarred him from joining in such intimate association as their absence from home and residence in a foreign land ought to have engendered.

He was grieved to see, also, how some gave themselves up to

intemperance, as if to drown in wine the memory of things they should have held most dear;—how others betook themselves to cards or dice, to pass away the monotonous hours of their long voyage; how these and other vices had already changed many whom he had at first been inclined to esteem sincerely, and forced him to contract gradually the association which he fain would have had intimate and general.

But there were nevertheless two with whom, though his intercourse had been slight at first, yet it had steadily progressed, and who returned his advances towards a sincere and unreserved friendship with corresponding warmth. One, Philip Dalton, was his equal in rank, and slightly his senior in age, and in the regiment. The other, Charles Balfour, his ensign, a youth even younger than himself, a fair and sprightly fellow, whose joyous spirit nothing could daunt, and over whom care had not as yet flung even a shadow of her sobering mantle.

Dalton was grave and religious, it might be even tinctured with superstition, at least with a belief in destiny; and while his spirit recoiled at once from those thoughtless or vicious companions by whom he was surrounded, whom he shunned the more as he perceived the uncontrolled licence they were prepared to give to their passions upon landing, and whose only conversation consisted in the prospects of indulgence which were opening upon them,—he soon grew into intimate association with Herbert, as well from a similarity of tastes and disgust of the others' wild revelry, as from seeing at once that he possessed a deep religious feeling, and gave expression to his sincere thoughts upon the subject, when it was openly ridiculed or sneered at among the others.

The three were standing in a group by themselves, and Herbert's busy and skilful pencil was rapidly sketching outlines of the mountains and views of the harbour as they successively presented themselves, with the new and curious forms of the boats and vessels around them.

'I envy you that talent, Herbert,' said Dalton; 'how valuable it would be to me, who feel that I shall so lack occupation that the time will often hang heavy on my hands; and how gratifying to those we love to send them even scraps of scenes in which we live and move!'

'Nay, Philip, you have never tried to use your pencil; I would have given you fifty lessons while we have been on board, but you have never expressed the wish. Here is Charles, who is already a tolerable proficient, and who sketches with most meritorious perseverance.'

'It is well for him, Herbert; it will help to keep him from vicious and corrupt society, and on his return to our dear England, you will both have the pleasure of comparing your graphic notes, and talking over these beautiful scenes together. But with me it is different: I feel even now that yonder glorious land will be my grave, that the name of Philip Dalton will live only for a while, and that some fatal shot or deadly fever will free me from this earthly existence.'

'Nonsense, Philip!' cried both at once; 'why should you be so gloomy amidst so bright and joyous a scene? As for me,' continued Balfour, 'I intend to defy bullet-shots and jungle-fevers, to become a major or a colonel at least, to serve my time out here, and then go home and marry some one. I don't intend to get bilious or brown or ugly, but to keep my own tolerable looks for ten years at all events. That bright land is an earnest to me of success; and as it now smiles upon us a hearty welcome, so do I feel my spirits rise within me proportionately. Why should I forbid them?'

'Ay, why should you, Charles?' said Dalton; 'I would that mine were as light as yours, but they are not so, nor ever have been; and I am thankful too for this, for I have been led to think more deeply of serious matters than I otherwise should have done, and thus in some degree to prepare for the change which must soon come to me. Your career will, I hope, be very different, and I trust that your own bright hopes will be fulfilled; but remember, that though the sky and land are bright and fair, fairer than our England, yet death strikes many more of our race here than there, and that we have to encounter dangers in the field—active and brave enemies—so that we had need to be prepared whenever the blow comes, either by a shot upon the battle-field, or by the slower but equally fatal disease. Is it not so, Herbert?'

'It is, Philip; and yet I would not allow, were I you, such dismal phantasies and thoughts to possess me. Surely, when God has thrown around us such beauties as these, our hearts should bid us rejoice, and enjoy them as they are sent, and we ought not to think gloomily upon the future, which may lead us insensibly into discontent and repining. Let us only continue this our unreserved and sincere friendship, whatever may be our position, and I feel confident that we possess in it the elements of much happiness, perhaps of mutual assistance in many difficulties.'

'With all my heart and soul I promise it, Herbert,' cried Dalton, and he was followed with equal enthusiasm by Balfour.

'There will arise many adverse parties in the regiment, I foresee, but we need know none; singly, we might be obliged to belong to one or other—united, we may be thought singular, but we are safe, and I for one am ready to brave all obloquy on this score in your society.'

'Then we are agreed, Philip,' said Herbert; 'if it be possible we will live together; it will take some time perhaps to arrange this, but if it can be done, are you willing?'

'Perfectly.'

'And you, Charles?'

'Certainly; there is nothing I should like better than to be near you both always, for I feel that my wild spirits might lead me to do things in company with many of the rest, who are very pleasant fellows, that I should feel ashamed of afterwards.'

'This is, then, a happy termination to our voyage,' said Herbert; 'one unlooked for at its commencement, one which already is a comfort to me; for I am assured that, whether we are safe in barracks, or in the danger of service, in action or in sickness, we shall be much to one another, and that we shall have always some one near us on whom we can rely in any strait.'

'I confess that many of my gloomy thoughts have passed away already,' said Philip; 'but let us for the present keep our own counsel, lest we be denounced as a party even before we go on shore. There, your sketch will do, Herbert; it is capital! And now put up your book, for I suspect we are not far from our anchorage, as the frigates are shortening sail; at anyrate, you should look about you.'

They had sailed gradually on under the light morning breeze, which was fast falling, and hardly served to carry them to their resting-place; but still they moved, and thus the enjoyment they felt at the novelty of the scene around them was insensibly prolonged. The fleet had now all drawn together, and many greetings were exchanged between friends on board different vessels, who had been unavoidably separated during the voyage. The ships one by one shortened sail, and as they watched with anxiety the movements of the leading frigate, they heard at last the splash of her anchor as it plunged from her bows; simultaneously a wreath of smoke burst from her sides, and the first gun of her cheering salute awoke the echoes of the islands and shores of the harbour; ere it was finished her sails were furled, and she lay peacefully upon the smooth water, 'a thing of life,' seemingly enjoying rest after her long and ceaseless travel. Her consort followed her example—then the ships of the fleet in rotation; and the fort and vessels in the harbour saluted in return, a joyful earnest of a hearty welcome.

Many a telescope was directed to the crowds of people who lined the shores, the piers, and the fortifications, and many were the speculations upon their varied appearance and costumes. All, at that distance, appeared bright and clean and cheerful, and the inmates of the vessels longed fervently to set foot upon the land once more. As they anchored, each ship became surrounded by boats; and the shrill cries of vendors of fruit, vegetables, fresh bread, with eggs and other refreshments, resounded on all sides,—a din which almost bewildered them.

Their turn came to be visited by the staff-officers from shore; their men were paraded, and each company, headed by its officer, was inspected. They were shocked by the appearance of their inspectors—sallow and pale—as if disease of the worst kind possessed them; they seemed more like men who had just arisen from their death-beds, than any in active performance of very onerous and fatiguing duties.

'To this must we come, you see, Charles,' said Philip Dalton, as the staff-officer, having inspected his company and complimented him upon its appearance, passed on to another; 'pale faces, death-like looks, seem to be the lot of all here who attain to blue coats, cocked hats and plumes. It was but just now that you said you *would* preserve yours, in spite of all climate; you see the result of time and hot weather better than I can tell you.'

'I cannot bear to think of it,' said Charles; 'but surely all cannot be so, Philip? However, we shall see when we get ashore. When are we to land?'

'This evening, I believe; they are preparing our barracks for us; till then we must admire at a distance.'

'More than we shall on shore, I daresay,' said his companion, and so indeed it proved.

The landing in the close warm evening,—the march through the Fort over the dusty roads,—the aspect of the narrow streets and oddly fashioned houses,—the heat, the flies, the smells of various kinds, some not the most fragrant,—particularly that of fish under the process of drying,—the discomfort of their first night on shore, passed in beds but ill adapted to defy the attacks of their bitter foes the musquitoes, completely dispelled all the romance which they had hoped would be attendant on a landing in the gorgeous East, but which they discovered, with no small chagrin, existed only in their imaginations. All their beautiful gardens and gilded palaces, their luxurious couches and airy fountains, had passed away, and given place to the bare and dull reality of a barrack-room ; not half so comfortable, they thought, as their old quarters in England, to which many of their thoughts wandered painfully.

CHAPTER XVII.

GRADUALLY, however, all became more and more indifferent to these discomforts, and the few days which passed in the barracks, previous to their second embarkation, were as fully occupied as soldiers' time usually is when preparations for service, and that too of an active and spirit-stirring kind, are undertaken.

The close of the year 1782 had brought with it an event of the most important magnitude to the British interests in India. When Madras was in a state of famine, its treasury exhausted, and its means even of defence at the lowest ebb, Hyder Ali, the most formidable and untiring foe the English had ever known, constantly victorious over the ill-commanded armies of the southern Presidency, and holding a position which, in case of a successful blow early in the next campaign, would render him master of the field, died at Chittoor.

The relief which this event gave to the minds of the public functionaries in the south was great; and a blow upon the army which had obeyed Hyder, might have been struck with advantage in the absence of any leader on whom it could have relied: that opportunity, however, was allowed to pass. Tippoo, the enterprising son of the deceased chief, was enabled to join it; and he assumed the command, and inheritance of his father's dominions, without opposition—nay, amidst the rejoicings of his future subjects. He had been employed in directing a successful opposition to the British invasion of his dominions from the westward, which had made much progress; and he had nearly succeeded in his object, when the news of his father's death was secretly conveyed to him. In order now to establish his authority, it was absolutely necessary that he should cross the peninsula, and proceed at once to Chittoor, where his father had died, and where the army lay. This absence from his command, which was longer protracted than the invaders had calculated upon, gave them renewed courage, and the war against the Mysore dominions was prosecuted by the Bombay force with a vigour and success which had long been strangers to the operations of the English.

During the time which Tippoo necessarily consumed in consolidating his authority in the eastern part of his dominions, and providing for the invasion there menaced by the force of the Madras Presidency, the Bombay army, which had been driven by him into the fort of Paniané, had received reinforcements, and in return was enabled to beat back its assailants, and to advance with some success once more into the enemy's country, though from a more northern position, whither it had proceeded by sea. Before, however, any expedition of magnitude, or that promised a permanent occupation of the country, could be undertaken from Merjee (now the position of the Bombay force) it was necessary that it should be reinforced largely—in fact reconstituted; and the opportune arrival of the large body of European troops, to which Herbert Compton and his companions belonged, enabled the Government to effect this in an efficient manner.

There were two ways also in which the dominions of Mysore could be assaulted; the one through the natural road, or gap, eastward from the town of Calicut, in the midst of which was situated the strong fort of Palghatcherry, and which led immediately into the rich provinces of Coimbatoor and Barah Mahal, bordering on the English possessions to the eastward; and another, by any one of the passes which led upwards from the level country between the Ghats and the sea, into the kingdom of Mysore. The southern route had been often attempted; but from the difficulty of the road, the dense jungles, and the facility with which the invading forces could be met by the Mysore armies, attacks had never more than partially succeeded. It was hoped that, when once the army reached the table-land above the mountains, it would not only hold a superior and commanding position for further operations towards the capital, in case of previous success, but it would possess the incalculable advantage of a cool and salubrious climate, of so much importance to the health—nay, existence—of the European troops.

Accordingly, when it was known at Bombay that the force had been enabled to escape from the fort of Paniané, where, as we have mentioned, it had been beleagured by Tippoo in person—that it had sailed—re-landed at Merjee, and was in condition to resume operations—it was determined that the whole of the disposable force, including the newly-arrived troops, should be sent to join it, and that operations should be commenced without delay.

Already prepared for active service, Herbert's regiment was

one of the first which sailed again from the island : its complete equipment, and the health and spirit of the officers and men, led the Government to place every dependence on its exertions in the coming arduous contest. It was followed on the same day by others ; and three or four days of delightful sailing down the beautiful coast brought the armament to its desired haven, and the troops landed amidst the cheers and hearty welcome of their future brethren in arms.

A very few days served to make preparations for the campaign : bullocks and stores had already been collected, with a few elephants to assist the guns in their ascent of the passes ; and, after the plans for the campaign had been determined by the leaders—Mathews, Macleod, Humberstone, and Shaw—the army moved from its camp toward its destination.

There was necessarily much of romance in the early campaigns in India : the country was unknown, and imagination peopled it with warlike races far different from the peaceable inhabitants of the coasts—men in whom the pride of possession, of high rank, of wealth, of fierce bigotry and hatred of the Christians, uniting, made them no less the objects of curiosity, than worthy enemies of the gallant bands which sought them in war. Those who were new to the country, and who, in the close atmosphere and thick jungles of the coast, saw little to realise their dreams of eastern beauty, looked to the wall of mountains spread out before them, with the utmost ardour of impatience to surmount them. Beyond them, they should see the splendour of Asiatic pomp, the palaces, the gardens, the luxuries of which they had heard ; beyond them, they should meet the foes they sought in the fair field ; there, there was not only honour to be won, but riches—wealth unbounded, the sack of towns, the spoil of treasuries, which, if they might believe the reports diligently circulated throughout the army, only waited their coming to fall into their possession ; above all, they burned to revenge the defeat and destruction of Bailie's detachment in the west, which was vaunted of by their enemies, and to retrieve the dishonour with which that defeat had tarnished the hitherto unsullied reputation of the British.

The spies brought them word that the passes were ill-defended, that the rich city of Bednore, with its surrounding territory, was unprotected, that its governor, an officer of Tippoo's, and a forcibly-converted Hindoo, sought earnestly an opportunity to revenge his own dishonour, in surrendering this the key of his master's dominions into the hands of his enemies. It is no wonder then, that, urged on by cupidity, and inflamed by an ardent zeal to carry the instructions he had received into effect, the commander, Mathews, looked to the realisation of his hopes with a certainty which shut out the necessity of securing himself against reverses, and hurried blindly on to what at first looked so brightly, but which soon clouded over, and led to the miserable fate of many.

It was a subject of painful anxiety to Herbert and his companions, so long as the destination of their regiment was unknown; for the army had to separate—part of it to reduce the forts and hold the country below the passes (a service which none of them liked in anticipation), and the other to press on through the open country to Bednore, the present object of their most ardent hopes. The strong fort of Honoor, however, which lay not far from their place of rendezvous, could not be passed; and to try the temper of the troops, and to strike terror into the country, it was assaulted and carried by storm, with the spirit of men whom no common danger could appal, and who, in this their first enterprise, showed that they had only to be led with determination in order to perform prodigies of valour. Nor was there any check given to their rapacity; the place was plundered, and thus their appetites were whetted both with blood and spoil for their ensuing service

Now, indeed, shone out the true spirit of many an one whom Herbert and his companions had even respected hitherto; and they saw rapacity and lust possessing them, to the extinction of every moral feeling; while unbridled revelry, habitual disregard of temperance, and indulgence in excesses, hurried many to the grave whom even the bullet and the sword spared. They were thankful to be thus knit in those bonds of friendship which the conduct of their associates only drew the closer. They lived in the same tents, marched together, fought together, and found that many of their duties were lighter, and their marches and watches the shorter, for the companionship they had made for themselves.

The commander, Mathews, a man of deep religious feeling, quite amounting to superstition, had early remarked the appearance of Philip Dalton; his high bearing, his steady conduct, the grave expression of his face, impressed him with a sense of his assimilation to himself in thought; and the excellent appearance of his men, and his attention to their comforts, with a high estimate of him as a soldier. Nor did Herbert escape his observation, nor the evident friendship which existed between them. On inquiry he found that both bore the highest character, though their habits of exclusiveness and hauteur were sneered at; yet, perceiving the cause, they rose the higher in his opinion on that account. For some time he weighed between the two; but gradually leaning to the side of Dalton, he at last determined to offer to him the post of aide-de-camp and secretary, which he accepted; and this, though productive of temporary separations between the friends, still gave them ample opportunities of association.

A few days after the storm and capture of Honoor, in which Herbert's regiment had borne a conspicuous part, and he, as commander of the light company, had been noticed by the general in orders, the army reached the foot of the pass, above which the fort of Hussainghurry reared its head, and from which it took its name. Of the defences of the pass all were in fact ignorant, but the native spies had represented them as weak and easily to be surmounted, and they were implicitly believed. A few straggling parties of the enemy had been met with during the day, and driven up the pass, without any prisoners having been made from whom an idea of the opposition to be encountered could be gained or extorted. The way, however, lay before them; the army was in the highest spirits; and, though the only road discernible was a rugged path, almost perpendicular, up the side of the immense mountain, yet to them there was nought to be dreaded—the morrow would see them on the head of the ascent, breathing a purer air, with the broad plains of India before them, to march whither they listed.

It was night ere the army was safely encamped at the foot of the pass; the regiments had taken up their ground in the order they were to ascend, and Herbert's company was in the van; upon it would rest, if not the fate of the day, at least the brunt of the ascent. Philip Dalton sought him after his duties were over, the final orders had been given, and the various officers had been warned for the performance of their several parts in the coming struggle.

'I am afraid you will have hot work to-morrow, Herbert,' he said, as he entered his little tent, where sat his friend writing very earnestly. 'I tried all I could to get the regiment another place, or at least to have the force march right in front, but it could not be done. Somehow or other the general had more than ordinary confidence in the light company of the —th, and was pleased to express a very flattering opinion of my friend; so—'

'Make no apologies, dear Philip; all is as it should be—as I wish it; I would not have it otherwise for the world. My gallant fellows are ready for the fray, and you know they are not easily daunted; besides, what is there to be afraid of? The people we have seen as yet have fled before us, panic-stricken, ever since the affair of Honoor, and I for one anticipate nothing but a pleasant walk up the mountain, or a scramble rather, for the road does not look over smooth.'

'There will be hot work, nevertheless, Herbert; we have the best information as to the defences of the pass; they are insignificant, it is true, but every rock is a defence, and a shelter from whence the steady fire of these fellows may be fatal; and we hear of a scarped wall or something of the kind at the top, which we cannot very clearly make out. Would that I understood the language of the country, and could make inquiries myself; it appears to me that those who pretend to know it make but a lamentable hand of it, and guess at half they ought to know.'

'It matters not, Philip—there is the road; we are to get to the top if we can. I presume no other orders will be necessary.'

'None.'

'Then trust me for the rest. I have a little memorandum here, which I was writing, and which, if you will wait with me for a while, I will finish. It is only in case anything happens, you know,' he added gaily, 'there are a few things I would wish to be done.'

I will not disturb you, so write on; I too had a similar errand, —ours is but an interchange of commissions.'

'There, my few words are soon finished,' said Herbert; 'these are addressed to you, Philip, but they are to be opened in case only of accident. Here are a few letters that I have written in my desk, which, with all my sketches, you must send home for me, or take with you if you go; for the rest, this will tell you fully all I wish to have done.'

'It is safe with me, Herbert, if I am safe myself, of which I have small hope.'

'Ah, so you said at Honoor; yet who exposed himself more, or fought better, nay hand to hand with some of the natives, than yourself? I shall use your own word destiny, and argue against you.'

'Nevertheless, I am more impressed than ever with the certainty that I stand before you for the last time, Herbert. I shall not seek danger, however; indeed, my post near the general precludes my doing so of my own accord; but in case of accident, here are my few memorandums; put them in your desk, where they can remain safely.'

'And so now, having deposited our mutual last commands with each other, let us not think on the morrow, Philip, but as one in which we may win honour. If God wills it, we may meet when all is over, and we are quietly encamped upon the top, and fight all our battles over again. I am glad, at all events, that I shall have Charles Balfour with me.'

'Ah! how is that?'

'Why, the picquets are ordered to join the advance guard, which is my company; he commands them to-day, and is yonder bivouacking under a tree, I believe; I was going to him when you came. Poor boy, I believe he is alone; will you come?'

'With all my heart.'

They took their way through the busy camp, where numerous watch-fires were gleaming, and groups of native soldiery gathered round them, warming themselves from the cold night air and dew which was fast falling. The spot on which the army rested was an open space at the very foot of the pass, surrounded by dense jungle, and mountains whose bulk appeared magnified by the dusk. Although the stars shone brightly, the fires which blazed around caused everything to appear dark, except in their immediate vicinity, where the light fell on many a swarthy group, among whom the rude hooka went its busy round, as they sat and discussed the chances of plunder on the morrow, or the events of the past day. Everywhere arose the busy hum of men, the careless laugh, the shout for a friend or comrade, many a profane oath and jest, and often the burden of a song to which a rude chorus was sung by others. The large mess-tent of the regiment, with its doors wide open, displayed by the glare within a group of choice spirits, who, over the bottle they could not forsake, fought their battles over again, coolly discussed the chances of promotion, and openly boasted of the plunder they had acquired, and their thirst for more. Herbert and his friend could almost guess from the gesticulations the nature of the conversation, and could see that the men who held those orgies were drowning in wine the cares and thoughts which the events of the coming day might otherwise press on them. They turned away to where the watchful sentinels, placed double, native and European, paced upon their narrow walk, and where, around the embers of fires which had been lighted, the picquets lay wrapped in their coats, taking the rest which should fit them for the morrow's arduous strife.

'Who comes there?' challenged the nearest sentry, one of his own company.

'A friend—Captain Compton; do you know where Mr. Balfour is?'

'Yonder, sir; the officer of the native regiment is with him; they are sitting under the tree near yon fire.'

Thither they proceeded—it was but a few steps off.

'Ah! this is kind of you, Herbert and Philip, to come to cheer my watch; not that it is lonely, for Mr. Wheeler here, who shares it with me, has a store of coffee and other matters very agreeable to discuss; but it was kind of you to come to me. Now be seated, camp fashion, upon the ground, and let us talk over the affairs of to-morrow; we are likely, it appears, to have some work.'

'How do you know? have you any late news?' asked Philip.

'Mr. Wheeler can tell you better than I; but a short time ago the sentry yonder challenged in the direction of the pass, and, no answer being returned, I took a corporal's guard and made a little expedition, which was in some degree successful; for we caught two fellows who looked marvellously like spies, but who, on being interrogated by my friend here, swore lustily they were deserters, who had come to give information. From them we learned that at least twenty thousand of Tippoo's valiant troops were prepared to make this a second Thermopylæ, that we should have to storm entrenchments, and perform prodigies of valour, and that we might possibly get near the top; but as to surmounting it, that was out of the question: was it not so, Mr. Wheeler?'

'It was as you have said: these fellows were very likely put forward to give this news, in order that we might be deterred from our attack, and thereby give them time to throw up some breastworks or stockades, at which they are expert enough. I fancy, however, the intelligence will have but little effect upon the general.'

'What have you done with the prisoners? Sent them to headquarters, of course, Philip? I thought you must have seen them ere this.'

'No, indeed, I have not; but it is time I should. I may be wanted, too, and I must bid you farewell. If I can, I will be with you early; if not, and we are spared, we shall meet to-morrow on the summit. So once more, God bless you both!'

'God bless you! God bless you!' both repeated sincerely and affectionately, as they wrung his hand. It might be they should never meet again; but they were young, and soldiers, among whom such thoughts are seldom expressed, though they are often felt.

Herbert as yet had formed no acquaintance with the officers of the native army. Taught by the tone prevalent among those of his own at that period, to consider them of a lower grade, he was both surprised and gratified to find Mr. Wheeler a man of very general information. In particular he found him to be excellent authority on many matters connected with the usages and customs of the native troops, which to Herbert's military eye had appeared quite out of rule; and the sensible explanations he gave of these and many other circumstances, not only amused Herbert and his companion during their watch, but threw much light on the objects and chances of success in their undertaking.

'Then you think the general has considered the end without the means to accomplish what he has in view?' said Herbert, questioning him upon a remark he hazarded.

'I do; I think too (and the thought is not original, but one of high authority that I could mention, only it is discreet not to do so) that the Government is wrong in the precipitancy with which they have urged this on, and are injuring it daily. Our force is not sufficient to keep any country against Tippoo's whole army, which, whatever others may say of it, is in a very respectable state of discipline; and if we succeed in reaching Bednore, we shall hardly get out of it with whole bones. Have we men to occupy the passes, to take forts, to secure the country, and to fight Tippoo besides?'

'We have little force enough certainly,' said Herbert; 'but then most are Europeans.'

'Ay, but they are difficult to support, and helpless if not supported. It is the fashion for you gentlemen of the royal army to cry down our poor fellows, who after all fight well and do all the drudgery. We may never meet again, Captain Herbert, but you will remember the words of a poor Sub of native infantry, who, because he knows more of the native character than your general, and more of the country, is very much disposed to prophesy a disastrous end to what is just now very brilliant.'

'I hope you are wrong; nevertheless, what is chalked out for us we must do; we ought to have no opinions but those of our superiors.'

'Ah, well! that is the acmé of discipline to which I fear we shall never attain,' said the lieutenant, laughing. 'I, for one, am willing to play my part in what is before us; for I am too inured by this time to hard blows and desultory fighting to care much for the passage of a ghat, where, after all, the resistance to be apprehended may only be from a few fellows behind a wall with rusty matchlocks.'

'You are right, Mr. Wheeler,' said young Balfour; 'I want to see my good fellows show the army the way to get up a hill; you, Herbert, will answer for their doing the thing in style.'

'I can, Charles; but remember you are not to be rash. As your superior officer, I shall beg of you to use discretion with your valour. Do I not advise well, Mr. Wheeler?'

'You do indeed, sir; I wish many higher than you in rank could think as calmly while they act as bravely. But here comes the field-officer of the night; we must be on the alert, Mr. Balfour. Good night, Captain Compton! we may renew this acquaintance.'

'I shall be delighted to do so whenever you please; you know where to find me, in the lines of the —th; I am seldom absent. And now, dear Charles, tell me before you go if I can do anything for you, in case of accident to-morrow? Dalton and I have exchanged little memorandums, which I felt to be necessary, as we are to bear the brunt of the business.'

'Ah, there is really no danger, Herbert: you see Mr. Wheeler says there is none; besides—'

'Do not say so, Charles; wherever bullets are flying, there is danger. I do not mean—God forbid I should think of any danger to you—but it is our duty to consider such matters, that we may be able to meet them calmly.'

'You are right, you are right, dear Herbert; I am glad you have spoken to me, for I dared not have mentioned it to you or Dalton. But in case I am—in case, you know, of any accident—you will write home about me, Herbert. You will find the direction pasted inside my desk—to my—my—mother—'

Poor boy! the sudden thought of her, linked with that of his own possible death, was too much for a heart overflowing with affection for his only parent. He struggled for a while with his feelings, and then, able to control them no longer, burst into tears.

Herbert did not check them. It was but for a moment, however; he quickly rallied. 'This is a weakness which I little thought to have displayed, Herbert; but just then my thoughts were too much for me. Will you do what I asked?'

'That will I, most cheerfully, if I live, Charles.'

'And just tell them,' he continued gaily, 'what sort of a fellow I have been. It will be a comfort for them to know perhaps that—but enough!—you know all. Wheeler has got his men ready, and yonder are the rounds: so good night! to-morrow we spend for a time, at all events, in company. I am glad you spoke to me—I feel all the lighter for it already.'

'Good night, Charles! get some rest if you can after the

rounds are past, you will need it; and all appears safe and quiet now around us.'

Herbert slowly returned towards his tent, picking his way amidst the prostrate forms of the native followers, which everywhere covered the ground, wrapped in deep sleep. All was now still, except the spot he had left, where the usual words of the guards challenging the rounds arose shrill and clear upon the night air; and the 'Pass Grand Round—all is well!' gave a sense of security, which, in the midst of a watchful enemy's country, was doubly acceptable. Once he thought, as he listened, that the challenge was answered from the pass by the shrill and quivering blast of the brass horn of the country; and he looked, lest there should be any stir discernible. But all was still; the giant form of the mountain apparently slept in the calm night air; a few mists were wreathing themselves about its summit, which was sharply defined against the deep blue sky glistening with stars; and here and there the bright twinkle of a distant watch-fire far above him showed that the enemy kept their watch too as carefully as their assailants.

The camp was quite hushed; here and there the sharp bark of a dog arose, but was as instantly silenced; or the screams and howlings of a pack of jackals, as they prowled about the outskirts of the camp in search of offal, awoke the echoes of the mountains. The drowsy tinklings of the cattle-bells, with their varied tones, and the shrill chirrupings of innumerable grasshoppers, were sounds which never ceased: but they were peaceful, and invited that repose which all needed and were enjoying.

CHAPTER XVIII.

LONG ere the morning's dawn had broken, the bugle's cheerful note had sounded the reveillé; from the headquarter tents the first blast arose, and its prolonged echoes rang through the mountains—now retiring far away among the dense woods—now returning and swelling upon the ear more near and more distinct than it had been at first. One by one the regiments took it up, and were followed by their drums and fifes, making the solitudes, which hitherto had known only the growl of the bear, the shrieking howl of the hyæna, or the bellow of the wild bison, resound with the inspiring and martial sounds.

Soon all were prepared; the regiments fell into the various places allotted to them; the light artillery, to which were harnessed the strongest and most active bullocks—each piece having an elephant behind to urge it over the roughest or most inaccessible places—brought up the rear. Each man was as lightly equipped as possible, that he might not be distressed by climbing; and, as a last order, might be heard the words 'Fix bayonets, with cartridge prime and load!' pass from regiment to regiment, succeeded by the rattling of the muskets and jingling sound of ramrods, as each sent home the ball which he firmly hoped might in its discharge bear with it the life of one of his enemies.

Herbert and his young friend Balfour had long been ready, and waiting for the signal to advance at the head of the column; their men were impatient, and their blood was chilled with the long detention which the preparation of so large a body necessarily occasioned. They were standing around a fire which one of the men had kindled with some dry leaves and sticks gathered from the adjacent thickets. All about them was obscure; for the thick vapour which had wreathed itself about the mountain-tops early in the night, had now descended, and occupied the whole of the narrow valleys in dense volumes, so that nothing could be seen beyond their immediate vicinity; they could only hear the bugle-sounds, as they arose one by one, and the measured tramp of many feet as the corps moved to take up their various positions.

'This is very tiresome, Herbert,' said Balfour; 'I wish we were off. I think we could do much under cover of this darkness; we might surprise the fellows above, and be at the top before they knew what we were about.'

'I rather think we shall wait for daylight; but what is your opinion, Mr. Wheeler?' he said to the young man who had just joined them.

'I think with you. The general most likely has heard that this fog will rise with the daylight, and screen us half way up, perhaps better than the night; but here is Captain Dalton, who looks as if he had orders for the advaneed guard.'

'Where is your captain?' they heard him ask of one of the sergeants; 'I have orders for him.'

'Yonder, sir,' replied the man, whose concluding words were unheeded in the cry of 'Here, here, by the fire!' which arose from the trio around it.

'Well, Philip, are we to move on? I suppose there will be no signal?' asked Herbert, as Dalton rode up.

'Not yet, not yet; we are to wait till daylight,' returned the other; 'the fellows who came in last night have offered to lead up two detachments, so that the whole force can advance and the columns support each other.'

'That is well, so far; but we are still to have the main path, I hope.'

'Oh yes, and the native company will lead the other—yours perhaps, Mr. Wheeler.'

'Yes, mine; and I am glad to hear it. Now, Captain Compton, we have a fair chance; natives against Englishmen in fair emulation.'

'Ah, here are the fellows! Will you take charge of one, Herbert? and you, Mr. Wheeler, of the other? If either of you find they have led you wrong, you are at liberty to shoot them upon the spot. Will you explain that fully to them, if you please?—though indeed they ought to know it pretty well already. And now good-bye, boys, and good success to ye all! the —th never yet yielded, and you have the post of honour to-day—so remember!'

These few words were received with a hearty shout by the sections around, and Dalton departed to deliver the other commands with which he was charged.

The short time which elapsed before the signal for advance, was passed by Herbert and his companions in examination of the men who were to lead them.

With very different feelings had these men sought the English camp. The one a Nair, a Hindoo of high birth, forcibly converted to the religion of Mahomedanism, burned for an opportunity of revenge. The other, a Mahomedan—a fellow in whose heart grew and flourished every base passion, more particularly that of gain, which had led him to proffer his services to the English commander for gold.

They had both been promised reward, which, while the one indignantly scorned, the other bargained for with the rapacity of his nature; the one was willing to hazard his life for his revenge, the other for the gold which had been promised. How different was to be the fate of the two!

Now in the presence of the two young English leaders, both were confronted and examined. The young Nair, a fellow of high and haughty bearing, ill brooked the searching and suspicious questions of the English officer; but he gave, nevertheless, clear and distinct information about the road, free from every taint of suspicion.

'What is to be thy reward?' asked Wheeler at last.

'My revenge for the insult upon my faith. I was a Nair once, yet am now a vile Mussulman. I need say no more, and it concerns thee not.'

'Thou art haughty enough, methinks,' returned his questioner.

'As thyself,' was his only reply.

'By Jove, he is a fine fellow!' said Herbert, who guessed at the conversation; 'let me have him with me.'

'As you will. Now let us see what account the other can give of himself. What is to be thy reward, good fellow?'

'I was promised two hundred rupees for this service. My lord will surely see his slave gets the money?'

'That depends upon thy conduct: if thou art false, I swear to thee I will shoot thee like a dog. I like not thy face.'

'Your slave's life is in your hands—may I be your sacrifice this moment—I will lead you safely; ask him yonder whether I will or no.'

'I cannot answer for him,' said the Nair haughtily; 'he guides you for gain: give me the post of danger. I know he is a coward at heart; let him take the back way, he will show it for fear of his life: I will fight for my revenge.'

'So be it then, Captain Compton; as yours is the main column, take you the best man. I leave you my orderly, who speaks enough English to interpret a little between you and your guide. And now to our posts, for the day dawns, I suspect.'

'How?'

'Did you not feel a breath of wind? That tells us that the new day has awakened; you will soon hear the bugle.'

Nor did they wait long. The long-expected sound arose from the centre of the force; it was answered by the others in front and rear; and the column, like a huge snake, began its steep and tortuous ascent in perfect silence.

Herbert had received orders not to hurry, and with some difficulty restrained the ardour of his men, and the impatience of his young friend, who, with himself, was with the leading section of the advance. Long they climbed up the narrow and rugged pass, which, though a rough one, possessed the form of a road, and as yet no obstacle had been met with. The mist still hung upon the mountain; but the gentle wind which had arisen was swaying it to and fro, causing it to wheel in eddies about them; and the now increasing light showed them the track, and gave them glimpses of the deep and precipitous ravines, upon the very edges of which they were proceeding,—giddy depths, into which the eye strove to penetrate, but filled with the whirling mists which, though in motion, had not yet arisen.

For nearly an hour did they proceed thus slowly, in order that the rear corps might fully support them; and they could hear the steps of the column on their right marching parallel with themselves at no great distance among the forest trees. At length the head of the column approached a rock, which formed an acute angle with the road. Motioning with his hand for them to advance slowly, the young Nair drew his sword and ran lightly on. They saw him crouch down and disappear.

'He will betray us!' cried Balfour; 'on—after him!' And he would have obeyed the impulse of his ardour but for his captain.

'Be still an instant, I will answer for his fidelity,' exclaimed Herbert. He had hardly spoken, ere the young man was seen again, waving his sword.

'Now, my lads, follow me!' cried Herbert, dashing forward. 'Promotion to the first who enters the defences!'

Ere the enemy could hear the cheer which followed these words, their assailants were upon them. Turning the angle, they beheld a wall of strong masonry, with loop-holes for musketry, one side of which was built against a precipitous rock—the other open. One or two matchlocks were discharged ineffectually from the rampart, but this was no check to them: hurrying on, they crowded through the side opening, where they were met by a few determined fellows, who opposed them for an instant. Vain endeavour! The deadly bayonet was doing its work; and a few slight sword-cuts only served to inflame those who received them to more deadly revenge. The Nair fought nobly. Cheered on by the soldiers, who took delight in his prowess, he threw himself headlong upon several of the defenders of the place in succession; and, though he too was slightly wounded, yet his deeply-planted sword-cuts told the strength of arm which inflicted them, and the deep hate and revenge which urged him on.

Now, indeed, ensued a scene of excitement and spirited exertion difficult to describe. The few musket-shots which had been fired, proved to those in the rear that the work had begun in earnest, and every one now strove to be the first to mingle in it. The column pressed on, disregarding order and formation, which indeed was little necessary, but which was preserved by the officers as far as possible. The gallant Macleod was soon with the leading sections, animating the men by his gestures and his cheers. They needed not this, however, for Herbert was there, and young Balfour, who emulated his example; and all hurried after the fugitives, from ascent to ascent, with various effect. Now one of their number would fall by a shot—now one of the Europeans, as the retreating enemy turned and fired. Now a wreath of smoke would burst from among the bushes and crags above them, and the bullets would sing harmlessly over their heads, or rattle among the stones around them :—again this would be answered by the steady fire of a section, which was given ere the men rushed forward with the more sure and deadly bayonet.

Herbert and his men, guided by the Nair, still fought on in the front, toiling up many a steep ascent : one by one the works which guarded them were carried ; and though in many cases obstinately disputed for a few moments, yet eventually abandoned—their defenders, panic-stricken, hurried after the horde of fugitives which now pressed up the pass before them.

At length a steeper acclivity appeared in view, the sides of which were lined with a more numerous body of men than had hitherto been seen ; and the sun, which now broke over the mountain's brow for the first time, glanced from their steel spears and bright musket-barrels.

'Let us take breath for a moment,' cried Macleod, 'and do all of ye load ; there will be tough work yonder—the last, if I mistake not, of this affair. The enemy has mustered his strength, and awaits our coming : we are within shot, yet they do not fire. You have behaved nobly, Captain Herbert, and your guide is a gallant fellow. Mr. Balfour too seems to have had his share, as appears by his sword. But come, we are enough together now, and the rest are pressing on us. Follow me, gentlemen, for the honour of Scotland !'

Waving his sword above his head, which flashed brightly in the sunlight, he dashed on, followed by the Nair and the others, upon whom the momentary rest had had a good effect. Their aim was more deadly, their footsteps firmer and more rapid.

Urged on by his impetuosity, the gallant Colonel did not heed the motions of the Nair, who, fatigued by his exertions, vainly strove to keep pace with the commander. He hurried on, followed by nearly the whole of Herbert's company and the young Balfour, up the broad ascent which invited their progress, but which it was apparent, from the position of the defenders, would be hotly contested. It was in vain that the Nair stormed, nay raved, in his own tongue : who heeded him ? or if they did, who understood him ?

'There is no road, there is no road there !' he cried. 'Ah fools, ye will be lost if ye persevere ! Follow me ! I will lead ye—I know the way !'

Fortunately at that moment Herbert happened to cast his eyes behind him. He had missed the young Nair with the advance, and had thought he was killed: he now saw his gesticulations, and that the orderly was beside him. A sudden thought flashed upon him that there was no road, from the confidence with which the attacking party was about to be received; and hurrying back to them, he eagerly demanded the cause of his cries.

'No road there!' 'no road!' 'he know the road!' 'he show the road!' was the answer he got through the orderly. But to turn any portion of his men, who heard nothing and saw nothing but the fierce contest which had begun only a few paces above them, was a matter of no small difficulty: a steady sergeant or two of a different regiment and some of his own men at last saw his intentions; and, with their aid, he found himself at the head of a small body, which was being increased every instant.

The Nair surveyed them half doubtfully. 'They will be enough!' he said in his own tongue, and dashed down a narrow path which led from the main road.

Following this in breathless haste for a few moments, and in fearful anxiety lest he should be betrayed, Herbert called to the men to keep together; and as they began again to ascend, he saw the nature of the Nair's movement. The wall which was being attacked by the main body, was built on one side up to a steep precipice, the edge of a fearful chasm; on the other to a large and high rock of great extent, which flanked the wall and defied assault from the front, but could evidently be turned by the path by which they were now proceeding. How his heart bounded with joy therefore, when, after a few moments of hard climbing, he found himself, with a greater number of men than he had expected, on the top of the rock within the enemy's position!

Pausing for an instant to take breath, he saw the desperate but unavailing struggle which was going on below him, in the vain attempts being made by the troops to scale the wall. What could they do against a high wall, with a precipitous rock on either hand, and a murderous fire in front? many had fallen, and others fell as he looked on. He could bear it no longer; he had scarcely fifty men with him,—in the redoubt were hundreds. 'Give them one steady volley, boys!' he cried to his men. "Wait for the word—Fire!—Now on them with the steel!'

Secure in their position, the enemy little expected this discharge, by which some dozen of their number fell; and as they cast a hurried glance up to the rock, it was plain by their great consternation how admirably had the surprise been effected.

Numbers in an instant threw away their arms and betook themselves to flight, while others, irresolute, hesitated. The British below soon saw their comrades above, and saluted them with a hearty cheer, while they redoubled their efforts to get over the wall; in this there was a sally-port; and, as the small party dashed down into the enclosure amidst the confusion and hand-to-hand conflict which ensued, one of them contrived to open it. Eagerly the assailants rushed in, and few of those who remained asked or received quarter.

Herbert's eye was fascinated, however, by the Nair, his guide, who from the first descent from the rock had singled out one of the defenders of the redoubt, evidently a man of some rank. He saw him rush upon him waving his reddened sword;—he saw the other defend himself gallantly against the attack;—even the soldiers paused to see the issue of the contest. The Nair was not fresh, but he was reckless, and pressed his opponent so hard that he retired, though slowly, along the rampart. Their shields showed where many a desperate cut was caught, and both were bleeding from slight wounds. By degrees they approached the platform of the precipice, beyond which was only a blue depth, an abyss which made the brain giddy to look on. Ere they were aware of it, the combatants, urging their utmost fury, and apparently not heeding their situation, approached the edge, exchanging cuts with redoubled violence; and now one, now the other, reeled under the blows.

On a sudden Herbert saw—and as he saw it he sprang forward, with many others, to prevent the consequences they feared—the chief, who had his back to the edge, turn round and look at his position. The next instant his sword and shield were thrown away, he had drawn a dagger from his girdle and rushed upon the Nair his adversary. A desperate struggle ensued; they saw the fatal use made of the knife; but still the Nair, dropping his sword, struggled fiercely on. As they approached the edge the suspense became fearful, for no one dared venture near the combatants; in another instant they tottered on the brink, still struggling;—another—and a portion of the earth gave way under their feet, and they fell! They saw for an instant a hand grasp a twig which projected,—that disappeared, and they were gone for ever! Herbert and many others rushed to the spot, and, shading their eyes, looked over the precipice; they saw them descending, bounding from every jutting pinnacle of rock, till their aching sight could follow them no longer.

'It was a deadly hate which must have prompted that man's exertions this day,' said a voice beside him, as

Herbert turned away sickened from the spot—it was Philip Dalton.

'May that Being into whose presence he has gone be merciful to him!' said Herbert, 'for he has fought well and bravely to-day, and guided us faithfully; without his aid, who could have discovered the narrow path by which I was enabled to turn this position?'

'You, Herbert? I thought it must be you, when I heard how it had been done. I envy you, while I admire your courage; you have saved the army; we should have lost many men at that wall but for your well-timed diversion.'

'Then you saw it?'

'I did; I was with the General, down there, when the welcome red coats appeared on the rock yonder; he hailed your appearance like that of an angel deliverer, and exclaimed that Heaven had sent you.'

'Not Heaven, Philip, but the poor fellow who lies in yonder chasm. I would to Heaven he had lived!'

'Do not think of him, Herbert, but as one who has fought nobly and died bravely—an honourable end at any time; but have you seen Charles Balfour?'

'He was with me, surely,' said Herbert; 'but no, now that I remember, I think he went on with the Colonel and the rest. Good God! he must have been in all that hot work: you saw nothing of him as you passed the sally-port?'

'No, but let us go and look; the bugles are sounding a halt, and you have done enough to-day; so trouble yourself no further; we have gained the ascent, and the enemy is flying in all directions.'

As they spoke, they passed through the sally-port into the open space beyond, where many a poor fellow lay writhing in his death-agony, vainly crying for water, which was not immediately to be found. Many men of Herbert's own company, faces familiar to him from long companionship, lay now blue and cold in death, their glazed and open eyes turned upwards to the bright sun, which to them shone no longer. His favourite sergeant in particular attracted his notice, who was vainly endeavouring to raise himself up to breathe, on account of the blood which nearly choked him.

'I am sorry to see this, Sadler,' said Herbert kindly, as he seated him upright.

'Do not think of me, sir,' said the poor fellow; 'Mr. Balfour is badly hurt. I was with him till I received the shot, but they have taken him yonder behind the rock.'

'Then I must leave you, and will send some one to you;' and Herbert and Dalton hurried on.

Behind the rock, almost on the brink of the precipice, and below the wall, there was a shady place, formed by the rock itself and by the spreading branches of a Peepul-tree which rustled gently over it. This served for a kind of hospital; and the surgeons of the force, as one by one they came up, lent their aid to dress the wounds of such as offered themselves.

There, supported by two men of his company, and reclining upon the ground with such props as could be hastily arranged around him, lay Charles Balfour—his fair and handsome features disfigured by a gaping wound in his cheek, and wearing the ghastly colour and pinched expression which is ever attendant upon mortal gun-shot wounds. Both saw at once that there was no hope; but he was still alive, and, as he heard footsteps approaching, his dim and already glazed eye turned to meet the sound, and a faint smile passed over his countenance, evidently of recognition of his companions. They knelt down by him gently, and each took the hand he offered.

'I thought,'—he said with much difficulty and very faintly,—'I thought I should have died without seeing you; and I am thankful, so thankful that you have come! Now, I go in peace. A few moments more, and I shall see you and this bright earth and sky no more. You will write, Herbert, to—to—' He could not say—mother.

'I will, I will do all you say, dear Charles; now do not speak—it hurts you.'

'No, it does not pain me; but I am dying, Herbert, and all is fast becoming dim and cold. It is pleasant to talk to you while life lasts. You will tell her that I died fighting like a man—that no one passed me in the struggle, not even yourself.'

Herbert could not answer, but he pressed his hand warmly.

'Thank you, thank you. Now pray for me!—both of you; I will pray too myself.'

Reverently they removed their caps from their brows, and, as they knelt by him, offered up in fervency prayers, unstudied perhaps and even incoherent, but gushing fresh from the purest springs of their hearts, and with tbe wide and glorious scene which was spread out before them for their temple. As they still prayed in silence, each felt a tremulous shiver of the hand they held in theirs; they looked upon the sufferer: a slight convulsion passed across his face—it was not repeated—he was dead!

Both were brave soldiers; both had borne honourable parts in that day's fight; yet now, as their eyes met, overcome by their emotions, both wept. Herbert passionately; for his mind had been worked up to a pitch of excitement which, when it found vent at all, was not to be repressed. But after awhile he arose, and found Dalton looking out over the magnificent prospect; the tears were glistening in his eyes it was true, but there was an expression of hope upon his manly features, which showed that he thought Charles's change had been for the better.

They stood almost upon the verge of the precipice; far, far below them was a giddy depth, the sides of which were clothed with wood, and were blue from extreme distance. Mountains of every strange and varied form, whose naked tops displayed bright hues of colour, rose in their precipices out of eternal forests, and formed combinations of beautiful forms not to be expressed by words—now gracefully sweeping down into endless successions of valleys, now presenting a bold and rugged outline, or a flat top with perpendicular sides of two or three thousand feet, which descended into some gloomy depth, where a streamlet might be seen chafing in its headlong course, though its roar was not even heard. There were many scathed and shattered peaks, the remains of former convulsions, which, rearing themselves above, and surrounded by mist, looked like a craggy island in a sea; and again beyond, the vapours had arisen in parts and floated gracefully along upon the mountain side, disclosing glimpses of blue and indistinct distance to which the mind could hardly penetrate—a sea of mountains of all forms, of all hues, blended together in one majestic whole, and glowing under the fervent light of the brilliant sun; and they looked forth over this with heart softened from the pride of conquest, more fitted to behold it, to drink in its exquisite beauty, from the scene they had just witnessed, than if in the exultation of victory they had gazed upon it from the rock above.

'Methinks it would take from the bitterness of death,' said Herbert, 'to part from life amidst such scenery, which of itself creates an involuntary wish to rise above the earth, to behold and commune with the Author and Creator of it; and if the taste of this, which we are permitted here, be so exquisite, what will be the fulness of reality? Poor Charles! his fate was early and unlooked for; yet with his pure spirit, in the hour of conquest, and here, without pain too, we may well think there was bitterness in his death.'

'There is never bitterness in death, if we look at it steadily, Herbert, and consider it as a change to an existence far more glorious. Charles has passed away from us,—the first of our little company, in this strange and gorgeous land,—perhaps not the last; but come, we may be wanted.'

And saying this, they turned from the spot, giving a few necessary orders for the care of the body of their friend; and with some cheering words to the poor wounded fellows, who were brought in every moment, they passed on to the other duties which required their presence.

CHAPTER XIX.

On the summit of the Hussainghurry pass, if the traveller turns aside from the beaten track into the thin brushwood to the left and near the edge of the mountain, from whence he will behold an indescribably sublime prospect, there are a few ruined tombs. They are those of the officers and men who fell in the assault, and who lie near the scene of their triumph,—sad yet honourable memorials of the event which even now is sung and described by the bards of the country in rude but expressive language.

Beyond these again is another, beneath a shady Neem-tree, which is in better preservation, and, by the hut near it, has evidently been taken under the care of an old Fakeer. He will always supply the thirsty traveller with a cup of cool water after his weary ascent, and though he could originally have had no interest in the tomb, has yet inherited the occupation of the spot from others before him, whom either death swept from the face of the earth, or, having rested there for awhile, have wandered into other and far-distant lands.

That tomb is Charles Balfour's; and whether it is that more than ordinary interest existed at the period in the fate of him who lies there,—whether any tradition of his youth and virtues descended with time—from its being apart from the others, or from the shade the tree afforded—that it has been selected from the rest, and held in sanctity,—we know not; yet so it is. Annually, a few flowers and a lighted lamp are offered up upon it, and often a love-sick maiden, or a mother beseeching health for her child or a propitious return to her absent husband, brings a lamp and a garland with her, and in a few simple prayers beseeches the spirit of him who rests there to aid her requests.

Certain it is they could not pray to the spirit of a purer being; and if the act itself be questionable, at least we cannot refuse, to the emotion which prompts it, our mental tribute of sincere sympathy.

Herbert and Dalton selected the spot themselves; and in the evening, after they had completed the few necessary preparations for the funeral, as the red glow of the declining sun was lingering upon the mountain-peaks, gilding the naked precipices till they shone like fire, and the huge mountains were flinging their purple shadows over the deep valleys and chasms, making their depths even more profound and gloomy,—the slow and sad funereal train which bore Charles Balfour to his grave issued from the camp, followed by most of the officers in the force and the men of his regiment; for the youngest officer in it had been a favourite with all, and his daring bravery on that day had caused a double regret for his early fate.

What more affecting sight exists than a soldier's funeral? the cap and sword, and belt and gloves upon the coffin, speak to the heart more than studied eulogy or the pomp of nodding plumes and silent mutes; the head which proudly bore the one, the arm which wielded the other, are stiff and cold. Earth has claimed her own; and it goes to its last narrow resting-place, not in the triumphal procession of hearses and lines of carriages, but with the solemn wail of the music for the dead, and with slow and measured tramp, so full of contrast to the vigorous and decisive step of military movement.

The mournful procession passed onward till it reached the grave; the funeral party which preceded the coffin performed its simple movement in silence; and as the lane was formed, and the men bowed their heads upon the butts of their muskets, many a big tear could be seen coursing down the cheeks of those who had fought beside him who had passed from among them for ever!

Soon all was finished: the rattle of musketry resounded in the still evening through the mountains; it died gradually away; again and again it was repeated; and the last honours being paid to their departed brother, all separated, and returned in groups to the camp, soon to forget, even amidst other excitements than those of action or constant service, the solemnity of the scene they had been engaged in.

Philip and Herbert remained however till the grave was filled in and stones and thorns were piled upon it; and by this time evening had far advanced, and spread her dusky mantle over the sublime scenery. All beyond the pass gradually became a dark void, wherein nothing was discernible save here and there a dim twinkling light, which showed where a shepherd kept his watch, or a few wood-cutters cooked their evening meal after the labours of the day. They could not remain long; the chill breeze which arose as night advanced, though it was pleasant to their relaxed frames, warned them to retire to the shelter of their tent; and if their evening there was spent sadly, at least they had the satisfaction of thinking that all the honours of a soldier's death had been shown to their young friend, and that he lay in a grave which would be unmolested for ever.

It is far from our intention to follow *seriatim* the operations of this campaign, which are already matters of history, except as they are necessary to the explanation of the positions into which the fate of Herbert Compton led him. It has been already stated that the rich town of Bednore, the capital of the province in which the army now was, had been from the first the object of the present campaign; accordingly Mathews, the day after the assault of the pass, pressed onwards with his whole force to Hyderghur, a strong fort on the way to Bednore. This place quickly yielded; and the governor, having been offered terms by the English commander, agreed to them, and delivered over the whole of the districts dependent upon the fortress. The fortress of Anantpoor soon followed, and the country was quickly occupied by small detachments, and the inhabitants yielded apparently quiet possession to their conquerors. Bednore was next approached; and as the minarets and white-terraced houses appeared to the view of the army, and it was known that its governor had deserted his post, all were clamorous to be led at once against it, both because it was to be their resting-place, after their fatiguing service, and was described to be full of treasure, which would become their lawful spoil.

The possession of it was the more urgent, because only six rounds of ammunition remained to each man in the whole army; with this miserable provision, no operation of any magnitude could be undertaken; there was no prospect of immediate supplies from Bombay; the communication from the coast was very irregular, but Bednore was before them; and, reckless almost of consequences, it was attacked and carried by escalade, with all the ardour of desperate men. The reduction of the forts of the country followed, and, in a mistaken idea, perhaps, all were occupied with small detachments; thus the army was rendered inefficient, and, in a great measure, the execution of these services gave notoriously such profit to the officers engaged in them, on account of the plunder they obtained, that they were with difficulty recalled. The dreams all had entertained of riches appeared to be realised, the spirit of rapacity pervaded all ranks, and each man was anxious to secure what he could of the golden harvest.

During the month of February, these and other operations below the passes took place; and when the army, or such part of it as could be assembled at Bednore, was collected, it was the general expectation that the immense booty would be divided, and, at all events, that the army would receive its pay, which to most of the troops was considerably in arrear. Herbert, however, had been prevented, by a wound received at the storm of Anantpoor, from taking any part with his regiment in the operations we have alluded to; he had received a severe sword-cut upon his right arm, which, though it did not confine him to his bed, yet rendered it impossible for him to accompany the regiment; and after the possession of Bednore, he remained there with the other sick and wounded. Dalton, on the contrary, continued to be most actively employed, and in all the affairs of the campaign bore a conspicuous part.

His constant association with the General gave him opportunities of observing his character narrowly. While he admired the courage and the perseverance with which he laboured to carry out to the letter the instructions of the Government, he could not but see that his blind reliance upon fate, his neglect of the most ordinary means of gaining intelligence, and of providing stores and supplies for his army,—while he denied them the power of purchasing for themselves by withholding their pay, which he had ample means to discharge,—would sooner or later be the causes of ruin to the expedition, which, so long as it was not menaced by the armies of Mysore, held efficient possession of the territory it had gained.

Nor was it to be doubted that Tippoo, with the whole resources of his kingdom at his perfect command, would make a decisive attempt for the recovery of this, his favourite and most fertile province. Dalton had repeatedly urged these considerations upon his commander with the utmost earnestness, but without effect, and the events which followed their return to Bednore were of a character to excite his most lively apprehensions.

No sooner had the chief commanders of the army re-assembled at Bednore, from their various expeditions, than a division of the plunder, or at any rate an issue of pay, was insisted upon by them, and by some of the officers; for the sum which had been collected was notoriously very large. The whole amount of the lately-collected revenue of the district had been seized in the Bednore treasury; and this, with the property and jewels, the plunder of the various forts, might have been considered available in part to the public service. With an obstinacy, however, peculiar to his character, Mathews refused any distribution; the small advances doled out to the officers and the men were dissipated as fast as given, and were totally inadequate to their wants; and a general spirit of discontent, little short of absolute mutiny, arose throughout the army.

After many scenes of violent recrimination, of mutual threats, of forcible suspension from the functions of their office between the General and his subordinates, the latter declared to him in the presence of Dalton and others of his staff, that they felt themselves perfectly justified, for the safety of the army and the furtherance of the public interests, to proceed at once to Bombay, and in person to expose his conduct.

Having come to this determination, Mathews made no attempt to shake it. Convinced, though mistakenly, that he was acting for the public good, he formally granted them the permission they would otherwise have taken, and requested Captain Dalton would hold himself in readiness to proceed with the three commanders, as the bearer of his despatches, which contained his reasons for acting as he had done, his requests for further aid, and instructions as to his ultimate proceedings.

This was a somewhat sudden blow to Dalton, who would have far preferred remaining with the General, to whom he felt a strong attachment, which was increased by the difficulties and dangers by which he saw him encompassed; and for a while he endeavoured to make a change in his determination.

There were others, he said, of the staff much more fit to execute the orders than himself; men who were acquainted with the authorities at the Presidency, and with the language of the country, so necessary in a rapid journey to and from the coast. But the General continued inflexible; his confidence in the manly and independent character of Dalton was not to be shaken, and Philip himself soon saw that it was useless to press him upon the point.

Once he suggested that his friend Herbert should fulfil the mission, and the mention of his name thus casually led to a request on the part of the General that he would undertake Captain Dalton's duties during his absence. This was satisfactory to both of them, to Philip particularly, for he felt assured in the talent and excellent military knowledge of Herbert, which he was daily increasing by study, that the General would have advice upon which he could depend.

'Then, Philip, you will be back within a month?' said

Herbert, as they sat together the evening before his departure.

'I think so. Macleod and Humberstone are very friendly to me, though we go upon opposite errands, for which I would to God no necessity existed; and they are determined to get back as soon as possible; indeed, you know it is absolutely necessary, for things cannot go on much longer in this state.'

'No, indeed. I regret sincerely that matters are thus; what in the world can make the old man so obstinate?'.

'I know not; it is in vain that I have represented the absolute necessity for a distribution of money, or for a prize-committee, in order that the army may know something of what was secured here and elsewhere. It is in vain; the old man is absorbed in the contemplation of this wealth; it occupies his thoughts incessantly; and, though it is not his, yet I verily believe he cannot make up his mind to part with it, merely because it is wealth.'

'It is most strange; one of those curious anomalies in human conduct which we often see without being able to give any satisfactory reason for it. I hope, however, the Government will decide the matter, and soon send you back to us, Philip.'

'Indeed, I hope so too. I very much suspect the General will be superseded, for in truth he is little fitted to command; but you will be able to judge of this yourself in a day or two.'

'Well, I shall see; at any rate he shall have my opinion upon the state of the fortifications, which I have often mentioned to you.'

'And I to him; but he relies so implicitly upon his fate, and is so sure of aid, which seems to me like a hope in a miraculous intervention in his favour, that I ceased to urge it.'

'There is no use in our speaking more now upon this vexatious subject, Philip, and I pray you to execute my commissions in Bombay. Here are a few letters for England, and some drawings among them; one for Charles's poor mother, and a sketch of the place where he fell, and his last resting-place, which please despatch for me. Perhaps you can get them into the Government packets; if so, they will be safer than in the ship's letter-bags. Here too is a packet of drawings of all our late scenes and skirmishes, till my wound prevented my sketching any more, which you may have an opportunity of sending by a private hand; and if not, any of the captains will take it for me, I have no doubt.'

'I will arrange all for you safely, Herbert. I have written some letters myself, and they can all go together. I doubt not I shall be able to get one of the secretaries to forward them, and your drawings besides, which are not very large. Anything more?'

'Nothing, except these trifling purchases.'

'Certainly, I will bring the contents of the list without fail. So now good-bye, and God bless you till we meet again! which I hope will not be further distant than three weeks or a month. Take care of the old commander; and if you can persuade him into parting with some money, and into vigilance and exertion, you will not only be cleverer than I am, but will deserve the thanks of all parties.'

'I will try at all events. So good-bye! Don't forget my letters, whatever you do, for there are those in our merry England who look for them with almost feverish impatience. God bless you!'

They wrung each other's hands with warm affection, and even the tears started to Herbert's eyes. He thought then that he should be alone, to meet any vicissitudes which might arise, and he could not repress a kind of presentiment of evil, vague and indefinite. If he had been Dalton, he would have expressed it; but his was a differently constituted temperament, and he was silent. Another warm and hearty shake of the hand, and Philip was gone.

The rest of that evening and night was sad enough to Herbert, and many anxious thoughts for the future rose up in his mind. Dalton was only to be absent a month; but in that time what might not happen? The army was inefficient, from being broken up into detachments, and the best commanders were about to leave; the authority would devolve upon others who were untried in such situations; disaffection and party spirit were at a high pitch. Should the enemy hear of this, and attack them, he feared they could but ill resist.

However, he thought he could do much by forcible entreaty with the general, whom he was now in a condition to advise; and, as he said, these thoughts are but the effect of circumstances after all. For how often is it that they who are departing on a journey in the prospect of novelty and occupation of thought, have spirits lighter and more buoyant than those who, remaining, can not only imagine dangers for the absent, but are oppressed with anxieties for their safe progress, and lest evils should come in which their aid and sympathy will be wanting!

But sad thoughts will soon pass away under the action of a well-regulated mind: and Herbert, in his ensuing duties, found much to occupy his, and prevent it from dwelling upon ideal evils. They were not, however, without foundation.

But a few days had elapsed after the departure of his friend, ere Herbert began to suggest plans to the commander for the general safety. Young as he was, he put them forward with much diffidence, and only when they were supported by another officer of the staff who could not blind his eyes to the critical state of the army. Leaving for a while the vexatious subject of money, upon which the general could not be approached without giving way to passionate expressions, they gradually endeavoured to lead his attention to the state of the fortifications, which, ruinous and neglected as they were, could not afford defence against any ordinarily resolute enemy. They next endeavoured to organise some system of intelligence; for of what was passing within twenty miles of Bednore—nay, even the state of their own detachments—they had no knowledge whatever. They urged upon their infatuated commander the necessity of establishing some order and discipline in the army, which from neglect, inactivity, and poverty, was becoming riotous and unmanageable.

But all was in vain. The more apparent the difficulties of his situation were made to him, the more he tried to shut his eyes against them; and when driven by absolute conviction to confess the peril, which daily increased, though as yet no enemy threatened, he declared that he had reliance in Almighty power to send succour, to perplex the councils of his enemies, to distract their attention from one who, having carried conquest so far, was destined (though certainly in some strait at present) to rise out of all his troubles triumphant, to confound his enemies and those who sought to dispossess him of his situation.

It was in very despair therefore that Herbert and the others, who had aided him in his plans, were at length obliged to desist from further importunity, and to settle down into a kind of dogged resolution to bear with resignation whatever might be hidden behind the dark veil of the future; and all hoped that news would speedily arrive of the supercession of the general, and the appointment of some other more competent person.

It will be remembered that two persons came into the English camp on the night before the storming of the pass. The fate of one will be fresh in the reader's memory. The other performed his part well: he led the column he guided steadily on one side of all the entrenchments, by narrow bypaths and difficult places: it reached the top in time to intercept the fugitives, who, driven from redoubt to redoubt, and finally from the last, as we have already mentioned, fled panic-stricken, and were destroyed in great numbers by the second column, which intercepted many of them at the summit of the pass.

This guide, whose name was Jaffar Sahib, therefore, received his full reward, and more; and as he was assumed to be faithful, so the general kept him about his person, and lent a ready ear to his suggestions. By him he had been informed of some secret stores of treasure, which he had added to the general stock. By him he was told of the terror with which his presence and conquest had inspired Tippoo and his armies, who would not dare to attack him; and if the unfortunate general ever ventured to express a doubt of the security of his position, he was flattered into the belief that there was no fear, and was told, in the language of Oriental hyperbole, that it was impregnable.

The interpreter between them was the general's personal servant, who—not proof against a heavy bribe, and greater promises—had lent himself to the deep designs of the other.

It was long before suspicion of this person entered the mind of Herbert; but a remark that fell from the general one day, that he had the best information of the proceedings of the enemy, when it was very evident he had none at all, led him to suspect that Jaffar Sahib was exercising with the general a fatal and as yet unknown influence. The man's conduct, however, was so guarded, his civility and his apparent readiness to oblige so great, that it was long before Herbert's suspicion led him to adopt any course to detect him.

But expressions, however light, will sometimes remain upon the memory, and oftentimes obtrude themselves upon our notice when least expected. During a nightly reverie, when the scenes of the short campaign were vividly present to his imagination, he remembered the tone of contempt in which the gallant Nair had spoken of Jaffar Sahib; and though he had not understood the words, yet he could not help thinking there was more implied in them than Wheeler had noticed. Early the next day he sought that officer, with whom he had been in constant association, and mentioned his doubts to him.

Mr. Wheeler readily repeated the words which the Nair had used; and remembering his tone of contempt, he was gradually led to think with Herbert that there was ground for extreme suspicion and watchfulness. Nothing, however, could be discovered against the man; and though they set others to watch his movements, they could not ascertain that he held communication with any one but the general's own servants, among whom he lived.

The first three days of April had passed, and as yet there was no news of the issue of the appeal to Bombay. All were anxious upon the subject, and party-spirit ran higher and higher in consequence. They had soon, however, matter for sterner contemplation. On the fourth morning, early, there arose a slight rumour that Tippoo's army was approaching. Three similar ones had been heard before, but nothing had followed; and Herbert flew with the intelligence to the general, accompanied by Wheeler; for their suspicions were roused to the utmost against Jaffar Sahib.

'Impossible!' said the general when he had heard the news. 'I have the most positive information that Tippoo is at Seringapatam, and purposes advancing in the opposite direction to meet the Madras army. Who is the author of this groundless rumour, gentlemen?'

'It was prevalent,' they said, 'in the bazaar.'

'Some scheme of the grain-merchants to raise the price of grain, I have no doubt. But here is Jaffar Sahib, the faithful fellow to whom we owe much of our success, and who would be the first to give this information if it were true: ask him, if you please, Mr. Wheeler, what he thinks.'

Wheeler put the question, and the man laughed confidently.

'It is a lie,—it is a lie! Look you, sir, as you speak my language so well, perhaps you can read it also. Here are letters which I have daily received from Seringapatam, through a friend, who thus risks his life in the service of the brave English. They contain the daily records of the bazaar there, and the movements of the troops.'

'We will have them read by a scribe, if you please, general,' said Wheeler. 'If thou art faithless, as I suspect,' he continued to the man, 'thou shalt hang on the highest tree in the fort!'

'My life is in your hands,' he replied in his usual subdued tone; 'I am not afraid that you should read.'

The letters were read, and were, as he described them to be, daily accounts from the capital, where the army was said to be quiet. The last letter was only four days old, the time which the post usually occupied.

'Now, gentlemen, are you satisfied?' cried the general in triumph. 'Have I not always told you that I possessed the most exact information through this my faithful servant? Contradict, I pray you, this absurd rumour, and believe me that there is no danger.'

But the next morning, as the day broke, a cloud of irregular cavalry was seen by those on the look-out, advancing from the southward; and amidst the confusion and alarm which followed, no efforts were made to check them—none to defend the outer lines of fortification, which would have enabled the English to have strengthened their position within. A few skirmishes occurred, in ineffectual attempts to retain their ground, and before noon the place was formally invested by the regular infantry and very efficient artillery of Tippoo's army.

Herbert and Wheeler made every search for Jaffar Sahib, but he was nowhere to be found. In the confusion, he and the general's servant, who had been his confidant and associate, had escaped.

Then only broke upon the unfortunate general a bitter prospect, and a sense of the misery he had brought upon himself and others. But instead of yielding to any despair, the courage and discipline of the army rose with the danger which threatened its very existence: animosities were forgotten: and while the siege of the fort was vigorously pressed by Tippoo, and with the most efficient means, its defenders exerted themselves with the intrepidity and spirit of English soldiers to repel their assailants.

With their insufficient means of defence, however—with broken and ruined walls—the gradual failure of ammunition and of food—their exertions at length relaxed; and after a vigorous assault, directed by Tippoo in person, they were forced to relinquish the outer walls, and retire within the citadel, where they were now closer and closer pressed, and without any chance of escape or relief. In this condition, and having done all that brave men could for the defence of their honour and of their post, the general was induced to offer a capitulation. The deputation was received with courtesy by Tippoo, the officers complimented on their valorous defence of an almost untenable post; and the articles of capitulation having been drawn up, they returned to their companions. The conditions were accepted with some modifications, after a day or two's negotiation, and the 30th of April was fixed as that on which they should march out with the honours of war; and after that, they should move with their private property to the coast. It was destined, however, to be otherwise.

By the articles of capitulation it was specified that all treasure in possession of the garrison was to be given up—that, though the private property of the officers and men was to be respected, yet all public stores and treasure were to be surrendered in good faith.

But the officers and men, whose means of subsistence—now that the army was to be broken up and disorganised, upon becoming prisoners of war—would entirely depend upon the charity of their conquerors, were little inclined to trust to so questionable a source; and the evening before the capitulation was to be carried into effect, a large body of the garrison, in a state of mutiny, surrounded the abode of the general, and with tumultuous cries demanded pay.

Herbert was with the old man, assisting him to pack up such articles as could most easily be carried away, when the demand was made. It was in vain that, by the general's order, he attempted to reason with the men to show them the dishonour of touching anything of what had been promised in exchange for their lives. They would listen to no reason.

'We are starving,' they cried, 'and there is treasure yonder: we will have it!'

But at last they were satisfied, on receiving the assurance of a month's pay to each man, and reluctantly the general surrendered the keys of the treasury.

The regiments were engaged in receiving the money, when some one bolder than the rest exclaimed, 'Why not have it all, boys? We may as well have it, as let it go to the enemy."

The cry acted at once upon their excited spirits. 'Let us have it all!' was repeated by hundreds; and ere they could be prevented, the contents of the treasury were plundered and distributed amongst them. Officers and men alike were laden with the spoil in jewels and money.

It was with bitter regret that this was seen by Herbert and many others, whose high sense of honour forbade their sharing in the work of plunder. It would be impossible, they thought, to conceal such an event from the Mysore chief; and as it was a direct breach of the articles they had solemnly agreed to, they but too justly anticipated a severe retribution for the act.

It was even so. On the morrow, as they marched out with the melancholy honours of war, a wasted band, worn out with fatigue and privation, they were surrounded by Tippoo's troops, while others took possession of the fort. The keys of the magazines and treasures had been given up with the rest, and there was an immediate search made for the valuables, of which the place was well known to be full—to Tippoo personally; for, as may have been anticipated, the guide Jaffar was the means of the intelligence which he possessed, and through whom he had been informed of every event which happened; though his share in the previous British success he had kept concealed from the Sultaun: indeed it was known to none except the British.

Disappointed at the issue of the examination, the English were at once suspected, and denounced by Jaffar. They were surrounded and rudely searched: on most was found a portion of the missing money and jewels; and, as it but too well fell in with Tippoo's humour, and gratified his hate against them, they were one and all decreed to captivity—which, from the horrors all had heard related of it, was in prospect worse than death.

CHAPTER XX.

ABDOOL RHYMAN KHAN, as may be imagined, quitted his wives in no very pleasant mood. Tired by his long march, and without having tasted food since the morning, the bitter insult he had received, their disrespect and their abuse, were the more aggravating, and sank deeply into his heart. Although not a man of wrath habitually, or one indeed who could be easily excited, he was now in very truth enraged, and felt that he would have given worlds for any object on which he could have vented the fury that possessed him.

'Alla! Alla!' he exclaimed, as he ground his teeth in vexation; 'that I should have been born to eat this abomination; that I, who have a grey beard, should be thus taunted by my women, and called a coward, one less than a man! I who, Mashalla! have slain men, even Feringhees!—that I should have to bear this—Ya Hyder! Ya Hoosein!—but I am a fool to be thus excited. Let them only fail to receive Ameena as she ought to be received—let me but have a pretext for what I have long desired, and now threatened, and they will see whether my words are truth or lies. Too long have I borne this,—first one, then the other—now Kummoo, now Hoormut—now one's mother, now the other's brothers and cousins; but, Inshalla! this is the last dirt I eat at their hands—faithless and ungrateful! I will send them back to their homes; I have often threatened it, and now will do it.'

His horse awaited him at the door, and springing into the saddle, he urged him furiously on through the Fort gate, into the plain beyond; and here—for the rapid motion was a relief to him—he lunged him round and round; now exciting him to speed, now turning him rapidly from one side to another, as though in pursuit of an imaginary enemy. This he did for some time, while his groom and Daood looked quietly on; the latter attributing to its true cause the Khan's excitement, the former wondering what could possess his master to ride so furiously after the long journey the horse had already performed that morning.

The Khan at last desisted—either from feeling his temper

cooling, or from observing that his horse was tired—and turning first towards the encampment, he proceeded a short distance; but apparently remembering something, he retraced his steps towards the Fort; indeed he had forgotten to report the arrival of his corps to the officer whose duty it was to receive the intelligence.

As he passed his house, he saw one of the women-servants, who used to go on errands or make purchases in the bazaar, issue from the door-way, and covering her face, dart on before him, apparently to elude his observation.

'Ha! by the Prophet, I will know what that jade is after,' muttered the Khan to himself, as he dashed his heels into his charger's flanks, and was up with her in a moment. 'Where goest thou?' he cried; 'Kulloo, think not to conceal thyself; I saw thy face as thou camest out of the door; what errand hast thou now?'

'May I be your sacrifice, Khan!' said the woman; 'I am only sent for the Khanum Kummoo's mother,—may her prosperity increase!'

'May her lot be perdition rather!' cried the Khan; 'an old devil,—but never mind me; go thy way; I know why she is called. May the Prophet give them grace of their consultation!' he added ironically; 'tell thy mistress that; and tell her too,' he continued, speaking between his teeth, and looking back after he had gone a little way, 'tell her to remember my words, which I will perform if there be occasion, so help me Alla and his Prophet —now begone!'

The woman was right glad to escape, and the Khan pursued his way to the office where he had to make his report, and to ascertain what was to be done with the prisoners whom he had escorted from Bangalore. This necessarily occupied some time: the officer was an intimate friend, and the Khan had not only much to learn, but much also to communicate. His own marriage, his journey, his double escape, and the gallantry of his young friend Kasim Ali were mentioned, and excited the utmost praise, with many expressions of wonder from the hearers; and all were anxious to see, and become acquainted with, the hero of so much adventure.

'And what news have you from Hyderabad for us, Khan Sahib?' said his friend, whose name was Meer Saduk, a favourite and confidential officer of the Sultaun; 'what news for the Sultaun? may his greatness increase! I hope you were able to gather the intentions of the court there, or at any rate can give us some idea of them.'

The Khan's journey to Hyderabad had not entirely been of a private description. A native of the place, when he asked leave to proceed there to see his family, he had been requested by the Sultaun to ascertain as far as he could the politics of the State, and the part the Nizam personally was likely to play in the drama of Indian intrigue and diplomacy; and he had performed his mission with more tact than could have been anticipated from his open and blunt nature.

'I have news,' he replied, 'Meer Sahib, which will gratify the Sultaun, I think; and from such good sources too, that I am inclined to place the utmost dependence upon them. No sooner was it known that I, as an officer of the Sircar Khodadad,* had arrived in the city, than I was sought by several of the nobles and Munsubdars of the court, who in truth were friendly to the last degree, when I did not well know how I should have fared with them; and it appeared from their speech that the Huzoor himself was well inclined to be friendly. This is all I can tell you, Meer Sahib, and you must not press me, for I have sworn to tell the rest to the Sultaun only; after he has heard it, I will let you know.'

'Enough, Khan, I am content; the Sultaun will be at the Doulut Bagh to-night, and to-morrow also; wilt thou come this evening?'

'Pardon me, not to-night; I am tired, and have to arrange my house after my journey; but, Inshalla! to-morrow evening, when I shall present my young Roostum, and solicit employment for him. Being the bearer of good news, I may be successful; but in any case I think Kasim Ali would be welcome.'

'There is not a doubt of it,' replied his friend. 'I go to the Durbar to-night, and will tell of thy adventurous journey; this will whet the Sultaun's curiosity to see the young Syud.'

The friends then separated. In spite of this amicable interview, the Khan's temper, which had been so violently chafed, was not completely soothed: the memory of the abuse which had been poured upon him still rankled at his heart, and he was at a loss what to tell Ameena of his interview with his wives, and of her having to meet them that evening.

The nearer he approached his tents in the camp, the more oppressive these thoughts became; and alternately blaming himself for having visited his wives so early after his arrival, and mentally threatening them with punishment should they continue insubordinate, he had gradually worked himself up to a pitch of ill

* 'The Government, the gift of God.'

temper, but little less than that in which he had left his house, and which he was ready to discharge upon any one.

The opportunity was not long wanting; for, as he entered his outer tent, which was used by Kasim and the Moonshees, as well as by any visitor or friends, he heard a violent altercation, in which Kasim's voice and that of the Moonshee, Naser-oo-deen, were very prominent.

'I tell thee thou art a cheat and a rogue!' Kasim was exclaiming with vehemence; 'this is the second time I have detected thee, and therefore instantly alter these accounts and repay the money, or I will tell the Khan.'

'I am no cheat nor rogue, any more than thyself, thou nameless base-born!' retorted the Moonshee, whose remaining words were lost in the violent passion of the other.

'Base-born! dog! thou shalt rue this,' cried Kasim; 'thou shalt not escape me, by Alla! I will beat thee with a shoe.' And a scuffle ensued.

'Hold!' exclaimed the Khan, who now rushed into the tent and parted them; 'what is the meaning of all this?'

'Khodawund!' cried both at once.

'Do thou speak, Naser-oo-deen,' said the Khan; 'thou art the oldest. What is the meaning of this disturbance? is this the bazaar? hast thou, an old man, no shame? Hast thou too lost all respect, Kasim Ali?'

'Judge if I have not cause to be angry, O Khan, at being called a rogue and a cheat by that boy," said the Moonshee; 'have I not cause to be enraged when my character is thus taken away?'

'Wherefore didst thou say this, Kasim, to a respectable man like him? these words are improper from such a youth as thou art.'

'Khan Sahib,' said Kasim, 'you have hitherto trusted me implicitly; is it not so? you have never doubted me?'

'Never; go on.'

'Alla is my witness!' he continued; 'I know no other motive in this but your welfare and prosperity, which first led me to inquire, in consequence of my suspicion. Since the Moonshee has provoked it, and my lord is present, know then why I called him rogue and cheat. At Bangalore, by making notes of the prices in the bazaars, I detected him in overcharging for grain and forage to an immense amount in the week's account; I found the papers here, while my lord was absent, and for lack of other occupation I began looking over the items. I see the same thing again attempted—he swears he will not alter the papers, and I was angry; he called me base-born—'

'Yes, I heard that, Kasim; but say, hast thou proof of all this?'

'Behold the daily memorandum I made of the rates, Khan, village after village, and day after day, written as I made the inquiry; the grain and forage was I know bought from the very people from whose lips I had the rates. Call them if you like—they are the bazaar merchants.'

'And so thou wouldst have cheated me, Naser-oo-deen,' said the Khan, his choler rising rapidly and obstructing his speech, and looking wrathfully at the trembling Moonshee; 'thou who owest me so much, to cheat me! Alla! Alla! have I deserved this? To what amount was the fraud, Kasim?'

'A hundred rupees or more, Khan, at least, even upon this week's account; I could not tell exactly without making up the whole difference.'

'I doubt it not, I doubt it not; and if this for one week or a little more, what for the whole time since thou hast had this place—the sole control of my horses' expenditure! what—"

'My lord! my lord!' ejaculated the Moonshee, 'be not so angry; your slave is terrified—he dares not speak; he has not cheated, he has never given a false account.'

But his looks belied his words; he stood a convicted rogue, even while he tried thus weakly to assert his innocence; for he trembled much, and his lips were blue from terror.

'We will soon see that,' said the Khan deliberately. 'Go!' he said to Daood, who stood by, 'bring two grooms with whips; let us see whether they cannot bring this worthy man to a very different opinion.'

It was not needed, however; the Moonshee, terrified almost to speechlessness, and not heeding the interference Kasim was earnestly making in his behalf, prostrated himself on the ground at the Khan's feet.

'I will pay! I will pay all!' he cried; 'I confess my false accounts. Do with me what thou wilt, but oh! save my character; I am a respectable man.'

'Good!' said the Khan; 'all of ye who are present hear that he has confessed himself a thief before he was touched, and that he says he is a respectable man. Ye will bear me witness in this—a respectable man—Ya Moula Ali!'

All answered that they would. 'Take him then,' he said to Daood and some of the Furashes who stood near, 'take him from my sight; put him on an ass, with his face to the tail; blacken his face, and show him in the bazaar. If any one recognises the *respectable* Naser-oo-deen, and asks after his health, say that he is taking the air by my order, for having cheated me. Enough—begone!'

The order did not need repetition; amidst his cries and protestations against the sudden sentence, the Moonshee was carried off; and in a few minutes, his face blackened, and set on an ass with his face to the tail, he was the sport of the idlers and vagabonds in the camp. He had richly deserved his punishment, however; for with a short-sighted cunning he had imagined that he could brazen out his false accounts, and that, as he had declared that any division of the spoil was at an end from the previous detection, he had made himself now sure of the whole. He had thought too that Kasim, contented with his first detection of overcharge, would not have continued his system of inquiry. Thus he was doubly disappointed.

Having vented his long pent-up rage, the Khan soon cooled down into his usual pleasant deportment, begging Kasim to explain to him minutely the whole of the Moonshee's system of false accounts. This Kasim did clearly, and showed him how much cause there was to suspect far greater delinquencies, for months, nay years past; indeed, it was but too apparent that the Khan had been defrauded of large sums, and that the Moonshee's gains must have been enormous.

'And this might have gone on for ever, Kasim, but for thy penetration,' said the Khan. 'Well, thou hast added another to the very good reasons I already have for aiding thee. Our reception is to take place to-morrow evening, against which time get thy best apparel ready; or stay—I have a better thought; wait here, and I will return instantly.' He did so, and brought with him a superb suit of cloth-of-gold, quite new.

'There,' he said, 'take that, Kasim, and wear it to-morrow; it is the best kumkhab* of Aurungabad, and was made for one of my marriage-dresses. Nay, no words, for thou hast saved me far more than the cost of it in the detection of yon scoundrel; and now prepare thyself. This may not fit thee, thou canst have it altered. I shall remove the Khanum to my house to-night, and sleep there; but come by the third watch of the day to-morrow; they will show thee where it is, and I will be ready to accompany thee. Inshalla! I have that news for the Sultaun which shall make him propitious towards us both.' And so saying, he left him, and went through the enclosure which separated the tents, into that which was appropriated to Ameena.

From a window in the tent, which was screened by transparent blinds, so that the immates could look out without being seen,

* Cloth-of-gold.

Ameena was sitting and gazing on the plain, which swarmed with men, elephants, horses, and camels, hurrying to an fro. Beyond was the Fort, from the gate of which every now and then issued a gay cavalcade,—an elephant, bearing some officer of rank, surrounded by spearmen and running footmen,—or a troop of gaily-dressed horsemen, who, as they advanced, spread over the plain, and amused themselves with feats of horsemanship, pursuing each other in mock combat, or causing their horses to perform bounds and caracoles, to the admiration of the beholders.

'A gallant sight! is it not, fairest? and a gallant and noble patron of soldiers do we serve—one who hath not his equal in Hind. Say, didst thou ever see such at thy city?'

'No, in truth,' said Ameena, who had risen to receive her lord; 'but thou knowest we lived in a quiet street of the city, so that few cavaliers passed that way; nevertheless, we have brave soldiers there also. I would I could live among such scenes always,' she added; 'it is pleasant to sit and look out on men of such gallant bearing.'

'I am afraid thou wilt not see so much within the Fort,' said the Khan; 'nevertheless, my house is in the main thoroughfare, and there are always men passing.'

'And when are we to remove there, my lord?' asked Ameena timidly, for she feared the introduction to the wives more than she dared express. 'Methinks I should live as well here as there; and I have been now so much accustomed to the tents, that a house would appear a confinement to me.'

'Why, fairest, thou shouldest remain in them, only that they want repair very much, and we have prospect of immediate service; besides, the house is all prepared for thee, and I long to make my rose mistress of what is hers in right; so we will go thither this afternoon. Zoolfoo has orders to prepare our evening meal.'

'And they—' she could not say *wives*—

'Fear not; they will be prepared to receive thee with honour. I have spoken with them, and bidden them be ready to welcome thee.'

'Alla bless them!' said Ameena, the tears starting to her eyes; 'and will they be kind to one whom they ought to hate? Alla bless them! I did not look for this, but expected much misery.'

'Fear not,' said the Khan, who winced under her artless remark, yet dared not undeceive her. 'Fear not, they will be kind to thee; Inshalla! ye will be sisters together.' Alas, he had but little hope of this, though he said it. But it is necessary to revert to the ladies themselves.

The Khan's two wives sat in anxious expectation of the arrival of the lady for whom they had dispatched the servant; they had held a hurried colloquy together after the Khan's departure in the morning, and had come to the resolution of abiding by the advice of the mother of Kummoobee, who was the wife of the head Kazee of Seringapatam, a wealthy but corrupt man, who, of good family himself, had married the daughter of a poor gentleman of long descent but of extreme poverty. She inherited all her father's pride of birth, and had married her daughter to the Khan, only because of his rank and known wealth; for she despised his low origin, which had become known to her—indeed it was not sought to be concealed.

As the ladies waited, they heard the sound of bearers, and in a few moments the jingle of the anklets and heavy tread of the old lady, as she advanced along the open verandah of the court which led to their apartment. They rose to welcome her, and the next moment she entered, and advanced towards her daughter—almost starting as she saw the Khan's other wife, knowing that they had been enemies; but returning her salaam very courteously, she proceeded to take the evil from her daughter by cracking her knuckles over her. Having done this, and embraced, she was led to the musnud; and being seated thereon, and her daughter's hooka given to her, she drew a long breath as if she had exerted herself very much, and looking from one to the other (for the slaves had been ordered out of the room), demanded to know what they had to say to her.

'We have news for thee, mother,' said Kummoo-bee pettishly.

'Ay, news, rare news!' added the other, who seemed as spiteful as suppressed anger could make her.

'Ajaib!' said the old lady, looking from one to the other, 'wonderful news? By your souls, tell me what news: what has happened that I know not of?'

'Of the Khan,' said Kummoo, edging nearer to her mother.

'Ay, listen,' said the other; 'Mashalla! it is worth hearing.'

'Of the Khan? most wonderful! Is he dead?—have ye all his money?'

'No!' ejaculated Kummoo passionately; 'it would be well for us and him if he were dead. Dead! no, he is returned, and well.'

'Well!' said the old lady, apparently relieved, 'there is nothing very wonderful in this—nothing particular to marvel at, that I see; if I had known I was to have been called from home only to hear this, I can tell you, you would have waited long. I had a thousand things to do when Kulloo came for me; I was going to cook a dish, and then I had the woman with bangles for my arms, and then the silversmith was coming, and—'

'Alla! Alla! how shall I tell this shame?' cried her daughter, interrupting her; 'how shall I utter the words, to make it fit for thee to hear or my tongue to utter? Alas! mother, he has returned, and brought a woman with him,—a woman who, Inshalla! is vile and ugly, and unchaste, and low-born, and who—'

'Punah-i-Khoda, a woman! thou didst not say a woman! Another wife?' cried the old lady, interrupting the torrent of foul names, which, once the subject of them had been named, followed rapidly enough.

'So he says, mother,' cried Hoormut, 'another wife. He dared not write this to either of us; he dared not tell us how he had misused us, how he had cheated us; he dared not tell us this; and we heard it only from my cousin, who discovered it at Nundidroog, and wrote to the family.'

'I will throw ashes on his beard—I will fill his mouth with earth! I will spit on him!' cried the old lady, who, having looked from the one to the other, was now excited to fury at this sudden intelligence; 'Ya Alla Kereem! What dirt has he not eaten? What abomination have ye also to bear, O my daughters? Married again? another wife? a young one, I'll warrant, the old lecher! Oh shame, shame on his grey hairs! may dogs defile them! And beautiful, too, I have no doubt! Is there no law? is there no justice? Inshalla! we will see to that. Is he to throw dirt on the family of the chief Kazee, and cause his daughter to eat grief? is he to mock us, to cheat us, to bring his vile women before our very faces, without we turn and strike again? Are we cows and sheep? Inshalla, no! but persons of good family, of a hundred descents; while he—pah! he is a poor, pitiful, low-born, ill-bred wretch!' And she paused, fairly exhausted from want of breath.

'Ay, mother,' said Kummoo-bee, 'and what is more, he has threatened to bring her here to-night—here, into this very house—to make us see her and welcome her—pah! I could cry with passion.'

'Here? it is a lie!' roared the old lady; 'it is a lie! this is some trick of yours, or joke; I will not believe that. Is he mad to do it?'

'It is the truth, however,' said Hoormut; 'and what is more, he swore by Alla and the Prophet's beard, if we did not receive her kindly, he would send us both home to our parents, and let them support us, for he would not.'

'At least *I* need not care about *that*,' said Kummoo, pointedly and spitefully; 'Inshalla! I shall always find food and clothes there; *my* people, Mashalla! are not poor.'

With the other it was different; for her family were poor, and had been ruinously extravagant; and even their mutual dilemma could not prevent this expression of spite from her richer sister-wife.

'I should like to know,' retorted Hoormut, tartly, 'who could not?'

At any other time a quarrel would have resulted to a certainty. But now Kummoo's mother spoke again, fortunately for the general peace.

'So he threatened that, did he? And what said ye?' added the old lady, more calmly; for, in truth, the sudden vision of her daughter's return to her house, which the words she had just heard caused, were not by any means agreeable.

'Mother, we could say nothing, for he left us,' replied her daughter; 'and we have sent for you to ask your advice as to what we should do,' said Kummoo, wiping her eyes with the end of her doputta.

'Humph!' said the old lady, after a pause, and some most vigorous pulls at the hooka, ending in a discharge of smoke through her nostrils; 'do you know whether the girl is beautiful?'

'We hear she is,' said Hoormut very reluctantly, and with an indignant toss of her head, which was repeated by the other lady.

'Then there is no use to resist, my daughters. The old fool is bewitched with her, and all you can do is to bear the insult—for such it is—until you can revenge it. Ay, revenge it: Thou art no daughter of mine, Kummoo, if thou canst bear this like a mean-spirited thing. I never suffered any one to come between me and thy father; he tried it more than once, but, Mashalla! he got tired of that.'

'And so thou wouldst have me bear it, mother,' said Kummoo, bursting into a torrent of tears, the effects of her vexation. 'I had expected different advice from thee. How can I bear to meet the vile creature, whom I could spit upon and beat with a shoe? how to lose my power, influence, money, clothes, jewels, attendants—all of which will be lavished on this child? How can I eat the dirt which the very seeing her will occasion? Mother, I tell thee true, I cannot and I will not bear it. I will appeal to my father, and to the Sultaun, if he will not hear me.'

'Patience, my child, patience!' said the old lady, soothingly. 'Not so fast—all in good time; it is better to eat dirt for one night than all thy life. Why shouldst thou be afraid? Mashalla!

thou art beautiful—thou art of perfect form—thou art not old. Inshalla! wait therefore; let this novelty wear off, and he will return to thee—to both of you, Inshalla! Inshalla! Meanwhile I will consult thy father. I will see if the law can avail thee aught. But for the present—for the sake of the Prophet—keep thy temper. Wouldst thou not eat dirt for ever—both of ye, I say—if he turned ye out to your homes? What would not be said? Verily, that ye were vile and worthless, and that he had detected you in his absence. Therefore wait: Inshalla and the Prophet! we will be revenged. I who am your mother say this, on him and her we will have our exchange for this, if charms or spells, or, what is better, women's wit, can effect this.'

'Quickly then, mother, by your soul! devise something. I shall live in misery till thou dost, and we will aid thee. Is it not so, sister?'

'I promise to do all ye wish of me,' returned Hoormut; 'I am in your hands. Alas! I have now no mother whom I can consult; you are my only mother, lady!' And she began to sob.

'Do not cry, daughter,' said the dame, rising majestically; 'Inshalla! we shall prosper yet. Alla Hafiz! I go to think over the matter, and consult my faithful Ummun; she is wise, and to her I am indebted for many a charm, without which it would have fared ill with me. I will send her to-morrow, and thou canst tell her what happened when he brought her, and what she is like;' and so saying, she left them.

'Since we are to see her,' said Kummoo, who had been hiding her vexation by looking out of the window to watch her mother's departure, 'and to behold her triumph over us, we must only eat our own vexation, and make the best of the matter; let us prepare the room—the Khan has ordered the repast—we will get some garlands and salute them. If we are not to be revenged at once by insulting them both, at least let us pretend civility, which may blind them to our ultimate purposes.'

'Excellent advice, sister!' said Hoormut, who, though the elder, yet had lost much of her authority to the younger and far handsomer Kummoo; 'let us make a rejoicing of it—sing and play to them, and put on our best clothes; we shall not fail to please the Khan.'

'Best clothes!' echoed Kummoo, 'alas! the time for those is gone. We may even have to wear *her* cast-off suits for want of better. No more clothes, no more jewels!' she added pettishly; 'but what matters it? revenge will follow. Hoormut, thy advice is good; we will prepare for the marriage-feast. Pah! I have no patience to mention it.'

And so they did. A clean covering was put upon the musnud; the crimson velvet pillows of state occasions laid upon it; the Khan's gold Pāndān and Uttrdān set out, and their costly hookas arranged near them. All the slaves were desired to put on clean clothes; and they themselves, dressed in their most sumptuous apparel and adorned with all their jewels, were seated about the time of evening in the room which on that morning had been the scene of so violent an altercation.

Trembling for the issue of the event, but cheered by the Khan to the utmost of his power, the gentle Ameena accompanied him about dusk to his abode in the Fort. The palankeen was set down in the court-yard; and the bearers having retired, she essayed to get out of it, but could hardly support her trembling limbs. One or two of the women servants, however, kindly assisted her, and a cup of cool water refreshed her. The Khan too had now arrived; and veiling herself closely, she followed him into the apartment which had been prepared.

The Khan had been uncertain what would be the issue, until he reached the room; but he had determined, if necessary, to carry his threat into execution. A glance, however, assured him that all was right. The ladies rose courteously, made them low salaams, and advanced to meet them; and as he led forward the shrinking girl, they took her kindly by the hand with many warm welcomes and blessings, and, despite of her protestations to the contrary, seated her upon the place of honour and themselves at her feet. This done, a slave advanced with a tray of garlands of the sweet Moteea, one of which they hung around her neck, while they again salaamed to her, and the slaves one by one did the same. The Khan too underwent these ceremonies with delight, for he had little expected such a greeting.

The ladies at last were seated, and Kummoo said, 'Let us, I pray thee, sister, see the face of which report hath spoken so warmly; unveil, I beseech thee, that we may look on our new sister.'

'It is not worth seeing,' said the timid girl, throwing back the end of her doputta; 'nevertheless your kindness and welcome is so great that I cannot refuse you.'

'Ya Alla!' cried one and all, 'how beautiful!' for they were really struck with her appearance, and could not restrain their sincere expression of admiration at her loveliness. 'Mashalla! the Khan has good taste.'

Kummoo, the principal speaker, and the youngest of the two wives, was beautiful too; but her flashing eyes, full person, and rather dark skin, though her features were regular, could but ill stand a comparison with the gentle beauty, exquisite though small proportions, and fair skin of Ameena; and the Khan's eye, which wandered from one to the other for a few moments, rested at last on Ameena with a look so full of admiration, that it did not—could not—escape Kummoo's notice. She of course said nothing, but the venom of her heart arose with more bitterness than ever.

'Ay, she is fair, Kummoo-bee,' said the Khan, 'and gentle as she is fair; I am thankful that ye seem already to love her as a sister. Inshalla! ye will be friends and sisters in truth, when ye know each other better.'

'Inshalla-ta-Alla!' said Kummoo-bee reverently; 'the Khanum (may her house be honoured!) is welcome; how sayest thou, Hoormut? hast thou no welcome for the lady?'

'By your head and eyes, you speak well, sister. If the love of such an unknown and unworthy person as I am be worth anything, the Khanum is welcome to it.'

'I am grateful,' said Ameena; 'ye are more than kind to one who hath no claim on ye; but I am alone here, and my people are far distant—very far. Your love will be precious to me during the years Alla may cast our lots together.'

There was something very touching in her sad and gentle tone; and as the old Khan's heart had been moved by his wives' unexpected kindness, he well nigh blubbered aloud.

'Ameena!' he said, 'Ameena! Alla, who hears ye say these words of affection, will give ye grace to abide by them.'

'But come,' said Kummoo, who thought these protestations of love going rather too far, 'we have some of our singers for thee to hear, lady: we of the south call them good, but we hear rare things of the Dōmnees of Hyderabad. Call them in,' she added to an attendant.

They came in, and, having tuned their instruments, began one of the usual songs of congratulation; it was followed by others, while the party sat and conversed cheerily on the adventures of the journey. An ample repast was shortly after spread; and at the end of the evening Ameena retired to her new apartments, believing, in her simplicity and goodness, that her sister-wives loved her in real truth, and enjoying those sweet sensations which ensue whenever doubt and mistrust have been removed from the heart. If the Khan felt any of his own doubts remaining, he did not seek to disturb Ameena's security by imparting them to her; and for the first time since she had heard of the existence of her sister-wives, Ameena felt happy.

CHAPTER XXI.

Kasim attended closely to the advice of the Khan, and spared no pains, on the day which was to fix his fate and rank in the service, to adorn his person to the best advantage. The splendid brocade suit which the Khan had given him—of crimson silk, with large gold flowers upon it, the most expensive the looms of Aurungabad could produce—he had found to fit him so nearly, that it required but few alterations, which were easily made.

This, therefore, he was able to wear. Around his head was a mundeel, or turban of gauze and gold in alternate stripes. The colour of the gauze was green, which marked his descent as a Syud; and it was an additional reason, beyond his own pride in the matter, for thus openly showing it, that the Sultaun, in his zeal for the Faith, was particularly partial to the nobly-descended race. The mundeel was of the richest and most expensive kind, and its costly fabric suited well with the appearance of the brocade suit. He had bound it, too, in the most approved and genteel form—that worn by the nobility of the Dekhan, and which is called *nashtalik.*

Under his chin, and tied on the top of his head, so as to protect the ears, he wore a Benares handkerchief—the gift of his mother—of purple and silver, the glittering ends of which fluttered in the breeze as he walked, while the colour contrasted well with his fair skin. His waist was girded by a crimson muslin doputta, or scarf, with gold ends nearly a foot long, richly embroidered, which hung down on one side, and were displayed to the best advantage. A pair of tight-fitting trousers of yellow mushroo, or thick satin, striped with crimson, completed a costume which for its splendour could not well be surpassed, and which displayed his striking figure and handsome face to the best advantage.

The baldric, which held his father's trusty sword, was tarnished to be sure, but that was a mark of its having seen service; and it was the more honourable in appearance on that account. Its gold inlaid half-basket hilt had been newly polished, and the crimson velvet scabbard renewed; and it looked, as indeed it was, a handsome as well as most formidable weapon, from its great length and breadth. Two or three daggers, with richly chased and ornamented handles, occupied a conspicuous place in his girdle; his shield hung loosely at his back; and thus accoutred, he mounted the gallant horse which the Khan had provided for him, and which had not only been more richly caparisoned than usual, but decked with a profusion of silver ornaments, and took his way into the Fort.

Many an eye was turned towards him as he passed along; for the proud animal he rode, apparently aware that the appearance of his rider warranted more than usual exertion, and excited by the clashing and jingling of the silver ornaments and tiny bells around his neck and upon his crupper, bounded to and fro, curvetted and pranced, as much to show off his own unexceptionable shape, as to display his rider's admirable and easy horsemanship to the best advantage.

'A gallant cavalier!' cried one, as he passed near the gate of the Fort, loud enough for Kasim to hear it; 'five hundred rupees would not buy his suit of clothes. Mashalla! this is the place after all where soldiers are patronised, and come to spend their money in adorning their persons.'

'Ay, brother,' said the man he was with; 'knowest thou who that is? it is Kasim Ali Patél—he who saved Rhyman Khan's life on—'

Kasim lost the rest of the sentence as he passed on; but it proved to him, and not unpleasantly, that the only action he had as yet performed worthy of note was known.

'If my fate favour me, it shall not be the last. Ya Nusseeb!' he cried, apostrophising his fate, 'thou art darkly hidden; but if it be the will of Alla, thou shalt yet shine brightly out.'

'Alla kereem! what a beautiful youth!' exclaimed a bevy of dancing girls, whose gaily-ornamented bullock-carriage obstructed the gateway of the Fort, and who in all the pride of gay and glittering apparel, and impudence of fair and pretty faces (their lustrous eyes even made more so by the use of soorméh), were proceeding to the Sultaun's Durbar.

'Alla, what a beautiful youth!' cried one; 'wilt thou not come and visit us?'

'Shall we see thee at the Durbar?' cried two others.

'I am stricken with love at once,' said a fourth.

'What a coat! what a horse! what eyes!' cried first one, and then another; until Kasim, whose horse had become uneasy at this volley of words, and at the jingling and clashing of the bells around the bullock's necks or attached to the posts and crimson curtains of the car—and had curvetted once or twice, so as to cause a few faint shrieks, and afterwards a burst of merry laughter from the fair ones—bounded on, and freed him from them.

Passing hastily through the gateway, he rode on into the Fort—first through an open space, where cannon-balls in heaps, cannon mounted on carriages, and soldiers moving in all directions, showed the efficient state of the Fort for defence. Beyond this was the bazaar—long streets of goodly houses, the lower parts of which were shops, and where all sorts of grain, rich clothes, tobacco, brazen pans, and arms of all kinds, were exposed for sale.

As he rode along slowly through the crowd—among which his appearance attracted much notice and many flattering comments—he could not but observe that every house was gaudily ornamented with paintings, which were a proof, if any was needed, in what hatred the English were held by all.

Here were represented a row of white-faced Feringhees, their hands tied behind them, and with their faces half blackened; while others were seated on asses, with their faces to the tail. Again there were some being torn to pieces by tigers, while men of the true faith looked on and applauded; others were under the feet or chained to the legs of elephants, one to each leg, while the beast was depicted at his utmost speed, his trunk raised into the air, and the Mahout evading him with a huge ankoos. Again another row were undergoing the rite of Mahomedanism at the hands of the Kazee; others were suffering torture; several appeared drawn up in a line, whose heads were all falling to the ground under one vigorous blow of the executioner—a man of the true faith, with a huge beard and mustachios curling up to his eyes, while streams of gore, very red and much higher and thicker than the sufferers themselves, gushed from the bodies.

Here again were a group of ten or twelve seated round a table, each with a fierce regimental cocked-hat upon his head, a very red and drunken face, and his right hand upraised grasping a huge glass filled with red wine; while others, overcome by inebriation, were sprawling under the table, and wallowing among the swine and dogs which lay at the feet of those who were yet able to preserve their equilibrium.

Kasim was amused at all this; and if he could not enter into the general hatred with all the zest of one of Tippoo's soldiers, perhaps it was that the remembrance of the young Englishman whom we have mentioned rose in his mind, as he looked on these disgusting and indecent pictures of his race, with far different feelings than they were calculated to engender in a Syud and a true believer.

As he passed on, the tall minarets of the mosque built by Hyder Ali Khan towered above him, which, pierced from top to bottom with pigeon-holes, after the manner of those in Arabia, were surrounded by thousands of pigeons of all colours and kinds, wheeling hither and thither in the air in immense flocks, whilst others sat quietly cooing in the niches and enjoying their abode unmolested. Soon afterwards he emerged from the narrow street into the square, the Futteh Mydan, or plain of victory, on one side of which was the long line of the Sultaun's palace, presenting nothing to the observer but a line of dead wall with many windows, whose closed shutters showed they were the Zenana. Around the gate, however, were many guards dressed in the striped tiger-skin-pattern calico in use among his bodyguard of regular infantry, interspersed with men in richer dresses and armour,—those of the irregular troops who were permitted to share the watch over the monarch's abode. In the centre of the square were a number of men under instruction, whose evolutions, with the words of command, were quite new to Kasim, and inspired him with great admiration. At the other side of the square the venerable forms of the ancient Hindoo temples reared their huge conical and richly ornamented roofs; and around their massy gates and in the courts lounged many a sleek and well-fed Brahmin, whose closely shaven and shining head, and body naked to the waist—having only a long white muslin cloth tied around his loins, with its end thrown over his shoulder—proved him to be in the service of the enshrined divinity, whose worship was not forbidden by the fanatical ruler of the Fort—nay, it was even whispered, shared in by him.

The Khan's house was not far from the temple, in one of the chief streets; and having announced his arrival to the gate-keeper, Kasim continued riding up and down before it till the Khan should issue forth to accompany him.

This was then the place where Ameena was secured, he thought; the gentle, lovely being on whose fair face his eye had rested only a few times; yet each glance, however short its duration had been, was treasured up in the inmost shrine of his heart. As long as she remained in the camp, he might have an opportunity of seeing her, even though for a moment, and of displaying the scarf she had given to him—a mute evidence which would prove to her she was not forgotten; for he had continued to wear it tied around his chest as at first, even though his slight wound was so far healed as to require nothing but a bandage underneath his vest.

It had been even a comfort to him to watch the arrival of her palankeen daily in the camp, and before that to busy himself in writing the despatch for the Furashes, who prepared the tents for her reception. Sometimes, as she got out of her palankeen, he would catch a glimpse of her muffled figure, or hear the chink of her gold anklets, and even this would be pleasant to him. But now there was no hope; she had passed within those walls which had, he thought, for ever shut her from his sight; and while his memory was busy with the past, he strove, under the weight of obligation with which the Khan had loaded him, and which that day would be augmented, to drive away the thoughts of his fair wife, not, however, with the success which ought to have attended his efforts.

Indeed, the beautiful image of her face was too deeply fixed upon his memory; and the fears that her lot, so young and gentle-tempered as she was, in the companionship of her lord's older and ill-tempered wives, would not be a happy one, made him again determine that in need or danger she might rely on one who would be true to her. Every now and then he cast up his eyes to the lattices to see if perchance any one looked out from thence; but there was no one, and he continued his slow pace to and fro.

In a short time, however, his reverie was interrupted by the cheerful voice of the Khan, who, fully armed, was splendidly dressed in a suit of bright chain-armour over a tunic of cloth-of-gold; a highly-polished steel cap glittered on his head, from the sides of which to his neck descended lappets of chain-links strengthened with scales; his long straight sword was suspended in an embroidered baldric, and his waist was girded by a green and gold scarf similar to that Kasim wore. He greeted Kasim heartily.

'By the Prophet! thou art no disgrace to me, and the Ulkhaluk becomes thee; a green mundeel too—that is well, as thou art a Syud, and hast a right to wear it. I would thou hadst a pair of Persian boots like mine—but no—better as thou art; they would not fit thee, nor suit thy dress. So now let us see thee make my Yacoot bound a little.'

As Kasim complied with his request, the delight of the Khan and his retainers, who had now assembled, was extreme; and cries of 'Shabash! shabash! Wah wah! Wah wah!' rewarded his exertions; indeed Kasim's horsemanship, like that of most Dekhanie's, was perfect; and he sat his excited horse with the ease and grace of one who was completely at home upon his back, in spite of his extreme spirit and violence.

As the Khan prepared to mount, Kasim happened once more to cast his eyes up toward the lattices which looked into the street: they were guarded with transparent blinds, but nevertheless he thought he could distinguish one or more female figures behind each, and his heart beat very rapidly as he thought

—nay was sure—that Ameena beheld him; it was not an unpleasant thought that she looked upon him, richly dressed and accoutred as he was, and had seen him exhibit his spirited horsemanship to the Khan.

Again he looked—and for a moment, with an apparent pretence of arranging the blind, the corner was drawn inwards: a face which was new to him—dark, yet very beautiful—appeared; and a pair of large flashing eyes threw a glance towards him, which met his. It was not Ameena's, and he was disappointed; but he could not the less remember afterwards the glance he had received from eyes so bold and so commanding, and the older yet beautiful face and remarkable expression, and involuntarily sought it again. The Khan, however, at the moment he saw it, called to him to proceed; and the spearmen and running footmen and grooms having arranged themselves in front, they set forward at a quick pace, followed by the Khan's retainers, who were almost as well mounted, though not so richly clothed, as themselves; those in front shouting the Khan's titles, and clearing the way, often with rude blows of the heavy spear-shafts.

They retraced Kasim's steps through the bazaars, where the profusion of salaams and compliments which greeted them, showed how greatly the Khan was respected and esteemed; and the various cries of the Fakeers, who appealed to him by name as they solicited charity, and mentioned many of his valiant acts in high-flown and laudatory terms, proved how well his brave deeds were known to all. Kasim also came in for his share; and as his connection with the Khan was mentioned truly, and the subsequent engagement with the Mahrattas, it was plain that it had become known to those rapid acquirers of topics for gossip, the Fakeers, and had already become the common talk of the bazaars.

Issuing from the Fort, they escaped from this in a great measure; yet here and there along the road sat a half-naked Fakeer, or Kalundur, with his high-pointed felt cap, and quilted chequered gown of many colours, who, with a sheet spread before him, upon which was a cup, solicited the alms of the true believers, alternately with prayers, threats, or abuse, as the quality of the passers-by warranted. Instead of taking the road to the right, which led to the camp, they struck off to the left, and after a few minutes' ride arrived at the gate of the garden of the Duria-i-Doulut, or Sea of Wealth, by the river side, where, for the day, the Sultaun held his court.

This palace, which had been erected by his father many years before, stood in the centre of a garden of great beauty, which, from the richness of the soil and plentiful supply of water, brought from the river by a deep water-course, flourished in the utmost luxuriance. Large trees, mango and tamarind, walnut, and the sweet-scented chumpa, with many other forest kinds distinguished for their beauty of growth, or the fragrance or luxuriance of their foliage and blossom, with large clumps of feathering bamboos, overshadowed the broad walks and long green alleys, and in the hottest weather formed an almost impervious shade, while the coolness was increased by the constant irrigation and consequent evaporation from the ground.

Passing through the gate, the Khan and Kasim rode down the avenue, at the end of which was the palace; they could not see the extent of it, nor was there anything remarkable in the outward appearance which corresponded at all with the splendour within. The building was two storeys high, the lower of which was occupied by kitchens, halls for servants, and long corridors—the upper contained the rooms of state; a projecting roof, which was supported by carved wooden pillars, formed a deep verandah, which was occupied by a crowd of persons—servants, and those who attended either with petitions or upon business, and whose rich and gay dresses contrasted well with the dark foliage which almost swept the ground near them.

'Behold the triumph of art!' cried the Khan, as they dismounted and approached the building, and Kasim could see that the walls were covered with paintings; 'there are not such paintings in Hind, thanks to Hyder Ali Khan—may his place in Heaven be blessed, and his grave honoured! Behold the whole of the rout of the kafir English at Perambaukum, where, praise be to Alla! the arms of the true believers were completely victorious, and thousands of the kafirs tasted of death at their hands. Yonder is Baillie and his troops; you can see Baillie in the centre. Mashalla! he was a great man: so indeed he and the other leaders appeared, for they were much larger than the troops. Yonder are the valiant Assud Illahee of the great Hyder, the disciplined troops before which the English battalions are only as chaff; behold, they are advancing to the attack, and bear down all before them. There are the guns too pouring fire on the devoted Feringhees, and the rockets flying in the air, which overwhelm them with confusion. In the midst of the fire the cavalry of the Sircar, led on by the young Tippoo, are charging, and Hyder himself is animating the attack by his presence on his elephant. And look there,' he continued, pointing to another part of the wall, after Kasim had expressed his admiration at the are skill of the artist, who had delineated so many figures; 'that is the end of the affair, as the end of all like affairs ever will be: the kafirs are being cut to pieces, while their blood is poured out upon the earth like water.' This indeed was pretty evident from the prostrate forms of the Europeans, and the figures of the Mahomedans hacking at them with swords rather larger than themselves; while large daubs of red paint showed how indeed the blood had been poured forth like water. The figures, being all in profile, had considerably exercised the ingenuity of the artist to express what he meant.

'Alla kureem!' ejaculated Kasim at last, who was mightily struck with the magnitude of the drawings, the lines of charging cavalry, all with their fore feet in the air—the bodies of infantry, which marched in all kinds of lines to the attack with their right legs uplifted—the smoke of the guns that obscured everything—the rockets flying in the air with fiery tails—the elephants, and the General's officers, some of whom were bigger than the elephants they rode—the horses and their riders—the whole battle, of which, from the peculiarity of the perspective, it was difficult to say whether it was on the earth or in the sky,—'Alla kureem! it was a great battle, and this is a wonderful picture—may the designer's prosperity increase!'

'Ay, you may well say that,' continued the Khan; 'and behold, here are the Feringhees in captivity, all wounded, but enduring life; there they are, brought before Hyder the victorious, who, seated on his throne, allows the officers to live, while the soldiers he orders to be dispatched to the regions of perdition by the executioner. Yonder are a row kneeling in terror, while the sword is brandished behind them which shall cause them to taste the bitterness of death. There again are others under torture, and those who are spared by the clemency of the exalted in rank, going into a deserved captivity!'

'Those we brought were then some of them,' said Kasim.

'No, I think not. I rather believe they were all discharged, or most of them, at the peace, four years ago. These are some who, if I mistake not, were taken at Bednore, when Mathews was surrounded, and obliged to yield himself to the Sultaun; however we shall soon know, for I have heard that judgment is to be done on them to-day. But come, the Durbar is open, we have much to do and to see; others are pressing on before us, and we shall lose our place.

So saying, he led the way by one side of the building to a flight of broad stairs under the cover of a verandah, and they ascended amidst the crowd of courtiers and military officers who were thronging to the Durbar; for proclamation was being made as they waited without, and the cries of the Chobdars of 'Durbar-i-Aum! Durbar-i-Aum!' announced to all that the Sultaun had taken his seat. The head of the stairs opened at once into the hall of audience, so that when they reached the top the scene burst fully upon them. To the Khan there was nothing new in it; but to Kasim, who had never seen anything grander than his own village, or at most the town of Adoni, the effect was dazzling and overpowering.

The room was large, but low in its proportions. The walls were of that beautiful stucco which is only to be seen in perfection in the south of India, and which, from its high polish and exquisite whiteness, so nearly resembles the purest marble. This was wrought into most elaborate designs of arabesque work; and the sharp edges of every flower, leaf, and line were picked out with a faint line of pure vermilion, here and there relieved with gold, which gave a peculiar but agreeable effect to the ornament. In the niches and compartments into which the walls were divided, upon the deep cornices, and especially around the open arched windows, the patterns were more intricate and delicate than elsewhere. The windows themselves were without frames, and were open to the garden, which in all its beauty and luxuriance could be seen through them; and they admitted the cool breeze to play through the room, which otherwise, from its crowded state, would have been insufferably hot. Heavy purdahs, or gilded curtains of crimson cloth, hung above them, which could be let down so as to exclude the air completely if required. The ceiling was covered with fret-work and arabesque patterns of stucco in chequers, from the intersections of which depended a small stalactite, decorated like the walls with red and gold; this, while it caused a heavy effect to the room, was nevertheless extremely rich and handsome. The floor was covered with rich carpets to about one half of its length, where commenced a white muslin cloth, on which none dared to venture but those whose rank or station about the monarch entitled them to that honour.

At the further end of the room was a raised dais, which was covered, like the floor, with white muslin; but in the centre of it was a square carpet of rich purple velvet, surrounded with soft cushions, also of velvet, upon which sat Tippoo, alike the pride and the dread of those by whom he was surrounded.

Kasim easily distinguished the bull-slayer of the previous day in the person before him; but he was dressed with extreme plainness in white muslin, and would not have been taken for the Sultaun by a stranger, except from the place he occupied, and the large and peculiarly-formed turban, with which every one was familiar from description.

On each side of him knelt two fair and rosy-faced youths, dressed in gorgeous apparel, the children of Europeans captured on various occasions, who, forcibly converted to Mahomedanism, always attended the Sultaun, and waved chowrees, formed of the white tail of the Tibet cow, with gold handles, on all sides of him, to drive away the flies. On each side of the dais, in semicircles, sat the officers of state and of the army, in their various costumes, leaving an open space in the centre, through which those passed who desired to present their nuzzurs to the Sultaun.

Some French officers were there in glittering uniforms, but whose tight-fitting clothes, bare heads and feet, without boots or shoes, looked meanly amidst the turbaned heads and more graceful costume of the courtiers. Behind all were a number of the royal Chelas, or bodyguard, splendidly dressed, and armed to the teeth, whose formidable appearance completely awed the assembly, if indeed the presence of the Sultaun himself was not sufficient to produce that effect.

The figure of the Sultaun was of middle height, and stout; his complexion was darker than that of most of those who surrounded him, and he sat with an affected air of royalty, which, though it at first impressed the spectator with awe, yet that passed away in a great measure upon the contemplation of his face, which wanted the dignity of expression that his body assumed. His eyes were full and prominent, but the whites of them were of a dull yellowish tint, which, with their restless and suspicious expression, gave them a disagreeable look, and one which bespoke a mind of perpetual but not profound thought; his nose was small and straight, and, with his mouth, would have been good-looking, except for the habitual sneer which sat on both; his eyebrows and mustachios were trimmed most carefully into arched lines, and he wore no beard. In his hand there was a large rosary of beautiful pearls, with emeralds at the regular distances, which he kept perpetually counting mechanically with the fingers of his right hand. Before him lay a straight sword of small size, the hilt of which was inlaid with gold and turquoise stones; and near him stood a gold spitting-cup, inlaid with precious stones, into which he incessantly discharged the saliva engendered by the quantity of pān he chewed, the red colour of which appeared upon his lips and teeth in a disagreeable manner; and a chased gold writing-case, containing some reed pens, ink, paper, and a pair of scissors to cut it to the sizes required, lay near his left hand.

The ceremony of presentation and of obeisance went on rapidly; almost all offered their nuzzurs of gold or silver, which the Sultaun took, and deposited beside him until there had accumulated a goodly heap, Kasim, at the distance he then was, could catch nothing of the conversation which was going on; for in spite of the loud cries of 'Khamosh! Khamosh!' from the attendants, there was more noise in the assembly than he thought befitting the presence of the Sultaun. After waiting some little time, and having advanced nearer and nearer to the musnud, the Sultaun's eye fell upon the Khan, who in truth was a remarkable figure, even among that richly-dressed assembly, being the only one who wore armour. As the Sultaun's eye met his, the Khan advanced, and bidding Kasim remain where he was till he should be called, he performed his obeisance, presenting, with the handle of his sword upon an embroidered handkerchief, his nuzzur of five gold mohurs, which the Sultaun received most propitiously.

'We welcome thee back, Khan Sahib, most heartily,' said the Sultaun; 'and it is pleasant in our eyes to see an old friend return in health; but thou art thin, friend, the effects of the journey perhaps. Praise be to Alla! his servant, unworthy of the honour, hath been given power of dreams such as no one else hath enjoyed since the days of the Apostle, on whose memory be peace! We dreamed last night—and the blessed planets were in a most auspicious conjunction, as we learned upon inquiry this morning as soon as we arose, which assures the matter to us—that we should see the face of an old friend, and receive a new servant, who should eclipse all the young men of our court in gallant bearing, bravery, and intelligence.'

As he looked around when he had said this, all those within hearing cried, 'Ameen! Ameen! who is favoured of Alla like unto the Sultaun? may he live a hundred years! whose knowledge is equal to his? not that even of Aflatoon or Sikundur.'

'Ay,' he continued, 'behold it hath come true; here has the Khan, as it were, dropped from the clouds, and with him a young man, who, Inshalla! is one whose bravery is great. Bring him forward, O Khan, that our fortunate glance may rest on him.'

'May I be your sacrifice, Huzrut!' said the Khan, 'he is unworthy the honour; nevertheless, I offer him unto your service, and can answer that he hath as stout an arm and as brave a heart as he looks to have. Mashalla! I have seen both tried, in circumstances of great peril to myself.'

'Good!' said the Sultaun, before whom Kasim had performed

the Tusleemât, or three obeisances, and now stood with folded hands. 'Good! by the Prophet, a fine youth! there is truth on his forehead—his destiny is good.'

'Ul-humd-ul-illa! who can discern character like the Sultaun?' cried several; 'behold all things, even men's hearts, are open to him.'

'He hath lucky marks about his face, only known to us,' continued the Sultaun; 'and the planets are auspicious to-day. A Syud too, his services will therefore be good, and beneficial to himself and us.'

'Ul-humd-ul-illa!' cried the court in ecstasy; 'what wisdom! what penetration! what gracious words! they should be written in a book.'

'Wilt thou take service, youth?' he continued to Kasim; 'art thou willing to strike a blow for the lion of the Faith?'

'Huzrut! your slave is willing to the death,' cried Kasim enthusiastically; 'prove him; he will not be unworthy of such exalted patronage.'

'Thou shalt be tried ere long, fear not. Enrol him,' he continued to a Moonshee; 'let his pay be twelve hoons, with allowance for a horse: hast thou one?'

'The Khan's generosity has already furnished me with one,' said Kasim.

'Good! thy business shall be to attend my person, and our friend the Khan will tell thee of thy duties. Enough! you have your dismissal.'

'I beg to represent that the Khan escorted some kafir prisoners from Bangalore,' said an officer who was sitting near the Sultaun; 'would your Highness like—'

'True, true!' replied the Sultaun; 'we had forgotten that;' and he added, as the expression of his countenance changed, 'Command silence, and let them be brought into the presence.'

CHAPTER XXII.

THERE hardly needed the order to be given that silence should be observed: as the words the Sultaun spoke fell upon the ears of the assembly, and they observed the sudden change in his countenance, the busy tongues ceased directly; there continued a little talking and some bustle towards the end of the room, but as the Chobdars called silence, and went hither and thither to enforce it, all became hushed except the Sultaun himself, who was inquiring from the secretaries whether any despatches had accompanied the prisoners from Bangalore.

'Huzrut!' said the Khan, again advancing, 'they are in the possession of your slave, who craves pardon that in the confusion of presenting his nuzzur, he forgot to deliver them.' And he laid the packets at the Sultaun's feet, who instantly tore open the envelope, and selecting one of the enclosures directed to himself, fell to perusing it with great attention.

'This speaks well of the prisoners,' he said at length to Syud Ghuffoor, who sat near him; 'the Killadar of Bangalore writes that one of them, a captain, is a man of knowledge, well versed in the science of war and tactics; that he understands fortification and gunnery, so that he is worthy of being offered our clement protection. Inshalla! therefore, though we need no instruction in these matters,—thanks be to Alla, who hath implanted a natural knowledge of them in our heart, which is not surpassed by any of the whoreson Feringhees—'

And all around interrupting him, cried 'Ameen! Ameen!'

'Inshalla!' he continued, 'as this is an auspicious day, we will offer life and service. If he accept it, well; if not, I will send him to hell, where thousands of his accursed and mother-defiled race await his coming: are not these good words?'

'Excellent—excellent words! They are not worthy to live! the race is accursed of Alla!' cried several; 'the Sultaun's clemency is great!'

As this ceased, the tramp of many feet was heard on the wooden staircase, and as the noise approached nearer, Kasim, who had been watching the Sultaun narrowly with intense interest, could see that he was far from being at ease; he fidgeted upon his musnud, the rosary passed twice as fast as usual through his fingers, his eyes winked sharply, and he stroked his mustachios from time to time, either with exultation or inquietude, Kasim could not distinguish which; at length the prisoners reached the head of the stairs, and their escort appeared to wait there for commands.

'Bid the officer advance,' said the Sultaun; 'the rest may be withdrawn for the present, we will send for them when this man is disposed of.'

The order was obeyed, and all were withdrawn but one, who, being desired to come forward through the lane which was opened for him to the foot of the musnud, advanced slowly, but with erect and manly gait and proud bearing, nigh to where the Sultaun sat.

'Salaam to the light of the world, to the sun of Islam! Perform thine obeisance here, and prostrate thyself on the ground,' said a Chobdar who accompanied the prisoner.

'I will salute him as I would salute my own monarch,' said the prisoner, in a voice audible to all, and in good Hindostanee, but spoken with rather a foreign pronunciation: and still advancing, he had placed one foot upon the white cloth which has been already mentioned.

'Kafir!' cried the Chobdar, striking him, 'son of perdition, keep back! dare not to advance a step beyond the carpet; prostrate thyself to the Sultaun, and implore his clemency.'

The Englishman turned in an instant, at the blow he had received, and raised his arm to strike again; the Sultaun observed the action and spoke.

'Hold!' he cried; 'do not strike, O Feringhee, and do some of ye seize that officious rascal, and give him ten blows upon his back with a cane.'

The fellow was seized and hustled out, while the Englishman continued standing where he had been arrested.

'Advance!' cried the Sultaun.

Some of those near tried to persuade him not to allow the Englishman to approach.

'Pah!' he exclaimed, 'I have caused the deaths of too many with arms in their hands, to fear this unarmed wretch. Advance then, that we may speak with thee conveniently; be not afraid, we will do thee no harm.'

'I fear thee not, O Sultaun,' said Herbert Compton (for so in very truth it was), advancing, and bowing stiffly yet respectfully, 'I fear thee not; what canst thou do to me that I should fear thee?'

'I could order thee to be put to death this instant,' said the Sultaun sharply; while others cried out fiercely that the speech was insolent, and reviled him.

Herbert looked round him proudly, and many a one among the crowd of flatterers quailed as his clear blue eye rested on them. 'I am not insolent!' he exclaimed; 'if my speech is plain and honest, take ye a lesson from it, cowards! who could insult one so helpless as I am;' and he drew himself up to his full height and folded his arms, awaiting what the Sultaun should say to him. His dress was mean, of the coarsest white cotton cloth of the country; his head was bare, and so were his feet; but in spite of this, there was a dignity in his appearance which inspired involuntary respect, nay awe to many.

The time which had elapsed had but little altered him, and if indeed there was a change, it was for the better! his appearance was more manly, his frame more strongly knit. His face was thinner and paler than when we last parted with him at the capitulation of Bednore, from whence, with the rest of his comrades, he had been hurried into captivity; but four years had passed since then, and his weary imprisonment, chequered by no event save the death or murder of a companion or a fellow-captive, would have utterly worn down a spirit less buoyant and intrepid than Herbert's.

Mathews had perished by poison almost before his eyes; he had been accused of having buried treasure, and persisting in the denial of this, he had been tortured by confinement in irons, denied food, subjected to privations of all kinds, which failing in their effect to force a confession of what had not taken place, he had been poisoned by the Sultaun's order. Numbers had been destroyed; numbers had died of hopelessness, of the climate, of disease engendered by inaction; many had been released at the peace of 1784, but still Herbert and a few of his comrades and fellow-prisoners remained, and had lingered on their wretched existence in the various prisons and forts of the country; for Tippoo hoped that long captivity and hardships at one time, and again indulgence and relaxation, would induce them to accede to his terms of service, which were offered from time to time, with alternate threats of death and promises of immense rewards.

Herbert's situation near the person of the General, and the plans of fortifications, books on the same, works on mathematics, on engineering, and his many drawings, all of which had been seized with him, had early marked him as an officer of superior attainment, and one whose services would be highly valuable. The others who were confined with him were for the most part men of the artillery, of whose experience and excellent skill as marksmen Tippoo had too often seen the fatal results to his own army not to be very anxious to get them to join him.

A few of the captives, from time to time, dazzled by promises which were never fulfilled and weary of imprisonment, had voluntarily become renegades, and others had been violently converted to Mahomedanism; these served in the army, and, though dissolute in their habits, were yet useful and brave when occasion needed; and the value of their services only made Tippoo more anxious to secure those of a higher grade and more extensive acquirements and education. With Herbert, and those who accompanied him, his many attempts had been vain; and while his desire to accomplish his ends became the more violent from their continued opposition, there now existed a necessity for urging their compliance, which will presently be made manifest. But we have digressed.

'Peace!' cried the Sultaun, 'we have not sent for thee, O Feringhee, to hear thy bold speech, but to advise thee as one who is a friend to thee, and has a true interest in thy welfare.'

'Dost thou understand the condescending speech of the Sultaun, or shall one of the Franceese interpret it for thee?' asked one of the Moonshees officiously.

'Peace!' again cried the Sultaun, 'he understands me well enough; if he does not, he will say so; and now, Captain Compton, since thus it is written is thy name, we have sent for thee from the Fort, not as a common criminal and one whose end is perdition, but with honour; we had thee seated on an elephant, lodged in a good tent, supplied with excellent food, and now thou art admitted into the presence, thou shouldest bow in acknowledgment of the condescension shown thee; nay, thou wouldst have done so, we are persuaded, but thy manners are not formed upon the model of those of the true believers. Now our good friend the Killadar writes to us that, weary of confinement, and induced by a sense of the obligations thou and thy companions are under to me, thou art in a frame of mind to accept our munificent offers of entertaining thee in our service, of raising thee to rank, of admitting thee to share—'

'Stop!' cried Herbert suddenly, while, as he spoke, the Sultaun fairly started at the suddenness of the interruption to his harangue and the boldness of the tone. 'Stop! when we are on equal terms thou canst offer me service; it is a mockery to tempt me with promises thou wouldst not fulfil.'

'By the gracious Alla and his Prophet, I would,' cried the Sultaun eagerly: 'say then, wilt thou serve me? thou shalt have rank, power, wealth, women—'

'I am in your hands, a helpless captive, O Sultaun,' replied Herbert; 'and therefore I cannot but hear whatever thou choosest to say to me: but if thou art a man and a soldier, insult me no more with such words. Nay, be not impatient, but listen. When Mathews was poisoned by thy order,—nay, start not! thou knowest well it is the truth,—I was given the choice of life, and thy service, or death upon refusal,—I chose death. Year after year I have seen those die around me whom I loved; I have courted death by refusal of thy base and dishonourable offers: thou hast not dared to destroy me. My life, a miserable one to me, is now of no value; those whom I love in my own land have long mourned me as dead. It is well that it is so—I am honoured in death. Alive, and in thy service, I should be dead to them, but dishonoured: therefore I prefer death. I ask it from thee as a favour; I have no wish to live: bid yonder fellow strike my head from my body before thine eyes. As thou lovest to look on blood, thou wilt see how a man, and an Englishman, can bear death. Strike! I defy thee.'

'Beat him on the mouth with a shoe! gag the kafir son of perdition! send him to hell!' roared many voices; 'let him die!' while scowling looks and threatening gestures met him on all sides.

'Peace!' exclaimed the Sultaun, who seeing that his words were not heard amidst the hubbub, rose from his seat and commanded silence. 'Peace! by Alla I swear,' he cried, when the assembly was still once more, 'if any one disturbs this conference by word or deed, I will disgrace him.' And then turning to Herbert, who with glowing cheek and glistening eye stood awaiting what he thought would be his doom, 'Fool, O fool!' he cried, 'art thou mad? wilt thou be a fool? Thy race mourn thee as dead; there is a new life open to thee, a life of honourable service, of rank and wealth, of a new and true faith. Once more, as a friend, as one who will greet thee as a brother, who will raise thee to honour, who will confide in thee, I do advise thee to comply. Thou shalt share the command of my armies—we will fight together: thou art wise—we will consult together: thou art skilled in science, in which, praise be to Alla! I am a proficient, and we will study together. Alla kureem, wilt thou not listen to reason? Wilt thou refuse the golden path which thine own destiny has opened to thee? Let me not hear thy answer now. Go! thou shalt be lodged well, fed from my own table; in three days I will again hear thy determination.'

'Were it three years, my answer would be the same,' cried Herbert, whose chest heaved with excitement, and who with some difficulty had heard out the Sultaun's address. 'I defy thee! I spurn thy base and dishonourable offers, with indignation which I have not words to express. When thou canst give me back the murdered Mathews, whose blood is on thy head—when thou canst restore to life those whom thou hast murdered, thrown from rocks, strangled—when thou canst do this, I will serve thee. For the rest, I abhor thy base and unholy faith.'

'Hog! son of a defiled mother! vilest son of hell!' screamed the Sultaun, almost speechless with passion, 'dost thou dare to revile the faith? Do ye hear him friends? do ye hear the kafir's words? Have ye ears, and do not avenge me? have ye swords, and do not use them?'

Fifty swords flashed from their scabbards as he spoke, and many were uplifted to strike the daring and reckless speaker, when Kasim, who had been listening with the most intense interest, and remembering his promise of succour, while he felt the high sense of honour which prompted the Englishman's defiance of the Sultaun, rushed forward, and with uplifted arm stayed the descent of the weapons, which would have deluged the floor with blood, and committed murder on an innocent person.

'Hold!' he exclaimed, with the utmost power of his strong voice,—'are ye men? are ye soldiers? to cut down a man unarmed, and who is helpless as a woman? Have you no regard for honour, or for truth, when you hear it spoken?

'Rash and foolish youth!' cried the Sultaun; 'is this thy first act of service? An act of disrespect and rebellion. And yet I thank thee for one thing—though he whom thou hast saved will curse thee for it—I thank thee for his life, which I have now to torture.'

'Thy death, kafir Feringhee,' he continued to Herbert, 'under the swords of the Moslims would have been sweet and that of a soldier—it shall now be a bitter one. Away with him to the Droog; no matter how he is carried thither, the meanest tattoo, the meanest dooly is enough. Here, do thou, Jaffar Sahib, see this done; travel night and day till it is accomplished: see him and his vile companions, or such of them as will now dare to refuse my offers, flung from the rock by Kowul Droog, and hasten back to report that they are dead. Begone!'

'Farewell, brave friend,' said Herbert to Kasim, as they laid hold on him roughly, and with violent abuse urged his departure; 'if we meet not again on earth, there is a higher and a better world, where men of all creeds will meet, but where yonder tiger will never come. Farewell!'

'Say, have I not acquitted myself of my promise to thee?' cried Kasim passionately, for he too was held by the Khan and others.

'Thou hast,' was the reply. 'May God reward thy intentions—' His last words were lost in the exclamations, threats, and obscene abuse of those who dragged him away.

The Sultaun re-seated himself on the musnud, and the tumultuous heaving of the assembly was after a short while once more stilled. No one spoke, no one dared to interrupt the current of the monarch's thoughts, whatever they might be. All had their eyes fixed upon Kasim, who, held by the Khan and another, waited expecting his doom in silence, but not with dread: yet his thoughts were in a whirl of excitement; and the remembrance of his mother, Ameena, the Englishman, and the acts of his own life, flashed through his mind, till he could hardly distinguish one from the other. But Kasim's earnest gaze was all the while fixed upon the monarch, who for a few moments was absorbed in a reverie, in which indecision and a feeling of mercy toward the young Englishman appeared to be struggling with the fiercely excited passion which still trembled about the corners of his mouth and his chin in convulsive twitchings. After a little time it passed away, and left only that stern expression which was habitual to him when a sneer did not occupy his features. His eyes had been fixed on vacancy; but on a sudden he raised them up, and they met those of Kasim, who, still held by the Khan, stood close to him.

'Ai Kumbukht!' he exclaimed. 'O unfortunate, what hast thou done? By Alla I would have loved thee, only for thy rashness. Knowest thou the peril of coming between the tiger and his prey? Knowest thou that I have but to speak, and, ere thou couldst say thy belief, thy young blood would moisten the grass yonder? Knowest thou this, and yet didst thou dare to brave me? Alla kureem! what dirt has not been ordained for me to eat to-day? Whose unlucky face could I have seen this morning when I awoke? Speak, slave! thou art not a spy of the kafir English, that thou wentest beside thyself in his behalf whom we have doomed to death?'

'May I be your sacrifice, O Sultaun!' cried Kasim, joining his hands and addressing Tippoo, 'I am no spy—I am not faithless—thou hast the power to strike my head from my body—bid it be done; your slave is ready to die.'

'Then why didst thou behave thus?' said Tippoo.

'The Englishman was helpless—he was unarmed—he was my friend—for I rescued him from insult at Bangalore,' replied Kasim; 'he told me his history, and I grieved for him: he besought me not to enter thy service, O Sultaun, but to join his race. I was free to have done so; but I despised them, and longed to fight against them under the banner of the lion of Islam. I swore to befriend him, however, if ever I could; the time came sooner than I expected, and in an unlooked-for form; and I had been faithless, craven, and vile, had I failed him when he could not strike a blow in his own defence. This is the truth, O Sultaun! punish me if thou wilt—I am thy slave.'

'Unhappy boy,' said the Khan to him in a whisper, 'thou hast spoken too boldly. Alla help thee, for there is no hope for thee that I can see. See, he speaks to thee.'

'Kasim Ali,' said the Sultaun, 'had one of these who know me dared to do what thou hast done, I would have destroyed him; had any one dared to have spoken as boldly as thou hast done, I would have disgraced him for disrespect. Thou art young—thou art brave; thou hast truth on thy forehead and in thy words, and we love it. Go! thou art pardoned: and yet for warning's sake thou must suffer punishment, lest the example should spread in our army, which—thanks to Alla! who hath given his servant the wisdom to direct and discipline it after a fashion, the perfection of which is not to be met with upon the earth—'

Here he paused, and looked around, and all the courtiers cried 'Ameen! Ameen! listen to the words of wisdom, to the oracle of the faith of Islam!'

'For example's sake,' continued the Sultaun gravely, 'thou must be punished. We had thy pay written down at twelve hoons—it shall be ten; thou wast to be near my person—thou shalt serve under the Khan, as he may think fit. If thou art valiant, we shall hear of thee with pleasure, and reward thee; and remember our eyes, which are as all-seeing as those of Alla and the angels, will ever be fixed upon thee. Remember this, and tremble while thou thinkest upon it!'

Kasim saluted the monarch profoundly and drew back; he had been rebuked, but mildly, and the honest face of the Khan was once more overjoyed.

'Inshalla! thy destiny is great,' he whispered; 'now had I, or any one else here, got by any accident into such a scrape, we should have been heavily fined, degraded, and Alla only knows what else; but thou hast come off triumphant, and, as for the loss of the money, thou needest not mind. Alla grant, too, there may soon be an opportunity of winning fame. Inshalla! we will yet fight together.'

Just then the loud cries of 'Khamoosh! Khamoosh!' again resounded through the hall, and the Sultaun once more spoke.

'Let every officer inspect his cushoon* minutely during the ensuing month,' he said; 'let the officers of cavalry look well to their horses: let those who have the charge of our invincible artillery look to their carriages and bullocks: let all the departments of the army be in readiness to move at the shortest notice: for we hear of wars against our detachments in Canara, and that the infidel Nairs (may their lot be perdition!) have again taken up arms, and are giving trouble to our troops. Therefore it was revealed to us in a dream, which we have chronicled as it appeared, and with which we will now delight the ears of our people.'

* A division of troops.

And feeling under him for a manuscript, he began to read it with pompous gravity.

'On the night before last, soon after this child of clay lay down to rest, an angel of light appeared to him, even like unto the angel Gabriel, as he manifested himself unto the blessed Apostle (may his memory be honoured !) and of whom this mortal is an unworthy imitator; and the angel said,—"The Nairs in thy dominions are becoming troublesome, therefore shalt thou destroy them utterly; their abominations and the loose conduct of their women are offences against the Most High, therefore they shall be punished,—they shall be all honoured with Islamism." And so saying the angel vanished, and this servant awoke, and recorded the dream as he had heard it.'

'Ajaib! Ajaib! Karamut! Karamut!* The Sultaun is the friend of Alla—the Sultaun is the apostle of Alla!' burst from the assembly, with many other ejaculations equally devout and flattering.

'Yes, my friends, even thus doth the providence of Alla overshadow us,' continued the Sultaun, 'and enable us to avert the evils which the infidels would bring upon the true faith. Inshalla! however, we will teach them a lesson, and one which they will remember while they have being. I have read you my dream, and behold, in confirmation of it, this morning's post brought letters from Arshed Beg Khan, our governor, which informs us of the disorders, and that he is making head against them with all the force he can muster: therefore we would have you all prepared should reinforcements be needed. And now, Rhyman Khan,' he added, 'what news hast thou for us from the court of Nizam Ali Khan?'

'Shall I speak it out, Protector of the Universe, or wilt thou hear it in thy closet?' said the Khan advancing.

'Here, friend, here; what secrets have I that my friends about me should not know? Mashalla! in the Sircar Khodadad all is as open as daylight.'

Amidst the murmur of applause which this speech produced, the Khan hemmed audibly, to ensure silence, and proceeded.

'I beg to represent,' said he, 'that Nizam Ali Khan is favourable to the Sircar—entirely favourable. The English pressed him to give up the province of Guntoor, which he is bound to do by treaty; but he is unwilling (and no wonder) to comply; things have advanced to almost a quarrel between them, and if he was sure of the feeling of this Sircar, I would pledge my life on it that he would declare war to-morrow, and thus the

* Wonderful! wonderful! a miracle! a miracle!

two Sircars could fight under the banner of Islam, and exterminate the unbelievers. But, Inshalla! there will be more proof than my poor words; for I heard from good authority that the Huzoor was about to select an ambassador, a man of tact and knowledge, who will explain all his wishes satisfactorily.'

'An ambassador! sayest thou, Khan? By Alla, rare news! He is then in earnest, and with his aid what may not be done? he can bring a lakh of men—cavalry too—into the field, and he has infantry besides. Alla grant he may come soon! let us only chastise these infidel Nairs, and thus make a step towards the extermination of unbelief from Hind. Let the Durbar be closed!' he cried suddenly and abruptly after a short silence; and rising, he retired into one of the smaller rooms, where, alone, he meditated over those wild schemes of conquest which were eventually his ruin.

CHAPTER XXIII.

Dragged away by his relentless guards, Herbert Compton had no leisure allowed him to speak with his companions; even the last miserable gratification of a hurried farewell was denied him; and as he passed them, a melancholy group, some standing or leaning against the building, others sitting upon the grass in dejected attitudes, he strove to speak; but every word was a signal for fresh insult, and he was pushed, struck with shoes, spit upon by the rabble of the courtiers' servants and grooms, to whom the sufferings of a kafir Feringhee were the highest sport that could be afforded.

A sad spectacle was Herbert's renewed captivity, in insult and suffering, to those of his fellow-countrymen who beheld it. They had seen him and several others of their body brought from Bangalore in decency, if not with honour; during their journey the utmost indulgence had been shown them, and all their hearts had been buoyant with excitement when Herbert alone had been sent for into the Durbar, for they were well assured that upon his fate would turn the issue of their life or death, continued captivity or release.

There had been many among them who had, in the buoyancy of hope anticipated a release; before whose minds visions of home, of return to those beloved, to those who had mourned them dead, had been rapidly and vividly passing; who, when a ray of hope had darted in upon their cheerless thoughts, had allowed it to illuminate and warm them till it had induced even extravagances of behaviour. Some had exulted to their more staid companions; others had sung or whistled joyfully; and the mockery of their guards and of the bystanders only served to excite them the more, and to cause them to anticipate their triumph by words and gestures not to be misunderstood by those to whom they were addressed. But when Herbert passed out, ruffled, insulted, dragged away without being allowed to exchange a word with them—apparently led to death, and followed by the jeers and scoffings of the crowd who thirsted for his blood—then did hope forsake them, and the memory of the deaths of former companions by poison, by torture, or by the executioner, came upon them suddenly, and caused a revulsion of feeling which had an almost deadly effect on the most sanguine. The more sober and less excited exchanged glances and a few words with each other, expressive of their awful situation, and that their last hope had fled.

They were, in bodies of three and four, led before the Sultaun in the evening Durbar, and, like Herbert, offered the alternative of death, or service and life. A few were found to prefer the latter, but by far the greater part braved the tyrant's wrath, and in despair chose to die.

That evening saw the return of a melancholy band to the fort of Nundidroog, the rigours of the captivity of which had been known to them before by report, as also the fate there of many a brave fellow European and native, boasted to them by their guards in the various forts and prisons in which they had been confined. Nor was it as if they had been led to death at once; those who could speak a few words of the language of the country had implored this of the Sultaun, but had been refused with exultation; and they had to endure a long march of many days, with every hardship and indignity which the unconcealed wrath and spite of the Sultaun, descending almost in a redoubled degree to his subordinate officers, could inflict upon them. Their food was of the coarsest description; bad water, where it could be found, was given them to drink; miserable doolies, in which it was impossible to lie at full length, or even to sit, and open so that the sun beat in on them, were given to some: they were carried too by the inhabitants of the villages, who were pressed from stage to stage, in order that they might travel with the utmost expedition; and as these men were unaccustomed to carry loads in that way, the exhausted men they bore were jolted, until excess of fatigue often caused faintness and even death. Blest were those who died thus! they were spared the misery the survivors had to endure.

Nor was the person under whose charge they travelled, Jaffar Sahib, one likely to make any amelioration in their condition; he had received his last orders from Tippoo at the evening Durbar, relative to Herbert Compton (in regard to whom his instructions were somewhat different to those the Sultaun had given in the morning), and also to the rest of the prisoners; and well mounted himself, and accompanied by an escort of his own risala, the Jemadar hurried on, travelling the whole day, with but short rests, when the exhaustion of some of the prisoners, or at times the want of a relay of bearers, caused an unavoidable stoppage. Everywhere it was made known that the Feringhees were going to death; and while crowds from many of the villages and towns flocked to see them as they passed by, they were everywhere met by bitter insults, abuse, and derision.

It was a bitter cup to quaff for Herbert Compton, who, in spite of all, was not cast down. His stout heart, on the contrary, prepared for death by long suffering and abandonment of all hope, looked to the termination of his journey with joyful feelings as the time when he should be released from his earthly troubles. Indeed, since the capitulation of Bednore, after they were all led away into captivity,—the frequent disappearance of his comrades and brother officers telling their untimely fates,—he had daily prepared himself for death, not knowing in what hour or by what manner he should be summoned to it. This had lasted so long, that the dim visions of hope which had now and then broken the gloom in which his future was wrapped, so far as life was concerned, were at an end; now a hope of death succeeded, which amounted to a certainty, and was even pleasant in contemplation.

At first, how bitter, how agonising had been his thoughts of home, of his parents—worst of all, of Amy, whom he could not help picturing to himself as worn down by sorrow, broken in spirit, and mourning his absence, most likely his death, in vain. His mother too, alas! what a world of thought was there not in her name who had so loved him, and whose tender nature could ill have borne so rude a shock as that of his death, for he was sure they must long ago have abandoned all hope of his being alive. And when at the peace some captives were given up, and it was told that the others were dead, though it was well known in India that there were many retained, yet they would be ignorant of this in England, and would conclude he was dead also. Thus he looked to the future, with a hope, a certainty of reunion in death with those he had best loved on earth, and this made him cheerful and calm, when many around him either held the stern silence of despair or mournfully bewailed their fate.

As they passed Bangalore the governor visited them, by order of the Sultaun; he had known Herbert, and supplied him with Hindostanee books, which was done by Tippoo's order, that he might in the solitude and *ennui* of prison-life learn the language of the country, which would fit him for the duties for which he designed him. He was grieved to see him, and advised him to comply with the Sultaun's request, which Tippoo, knowing that he had been kind to the young Englishman, and thinking he might be able to turn him aside from his purpose, had advanced to him. The brave soldier, who not long afterwards met a warrior's death in defence of the fortress, used his utmost persuasion to alter Herbert's resolution, but in vain,—it was deeply rooted; the alternative proposed was too dishonourable in prospect, and the event so nigh at hand too welcome, for his resolution to be shaken. He bade Herbert farewell, with an expression of deep feeling and interest which gratified him, and which his friend did not seek to disguise. With one or two of the captives, however, the governor was more successful; the near approach of death, and the inability to look on it continuously for many days, was more than they could bear, and they yielded to solicitation which they little hoped would have been used. There were still a few, however, whom the example of Herbert, and their own strong and faithful hearts kept steady to their purpose, men who preferred death to dishonour in the service of their country's foe.

The Killadar caused nearly two days to be spent in the negotiations with the prisoners, in despite of the inquiry of Jaffar Sahib, who pretended to be full of zeal in the execution of the Sultaun's orders; but on the third morning after their arrival, there was no longer pretence for delay, and the party again set forward.

The day after Herbert knew they should arrive at the fort of Nundidroog, and their place of execution was then but at a short distance. Another day, thought he, and all will be over!

Already the dark grey mass of the fort appeared above the plain as they approached it; its immense height and precipitous sides rose plainly into view. That evening they passed over the large tank to the southward of the fort on the Bangalore road; and as its huge bulk appeared to sleep peacefully reflected on the waters, making its perpendicular sides and immense height the more apparent, Herbert thought the death to which he was doomed would be easy and sudden, and that it was a more merciful one than that of Mathews, or the lingering torment or strangulation of so many others.

Herbert observed during the journey that the officer who commanded the large party which escorted them kept aloof from him in particular; he had seen him address the others, and heard from them that he endeavoured to reason them into acceptance of the Sultaun's offers; to himself he had never spoken, but concealed his face from him; he had, however, seen it several times, and on each occasion was inclined to think that it was familiar to him; but, on reflection, he could discover no clue to the supposition in his mind, and he vainly strove to dismiss the idea from his thoughts.

The town of Nundidroog was in sight; it was evening, the mountain flung its broad shadow over the plain under the declining rays of the sun, and the warm red light of an Indian sunset covered every object with splendour. The herds of cattle, and of sheep and goats, were hastening home from their pasture with loud lowings and bleatings, and the simple melody of the shepherd's pipe arose, now far away, now near, from the various herds they passed. On their left towered the huge rock almost above their heads; its fortifications, built on the giddy verge full eight hundred feet above the brushwood and rocky declivity out of which it rose naked, appeared ready to topple over the precipice. There was one huge round bastion in particular, on the very edge of the steepest and highest part, and Herbert speculated whether or no that was the spot; he was looking so intently at it that he did not heed the approach on his right hand of the leader of the party, who, speaking to him suddenly, almost startled him by the familiar accent of his voice.

'Dost thou see yonder bastion, Feringhee?' said the officer, pointing to it—'yonder round one, from which the flag of the Sultaun floats proudly upon the evening wind?'

'I do,' replied Herbert; 'it is a giddy place.'

'Many a kafir Feringhee,' continued the man, 'has been flung from thence, while a prayer for mercy was on his lips, and his last shrieks grew fainter and fainter as he descended to perdition: many an unworthy Moslim and kafir Hindoo, taken in arms against the true believers, have wished they had never been born, or had never seen your accursed race, when he was taken to the edge and hurled over it.'

'Death will be easy from thence,' said Herbert calmly. 'I can look on it, and think on it with pleasure; is that the place where—'

'No,' cried the man exultingly interrupting him, 'that is too good for thee and thy obstinate companions. Dost thou see yonder lotos-shaped hill?' And he pointed to one around which the evening vapour was wreathing itself in soft fleecy masses, while the red sunlight lighted up its rugged sides and narrow top.

'I see it,' said Herbert.

'Beneath it,' continued the man, 'there is a rock; thou wilt see it to-morrow—till then farewell.'

'Stay!' cried Herbert, 'tell me, if thou wilt—for it matters little to one so near death—tell me who thou art; surely I have met thee ere now; thy voice is familiar to my ears.'

'Thou shalt know to-morrow,' was the only reply the man gave, as he touched the flanks of his horse and galloped to the head of the detachment.

The wearied prisoners were glad when they reached the ancient Hindoo cloisters, where we have before seen the Khan and Ameena with his risala encamped; and though the evening wind, which had arisen sharply, blew chill around them and whistled through the ruined arches and pillars, they were glad to eat their humble meal of coarse flour cakes and a little sour curds; and wrapping themselves in the horse-cloths which were flung to them out of pity by the grooms, they lay down on the hard ground, each with a stone for his pillow, and exhausted nature claiming its repose, they slept soundly.

But Herbert only for a while; he had dreamed vividly and yet confusedly of many things, and at last awoke, fevered and unrefreshed. A jar of water was beside them; he arose, drank some, which revived him, and sat down on a broken pillar, for he could not sleep again; thought was too busy within him. There was no one stirring except the men on watch, who lazily paced to and fro close to him, talking in short sentences: he strove to listen to their conversation.

'And do you think he knows where it is? they say the Feringhees buried it when the place was taken,' said one.

'Willa Alum!'* said the other, 'the Jemadar says he does, and that he will make him tell where it is before—'

Here Herbert lost the rest, and they did not return to the subject again, but wandered away to others which to him had no interest. The night was very chill, and a keen wind blew, raising the fine dust which had accumulated in the place, and blowing it sharply against his face; there was something melancholy in the sound, as it whistled and moaned through the

* 'God knows!'

ruins, and through the branches of an old blasted peepul-tree which, blanched with age, stood out a ghastly object against the dark sky. At length, after some time of weary watching, a cock in the town crew; another answered his call; and as Herbert looked into the east, the grey flush of dawn was apparent, and he was glad the day had come, though it was to be, as he thought, his last.

The whole party were soon astir, the unhappy sleepers aroused, and, as one by one they awoke to consciousness, with the light that greeted them, miserable thoughts of death poured into their hearts, and occupied them to the exclusion of every other idea. One sat motionless, and apparently stupefied, as though he had eaten opium; another prayed aloud wildly, yet fervently; others laughed and spoke with a feverish excitement; and there were one or two who blasphemed and cursed, while they bewailed their early and fearful fate.

For some hours they waited in the cloisters, and the sun was high and bright, ere a body of men on foot, the soldiers of the country, armed with sword and matchlock, marched into it. It was plain that their escort was to be changed, and that the respectable men who had been with them were no longer to accompany them, but had given place to some of the lowest description of Tippoo's troops, who were usually composed of the unclean castes of the country. Their appearance was forbidding, and in vain the prisoners looked for a glance of pity from the half-naked and savage-looking band to whom they were given over; they appeared used to the scenes which were to ensue, and regarded the miserable Englishmen with a cold stare of indifferent curiosity.

But little communication passed between the prisoners; Herbert had for some days spoken to them, and advised them to prepare for death by prayer and penitent confession to God; he had reasoned with several, who had from the first shown a foolhardy and light demeanour, on the madness of attempting indifference to their fate; but as the time drew near, he was too fully occupied with his own overpowering thoughts to attend to the others, and he had withdrawn to as far a distance as possible from them, where he sat moodily, and contemplated with bitter thoughts his approaching death.

While he was thus occupied the Jemadar entered the court, and having given some orders to the men who remained behind, he directed the legs of the prisoners to be tied. This having been executed, they were placed in the doolies, and the whole again proceeded.

Passing the outskirts of the town of Nundidroog, they travelled for two or three miles through the avenues of mango-trees, which in parts line the road: could they have had thought for anything around them, they would have admired the varied prospect presented to them by the rugged rocky hills, and their picturesque and ever-varying outlines: but one idea absorbed all others, and they were borne along in a kind of unconscious state; they could see nothing but death, even though the bright sun was in their eyes, and the glad and joyful face of nature was spread out before them.

At length the leading men turned off the road by a by-path towards a huge pile of rocks in the plain, about half a mile distant, and the others followed; it was plain to all that this was their destination. Then it flashed across their minds that the rock was not high enough to cause death instantaneously; and while some demanded in haughty words of expostulation to be taken to the fort itself, or to the summit of the conical mountain, which arose precipitously on the right hand,—others besought the same with piteous and plaintive entreaty, in very abjectness compared with their former conduct. They might as well have spoken to the wind which blew over them in soft and cool breezes as if to soothe their excited and fevered frames. Ignorant of the only language of which the Europeans could speak a few words, the rude soldiers listened with indifference, or replied with obscene jests and mocking gestures and tones.

They reached the foot of the rocks; the bearers were directed to put down the doolies, and the prisoners were dragged from them with violence. A few clung with fearful cries to the wretched vehicle, which had been their wearisome abode for so many days, and one or two resisted, with frantic efforts, to the utmost of their power, the endeavours of their guards to lead them up the narrow pathway; they were even wounded in their struggles; but the men they had to deal with were far stronger than the attenuated Europeans, and had been accustomed to the work too long to heed cries or screams; they were the far-famed guard of the rock, even now remembered, who had been selected for their fierce behaviour, strength, and savage deportment, to carry into execution the decrees of the Sultaun.

All the while they had been accompanied by the Jemadar, who, having ridden in advance of the party, now awaited their coming at the top of the rock. Herbert was the first who arrived there, led by the rope which, tied to both his arms, was held by one of the guards, while others with drawn swords walked on each side of and behind him. He had been cast down in heart since the morning, and faint and sick at heart; but now his spirit seemed nerved within him. One plunge, he thought, and all would be over; then he should be released from this worse than death. Prayer too was in his heart and on his lips, and his soul was comforted, as he stepped firmly upon the level space above and looked around him.

The Jemadar was there, and a few other soldiers; the terrace was a naked rock, which was heated by the sun so that it scorched his bare feet. There were a few bushes growing around it, and on one side were two mud houses, the one close, the other open for the guard. Besides these, there was a hut of reeds, which was used as a place for keeping water.

'Thou art welcome, captain,' said the Jemadar with mock politeness. 'Art thou ready to taste of the banquet of death?'

'Lead on,' said Herbert firmly, 'and molest me not by thy words. I am ready.'

'Not so fast, sir; the Sultaun's orders must first be obeyed. Say, art thou ready to take his service, or dost thou refuse?'

'I have already told him my determination, and will waste no words upon such as thee,' was Herbert's reply.

'It is well!' said the Jemadar, 'thou wilt learn ere long to speak differently:' and he turned away from him to where several of the others were now standing. He regarded them for a few minutes steadily and exultingly, as one by one the miserable beings were led up; and some, unable from mental and bodily exhaustion to support themselves, sunk down on the rock almost insensible.'

There was one youth, a noble and vigorous fellow. Herbert had remembered him when he was first brought to Bangalore from some distant fortress—high-spirited and full of fire, which even captivity had not tamed. But the long and rapid journey, the bad food, the exposure to scorching heat and chilling dew, had brought on dysentery, which had exhausted him nigh to death. He was almost carried by the guards, and set down apart from the rest. His languid and sunken eye and pallid cheek told of his sickness; but there was a look of hope in the glance which he cast upwards now and then, and a gentle movement of his lips, which showed that his spirit was occupied in prayer.

The Jemadar's eye rested on him. 'Let him be the first—he will die else!' he cried to some of the guards, who, having divested themselves of their arms, stood ready to do his bidding.

A cry of horror burst from the group of Englishmen. There were two or three of the strong men who struggled firmly with their captors, as their gallant hearts prompted them to strike a blow for their suffering comrade. But, bound and guarded, what could they do?

They saw the young man lifted up by two of the executioners, and borne rapidly to the further edge of the rock, not twenty yards from them. He uttered no cry; but looking towards them sadly, he bade them farewell for ever, with a glance even more eloquent than words. Another instant, and he was hurled from the brink by those who carried him.

Almost unconsciously each bent forward to catch even a passing sound, should any arise; and there was a dead silence for a few moments, as the men who had done their work leaned over the edge to see if it had been surely effected. But none arose: the sufferer had been quickly released from his earthly pain.

'Dost thou see that, Captain Compton?' said the Jemadar. 'Thy turn will come.'

'Now,' was the reply; 'I am ready.' And Herbert hoped that his turn would be the next. His energies were knit, and his spirit prepared for the change.

'Not yet,' said the Jemadar: 'I would speak with thee first. Lead the rest away into the house yonder,' he continued to the guard, 'loose them, and lock the door.' It was done, and Herbert alone remained outside.

'Listen!' he said, addressing Herbert, 'does thou remember me?'

'I said before that I thought I knew thee; but what has that to do with death?' said Herbert. 'I am ready to die; bid thy people do their office.'

'That will not be for many days,' he replied; 'I have a long reckoning to settle with thee.'

'For what? I have never harmed thee.'

'When Mathews was in Bednore, and there was alarm of the Sultaun's coming, thou didst suspect me, thou and another. Thou didst insult and threaten to hang me. We are even now, —dost thou understand?'

'What! Jaffar Sahib, the guide, the man who betrayed the salt he ate?'

'Even so. Ye were owls, fools, and fell into the snare laid for you.'

'Has thy resentment slumbered so long then?' said Herbert. 'I pity thee: thy own heart must be a hell to thee.'

'Kafir! dare to speak so again, and I will spit on thee.'

'It would befit thee to do so; but I am silent,' was Herbert's reply.

'Where is the money that thou and that old fool, who is now

in perdition, buried in Bednore? Lead me to it, and I will save thy life. The coast is near, and thou canst escape. Fear not to speak,—those around do not understand us.'

'Thy master has been told by me, by Mathews, who lost his life in that cause, and by every one, that there was none but what he found. We hid no money—thou well knowest this: why dost thou torment me?'

'Thou wilt remember it in three or four days, perhaps,' said the man; 'till then I shall not ask thee again. Go to the company of thy people.'

Herbert's mind had been strung up to its purpose, and he coveted death at that moment as the dearest boon which could have been granted. But it was denied him; and he could only gather from the leader of the party that further suffering was in store for him. In spite of his utmost exertions to repel the feeling, despondence came over him,—a sickening and sinking of his heart, which his utmost exertion of mind could not repel.

The day passed away, and the night fell. As the gloom spread over their narrow chamber, the men, whom the light had kept silent or cheering each other, now gave way to superstitious terrors; and, as they huddled together in a group, some cried out that there were hideous spectres about them; others prayed aloud; and those who were hard of heart blasphemed, and made no repentance. As night advanced, some yelled in mental agony and terror, and the thought of those who were to die on the morrow appalled every heart. None slept.

Four days passed thus; on every morning a new victim was taken, while the rest were forced to look on. Sometimes he went gladly and rejoicing, sometimes he had to be torn from his companions, who in vain strove to protect him: two suffered passively—two made desperate resistance, and their parting shrieks long rang in the ears of the survivors. On the fourth day the Jemadar arrived. 'Come forth,' he said to Herbert, 'I would speak to thee. Wilt thou be obdurate, O fool? wilt thou longer refuse to tell of the money, and the Sultaun's benevolence? Bethink thee.'

'Thou couldst not grant me a greater favour than death,' said Herbert; 'therefore why are these things urged? If there was money hidden thou shouldst have it; I know it is thy god. But there is none, therefore let me die. I tell thee once for all, I spurn thy master's offers with loathing.'

'Dost thou know what this death is?' said the Jemadar; 'thou shalt see.' And he called to several of the guards who stood around. Herbert thought, as they led him to the brink, that his time was come. 'I come, I come, Amy!' he cried aloud—'at length I come! O God, be merciful to me!'

They led him passively to the brink; the Jemadar stood there already; it was a dizzy place, and Herbert's eyes swam as he surveyed it.

'Thou art not to die, Feringhee,' said the Jemadar; 'but look over. Behold what will be thy fate!'

Herbert obeyed mechanically, and the men held him fast on the very verge, or the temptation would have been strong to have ridden himself of life. He looked down: the hot and glaring sunlight fell full on the mangled remains of his comrades, which lay in a confused heap at the bottom: a hundred vultures were scrambling over each other to get at them, and the bodies were snatched to and fro by their united efforts. The Jemadar heaved a fragment of rock over, which, rebounding from the side, crashed among the brushwood and the obscene birds; they arose screaming at being disturbed, and two or three jackals skulked away through the brushwood. But Herbert saw not these; the first glance and the putrid smell which came up had sickened him, weak and excited as he was, and he fainted.

CHAPTER XXIV.

'He has fainted, or is dead,' cried the men who held him, to the Jemadar, who was busied in heaving over another fragment of rock. 'He has fainted; shall we fling him over?'

'For your lives do not!' cried the Jemadar; 'draw back from thence—let us see what is the matter.'

They obeyed him, and laid Herbert down softly upon the rock, while the Jemadar stood over him. His hand was powerless and cold, his face quite pale, and he looked as though he were dead.

'He has cheated us,' said the Jemadar to those around; 'surely he is dead. Who prates now of the valour of the Feringhees? Even this leader among them could not look on a few dead bodies without fainting like a woman: Thooh! I spit on the kafirs: I marvel that the Sultaun so desires him to enter the service, and is at such trouble about him.'

'He will die,' said one of the men; 'his hand grows colder and colder.'

'He must not die yet, Pochul,' said Jaffar Sahib; 'what would the Sultaun say to us? Away! get some water; he may revive. This is only a faint, the effect of terror; he will soon speak again.'

The man obeyed the order, and brought water. They dashed some on Herbert's face, and opening his lips, poured some between his tightly closed teeth. But it was in vain; he moved not, nor showed signs of life for a long while; and was it not that his body continued warm, they would have thought him dead. At length he sighed, and opening his eyes, gazed wildly around him. The effort was greeted with a shout from those about him, which he appeared not to hear, but sank back again insensible. Again they essayed to revive him as they best could; and after a long time partially succeeded as before; but it was only to see him relapse again and again. Once or twice he spoke, but incoherently.

For some hours he continued thus. At last a violent shivering commenced; and seeing him so affected (for the Jemadar had left them for a while, having given the men strict orders to look carefully to Herbert, and to remove him to their guard-house), as they were aware he was a person of more than ordinary consequence, they used what means they could to alleviate his sufferings. One lent him his rozaee, or quilted counterpane; another kneaded his limbs or chafed his hands; a third heated cloths and applied them to his back and head. But it was in vain: the shivering continued, accompanied at times with dreadful sickness. After being in this state for awhile, he broke into a violent heat—a burning, exhausting heat—which excited him furiously. Now he raved wildly: he spoke sometimes in English, sometimes in Hindostanee; and as none of the men around him understood either, they held a hurried consultation among themselves, and came to the resolution of selecting one of the prisoners to remain with him, and minister to his wants. The office was gladly accepted by the man they chose, whose name was Bolton, and whom they fixed on because he had been seen in conversation with Herbert more than the rest, and could speak a few words of their language, Canarese, which he had learned where he had been last confined.

All that night was passed by the unfortunate young man in violent raving, the consequence of the raging fever which consumed him. He tossed incessantly to and fro in the small corded bed upon which he had been laid; now yelling forth, in the agony he suffered from his head, which he held with both his hands; and now moaning piteously, so that even the rough guards felt compassion for the young and helpless Englishman. 'Water!' was the only coherent word he could utter; the rest was a continued unintelligible muttering, in which some English words and names were sometimes faintly discernible.

Poor Bolton did what he could, but it was in vain; and when the Jemadar returned in the morning for the purpose of adding another victim to his last, he found Herbert in such a state as to alarm him; for the Sultaun had sworn he would have life for life if aught happened to him.

'He must be removed instantly,' he said. 'Away, one of ye, for a dooly! Bring it to the foot of the rock—we will carry him down thither, and he must be removed to the town.'

In the end too he was merciful, for he took Bolton with him to attend on Herbert while he should live; it could not be long, he thought, for he raved incessantly, until exhaustion ensued, and he gained fresh strength for further frantic efforts.

And they left the fatal rock soon afterwards, the only two of that numerous company alive; nor was the fate of the rest long protracted. They were murdered as the rest had been; and the bleached bones and skulls, and fragments of clothes which had no shape to tell to whom they had belonged—for they had been stripped from the dead by the beaks of vultures and teeth of jackals—proved to those who long afterwards looked on the place, that the tales they had heard of the horrors of that fatal rock, and which they had in part disbelieved, were not unfounded.

It was on a mild and balmy evening that Herbert awoke to consciousness, about a week after he had been removed. He looked languidly around him, for he was so weak that even the effort he made to raise himself caused a giddy faintness; and for an instant the remembrance of his last conscious moment upon the brink of the precipice flashed across his mind, and he shuddered at the recollection of what he had seen. Again he looked around, but he was not upon the rock; the fatal and wretched abode in which he had passed five days—such days of enduring agony as he could not have believed it possible to sustain—with its bare walls scrawled all over with the names of its miserable inhabitants, and their care-worn, despairing, and almost maniac faces, were around him no longer. He lay in the open air, under the shade of a wide-spreading peepul-tree, upon a mound of earth surrounding a tomb; which, from its clean white-washed state, and the garlands of flowers which hung upon it, was evidently that of a Mahomedan saint or holy martyr. At a short distance was a small mosque, exquisitely white and clean, behind which rose some noble tamarind-trees, and with them cocoa-nut and plantains, which formed an appropriate background to the pureness of the building, their foliage partly shaded and intermingled with the minarets and ornamented pinnacles of the mosque. Before it was a little garden, where flourished luxuriantly a pomegranate-tree or two, covered with their bright scarlet blossoms—a few marigolds and cockscombs, intermixed with mint and other sweet herbs, which appeared to be cultivated with care. The space around the tomb and before the mosque, and for a considerable extent all round, was carefully swept; and the branches of the peepul and tamarind-trees, which met and interweaved high above, formed a cover impenetrable by the rays of the fiercest sun at noon-day; but it was now evening, and the red light streamed in a flood between the stems of the trees, lighting up the gnarled branches of the peepul and the thick foliage beyond. Innumerable parroquets and minas screamed and twittered in the branches above him, and flew from place to place restlessly: but the only sound of man was from one drawing water for the garden, by the aid of the lever and bucket common to Mysore, whose monotonous yet not unmusical song and mellow voice ceased only to allow the delicious sound of the rush of water to reach Herbert's ear, as the bucket was emptied from time to time into the reservoir which supplied the garden.

He lay in a half unconscious state, in that dreamy languor, which, when fierce fever has subsided, is almost painful from its vagueness; when the mind, striving to recal the past, wanders away into thoughts which have no reference to it, but which lose themselves in a maze of unreal illusions too subtle and shifting to be followed, and yet too pleasant to excite aught but tranquil images and soothing effects.

The sun sank in glory,—in such glory behind the mountains beyond as Herbert had never before witnessed, save once, when he was at sea, and the land which held him a prisoner, and was his living grave, appeared in sight. As the evening fell, and the golden tints of the west faded, giving place to the rich hues of crimson and purple which spread over it, the sonorous voice of the Muezzin, from a corner of the enclosure, proclaimed the evening worship; and in the melancholy yet melodious tone of the invitation, called the Believers to prayer. A few devout answered to it, and advancing from one side, performed their ablutions at a little fountain which cast up a tiny thread of spray into the air; this done, they entered the mosque, and, marshalled in a row, went through, with apparent fervour, the various forms and genuflexions prescribed by their belief

Afterwards two advanced towards Herbert,—one, a venerable man in the garb of a Fakeer, the other a gentleman of respectable appearance, who, from the sword he carried under his arm, might be an officer.

Herbert heard one say, 'Most likely he is dead now; he was dying when we last saw him, and his attendant went with Jaffar Sahib to purchase his winding-sheet; poor fellow, he was unwilling to go, but the Jemadar forced him away.'

'I have hope,' said the old Fakeer, 'the medicine I gave him (praised be the power of Alla!) has rarely failed in such cases, and if the paroxysm is past he will recover.'

Herbert heard this and strove to speak; his lips moved, but no words followed above a whisper: he was weaker than an infant. But now the Fakeer advanced to him and felt his hand and head; they were cool and moist, and Herbert turned to look on them with a heart full of gratitude at the kindness and interest which their words and looks expressed.

'Ya Ruhman! ya Salaam! Oh he lives! he is free from the disease (blessed be the power of Alla!)—he is once more among the living. Therefore rejoice, O Feringhee,' exclaimed the Fakeer, 'and bless Alla that thou livest! for He hath been merciful to thee. Six days hast thou lain in yonder serai, and the breath was in thy nostrils, but it hath now returned to thy heart, so be thankful.'

'I am grateful for thy kindness, Shah Sahib,' said Herbert, speaking very faintly,—for he had learned the usual appellation of all respectable Fakeers long before—'Alla will reward thee; I pray thee tell me who thou art, and where I am. Methinks I was—'

'Trouble not thyself to think on the past,' he replied; 'it was not destined to be, and thy life is for the present safe; thou art in the garden of the poor slave of Alla and the apostle, Sheikh Furreed, of Balapoor.'

'A worthy Fakeer, and one on whom the power to work miracles hath descended in this degenerate time,' said his companion; 'one who may well be called "Wullee," and who will be honoured in death.'

'I have an indifferent skill in medicine,' said the Fakeer; 'but to the rest I have no pretensions, Khan Sahib; but we should not speak to the youth; let him be quiet; the air will revive him; and when they return he shall be carried back to the serai.'

They left him; and ere long he heard footsteps approaching; a figure was running towards him—he could not surely be mistaken—it was an English face: he came nearer—it was Bolton.

The poor fellow sobbed with very joy when he saw his officer released, as it were, from the jaws of death; he hung over him, and bathed his hand with tears; he little expected ever to have heard him speak again. Now his officer lived, and while a load of sorrow was removed from his heart, he blessed God that He had been so merciful.

'I have carried you forth day by day in my arms, and laid you yonder,' said the faithful fellow, as he lifted him up like a child: 'they said you would die, and I thought if you were sensible before that time came, you would like to be in this shady cool place, where the light would not be too strong for you, the fresh air would play over you, and you could look around upon the green trees and gardens ere you went hence.'

Herbert could only press his hand in silence, for his heart was too full to speak; indeed he was too weak also; for in being carried to the serai once more, he fainted, and it was long ere he recovered. But that night a few mouthfuls of rice-milk were given him, and he slept peacefully,—that noiseless, almost breathless sleep, which is attendant on extreme weakness, when dreams and pleasant phantasies flit before the imagination like shadows chasing each other over beautiful prospects, when the day is bright and soft. Herbert's visions were of home, of walks in the twilight with Amy, of her soft words, of the plashing of the river in their well-known haunts, sacred to him by the dearest and holiest ties,—and he woke in the morning refreshed and strengthened.

He could now speak; he could converse with the soldier who had watched over him so devotedly, and he learned from him all that had occurred.

'You were delirious, sir,' he said; 'and I was sent for from among the rest; poor fellows! I hear they are all murdered. I thought you had been struck by the sun, for you were bareheaded; perhaps it was so, for you were quite mad and very violent. They brought you here in the dooly, which was sent for by the Jemadar, and at first no one would receive you. You lay raving in the bazaar, and people avoided you as they would have done a devil,—they even called you one. But the good Fakeer who lives here saw you by chance, and took you away from them, and he has watched you and given you various medicines, which have made you, I fear, very weak, sir; but you are better now.'

'So they were all murdered?' said Herbert, his thoughts reverting to the past.

'They were, sir; but why think of that now? it will distress you—you should not; there are brighter things in store for you, depend on it.'

'Alas!' said Herbert, 'I fear not, Bolton; but since God has spared me from that death, and protected me through this dreadful illness, of which I have a confused remembrance, surely it is not too much to hope.'

And he did hope, and from his soul he breathed a fervent prayer; for through the future there appeared a glimmering ray of hope on which his mind loved to rest, though clouds and dark vapours of doubt and uncertainty would rise up occasionally and obscure it. Day by day, however, he recovered strength, and the old Fakeer sate by him often, and beguiled the time with tales and legends of the mighty of the earth who were dead and gone. It was a dreamy existence, to live weak and helpless among those shady groves, to lie for hours listening to the ever-sighing trees, as the wind rustled through their thick foliage, watching the birds of varied plumage as they flitted among their branches, while his ear was filled with wild legends of love, of war, of crime, or of revenge.

But this had an end—it was too bright, too peaceful to last. When a week had elapsed, the Jemadar who had avoided him studiously during his recovery, came to him with the Fakeer; for knowing Herbert's detestation of him, he had not dared to venture alone.

'The Jemadar hath news for thee, my son,' said the old man; 'fear not, he will not harm thee—I would not let him do so. He hath shown me the Sultaun's letter to him, which arrived a short time ago by an express.'

'Listen, Feringhee!' said Jaffar Sahib; 'the Shah Sahib will bear me witness that there is no wrong intended thee; my royal master doth but seek his own, and still asketh thee for the treasure.'

'Shah Sahib,' said Herbert, 'hear me say, and be witness, that as Alla, whom we both worship, sees my heart, that it is pure of deceit,—I know nought of it. Unlike those who loaded themselves with money, and plundered the treasury at Bednore, I and a few others never touched it. Canst thou not believe that, to save my life, I would have told if I had known aught of it?'

'I believe that thou wouldst, my son, but—'

'There must have been lakhs of money and jewels buried there or destroyed,' said the Jemadar; 'else, where is the treasure? Every one was searched, and yet not half was found that I myself saw there before—'

'Before what?' asked the Fakeer, whose curiosity was raised.

'Let him tell his own tale of shame if he can,' said Herbert;

'I would not so humble him, though he is my enemy, for some reason that I know not of.'

'Thou knowest well I have cause to be so,' said the Jemadar, with bitter rancour in his tone; 'but this is foolishness; here is the Sultaun's letter; thou must either tell of the treasure, or go again into confinement;—tell of it, and thou wilt be freed and sent on an embassy to thine own people,—refuse, and the alternative is thy doom. Choose then—in this at least there is no tyranny.'

'Alas! I am but mocked,' said Herbert sadly; 'I have given thee my answer so many times, that this is but torment, exciting hope that makes me dream of joy I can never realise. My own people—alas! to them I am dead long ago, and— But why speculate? I tell thee, before this holy witness, my kind and benevolent friend, that I have no other reply to give than that thou knowest.'

'It is well, Sahib,—thy fate is cast; the old prison at Bangalore awaits thee, where, if Alla give thee long life, thou art fortunate, but where speedy death will be thy most probable fate.'

'It will be welcome,' said Herbert; 'but while I have life, I will remember thee, O Fakeer, who hast been to me a friend in bitter adversity, when to all others I was accursed. When am I to travel?'

'To-morrow,' replied the Jemadar; 'the letter is peremptory, if thou art strong enough to bear the journey.'

'He is not,' said the Fakeer, 'he is still weak. On my head be the blame of his remaining longer.'

'No,' said Herbert, 'I am feeble, it is true, but let it be as the Sultaun wills. I am too long accustomed to hardship to resist or object, and thou, my friend, wouldst only bring down his wrath upon thee by keeping me here: yet think, when I am gone, from this our short acquaintance, that our race can be grateful, and when thou hearest us reviled, say that we are not as our slanderers speak of us. For myself, while I have life, I will remember thee as a kind and dear friend; and if Alla wills it, we may meet again.'

'If Alla wills it?—Ya Moojeeb!* ya Kubeer!† ya Moota-alee!‡ grant that it may be that we may meet again.'

And, full of regret, of pain at parting with his old and true friend,—even shedding tears, for he was weak in body and in mind, as he left those quiet, peaceful groves and green shades,—with the memory of his fearful illness, his kind nursing, and the devotion of their possessor fresh and vivid in his thoughts,—Her-

* O answerer of prayer! † O Lord of power! ‡ O most sublime!

bert left the place the next day, accompanied by his comrade in captivity, whose only hope now was, that they should never again be separated. In the secrecy of friendship, he had procured a pen and paper from the old Fakeer, and had written a few lines to the Governor of Madras, stating who he was, and that he still lived; this the old man promised to send whenever an opportunity occurred; but he was over-cautious, Herbert thought, and there was but little hope that it would ever reach its destination.

The journey did not fatigue him as he had expected; in contrast to the hurried travel in coming, they returned to Bangalore in three days, and Herbert was even stronger and better for the exertion. He expected once more his old cell, and the company of books, even sometimes a word with his kind friend the Killadar; but there was another trial in store for him, of which he could have had no idea—it was terrible in contemplation.

It would seem as if the capricious mind of the Sultaun was never settled to one point about Herbert; order after order was revoked, and others substituted; the last, which met him at Bangalore, was that Herbert should be taken to a solitary mountain fortress beyond Mysore, in a region which was known to be inclement, and from whence tidings of his existence could never find their way. He had been passive in the hands of his captors now for years, and this fresh mark of tyranny was nothing new, nor the changes in the Sultaun's designs for him to be wondered at. A few days' delay occurred at Bangalore, where some suits of coarse but thickly quilted clothes were given to him, two or three blankets, a counterpane, and a few other necessaries; and he once more journeyed onwards. A bitter pang to him was the loss of his faithful friend and attendant Bolton, who was not permitted to accompany him. They separated in sorrow, but they exchanged written memoranda of each other's history, to be made known to their countrymen in case either had ever an opportunity.

Herbert travelled many days; following at first the road to Seringapatam, the party struck off to the left when near the city; there he was rid of the hateful presence of the Jemadar, who to the last urged him to confess the existence of the treasure, and repeated his offers of conniving at his flight, should he disclose it.

At length a blue wall of mountains appeared in the far distance; their bases were wreathed with vapours, which rolled along their sides but never appeared to reach the summit. Day after day, as they approached them nearer, their giant forms displayed themselves in grander and more majestic beauty. What had appeared chasms and rents in their sides, when the light rested on them, now revealed valleys and thickly wooded glens, into which imagination strove to penetrate, in speculation of their real loveliness.

At length they reached the pass, which from the table-land of Mysore descends into the plain of Coimbatoor; and from thence the boundless prospect which met Herbert's eye filled his mind with delight and rapture. The blue distance melted into the sky, by a succession of the tenderest tints: away through the plains rolled the Bhowanee, a silver thread glittering amidst the most exquisite colours. The huge mountains were on his right,—blue and vast—their rugged sides, here hewn into deep chasms, and again clothed with woods of a luxuriance which he had never before seen equalled. In the distance of the lofty chain, one mountain of peculiar form, whose sides were naked precipices, stood out boldly against the blue plain. The soldiers pointed to it exultingly, and when he asked them the reason, he was told that it was his destination.

They descended; everywhere the same noble views, the same glory of the works of Heaven, which Herbert worshipped in his heart, met his gaze. Having passed along the foot of the mountains for two days, and approached them nearer and nearer, they began to ascend. Below the rugged pass, the mighty forests, the huge bamboos, the giant creepers, and their lovely flowers, had filled Herbert's mind with wonder and awe; as he ascended, this gave place to feelings of delight. The path was rugged and stony, and the pony he rode (for which the dooly had been exchanged beneath the pass) climbed but slowly, and he was obliged to rest him occasionally, while he turned round to enjoy the mighty prospect. How grand it was to see the high table-land of Mysore breaking into the plain in mountains of four thousand feet high, of every conceivable form, and bathed in the bright light of an Indian sun, while the boundless plains stretched away from their feet!

As he ascended, the air blew cooler and cooler, and plants and beautiful flowers new to him grew profusely by the wayside; at last he saw—he could not be mistaken—some fern! How his heart bounded as he plucked it, and kissed its well-remembered form. A little higher there was a bed of blue flowers peering from among the luxuriant shrubs; they had familiar faces,—he stopped, and dismounting ran to them. They were violets,—the same as those with which he had a thousand times filled his

Amy's lap in summer time, when they were children;—how full his heart was!

Further on, a brake of brambles met his eye; the ripe black fruit was a luxury to him, such as he had not dreamed of; and below them a bed of wild strawberries, the same as they had grown in the Beechwood groves and round the Hermitage. He was now near the summit; the air was cold and fresh like that of England, the sky was bluer than below, and a few light fleecy clouds floated about the mountain-top, veiling its beauty. They still advanced, and he was in rapture: he could not speak, his thoughts could only find vent in thanksgiving. A familiar flower caught his eye in a bush above his head; it was woodbine—the same, and as fragrant, as in England. Herbert's heart was already full to overflowing, and thoughts of the past increased by these simple objects were too powerful for him to bear calmly; he could resist nature's best relief no longer, and wept—tears which soothed him as they flowed; and while he sate down, and with dim and streaming eyes gazed over the almost boundless prospect, he felt that if he could have passed away to another existence with those feelings, it would have been bliss.

CHAPTER XXV.

SOME years have now elapsed since Philip Dalton parted from his friend Herbert at Bednore, upon the mission of the unfortunate Mathews; and it becomes necessary to revert to him for a while, in order to present successively the various events which belong to our history, in such a manner as may best serve to fix them upon the reader's attention, and which from their connection, though at considerable distances of time, it is needful to follow to the end in their true order.

Philip's journey to the coast was rapid, but he had time once more to tread the ground which was the scene of that spirited conflict, once more to visit the grave of his young companion, which was undisturbed; and he saw with satisfaction that the simple monument which they had ordered to be erected over it, to preserve it from being molested as well as to mark the place, was in a state of forwardness and would soon be finished. In a few days more the party were at the coast, and finding vessels there belonging to the Government, they embarked, and with the soft and favourable breezes of the season, soon reached their destination in safety.

Here now ensued a scene of bitter contention among the friends of both parties, and opinions ran high on both sides. While the one urged the incompetency, the neglect of orders and caution, and the obstinacy of Mathews, in not listening to the advice of those well calculated by their rank and experience to give it, there were also those who argued, that in all his acts Mathews was fully justified,—that, should disaster come, the Government of the island was alone to blame, in having directed him to undertake operations of such magnitude with means so insignificant, which, though they had been eminently successful, he could not be expected to maintain without large and speedy reinforcements.

Before the council, however, the affairs were argued with calmness and temper; the letters of Mathews certainly threw no light upon his position, his means of defence or intelligence of the enemy; and though Philip Dalton defended his commander with zeal and temper, he was forced to acknowledge that there were many points on which he, in common with others, had offered advice that had been disregarded—points, the neglect of which could not be otherwise than injurious to the discipline of the army, which had already suffered in a great degree.

The arguments against Mathews finally prevailed, and the orders for his supercession in the command were given to Macleod, who, with Shaw and Humberstone, already mentioned, took a speedy departure from Bombay. A severe indisposition prevented Philip's accompanying them, as he had intended; for Macleod, aware of his talent, zeal, and military skill, had offered him the same office on his own staff which he had filled with Mathews, and he had accepted it; and as the Government had promised a reinforcement, which the commanders represented as absolutely necessary to enable them to hold the ground they had acquired, there was an opportunity for proceeding with troops. This, besides being more agreeable to Philip, would enable him to be of use to the officer who was nominated to the command, from his knowledge of the road and of the country.

But he was destined never to proceed: the three commanders, who had sailed from Bombay in a small armed vessel belonging to the Government, were attacked off the Mahratta fort of Gheriah by some heavy Mahratta vessels, for which they were no match. The officers defended themselves and their charge bravely, and made a determined though ineffectual resistance, in which one of their number, the gallant Humberstone, lost his life;

the others, with the crew and vessel, were carried into Gheriah, and it was not until after a long lapse of time that their release was effected. When the news of this disaster reached Bombay, it retarded the preparations for embarkation which were being made for the troops; and ere many weeks had passed, the sad intelligence of the disaster at Bednore completed the distress and consternation of the Presidency.

From the few that escaped, who magnified the terrors of the event, and described in fearful terms the miseries endured by the prisoners,—and from the reports of the cruelties exercised upon them, which had long been prevalent, and were known to be well founded—Philip had despaired of ever gaining intelligence of his friend Herbert; and while he wrote to his family, whose direction he was in possession of, to inform them of the sad event, and to tell them that Herbert was known to have been in good health when he was taken with the rest, he could give them but little hope as to the final issue; indeed upon this point he was quite silent, as, having no hope himself, he was unable to impart any to them.

He did not, however, write for several months after the intelligence had been received at Bombay; for the letters he had dispatched for Herbert immediately on his arrival would, he hoped, prevent his family from being over anxious; and he thought that perhaps news might arrive of the prisoners, of their health and condition, which would be acceptable, or that some treaty might be arranged between the English and Mysore Governments which would put an end to their captivity; indeed it was in the latter confident hope that he wrote, when all prospect of an immediate release was out of the question.

The letters which Herbert had dispatched had reached England, and by them his family were informed of the issue of the war as far as the capture of Bednore; and he then wrote in the highest spirits, like a young and gallant soldier, of the prospects of the campaign, made light of his wound, and was eagerly looking for fresh encounters with the enemy, in which distinction and promotion were to be won. This account greatly soothed his parents and Amy, who was especially tormented by agonising fears and apprehensions regarding him, in spite of his often repeated but playful assurances that he was safe and well.

'He cannot be safe,' she used to argue to herself, 'when there are such desperate engagements as that of which he writes us word, and where he has too the baneful climate to contend against; but God is over all, and to Him I commit the future in hope and confidence.'

And so she continued—a vague dread of future misery striving for mastery in her heart with deep religious reliance; and during this struggle her parents became, from her altered appearance, so anxious for her, that they would fain have removed her to one of the watering-places for change of air and scene.

She firmly opposed the proposal, for she clung with increasing attachment to her home, and apparently to the pursuits which Herbert had shared with her. But if they looked at her sketches, there used to be little advance made from day to day; she would sit for hours seemingly engaged on them, whilst her eye was fixed upon vacancy, or gazing upon the familiar spots she was delineating, where she had often watched his figure, or realising to her tenacious memory all the words she had heard him speak there.

And thus the time passed; her companionship with the family of Herbert increased, and she would spend days in conversing with them, especially with Mrs. Compton, about him, listening to every tale of his life,—to every incident even of his childhood with delight, and an interest which appeared to increase in their repetition. But the suspense after the receipt of his last letter—the one dispatched by Philip Dalton—grew day by day more insupportable; several vessels arrived, but there was no intelligence from Herbert. Many of the newspapers of the day mentioned the expedition, with some criticisms upon its object, and prophesied an ill termination to its exertions: and at length, when the ship arrived by which she had expected a long despatch, and there was none, and the letter was read from Mr. Herbert's agent, as we have before recorded, wherein he stated broadly that there was bad news from India—the poor girl's brain reeled under the shock of having her worst fears confirmed. Her active and already excited mind in an instant presented to her the being in whose existence her own was wrapped up, as if in death, ghastly, with disfiguring wounds; and the thought, suddenly as it had come into her mind, for the time paralyzed her faculties; her body was not strong enough to resist its influence, and, yielding at once, she had fainted under the overpowering weight of her misery. News, however, there was of Herbert, which in some measure relieved their worst fears and gave room for hope; although sickening in its uncertainty, it gave room for hope, to which every member of both families clung with the tenacity naturally inspired by their affection.

The newspapers gave such accounts as could be gained of the disaster, and the name of Herbert was mentioned among those who were known to be in captivity. But they nowhere saw that of Dalton, whom Herbert had so constantly mentioned in his letters, and they concluded that he had been killed in one of the engagements: this was an additional source of pain to them, that Herbert had lost his dearest friend.

However in a few months after, the first letter from Philip arrived at the rectory, and despite its melancholy tone, it gave the family good reason to hope. Philip was one who could not believe implicitly in the constant ill-treatment said to be exercised by the Sultaun upon his prisoners, and he could plainly see that such statements were encouraged by the Government, in order to induce those favourable to their cause to lend their aid in the struggle. And perceiving this, he wrote that he hoped the treaties about to be drawn up between the two nations would be productive not only of Herbert's release, but of that of his fellow-captives;—he undeceived them, too (which was necessary), as to the natives of the country being savage, assuring them, on the contrary, that they were polite and courteous; and as the hopes of peace continued to be confirmed from time to time by Philip, who wrote by every opportunity, as well as by the papers, they remained in a most pitiable state of excitement, which was doomed to be bitterly disappointed.

The peace of 1784 came. Many a man whose existence had been despaired of by his long-expecting and wretched family reappeared, and that of the rectory now looked forward with intense eagerness to the receipt of letters from Herbert or from Philip Dalton, announcing their reunion, and the prospect of their speedy return home.

Alas! while others rejoiced, they were plunged into deeper despair than ever; for, as Herbert's name did not appear in the lists of those who had been given up, Philip did not immediately write his bitter disappointment that his dear friend was not among their number.

Who could paint the withering effect of this miserable intelligence upon the unhappy Amy? She had striven, and successfully, against her own despairing heart; whilst a ray of hope broke in upon her gloomy future, she cherished it, and strove to dispel the clouds which doubt would, in spite of her exertions, accumulate before her. She was cheerful, and when Mrs. Compton mourned her son's early fate in bitter grief, and almost refused comfort, Amy would soothe her, and raise her to hope again. But from the last news there was no comfort to be gained. Had Herbert been alive, he would have been given up like the rest; and though it was suspected at the time that many prisoners were retained by Tippoo in defiance of the articles of treaty, still that was so uncertain, so vague and wretched a hope, that it was abandoned as even sinful to indulge in, and Herbert was mourned as dead.

It was happy perhaps for Amy that her own grief was in a measure diverted by the long illness of Mrs. Compton, whom the violence of the affliction brought to the very verge of the grave. For many months did the gentle and patient girl minister to her who was to have been her mother, with a devotion of affection which hardly found its equal in that of her own daughter. From no one's hand did the sufferer take the remedies prescribed so readily as from Amy's; none could smooth the pillow of the languid invalid like Amy—none read to her so sweetly, none conversed with her upon their favourite subject—him who was lost to them both—so eloquently and so devotedly as Amy. And her beauty, which had grown up with her years, until it was now surpassingly bright—her meek and cheerful resignation, after the first pang of sorrow was over—her unceasing and untiring benevolence—made her an object of peculiar interest to the neighbourhood of all ranks, to whom her sad story and early trials were known.

Calm and cheerful as she usually was in the society of her family and at the rectory, no one but her mother knew the bitter bursts of grief to which nature would force her sometimes, when the memory of him they thought dead was more prominently excited. Herbert was constantly the subject of their conversation; for this Amy loved, and it often soothed her to hear him spoken of or alluded to. But it was not this that affected her; it was often the merest trifle and sudden thought, the sight of a flower, a word or tone from Charles, who now strongly resembled his brother, that caused these paroxysms, which, violent as they were, prostrated her for the time, only to rise with renewed cheerfulness, resignation, and affection for those she loved.

They continued to hear from Philip Dalton, who, restless under the belief that Herbert still lived, spared neither money nor pains to get information. As time flew on, it became known that some Europeans were in confinement, and Philip had dispatched one or two trusty emissaries to endeavour to discover Herbert. All had, however, ended in disappointment, and he was baffled in every inquiry. He did not assert to Herbert's family that he lived, but from time to time he renewed the supposition. After the lapse of nearly four years, they heard from him that he was about to return home on leave, and that he would take the earliest opportunity of visiting the rectory. His coming was earnestly and impatiently expected for many months; for how much should they not have to hear of their long-lost Herbert from his most devoted friend! how many particulars of their short service together and its fatal result, which, though the themes of many letters, were incomplete in comparison with what they should hear from him in person!

At length his arrival in England was announced by him, and though he could not say when he should be at liberty, he declared it would not be long ere he performed his promise. Philip had thought it better thus to leave them in uncertainty, lest, having their attention fixed upon any particular day, the contemplation of the excitement which would necessarily follow would be more than the female part of the families could endure.

But he did not, he could not delay long; he was impatient to communicate his suspicions, his hopes that Herbert existed, which every day's experience and reflection told him were reasonable; and hardly a fortnight had elapsed, ere he took the mail to the town of ——, where the regiment had been quartered, and where he had now a friend. Leaving his portmanteau at the barracks, he took with him a change of linen, and late in the afternoon rode his friend's horse over to the rectory.

It was a lovely autumn evening; the twilight had begun to deepen the shadows of the luxuriant woods of the park, and the rectory groves appeared dark and solemn at that hour. A few leaves had already fallen upon the smooth and beautifully kept entrance avenue, which passed under some huge elms, on whose tops the noisy rooks still sat cawing, or rising suddenly with eccentric and rapid flights large bodies of the colony sailed through the air, alighting only to dispossess others of a more favoured place or one more coveted. Beyond a turning in the avenue, the house opened upon his view—an old edifice of red brick, of the age of Elizabeth; the large oblong windows of the drawing-room, with their diamond panes, were a blaze of light; and even as he rode along he could distinguish the forms of many within, and the cheerful notes of music came to him through the open casement.

A pale elderly lady lay on the sofa working—he felt sure it was Herbert's mother. There were several standing round a piano-forte: he listened for a while with deep pleasure, as the sounds of music now rose, now fell upon the evening air, and affected him the more powerfully as the air was one he well remembered Herbert to have often sung, and now the place he had occupied there was vacant, perhaps for ever.

As he listened, the voice of a female arose in a solo part, so liquid, so melodious, so exquisitely modulated, that he drew closer to hear it better. Could it be that of Amy? he thought, or one of Herbert's sisters, of whom he had heard him speak so often that he fancied he almost knew them?—Ellen perhaps, his favourite; but it was useless to speculate—he should soon know all. The solo ceased; again arose a full swell of voices, attuned by constant practice, and assisted by the instrument and a bass violin, which was played by an elderly gentleman. It lasted for a while, then ceased entirely—the party broke up cheerfully, and the sound of their merry voices caught his ear—a change, perhaps an abrupt one, from the melody he had heard, which he would have wished had been followed by silence, for his feelings were mournful, and the image of his lost friend was painfully vivid to his imagination; they might have arrived together he thought.

Again he cast his eyes around him; the house, with its deeply embayed windows and quaint projections, was covered with roses and creepers, which entwined thickly around the drawing-room; beside there were a pear-tree and a large fig-tree which were trained over the wall, and almost hid it with their luxuriant foliage, showing here and there the large black crossbeams which appeared through the masonry of the wall, and added to its venerable appearance. Before the house there was a flower-garden, which bloomed with a profusion of flowers, whose rich perfume arose in the evening air. On one side a long conservatory, and beyond it a thick and closely kept hedge that partly screened a wall which led to other gardens. On the other side was a lawn, close and mossy-looking, which stretched a short distance to a sunken fence, beyond which was a field with a few single teres, and the deep woods of the park made up the distance. The hall-door was low and deeply screened by a porch, around which roses and clematis flourished in luxuriance.

Dismounting from his horse he rang the bell, which was quickly answered; and desiring the servant to inform Mr. Compton that a gentleman wished to speak to him, he remained in the porch.

'Who can it be?' said some, as the servant announced the message. In another instant it had flashed into the minds of all that it might be Captain Dalton; and with him came the memory of poor Herbert, now to be so freely awakened.

'If it should be he, Maria,' said Mr. Compton to his lady, who at the announcement had risen from the sofa, 'can you bear to see him?'

'Yes, love—yes, here—but with you only. Go into the dining-room, my children, we will call you after a while.'

They obeyed instantly, and Mr. Compton hurried into the hall to receive the stranger, while his lady prayed fervently for support in the coming interview; for she trembled exceedingly, and her conflicting emotions almost overpowered her.

The servant was holding Philip's horse, and he himself was pacing slowly up and down the narrow porch. As Mr. Compton advanced, Philip turned to meet him; and his first glance assured him that the friend of his lost son was before him.

'You need not mention your name, my dear sir,' said the old gentleman, as he clasped his hand most warmly and affectionately in his own, while his trembling voice showed how deeply he was agitated; 'I am convinced that I now welcome our long-expected and already very dear Captain Dalton. We have been long expecting you and I need hardly say how anxiously we have looked for the arrival of one who was so dear to—' and he hesitated for an instant; but mastering his emotion, he continued —'to our poor Herbert, from whom we heard so much of you. God bless you, sir! that you have come to us so soon, when you must have had so many claims upon you from your own family.'

'I thank you, sir, heartily, for this warm welcome,' said Philip. 'But before I proceed further, tell me candidly whether Mrs. Compton is able to see me. That I have seen you, will be a comfort to me, and for the present I will leave you, and give her time for any preparation she may wish to make.'

'By no means: she is already aware that this visit could be from no other but yourself, and she will be better when she has seen you. You must make some allowances for a mother's grief—a fond mother's too—Captain Dalton.'

'I know all, sir,' said Philip, pressing his hand; 'and Miss Hayward?'

'She is fortunately not with us to-night,' replied Mr. Compton, 'and we will speak upon the subject with her parents before we tell her that you are come.'

They were at the drawing-room door, and Philip's heart beat faster than he had ever remembered it to beat before. The suspense and anxiety he was in, as to the issue of his meeting with Mrs. Compton, almost overcame his habitual self-possession; and he would have given worlds could he have ensured her equanimity, which was little to be expected. She, too, was not less excited; and a feeling of faintness came over her as she heard the hand of her husband upon the lock. She made a strong effort, however, to repel it, and the next moment he and Dalton were before her.

'This is Captain Dalton, Maria,' were all the words Mr. Compton had time to utter ere his lady advanced to meet him. It needed not his words to assure her that the tall, manly, and soldier-like figure of the young man was Philip; and as she eagerly took his proffered hand, while her eyes were full of tears, she in vain strove to speak. She read in the expression of his fine features, as she looked into his face, that her own grief was reciprocated, and she could no longer restrain the utterance of her feelings, nor the impulse of her affectionate heart. She threw herself into his arms, as she would have done into her own son's, and wept; the tears and bitter sobs of a mother's grief could not be restrained, and she yielded to them freely.

For a while his reserved demeanour, under which was concealed as kind a heart as ever beat, struggled with his awakened sensibilities; but nature asserted her power; Philip's tears mingled with hers, and she could feel them falling fast upon her cheek, though silently, as he bent over and supported her. Mr. Compton did not interrupt them; he was too glad to see her emotion find so natural and easy a vent, for he had anticipated a much more violent effect. Mrs. Compton soon rallied.

'You will forgive this welcome of one who is so dear to us, Captain Dalton,' she said, speaking with difficulty; 'but you know that with you are associated many, many painful recollections. Bear with me,—I shall be calm soon. I feel that my heart has already been relieved and is lighter.'

Philip could not then say much in reply; but soon their conversation flowed more naturally and calmly; and ere long the rest of the family were admitted, and he was introduced and received as a brother among them.

Gradually their conversation turned upon him they thought dead. Philip had to answer a thousand questions, and to give the minutest particulars to the eager and loving inquirers; and though the tears of all flowed silently and fast, even as they spoke, yet Mrs. Compton felt, when she retired to rest at a late hour, as if some portion of the load which had oppressed her had been removed, and she fervently blessed God who had sent her such a friend and comforter.

CHAPTER XXVI.

THE first constraint of ceremony having been broken, and the subject so near to the hearts of all touched upon even on the first night of their acquaintance, as every succeeding day passed they became more attached to each other—the parents, to one they looked upon and loved as a son—the children, to their poor brother's friend and dearest companion. Day by day the subject of poor Herbert's fate was the theme of conversation; they were never weary of it, and Philip unfolded to them gently but unreservedly his convictions that Herbert still lived—confined perhaps in some lonely hill-fort, away from the capital of Mysore, or engaged in the hated service of the ruler of the country. For many others were known to have submitted to Tippoo's will in this respect, in the hope that some opportunity would be afforded for escape, or some action with their countrymen would facilitate their desertion.

Poor Amy! the bitterest trial she had endured since the news of Herbert's captivity, and next to his supposed death, was the meeting with Philip, and receiving from his own hands the little packet which Herbert had entrusted to him in case of his death, and which he had retained. For many days she could not see him; but at length she fixed a day and hour, and he walked over to Beechwood. He had not seen her except at church, where he had caught a glimpse of her graceful figure, dressed in simple mourning: this only excited his curiosity to know more of one whom his poor friend had loved with such intensity of affection—a love so faithfully reciprocated.

Mrs. Hayward received the young soldier, and in a short conversation with him justly estimated the strength and delicacy of his feelings; it was impossible for any one to have been more deeply aware of the difficult part he had to perform, nor to have evinced more tenderness in the manner in which he executed it.

'I would not have pressed Miss Hayward upon the subject,' he said; 'I would not willingly distress her, nor excite thoughts which must violently affect her; but I made a promise solemnly to Herbert, and I have come to fulfil it: and it will be a gratification to me if I am allowed to do so. Still, if she declines an interview with me, I would leave the packet with you, Mrs. Hayward—convinced that it will be in safe hands, and it can be delivered or not to Miss Hayward as you please.'

'If you will remain here, Captain Dalton, I will see Amy, and state what you say to her,' replied the old lady, 'but I can promise nothing: she is usually calm and strong-minded, but your coming may have such an effect upon her as to unfit her for receiving you. You shall, however, soon know the truth.' And so saying she left the room.

Philip looked around. There were books, Italian and Spanish poets open upon the table, with some beautiful embroidery, which showed that Amy must have been there when he was announced. On a side table was an unfinished landscape—a large tree, a few sheep, and a mossy bank, beautifully painted; and the colours and water which stood near it proved that she had lately been engaged upon it. Philip went to examine it, and while admiring the freedom and vigour of the drawing, and the keen perception of nature evident in the colouring, the door gently opened, and a lady entered, whose appearance caused in his heart a thrill of excitement, and a confusion in his address which he had little expected.

'Miss Hayward, I presume,' he said, advancing to her with hesitation; for her beauty, the sweet expression of her face, and her mild blue eyes, fixed his attention, and rendered his manner involuntarily constrained.

Amy could not reply, her heart was full even to choking; she had in vain tried to compose herself when his name was announced; but unable to do so, she had left the room; and it was only on hearing the message her mother had delivered, that she determined to see the friend of her Herbert, to speak to him who had received his last message for her; and she came down alone to meet him. She had, however, taxed her powers of endurance to the utmost: the sight of the tall and manly figure of Philip, his dark and expressive features—bronzed somewhat by an eastern sun, yet preserving the ruddy glow of health—his soldier-like form and bearing—all caused at first a rush of remembrances almost too powerful to endure; and her imagination, despite of her efforts not to yield to such thoughts, could not help picturing to herself how Herbert would have been improved—how he would have looked, how he would have met her after their long absence! She could not speak to Dalton, but trembled exceedingly, and would have fallen; but, seeing her agitation, he assisted her to a seat; she sank into it, and, unable to speak, buried her face in her hands. Philip sat silent for a while, but he saw that further delay would only be a protraction of her misery.

'Miss Hayward,' he said very respectfully, 'I am the bearer of a small packet for you, which I promised to deliver; if you will receive it from my hands, I shall be gratified, as you will have enabled me to fulfil a promise I have looked on as sacred.'

Again Amy endeavoured to reply, but her words failed her, and her hand trembled so much as she stretched it out to him, that he feared the consequences of her emotion.

'I implore you to be calm, Miss Hayward; shall I ring for water—for your mother? can I do aught to assist you?' he continued, as he gave her the little packet, which she received with extreme agitation, and not daring to look at him.

'No, I thank you, Captain Dalton,' she said at length, after a severe effort to repress her feelings, in which she partly succeeded. 'I am better now, and will hear whatever he—whatever you have to say—it will be better than to delay.'

But Philip feared the result, and urged that her mother at least should be present.

'No,' she replied, 'it is better thus; with her I should fail, alone, I think, I can be firm; therefore proceed.'

And he obeyed her: he told her of their last service—of the events of the war; and when she appeared to listen calmly, he mentioned their last few days' intercourse, their last interview, their farewell, and their mutual promises in case of the death of either. There was no message in particular to herself—the packet would explain all, he said; he had been desired to mention to her the events that had occurred before he received it, and he was thankful he had been spared to deliver the message himself.

Amy listened patiently, and grew calmer as he proceeded; he could not see her features, for her hand covered them as she leaned back; but at length, before he ceased, he could perceive that his simple narrative had soothed her; for a silent tear forced its way between her slender fingers, and trickled over her fair hand; she appeared not to be aware of it, and others followed rapidly; nature had yielded her most gentle remedy for a troubled spirit—silent tears, which flow without pain or sobbings.

He did not disturb her thoughts, which appeared entirely to absorb her, and he fancied that she prayed mentally, for her lips moved. He arose, and stealing to the door, opened it very gently and quitted the apartment; it was enough that he had seen and spoken to her. Mrs. Compton stood without, anxiously awaiting the issue, should there have been occasion for her aid; he told her how touchingly, how beautifully she had heard him; and the mother was glad that Dalton had seen her, that the crisis had passed so calmly.

'She will be better for this hereafter,' she said, and judged rightly. Amy was more cheerful, and more equably so from that day.

Mrs. Hayward accompanied Philip to her husband's study, to bear him the happy tidings that had so rejoiced her; and here they long and earnestly talked over Philip's hopes, his almost certainty that Herbert lived. There was much which appeared to both Mr. and Mrs. Hayward improbable in what he thought—much that they could not understand, from their ignorance of the habits of the natives, and of their highly civilised and cultivated character. In the end, however, they could not but encourage the glimmering of hope which had entered their minds—dimmed, it is true, by doubts and fears, but still abiding there. It would have been cruel, however, to have mentioned this to Amy, and for the present she was ignorant of it.

Amy sat long so absorbed in thought that she had not noticed the departure of Philip Dalton; and when she spoke, not daring to withdraw her hands from her eyes, and received no answer, she looked around and saw that she was alone. Then she thanked Philip in her heart for his tender consideration of her, and long remembered the act, simple as it was, with gratitude. She held the packet she had received, and once more dared to look on the well-known handwriting. She knew that it could be of no later date than the letters she had already in her possession; but it was not opened, it was to be given her only in case of his death; and her mind was oppressed with feelings of awe, as she almost hesitated to break the seal and peruse its contents. It is a period for solemn thought when we open a letter from one known to be dead—to think that the hand which traced the characters is cold and powerless, that the mind whose thoughts are there recorded is no longer constituted as ours. This carries us involuntarily into a deep train of thought and speculation, vague and indefinite—leading to no end but a vain striving for knowledge of what is better hidden in futurity. Or if the writing be that of one dear or familiar to us, how many reminiscences crowd instantly into the mind! tokens of affection, in which nature is prolific, soothing the thoughts of the survivor, while they hallow the memory of the dead.

Amy's packet was precious indeed; Herbert had written to her gravely and thoughtfully, yet here and there with passionate love, as though he had at times failed in checking the expression of feelings to which, when she received the letter, he could no longer respond. He had enclosed a little locket, which contained his hair, and implored her with an earnestness which his strong sense of honour prompted, but which cost him pain to write and her to peruse, while she honoured his memory in death, not to refuse that station in life to which she would be solicited by many. She appreciated these expressions with a just sense of the feelings under which he had written them; but while she read them, she more strongly than ever clung to his memory with grateful and devoted, yet mournful affection. And could Philip have seen her as she rose from the perusal of that letter, with eyes dim and glistening with tears, and advancing to the window, look forth in her calm and gentle beauty over the broad and glowing landscape—he might have worshipped her in his heart as a personification of one of those pure beings who do service in heaven, and who, touched with our infirmities, can be supposed to feel in some degree the sorrows of an earthly existence.

From that day forth there was no reserve on Philip's part towards the Beechwood family, with whom he was ever a welcome and a sought-for guest. His own affairs, and a visit to his elder brother (for his mother, his only surviving parent, had died while he was in India), occupied him for a month after his departure from the rectory; and when this period had arrived, he was only too glad to avail himself of the pressing invitations of both families to return and spend some time alternately with them. The young Haywards too had returned home; the one from Scotland, where he had been on a visit; the other from Oxford, where he was studying for a degree.

CHAPTER XXVII.

In this delightful society Philip's time flew rapidly and happily; he was fond of the chase and of shooting, and in the noble stud of Beechwood, and over its broad manors and preserves, there were ample resources for both pursuits, and the young men became intimate and inseparable companions. Among themselves they often talked of Herbert as of a departed brother, and Philip at length unreservedly opened his heart to them on the subject which, except one of later growth, was nearest to it.

Our hearts often take strong impressions from the veriest trifles;—how much more when they are assisted or coloured by adventitious circumstances! As Philip listened to the sweet voice he had heard singing as he rode up to the rectory on the evening he first arrived there, his sensibilities had been powerfully excited towards the songstress, either because she might be the affianced, or the sister of his friend.

He had been introduced to all the family in succession on that evening, and he was at once struck with the beauty of one of the young ladies, and her great likeness to his friend; she had the same large and expressive blue eye, regular features, and brown hair, falling upon her shoulders in luxuriant curling tresses; she was taller in proportion than he was, but her figure was remarkable for its grace and beauty of contour. He then hoped she might be the songstress; why, he could hardly have told.

He heard her repeat the air to which he had first listened, for it was often afterwards sung by the small but well-trained band, and distinguished by the name of Captain Dalton's favourite; night after night did Philip sit listening with increasing delight to Ellen's rich voice as she sang either alone or in parts. Indeed she was a thorough mistress of the art, in which she had from the first been well grounded; and her execution evinced a pure taste, which, entering into the spirit of the composer, sought rather to draw gratification from giving expression to his thoughts, than to indulge in the poor vanity of exhibiting her own powers. She was by no means insensible to the marked pleasure which her singing gave to the young soldier; and from this commencement, there gradually sprang up a warm and increasing attachment, which her parents observed with sincere pleasure.

Philip found, on a further knowledge of her character, that she possessed many tastes and feelings in common with his own; and he observed with delight her extensive charity, her visits with Amy to the sick and poor of the neighbourhood, and their close and affectionate friendship. Somehow or other, he oftener spoke to her than to the rest, and she listened (so he thought) with more interest than the others to his tales of foreign climes and hard service; he oftener found something to do for her, oftener walked with her, or escorted her and Amy upon their charitable visits. A thousand kindnesses passed between them, which in others would have been forgotten, but with them were treasured up, and remembered vividly when they were separated.

We do not intend to be the chroniclers of this tale of mutual attachment, which steadily increased, and—as there was no opposition from her parents, but on the contrary the utmost desire that it should progress steadily and uninterruptedly—was in the end successful. Philip waited, however, until he had known her for nearly a year; and when he felt sure that his offer would be accepted, he made it, and was rewarded. The gentle and lovely girl had long been his, and she now gave herself up to the ardent feelings of her loving heart.

They were married: early in the spring of the year succeeding the one in which Philip had arrived, the joyous bridal took place —on one of those bright and sunny days when hardly a cloud dims the serenity of the sky, when the buds are just bursting into life, and nature, having rested through the winter, is about to resume her robe of luxuriant foliage, ere she rejoices in the genial sun and the warm winds of summer.

Amy consented, with much fear and many doubts of her ability, to go through her simple duties as one of the bride's-maids; and she appeared that day in more than her usual beauty, having thrown off her garb of mourning. Ellen's sisters, and Philip's only one, were the others; and as the joyous procession wound down the broad aisle of the old church, and the light streaming through the painted windows rested upon the group collected around the altar, assuredly on a gayer bridal party, or one whose hearts were more linked together by affection, the bright and glowing sun never shone. Nevertheless, there were a few among them on whom the hand of sorrow had lain heavily, and who, if they did not join in the exuberant joy of the rest, were as sincere and as fervent in their prayers and wishes for the happiness of those who plighted their vows in their presence.

Some months—nearly a year—passed, and, what Philip had wished so much, the purchase of a majority in a regiment then in India, was at last within his attainment; for he had not concealed from Mr. Compton nor from his wife, that he still looked to that land for distinction and advancement in his profession, and also for the chance of sooner or later discovering a clue to the fate of him whom all still mourned. The handsome portion which he had received with Ellen had enabled him to meet the outlay for this advancement with perfect convenience, and in a short time he was gazetted as Major in the —th, then serving in the Madras Presidency; and being anxious to join his regiment, he prepared without delay.

This was, however, productive of another incident in the family circle of Beechwood. In the mind of the youngest of Amy's brothers, Philip's wild tales of adventure—of battles, of marches, of the gorgeous country, and its curious and interesting inhabitants—of their ceremonies and their various faiths—of tiger and wild-boar hunts—had excited a restless curiosity to behold them, and to become an actor in the stirring scenes which were every day taking place. But when Philip spoke of Herbert, and of his own hope that he would be eventually recovered, Charles Hayward's enthusiasm was warmed by his affection, and his waking thoughts and dreams were alike incessantly occupied with speculations upon the subject, which unfitted him for study, and rendered him restless and uneasy. Long before Philip had declared his intention of returning to India, Charles had determined upon requesting his father's permission to enter the army in a regiment serving as near the scene of Herbert's disappearance as possible.

Charles, too, loved his sister with an intensity which would have urged him to make any sacrifice for her sake, and it was anguish to him to see her bowed down by mental suffering, and clinging with fond tenacity to the memory of the dead, when his own exertions, guided by the experience of their friend Dalton, might, under the aid of Providence, be instrumental in restoring her to her usual health and joyous spirits. It was true she had expressed no thought or hope of Herbert's existence to any of them; and the youth, as he roamed with her through the park, or sat with her in her own little study, where she was surrounded by precious memorials of Herbert, often longed to tell her of Philip's suspicions, and his own wild yearnings towards that distant land.

Had he done so, there is little doubt that she would have disclosed to him, sooner than she did, the hope she secretly cherished, that Herbert still existed and would return. No sooner had Philip openly declared his intention of revisiting India, than Charles' determination was formed to break the matter at once to his father, and to proceed with Philip, should no opposition be made—some objections he certainly anticipated, but he thought he could overcome them. Before he broached the subject to his parents, he held a long and anxious conversation with Philip, and was delighted to find that he not only coincided in his views, but was prepared to aid them by his interest in the purchase of an ensigncy in the regiment to which he now belonged, in which there was a vacant commission.

His proposal, as he had anticipated, was met by many objections and much distress on the part of his parents and sister. Loving him tenderly as she did, Amy could not bear the thought which at first obtruded upon her, that India would be his grave, as it had been that of Herbert. But the young man was resolute; and, after exhausting all his arguments, he called Philip Dalton to his aid, who not only promised to be a guardian to him, but declared he would let slip no opportunity of bettering his station and prospects in his profession. All opposition, therefore, ceased gradually, partly because Charles appeared to relish the prospects of a military life more than any other, and partly because there appeared a likelihood of rapid advancement in the regiment while it remained on its eastern service.

The day at last arrived when he was to leave home for his long absence; to all it was a source of bitter grief, but the most so to his mother and to Amy; and ere the hour came when he was to depart from them, Amy led him away from the house, and, wandering together, they talked over the future—to him bright with promise—a contrast, and a sad one to hers, which was so overcast. They wandered on through the parks, and by the stream, where years before she had roamed with Herbert. Charles knew that she must be thinking of him whose fate was wrapt in mystery, and he longed to know and to share all her thoughts and feelings on the subject. Gradually he led her to speak of Herbert; and as their conversation warmed, the devoted girl could no longer refrain from unburdening her heart, and confessing the hopes which only her God, to whom she addressed them night and morning in fervent prayer, knew to exist.

Still, however, Charles was sorely perplexed, and his judgment and affection were at variance; but the latter prevailed under her artless confidence, and he told her in hesitation and fear of Philip Dalton's hopes of the chances of Herbert's life, spoke to her of the folly of cherishing hope only because they had not heard he was dead, but nevertheless declared how this had preyed on his mind till it almost amounted to an earnest of success.

She listened with breathless interest to his narrative—it was too much in accordance with her own thoughts to be slighted. She did not blame her brother that he had kept it from her, and she could not have borne it from Dalton: now she believed all—not rashly, however—for her mind was strong and tempered by affliction; but there was more room for hope than ever, and she felt as though the hand of Providence was discernible in the matter, guiding her brother onward in the track of her lost Herbert. Now that their most secret thoughts were in common, she felt that she could part with Charles more easily; and he left her at last in their little summer-house, where she loved to sit, and where they had been conversing—afflicted, yet with hope in her heart.

His mother bade him farewell, with many tears and many prayers for his safety; and, accompanied by his father and his elder brother, Charles was rapidly whirled away from his home, to enter upon the life of danger and adventure he had chosen for himself. In another week, he, with Philip Dalton and his wife, had left their native shores for a long and perhaps perilous absence.

Six months had now passed at Seringapatam, during much of which time Kasim Ali had been absent on the various duties connected with his new situation. He had risen in rank, and from the steadiness of his conduct, the Khan would have been glad to have kept Kasim always with him; but this was impossible, for the Sultaun's eye was upon him, although, remembering the scene in the Durbar, he had wished to see little of one who had behaved so boldly before him, yet whom he respected from the lucky appearances he believed Kasim to possess, and which he had given himself credit for having discovered. He would often say to his favourite, Syud Sahib, that he was sure Kasim Ali, notwithstanding he was in disgrace, would be of service to him in the end, and that it was better he should be checked at first, and thus inspired with a thirst for distinguishing himself, than spoiled by too early notice or promotion.

But he had nevertheless given a strong proof of his reliance on the young man's ability and courage. Hardly a month had passed after his disgrace, and Kasim was fast sinking into a state of apathy at his dim prospects, which at first were so brilliant, when the Sultaun entrusted him with a mission requiring much delicacy and tact in its execution. It will be remembered that the Khan had stated in the Durbar, that he had heard of an embassy to Seringapatam being meditated at the Nizam's court; and this Tippoo so earnestly desired, that his restless mind was in a constant state of irritation upon the subject. Could he only detach the Nizam from the alliance of the hated English—could the Afghan monarch only see the two great Mahomedan powers of the south united in a close alliance—he would pour his hardy followers upon their northern possessions—there might be a second battle of Paniput! And, with such a result, what was to prevent the northern army joining with the Nizam's—with his own—and, falling in one overwhelming mass upon the English possessions,—their driving the hated race into the sea for ever? A month passed, and still no embassy arrived, nor was there any intelligence of one; to gain news therefore of the Nizam's court, he dispatched Kasim, attended only by a horseman or two, to travel by rapid marches to Hyderabad, and to discover, as far as lay in his power, the sentiments of the Court and the feeling of the people.

Kasim was gratified beyond expression by the selection of him above others of known sagacity for such a mission, and he determined to spare neither exertion nor zeal in his master's cause, in order to regain his favour. By the most rapid marches he traversed the nearest road to Bellary—that to the westward of

Nundidroog; and resting only a night at his own humble but not less dear home, where he found his mother well and his affairs continuing prosperous, he pushed on to Hyderabad; where, as soon as he arrived, he set himself to work to gain information.

For nearly three months did he wait there, expecting with anxiety the determination of the vacillating prince. At one time he heard that an embassy would soon set off, and that a nobleman was appointed ambassador; this was again contradicted, and it was rumoured that the Nizam had entered into a fresh league with the English. But in the end there was no doubt that an embassy would be sent to try the temper of the Mysore chief; and Kasim, hearing from undoubted authority the name of the gentleman who had been nominated, Ali Reza, waited on him, disclosed the subject of his mission, and having given such an account as he was able of the Sultaun's anxiety, received in return the purport of the proposed embassy, which was in effect what Tippoo looked for. Having obtained this, and being assured by Ali Reza that they should meet again in a short time, Kasim left Hyderabad, and, with the same expedition, returned to Seringapatam. Again, on his way, he stayed with his mother; again he visited the spot, which continued dear to him from the memorable night's adventure,—the trees were growing up, and the tomb of the poor soldier was neatly kept. He had to answer a thousand questions to his mother respecting their journey and Ameena, of whom Kasim could now tell her nothing, except that the Khan, whenever he inquired after her health, said she was well and happy.

CHAPTER XXVIII.

THE Sultaun was delighted at the news he received, which, while it surpassed his expectations, apparently confirmed him in his immediate plans of action. As the rainy season of 1788 closed, large bodies of troops were despatched to Coimbatoor, for the purpose of prosecuting the war against the rebellious Nairs, who, in the jungles and forests of Malabar, continued to defy the governor's power, and the forces from time to time sent against them. Among the latter was Kasim, soon after his return from the mission to Hyderabad, from the success of which he had hoped to have re-occupied his place near the Sultaun's person: but the wrong he had done had not been entirely forgiven or forgotten.

Nor was the Khan his companion; he was detached with the other half of the Khan's risala, which was commanded by Dilawur Ali, an officer somewhat like the Khan himself, but older—one of Hyder Ali's earliest adherents, who had been spared through many a hard fight and rough service; to him Kasim was of the utmost use, both as an excellent secretary, and an intelligent and upright adviser.

The Sultaun took the field in person against the Nairs in January of the ensuing year, and prosecuted the war against them with the utmost energy. In one fort alone, two thousand of them capitulated, who were converted, under the threat of death if they refused the rite of Islam: complying therefore, they publicly ate of beef, which, abhorrent as it was to them, they were obliged to partake of. The war prospered, and, ere the rains had set in, the territory was subdued by the ravages of the Mysore army; for the war had been proclaimed a holy one by the Sultaun, who, with mad fanaticism, everywhere destroyed temples, broke their images and plundered their treasures. Those Nairs who would not accept the conversion offered, were hunted like wild beasts and destroyed in thousands.

The army at Coimbatoor heard of these events one by one as they happened, and of the marriage of the Sultaun's son to the beautiful daughter of the lady ruler of Cannanore; and he soon afterwards arrived in triumph at Coimbatoor, having left a large detachment to complete the destruction of the Nairs.

Great were the rejoicings upon the victories that had been gained; the army had tasted blood, and, like their tiger leader, thirsted for more. Here was celebrated the Mohurrum, the sacred anniversary of the deaths of Hassan and Hoosein, with all the pomp and with all the zeal to which an army of fanatical Mahomedans could be excited by the example of their bigoted Sultaun. At this time was issued the proclamation that the kingly Noubut was to be performed five times on every Friday, because that day was the sabbath of the faithful—the day on which the flood happened—the day on which the Heaven was created. The Sultaun and his astrologers observed the aspect of the stars; and in a fortunate hour when the Moon was in Taurus, Mercury and Venus in Virgo, the Sun in Leo, Saturn in Aquarius, and Venus in opposition to Libra, it was proclaimed with pomp in the mosques that the music would be played and royal state observed. Then the deep tones of the huge kettle-drums burst from the neighbourhood of the Sultaun's tent, and the assembled army broke into loud acclamations and hoarse cries of 'Deen! Deen! the Sultaun is the apostle! the Sultaun is the conqueror!'

A few days afterwards the long looked-for embassy arrived from Hyderabad, and Kasim once more welcomed his friends. They were presented to the Sultaun in a full durbar of his officers, native and European, with all the pomp of regal state. They were at once disgusted with the assumed consequence of one whose state was less than that of their prince; but they presented the splendid Koran they had been entrusted with, upon which it was said that the Nizam had sworn to aid Tippoo with his whole army and power against the English. The letters they bore were cautious and dignified; yet, through the overwhelming flow of Eastern compliment, could be discovered the hidden meaning which Tippoo had so long and so earnestly expected. The ambassadors were dismissed for the present with honour, and the whole army rejoiced that such an alliance would be entered into.

A long conference did Tippoo hold that night, with the officers whom he habitually consulted, upon the subject of the embassy. He had long been solicitous of allying himself by marriage with the princely family of the Dekhan, but had never had an opportunity of proposing it; now, when the Nizam had sought him—when, humbled by the English and in dread of the Mahratta power, that prince had asked aid against both from his brother in the faith—he thought he could make that a condition of compliance. It had been his favourite project for years, and he was now determined to urge it.

It was in vain that those who wished his cause well, advised him bluntly and honestly to forego his request for the present; there were others who listened to his rhapsodies about the stars, to the records of his dreams, until they were carried on to support the demand; and it was made as proudly by the vain and inflated Sultaun, as his receipt of the embassy had been ostentatious and offensive.

But the Nizam's ambassadors were men of sound judgment; they knew that their prince had lowered himself already in sending the embassy to a self-constituted Sultaun—a low-born upstart; and, men of high family themselves, they could well appreciate the situation in which he would feel himself placed by the proposal. They answered the demand in cold and haughty terms, and, requesting their dismissal, soon after left his camp.

It was in vain that the Sultaun's best friends urged their recall as of vital importance to himself,—and to the cause of Islam, the ambassadors were allowed to proceed on their return to Hyderabad. The Saltaun's message was received with indignation by the Nizam, whose pride instantly rose against the degradation of the proposed matrimonial connection. An embassy from Tippoo, which followed, was dismissed with a flat refusal; and the Nizam, throwing himself now entirely into the cause of the English, pressed them for the execution of the treaty of 1768, which involved the conquest of Mysore.

Those who were near the Sultaun when he received the reply, for he had waited the issue of his demand ere he commenced the operations he had long ago determined upon, saw how nearly the refusal had touched his pride, and expected some outbreak of violent passion. But he stifled his feelings for the time; or perhaps, in the pride of possessing the fine army he commanded, and the slavish adoration which it paid him, he did not heed the slight. He was only heard to say, 'Well, it is a matter of no consequence; we, who are the chosen of Alla, will alone do the work which lies before us, marked out so plainly that we cannot deviate from it. Inshalla! alone we will do what Nizam Ali Khan will wonder at in his zenana, as he sits smoking like an eunuch. Ya, kureem Alla! thou art witness that thy servant's name has been left out from among those who are not to be attacked; Nizam Ali and the base infidel English have done this. But let them beware; thou canst revenge me on them both if thou wilt!'

His army too felt the slight which had been offered, and in their mad zeal might have been led to the gates of Hyderabad or those of Madras, but that was not the Sultaun's plan; he had resolved on one which had been sketched out by his father, and which he thought he had now matured. The possession of Travancore had long been coveted by his father, but he had been repulsed in his attacks upon it; and as many of the conquered Nairs had taken refuge in the Travancore territory, the Sultaun now demanded that they should be given up as rebellious subjects. This being indignantly refused, as he expected, he at length marched from Coimbatoor at the head of thirty-five thousand men, the flower of his army.

The Khan had arrived with the remainder of the corps from Seringapatam, and had brought Ameena with him, to the disgust and chagrin of his other wives, who, during his stay, had vainly endeavoured to begin their scheme of tormenting the gentle girl. She had hitherto been unmolested, and as happy as it was possible for her to be with these companions, and such others as she became acquainted with from time to time.

The friends were now once more united, and looked forward

with ardour to sharing the events and dangers of the campaign together. Kasim, in the daily march, often watched the well-known palankeen of Ameena to its destination, and, as often as etiquette permitted, inquired after her. He heard she was well, and it would have been pleasant to him could he have known the truth—that he was often the subject of interesting conversation between her and her lord, and that she remembered him gratefully and vividly.

Through the plain which extends westward to the ocean, between the huge and precipitous Neelgherries on the one hand, and the lofty and many-peaked Animallee range on the other, the host of Tippoo poured. Day by day saw an advance of many miles; and the season being favourable, they marched on without a check. The Sultaun was always at the head of the column of march, sometimes on foot with a musket on his shoulder, showing an example to his regular infantry who followed in order, relating his dreams, and pretending to inspiration among his sycophants who marched with him. At other times he appeared surrounded by his irregular cavalry, whom of old he had led against the English at Perambaukum,—a gorgeous-looking force, consisting of men of all descriptions—the small and wiry Mahratta, the more robust Mahomedan, men from Afghanistan and from the north of India, whom the splendid service and brilliant reputation of the Sultaun had tempted from their distant homes.

Sometimes he would be seen to dash out from among them as they rode along—a wild and picturesque-looking band—and turning his horse in the plain, would soon be followed by the most active and best-mounted of his officers, whose bright costumes, armour, and gaudy trappings glistened in the sun as they rode at one another. Then would ensue some mock combat or skirmish, in which the Sultaun bore an active and often a victorious part, and in which hard blows were by no means of rare occurrence. Ever foremost in these mock encounters were Kasim Ali and the Khan his commander; the former however was always the most conspicuous. He was usually dressed in a suit of chain-armour, which had been given him by the Khan, and which he wore over his usual silk or satin quilted vest; on his head was a round steel cap, surmounted by a steel spike, and around it was always tied a shawl of the gayest red or yellow, or else a mundeel or other scarf of gold or silver tissue. He usually carried a long tilting-lance of bamboo, with a stuffed ball at the end, from which depended a number of small streamers of various colours; or else his small inlaid matchlock, with which from time to time he shot at birds, or deer as they bounded along in the thickets which lined the road. He had expended all the money he could spare in purchasing handsome trappings for his horse; and indeed the Khan's noble gift well became his silver ornaments and the gay red, yellow, and green khogeer,* the seat of which was of crimson velvet, with a deep fringe cut into points, and hanging far below its belly.

Tippoo often noticed the young Kasim since his mission to Hyderabad, and as he attended the Khan (who was always among the crowd of officers near the person of the Sultaun) he frequently had an opportunity of joining in these *melées*, in which he was dreaded by many for his strength, perfect mastery of his weapons, and beautiful horsemanship. Indeed the Sultaun had himself, or more than one occasion, crossed spears with the young Patél, and been indebted for victory to the courtesy of his antagonist rather than his own prowess. He never addressed to him more than a word or two during these mock encounters, noticing him however to the old Khan, by whom the gracious speeches were related to Kasim in his tent.

Kasim had been more than usually fortunate one morning, a few days after they had left Coimbatoor; he had engaged rather roughly with another officer, and had overthrown him, and the Sultaun expressed himself with more than usual warmth to the Khan.

'By the Prophet, we must forgive thy young friend,' he said, 'and promote him; didst thou see how he overthrew Surmust Khan just now, Khan Sahib? there are few who could do that. We had much ado to persuade the Khan that it was accidental; thou must tell the youth to be more discreet in future; we would have no man his enemy but ourselves.'

'May your condescension increase!' cried the Khan; 'I will tell the youth; but did my lord ever see him shoot?'

'Ha! can he do that also, Khan? could he hit me yonder goat, thinkest thou?' exclaimed Tippoo, as he pointed to one, the patriarch of a herd, browsing among some craggy rocks at a short distance, and which, interrupted in its morning's meal, was bleating loudly, as it looked over the glittering and busy host which was approaching.

'It is a long shot,' said the Khan, putting his forefinger between his teeth and considering; 'nevertheless, I think he could.'

'Wilt thou hold me a wager he does?' cried the Sultaun; 'I will bet thee a pair of English pistols against that old one of thine, he does not hit it.'

* Stuffed saddle.

'May your favour never be less upon your servant! I accept it,' cried the Khan; and he turned round to seek Kasim, who was behind among the other officers. The Sultaun stopped, and those around him cried out, 'A wager! a wager! Inshalla, the Sultaun will win, his destiny is great!'

Kasim was brought from the rear after some little time, to where the Sultaun stood awaiting him; the Khan had not told him why, and he appeared to ask for orders. All was soon explained to him; but the distance was great, and he doubted his power; however, not daring to disobey, he addressed himself to his task. The goat continued steady, and after a long aim he fired. It was successful; the animal lost its footing, rolled from its high place, and ere any one of the grooms could reach it with a knife, or pronounce the blessing before they cut its throat, it was dead: the ball had broken its neck. 'Mashalla! Wonderful!' passed from mouth to mouth, while some wondered at, and others envied the young Patél's success.

'It must have been chance,' cried the Sultaun good-humouredly; 'even we, who are by the blessing of Alla a sure shot, could not have done that. Nevertheless thou hast won the pistols, Khan, and shalt have them. But what say you, my friends, to a hunt; yonder are the Animallee hills, and it is strange if we find no game. We will prove thee again, young sir, ere we believe thy dexterity.'

'A hunt, a hunt!' cried all; and the words were taken up and passed from rank to rank, from regiment to regiment, down the long column, until all knew of it, and were prepared to bear their part in the royal sport. Preparations were begun as soon as the army arrived at its halting-place; men were sent forward for information of game; all the inhabitants of the country round were collected by the irregular horse to assist in driving it towards one spot, where it might be attacked.

For a day previously, under the active superintendence of the royal huntsman, the beaters, with parties of matchlock and rocket-men, took up positions all round a long and narrow valley; its sides were thickly clothed with wood, but it had an open space at the bottom through which it was possible to ride, though with some difficulty, on account of the long and rank grass. The ground was soft and marshy in places, and had been, at one time, cultivated with rice, as appeared by the square levels constructed so as to contain water. Large clumps of bamboos arose to an enormous height here and there, their light foliage waving in the wind, and giving them the appearance of huge bunches of feathers among the other dense trees by which they were surrounded. Where the ground was not marshy, it was covered with short sward, in some places green, in others parched by the heat of the sun. The sides of the valley arose steeply for five or six hundred feet, sometimes presenting a richly coloured declivity, from which hung the graceful leaf of the wild plantain, creepers innumerable, smaller bamboos, and other light and graceful foliage, amongst which was mingled the huge leaf and sturdy stem of the teak.

Far above the head of the valley—terminated by an abrupt rock, over which a rivulet flung itself in a broken waterfall—hill after hill, mountain after mountain towered into the fleecy mists and clouds—not so lofty as the Neelgherries, which, in the distance on the right, appeared like a huge blue wall, except where the sun glistened upon a precipice of many thousand feet in height, or where a vast chasm or jutting shoulder threw a broad shadow over the rest—but still very lofty, and wooded almost to the summit. A strong body of infantry had been placed across the mouth of the valley, with directions to throw up stockades in the elephant paths; and what game it was possible to drive in from the plain had thus been compelled to enter, and lay, it was thought, securely in the valley. One or two elephants had been seen, which gave hope of more.

Upon the back of that noble white-faced elephant Hyder (which was taken at the siege of Seringapatam, and still adorns, if he be not recently dead, the processions of the present Nizam), in a howdah of richly chased and carved silver, lined with blue velvet, sat Tippoo—his various guns and rifles supported by a rail in front of him, and ready to his hand. Only one favourite attendant accompanied him, who was in the khowass, or seat behind, and had charge of his powder and bullets. The Sultaun's dress was quite plain, and, except for his peculiar turban, he could not have been distinguished.

His cortége was gorgeous beyond imagination. As soon as the usual beat of the kettle-drums had announced that he had mounted his elephant, all who had others allowed them hurried after him, dressed in their gayest clothes and brightest colours. Fifty or sixty elephants were there of that company, all rushing along close together in a body at a rapid pace; around them was a cloud of irregular cavalry, who, no longer fettered by any kind of discipline, rode tumultuously, shouting, brandishing spears and matchlocks, and occasionally firing their pistols in the air. The hoarse kettle-drums sent forth their dull booming sound, mingled with the trampling of the horses, and at times the shrill trumpeting of the elephants. The army had cast aside its uniform for the day; officers and men were dressed in their gayest and most picturesque apparel—turbans and waistbands, and vests of every hue, and armed with weapons of all kinds, swords and shields, matchlocks and heavy broad-bladed spears; such as had not these, brought their own muskets and ammunition.

Thousands had gone on before, and were seen crowding the sides of the entrance to the valley, but kept back by the exertions of the huntsmen, in order that the Sultaun should enter first, and take up his position in the most open place, while the game should be gradually aroused and driven towards him. From the shape of the valley, and its almost perpendicular sides, it was impossible to surround it so as to make a simultaneous advance from all sides.

One of the Sultaun's own elephants had been sent for the Khan and Kasim, who were desired to keep as near him as the crowd would allow. They reached the entrance of the glen at last, and by the streamlet they met the chief huntsman, who was ready to lead them to the spot they should occupy, but the Sultaun would not permit this.

'Let us advance together,' he cried; 'I see the end of the glen is occupied by men, so nothing can escape us. Bismilla! let the signal be given to proceed.'

It had been previously agreed upon; and the discharge of a small field-piece, which had been dragged to the spot, awoke a thousand echoes in the quiet glen, and the merry thousands with one hoarse shout rushed forward.

CHAPTER XXIX.

It was a heart-stirring and magnificent sight to see the advance of that mighty hunting party into the glen. Scarcely a quarter of a mile across, the numerous elephants and horsemen were so closed together that it was impossible for anything to escape the line which now slowly but steadily advanced. The distance from the mouth to the waterfall was not more than three quarters of a mile, and nearly straight, so that the greater part of the intervening distance could be seen disticntly—in some places presenting a thick and impenetrable jungle, in others open, as we have before stated. Along the most abrupt sides, and in advance of the royal party, men were stationed, who, as the line advanced, discharged rockets, which whizzing into the air descended at a short distance among the trees and brushwood, and urged on the game to the end, where it was met by other discharges. Hundreds of men bore large flat drums, which they beat incessantly with sticks; and from time to time the broken and monotonous sound of the kettle-drums which accompanied Tippoo, and showed where he was, mingled with the din of shouts, screams, halloos, the shrill blasts of the collery horn, the shriller trumpetings of the elephants, and the neighings of the wild and frightened horses. All these noises collectively reverberated through the narrow glen, and from the echoes there arose one vast chaos of stunning sound, the effect of which was assisted by the clear air, while it produced the wildest excitement among the hunters.

At first no game was seen, except the wild hog of the country, which in hundreds arose from their resting-places, ran hither and thither confusedly among the crowd,—sometimes upsetting and seriously wounding a man or two; or a timid deer occasionally, unable to escape up the sides and terrified by the din, tried to break the line and perished in the attempt.. Innumerable peafowl arose, and with loud screaming flew onwards, or alighted upon the sides of the glen, and thus escaped; and birds of every plumage darted from tree to tree; large flocks of parroquets flew screaming into the air, and after wheeling rapidly once or twice alighted further on, or rising high took at once a flight over the shoulder of the glen and disappeared.

At length two huge black bears were roused from their den among some rocks which overhung the little stream, and with loud roars, which were heard by all, strove to pass through the line; they were met by the swords and shields of fifty men upon whom they rushed, and, though they strove gallantly for their lives and wounded several, they were cut to pieces.

The party had now proceeded about half way, and there was before the Sultaun's elephant a patch of dry rank grass which reached above its middle—even above old Hyder's, who far exceeded all the rest in height; it was of small extent, however, and was already half surrounded by elephants with their gay howdahs and more gaily dressed riders.

'Hold!' cried the Sultaun, 'we would try this alone, or with only a few; it is a likely place. Come, Khan, and you Meer Sahib, and you Syud Ghuffoor, see what ye can do to help us; now, Kasim Ali, prove to me that thou canst shoot—Bismilla!'

'Bismilla!' cried one and all, and the Mahouts urging on the noble beasts, they entered the long grass together. They had not gone many yards, when Hyder, who led, raised his white trunk high into the air, giving at the same time one of those low growls which proved there was something concealed before him. 'Shabash, Hyder!' cried the Sultaun, 'thou shalt eat goor for this; get on, my son, get on!'

The noble beast seemed almost to understand him, for he quickened his pace even without the command of the Mahout. At that moment a rocket, discharged from the side, whizzed through the grass before them. The effect was instantaneous; two beautiful tigers arose at once. One of them stood for an instant, looking proudly around him, and lashing his tail as he surveyed the line of elephants, several of which were restless and cowardly; the other tried to sneak off, but was stopped by a shot which turned him; and with a terrific roar, which sounded clear far above the din of the beaters, it charged the nearest elephant. It was beaten off, however, receiving several shots, and was then followed by a crowd of the hunters.

Kasim and the Khan had a mind to pursue it too, but the former's attention was at once attracted to the Sultaun, who, having fired and wounded the other tiger, had been charged by it, and had just fired again; he had missed, however, and the animal, excited to fury, had sprung at old Hyder—a far different foe to that his companion had attacked. Hyder had received the onset firmly, and as the tiger strove to fasten upon his shoulders had kicked him off; but at the second charge, when the Sultaun could not fire, the tiger had seized the elephant's leg, and was tearing it with all the energy of rage, which now defied his exertions to shake him off.

In vain did the Sultaun try to fire; he could see the tiger only for a moment at a time, and as Hyder was no longer steady, he again missed his aim. Kasim was, however, near, and with others was anxiously watching his opportunity to fire; but ere he could do so, one of the men on foot, a stout brawny soldier, with sword drawn and his buckler on his arm, and to whom death had no terror in comparison with gaining distinction under the Sultaun's own eye, dashed at the tiger, and dealt him a fierce blow on the loins. The blood gushed forth, and the brute, instantly quitting his hold, turned upon the man with a roar which appalled all hearts; the latter met him manfully, but was unskilful, or the beast was too powerful. All was the work of an instant: the tiger and the man rolled upon the ground,—but only one arose; the lacerated and bleeding body of the brave fellow lay there, his features turned upwards to the sun, and his eyes fixed in the leaden stare of death. Now was Kasim's opportunity; as the tiger looked around him for an instant to make another spring—

he fired; the brute reeled a few paces to the foot of the Sultaun's elephant, fell back, and his dying struggles were shortened by the vigorous kicks of the old elephant, who bandied the carcass between his legs like a football.

'Bus! bus! old Hyder,' cried the Sultaun, who had been soundly shaken. 'Enough! enough! he is dead—thanks to thy friend yonder;—what! not satisfied yet? Well, then, this to please thee,' and he fired again. It was apparently sufficient, for the noble beast became once more composed.

While the Mahout * dismounted to examine the elephant's wounds, the Sultaun made some hurried inquiries regarding the man who had been killed. No one, however, knew him; so directing his body to be borne to the rear, and the Mahout having reported that there was no injury of consequence done to Hyder, the Sultaun, and with him the whole line, once more pressed forward.

As he passed Kasim, the Sultaun now greeted him heartily. 'Thou didst me good service, youth,' he cried; 'but for thee my poor Hyder would have been sorely hurt. Enough—look sharp! there may be more work for thy gun yet.'

So indeed there was: at every step, as they advanced, the quantity of game appeared to increase; another bear was aroused, and, after producing a vast deal of merriment and shouting, was slain as the former ones had been. Several hyænas were speared or shot; guns were discharged in all directions at the deer and hogs which were everywhere running about, and bullets were flying, much to the danger of those engaged in the wild and animated scene: indeed one or two men were severely wounded during the day.

Suddenly, when they had nearly reached the head of the glen, the Sultaun, who was leading, stopped; the others hastened after him, as fast as the thick crowd would allow, and all beheld a sight which raised their excitement to the utmost. Before them, on a small open spot, under a rock, close to the right side of the glen, stood three elephants; one a huge male, the others a female and her calf, of small stature.

No one spoke—all were breathless with anxiety; for it was impossible to say whether it would be advisable to attack the large elephant where he stood, or to allow him to advance. The latter seemed to be the most prevalent opinion; and the Sultaun awaited his coming, while he hallooed to those in advance to urge him on. The noble monarch of the forest stood awaiting his foes—his brethren, who were thus trained to act against him.

* Elephant-driver.

His small red eye twinkled with excitement; his looks were savage, and he appeared almost resolved upon a rush, to endeavour to break the line and escape, or perish. He did not move, but stood holding a twig in his trunk, as if in very excess of thought he had torn it down and still held it. However, there was no time for consideration. As the Sultaun raised his gun to his shoulder several shots were fired, and the noble beast, impelled by rage and agony, rushed at once upon the nearest elephant among his enemies. A shower of balls met him, but he heeded them not: he was maddened, and could see or feel only his own revenge. In vain the Mahout of the elephant that was attacked strove to turn his beast, which had been suddenly paralysed by fear; but the wild one appeared to have no revengeful feelings against his fellow. While they all looked on, without being able to afford the least aid, the wild elephant had seized in his trunk the Mahout of the one he had attacked, wheeled him round high in the air, and dashed him upon the ground. A cry of horror burst from all present, and a volley of bullets were rained upon him; it had the effect of making him drop the body: but though sorely wounded, he did not fall, and retreating, he passed from their sight into the thick jungle.

'Pursue! pursue!' cried Tippoo from his elephant. 'Ya Mahomed! are our beards to be defiled by such a brute? Inshalla! we will have him yet. A hundred rupees to him who shoots him dead.'

The crowd hurried on; their excitement had reached almost a kind of madness; and the reward offered by the Sultaun, and the hope of his favour, had operated as a powerful stimulus. Everyone scrambled to be first, horsemen and foot, and those who rode the elephants, all in confusion, and shouting more tumultuously than ever. All other game was disregarded in the superior excitement; even two panthers, who, roused at last, savagely charged everybody and everything they came near, were hardly regarded, and were killed after a desperate battle by those in the rear. Those in the van still hurried on—the Sultaun leading, the Khan and Kasim as near to him as etiquette would allow, and the rest everywhere around them.

They were close to the top of the glen; the murmur of the fall could sometimes be heard when the shouting ceased for an instant, and its white and sparkling foam glistened through the branches of some noble teak-trees which stood around the little basin. The ground underneath them was quite clear, so that the elephants could advance easily.

'He is there—I see him!' cried the Sultaun, aiming at the

wounded elephant, and firing. 'Holy Alla, he comes! be ready —Fire!'

The noble animal came thundering on with his trunk uplifted, roaring fearfully, followed by two others, one a large female, who had a small calf with her, not larger than a buffalo; the other a male not nearly grown. It was a last and desperate effort to break the line; the blood was streaming from fifty wounds in his sides, and he was already weak; with that one effort he had hoped to have saved himself and the female, but in vain. As he came on, the Khan cried hurriedly to Kasim, 'Above the eye! above the eye! you are sure of him there.' He was met by a shower of balls, several of which hit him in the head. He seemed to stagger for a moment; his trunk, which had been raised high in the air, dropped, and he fell; his limbs quivered for an instant, and then he lay still in death. Kasim's bullet had been too truly aimed.

'Shabash, Shabash! he is dead!' shouted the Sultaun, wild with excitement; 'now for the rest. Spare the young one; now for the female—beware, she will be savage!'

But she was not so at first; she retreated as far as the rock would allow her, and placing herself between her enemies and her calf, which, unconscious of danger, still strove to suck her milk, she tried to protect it from the shot, that hit her almost every time. Now and then she would utter low plaintive moans, which if those who fired at her possessed any feeling, would have pleaded with them to leave her unmolested. At times, goaded on by maddening pain, she charged the line, but only to be driven back foiled and disheartened.

'Ya Alla!' cried Kasim, 'will they not let her go free—she and the young one? Listen, Khan, to her moans. By the Prophet I will not fire—I cannot.'

But the others continued the attack; and it was evident that she could not hold out much longer. She made one more desperate effort, but was beaten back by loud shouts and rockets, and her moans, and the cries of the calf, became more piteous than ever.

'For the sake of Alla put her out of pain!' said the Khan. 'Aim now again just over the eye, in the temple; be steady, the shot is sure to kill. Now! see they are going to fire again at her.'

Kasim raised his unerring matchlock: the firing had ceased at the moment—all were loading. One sharp crack was heard, and the poor beast sank down without a moan or a struggle.

A crowd rushed forward to seize the calf, which was pushing

its mother with its proboscis and head, as if to raise her up, uttering even more touching and piteous cries than ever. Alas! to no purpose. It had by a miracle escaped the shower of balls, and was strong enough to give much trouble to its captors ere it was secured. The Sultaun, who had looked on in silence, now dismounted to examine it; and all his officers and courtiers, Mahomedan and Hindoo, followed his example. The scene was a striking one, as that splendidly-dressed group stood beneath the shade of the noble teak-trees, by the waterfall and the clear stream which murmured over shining pebbles. Behind them was the rock, a sheer precipice of fifty feet, covered with flowers and creepers and beautiful mosses; by it lay the dead female, and near her the male elephant, whose length some were measuring and registering.

Already more than one had tried the temper of his sword upon the dead elephant's carcass, and the Sultaun stepped forward to see the exercise, which requires a strong and steady hand, and a fair cut, or the sword would bend or break.

Many had performed the feat with various success—none better than our friend Kasim; and many others were awaiting their turn, when the young elephant, bound and secured, was brought before the Sultaun. Instantly it appeared to Kasim that his eye lighted up with the same cruel expression he had once or twice noticed, and his countenance to appear as if a sudden thought had struck him.

'Bind it fast!' he cried to the attendants, 'tie it so that it cannot move.' For the poor thing was bleating and crying out loudly at its rude usage, while its innocent face and tremblings expressed terror most strongly. The order was obeyed—it was bound with ropes to two adjacent trees.

'Now,' cried the Sultaun, looking around him proudly, and drawing his light but keen blade, 'by the blessing of the Prophet we are counted to have some skill in our Qusrut—let us prove it!' So saying, and while a shudder at the cruelty of the act ran round the circle, and the Hindoos present trembled at the impiety, he bared his arm, and advancing, poised himself on one foot, while the glittering blade was uplifted above his head. At last it descended; but being weakly aimed, the back of the poor beast yielded to the blow, while it screamed with the pain. Almost human was that scream! The Sultaun tried again and again, losing temper at every blow, but with no better success.

'Curse on the blade!' he cried, throwing it upon the ground; 'it is not sharp enough, or we should have cut the beast in two pieces at a blow.' Several stepped forward and offered their swords; he took one and looked around—his eye was full of wanton mischief. 'Now Ramah, Seit,' he cried to a portly Hindoo banker who was near, 'thou shalt try.'

'May I be your sacrifice,' said the banker, joining his hands, and advancing terror-stricken, your slave is no soldier; he never used a sword in his life.'

'Peace!' exclaimed the Sultaun, stamping on the ground, 'dost thou dare to disobey? Take the sword, O son of perdition, and strike for thy life, else it shall be worse for thee.'

'But your slave is a Hindoo,' urged the trembling banker, 'to whom shedding the blood of an elephant is damnable.'

'It is right it should be so,' cried Tippoo, whose most dangerous passion, bigotry, was instantly aroused by the speech; 'what say ye, my friends? this is a kafir, an enemy of the true faith; why should he not be made to help himself on to perdition?' and he laughed a low, chuckling, brutal laugh, which many remembered long after.

'A wise speech! Ah, rare words! Whose speech is like the Sultaun's?' cried most of those around; 'let him obey orders or die!'

'Therefore take the sword, most holy Sahoukar,' continued the Sultaun, with mock politeness, 'and strike thy best.'

The poor man, in very dread of his life, which indeed had been little worth had he disobeyed—advanced and made a feeble stroke, amidst many protestations of want of skill. His excuses were received with shouts of laughter and derision by the ribald soldiery, who, with many of his flatterers, now surrounded the Sultaun, and urged him on. The man was forced to repeat the blow many times, nor was there a Hindoo present who was not compelled to take a part in the inhuman barbarity.

Why dwell on the scene further? The miserable animal was hacked at by the strong and by the weak—bleating and moaning the while in tones of pain and agony, which grew fainter and fainter, until death released it from its tormentors. Then only did the Sultaun remount his elephant; and the human tiger, sated for that day with blood, hunted no more.

'By Alla and his Prophet!' said Kasim to the Khan as they returned, and unable any longer to keep his indignant silence, 'should there be a repetition of this, I vow to thee I will forswear his service. This is the second instance I have seen of his cruelty: hast thou forgotten the bull?'

'I have not,' said the Khan; 'I well remember it; but this is the worst thing he has ever done, and is the effect of the refusal of the marriage. He is ever thus after being violently provoked; but it is much if Alla does not repay him for it with reverses—we shall see.'

Their horses were at the entrance of the glen, and alighting from their elephant, they mounted them, and rode on towards the camp, which, with its innumerable white tents, could be seen from the elevated ground on which they then stood, at about two miles distant, backed by the blue distance, and the noble range of the Neelgherry mountains. Here and there groves of date or palm-trees studded the plain, and in places were seen dense jungles, between which were open patches of cultivation, and little villages with their white temples or mosques. The thousands who had come out for the sport were now returning, some in crowds together, singing a wild song in chorus, others in smaller groups chatting upon the events of the day. Here and there was a palankeen, its bearers crying their monotonous song as they moved, bearing to the camp either some one too indolent or too grand to ride on horseback, or else the fair inhabitant of the Sultaun's or some other harem, who had been allowed to see as much as was possible of the amusement of the royal hunt.

'That is surely the Khanum's palankeen,' said Kasim, as its well-known appearance met his view at a turn of the road.

'Yes,' said the Khan, 'she has been dull of late, and I begged her to come out; she could have seen nothing, however, and 'tis well she could not, for that butchery was horrible. Bah! how the creature bleated!'

'I wish it had not been, Khan, but there is no use speaking of it now. But how is it that the Khanum is unattended in such a crowd as this? Some loocha* or shoda* might insult her, or say something disagreeable.'

'By the Prophet! well remarked—the horsemen must have lost her; let us ride up and see.' They urged their horses into a canter, and were soon with her.

'How is this?' cried the Khan to the Naik of the bearers; 'how comes it that thou art alone?'

'Khodawund!' replied the man, 'we lost the escort, and so thought we had better return by ourselves, for we knew not where to look for them in such a crowd.'

'We had better stay by the palankeen ourselves, Khan Sahib,' said Kasim; and Ameena well remembered the tones of his voice, though she had not heard it for some months; 'it is not safe that the lady should be here alone.'

'Be it so then, Kasim; we will not leave her.'

In a few minutes, however, the Sultaun, who they thought

* Disreputable fellow.

was before, but who had lingered behind to shoot deer, advanced rapidly on horseback at the head of the brilliant group of his officers;—a gay sight were they, as the afternoon sun glanced from spear and sword, from shield, matchlock, and steel cap, and from their fluttering scarfs of gay colours and gold and silver tissue. A band of spearmen, bearing the heavy broad-bladed spears of the Carnatic ornamented with gay tassels, preceded him, calling out his titles in extravagant terms, and running at their full speed. Behind him was the crowd of officers and attendants, checking their gaily caparisoned and plunging horses; and quite in the rear, followed the whole of the elephants, their bells jingling in a confused clash, and urged on by their drivers at their fullest speed to keep pace with the horses. The Sultaun sat his beautiful grey Arab with the ease and grace of a practised cavalier, now checking the ardent creature and nearly throwing him backwards, now urging him on to make bounds and leaps, which showed how admirably he had been taught his paces, and displayed his own and his rider's figure to the best advantage.

'By Alla, 'tis a gallant sight, Kasim!' said the Khan; for they had drawn up to one side, as the cavalcade came thundering on over a level and open spot, to let it pass; 'looking at them, a soldier's eye glistens and his heart swells; does not thine do so? Look out, my pearl!' he cried to Ameena; 'veil thyself and look out—the Sultaun comes.'

'My heart beats,' said Kasim, 'but not as it would were he who rides yonder a man whom I could love as well as fear.'

'Inshalla!' cried the Khan, 'thou wilt forget to-day's work ere long, and then thou wilt love the Lion of the Faith, the terrible in war, even as I do. Inshalla! what Sultaun is there on the earth like him, the favoured of Alla, before whom the infidels are as chaff in the wind? But see, he beckons to me; so remain thou with the Khanum, and bring her into camp.' And so saying, the Khan gave the rein to his impatient charger, and bounded onwards to meet the Sultaun, who appeared to welcome him kindly.

Kasim saw the Khan draw up beside him; joining his hands as if speaking to him; and as the wild and glittering group hurried by, horses and elephants intermingled, he lost sight of him among the crowd, and the cavalcade rapidly disappeared behind a grove of trees.

And now she, who for many months had often filled his dreams by night, and been the almost constant companion of his thoughts by day, was alone with him. He had seen her fair and tiny hand shut the door of the palankeen, which was an impenetrable screen to his longing eyes; and he would have given anything he possessed for one glance—to have heard one word, though he dared not have spoken to her.

And in truth, the thoughts of the fair inmate of the vehicle, which was being borne along at the utmost speed of the bearers, were busied also in a variety of speculations upon her young guardian. Did he remember her still? had he still the handkerchief with which his wound had been bound? for he had never returned it. Did he remember how she handed him matchlock after matchlock, to fire upon the wild Mahrattas, and cried with the rest Shabash! when they said his aim was true? She had not forgotten the most trivial incident; for her heart, in the lack of society, had brooded on these occurrences; they were associated too, in her youthful mind, with the appearance of one so noble and gallant, of whom she heard such constant and florid encomiums from the Khan her husband, that it would have been strange had she not dwelt on this remembrance with more than friendship for the author of them. But the current of these thoughts—when his noble figure was present to her imagination—as he had dashed on hotly in pursuit of the Mahrattas,—was suddenly and rudely interrupted by a hubbub, the reason of which she could not at first comprehend.

The bearers were proceeding rapidly, when, at a turning of the cross road which they had taken for shortness, they perceived an elephant, one of the royal procession, which, either maddened by the excitement of the hunt, or goaded to desperation by its driver, was running hither and thither upon the road in the wildest manner. The Mahout repeatedly drove his sharp ankoos * into its lacerated head; but this appeared to enrage, and make it the more restive, instead of compelling it to go forward, as was evidently his wish.

The bearers stopped suddenly, and appeared irresolute; to attempt to pass the infuriated animal was madness, and yet what to do immediately was difficult to determine, for the road was bounded by a thick and impenetrable hedge of the prickly pear. It was in vain that Kasim shouted to the Mahout to go on, for he did not immediately comprehend the cause of the elephant's behaviour; the obstinate beast could not be moved in the direction required—it was impossible to force him through the hedge, and it was frightful to see his behaviour, and to hear the wild screams and trumpetings he uttered when struck with the sharp goad. Kasim saw there was danger, but he had little time for thought; he however drew his sword, and had just ordered the bearers to

* Pointed goads with which elephants are driven.

retreat behind the corner, when the elephant, which by a sudden turn had seen what was behind, uplifted its trunk, and with a loud cry dashed forward.

Kasim was brave and cool; and yet there was something so frightful in the desperate rush of the maddened animal, that his heart almost failed him; nor could he discover whether it was himself or the palankeen that was the object of the elephant's attack; but he had confidence in the activity of his horse,—his sword was in his hand, and he little feared for himself. The elephant's advance was instantaneous; Kasim saw the palankeen was his object, and dashing forward almost as he reached it, he struck with his whole force at the brute's trunk, which was just within reach. The blow and pain turned the animal from his purpose, but his huge bulk grazed the palankeen, which, with its terrified bearers, fell heavily and rudely to the ground, and rolled upon its side.

Kasim heard the scream of Ameena (who had been unable to discover the cause of the alarm, and was afraid to open the door) the moment the shock was given, and throwing himself from his horse he hurried to her assistance, for he was certain she must be severely hurt. This was no time for ceremony; in an instant the palankeen was set upright, the door opened, and seeing the fair girl lying, as he thought, senseless within, he cried out for water, while he supported her inanimate figure, and poured forth a torrent of passionate exclamations which he could not restrain.

But no water was there to be had, and it was fortunate that the lady had received no serious injury; she was stunned and extremely terrified; but a few moments of rest, and the consciousness of Kasim's presence, revived her. Instantly a thought of her situation, and her own modesty, caused her to cover herself hurriedly with her veil, which had become disarranged; and, not daring to look upon Kasim, whose incoherent inquiries were sounding in her ears, she implored him in a few broken sentences to leave her, and to have her carried onwards. He obeyed, though he would have given worlds to have heard her voice longer, broken and agitated as it was; he withdrew sadly, yet respectfully; and the danger being past—for the elephant had fled madly down the road by which they had come—they pursued their way to the camp.

CHAPTER XXX.

'But he saw my face—he must have seen it,' cried Ameena; as, after relating the adventure to her lord, she was lying upon the soft cushions which had been spread for her. 'I was not sensible, and he thought I must be hurt. Ah, what wilt thou not think of me, my lord!' And she hid her burning face in her hands upon the pillow.

'What matter, fairest?' replied the Khan, as, bending over her with much concern in his countenance, he parted the hair upon her forehead and kissed it tenderly. 'What matter? had it been another, indeed, who had opened thy palankeen, the officious rascal should have paid dearly for his temerity: but Kasim—why should it concern thee? did he not save thy life? and is he not my friend? and now again have we not cause to be thankful to him? Let this not distress thee therefore, but praise Alla, as I do, that thou art safe.'

It was not, however, the simple gaze of Kasim upon her face that had disturbed the agitated girl, though in confessing this to her lord she sought ease from other thoughts which were engrossing her. He had seen her face; happy were it if that had been the only result of the accident; but the passionate words which in his anxiety for her he had uttered, had fallen upon her ears, and but too readily accorded with her own previous thoughts; she remembered, too, as she looked around with returning consciousness after the shock, how she had seen his expressive eyes, lighted up with enthusiasm and anxiety, gazing on her; and she had read in them, even had he not spoken, that he loved her. And when she repeated to her husband again and again that Kasim had looked upon her face, that was all she dared to tell him of what had happened.

Poor Ameena! the Khan's constant theme of conversation had been Kasim Ali, as from time to time any new feat of arms, of horsemanship, any new weapon or gay dress he had worn, attracted his attention; he would delight to relate all to her minutely, to recount how adroitly he had foiled such an one, how handsome he had looked, and to dwell upon these themes with expressions of praise and satisfaction at Kasim's daily proving himself more and more worthy of his patronage. Often would he foretell an exalted station for the young man, from the Sultaun's early selection of him to fulfil so delicate a mission as that to Hyderabad; and on that very day, when he had been beckoned by the Sultaun, it was to hear the praises of Kasim Ali, to be asked whether it was not he who had won the reward he had offered; and, upon his answering in the affirmative, the Sultaun had graciously bidden him bring Kasim to the morning Durbar, when he should be enrolled once more among his personal attendants.

Ameena was obliged to listen to all this; and after listening, she would brood over these discourses upon his noble qualities, until her heart grew sick at the thought that to *her* none such would ever be—and her dearest hopes, for one to love her in whom should be united all those qualities which she heard he possessed, had long ago been blighted for ever. She needed no new event to remind her of Kasim's first service, nor to impress more strongly upon her mind his noble but melancholy features; which, except when lighted up by the hot excitement of battle, habitually wore a sad expression. And yet the last adventure had come, like the first, unsought and unexpected, and the consequences were sad to both. In Ameena, producing an inward shame, a consciousness of harbouring thoughts she dared not reveal—a vain striving between her honour to her lord and her love for the young man his friend. In Kasim, a burning passion —which, as it exists in Asiatics, is almost irrepressible—struggling with his high feelings of rectitude, of respect, nay of affection for him he served, which was hardly to be endured.

And thus it continued, producing misery in both; except in forgetfulness, there was indeed no alleviation; and that was impossible, for they thought of little else than of each other, through the long hours of the days and nights which followed.

The Sultaun had ordered the Khan to bring Kasim Ali before him in the morning after the usual march, but it was in vain that his messengers sought him, to apprise him of the order; he had been seen to ride off after the arrival of the Khanum, and was not to be found. In truth, the young man felt himself unable to meet the Khan with any composure after what had happened, and he also dreaded (if Ameena had heard the expressions he uttered) that she was offended. He had no possible means of ascertaining this—of imploring her not to denounce him to the Khan, as faithless and treacherous; and under the influence of these mingled and agitating feelings, the young man continued to ride hither and thither as if without a purpose—now in some level spot urging his horse into a furious gallop, to gain release from the thoughts which almost maddened him—again allowing him to walk slowly, while he brooded over the exquisite beauty and gentleness of her whom he had twice saved from injury, perhaps from destruction.

But the hour for evening prayer drew nigh, and he turned his horse towards the camp: its many fires were everywhere twinkling upon the fast darkening plain, and the deep sounds of the evening kettle-drums, mingled with the dull and distant murmur of thousands of voices, were borne clearly upon the evening wind.

He quickened his pace, and as the sonorous and musical voices of the Muezzins among the army, proclaiming the Azan,* called the faithful into their various groups for prayer, he rode up to the Khan's tent, where the usual number had their carpets spread, and awaited the proper moment for commencement. Kasim joined them, but the act of supplication had little effect in quieting his agitation; the idea that Ameena might have told all that had passed precluded every other thought, and caused a feeling of apprehension, from which he could not release himself.

When the prayer was ended, the Khan addressed him in his usual kind and hearty manner, and calling him into his private tent, poured out his thanks, and those of Ameena, for his timely and gallant assistance in her late extreme danger. As he spoke, Kasim at once saw there was no cause for suspicion; and as the dread of detection passed from his heart, a feeling of tumultuous joy, that his words had not been ill received by her to whom he had addressed them, on the instant filled its place, and for a while disturbed those high principles which hitherto had been the rule of his conduct.

'And now,' said the Khan, after he had fairly overwhelmed the young man with thanks, 'I have news, and good news for thee! thou art ordered to attend the morning Durbar, and I suspect for thy good. The Sultaun (may his condescension increase!) has looked once more with an eye of favour upon thee; he means to give thee a command among his guards, and to attach thee to his person. I shall lose thee therefore, Kasim, but thou wilt ever find me as sincere and devoted a friend as thou hast hitherto done. We may soon be separated, but so long as we march thus day after day, indeed so long as this campaign continues, we may at least associate together as we have been accustomed to do.'

Kasim could hardly reply intelligibly to the Khan's kind expressions. That he had been exerting his influence with the Sultaun on his account, he could have no doubt; and this, with the affectionate friendship he had professed, again very powerfully brought all the young man's best feelings to his aid, and he went

* Call to prayer.

from his presence late in the evening, with a determination to seek Ameena no more, and, if possible, to drive all concern for her from his heart. Vain thought! Away from the Khan, his excited imagination still dwelt upon her, and his visions that night of their mutual happiness almost appeared to him an earnest that they would be ultimately realised.

He accompanied the Khan as usual during the march, for the army proceeded the next morning on its way, and at its early close he rode with him to the place where the Sultaun held his morning Durbar, in some anxiety as to what would happen. The tents of the monarch had not been pitched, for under the thick shade of some enormous tamarind-trees there was found ample space for the assembly; and pillows had been placed, and soft carpets spread for his reception. One by one the different leaders and officers of rank arrived, and dismounting ranged themselves about the place which had been set apart for the Sultaun: their gay dresses somewhat sobered in colour by the deep shade the trees cast upon them, and contrasting powerfully with the green foliage, which descended in heavy masses close to the ground. On the outskirts of the spot the grooms led about their chargers, whose loud and impatient neighings resounded through the grove. On one side the busy camp could be seen, as division after division of horse and foot arrived in turn, and took up their ground in regular order.

At last the Sultaun's kettle-drums were heard, and in a few minutes he galloped up at the head of a crowd of attendants, and immediately dismounting, advanced into the centre of the group, and returned the low obeisances of those who hastened to offer them. There were a few reports to be listened to, one or two summary and fearful punishments to be inflicted; and these done, the Sultaun turned to Rhyman Khan, who stood near him.

'Where is the young man?' he said; 'we have thought much of him during the night, and our dreams have confirmed the previous visions we have mentioned regarding him. Therefore let him be brought, we would fain do justice in his case: this is a fortunate day and hour, as we have read by the stars; and the planetary influences are propitious.'

Kasim was at hand, and amidst the crowd of courtiers, sycophants, and parasites, who would have given all they possessed to have been so noticed, he advanced, performed the Tusleemât, and then stood with his hands folded in an attitude of humility and attention.

'Youth!' cried the Sultaun, 'we have heard that it was thou

who killed the mad elephant yesterday, when our royal hand trembled and our gun missed fire. We offered a reward for that deed—dost thou claim it?'

'May I be your sacrifice!' replied Kasim, 'I know not; what can I say?—let the Khan answer for me.'

'He has already told me all,' cried the Sultaun, 'therefore we have sent for thee. Hear, then, and reflect on what we say to thee. Thou shalt be raised higher than thou wast before, and we will arrange thy pay hereafter. It will be thy business to attend on and accompany us; and in the coming battles, in which by the aid of the Prophet we intend to eclipse our former achievements, which are known to all—'

Here he looked around, and cries of 'Wonderful! The Sultaun is great and valiant! he eats mountains and drinks rivers! before his eye the livers of his enemies melt into water!' passed from mouth to mouth.

'Therefore,' he continued, after a pause, 'do thy service well and boldly, and it shall be good for thee that thou hast eaten the salt of Tippoo. Thou art Jemadar from this time forth, O Kasim Ali! and hear all of ye that it is so ordered.'

The congratulations of all fell upon the gladdened ears of the young Patél, who, in truth, as he bowed lowly and fell back among the crowd, was somewhat bewildered by his new honour, so great and so unexpected. Now he should rank with the men of consequence,—nay, he was one himself; and he felt, as was natural, proud and elated at his promotion.

The Khan's joy knew no bounds. 'I thought,' he said, 'thou wouldest be taken into favour, and have thy pay increased, but this is most excellent. By Alla! Kasim, say or think what thou wilt, the Sultaun has a rare discrimination. Wilt thou *now* forget the scene of yesterday, and the young elephant?'

'I shall never forget it,' said Kasim, 'but I pray Alla it may never be repeated.'

'Ameen!' responded the Khan; 'yet listen—the Sultaun speaks.'

And the voice of the Sultaun was again heard, interrupting the Khan. 'Proclaim silence!' he cried to the attendants; and after the loud cries of 'Khamoosh! khamoosh!' had in some degree subsided, he addressed the assembled officers, whose number was every moment increased by other wild and martial figures from the camp, who crowded behind the rest on tiptoe to hear his address.

'Ye all know,' he said, 'how the infidel Rajah of Travancore —who has his portion already with the accursed—has allowed our rebellious and infidel subjects the Nairs to have shelter in his territory. We have demanded them from him, and have met with insult and scorn in his replies; are we, who are the chosen of Alla, to bear this patiently?'

'Let him die! let him be sent to hell!' cried the assembly with one voice, their passions suddenly aroused by this abrupt address.

'Stay!' continued Tippoo—his visage becoming inflamed, and his eye glistening like that of a tiger's chafing into fury,—'we, by the favour of Alla, possess accurate knowledge of the councils of the unbelievers and of the kafir English. We know that this miserable Rajah is upheld by them in his contumacy; but we have ere now humbled their pride. Baillie and Mathews, with their hosts—where are they? and we will, Inshalla! humble them again, and drive them into the sea! They have threatened us with war if we attack the wall which this Rajah hath built upon our subjects' territory, and over which we have a right to pass to Cochin, whither it is our pleasure to go. Say, therefore, my friends, shall there be peace? Shall we, who wear swords on our thighs, eat dirt at the hands of these lying and damnable kafirs? or shall—'

The remainder of his speech was lost. The cry for war was as one voice. He had appealed to the fierce passions of his officers, who saw only victory in prospect, and they had responded as warmly as he could wish.

'Be it so,' cried the Sultaun, when the tumult was stilled; 'in a few days we shall see this wonderful wall, of which we hear things that would produce terror in any mind less strong or valiant than our own; and then, Inshalla-ta-Alla! we will see what can be done by the army of the Government, which is the gift of Alla, led by him who is an apostle sent to scourge all kafirs and sceptics. You have your dismissal now;—go, and prepare your men for this service. Mashalla! victory awaits our footsteps!'

In a few days afterwards the army arrived within sight of the wall; it was of considerable height and thickness, had a broad and deep ditch in front, and presented a formidable obstacle to the invading army. It is probable that, had Tippoo attacked the wall at once, he might have carried it by escalade; but he was evidently uncertain as to the result of his negotiations; he hesitated for a time to strike a blow which must inevitably embroil him with the English, and therefore drew off a short distance to the northward; where, engaged in correspondence with the English and Travancore Governments, he passed most o. his time, thus allowing his enemy every opportunity to increase his force and prepare for resistance.

Kasim's post near the Sultaun's person led him into daily and close communication with the monarch, and he gradually gained an insight into his extraordinary character. Sometimes, when he uttered the noblest and loftiest sentiments of honour, he would love and respect him; again some frivolous or ridiculous idea would get possession of his imagination, and drive him into the commission of a thousand absurdities and terrible cruelties. It was no uncommon thing to see beyond the precincts of the camp a row of miserable Hindoos hanging upon trees, who had defied the Sultaun's efforts at conversion, and had preferred death rather than change the religion of their fathers. For Shekh Jaffur had arrived in camp with a division of the army which was ordered to join from the Canarese provinces, where he had been particularly active against the Nairs; and to him Tippoo delegated the direction of the torture and punishment of those Hindoos, whom, on the slightest pretext, either of rebellion, disobedience, or denial of supplies, they could get into their hands. With this duty Kasim Ali had no concern; but he observed that under the other it flourished, and that day after day some wretched beings were dragged before the monarch, whose death appeared to stay his appetite for slaughter till the negotiation should end, as he expected, by his letting loose his army upon the defenders of Travancore.

But month after month passed, and the season was advancing; the immense preparations of the English, the Nizam, and the Mahrattas, to join in one common league for his destruction were everywhere reported; it was necessary for him to strike some blow, else, after the preparations he had made and the threats he had promulgated, his conduct would appear in a weak and puerile light to his enemies. To Kasim Ali this state of inactivity was insupportable; he had hoped from the Sultaun's address that the army would at once have been led to battle, and he was disappointed beyond expression when, after a trifling skirmish before the wall, the whole drew off to that ground it was destined to occupy for so long. Instead of active employment in the field, in the excitement of which he might for the time forget Ameena, or strengthen his resolution to think no more of her with love—there was absolute stagnation.

The life he led was entirely the opposite of what he wished it, and during the days of idleness and inactivity he had little else to do than dream of her. But he refrained from seeking her, even when opportunity was afforded by the return of his old friend the cook Zoolficar, who, having been left at Seringapatam by the Khan, had been sent for upon the misconduct and discharge of the one he had brought with him.

His arrival was heartily welcomed both by the Khan and Ameena; by the first, because he could once more enjoy his excellent cookery and most favourite concoctions; by the lady, because his sister, the old servant of her family at Hyderabad, who had joined the worthy functionary at Seringapatam, accompanied him to the camp. She was gladly welcomed by Ameena, who, among the women that attended upon her, had no one to whom she cared to open her heart; for they were all natives of the south, with whom she had little communion of thought and feeling, and who spoke her language indifferently.

With Meeran, however, almost a new existence commenced; while alone the most part of the day—when the Khan's duties and attendance upon the Sultaun kept him away from her—she had few occupations except her own thoughts, which were sad enough; yet in Meeran's society, humble though she was, she could ever find topics of conversation—of her home, her family, her friends and acquaintance; old subjects long gone by were revived and dwelt upon with all the zest of fresh occurrences; and the incidents of her travel to the city, and every event connected with herself since she left her home, were repeated again and again with that minuteness which is commonly the result of a want of other occupation.

It hardly needed the very quick penetration common to a woman whose wits had been sharpened by a residence in such a city as Hyderabad, to discover very soon that her young and beautiful mistress was unhappy; and Meeran heard so often of the young Patél, as Ameena still called him, and found that she so evidently delighted to speak of him and his acts, that she very naturally concluded that much of her unhappiness was attributable to the young man, however innocent he might be of the cause. For, after speaking of him, and describing his noble appearance as she had seen it on several occasions, and repeating the constant eulogiums of her lord, Ameena would often involuntarily find a tear starting to her eye, or a deep-drawn sigh heave forth, which she fain would have suppressed, but could not.

Now Meeran had from the first, and while there was yet a chance of averting the evil, protested against the giving away of her child (for so she called Ameena) to a man as old as the Khan for a sum of money; and though she had every respect for him, yet she could see no harm, after a little consideration, and the overcoming a few scruples, of striving to help the lovers. She had nursed Ameena at her own breast, she had tended her from infancy, had been the confidant of all her secrets, and, if the truth were known, had helped the young girl to form exactly such an idea of a lover as it appeared Kasim was—young, gallant, handsome, and of a fine generous temper.

Kasim had renewed his acquaintance with the good-natured Zoolficar, and on several occasions the man had come to his little tent upon one excuse or another; sometimes to talk over their journey, sometimes to cook him a dish he liked, when the Khan was employed elsewhere, and they did not dine together. Often had their conversation fallen upon Ameena; and though at first the mention of her name had been avoided by the young Jemadar, yet the theme was so pleasant a one, that he insensibly dwelt upon it more and more. Soon Kasim heard from the cook that his sister was with his young mistress, and that she was happier in the society of her old nurse than she had been before her arrival.

Habitual indulgence in conversation about her naturally begat a craving in the young man to know all the particulars of Ameena's daily existence. The most trifling circumstances appeared to be welcome to him; and it was not long ere Zoolficar, finding that he could not give the information so greedily looked for as minutely as was required, proposed that his sister should supply it. This, however pleasant, was nevertheless a matter of more difficulty, and one that required concealment; for it would have been at once fatal to Ameena's reputation, had her favourite servant been seen in private conversation with one like Kasim Ali. Despite of obstacles, however, they contrived to meet; and on the first of these interviews the nurse saw clearly enough how passionately devoted Kasim was to her fair mistress, and how precious to him was every detail of her life, of her meek and gentle temper, and of her loving disposition. The nurse would often bewail her unhappy destiny, in being cut off from all chance of real happiness in company with the Khan; and she could appreciate, from the evident agitation of the young man, and his half-suppressed exclamations, how difficult it was for him to withhold an open declaration of his thoughts. Yet she could not help seeing that through all this there was nothing breathed of dishonour to the Khan, no wish to meet her whom she was sure he so passionately loved.

It was not until after some time and many such conversations with the young Jemadar, that Meeran dared to mention to Ameena that she had seen him. She had heard from Kasim the account of his protection of her from the enraged elephant, and he had confessed what he had then uttered.

'She knows of his love, then,' said Meeran mentally, 'and she dares not mention it to her old nurse. We shall see whether this humour will last long. Inshalla! they shall yet be happy in each other's society.'

She could not appreciate the nice morality either of Kasim or her young mistress: she knew that neither was happy, and believed she had in her power the means of making both so. 'Could they but meet,' she used to say, 'they might speak to each other, and even half the words that I hear, spoken by one to the other, would set their hearts at rest for ever.'

But Ameena grew really angry with the woman, that she had dared to think of such a step, much less to speak of it. Meeran bore all good-humouredly, but she determined to persevere, convinced that she was acting for their mutual good.

Time passed on; the army advanced nearer to the wall, and at length the Sultaun, tired of inactivity or protracted negotiation, determined to strike the first blow in the strife, which it was useless to disguise to himself was fast approaching; and could he but possess himself of Travancore, his operations against the English would be materially aided. His resolution was, however, suddenly and unexpectedly made. Kasim with some men had been directed to examine a part of the defence where the wall joined a precipice, some miles from the camp, and to report the practicability of its assault. His statement confirmed the Sultaun's previous intentions, and he gave orders for the attacking parties—ten thousand of the flower of his army—to prepare for immediate action.

Kasim was aware that his post would be one of danger, for the Sultaun was determined to lead the attack in person, and it was more than probable that he would be bravely opposed by the defenders of the lines; among these were many of the fugitive Nairs, who burned for an opportunity of revenging upon the Sultaun's army the many insults and oppressions they had suffered.

Much, however, was hoped from so powerful an attack on an undefended point; and the Sultaun's order was delivered to the army on the afternoon of Kasim's report. The divisions for the assault were ordered under arms after evening prayer, and all were in readiness, and exulting that ere that time on the morrow the barrier before them would be overcome, and the dominions of their enemy open to plunder.

The night was bright and clear and cool: there was no wind,

and the melancholy and shrill notes of the collery horn came up sharp upon the ear from all parts of the wall before them, which extended for miles on either side. Lights were twinkling here and there upon it, showing that the watchers did not sleep, and sometimes the flash and report of a musket or matchlock appeared or was heard, fired by one or other of the parties. The camp of the Sultaun was alive with preparation, and the busy hum of men arose high into the still air. Soon all was completed; and when it was no longer doubtful that darkness veiled their preparations, the mass of men moved slowly out of the camp, and led by Kasim, took their way to the place he had discovered.

CHAPTER XXXI.

THE huge column moved slowly and silently onwards, aided by the light of a brilliant moon. The Sultaun, at its head, sometimes on foot, at others on horseback, or in bad places upon his elephant, cheered on his men and officers with words he knew would best arouse their zeal and spirit. There was hardly need, however, for the army proceeded as fast as the nature of the ground would permit. All night they marched, but slowly enough, through the narrow and rugged road, and sometimes through the thick jungles; and often the Sultaun would turn to Kasim, and question him about the path, evidently thinking that he had lost it, and that the expedition would be in vain. But the young Jemadar was sure of the way; the guides he had taken with him when he explored the path in the first instance were also confident; and as morning broke, the dull grey light disclosed the precipitous rock which was their object, close before them.

'Art thou sure this is the place, Kasim Ali?' said the Sultaun, as he rode backwards and forwards, vainly endeavouring to find the path which led to the summit. 'Art thou sure? By the Prophet, it will be worse for thee if thou hast led us wrong!'

'May I be your sacrifice,' said Kasim, 'this is the place. Let the army halt here for a short time; your slave will take a few of the pioneers and see if it be clear of the enemy; but it is not probable they would defend it, so far from the gate, and in this wild jungle.'

'I will accompany thee,' replied the Sultaun; and despite the entreaties of the numerous officers by whom he was surrounded, he rode after Kasim. A strong body of infantry supported them in case of danger.

There was however none: the path, which was concealed from view by a large tree, and ran up between two high rocks, was undefended. A few men might have disputed it against a host, but the Sultaun's threatening disposition of troops in front of the gate, which was many miles distant, had drawn all the defenders to that spot; and where the wall terminated against the rock there was no one left to guard it.

Accompanied by a few of the household slaves, sword in hand, Kasim advanced slowly and cautiously up the path. There was perfect silence, except when a jungle fowl, scared from its roost by the unusual sound of men's feet, flew with a loud whirr into the dense thickets beyond the pass; or when the ravens, aroused from the trees below, flew before them from bush to bush, croaking their dismal welcome to the feast they seemed to anticipate.

They gained the top without interruption; and Kasim, sending word to the Sultaun (who had not ventured with the leading party up the pass) that all was safe, went on to the edge of the precipice, and looked over the scene before him.

The night mists still lay quietly in the hollows, looking like unruffled lakes in the dim light; and here and there a huge rock, like the one on which he stood, was surrounded by them, and appeared like an island. Immediately below him all was clear, and the long columns and crowds of persons—the elephants moving majestically about, and horsemen here and there appearing where the jungle was thin or open—was a sight at which the young soldier's blood danced briskly through his veins; for all were now pressing forward towards the pass, and he hoped that the leading divisions would soon be at the summit. Away to the left, the line of wall, with its bastions and towers, which so long had been their object of desire, stretched over the undulating ground; but it was deserted, except at a distant point, where two or three faintly twinkling lights showed that a watch was kept.

'By the Prophet, thy road is a rare one, Kasim Ali!' said the Sultaun, who had come up to him unobserved, and touched his shoulder; 'the army will soon be up, though it is somewhat narrow. Dost thou see any one stirring on the wall?'

'No one, my lord; they have all been deceived by the troops before the gate, and imagine the attack is to be made there.'

'Yes,' said the Sultaun, 'we are unrivalled in such stratagems; it was ourself who planned the ambuscade which ended in the discomfiture of Baillie and his kafirs; and we have ever exercised the talent which Alla hath confided to us, among many others, of military skill, in which we surpass the English and French—may their races be defiled!'

How long the Sultaun might have continued the theme of his own praises, which was always a most pleasant one to him, it is impossible to say, but his harangue was rather rudely interrupted by two shots, discharged in quick succession from a distant part of the wall before them, one of which whistled over their heads (for they were standing upon the crest of the rock)—the other struck the ground a little below them.

'Ha! so the rogues are awake,' cried Kasim; 'I beseech you, my lord, to turn back, and not to expose yourself to danger. Your slave will lead the way, and send these infidels to perdition.'

'Inshalla!' cried the Sultaun, yielding to the solicitations of all around him, and retiring a few paces, 'Inshalla! many will see the angel of death ere night. On with ye! victory is before—cry Alla Yar! and set on them. Think that ye fight for the faith, and that your Sultaun is beholding your deeds of prowess.'

'Alla Yar! Deen! Deen!' was now shouted by the hoarse voices of the crowd which occupied the top of the rock, and the cry flew from division to division down the pass and into the plain; thousands shouted 'Alla Yar! Alla Yar!' the Sultaun's war-cry, and strained every nerve to press onwards.

The shout of the army was answered by several single shots from the same spot as before; and an officer of the regular infantry, who had been standing on the very brink of the precipitous rock, was seen to toss his arms wildly into the air, and, ere he could be caught by several who rushed to his assistance, had fallen headlong into the thicket below.

'Follow Kasim Ali Patél!' cried the daring young man—for he was the foremost, and the path was not at first apparent to the rest. Drawing his sword and putting his arm through the loops of his shield, he dashed down it, followed by a hundred of those who waited the signal of attack.

They scrambled down the side of the declivity on to the wall—there was nothing that could be called a path for soldiers—and it was still so dusk that objects could but ill be discerned. Once on the wall, however, all was fair before them: the parapet was broad enough for three or four men to pass abreast; but Kasim and the rest were obliged to wait a while ere they were joined by a sufficient number to press on.

'We shall have hot work ere long,' said the officer who had

accompanied Kasim, 'and this is no place for infantry to fight in —a narrow wall, with a deep ditch on the one hand, and a thick jungle, with only a narrow path through it on the other. By Alla, I like it not.'

'Art thou a coward?' said Kasim, turning on him with some contempt in his voice; 'thou hadst better in that case go to the rear. Fie on thee to speak thus! do we not eat the Sultaun's salt? Come on, in the name of the Prophet! there are enough of us—more are coming every moment, and the top of the rock is already crowded.'

'Thou shalt see I am no coward,' cried the officer, darting forward; but he was stopped by another deadly shot, and fell on his face without uttering a word or cry.

His fate did not, however, check the assault. 'Alla Yar! Alla Yar!' was still the shout, and the whole body hurried on. impelled forward by the pressure from the rear. There was no retreating; on the one hand was the impassable ditch, on the other the jungle—here and there open, and with paths through it running parallel to the wall, by which many rapidly advanced. They saw nothing of the defenders, though from time to time a fatal shot struck the dense mass, and one of their number fell headlong from the narrow path, or sinking down wounded, was thrown over by his comrades. The thick jungle hid the defenders of the wall, who retreated as the others advanced; for they were as yet too few to offer any resistance. But gradually the noise of the shouting and firing was heard along the line of wall, and its defenders hurried along to the right to meet their enemies, judging that their flank had been turned, and that there was little hope of retaining their post if the Sultaun's army should succeed in advancing. In this manner parties joined together and gradually succeeded in arresting the rapid approach of their enemies, who had now to fight for every foot of ground. Tower after tower was desperately disputed; the day was advancing, many of the men were already exhausted by their long night march, and to stop or retreat was impossible.

'At this rate we shall never reach the gate,' cried the Sultaun, who had entered a tower which had just been taken, and where Kasim and many others were taking breath for an instant ere they recommenced their advance. 'We shall never gain the gate—it must now be nearly three coss from us;' and he looked from one to the other of those assembled.

'And the men are very weary,' said Kasim, for he spoke boldly.

'Ya, Alla kureem!' exclaimed the Sultaun, 'dost *thou* despair, Kasim Ali?'

'Alla forbid!' was his reply; 'by the favour of the Prophet we shall prevail; but my lord sees that it is tedious work, for the kafirs have heard the firing and are collecting more and more in every tower; and though they pay dearly for their temerity in resisting the power of the Lion of the Faith, as these unblessed bodies testify, yet the taking of every succeeding tower is a work of more labour, and many of the faithful have tasted of death.'

'A thought strikes me,' said the Sultaun; 'what if the wall were thrown down? we should then possess a breach, by which we could enter or go out at pleasure.'

'A wise thought! Excellent advice! What great wisdom!' was repeated by the whole circle, while the Sultaun stood by silent, apparently in further consideration upon the subject.

'Yes,' he continued, after holding his forefinger between his teeth in an attitude of deliberation for some time,—'yes, it is a good thought; and we charge you, Syud,' he added, to his relative, 'with its execution; collect the pioneers, heave over the battlements into the ditch, fill it up level with the plain. Inshalla! there will be a broad road soon. Be quick about it; and now, sirs, let us lose no more time, but press on; our swords are hardly red with the blood of the infidels, and they appear to be collecting yonder in some force.'

'But,' said the Syud, 'this is a pioneer's work: in the name of the Prophet, leave me not with them.'

'I have spoken,' replied the Sultaun, frowning. 'Enough! see my command obeyed, and be quick about it.'

'We may need the road too soon,' said a voice: but, although they tried hard, they could not discover whose it was.

Once more then they resolutely set forward, and the Sultaun was on foot among his men, who were full of animation as he often spoke to them, and reminded them that those who fell were martyrs, who would be translated to Paradise, and those who survived would win honour and renown. But it was easy to see that, tired and exhausted as they were, the men had not their first spirit; and some hours of constant fighting, with no water to refresh them, had been more than they could support; the opposition every moment became more and more certain and effective, and each step was disputed.

Meanwhile the road over the ditch progressed but slowly. The Syud had thought himself offended by being left behind to see it done, and looked sulkily on without attempting to hasten the operation. The pioneers were too few to effect anything rapidly; indeed it would have been impossible to have done what the Sultaun had ordered, even had the whole force joined in the work; for the ditch was wide and deep, full of thorns, briars, matted creepers, and bamboos, which had been planted on purpose to offer a hindrance to an enemy. A few stones only had been displaced, though the work had gone on nearly an hour, when it was suddenly and rudely interrupted.

The advancing party had proceeded hardly half-a-mile, with much labour, when on a turn of the wall they perceived a square building filled with the enemy, who in considerable numbers had taken post there, and were evidently determined to dispute it hotly.

'Ah! had we now some of my good guns,' cried the Sultaun, as he beheld their preparations for defence, 'we would soon dislodge those unblessed kafirs. By Alla, they have a gun too! there must be some one yonder who understands fighting better than those we have yet seen.'

'May their mothers be defiled!' cried a gasconading commander of a battalion of infanty, who was well known for his boasting. 'Who are they that dare oppose us? my men are fresh' (for they had just come up from the rear), 'and if I am ordered I will go and bring the fellow's head who is pointing the gun yonder.'

'Ameen!' said the Sultaun, quietly; 'be it so—thou hast volunteered—go! Stir not thou, Kasim Ali, but remain here; we may require thee.'

The officer addressed his men for a few moments, formed them as compactly as he could on the narrow wall, and placing himself at their head, with loud cries of 'Alla Yar!' they dashed on, followed by many who had collected during the pause. Those in the enclosure reserved their fire till they were near.

'They have no ammunition,' cried the Sultaun; 'Ya Fukroo-deen! Ya Nathur Wullee! I vow a covering for both your tombs if they take the place.' But as he made the invocation, they saw (for all were looking from the tower where they had stayed in intense eagerness) one of the men inside the enclosure lift a match to the gun, and apply it;—it would not ignite.

'Ya Futteh-O!' cried Kasim, snatching a matchlock from a fellow who stood near, and aiming; 'it is a long shot, but, Bismilla!' and he fired.

The man was raising his hand again when the shot struck him; he fell back into the arms of those behind him.

'Another, for the sake of the Prophet, or it will be too late!' cried Kasim, not heeding the cries of 'Shabash! Shabash!' which all poured forth.

It was indeed too late: the success of the first shot had gained the advancing party a moment, but ere he could be sure of his aim a second time, the fatal match was applied, and with the explosion half of the leading division fell as one man.

'May perdition light on them!' cried the Sultaun, in agony; 'may hell be their portion! My men waver too. Ya Kubeer! Ya Alla kureem! Support them—Ya Mahomed!—against the infidels!'

But his wild invocations were of no use; the commander of the party had fallen; and the men, having fired a volley at random, turned and fled as hastily as they could on that narrow, crowded way.

'Cowards!' exclaimed Kasim. 'Ah, had I here fifty of the youth of my country, and their good swords—Inshalla! we would see whether we were to eat this abomination.'

The Sultaun was speechless with rage for some moments. 'Order on the next corps!' he shouted at last; 'that unworthy one shall be disgraced. Before my very eyes to behave thus! Do not stay to fire,' he cried to its commander who came up; 'upon them with the steel! were ye English, ye would carry the place—ye are of the true faith, will ye not fight better? Ya Karwa Owlea! Ya Baba Boodun! grant me your prayers.'

'Let me head this attack,' cried Kasim, for others appeared to hang back; 'on my head and eyes be it—I will carry the place or die in the effort!'

'Remain here!' exclaimed the Sultaun fiercely; 'art thou, too, rebellious? remain and shoot if thou wilt, we may need thee. Let them go whose duty it is.'

'Jo Hookum!' exclaimed the officer who had been addressed; 'I will either carry it or die.'

Again the advance was made, while those in the tower kept up an incessant fire, the Sultaun himself aiming frequently; but they had now to face men emboldened by success. The division was allowed to advance nearly to the same place as the former had done; and again the fatal cannon, loaded almost to the muzzle with grape, was fired. A loud shout from the enemy followed. The execution was terrible; the survivors hesitated for a moment, then turned and fled, leaving a heap of mangled and writhing forms between them and the enemy. At this moment too, a body of men from an eminence on the flank, who had hitherto been concealed, poured in a destructive volley, which added to the terror. The retreating body met another which was hurrying on to their assistance, and the confusion became irretrievable. Blows and bayonet-thrusts were even exchanged on the narrow wall, and many a man fell wounded or maimed by the hands of his fellow-soldiers, while only the powerful could keep possession of the passage. On a sudden arose a cry of 'The road! the road!' and as if the means of escape were thus open, the whole, for a great distance down the wall, turned and fled.

The Sultaun saw the action; it was in vain that he tore his hair, threw his turban on the ground, raved, swore, implored the assistance of the Prophet and all the saints in one breath, and in the next wildly invoked the vengeance of Heaven upon his coward army. It was in vain that he threw himself, accompanied by Kasim and his personal attendants, into the crowd, and upon the narrow path strove to withstand the torrent which poured backwards. It was in vain that he shouted—screamed till he was hoarse: his voice was lost in the mighty hubbub, in the cries of thousands, the oaths, the groans, and rattle of musketry from behind. It was in vain that, drawing his sword in despair, he cut fiercely at, and desperately wounded, many of the fugitives, and implored those around him to do the same. He was at last overpowered, and accompanied by Kasim and a few of the strongest of his slaves, he was borne on with the crowd. No one heeded him; in the *mêlée* he had lost his turban, by which he was usually known, and he became undistinguishable to his soldiery from one of themselves.

Thus it was that the throwing down of the wall was interrupted; the cry from the panic-stricken multitude, re-echoed by the advancing troops, rose almost instantaneously upon the air with a deafening sound. 'The road! the road!' all shouted, and hurried to where they expected to have seen it completed. The narrow stream met from two opposite directions, pouring on, urged by the energy of despair from behind. The two extremes met; there was no time for thought—not a second; those who were first had hardly looked into the ditch, and seen there only a heap of stones instead of a road, and those thirty feet below them, ere, with one wild cry to Alla, they were pushed into it by those behind, whose turn was to come next. A few there were—men of desperate strength—who clung to the battlements with the tenacity of despair; a few who, drawing their swords, turned and tried to cut their way through the mass. Vain effort! force was met by force, for the danger was not perceived till the men were on the brink and were pushed over; those in the rear thought they had escaped, and no warning cry was heard, or, if heard, attended to or understood.

The multitude poured on. Ten thousand men had to pass by that place. Those who leaped, lay at the bottom, many maimed, others crushed and entangled amidst the thorny briars and thick grasses. The mass at the bottom of the ditch gradually increased; and a road arose, not of the ruins of the wall, but a mass of human bodies: those uppermost struggling in agony for life, those underneath already at rest in death—a quiet foundation for the superincumbent structure.

The Sultaun and his companions were hurried on. Kasim had a dread of what he should see—a sickening feeling, as the shrieks and imprecations which arose from that horrible spot fell upon his ear as they approached; they could do nothing however, for to turn was impossible; to leap from the walls into the midst of the enemy would have been death, for they pursued the flying army with exulting shouts, and pressed close upon the flanks and rear with their long spears. By the road there was a chance of life—a chance only—and that was clung to as a reality at that moment.

They reached the brink. 'Way for the Sultaun! aid the Sultaun! rescue your King!' shouted Kasim with his utmost energy, while he dealt blows right and left, as did also the others with him, to stay the crowd even for an instant. The Sultaun looked down on the horrible heap, which, wildly agitated, was heaving with the convulsions of those beneath it; he appeared to turn sick and stagger, and Kasim observed it.

'For your life,' cried he, 'Lall Khan and some more of ye, keep together, or he is lost! Now leap with me!' and as the Sultaun still hesitated, Kasim seized him by the arm and threw himself from the brink.

Now began a fresh struggle—one for life or death, in which only the strongest prevailed. For an instant Kasim was stunned by the shock, but he saw Lall Khan trying to help on the Sultaun, whose features wore the hue of despair, and he made a mighty effort to aid him. The footing upon the heaving mass was unsteady and insecure; in the wild despair of death, the struggling beings below clung to the legs of those above them, and thus the weak were drawn down to destruction. But Kasim Ali and those who followed him were powerful men, and raising the almost senseless body of the Sultaun in their arms, and spurning many a feeble and exhausted wretch beneath their feet, they bore it with immense exertions across the ditch.

There remained, however, the counterscarp to surmount. Here many a man who had passed across the ditch failed to ascend, for it was of rock, and so rugged and inclining inwards as to afford no footing. It was vain attempting to raise the Sultaun to the top, without he made some exertion, and Kasim shouted his danger in his ear, while he pointed to the place.

The Sultaun at last comprehended the peril, and being raised by Kasim and the others on the shoulders of the tallest of his slaves, he twice essayed to mount the bank, and twice fell back among the writhing and crushed wretches at the foot, upon whom they were standing.

The second time he was raised he was evidently much hurt, and could not stand; what was to be done? Motioning to the others—for to speak was impossible—Kasim mounted by their aid to the top; and the Sultaun being once more lifted, was received by the young man, who supported him a few steps, and then laying him down, groaning heavily, he flew to the rescue of those who had so nobly aided him.

One by one they had ascended by his and their mutual aid, and the generous fellow had stretched his hand to several despairing wretches, who were weak with their efforts and previous fatigue, and rescued them from death; when, seeing the enemy now lining the wall and about to fire upon the bank opposite to where he stood, he turned away in order to remove the Sultaun, who still lay where he had placed him, out of danger. He had gone but a few paces, when he heard a sharp discharge of matchlocks, and felt a cold stinging pain in his shoulder and all down his back; the next instant a deadly sickness, which precluded thought, overpowered his faculties, and he sank to the ground in utter insensibility.

CHAPTER XXXII.

WHILE the principal division of the army was displaying its choicest manœuvres in front of the gate of the wall, now and then venturing within shot, and giving and receiving a distant volley, the noise of the firing came faintly to those engaged, and, as it was expected, caused no sensation, except of anxiety for the moment when their victorious Sultaun should arrive, driving before him the infidel defenders; and when the gates should be opened, and the mass of cavalry should rush in to complete their rout and destruction. Many a man there anticipated the pleasure of slaughtering the flying foe, of hunting them like wild beasts, of the fierce gratifications of lust and unchecked plunder; but hours passed and no victorious army appeared; the defenders of the fort called to them to come on, with insulting gestures and obscene abuse, and shook their swords and matchlocks at them in defiance. This was hardly to be borne, and yet they who mocked them were beyond their reach; at length, as they looked, several horsemen approached them with desperate speed, their horses panting with fatigue and heat. The Khan and many others rode to meet them.

'Ya Alla kureem,' cried all, 'what news? where are the army and the Sultaun? why do you look so wildly?'

'Alas!' answered one who was well known to the Khan as a leader of note, 'the army is defeated, and we much fear the Sultaun is lost; he was in the van leading on the attack with Syud Sahib, Hussein Ali, Bakir Sahib, and the young Patél, who was fighting, we heard, like a tiger, when Alla only knows how the army took a panic and fled.'

'And you were within the walls?' cried many voices.

'We were, and had marched some miles. Alas! it would have been better had we never entered.'

'And how did you escape?'

'The ditch was already filled with our companions,' said the horseman, 'and we scrambled over their bodies; I found a horse near, and have ridden for my life to tell the news.'

They asked no more questions, and each looked at his fellow with silent shame and vexation that this should have been the end of all their hopes. One by one the leaders drew off, and in a short time division after division left the ground, and returned towards the camp; a few only daring to meet the discomfited host, which soon began to pour by hundreds into it, exhausted, humbled, full of shame and mortification.

Among the first was the Sultaun; for the elephants had, at a little distance, kept a parallel line with the wall. One was easily procured for him, and having been lifted upon it, he was rapidly borne to the camp; but he was unattended, and arrived at his tents almost unknown and unobserved.

But the loud nagara soon sounded, and men knew that he was safe; and though it was the signal that the Durbar was open, and that he expected their presence, few went to him, or cared to meet him in the temper which they knew must possess him. The Khan was among the first who entered; his low salaam was almost disregarded, and he took his seat, pitying the Sultaun's shame and mortification, which was fully expressed on his sullen countenance.

One by one, however, the leaders of the divisions which had remained behind entered, and took their places in silence; none dared to speak; and the restless eyes of the monarch, the whites of which were yellow and bloodshot, wandered from one to another round the assembly, as if searching for some pretext to break forth into the rage which evidently possessed him, and which was augmented by the pain of the sprain of his ankle. There was a dead silence, so unusual in his Durbar; and the words which were spoken by the attendants to one another were uttered in a whisper. Now and then the Sultaun rubbed his ankle impatiently, and knit his brows when a severe paroxysm of pain passed through it: or else he sat silent, looking round and round; —the bravest of those present used to say afterwards that they waited to see who would be first sacrificed to his vengeance. The silence was insupportable; at last Nedeem Khan, his favourite and chief flatterer, ventured to speak.

'May Alla and the Prophet ease the pain thou art suffering, O Sultaun!' he said; 'can your slave do aught to relieve it?'

'Oh, rare bravery to speak!' cried the Sultaun with bitterness; 'thou wert not with me, Nedeem Khan, to partake of the abomination we have eaten this day at the hands of our own friends and those infidel Hindoos—may their ends be damnation! No, thou didst volunteer to be with the division without the gate, that thy fine clothes and fine horse might be seen by the defenders of the wall. Verily thy destiny is great, that thou wert not among that crowd, nor struggling with that heap of— Pah! where is Kasim Ali Patél?' he continued after a pause; 'why is he not present? and Lall Khan also?'

'Kasim Ali Jemadar Huzrut!' cried Lall Khan advancing, 'has not been seen since—'

'Not been seen!' thundered the Sultaun, attempting to rise, and sinking back in pain,—'not been seen! and thou to tell me this! Oh kumbukht! By Alla, Lall Khan, hadst thou not too aided me, thou shouldest have been scourged till the skin was cut from thy back. Begone! thou and thy companions—seek him, dead or alive, and bring him hither to me.'

'Asylum of the world! he lies, if he be killed, among the dead upon the edge of the ditch, and the enemy is in possession of the walls, and—'

'Begone!' roared the Sultaun; 'if he was in hell thou shouldest bring him. Begone! thou art a coward, Lall Khan.'

'Huzrut!' said the old Khan, rising and joining his hands, hardly able to speak, for his grief was choking him; 'if your slave has his dismissal, he will accompany Lall Khan in search of—' He could not finish the speech, and the big tears rolled down his rough visage upon his beard.

'Go, Rhyman Khan,' said the Sultaun, evidently touched by

his emotion; 'may you be successful.' And again he relapsed into silence, as the two officers departed on their almost hopeless errand.

'The tiger will have blood ere he is pacified,' whispered Bakir Sahib, who had arrived, and now sat near Nedeem. 'I pray Alla it may be none of this assembly!'

'Will they find Kasim Ali?' asked the other.

'Willa Alum,' responded his friend, 'I think not; but he will be no loss to us.'

'None—but what is this?'

As he spoke there was a noise without, and suddenly a man, evidently a Hindoo, rushed bare-headed into the assembly, crying out, 'Daad! Daad! Daad!'* and advancing threw himself on the ground, and lay at full length motionless before the Sultaun.

'What ho, Furashes! Chobdars!' roared the Sultaun, his face quivering with rage; 'what is this hog—this defiled father of abomination? were ye asleep to allow our Durbar to be polluted by his presence? who and what art thou?' he cried to the trembling wretch, who had been roughly raised by the Furashes; 'speak! art thou drunk?'

'You are my father and mother—you are my Sultaun—you are my god!' cried the man; 'I am a poor Brahmin; I am not drunk—I have been plundered—I have been beaten by a devil they call Jaffar Sahib; he seeks my life, and I have fled to your throne for mercy.'

'Thou shalt have it,' said the Sultaun quietly, with his low chuckling laugh, which not even his officers could listen to without feeling their blood curdle; 'thou shalt have it. Away with him, Furashes!' he cried, raising his shrill voice, 'away with him! I see an elephant yonder; chain him to its foot, and let him be dragged to and fro before the place he has defiled.'

The wretched man listened wildly to his sentence—he could not understand it; he looked on the Sultaun with a trembling smile, and then with a feigned laugh round the assembly; nought met his eye but stern and inexorable faces; there were many who felt the horrible injustice of the act, but none pitied the fate of the Brahmin after the event of the morning.

'Do ye not hear?' cried the Sultaun again; and, ere he could say a word, the Brahmin was borne shrieking out of the tent. All listened fearfully, and soon they heard the shrill scream of the elephant, as, after the wretched man had been bound to his

* Complaint.

foot, the noble and tender-hearted animal—it was old Hyder—was unwillingly goaded into a desperate run, and, dashing forward, soon put an end to his sufferings. They looked, and saw something apparently without form jerked along at the end of a chain by the foot of the elephant at every step he took in the rapid pace into which he had been urged.

'The Durbar is closed,' said the Sultaun after a time, during which he had not spoken, but continued moodily to watch the door of the tent for the elephant, as it passed to and fro. 'Ye have your dismissal, sirs, we would be alone.'

They were glad to escape from his presence.

'I said how it would be, Khan,' said Bakir Sahib, as they passed out; 'Alla knows what would have happened if that Brahmin had not rushed in.'

'Alla knows!' said the other; 'I trembled for myself, for he was savage to me. After all it was the Brahmin's fate—it was written—who could have averted it?'

The glaring day waned fast. Kasim had been wounded about mid-day, and still lay near the same spot, enduring almost insufferable agony. At first he had been insensible, but when he recovered and was enabled to look around him, the place was deserted, except by a few of the enemy at a distance, who were busily employed in stripping the dead and wounded of their arms and clothes. He found his sword, his shield, and daggers were gone,—his turban and waistband, and upper garment also: his head and his body were bare, for they had thought him dead, and the fierce rays of the burning sun descended in unmitigated fury upon him, increasing to an agonising degree the torment of thirst.

'Water! water!' he cried to those whom he saw afar off; 'Water, for the sake of your mothers and your children!—will ye suffer me to die?'

Alas! they heard him not; they were too busy in their work of plunder; and if they had, it would have been only to return, and with a thrust of a spear or a sword to have ended his sufferings. To him death would have been welcome, for his agony was past enduring, and he had no hope of alleviation till he died. But his voice was too weak for them to hear; and if he exerted it there came a rush of blood into his mouth which almost choked him.

He tried to move, to drag himself under the shade of a bush which was at a short distance; it was impossible,—the pain he suffered became excruciating; and, after making several desperate but ineffectual attempts, he fainted. This temporary oblivion, at least, brought absence from pain, and was welcome,—but it did not last; and as the returning life-blood poured through his heart, his agony of body was renewed, and thoughts too rapid and too vague to assume decisive forms—a weak delirium, in which his mother, Ameena, his friend, the Sultaun, the dreadful passage of the ditch, and the heaps of struggling forms—were incoherently mingled in wild confusion. Now his distempered fancy caused him to imagine that he again bore on the Sultaun,—now his form would seem to change into Ameena's, and he would shout his despair, and cry the war-cry of the faith as he strove for life and mastery among the thousands who fiercely struggled with him; but his fancied shouts were only low moans, which from time to time escaped him, as he lay to all appearance dead.

And again the thirst, the heat, and the pain slowly but surely brought on frenzy—fierce ravings of battle and hot contest; and words of encouragement to those around him: defiance of the enemy, with wild invocations of Alla and the Prophet, broke from his lips in faint murmurs, though passionately uttered; he thought them shouts, but they could scarcely have been heard by one standing over him. At times the sweat poured from him in streams, or stood in big drops on his brow; again his frame would seem to dry up, till he thought it would crack and burst.

In a lucid moment he found he had dragged himself, during a paroxysm of delirium, under the shade of the bush; it was grateful to him, and soothed his burning head and skin; and with the coolness came visions of quiet shady groves—of fountains, whose ceaseless plashings, mingling with the gentle rustling of leafy boughs, were music in his ears—of bubbling springs, whose waters flowed up to his lips and were dashed thence by malignant forms which his excited brain created. By turns despair and hope possessed him, but in his quiet moments he prayed to Alla for death, for release from suffering, and from the deadly sickness caused by a burning throat and loss of blood. He could feel that he had been shot through the body, and he wondered how it was possible to retain life in such a state.

As often as he looked for a moment over the open space, he saw in hundreds the horrible birds of prey, ravens and kites, and the filthy and powerful vultures, tearing the hardly cold bodies, and disputing with each other over their sickening banquet, while th ers wheeled and screamed above them ready to take the place of any who should be driven by the rest from their meal. Wherever he looked, it was the same; there were hundreds of ohe obscene birds, struggling, scrambling, fighting with each other, while thousands of crows, in clamorous and incessant flight, hovered over, alighting where chance threw in their way a coveted morsel; and now and then some prying raven would approach him with long hops, croaking to his fellows, his keen black eye glistening brightly in anticipation, and would hardly be scared away by the faint gestures and cries of the sufferer.

The night fell gently—that night, which many an one would spend in luxury, in the enjoyment of voluptuous pleasures, surrounded by objects which enthral the senses, lying upon the softest carpets, while burning incense filled the air with rich perfume, and the soft sighs of women and the gentle tinkling of their anklets sounded in their ears—that night he would pass in terror, surrounded by the ghastly forms of the dead.

The sun sank in glory, the hues of the brilliant west faded dimly on his aching sight, and from the east over the wooded hills the yellow moon arose, dim at first, and seemingly striving to maintain the waning daylight. Soon, however, that faded away, and the melancholy and quivering wail of the brass horn, and the deep sound of the evening kettle-drums from the wall, showed that the enemy were setting their night-watch. The gorged birds of prey flapped their broad wings heavily in their short flights to the nearest trees, to roost there till the morrow should break, enabling them to recommence their glutting and bloody feast.

They were succeeded by beasts of prey: one by one jackals issued from the jungle, and looking carefully around, first one and then another raised his nose into the air, and as he sniffed the banquet, sent forth a howl or shriek which ran through the unfortunate Kasim's veins like ice. Now he could see many, many, running to and fro in the moon's bright light, and their cries and screams increased fearfully. To his excited and delirious spirit—for his senses fled and returned at intervals—the place he thought was the hell he had read of, and the howls like those of the damned. Now stalked abroad the stealthy wolf, and the gaunt and fierce hyæna mingled his horrible howl with those of the innumerable jackals which hurried on in packs to the ditch; and Kasim could hear the distant bayings of others as they answered the invitation from afar. How he prayed for death! Had he possessed a weapon, he would have rid himself of life; but he had to endure all, and he shrank into the bush as far as he could, to screen himself from the notice of the wild animals, lest he should be torn in pieces by them ere he was dead. Some even came and sniffed at him, and their bright and wild eyes glared upon him; but seeing that he yet lived, they passed on to where in the ditch carcases lay in heaps inviting them to feast.

On a sudden, while he lay in utter despair, he thought he heard the clashing sound of an elephant's bells, and the peculiar and monotonous cry of palankeen-bearers. Could it be? or was it only a mockery of his senses, such as had raised water to his lips and spread before him delicious and juicy fruits? He listened in fearful suspense; he did not hear it for a time, and hope, which had arisen strong within him, was dying away, when it came again on the soft night breeze that had just arisen, and he could hear it clearly above the yells and howls of the beasts around him, who were fighting savagely over the dead.

Alla! how he panted, as the welcome sound came nearer and nearer; and how his spirit sank within him as he thought it might only be travellers by some by-road he knew not of. Now his faculties were all sharply alive; had he possessed the power of motion, how gladly would he have hurried to meet them; he tried to move, to raise himself, and fell back helpless. 'Alas!' he said aloud, 'it is but a delusion; they will pass me, and the light of morning will never shine on Kasim Ali alive.' His own voice seemed awful in the solitude, but he could speak now, although very faintly, and if they passed near him he was determined to exert his utmost energy in one cry, should it even be his last effort.

A horse's neigh now rang shrill and clear in the distance, and the clash of the elephant's bells became more and more distinct. They were coming!—they were surely coming—perhaps for him—perhaps it was the Khan—perhaps the Sultaun had thought of him—how tumultuous were his thoughts!

Now he even thought he could hear voices, and presently there was another loud snorting neigh, for the horses had smelt the dead afar off. He crawled out from his hiding-place, and looked with intense expectation; there was a twinkling light far away among the jungle. It blazed up.

'Ya Alla kureem! it is a torch—they come, they come!' cried the poor fellow. He heard a confused sound of voices, for the yells of the beasts had ceased: he could see many slinking off into the thickets, and there was perfect silence. Now the red light illumined the trees at a little distance—they were descending one side of a hollow towards him—he could track their progress by the light upon the trees—he lost it for a time, as they ascended the other side—again it gleamed brightly, and on a sudden burst like a meteor upon his glance, as the body of men, with several torches, the elephant, the palankeen, and some horsemen appeared for a moment on an open spot pressing towards him.

He could not be mistaken: but Kasim now dreaded lest the garrison should make a sally over the ditch; he looked there—all was dark, but in the distance a few lights on the wall were hurrying to and fro, as though the alarm was given, and a shrill blast of the collery horn was borne to his ear. 'They will not come!' he thought, and thought truly; they would not have dared to face the ghastly spectacle in the ditch.

The voices were real, and the lights were but a short distance from him: the party had stopped to consult, and the poor fellow's heart beat wildly with suspense lest they should advance no further; he could not hear what they said, but on a sudden a cry arose from several, 'Kasim Ali! Kasim Ali! ho!' which resounded far and wide among the still jungle.

He strove to repeat it, but the blood gushed into his throat: he fell back in despair. They came nearer and nearer, shouting his name.

'It was near this spot,' said one; 'I am sure of it, for here is a corpse, and here another: let us look further.' And they continued to track the way of the fugitives by the dead.

'Kasim Ali! Kasim Ali! ho, hote!' shouted a voice which thrilled to Kasim's very soul, for it was the Khan's: how well he knew it—an angel's would have been less welcome. One torch-bearer was advancing, hardly fifty paces from him; he waited an instant, then summoning his resolution, 'Ho! hote!' he cried, with all his remaining power. The sound was very faint, but it was heard.

'Some one answered!' shouted the torch-bearer.

'Where? for the sake of Alla,' cried the Khan from his horse.

'Yonder, in front.'

'Quick, run!' was the reply, and all hurried on, looking to the right and left.

Kasim could not speak, but he waved his arm; as they came close to him, the broad glare of the torch fell on him, and he was seen.

All rushed towards him, and the old Khan, throwing himself recklessly from his horse, ran eagerly to his side and gazed in his face. Kasim's eye was dim, and his face and body were covered with blood; but the features were well known to him, and the old soldier, unable to repress his emotion, fell on his knees beside him, and raising his clasped hands wept aloud.

'Shookur-khoda! Ul-humd-ul-illa!' he cried at last when he

could speak, 'he lives! my friends, he lives! I vow a gift to thee, O Moula Ali, and to thee, O Burhanee Sahib, for this joy; I vow Fatehas at your shrines, and to feed a hundred Fakeers in your names.'

'Do not speak, Kasim Ali, my son, my heart's life. Inshalla! you will live. Inshalla! we will tend thee as a child. Do not stir hand or foot:' (Kasim had clasped the Khan's hand, and was endeavouring to raise it to his lips:) 'no thanks, no thanks—not a word! art thou not dear to us? Ay, by Alla and his apostle! Gently now, my friends, gently; so, raise him up—now the palankeen here, 'tis the Khanum's own, Kasim—never heed his blood,' he added, as some of the bearers strove to put their waistbands under him. 'Aistee, aistee!*—kubardar!†—well done! Art thou easy, Kasim? are the pillows right?—what, too low? thou canst not breathe?—now, are they better?—nay, speak not, I understand thy smile;' and truly it was one of exquisite pleasure which overspread his face.

'What, water?' he continued, as Kasim motioned to his open mouth, 'Ya, Alla! he can have had none here all day. Quick, bring the soraee and cup! There,' he said, filling a cup with the sparkling and cool fluid, 'Bismilla, drink!'

The fevered Kasim clutched it as though it had contained the water of Paradise; cup after cup was given him, and he was refreshed. The flower of life, which had well nigh withered, was revived once more, and hope again sprang up in his breast.

'Go on with easy steps,' cried the Khan to the bearers,' I will give you a sheep to-morrow if ye carry him well and quickly.'

'On our head and eyes be it,' said the chief of the bearers, and they set forward.

The men on the wall fired a few random shots at the party, but they were too distant to aim with effect, and it proceeded rapidly. The journey of some miles was a severe trial to the exhausted Kasim, and they were several times obliged to rest; but they reached the summit of the last declivity after some hours, and the welcome sight of the huge camp below, the white tents gleaming brightly in the moonlight, among which hundreds of watchfires were sparkling, greeted the longing eyes of Kasim. In a few minutes more they had arrived at the Khan's own tent, and he was lifted from the palankeen into the interior, and laid on a soft bedding which had been prepared within. The place was cleared of those who had crowded round, and although Kasim's eyes were dizzy, and the tent reeled before him, he was conscious that the gentle voices which were around him, the

* Easy, easy! † Take care.

shrouded forms which knelt by him, and the soft hands which washed the hard and clotted blood from him, were those of Ameena's women.

CHAPTER XXXIII.

THE excitement of the day had prevented the Sultaun from feeling the pain of the severe sprain until late, when it became insupportable: in vain it was fomented and rubbed; that seemed only to increase the swelling and stiffness; but when he heard that Kasim had arrived in the camp badly wounded, he could not withstand the desire of seeing him to whom he owed the preservation of his life; accordingly he was lifted into a chair, and, entirely unattended, directed his bearers to carry him to the Khan's tent, where he sent orders for his chief physician to meet him.

Such an honour was entirely unlooked for by the Khan and his household; nevertheless he was received with respect, carried into the tent where Kasim was, and set down by the side of the sufferer, who lay almost in a state of insensibility, showing consciousness only at intervals. The women servants who had been fomenting the wound, and had arisen at his entrance, now resumed their occupation; for though Daood and his other men had offered their services, the Khan had thought truly that there was more lightness and softness in the hand of woman; and Ameena's nurse, Meeran, had set the example to the rest, aided by the instructions of her brother Zoolficar, who was busy preparing a poultice of herbs for the wound.

The Sultaun regarded Kasim intently before he spoke to the Khan, and several times stooping down felt his pulse and head.

'Inshalla! he will yet live,' he said; 'we, the chosen of the Prophet, are counted to have much skill in the treatment of wounds, and therefore we say, Inshalla! he will live; his pulse is strong and firm, and he is not going to die.'

'Alla forbid,' echoed all around.

'Whose advice hast thou got for him, Khan?' asked the Sultaun.

'None as yet, Asylum of the World! My Khanum's women here have been fomenting the wound, and a slave of mine who has skill in such matters, for he was a barber once, is preparing a poultice.'

'We desire to know what is in it,' said the Sultaun; 'there is much in having lucky herbs boiled under the influence of salutary planets; send for him.' The replies of Zoolficar were deemed satisfactory by the Sultaun, who desired him to proceed with the work. The Hukeem too shortly afterwards attended, and began carefully to examine the patient; he had evidently but little hope, and shook his head with a melancholy air when he had made his survey.

'There is no hope of his life,' said the old man. 'I have seen many shot, but a man never survived such a wound—his liver is pierced, and he must die.'

'I tell thee no! Moorad-ali,' said the Sultaun; 'we have had dreams about him of late, his destiny we know is linked with our own, and we are alive—Inshalla! we shall yet see him on horseback.'

'Inshalla-ta-Alla,' said the Hukeem, 'in him alone is the power, and we will do what we can to aid any merciful interference he may make.' But his directions for an application were little different from the mixture of the cook, which was shortly afterwards applied. The Sultaun waited a while in the hope of hearing Kasim speak, but he continued to lie breathing heavily and slightly groaning, when additional pain caused a pang.

'We can do no good,' he said to the Khan; 'let us leave him to the care of Alla, who will restore him to us if it be his destiny. Come then with me to the morning Durbar; we will summon the leaders, and settle some plan for the future, which we were too disturbed to arrange yesterday.'

The Khan followed him, charging the women strictly with the care of the poor sufferer until he returned; he was soon afterwards engaged in deliberation with the Sultaun and his officers. One of two alternatives presented themselves to Tippoo; either to abandon the undertaking suddenly, and while the English should think him engaged there to fall upon their territory with fire and sword,—or to send for heavy guns from Seringapatam, and breach the barrier, when an assault, such as could not be withstood by the besieged, might be made with success. The latter was in the end adopted; the army serving in Malabar was desired to join the Sultaun by long forced marches; heavy batteries of guns were ordered directly from the city; and his officers, from his manner and the eagerness with which he entered into the matter, saw how intent he was on providing for the emergency.

The pain Tippoo had suffered the whole night was intense; but the excitement of the Durbar, the dictation of the letters to his officers, and the deliberation, had prevented him from betraying it more than by an impatient gesture or ill-suppressed oath. At last he could bear it no longer, and sank back upon his musnud, cursing terribly the infidels who had caused his defeat and suffering; but he rallied again immediately, and started up to a sitting posture, while he exposed and pointed to his ankle, which he had hitherto kept concealed under a shawl.

'Ye see what pain and grief are devouring us,' he cried, 'and we call upon ye to revenge it.'

'We are ready—on our head and eyes be it!' cried all.

'For every throb of pain,' continued the Sultaun, speaking in suppressed rage from between his closed teeth, while he held his ankle, 'we will have a kafir's life; we will hunt them like beasts, we will utterly despoil their country. Ya, Alla Mousoof! we swear before thee and this company, that we will resent this affront upon thy people to the death—that we will not leave this camp, pressing as are our necessities elsewhere, till we have sent thousands of these kafirs to perdition; and ye are witness, my friends, of this.'

'And I swear to aid thee, O Sultaun!' cried the Khan with enthusiasm, 'and to revenge that poor boy if he dies.' 'And I! and I!' cried all, as they started to their feet in the wild spirit of the moment; 'the kafirs shall be utterly destroyed.'

'I am satisfied now,' cried the Sultaun; 'what has happened was the will of Alla, and was pre-ordained; whatever a man's fate is, that he must suffer;' and the assembly assented by a general 'Ameen!' 'However, Inshalla!' he continued, 'we have seen the last reverse; and we are assured by comforting thoughts that the army of the faith will be henceforth victorious. Ye have your dismissal now, for we are in much pain and would consult our physician.'

During the absence of the Khan, the attentions of the women to poor Kasim had been incessant, and everything was done that kindness could suggest to procure any alleviation of his pain. His wound was fomented, his limbs kneaded, his still parched and fevered lips moistened with cool sherbet. Meeran had striven to comfort her young mistress for some time, but in vain: she had not been able to repress her emotions when he was brought in wounded, although she dared not in presence of her lord give full vent to her feelings; but when she knew that he had left the tent with the Sultaun, she could no longer restrain herself, and gave way to a burst of grief, which would have proved to Meeran, had she not before known of her love for him, how deep and true it was.

'I must see him, Meeran,' she said at length; 'the Khan is gone now, and canst thou not devise some means? Quick! think and act promptly.'

'I will send away the women, my rose,—thou shalt see him,' said the attendant; 'when I cough slightly do thou come in; they say he cannot speak, and lies with his eyes shut.'

'Ya, Alla kureem!' cried Ameena; 'what if he should die ere I see him? Oh grant him life,—thou wilt not take one so young and so brave. Quick, good nurse! I am sick at heart with impatience.'

Meeran found but little difficulty in sending away the women upon some trifling errands, for Kasim slept, or appeared to dose; so taking their place by his side, she coughed slightly, and Ameena, who had been waiting anxiously behind the screen which divided the tents, withdrew it hastily and entered.

She advanced with a throbbing heart; she could hardly support herself, as well from her despair of his life as of her own feelings of love for him, which would now brook no control; her mind was a chaos of thoughts, in which that of his death and her own misery were the most prominent and most wretched.

Nor was the sight before her, as she drew near Kasim, at all calculated to allay her fears; he lay to all appearance dead; his eyes were closed, and his breathing was so slight that it scarcely disturbed the sheet which was thrown over him; the ruddy brown of his features had changed to a death-like hue, and his eyes were sunken.

Ameena was more shocked than she had anticipated, and it was with difficulty that she could prevent herself from falling to the ground when she first saw his features, so deadly was the sickness which seemed to strike at her heart; but she rallied after an instant of irresolution, and advancing sat down by her nurse, who gently fanned the sleeper.

'He sleeps,' she whispered; 'Zoolficar has bound up the wound, his remedies are always sure, and there is luck with his hand. Alla kureem! I have hope.'

'Alas! I have none, Unna,' said Ameena; 'I cannot look on those altered features and hope. Holy Alla! see how he looks now—what will happen?' and she gasped in dread, and put her hand before her eyes.

'It was nothing—nothing, my life, but a slight spasm, some pain he felt in his asleep, or perchance a dream; but it is past; look again, he is smiling!'

His features were indeed pleasant to behold. Even in a few minutes a change had come over them; he had been dreaming, and the excitement and pain of one had been followed, as is often the case, by another of an opposite nature—one of those delirious visions of gardens and fountains which had mocked him as he lay on the battle-field again arose before him, and he fancied that Ameena was beside him, and they roamed together. They saw his lips moving, as though he were speaking, yet no sound came, except an indistinct muttering; but Ameena, whose whole soul was wrapt in watching him, fancied that the motion of his lips expressed her name, and mingled emotions of joy and shame struggled within her for mastery.

Again the peaceful vision had passed away, and his brow contracted; his nervous arms were raised above the covering over him, and his hands were firmly clenched; he ground his teeth till the blood curdled in their veins, and his lips moved rapidly. 'Oh that I could wake him, Unna!' said Ameena; 'that I could soothe him with words—that I dared to speak to him. Hush! what does he say?'

'Water! water!' whispered Kasim hoarsely. The rest they could not hear, but it was enough for Ameena; a jar of cool sherbet stood close to her; with a trembling hand she poured out some into the silver cup and held it to his lips. She only thought of his pain, and that she might alleviate it, and Meeran did not prevent the action. The cool metal was grateful to Kasim's dry and heated lips; they were partly open, and as she allowed a little of the delicious beverage to find its way into them, the frown from his brow passed away, the rigid muscles of his face relaxed, and as she softly strove to repeat the action, his eyes opened gently and gazed upon her.

For an instant, to his distempered fancy, her beauty appeared like that of a houri, and he imagined that he then tasted the cup of heavenly sherbet with which the faithful are welcomed to Paradise; but as he looked longer, the features became familiar to him, and the eyes—those soft and liquid eyes—rested on him with an expression of sympathy and concern which they could not conceal. For an instant he strove to speak—'Ameena!' The name trembled on his lips, but he could not utter it; he suddenly raised himself up a little, and coughed; it was followed by a rush of blood, which seemed almost to choke him.

Ameena could see no more; her sight failed her, and she sank down beside him unconsciously. Meeran, however, had seen all; she raised her up, and partly carrying, partly supporting her, led her away, while she called to her brother, who stood at the tent-door to watch, to come to Kasim's assistance.

'Thou must keep a stouter heart within thee, my pearl!' she said to Ameena, after having with much assiduity recovered her

'Holy Alla! suppose the Khan had come in then, when thou wert lying fainting beside him—what would he not have thought? I shall never be able to let thee see him again if thou canst not be more firm.'

'Alas!' sighed Ameena, 'I shall see him but little again; his breath is in his nostrils, and there is no hope: this night—tomorrow—a few hours—and he will cease to live, and then I shall have no friend.'

'Put thy trust in Alla!' said the nurse, looking up devoutly; 'if thy destiny is linked with his, as I firmly believe it is, there will be life and many happy days for you both.' But her words failed to cheer the lady, who wept unceasingly, and would not be comforted.

Days passed, however, and Kasim Ali lived; his spirit of life within him would one while appear to be on the verge of extinction, and again it would revive, and enable him to exchange a few words with those by whom he was tended. It was in vain that he entreated the Khan to allow him to be removed to his own tent; his request was unheeded or refused, and he remained. Gradually he regained some strength; and with this, a power of conversing, which he was only allowed to exert at intervals by the physicians, and by the kind old cook, who, with the Khan's servant Daood and Ameena's nurse, were his chief attendants. As he lay, weak and emaciated, he would love to speak with Meeran of her who he knew had visited him on the first night of his wound, and to hear of her anxious inquiries after his progress towards recovery.

To Ameena the days passed slowly and painfully; sometimes, when the Khan spoke of Kasim, it was with hope,—at others, as if no power on earth could save him; but she believed her nurse more than him, for her hope never failed, and she was assured by Zoolficar that the crisis had passed favourably, that all tendency to fever had left him, and, though his recovery would be slow, yet that it was sure; and on this hope she lived. Day and night her thoughts were filled with the one subject, and she conversed upon it freely with the Khan, who loved to speak of Kasim, without exciting any surprise in his mind.

And often would she steal softly on tiptoe to the place where Kasim lay asleep, at such times as she knew he was attended only by Meeran; and looking upon his wasted features, to satisfy herself that he was advancing towards recovery, she would put up a fervent prayer that it might be speedy. But Kasim knew not of these visits, for Ameena had strictly charged her nurse not to mention them, lest they should excite him or he should look for their continuance. Often would the old nurse rally her upon her caution, and urge that it would gratify Kasim, and aid his recovery, to speak with her, but Ameena was resolute.

'I should fail in my purpose,' she would say. 'Meeran, I dare not risk it; to look on him daily, even for an instant, is happiness to me which thou knowest not of, and such as I may indulge in without shame; but to speak to him, knowing his feelings and mine, would be to approach the brink of a giddy precipice, from whence we might fall to perdition. Am I not the Khan's wife? he is old—I cannot love him, Meeran, but I honour him, and while he lives I will be true to him.'

'Alla send thee power, my child!' Meeran would reply; 'thou art but a child, it is true, but thou hast the faith and honour of an older woman, and Alla will reward thee.'

But it was a sore temptation to Ameena, and as she gradually became habituated to her silent and stealthy visits, the thought rose up in her heart that it would be pleasant to sit by him for a while, to watch his gentle and refreshing slumbers, even to tend him as Meeran and the others did, above all, to listen to his converse; but she put these thoughts from her by a violent effort, and when once conquered they returned with less force.

Nor did Kasim occupy a less dangerous position; but his principle of honour was high, and, experiencing the constant kindness of the Khan, shown daily in a thousand acts, could he plot against his honour? His passion had imperceptibly given place during his long and great weakness to a purer feeling, which his best reflections and gratitude to his benefactor daily strengthened.

Weeks, nay months, passed. Kasim's recovery was slow and painful; it was long ere he could even sit up, and speak without pain and spitting of blood. But as his strength enabled him to do so, he was allowed to sit for a while, then to crawl about, a shadow of his former self! He was pitied by all, and there was hardly a man in that camp who did not feel an interest in the life and recovery of the Patél. Often, too, would the Sultaun visit him, and overpower him with thanks for his preservation; and he showed proofs of his gratitude, in advancing him to higher rank, and to a place of trust near his own person.

But the life of dull inaction that he led was irksome to Kasim Ali; the noise of the cannon thundered in his ear, and from the Khan's tent he could see the batteries day after day playing upon the wall, that had hitherto defied them. There was now a huge breach, through which the whole army might have marched, with little chance of opposition; the ditch became gradually filled up by the rubbish, and the fire of the besiegers was but faintly returned by those within; still, however, at times they showed a bold front, and often sallying forth, would do mischief to the advanced posts of the army.

Day after day reports of the progress of the siege, the camp gossip, the arrival of the remains of that splendid embassy which the Sultaun had sent to Constantinople, and the failure of its purpose, and the immense sums it had cost, were retailed to Kasim by the Khan and others; but he was helpless, and, though he longed again to mix in the strife and to strike a blow for the faith, the power was denied him.

Meanwhile the Sultaun had been a severe sufferer; the sprain of his foot was acutely painful, and subsided only after a tedious confinement, during which his temper had been more than usually capricious. The failure of his noble embassy to Turkey, the immense sum it had cost him, without any equivalent, except a letter of compliment from the Sultaun of Constantinople, the true value of which he could justly appreciate—the continued preparations of the English, the Mahrattas, and the Nizam, and their united power—pressed on him with force and occupied his thoughts by day and his dreams by night.

He had summoned the heaviest of his artillery from Seringapatam, and in time he had completed a breach, some hundred yards in extent, which invited attack; at length it was made. Opposition there was none, and the army, thirsting for revenge and plunder, poured upon the now defenceless territory of Travancore. Impelled by a smarting sense of the degradation they had suffered in the attack on the wall, and in the subsequent delay which had occurred before the storming of the breach, the army now gave itself up to frightful excesses. The inhabitants were hunted like wild beasts, shot and speared by the merciless soldiery—their women and children destroyed, or sent into a captivity, to which death would have been preferable. Thousands were forcibly made to profess the faith, and amidst the jeers of the rabble were publicly fed with beef and forced to destroy cows, which they had hitherto venerated.

But the necessities of his position began at length to press hard upon the mind of the Sultaun; he was far from his capital; in his present condition he was unable to strike a blow against his enemies; and, though he had endeavoured to mislead the English by plausible letters, and protestations of undiminished friendship, yet he could not disguise from himself that there was a stern array of preparation against him, which required to be met by decisive and vigorous operations.

'They shall see—the kafir English!'—he exclaimed in his Durbar, after the receipt of a letter from his capital, which warned him of danger; 'they shall see whether the Lion of the Faith is to be braved or not. Mashalla! we have hitherto been victorious, and the stars show our position yet to be firm; our dreams continue good, our army is faithful and brave, and those who remember the triumphs of Perambaukum and of Bednore will yet strike a blow for the Sultaun.'

These addresses were frequent, and the army was in daily expectation of being ordered to return, but as yet it did not move; the most sagacious of his officers, however, urged it at last with such force upon the Sultaun's notice, that he could no longer delay. 'We must utterly destroy the wall,' he replied to them; 'then we will return.'

And this was done. It was a magnificent sight to see that whole army, headed by the Sultaun himself, advance to the various positions upon the wall, which had been previously assigned, for the purpose of razing it to the ground. As the morning broke, the various divisions, without arms, moved to their posts, where pickaxes and shovels had been already prepared for them. All the camp-followers, the merchants, grain-sellers, money-changers, men of all grades, of all castes, were required to join in the work, and in the enthusiasm of the moment rushed to it eagerly. The Sultaun himself, dressed in gorgeous apparel, and surrounded by his courtiers, his chiefs and slaves, quitted his tent amidst a discharge of cannon which rent the air, the sound of kettle-drums and cymbals, and the shouts of assembled thousands, 'Alla Yar! Alla Yar! Deen! Deen!'

Tippoo rode on Hyder, his favourite elephant: the umbaree he sat on was of silver gilt, the cushions of crimson velvet, and the curtains of the finest cloth with gold fringes. The housings of the noble beast, of crimson velvet trimmed with green, swept the ground. Around him were all his officers, on a crowd of elephants and horses, decked with their richest trappings, and wearing cloth-of-gold or muslin dresses, with turbans of the gayest colours, red and pink, white, lilac, or green, sometimes twisted into each other.

The Sultaun dismounted from his elephant, for which a road had been made across the ditch, and seizing a pickaxe ascended the wall. For a while he stood alone, high upon a pinnacle of a tower, in the sight of his whole army, whose shouts rose to the skies, with pride in his heart and exultation flashing from his eye: his favourite astrologer was beneath him, busied with calculations.

'Is it the time, Sheikh?' he asked: 'surely it is near?'

'My art tells me it will be in a few minutes,' was the reply.

There was a breathless silence; at length the Sultaun's arm was uplifted to strike—the fortunate moment had arrived!

'Bismilla-ir-ruhman-ir-raheem, in the name of the most clement and merciful! Strike, O Sultaun!' cried the Sheikh.

The blow descended, and a shout arose, which mingling with the cannon and the drums, almost deafened the hearers; while each man of that great host applied himself to the task and tore down portions of the wall. Gradually, but rapidly, the long extent within sight disappeared, and in six days the whole for nearly twenty miles had been so destroyed as to make it useless for any purpose of defence. This completed, the army began to retrace its steps toward the capital, soon to enter upon new and fiercer scenes.

CHAPTER XXXIV.

WE must not linger by the way, but at once proceed to the city, where the army has arrived a few days. And now there is bustle, activity and life, where of late all was dull and spiritless. Its arrival has brought gladness to many, but none to her whom we now introduce to the reader.

'And thou hast seen him, Sozun?' said Kummoo, the Khan's wife who has been before mentioned, to her servant, who had always enjoyed her confidence—a woman with a cunning visage and deep-set twinkling eyes; 'thou hast seen him—and how looked he? They say he was terribly wounded, and even now is pale and emaciated.'

'They say truly, Khanum,' said the woman; 'your slave watched for him at the door of his house, and pretending to be a beggar asked alms of him in the name of the Beebee Muriam and Moula Ali of Hyderabad; and when he asked me if I were of Hyderabad, I said yes,—may Alla pardon the lie—and he flung me a few pice; lo, here they are. Yes, lady, he is pale, very pale: he looks not as if he could live.'

'Ya Alla spare him!' cried the lady: 'when I last saw him he was a gallant youth; he was then going with the Khan to the Durbar; and as I beheld him urging his noble courser to curvet and bound before this window, my liver turned to water, and, as I live, his image hath been in my heart ever since.'

'Toba! Toba! for shame! Beebee,' said the woman in a mock accent of reproof. 'How can you say so—and you a married woman?'

'And if I am married,' cried the lady, while her large lustrous eyes flashed with the sudden light of passion, and her bosom heaved rapidly, 'if I am married, what of that? Have I a husband, or one that is less than a man? Have I children, have I love? have I even a companion? Have I not hate where there should be love—barrenness, where children should have blessed me—a rival, whose beauty is the only theme I hear, to insult me? Have I not all these, Sozunbee? Thou hast had children—they have loved thee, their merry prattle hath sounded in thine ears, they have sucked their life from thee. Thou wast ground by poverty, and yet wast happy—thou hast told it me a thousand times. I am rich, young, and beautiful; yet my lord hath no pleasure in me, and I am a reproach among women. Why should I honour him, Sozun? I love—why should I not be beloved? Ya Alla kureem! why should I not be beloved?'

'It is possible,' said the dame.

'Possible!' echoed the lady, panting with excitement; 'I tell thee it must be. Listen, Sozun—thou canst be secret; if thou art not, were I turned into the street to-morrow I would dog thee to thy death, and thou well knowest my power is equal to my determination. I love that youth: he is noble, his large eyes speak love, his form is beautiful—Mejnoon's was not more fair. I could sit and gaze into his eyes, and drink in the intoxication of this passion for ever. Dost thou hear? He must know this; he must feel that I will peril life, fame, all for him. Thou must tell him this, and bring him here, or take me to him,—I care not which.'

'There will be peril in it, my rose,' said Sozun.

'And if there is, dost thou think that would deter me?' cried Kummoo, in a tone of bitter scorn; 'were there a thousand more perils than thou, whose blood is now cold, canst see or imagine in my path, I could see none. If thy heart burned as mine doth, Sozunbee,' she added, after a pause, 'thou wouldst think on no peril—thou wouldst only see a heaven of bliss at the end—the path between would be all darkness and indifference to thee.'

'I have felt it,' said the woman with a sigh.

'Thou?'

'Yes, Beebee. I thought no one would have ever known it but he and I; and he long ago died on the battle-field. Thou hast surprised me into confessing shame.'

'Then thou wast successful?'

'Even so,' replied the woman, covering her burning face from the earnest gaze of her mistress. 'I was young as thou art; he loved me, and we met.'

'Then by that love, by the memory of that hour, I conjure thee, Sozunbee, as thou art a woman, and hast loved, aid me in this, and my gratitude shall know no bounds; aid me, and I will bless thee awake and asleep—aid me, or I shall go mad. I have endured thus long without speaking, and methinks as I now speak my brain becomes hot, and it is harder to bear than if I had been silent.'

'I will, Khanum, I will,' cried the woman; I will do thy bidding, and only watch my opportunity. At times he walks on the northern rampart alone—I will meet him there.'

'Give him these, then, and thou needest not speak much; he is learned, and will understand them. There is a clove, that will tell him I have long loved; there is a pepper-corn, to bid him reply quickly. Now begone; come to me when thou hast seen him, but not till then. I shall burn with impatience, but I can wait. May Alla speed thee!'

The woman took her departure, and Kummoo, looking from her lattice window, watched her across the large square, till she disappeared behind some buildings.

'Ya Alla, should he despise me, should he spurn me!' she thought; 'should he— But no, he will not; he is young, he will hear I am beautiful, and his blood will burn as mine does now. Then he shall know what woman's love is, and we will fly together, whither I care not.'

'Kummoo, sister!' said a voice behind her, at which she started, and the blood rushed to her face.

'Why, Hoormut, is it thou? How thou didst startle me. I thought—but no matter: what seekest thou?'

'Hast thou seen Ameena since she arrived?'

'No—why dost thou ask me of one so hateful? Dost thou think I would go to seek her?'

'I know thou wouldst not; but I heard that she had received rich presents from the old dotard, and I went to see them. It was true, they are superb.'

'Holy prophet! what are they? Presents! and we have not even clothes fit to wear.'

'There were shawls and brocades, and jewels too,' returned Hoormut; 'and a goldsmith sat in the verandah making gold anklets, whose weight must be immense. I tell thee we are fools to bear this, and to preserve a civil demeanour to them. Hast thou seen the Khan of late?'

'No,' replied Kummoo, 'we are thrown by and neglected now, for her. It was to be expected that it would come to this, when we received her as if she was welcome, instead of making the Khan eat dirt as he deserved.'

'And yet thy mother counselled that it should be so.'

'She did; she thought that by means of the law we might get rid of her; but it seems there is no hope, for a man may have four wives lawfully, and this was a regular marriage; the Khan has the papers. But my mother will aid us; trust me that she loves me too well not to resent the insult which has been offered me. By the Prophet, that should be her palankeen crossing the square! it may be coming hither. It is—it is!' she exclaimed, as she looked from the window; 'it has stopped at the gate. She must have news for us, that she comes out from home.'

The old lady's heavy tread was soon heard on the stairs, and both flew to meet her at the door. As she entered she embraced both cordially, and they led her to the seat of honour.

A hooka was quickly brought, and as soon as she had taken breath, she began to smoke and to speak.

'And art thou well, Kummoo-bee?' she said to her daughter. 'Thou art thin: Mashalla! time was when thou wert fatter. Sozun came to me a short time ago, and said thou wert low-spirited, so I have come to see thee.'

'I have little to do but eat vexation,' said Kummoo with a pout; 'have I not a rival? and is not that enough to make my days unhappy and my nights sleepless?'

'And one who is loaded with rich gifts, while we are denied new clothes,' said Hoormut, joining in. 'O mother, canst thou listen to our shame and not aid us? once thou didst promise thou wouldst.'

'It is her beauty which makes that old dotard fond of her,' said Kummoo. 'For she has no spirit—she is like a sheep; if that were blighted, he would shake her off at once.'

'Is there no means of turning him from her?' said Hoormut, drawing nearer; 'you, my mother, once said you had a woman servant who was wise and could command spells; could she not aid us?'

'She is ill,' said the old lady; 'then she was well. She was preparing the incantations necessary for her purpose when the Khan left this on service; they have been neglected since then, but she may be able to resume them. I will inquire of her.'

'Couldst thou not send for her, mother?' said Kummoo.

'She is ill—nevertheless she may come. Yes, let the palankeen go, and here is my ring: let her know that she is wanted.'

Kummo hurried to the door, and dispatched a slave with the ring and a message in her mother's name: they soon heard the bearers depart.

Not much conversation passed till the return of the palankeen, for the subject was not an agreeable one to any of them, and the ladies had nothing but their own fancied insults and neglects to reflect upon. At last the palankeen arrived, and they soon had the satisfaction to behold the old woman hobble into the room, supporting herself on a stick.

Kummoo and the other flew to assist her. 'Welcome, mother!' cried both; 'your coming is happiness, may your steps be fortunate!'

'Alla kureem!' sighed the old woman, as she sank down on some soft cushions which had been spread for her. 'Alla kureem! I bless the Prophet and the Imaums and the spirits of good that I am here in safety; it is a fearful thing for one so old to venture forth. Art thou well, Kummoo-bee?' she asked, peering into her face with her yellow eyes, and into Hoormut's also, who now sat by her.

'As well as may be, mother,' said the girl, 'when I am not loved nor honoured in my house; hast thou no charm to preserve the love of men—none to destroy a rival?'

'Then this is why thou wouldst see me,' exclaimed the old woman; 'in trouble only Kureena is sure to be sent for and consulted; is it not so?'

'Thou knowest, for my mother says she has told it you, of the shame, the neglect, the insult, and bitterness which we endure daily. We have no honour as wives—we are as faded flowers, thrown aside for a fresh one which he hath lately taken to his bosom.'

'Thou art not faded, Kummoo,' said the crone, patting her cheek; 'thy hand is soft and warm, thine eye is lustrous and full of fire, thou art not faded.'

'No, Mashalla! I am not; but cease this trifling: wilt thou aid us? hast thou spells? hast thou blighting, withering curses, to fall on one who has despoiled us of our honour and made us a mockery among women?'

'Ay, Alla knows!' joined in Hoormut-bee; 'wherever I go I am taunted with this shame; one tells me the Khan's new wife is beautiful—another speaks of the magnificent gifts she has received, and I feel that I could eat my very fingers for shame. Mother, for the sake of the Prophet, aid us!'

'Thou seest the strait they are in, Kureena,' said Kummoo's mother.

'Can they do like me?' cried the old woman in a cracked tone; 'can they keep fasts and do penances to fit them for the work, to make the spells sure? can they dare to be present while these are said in the silence of the night, and when the spirits who obey them are hovering near to receive them?'

The women shuddered; superstitious terror for the moment asserted its full sway over them: but Kummoo's was a daring spirit.

'I can, mother!' she cried, striking her breast; 'I dare to follow thee, were there a thousand devils in my path, so that I had my revenge.'

The woman peered into her face. 'I thought I had been stout-hearted myself,' she said; 'but, young and ignorant as thou art of this matter, I should have trembled; thou dost not fear?'

'I know no dread when I have a purpose before me,' said the lady proudly; 'art thou thus minded, Hoormut-bee?'

'Inshalla! I will do as thou dost,' returned the other; 'whither thou leadest, I will follow.'

'Enough!' cried the crone; 'can we be alone here when the time comes, of which I will forewarn ye?'

'We can,' said Kummoo, 'without a chance of interruption.'

'Good—but no, it will be better done yonder, at thy mother's: there all can be prepared.'

'It will be less dangerous there,' said the old lady; 'thou canst do thy work in the closet which is off the private room. And when, Kureena-bee, shalt thou be ready?'

'In a month, perhaps: the spell is a heavy one to work, and requires preparation and thought, lest anything should be omitted. Ye must send Fatehas to the shrine, feed Fakeers in your presence, eat cooling victuals, and abstain as much as may be from meat. Thus ye will be prepared; but on me will fall the sore fast and penance: it is hard for an old woman to endure, but ye are in an evil strait, and I were ungrateful for years of protection from your house, Kummoo-bee, and for the salt I have eaten, did I refuse you my aid. And now bid me depart, for I have much to do ere night.'

'Not till you have eaten,' cried Kummoo; 'Mashalla! are we inhospitable?'

'Not a mouthful, not a taste,' said the old woman rising. 'No food must pass my lips, save what is cooked by my own hands till the spell is finished; the vow is upon me, and I must begone.'

'Alla Hafiz!' then cried both the ladies, leading her to the door, 'we trust to thee, mother; do not forget us.' In a few minutes the sound of the bearers was heard, as they rapidly traversed the street below them.

'She is as true as a soldier's sword,' said Kummoo's mother, who had been almost a silent listener to the conversation; 'she will not disappoint ye. Many a time hath she protected thee, Kummoo, from the evil eye, when it was upon thee—many a time wrought a spell for me, by which thy father's love returned when I had fancied it was grown cold; and thou hast more courage than ever I possessed—thy work will be the surer.'

'Inshalla!' said Kummoo, 'I feel as though I had that hated girl within my grasp, and could crush her.'

'Hush!' said her mother, 'thou shouldst not hate so.'

'I hate as I love, mother; and those who reject the one, provoke the other; thou shouldst know me by this time.'

Her mother was silent; she knew well the temper of her daughter, and her uncontrollable passions. 'It is their destiny,' she thought, 'let them work it out; I dare not oppose it.' And when the palankeen returned, she took her leave.

Meanwhile the object of this unprovoked hate was daily becoming more and more precious to the Khan. Returned from active service, while his risala continued absent under the command of his two subordinates, in the seclusion of the zenana he delighted to pass most of his time in Ameena's company, and his sole study seemed to be to provide for her comfort, to deck her with the costliest robes, to have jewels made for her of extreme value, to get up entertainments, to which the other wives were sometimes, but rarely invited; he could not bear the remembrance of the bitter days he had passed with them, when Ameena, in her beauty and purity, and mild and gentle disposition, was before him

Ameena's beauty too now appeared to increase daily; for in the cool and shady zenana her complexion had assumed a more delicate tint, and her skin become softer and more polished. It was ravishing to the Khan to behold her, as she moved about the court of her zenana, tending her few flowers, that bloomed beside a small fountain which always threw up a tiny column of spray, or ministering to the wants of her various favourites. Above her the broad matted leaves of the plantain mingled with the lighter sprays of the cocoa-nut and betel-palm, and a huge tamarind-tree threw its broad shadow over all, forming that refreshing green light so grateful to the eye. The walls of the court were kept carefully white-washed, and the area spread with the finest gravel.

On two sides there were open rooms, supported upon rows of pillars and arabesque arches, which were carved and painted in quaint devices; costly carpets were spread upon their floors, and in the centre was placed a musnud, covered with white muslin, upon which rested soft cushions of crimson velvet. On a perch was a gorgeous looree, whose brilliant plumage glittered in hues of gold and blue and scarlet; and there were two or three cages hanging within, wrapped round with muslin cloths, and gaily decorated with coloured beads and bells, from which larks poured their merry song, now trilling their own joyous notes, now imitating a hundred sounds of other birds with which they had become familiar. A young gazelle, with a collar of red velvet about its neck, with tiny bells sown to it and fastened around its fore legs above its knees, frisked here and there in merry play; and high above the trees soared a number of beautiful pigeons, enjoying the bright and glowing sun and the fresh air in which they sported.

These were daily sights, and the Khan would lie beholding Ameena's graceful actions, now and then bursting out into a torrent of praise of her beauty, and now joining in her tasks of feeding her birds or her pigeons, or would call them for her when they appeared to fly far away from her gentle voice. And their time passed peacefully on, marked by no occurrence whereby they could remember its flight—a continued stream of quiet pleasure, down which the Khan suffered himself to glide, enjoying the peaceful contrast to the life of turmoil he had passed in the camp; the more so as it showed to him the character of Ameena in its true light, that of domestic intercourse, freed from the interruption of others.

Kasim Ali too was his constant guest and companion; his wound had healed after tedious months of suffering; long after the army had arrived at Seringapatam he was unable to resume any duty or his attendance upon the Sultaun, and his time was passed mostly in company with the Khan, assisting him in the business of his risala, writing letters for him, or examining his accounts. He still retained too the happiness of occasional intercourse with Ameena, by means of the old servant; and as often as he received fruit, or any delicacy she thought acceptable to his weak condition, the gift was accompanied by kind messages, which Meeran would fain persuade him meant more than was apparent.

To Kasim Ali her love was too precious a thought to part with easily, and he clung to it with all the ardour of his soul, for he felt himself alone among that host. He possessed acquaintances, it was true, but they were either the wild and debauched characters of the army, whom he had met now and then on service, and in his attendance at the Durbar, with whom he had no congeniality of feeling—or the friends of the Khan, elderly men, who looked on him as a youth of inexperience, and with whom it would be beneath their importance to associate. But Kasim was content as it was. In the business the Khan provided for him there was enough of employment, and his weak state and constant ill health prevented him from seeking other society. Day after day he was seen in the Khan's Durbar, acting as his secretary, and fulfilling the duties of that important trust far more efficiently than the Mutsuddees* whom the Khan had hitherto employed.

We have before mentioned the extensive system of peculation practised by Jaffar Sahib, of whom indeed we have long lost sight; but as he was employed in a different sphere from the persons who belong to our history, we have not thought it worth our while to follow him into his career of oppression and spoliation, where he revelled in all the opportunies of gratifying his worst passions; nor was he a singular instance in the army of the Sultaun. Bigots in faith, zealots in the practice of it, there was no greater enjoyment to hundreds than the destruction of the Hindoos in those provinces of Malabar which had gradually been driven into rebellion, and afterwards conquered by the Sultaun, as we have already mentioned.

Employed with a portion of the risala, he had carried out to the letter the instructions which the Sultaun had personally communicated to him. Burn, slay, destroy, convert, were the reiterated orders, and they were literally obeyed. Jaffar Sahib had been with the camp only for a few days, when the storming of the breach was expected; and that having taken place, he was sent, with the rest of his own character, to finish the work in the defenceless territories of Travancore. But he had at last been withdrawn from thence, and was now attached to the large cavalry force which held possession of the plain of Coimbatoor, and guarded the passes into the table-land of Mysore.

To the Jemadar's system of deception, however, Kasim Ali fancied he had at length gained a clue, when it was prominently brought to his notice by the Khan himself, who, much disturbed upon the subject, one day handed him a letter he had received

* Clerks.

from the Bukhshee* of the army, who, it seemed, had detected the false accounts the Jemadar had furnished.

'The worst of all is,' said the Khan, after they had spoken a long while upon the subject, 'the demand which the Government will make upon me for the arrears of this peculation, for it would appear that it has gone on for a long time.'

'For years, Khan Sahib,' replied Kasim; 'here they give you the dates. I think I had better go over to the Bukhshee, and get access to the whole of the accounts which have been made out; we may perhaps detect the whole matter, and trace it to its source.'

'A wise thought, Kasim—I will go with thee. But that the honour of Rhyman Khan is too well known, this might brand me for ever with infamy.'

They went. The Khan was too well known to have such a request refused; and day after day did he, with Kasim and secretaries, pore over the accounts, sometimes thinking they had discovered the cheat, at others almost despairing, so cleverly had the matter been managed. The delay and consequent vexation was beginning to have a serious effect on the Khan; when, after a day of severer toil than usual, Kasim had no doubt remaining that the whole of the papers had been written by the Moonshee, whose disgrace we have mentioned, though the handwriting was feigned and altered in all; and he mentioned his suspicion to the Khan.

This seemed to throw a new light upon the subject; they knew that the Moonshee was still attached to the person of Jaffar Sahib as a kind of secretary, for he could not write himself, and it became a matter of paramount importance to separate him if possible from the Jemadar; nor was this difficult to manage. A few men of the risala always remained with the Khan, under the charge of Dilawur Ali Duffadar, the rough old soldier we have before mentioned. He bore the Jemadar no very good will, and readily undertook to carry off the Moonshee, unknown to his protector, and bring him to the city.

Accordingly, he took his departure the following morning with six resolute fellows, and by rapid marches soon gained the camp. Here, however, it was no easy task to apprehend the person they sought, for he kept constantly with the Jemadar, and it was necessary he should not know of the proceeding; but they succeeded at last. The Moonshee was decoyed to the outskirts of the camp by one of the men disguised as a Fakeer, where they were met by the Duffadar and his mounted party, and in

* Paymaster.

spite of his prayers, protestations, and threats, he was carried rapidly towards the city.

The rage of Jaffar Sahib was excessive when he fancied himself deserted by his dependent; no one could tell how he had disappeared or whither he had gone; the last known of him was that he had been seen in the company of a Fakeer, going in a certain direction. Jaffar Sahib was seriously uneasy at his supposed defection, not only because he had now no one on whom he could depend to transact his intricate business, but because this man knew more of his secret transactions than he cared to entrust to any one else, and which if divulged would be his ruin.

The arrival of the Moonshee was a source of true joy to the Khan and Kasim; at first, as might be expected, he knew, or pretended to know, nothing about the matter; but the suspicion was so strong against him, that the Khan, by a short mode of doing justice often practised in India, directed that no water should be given to him till he confessed the whole.

The threat was in the end sufficient; the fellow held out most vehemently for about a day, and then, overcome by terror at their determination, and threats that this was only the commencement of his punishments, declared he would confess all; and he unfolded secretly to the Khan and Kasim the whole of the deceits which had been practised from the first. Every account was gone through, and a fearful array of peculation registered against the Jemadar, who was written to, to make the best of his way to the city to answer the complaint against him. Ere the messenger reached the camp, however, the Jemadar had arrived at the city; for his active emissaries had traced the arrival of Dilawur Ali and his party, and their sudden departure, and it was evident that they must have carried off the Moonshee.

CHAPTER XXXV.

THE detection of his long concealed and successful peculations was a thunderbolt to the Jemadar. The Khan refused to see him, or to hear any exculpation he had to urge; and then, knowing the influence Kasim Ali possessed with his commander, he sought him, and implored him to use his influence with the Khan for pardon and for silence on the subject; he became abject, he even threw himself at the young man's feet, and when these failed, offered him a bribe to accede to his terms. It wanted but this to excite Kasim Ali's full indignation: he had despised the man for his meanness, but the insult aroused him, and he spurned the offer fiercely.

'Cheat and rogue!' he cried, 'many a man is whipped through the bazaars for less than this. Inshalla! I shall live to see this done upon thee. I have not forgotten thee, and thou art too well known in the army for any good men to feel regret at thy fate. Men say that thou art a devil, and not a man. By Alla I believe them. Begone! wert thou the Sultaun's son I would spurn thee.'

There was no one near, and the Jemadar eyed Kasim as the thought flashed into his mind that a thrust of his sword or dagger would silence him for ever, and that without his aid the Khan would easily be persuaded to drop the prosecution. Kasim was weak too, and might easily be overcome, and his hand stole to his sword-hilt; but the string which secured it to the scabbard was fast, and he could not draw it; with a muttered curse he clutched a long knife he wore in his girdle, and, on pretence of repeating his request, advanced a step; his eye glistened like that of a tiger about to spring; another moment might have been fatal to Kasim Ali, but he saw the action, and instantly seizing his sword which lay before him he started to his feet.

'I see thy cowardly intention, Jemadar,' he said; 'as yet, I will not draw this weapon, which would be polluted by a coward's blood; but advance one step, and by Alla and the Apostle thou mayest say the Kulma, for thou diest. Begone! in the name of the Prophet, and seek not thine own death.'

The coward attempted to stammer out an excuse, to protest that he had been misunderstood; but he could say nothing intelligible, and he slunk away defeated and mortified, with deadly hate rankling at his heart and urging him to revenge.

'That I should have been foiled by that boy!' he said aloud as he quitted the house; 'that I should have been destined to devour such abomination! that I, Jaffar Sahib, should have been thus trampled upon! Ya Ali! ya Hoosein! grant me power of revenge. Yea, his blood will hardly wipe out the insult I have suffered. Yes, tell him so,' he cried to a woman who he thought watched him; 'tell him so—tell him Jaffar Sahib curses him, and, as there is a light in heaven, will have his revenge for what has happened.'

'Jaffar Sahib!' cried the woman, rushing forward; 'thou canst not be he? thou canst not be he whom I thought dead years ago?'

'Begone! I know thee not; thou art one of his followers, and I curse thee;' and flinging her off, for she had clung to his arm, so violently that she stumbled against a stone and fell, he strode on at a rapid pace.

She arose slowly, and looked after him as he hurried on. 'Holy Prophet!' she said, as she brushed away the dust and her loose hair from her eyes, 'it must be he; his look when he was excited, his very tones, his name too, all are his. Jaffar Sahib! that name hath not sounded in mine ears since we met last, when the bright moon was above us, and the trees casting their deep shade over us veiled that from her prying glare which even now shames me to remember. Holy Alla! he did not remember Sozun! how should he? Years have passed since we were young, and they have not been without effect; and to meet thus, when I had thought him dead long, long ago, and mourned him in my heart! Ya Alla! what destiny is this before me? Be it what it may,' she continued, walking a few paces, 'I will see him, and he shall know that Sozun still lives.'

Jaffar Sahib had but one resource left; and as he hurried along his mind became resolutely bent upon attempting it. To urge the Khan again was impossible, and against Kasim his desire of revenge became more wild and implacable every moment. 'My only refuge is in the Sultaun; I will go to him and confess my fault. If I am fortunate—and who shall dare to say that the destiny of Jaffar Sahib is evil?—there is no worse to be apprehended than if I were proceeded against publicly. I may be fortunate and prevent all.' And thus saying and meditating how he should open his statement, he arrived before the gate of the palace, and entered it hastily; being well known no opposition was made to him, and he passed on to the appartment of those who waited upon the Sultaun, for he well knew that at that hour he must be alone, or in consultation with Purnea, or Kishun Rao, his advisers and ministers.

'Is the Sultaun alone, Abdool Hoosein?' he said, addressing the monarch's chief and confidential attendant, who, with a crowd of others, waited without.

'He is engaged in writing,' said the functionary; 'it would be as much as my life is worth to disturb him. This day he has received letters which have sorely distressed him, and he is not in his right senses.'

'I must see him,' said the Jemadar; 'my business is of the utmost importance.'

'You must write then, for it is impossible for me to mention it,' returned the man doggedly.

'Abdool Hoosein,' said Jaffar Sahib, taking him aside, 'thou knowest we have been friends hitherto, and, Inshalla! mean to continue so. I cannot write what I have to say—it would be impossible; but here is a trifle;' and he slipped a gold coin into his hand.

'It is not enough,' said the attendant, glancing his eye from the money to the giver, for he well knew with whom he had to deal; 'it is not enough—take it back.'

'Nay, be not hasty,' returned the other; 'here is more, but I have no gold.'

'Tis the worse for thee, Jaffar Sahib; I do not move under three gold pieces, and no one else dares to—"

'Take them then in the name of the Shitan,' cried the Jemadar. 'Go! say that I am here, and have a petition to make.'

'The Sultaun thinks thou art at the camp,' said the attendant; ''twas but yesterday he spoke of thee.'

'He will soon know why I am here,' replied the Jemadar; 'but begone! I have neither time nor inclination to bandy words with thee.'

The man went and returned. 'Go,' he said, 'in the name of Sheikh Suddoo, the father of mischief; I would not be present at your interview with the Sultaun for much. Away! he hath sent for thee.'

How the heart of the coward beat as he heard these words; but there was now no means of retreat, and he proceeded.

The Sultaun sat in a small room which communicated with the private apartments of the palace; the walls were plain, but the ceiling was richly painted and ornamented, and the casements and shutters of the windows also. On the floor there was spread a clean white calico covering; and at one end, upon a carpet supported by cushions, surrounded by heaps of papers, and holding in his left hand a stiff leather case, which supported the paper on which he was writing, sat the Sultaun.

Jaffar Sahib hesitated for a moment at the door, for he had looked through a chink, and seen that there was a frown on the Sultaun's brow, and that peculiar expression about his mouth which was always the precursor of mischief; but there was no time allowed him for reflection. The Sultaun had heard and called to him; and the Jemadar, hastily entering, at once threw himself at full length flat on the ground before him, with his arms and legs extended, and lay there motionless and silent.

'Why, Madur-bukht, what ails thee? in the name of the Prophet speak and tell; we thought thee at the camp. Why hast thou come here without leave? why hast thou transgressed orders, and the regulations of our army, which were drawn up with our own wisdom and are perfect models of military knowledge. Speak, O Kumbukht! O man without a destiny! why art thou come?'

'Pardon, O Asylum of the World!' cried the Jemadar, not daring to look up; 'thy slave's fault is great, and his liver is turned to water; I crave forgiveness ere I can tell my errand. My lord is generous—he will forgive magnanimously and will not punish the error of his slave.'

'Get up, in the name of the Prophet! and tell thy tale; do not lie snivelling there like a Hindoo: by Alla! thou remindest me of the Brahmin who said thou hadst plundered him, and whom we—but no matter. Get up! or by the Apostle I will prick thee with my sword;' and he drew it.

'Alla and the Prophet be my refuge, and the saints Hassan and Hoosein!' cried the man, rising up and joining his hands, while he trembled fearfully; 'if thou art against me, O Sultaun, I have no refuge in the world; may I be your sacrifice! I will speak the truth; why should I tell a lie?'

'Speak, then, and say it, Madur-Bukhta!' cried the Sultaun impatiently; 'dost thou think that we, the beloved of Alla, on whom rest the cares and protection of this kingdom, and of the true faith in Hind—dost thou think that we have nought to do but listen to thy prating? Quick!'

'Huzrut!' said the Jemadar, his agitation almost denying him utterance; 'thou mayest order me to be blown away from a gun, if what I say be not true.'

'Well!' exclaimed the Sultaun, 'what more?'

'I am disgraced—my character is gone—I have no friend—no, not one. Rhyman Khan and his minion Kasim Ali have leagued together to blast my reputation and to ruin me.'

'Hold!' cried Tippoo; 'the one is a man I am proud to call my friend, the other saved my life; beware how thou namest them.'

'May I be your sacrifice! thou mayest hang me if it be not the truth; listen and judge:—when I was with the camp, engaged in the Sircar's affairs, my Moonshee, a humble man, disappeared; your slave thought he had been murdered, and became uneasy; he discovered in a few days that the Khan had sent a party of the risala and carried him away privately; since then he and Kasim Ali have kept him here, tortured him, and made him draw up a declaration that your slave had made false accounts.'

'Ha!' said the Sultaun; 'but go on.'

'Yes, false accounts, protector of the poor! I who have fed on the Sircar's bounty, I who have eaten the Sircar's salt, who am a Khanazad,*—that I should do so base an act!'

'Peace!' exclaimed the Sultaun; 'I see by thine eye, Jaffar Sahib, that thou art guilty; there is no hiding truth from me. As I slept one night, the dream is recorded, the angel Gabriel appeared to me. "Thou art a Sultaun," he said, "and the destinies of thousands and millions are in thy hands; thou shalt be able from henceforth to detect a lie at once," and so saying he vanished: and I, who am a child of clay, and not worthy of the honour, feel that he said truly. Dost thou not tremble as I read thy heart in thine eye, and see that thou art a thief? yes, thou dost wince—the thief of the Sircar Khodadad.† Shall I have thee taken into the square, Kumbukht, and set in a high place, and a proclamation made that thou art a thief? Toba! Toba! wert thou not content with the plunder of the infidels, but thou must needs steal from us? Ya Alla kureem! grant us patience to bear this.'

'Enough! enough, O fountain of mercy!' said the trembling wretch; 'enough; I beseech you by my long and faithful service to forgive me, to pardon the past, to keep me from shame. I am your slave, I lick the dust of your feet! Holy Alla! be my aid, and ye saints and martyrs in whose name I have slain and despoiled infidels!'

'Who is this grovelling wretch?' said Meer Sadik the Dewan, and Kishun Rao the Treasurer, who then entered.

'Ay, who is he? ye may well ask,' replied the Sultaun; 'one who, Inshalla! has owned himself to be a thief,—to have taken the Sircar's money,—to have been unfaithful to his salt.' And then, though the miserable Jemadar pleaded hard for mercy, he told all he had guessed at, and invented the rest, joking the while upon the affair, at the expense of the culprit, who could have borne wrath, but not the cold and bitter irony of the Sultaun, and those who heard it.

'Alla! Alla! this is worse than death,' he cried at length; 'bid me be blown away from a gun, it will be an end to all misery and persecution.'

'Not so fast, Jaffar Sahib,' said the Sultaun; 'we intend, Inshalla! to make thee pay back the money thou hast taken, and to keep thee alive to serve us and eat our salt. What say ye, sirs?' he cried to the others.

'I beg to represent,' said Kishun Rao, 'that your slave hath learned with grief of the peculation which has been discovered in

* One born in the family. † The Government, the gift of God.

the department of the paymaster, from the false accounts of the risalas and the infantry, and was about making a report upon the subject; but enough; here is one culprit, let him smart for it, and the rest will be more careful.'

'Not so! Rao Sahib,' said the Sultaun; 'not so; this man we will pardon, because we have the memory of many of his services in our heart, where, Shookr Khoda! the services of each man of our invincible army is treasured up; this time we will spare his fame. Dost thou hear?' he cried to Jaffar Sahib; 'thou art free to go, and we shall desire Abdool Rhyman Khan to suspend his proceedings; but thou shalt pay to our treasurer two thousand hoons * by to-morrow at this time, if not, it will be worse for thee.'

'I call the Prophet to witness,' cried Jaffar Sahib, 'I have not half the quarter of that sum; five hundred I might perhaps—'

'Peace!' exclaimed the Sultaun; 'how darest thou to swear to a lie in the presence of the friend of the Apostle? I have spoken.'

'I have it not—where am I to find such a sum?'

'In hell!' roared the Sultaun, 'where I will send thee to seek it, if thou delayest one moment beyond the time. Begone! Look thou to this, Kishun Rao—we have spoken, and we will be obeyed; we shall expect thy report punctually.'

Jaffar Sahib silently made his obeisance, and retired burning with shame and anger, and renewed threats against Kasim, the author of all. Alone he could have borne the Sultaun's irony and bitter words, but that others should know of his detection and disgrace was more than he could endure. He did not wait to speak to those in the ante-chamber, but hurried at once to his temporary lodging in the bazaar.

'We have sent for you, my friends,' said the Sultaun to his ministers, after a short pause, 'to advise with us regarding momentous affairs which press upon our notice; not that we need advice—for, by the blessing of the Prophet! whose agent we are upon earth, and the favour of the Most High, we receive such intimations of our destiny in dreams, and by secret and holy communings with the saints, that our path is clearly marked out for us; but there are, nevertheless, matters which we have heard of within the last few days that disturb our rest. The kafir Feringhees of Madras have written to us, and remonstrated sharply for our atttack upon Travancore; they have the insolence to demand satisfaction for it, and the price of what was destroyed. Vain arrogance! they should know us better, than

* A hoon is about four rupees.

to think a mere threat could disturb the ruler of the kingdom which Alla hath given into our hand. They are making mighty preparations for war; they have incited the kafir Mahrattas (may their end be perdition!) and the imbecile ruler of Hyderabad to join against me. Nay, be not surprised; for though these have been the reports of the bazaars for months, yet we did not believe them; but here are the proofs:' and he handed to them the letters he had received, containing the intelligence, which they perused in silence.

'And now listen,' he continued, his mean features lighting up with a sudden excitement; 'listen to the revelation we have had from Alla himself. These letters arrived but yesterday; and as we lay cogitating upon their contents, and praying to Alla to enable us to devise some means of extrication from the difficulty, our eyes closed and we fell asleep. Soon, however, gorgeous visions began to crowd upon us, and shapes of glory, which, though almost indefinite, yet hovered around, filling the mind with wondrous delight; as we looked, we heard a voice which said, "Art thou hungry, O Sultaun?" and then I bowed down and cried, saying, "I lack food, O Alla! but it is revenge for the blood of the martyrs shed in thy cause, and I am hungry for aid, that all thine enemies may be subdued, and the banner of the faith float proudly over the realms of Hind, even as it did of yore under the power of Delhi;" and then, even as I finished speaking, three trays, whose surface sparkled with the light of Heaven, and upon which were piled fresh dates, the food of the true believers in paradise, descended to me, and the angel said,—"Eat, O beloved of the Apostle! and thou wilt be able to discern the hidden meaning of this vision:" and I ate; and lo! there came light into my heart, and I know that the three trays of dates were the dominions of the three confederates my enemies, and they were sweet to the taste, even as victory is sweet to the soldier.'

'Ajaib! most wonderful! most extraordinary!' echoed the two listeners, who were provoked enough at this puerile harangue. 'Inshalla! there is no fear.'

'Fear!' cried the Sultaun bitterly; 'fear! no, there is no fear; there is joy that at last we shall have them in our power. In a few months the King of the Afghans will rise in our favour, and, leagued with the Rajah of Nipaul, and the rulers of Joudhpoor and Jynuggur, who shall be able to withstand them? The French will rise with ten thousand men; our valiant troops are a lakh and more. Pressed on all sides, our enemies will fall; and then for revenge and plunder!' As he spoke his eyes flashed fire, his action was high and restless, and even that sedate counsellor the Dewan caught a portion of his excitement.

'Upon them then,' he cried, 'in the name of Alla! Syud Sahib is below the passes with all the cavalry. Bangalore hath a gallant commander, and the garrison is staunch and true; there is plenty of powder and ball; to the north are all the Droogs,* for the Mahrattas and Nizam to break their force against. Inshalla then! unfurl the standard of the faith in Durbar this night, and cry Alla Yar! He who is faithful to his creed and his Sultaun will follow thee to the death.'

'Asylum of the World!' said an attendant, entering; 'these letters have just arrived, and are said to contain news from the army; there hath been fighting.' And he laid them at Tippoo's feet.

'Ha!' cried the Sultaun exultingly, taking them up and tearing the covers off as he looked at the seal; 'Syud Sahib! then the English must have advanced. Now listen, my friends, to news of victory. Inshalla! the Syud is a brave man and a skilful general—' But, as he read silently, they saw his features change in expression; his brow contract; his lips become compressed; a nervous twitching of his face commenced, which always expressed his violent agitation, and they exchanged significant glances with each other. At last he was no longer able to bear his vexation, and broke out into a paroxysm of rage.

'Ya Futteh-o! Ya Alla Mousoof! A hog, and not a man, hath done this—a coward and a fool! not Syud Sahib, but Syud Ahmuk!—beaten—disgraced—foiled by the kafir English—forced to retire beyond the Bhowanee, and he is now close upon the Guzalhuttee pass. O saints and martyrs! grant me patience to read, to hear all;' and he read on. 'Reinforcements? infantry and guns?—that they may be led into evil, and lost to me! Never, by the Prophet! never, by the soul of my father!—may his sepulchre be honoured! Thou mayest even fight it out, Syud, or return disgraced; thou shalt have the option. What think you, sirs?'

'It is heavy news,' said Meer Sadik, 'and enough to ruffle my lord's temper; but the Syud is wary and cautious. Perhaps the English force is overwhelming, and he has wisely retired before it, drawing them into a snare, from whence it will be impossible to escape.'

'Ha! thinkest thou so? By Alla! a good thought; he shall have the men and the guns; we will write the order now

* Hill-forts.

to the commanders of the Cushoons* to attend the evening Durbar.'

'I beg to represent,' said Kishun Rao, 'that in such an undertaking there is no one like thyself, O Sultaun; under thine own eye all will go well; without thee, there is fear and hesitation, for the responsibility is great.'

'Well spoken,' responded the monarch; 'we have—blessed be the Dispenser of Wisdom!—such military skill, that before it the genius of the kafir English is nothing, and their livers become water. Was it not so in Baillie's affair? Inshalla! then, we will lead this expedition, and there will be many such.'

'And,' continued the Rao, 'what is there to prevent the victorious army, when it has driven the English beyond the boundary, to follow them to the gate of Madras—to burn, to slay, to plunder, and destroy all? The French, their bitter enemies, will rise upon them; and when the success is noised abroad, the Mahrattas, who hate them, and the Nizam, who is now under their power, will cast them off; and then what is to prevent the army of the Sircar Khodadad from driving them into the sea, and, with the power thus gained, of turning upon the faithless Nizam and destroying his power utterly? then shall Madras be the seaport of the Sultaun, and he may pitch his tents on the plain of Surroonuggur, and take his pleasure in the palace of the proud ruler of Hyderabad.'

'Mashalla! Mashalla! Inspiration! Inspiration!' exclaimed the Sultaun in rapture; 'it shall be done; the thing is easy. Our dreams forewarned us of this, and behold, our destiny points to it. One victory gained, and the Mahrattas are on our side; Sindia and his power can be thrown into the scale: then with the Afghans, the Rohillas, the brave men of the Dekhan, the Assud Illahee, and the French—Ya Futteh-o! thou wilt grant victory, and our power will reach a pitch such as men will wonder at and admire.'

'But stay, whose letter is this by the same post?' and he opened the envelope. The look of exultation at once gave way to passion. 'Here is another coward, another traitor!—Palghatcherry has fallen! the place we ourselves saw provisioned and garrisoned with the best troops;—shame on them! shame on them! they are women, not men. By Alla! I have women in the Mahal who would have died ere they had suffered a kafir to enter. Now there is a road opened from sea to sea, and the infidel English will not be slow to avail themselves of it. Yet this does but hasten our intentions. Ye have your leave now to

* His division of regular infantry were so called.

retire, my friends. Go, and say there will be a Durbar to-night,—no, to-morrow at noon; for, by the blessing of the Prophet! ere then a new dream may be vouchsafed for our guidance, Khoda Hafiz!'

They withdrew with many obeisances, and the strange being was left to his meditations, and to the wild visions of conquest, which the words of the Rao had resolved into matters apparently within his grasp.

Jaffar Sahib reached his abode with feelings it would be difficult to describe; the money was but a trifle to him in amount, for in his career of rapacity and plunder he had amassed thousands; but it was so lent out among bankers, suttlers, the men of the risala, and those of the bazaar, that he feared he should hardly be able to raise it in time to meet the Sultaun's demand, and without it he had little hope that mercy would be extended to him. As he dismounted from his horse, his attendant Madar met him.

'A woman is within,' he said, pointing to the door of the apartment; 'she came here a short while ago, and would take no denial, saying she would wait for thee.'

'A woman! in the name of the Shitan what doth she want?—is she young and fair?'

'Willa-alum!' replied the man, grinning, 'your worship will see; she is veiled from head to foot.'

'Most strange! Away with ye all from hence, it may be the matter is private, and we would be alone.' As he spoke, he entered the door. There was a small room at the back of the open shop he had hired; a door led from that into a small court, where was a shed for cooking or bathing, and a low verandah. There was no one in the room; he opened the door, and looked around. Close beside it, in the verandah, sat a woman, veiled from head to foot in a thick sheet; she appeared to be trembling violently, for the covering was much agitated.

'Who, in the name of Satan, art thou,' cried the Jemadar, 'who comest at this unseasonable hour?' She did not reply, and he spoke again more roughly.

'Alla be merciful to me! Jaffar,' she exclaimed, throwing herself at his feet, and clasping his knees, while she cast the veil from her, 'it is indeed thou! hast thou forgotten Sozun?'

'Sozun! Sozun!' he repeated, as he drew his hand across his forehead, 'she of Salem? Holy Alla! hast thou risen from the dead? is this a dream?'

'No! no! look on me. My features are wasted, but I am the same; thou didst spurn me a while ago like a dog, and my heart was broken. There was kindness between us once, Jaffar!' and she sighed deeply.

'I knew thee not,' he said, raising her up, and, for the moment yielding to a softer feeling, caressed her. 'I had been maddened! insulted by that dog of a Patél, Kasim Ali. I knew thee not, Sozun.'

'Ha! dost thou know him?'

'To my cost; he and his dotard patron, Rhyman Khan, have despoiled me of money—villified my character; but enough, 'tis no affair of thine. Why dost thou ask?'

'I have too a reckoning to settle with him, but let it pass; we will speak of that which once was pleasant to us. Thou hast not forgotton me then, Jaffar?'

'Alla is my witness—never! But canst thou come hither this night at dusk, unobserved? then we will speak of past times uninterruptedly; now I have affairs of moment to settle, and must begone.'

'I will come surely,' was the reply; 'thy voice is music in mine ears after so long a separation.'

'Follow me then, and I will dismiss thee openly before my servants; but be sure thou dost not fail to-night.'

CHAPTER XXXVI.

LOOKING from her latticed chamber sat Kummoo-bee, her heart beating so that its pulsations seemed audible to her own ear, her bosom heaving as though it would almost burst the bounds of the light boddice which enclosed it, and her eye flashing brightly, as she thought upon the sure success of her mission. Little she heeded the soft and chastening light which the moon's rays cast upon every object around, silvering the tall white minarets of the mosque, till they stood out in perfect relief against the deep blue of the sky, and resting upon the sharp pinnacles of the ancient temples, where all else was lost in shadow. The large courts around them, into which she looked in the day-time, then filled with busy throngs, were now deserted, save by the broad giant shadows which the temple and the trees around it cast across them. Now and then the shrouded form of a Brahmin would pass noiselessly through them, the moon's light resting brightly upon the white drapery around him; but as he hurried on the deep black shadow seemed to enshroud him, and he was no longer discernible within its influence.

As Kummoo sat thus, she would idly speculate, with vacant eye fixed upon some figure in the square beyond, or listen to the hoarse and distant noubut, which, as the night advanced, beat at the tomb of the Sultaun's father, or to the wailing and quivering sound of the brass horns which arose from the camp, when the watch was being relieved. She heeded not the luscious perfume of orange-flowers and tube-roses, which, loading the air, came in at her open window from the garden beneath; but her whole senses were absorbed in one object, which she rather wooed than strove to turn away from her mental vision; at times too a tear would fill her large lustrous eye, and, welling over the lid, trickle down her face unheeded—a tear of burning passion—no soother to her excited mind, but rather aggravating those feelings which had now become almost too painful to be borne.

'What can delay her?' she said, speaking half aloud to herself; 'by this time I might have been with him. Ya, Fatima, aid me! my liver is burnt with passion, and the air which comes to me seems hot—hot with my own breath; I can bear this no longer. Why does she tarry?—she is old, or she might be dallying with him. What if she were? but no, that cannot be—she dared not. She knows well I would tear her limb from limb if she harboured even a thought of his love; and she is faithful too. I must wait; he was away perhaps—he may have been here—here, under this roof, where he little dreamed there existed one whose greatest happiness would be to die at his feet. Holy Alla! who is that?' she cried, as a long train of musing into which she had fallen was suddenly interrupted by the opening of her chamber door. 'Who comes?'

'Sozunbee,' was the reply.

'Sozunbee!' she said, while the blood poured through her frame in wild pulsations; 'and 'tis thou at last! Hither, quick! quick! sit here, and tell me all. I have long, long looked for thee; why hast thou tarried? I am ready now—even now; come, let us haste—what? thou dost not speak! Woman! hast thou done my bidding?—hast thou seen him?—if not, tell me, and I shall be cool—now I am burning!—Ya Alla kureem, burning!' and she fanned herself violently, while her articulation showed that her mouth was quite parched. 'Speak! why dost thou not speak?'

'I have seen him,' was the reply.

'Well! Oh for patience to listen! By Alla! thou canst never

have loved, Sozunbee, or thou wouldst know what it is to have fire within thee—fire!—wilt thou not quench it?'

'It will be hard for thee to hear all, lady; shall I tell it?'

'All—all! thou sawest him—well! why dost thou hesitate?'

'I would spare thee pain; go now to rest, thou wilt be calm to-morrow.'

'Pain! what dost thou mean? Pain!—he cannot—' she almost gasped in a hoarse whisper, while her eyes flashed so that Sozun could hardly bear their intense gaze; 'he cannot have denied me! he dare not have flung aside love like mine! Holy Prophet! Sozun, thou dost jest!' and she laughed wildly.

'May the holy Mother of Ali, and the Lady Murium, and the saints aid thee, my life!' said the woman, rising and passing her hands over her head, to withdraw the evil from her. 'May they give thee peace! As I live I saw him and spoke with him, but thou must be calm ere I tell it thee.'

'I am calm—see, I am quite calm,' she said, making a violent effort to swallow; 'feel my hand—it is cool—I can listen.'

But her hand belied her words; it burned as though she were in a fever, and the quick and strong pulsations of her blood were distinctly perceptible; to delay, however, was but to excite her more.

'I went,' said Sozun, 'to his abode; long I watched at the door: men came and went; the Khan was there; there was haste and bustle, and much deliberation. At last all departed; a Khitmutgar* observed me, and asked me what I did there? I said I would speak with the Syud, that I had a matter to tell him of; he went in, and I followed. I was closely veiled. "Wait here," said the man, "I will inform him." I waited; the moments were like hours. "Go in," said the man when he returned, "he is alone." I trembled as I proceeded, and found myself in his small apartment ere I was aware. The Syud was writing. "Stop! who art thou?" he asked, and his words were sweet as the sound of children's voices at play. I salaamed thrice.'

'Quick! quick! good Sozun, what said he?' asked the lady eagerly. 'I care not what thou didst.'

'Thou shalt hear. "I am your slave," said I, "and bring thee a message—wilt thou listen?" "Say on," he replied, "I hear thee; sit down and speak; hast thou any complaint?" "No, no!" I said, "I have none; cease writing, and listen." He did so: then I untied the corner of my dooputta, and gave him what thou hadst sent. "Dost thou understand the tokens?" I asked.

* Attendant.

'Beebee! he looked sorrowfully on them. "They speak of love," he said; "why hast thou brought them to one who is dying?"

'"She is fair," I said—"most lovely. Her eyes are large, her lips are red; in beauty she is like a rose when it opens to meet the morning sun which drinks the fragrant dew from its cup. She has seen thee, O Syud, and her liver has become water."

'"What misfortune is around me?" he said. There was no anger in his tone, but sorrow. "I have no love now but for one; but let that pass. Go to her who sent thee: say I pity her—say, as we have never met, and I know her not, so let her turn her thoughts to another; she will see many in the Durbar."

'He had thought thee one of the palace dancers; thou knowest they are high and proud, and men account themselves fortunate to win a smile from them: I eagerly undeceived him.

'"She is no Tuwaif," I said; "she is a householder, and as far above them in beauty as the moon is above a star."'

'And what said he, Sozun?'

'Then he grew grave, my pearl, and said sternly,—"Such love is sinful—it is impure; bid her forget it. She hath a lord—what am I to her? Why hath she looked on me with eyes of passion? Begone! say to her, Kasim Ali Patél is no man of dishonour, but pure and unstained; as yet, no dissolute or debauched gallant. Away! thou art an offence to me." Beebee! I tried to speak; he would hear nought. "Begone! begone!" alone sounded in mine ears, and his eyes were so large and so severe that I trembled.'

'And was this all, Sozun? was this all? Ah fool! ah fool! why didst thou not say I was a Tuwaif—anything—a slave—he would have heard thee. Ah fool! couldst thou not have pleaded for me in words—hot, burning words, such as would have inflamed his heart, dried up the cold dew of his virtue, and turned him to me with a love as violent as mine own? Couldst thou not have said that I live upon his look?—one look I had, only one, which mine own thoughts have magnified into years of intercourse—couldst thou not tell him that I am one who will brook no control? Ya Rehman Alla! couldst thou—'

'But he said he loved another,' interrupted Sozun, vainly endeavouring to stem the torrent of her mistress's words.

'What, another! O woman, thou didst not say so—thou didst not dare to say it. He loves another! Then he *can* love, if he has loved another. Who is she? couldst thou discover her, O dull one? A Tuwaif perhaps—some vile and worthless one, some scum of perdition! No, he is too noble for that.—Water, Sozun, water! By Alla, I choke! Enough—now take the vessel. Thou saidst another. Ha! if it were she! *if* it were she! What dost thou think?'

'Who?'

'Ameena! it must be—it can be no other. She is beautiful, very beautiful; he hath saved her life, twice saved it. They have been in camps together, and he must have met her, and then— Dost thou not see all, Sozun, clear to thine eye as daylight? Does it not all open gradually upon thee, as when the dawn of morning dispels the darkness, objects that were before dim and shadowy assume palpable forms?'

'There is suspicion surely, Khanum, but we have never heard aught breathed against her.'

'No, she hath been discreet; but may it not be so? I ask thee calmly, when Alla knows my heart is on fire.'

'It may, but—'

'Enough! enough! we will watch: and she who was born to be my curse—she who hath thrown me from my seat of pride, and intruded between me and my rights—may perchance be rudely thrown from her elevation. Grant it, O Prophet! O ye saints and holy men, grant it! Yes, we will watch now, Sozun; wilt thou not aid me?'

'To the last.'

'Enough then now; this hath calmed me somewhat for the while: revenge is dimly seen in the distance, but it will come, it will come! Now lie down beside me and sleep; the night is far spent, I am weary of watching, and my heart aches, Sozun.'

'Alla keep thee, lady!' returned the other; 'I will watch beside thee for a while, for I feel not sleepy, and the air is pleasant.'

And she watched silently, for her thoughts were busy with the events of that night—her strange meeting with Jaffar, his now apparently reckless character, and the threats he had held out against the young Patél; for she had been with him long, and if they had not renewed the passionate love of former years, he had caressed her, and vowed to befriend the only being for whom he had ever felt affection.

The fresh breeze of night, laden with perfume from tree and flower, poured in gentle whispers through the casement, murmuring and sighing above it amidst the slender leaves of the palms. Abroad all was still, except now and then the bark of a dog, or the call of the sentinels upon the walls to each other that all was well. Gradually the moon's glorious light crept round to the window, and stealing into the room, it wandered over the recumbent figure of the lady till it rested upon her face. 'She sleeps now,' thought Sozun, 'or the light would disturb her; peacefully too! and oh, how lovely her features and those long lashes appear, as the light plays among them, and kisses them in very wantonness. I would he could see her now—he, with those glorious eyes so full of expression, into which no woman could look without love! her fate is in the power of her destiny. May it be propitious! Our paths are dark and rugged before us, yet we must walk on without a light or a guide. And now I will to rest also, for mind and body are both weary.'

Men poured into the Fort from every side the following morning, both officers and men; for the order had gone forth for all to hear the determination of the Sultaun upon the crisis. Elephants and horses, gay palankeens, their bearers striving with each other for precedence, proceeded to the Durbar, exerting their utmost speed with loud cries; and glittering armour, cloth of gold and silver, and the most brilliant silks, satins and muslins, shone in the bright sun, as the turbans, the vests, or the scarfs of the wearers. Rumour had gone forth that the Sultaun himself would proceed against the infidels, and every man was eager to be led to war and plunder—victory in the one, and rich booty in the other, being his by anticipation.

Crowds hurried on. The hall of audience in the palace had long been filled, and the people reached from the entrance far beyond into the courtyard. Cries of 'Deen! Deen! Alla Yar! Alla Yar!' rose perpetually from among the mass, and mingled with the sound of the kettle-drum and shrill pipes, which continued playing while the Durbar was open. The Sultaun was seated upon his throne, over which, suspended by a fine wire, so as to appear really to flutter over him, was hung a golden bird, whose wings and tail, set with precious gems, glittered as the wind stirred it to and fro. This was the Humma, or sacred bird of Paradise, whose shadow, so long as it falls upon a monarch, prevents his sustaining any injury, and to which many miraculous powers were ascribed by the lower order of soldiery, or those who had risen from it. Around Tippoo—some engaged in fanning him, others gently moving peacocks' feathers or tails of the Thibet cow to and fro, to prevent the flies from settling on him—were a number of fair and youthful creatures, whose ruddy or pale cheeks showed their origin to have been in the cold and distant climate of the West. They were all dressed sumptuously as women, they had been instructed in the arts of music and dancing, and were thus held up to the scorn of the people generally, who were taught, by frequent allusions to them, that all English were effeminate cowards, fit only to be dressed as women, and to be engaged in such frivolous occupations. Some of the boys were young, and had known no other existence than that debased slavery. These took pride in their gorgeous dresses, and moved about to display them; others, apparently overpowered by shame at their disgraceful situation, hung down their heads and strove to conceal their faces from the prying glances of the spectators. A miserable lot was theirs: many of them retaining a vivid remembrance of their countrymen, their faith, and their freedom, were obliged to perform a routine of bitterly degrading duties, dancing and singing before the Sultaun for the amusement of the Court; and although many of the spectators pitied the poor boys and their sad fate, yet no one dared to utter a word of sympathy in their behalf, while there were too many who rejoiced in their abject condition.

Seated near the monarch were his sons, three fine youths; and in double and treble rows from the throne, the officers of the army, of the state, his own flatterers and sycophants, and a host of others, as closely packed as it was possible to stand or sit. From time to time some of the boys would perform a dance before him, or a few jesters, buffoons or actors, exhibit some ribald scene: the more their language was indecent and keenly directed against the English, the more applause it received from those present, particularly from the Sultaun, who encouraged them by words and promises of liberal reward; while shouts of laughter would resound through the hall at any successful sally or witty allusion.

The moments were, however, precious; and when the Sultaun observed that the hall was full, the dancers and jesters were dismissed, and silence commanded. The order was obeyed, and all looked with impatience to hear the real result of their monarch's deliberation, in regard to the matter of peace or war, which had so long appeared to be doubtful. For a while he appeared to meditate: then, partly raising himself up, he selected a small paper from among the heap before him, and, ere he read it, spoke to those immediately around him.

'We, whose government is the gift of Alla,' he said, 'desire no concealment in our affairs; therefore listen, O ye faithful, and my friends—we are about to read you a revelation which was vouchsafed to us last night, and which on awaking we recorded; it hath since pleased the author of power to afford our mind a clue to the unravelment of the mystery, and this too we will unfold to you. As we lay asleep soon after midnight, we thought we stood on the shore of the sea, and afar off sailed many great and powerful ships which bore the colours of the English. As we looked, behold a little cloud arose, and soon there was a mighty wind, before which all was scattered, and those who were on the seashore awaiting their arrival returned to their homes dejected and dispirited. These were the kafir Feringhees (may their graves be unblessed !)—they are helpless now ; and, by the favour of the Prophet, as they have provoked a war by their own imprudence and bad faith, they shall find that the men of Islam are ready and willing to fight for their faith.'

'We are ready! we are ready!' cried the assembly with one voice; 'lead us to battle! we are your children—we will fight with you to the death.'

'Listen further,' he continued; 'there was yet another vision more wonderful than the last vouchsafed to us, which proves that all those Moosulmans who fight against us in the armies of the English become hogs when they are stricken with death.'

'They deserve it—they are faithless and treacherous—they sin against the holy Prophet (may his grave have rest !)—so may their ends be perdition and unholy!' shouted many of those who listened, while the rest cried, 'A miracle! a miracle! that such revelations should be made to our Father and our Sultaun!'

'But that was not all,' continued Tippoo; 'for, to prove his words, the angel withdrew a film from before mine eyes, and I beheld a most extraordinary spectacle—one which filled me with amazement: before me stood a man with a hog's head, who, when he saw me, advanced to meet me. "Who art thou?" I said. "I am one of the true faith of Islam," he cried, "but I no longer desire to be called one, for I fought against it under the banners of the infidels, and now I suffer for my indiscretion and faithlessness. I am, as you see, a hog; and these men have all been transformed into hogs; they also were killed in the various engagements with the kafirs; we are in the dreary land of spirits, and thine is permitted to hold communion with ours here, in order that the glory of the faith may be upheld, and the terror of our example made known among thine armies."

'Then methought all became dark and dreary, and a cold wind blew, and before us were shadowy objects which the eye could not determine at first; but as we looked upon the scene, dim forms were seen advancing towards us in lines, even like unto regiments, and the spirit which had spoken to us began to manœuvre them after the manner of the English, with whose system it appeared to be acquainted. But, O my friends, as I looked, all had hogs' faces! and the words of him they obeyed sounded like grunts in our ears. Wherefore we beseech you to consider this thing, and whether it is better to live and die in a natural state—the beloved and chosen of Alla—or whether ye would also be hogs, and wallow in the filth of your own abomination, like unto the Christians and those who serve them?'

'Miracles! miracles!' shouted the assembly; 'the Sultaun is the beloved of Alla! To him alone are now revealed visions and wonderful dreams! for him we will fight, and for the faith!'

'Ay, ye say right,' cried Tippoo; 'very wonderful are the manifestations of Alla to his servant; therefore we shall this day begin our march, for we have heard that the kafirs are below the passes: Inshalla! a few days will bring us up to them, and then we will see whether their pride and haughtiness cannot be humbled. Let us, therefore, join together and send these infidels to the regions of perdition; and if ye be crowned with victory, ye will be full of honour and renown, and become the envy of the world; while to those who fall, martyrs in the cause of Islam, hear what the Prophet (blessed be his name!) hath promised. "They shall enter into pleasant places, where many rivers flow, and curious fountains send forth most murmuring streams, near which they shall repose themselves on soft beds, adorned with gold and precious stones, under the shadow of the trees of Paradise, which shall continually yield all manner of delicious fruits. And they shall enjoy beautiful women, pure and clean, having black eyes and countenances always fresh and white as polished pearls, who shall love none but themselves, with whom they shall enjoy the perpetual pleasures of love, and solace themselves in their company with amorous delights to all eternity; drinking with them most delicious liquors without ever being overcharged by them, which shall be administered by beautiful boys, who shall be continually running round their beds to serve them up to them in cups of gold and glasses fixed on diamonds."'

'We will follow the good path!' cried hundreds, with flashing eyes and fierce gestures; 'show us the infidels, and we will fall on them and annihilate them for ever!'

'Bismilla, so be it!' returned the Sultaun; 'every man to his post! pay shall be issued to all, and to-morrow we shall advance. The planets are in a fortunate conjunction, and the kafirs shall tremble once more at our terrible war-cry of Alla Yar.'

CHAPTER XXXVII.

'NAY, cheer thee, beloved! thou must be now as thou wert ever wont to be, stout of heart and fearless for the future,' said Rhyman Khan to his fair wife, as, on the evening of that day, he sat with her in their quiet secluded apartments, with the moon's broad light playing on the slightly agitated fountain before them, and the cool wind rustling amidst the leaves above their heads. 'Thou must not fear; what is there to dread? Hast thou not thine own nurse with thee, and my household, who are devoted to thee? hast thou not these apartments, where no one dares to intrude without thine especial leave, and a guard of my most faithful men around thee? why shouldst thou fear?'

'My lord,' she said, looking up to him—and it was hard to resist those pleading eyes—'I know I am not worthy to share the fate of one who is honoured in the councils of the Sultaun, and who is respected in the assemblies of the great; yet, if thou art ill, who will tend thee like Ameena? if thou art wounded, who will soothe thy pain? Thou wouldst have no one to cheer thy dulness; even the Patél would fail thee—thou wouldst think of Ameena!'

'But the English, fairest—men affect to despise them, but the Sultaun well knows their power, though he denies it to all, and scoffs at it (I pray Alla, he may feel it not soon)—'tis the English I dread for thee. Fighting with them is not like fighting with the infidel Hindoos, who are slaughtered like sheep, but the war of men against men—the shock of contending armies—the roar of artillery—the rattle of musketry; this thy gentle heart cannot bear.'

'Bid me go before thee into the battle—bid me attend thee as thy servant—bind a turban on my brow and a sword to my waist, and see if Ameena will not follow thee to the death!' she cried, hastily rising. 'If the Mahratta women have done this many a time, thinkest thou that a Moghul of the old and proud blood of Delhi dares not?'

A sudden cry of admiration broke from the Khan. She had arisen from her seat and advanced towards him; her always soft and loving eye was filled with a daring and flashing light; her bosom heaved, and her slight and beautiful form was drawn up to its full height, as she stood almost panting, when she ceased to speak.

'By Alla and the Prophet, thou art fit to be a soldier's wife!'

he cried, starting to his feet; 'one who feels so keenly a soldier's honour and his fame, ought to share it with him. I had not thought that this spirit dwelt within thee. Come to me, girl—henceforth thou needst not fear; come evil or good, thou shalt share it with Rhyman Khan. I swear by thine eyes I will not leave thee; art thou content now?'

'Thou art too kind!' she murmured, as she bowed her head upon his shoulder; 'thou knowest I have none here but thyself, and my home is afar off; thou art father, mother, husband—all to me. I bless thee that thou hast heard my prayer, and that I am not to be left tormented by a thousand fears for thee, and dreads (may they be visionary!) of coming evil.'

'Of evil, Ameena?'

'Ay, my lord; hast thou not felt often, upon the eve of some event in thy life, when, as yet, it had not burst from the womb of futurity, an unknown, undefinable sense of dread which pervaded thy senses, causing thought to be painfully acute, and to run into a thousand channels too intricate to follow for a moment, till it was lost in vague, oppressive conjecture leading to no end?'

'Never, Ameena; I have never troubled myself to think much, but have been content to take events as it pleased Alla to send them.'

'I may be wrong then,' she returned; 'these may be the offsprings of my own imagination only, and not common to others. It is well it is so; they are not enviable.'

'There will be danger, Ameena,' said the Khan, who misapprehended her; 'bethink thee again upon going with me into the rough camp; remember, Kasim Ali will be here, and will protect thee, as he hath done before.'

'Oh no! no! I would not stay—I would not stay with him, but go with thee, my noble lord,' she said, averting her burning face from him; 'for the sake of the Prophet do not mention that again; thou hast already said thou wouldst let me accompany thee.'

'Bismilla! then be it so; yet why turnest thou away? art thou angry that I doubted thy firmness? I never doubted that, girl, since the night when we looked from the tower upon the burning village and those fierce Mahrattas; dost thou remember them?'

Alas! she remembered but too well; and even then the temptation had arisen within her to remain where Kasim Ali was, to be left under his care; but she had put it back with a struggle, and the Khan's doubt of her bravery had rallied her spirit, and with it her best feelings had come to her aid.

'I remember, Khan,' she said carelessly; 'but I would now prepare the few things I shall require, and warn Meeran to accompany me.'

'Go then; I had told the Patél he would have to look after thee, and, strange enough, he thought thou wouldst be better with me as he was not to go. Perhaps he may be in the Dewan Khana, I will go there and seek him.'

Ameena was left alone; how strange it was, she thought, that Kasim should have advised what she herself had suggested; perhaps his dread had been the same as hers, and the very idea brought painful blushes to her face, and led her into a reverie which well nigh upset her resolutions; it would be so easy to change her determination, to confess her fears, to have him near her, to rely on him in all dangers; this would be happiness. But Ameena's virtue was strong, far stronger than her servant's, who at first almost reproached her for the voluntary loss of the opportunity, which, as she said, destiny had presented. Meeran's sophistry was unable, however, to contend with the honest purpose of her youthful mistress, and she at length, but not without some difficulty, yielded to her whim, of which she protested she would be tired enough when the English cannon roared in her ears, and the balls whizzed through the camp.

Ameena might not, perhaps, have held out long against the combined effects of her own inclination and the terrible stories her nurse told her of the furious English; but there was little time for discussion—they were to move on the morrow; preparations for absence, though small, had to be made that night, and long ere noon the following day the army had left the city, for a longer absence than was at first contemplated.

But it is beyond our province to follow with the minuteness essential to history every event connected with the campaign, and we assume to ourselves, upon the precedents of many veterans who have toiled before us in the field of literary pursuit, the right of slightly sketching those details of historical occurrence which, however necessary to the historian, can be omitted, or merely glanced at, in a tale of the present character.

The Sultaun, at the head of his noble army, proceeded down the Guzulhuttee pass, the one in the angle formed where the grand range of the Neelgherries joins the table-land of Mysore, and where a tributary of the Bhowanee pours its rapid waters into the plain. On their right, as we have described when we took Herbert Compton to his lonely prison on the Neelgherries, rose their vast and blue chain, stretching far away into the distance; on the left, the wide plain, and the table-land breaking away into it in a series of giant ravines and gloomy depths. But for these the monarch had no eyes; a gloomy presentiment of evil appeared to possess him, and the constant succession of messengers with bad tidings, of the news of fall after fall of strongholds, forts, towns, and whole districts before the slight force of the English, inspired him with a dread which the confidence of the officers around him could not restore. Still if he could strike a decisive blow, he thought all would yet be well; and the fame and terror of the lion of Mysore, once more spread through the country, and reaching the ears of the English and their confederates the Nizam and the Mahrattas, would divert them from their alliance or convert them into positive friends.

The Bhowanee was full, but the army crossed in basket-boats, and, in the action which followed, met their enemies in such force and spirit, that the issue of the conflict compelled the English commander to draw off his force during the night, and to retreat, in the hope of effecting a junction with the commander-in-chief, whose force was daily expected. His movement was aided, as if providentially, by a violent rain, which, falling in the Sultaun's camp, caused confusion not easily to be remedied in the morning, when the escape of the English was known.

Frantic with rage, Tippoo ordered an immediate pursuit, which, though gallantly performed by his troops, was ineffectual, as well from the nature of the ground, and the protection afforded to the English by the thick prickly pear-hedges, as from the resolute determination and patience with which it was met. At the small village of Shawoor the English commander determined to make a stand, for his men were worn out by fatigue and excitement; and this place—where as memorable a display of obstinate British valour against overwhelming odds as took place at Korygaum or Seetabuldee might have occurred, was not fated to be so distinguished. A false rumour arose of the advance of the main body of the army under Meadows, which, while it gave new energy to the English, inspired the Sultaun with dread; a vigorous charge by the English cavalry determined the day and the campaign; and the Sultaun, dispirited by this and by the death of a favourite and gallant officer of rank, drew off his troops; he could not be persuaded to resume the attack, but retreated southwards towards Errode, on the river Cavery.

Meanwhile the two English armies had united, and now advanced upon the Sultaun, who again retreated towards Coimbatoor; but imagining danger in that quarter, he turned again northwards, and falling upon the town of Darapoor, in which were some English sick and details, he captured it, and exacted a fearful revenge for his defeats and vexation. From hence, hearing of the advance of the English in the direction of Salem, and knowing the passes into Mysore in that direction to be easy and unguarded—in fact, only a series of undulations—he hurried thither, accompanied by all his cavalry, leaving a large body of his best infantry to hold the English in check, and, if necessary, to occupy the high and rugged passes that led directly to the capital.

The English armies were in possession of the country around the Tapoor pass, which leads from the fine town of Salem and farther to the south from Trichinopoly into Mysore; and it was evident to the Sultaun that their territories to the south must be inefficiently protected, considering the large amount of force which had been dispatched for the invasion of his dominions. His whole mind was now bent upon striking a blow in the rear of the advanced force, which should turn their attention from their meditated object to the defence of positions and districts; by this means time would be wasted, and the season for active operation pass away. Acting, therefore, upon this suggestion, he dexterously avoided the English army, though passing within sight of it; and leaving the magnificent range of the Shevaroy mountains to the left, he took the direct road through the beautiful valley in which Salem is situated to Trichinopoly. It was on the noble temple of Seringham that his fury first fell; and by the desecration of its sacred images, the plunder and forcible conversion of its priests, and the uncontrolled licence given to his bigoted soldiery to mutilate and destroy, a spirit of revenge was actively aroused against him in the minds of his Hindoo adherents, which had long been excited by his acts of horrible oppression and cruelty to their unhappy brethren the Nairs.

From Seringham ruin and devastation was mercilessly carried through Coromandel: each man had licence to plunder as he listed, and neither youth nor age was spared; the savage Pindharees of later years were not more destructive than the army of Islam, led on by its champion; and, although repulsed from the fort of Tiagar by a mere handful of British soldiers, yet that of Trinomallee was less fortunate in its defence, and on its unhappy garrison and inhabitants were vented in cruelties and tortures all the spleen that mortified vanity and ill success could prompt.

Tippoo had hoped too to arouse the ancient animosity of the French against the English, and to have involved them in the war; but his overtures for assistance were rejected or evaded by the Governor of Pondicherry, and his negotiations for an embassy to the Court of Louis XVI. met with no encouragement. Foiled in these attempts, he renewed his correspondence with many English officers, in the same hollow strain of attempted complaint and wonder at the commencement of hostilities that had before proved unsuccessful. But he had more able diplomatists and more wary commanders to deal with now than formerly; and having been unable to put into execution his threat of burning Madras, he abandoned the design, and hurried to meet the storm which now threatened to burst forth from the Nizam and the Mahrattas on the north, and from the English on the east; for Lord Cornwallis was already at Vellore, and the army assembled there were prepared to advance. But the Sultaun, although the force with him used the most strenuous exertions, failed to arrive in time to occupy the passes, and the English ascended to the table-land of Mysore without opposition.

During the period of our tale hitherto, the Sultaun had been separated from the ladies of his harem, which had remained in Bangalore, nor had he held much communication with them for some years. The places of his lawful wives were supplied from time to time as caprice willed the change, by numbers—some rudely torn from their families by his agents—others captives taken from among the Nairs and Hindoos of the coast, where his excesses had been most dreadful, to remain in favour for a while, and to be flung aside when their novelty palled upon his senses. But the mother of his children and his own mother remained dear to him—dear as any could be to one of so cold and heartless a temperament, which warmed only at the trumpet-call of bigotry, and felt none of those endearments common to men of all ranks in the intercourse of their families. His anxiety was excited upon their account from the near approach of the English, which he was unable to check, though he several times attempted it by distant cannonades and threatening displays of large bodies of cavalry. It was therefore absolutely necessary that they should be removed; and having sent orders for them to prepare, the next day, at the head of his whole army, he escorted them from the fort to his encampment, and preparation was made for sending the harem on to the capital.

But while these stirring events proceeded in the camp, and men's minds were gradually filled with alarm at the progress of the English and the formidable nature of their attack, events had occurred at the city which demand that we should notice them.

The army had left some days, and all was quiet within the fort, which but a short time before had resounded with the continuous beating of the Sultaun's kettle-drums, the exercise of the soldiery, and the bustle of the thousands attendant upon the Sultaun. But the work of the arsenals and foundries continued in full vigour, and it was plain to see that if the worst was feared, there was at least preparation made to meet it. In the midst of this, however, with which he had no concern, Kasim Ali, formed for the active occupation of the camp, led a life of inaction, from which he saw no hope of release until he should once more resume his post near the Sultaun, and lead into battle against the English his own gallant fellows, who had often sworn to follow him to the death.

There was one, however, to whom his every movement was an object of intense interest, and who, tormented by a thousand contending passions, now vowed revenge against him because her suit had been rejected, now implored her attendant again and again to go to him. But after her first refusal, Sozun had no mind to encounter the stern looks of the young Patél, and as often as she was sent, she would return with a lie that he had repulsed her.

It was night—quite dark, for the heavens were overcast with thick clouds, and the wind sighed and moaned within the trees above the Khan's dwelling; every now and then a gust would whistle round the apartment where the lady Kummoo sat, shaking the latticed windows and shutters which were carefully closed. She was alone with Sozun, and the theme had long been Kasim Ali and her wild, ungovernable passion for him.

'I tell thee I will bear this no longer, Sozun,' she said, as she arose, and opening the shutter looked forth. 'The night is dark—it is fit for the venture; no one will see us, or if they do, we shall not be known.'

'Holy Alla!' exclaimed the woman, 'thou wilt not go to him, Khanum?'

'Ay will I, Sozun; my heart burns, my soul is on fire! can I bear this for weeks and months? am I a stone? I tell thee nay; but a daring, loving woman, whose thoughts, night and day, are fixed on one object; it is now within my grasp, and the moment urges. Come, I am ready; take thy sheet and wrap thyself—thou knowest the way.'

'It is in vain for thee to go, Khanum; wilt thou eat shame? hast thou no pride?—a woman to seek him who spurns her love!'

'Peace, fool! he has not seen me yet. Come, and delay no longer. I command thee; the way is short, and methinks I am already in his embrace. Quick! see, I am ready.'

'If thy absence should be discovered, lady?'

'I care not; I will say boldly I go to my mother; come, why dost thou delay?'

Sozun knew her mistress's character too well to dare a refusal, and she wrapped herself closely and preceded her. As they descended the stairs they met a servant. 'I go to my mother's for a while—let no one follow me,' said the lady, and passed on. In a few moments they had quitted the house and were in the open street.

'Lend me thine arm, Sozun,' said the lady in a whisper: 'I tremble much, and the night is dark, very dark; I did not think it would be so fearful. Alla! how the clouds scurry along the heavens, and how the wind moans and sighs.'

'We had better return, Khanum.'

'No, no, not for worlds! I must see him;—quick! give me thine arm and lead on!'

Hastily traversing a few streets, Sozun stopped at a small door in a wall. 'This is the place,' she whispered; and as she said it she felt the arm within hers shake as if with ague.

'For the sake of the Prophet, let us turn back—it is not too late—I have not knocked—thou art not fit to meet him,' said the woman in broken sentences.

'Peace, fool! in a few moments I shall see him; dare I not this? Knock, and say he expects us.'

Thou art a bold woman, thought Sozun, and she knocked loudly. The door was opened instantly; two men stood within.

'We are expected,' said Sozun, in a disguised voice, without waiting to be questioned, and they proceeded.

'The Patél hath good company,' said one fellow.

'I marvel at this,' said the other; 'I have served him long, and have never known the like of this before.'

The women lost the rest as they passed hastily on. Kummoo's knees could hardly support her, but she followed Sozun mechanically, her heart beating violently, and her thoughts striving to arrange a few sentences for the interview; vain effort! they rose one upon another in wild confusion, defying retention.

Sozun knew the way; she entered the open verandah and looked through the door into the next apartment; Kasim was there, reading, as she had first seen him. 'That is he,' she whispered gently; 'enter!'

Kummoo was a bold and daring woman, but now her heart almost failed her—for a moment only, however—and she entered and stood before him.

'Who art thou?' he cried; 'and who has dared to admit thee?'

She could not reply; a few broken words escaped her; and unable any longer to stand or to control herself, she fell at his feet, and clasping his knees sobbed aloud.

'Thou art fair—very beautiful,' he said, as he raised her up and gazed upon her features, for her veil had fallen; 'who art thou?'

'One who has loved thee long! I saw thee once—I have lived upon thy look,' she said confusedly.

'Thou art not a tuwaif; thy speech is not like theirs.'

'I am not.'

'Thou art a wife then, or thou wouldst not wear that ring?'

'Why should I tell a lie?—I am; my lord is old—he is absent—he loves me not—he has neglected and thrown me aside for another. I have seen thee, O Patél, and my liver is become water; I have come to thee—pity me and love me, as I would love thee!'

Kasim was sorely tempted; her beauty, her large lustrous eyes sparkling with passion, shone upon him; she hung on him; her hand, as it touched his, was hot and trembling. He raised her up and caressed her, and she threw herself upon his broad chest and again sobbed—it was with passion.

Then, even then, a thought flashed into his mind, quicker than light; could she be the Khan's wife; could he be the man, old, absent, who had flung her aside for another? his heart felt as though it made a mighty bound within his bosom. 'Tell me,' he cried, 'by your soul—say, for my mind misgives me—tell me, art thou not the wife of Rhyman Khan?'

She could not reply—she burned—her mouth became parched and her eyes swam.

'Speak,' he cried, 'for the sake of Alla!' But no reply came; confusion was evident on her countenance; as he held her from him, suddenly her head drooped, and her form relaxed within his grasp; had he not supported her she would have fallen; for the sense of sudden detection had overpowered her already too excited feelings, and she had fainted.

'Holy Prophet! what is to be done?—she is insensible,' exclaimed Kasim aloud; he was heard by Sozun, who entered.

'Tell me, by your soul, if she is the Khan's wife?' he cried in agitation not to be repressed.

'What matter if she is, Patél? she loves you, your destiny is bright; shall I retire?'

'It is as I thought then. Holy Alla! I bless thee that this was spared me! See, she is recovering; yonder is water—take her hence speedily, her secret will die with me; assure her of this, and tell her the Khan is my friend and benefactor.' And so saying, he opened a small door and disappeared.

'He is gone,' said Sozun, as her lady recovered and looked wildly around her: it was enough. They did not wait more than a few minutes; then Kummoo returned to her distasteful home, filled with rage and shame, and burning for revenge.

CHAPTER XXXVIII.

MONTHS had passed, and Herbert Compton remained in the lonely fastness to which he had been doomed. He had no hope of release—none of escape. As he looked forth over the vast plain beneath his feet, he could see the interminable forests spread out before him, through which he well knew there was no path, or, if any, one known to the inhabitants only of the hills—intricate, and utterly unattainable by himself. The Fort itself occupied a round knoll on the very verge of the range, and jutted out, a bold promontory, into the plain, forming evidently one of the extreme angles of the chain of mountains upon which he was; its sides were dizzy precipices of five thousand feet almost perpendicular to the bottom, where they rested amidst forests, the waving even of which could not be seen from the top. Looking eastward was the plain of Coimbatoor, stretching away to a dim horizon, where, at the distance of a hundred miles, were seen the rocky ranges of the Barah Mahal hills, broken at first, but gradually appearing to unite and form a continuous chain away to the left, till, increasing in height in the immense circle, they joined the huge mass on part of which stood his prison.

Through this the Bhowanee, the Baraudee, and several other streams which escaped from the mountains, wound their silent course, glistening in the bright sun like silver threads, away to the broader Cavery, a faint glimmer of which might now and then be seen, as the early rays of the morning sun shone upon the plain. Away to the south and west the mountains recommenced with the triangular peak of Dindigul, which could sometimes be seen, and continued, range over range, of every form, of every hue with which a brilliant sun, acting upon a dry, a damp, or a hot atmosphere, could clothe them—hues of sombre grey, of violet, of brilliant purple, till in the nearer range of the Animallee hills they assumed more positive colours and forms.

To the west lay the broad valley, filled with wood, the only road to the sea; and thence Herbert's sad thoughts often wandered in vivid remembrance of the past, to the land where those most dear to him on earth mourned him as dead. He could not think that they could retain any hope that he lived; years had fled since they had heard of him, and he was become to them as one in the grave; one for whom—when any trivial incident, a word, a look, a tone, recalls the dead to present association—regrets, mingled with hopes for the future, are the spontaneous expressions of undying affections, and a tear is silently dropped, the overflow of some heart which clings to the memory of the dead with fondness which even time does not impair.

To the north and west Herbert looked across the tremendous chasm through which the military road now winds its gradual and easy ascent up to Coonoor, upon the verdant and sunny hills beyond. It was clothed with wood here and there, as though planted with the most consummate taste, occupying now the side, now the gorge of a tiny valley, through which a small stream leaped from rock to rock, till, joining some larger one, it dashed down the precipitous sides of the chasm, into the foaming stream of the Baraudee, the roar of which sometimes reached his ear. At times he could distinguish noble herds of elk browsing upon the smooth, verdant sides of the declivities, and would watch their motions for hours with curious interest; or huge herds of buffalos, tended by a few herdsmen, who appeared to be the only inhabitants of those lovely regions, where the cool climate of his beloved country was joined to the brightness and radiance of an eastern sun.

But though he lived amidst the most exquisite scenery that it is possible to conceive, it was but a poor compensation for liberty; true, under the rigour of a burning climate, captivity would have been more difficult and painful of endurance than here, where he might almost fancy himself in his own land; and could he have enjoyed the happiness of wandering about as he listed over those beauteous hills, through the valleys and beside their bounding streams, it would have sufficed to him to have thus dreamed away his existence. Poor Herbert! his guards might have set him free; for escape from those mountains, through untrodden and pestilential jungles, into a country where death would await him if he were discovered, was guarantee enough that he would have remained; but they were answerable for him with their lives, and every kindness consistent with his safety was shown him; and though their food was coarse barley bread, rice, and the flesh of elk or wild hog, or jungle game,—yet his health and strength seemed to increase, and he had never felt greater vigour.

There were often changes in the little garrison: new comers brought such spices and condiments as were needed, and among them at last arrived one who spoke a few words of Hindostanee. That he should be able to speak intelligibly with any one was a subject of inexpressible delight to Herbert; but soon a new hope sprung up in his heart, which though slowly admitted, yet was, or might be, practicable—escape. Without a guide it was a useless risk of life to attempt it; with one who knew the country and the roads, either to the coast or to Madras, it was a matter, he thought, of difficult but not impossible attainment. Long he watched his opportunity to converse with his friend, for the man, he thought, was civil and obliging beyond his fellows; but he was evidently afraid to speak before them, lest he should at once be suspected and dismissed; but the time came at length.

Herbert, as was his wont, lay upon the green sward on the highest point of the Fort, basking in the warm sun, watching the shadows which chased each other over the beauteous and many-hued plain—now sailing over what appeared endless forests—now dimming the sparkle of the Bhowanee for a moment, which again glittered brightly as the shade passed away: again they appeared to creep up the face of some precipitous hill, or hang among its woods, while the sunlight toyed with the green slopes and mossy banks. Sometimes he speculated idly upon the scene below, and tried to make out the forms of villages among the groves which everywhere appeared amidst the cultivated parts. All was quite still, and not even a leaf rustled to disturb the silence; only the drowsy hum of a bee was heard now and then, as one flew by to its nest under a precipice, laden with sweets. Suddenly, as he listened, he thought he heard the roll of musketry: it was very faint, but it came to a soldier's ear with distinctness enough to be heard. He started to his feet, and listened with painful eagerness, while his eye travelled in the direction of the sound. His whole action was so sudden, and his attitude so wrapt, that his attendant, who had been basking beside him, was thrown completely off his guard.

'What dost thou hear, Sahib?' he said eagerly in Hindostanee. 'What dost thou see?'

'Hush!' cried Herbert; 'listen! there was a gun, and then musketry; hark—a gun again! What can that mean?'

'Alla knows!' said the man; 'but it is even so. Look! was that smoke? By Alla, it is; at Coimbatoor too—thou canst see the minarets of the mosque gleaming brightly.'

'Thou speakest well in thy new tongue,' said Herbert. 'Why hast thou not spoken to me before?'

'I dared not: even now do not, for the sake of your faith and mine, venture by word or sign to speak to me before the others, or it may cost me my life.'

'I will be discreet, and risk nothing; where are they?'

'Some are hunting, some are at the house. Enough—listen!' The sound came again. 'Dost thou not see the smoke?' inquired he.

'No, I see none,' said Herbert, straining his eyes.

'The Sultaun must be there, and they are firing,' said the man. 'It is wonderful that sound should come thus far.'

For some time they continued to hear it; for Ahmed, Herbert's acquaintance, called his associates, and they all listened and speculated, but could come to no conclusion; and then the wind arose, and they heard no more. But they were evidently perplexed, and continued to speak of it during the evening. At last one went out, and returned with an expression of wonder upon his countenance: he spoke to his companions, and some got up and followed him, Soon these sent for the rest, and they took Herbert with them.

It was quite dark. Near them a few objects were distinguishable when the eye became accustomed to the darkness, but overhead the sky was quite overcast and black; and though there was no wind, yet the cold air of night was chill and piercing at that height. They advanced to the place where they had been in the morning; it was within a stone's throw of the brink of the precipice, which descended full four thousand feet before it met even any of the projecting buttresses which appeared to support the mighty fabric. With difficulty they could see to the edge; beyond that all was black—a vast void, into the depths of which the eye strove to penetrate, as the mind into illimitable space and eternity, and felt as if it were thrust back and checked for its presumption by the awful profundity. It seemed to Herbert as though the ground they trod had no support, and was sinking into the gloomy abyss. There seemed to be no horizon, no sky. Instinctively the group closed together, and seemingly awestricken spoke hardly above their breath.

'We saw it awhile ago,' said one to another of those who had just arrived with Herbert.

'What did ye see?'

'Lights,—sparks in that black darkness. Look carefully, ye may see them again.'

'There! there!' cried several. 'Look! what can they be?

Herbert saw where they pointed; in the direction where he had heard the firing in the morning, and in the middle of the void before him, for an instant or two were several bright flashes; he rubbed his eyes, which ached from gazing, and from the effect even of those transient flashes. Again he looked and listened; there was no sound except the sigh of the night breeze in a tree near him; but again there were flashes in the same place. And now, while they gazed, a light arose, soared in a little circle into the air, and descended. Another and another. Herbert knew what they were, and his heart bounded within him with a quickness of pulsation it had not known for years. *If* they should be his countrymen!

His guards turned to one another, and spoke rapidly among themselves with eager gestures. At last Ahmed addressed him.

'They bid me ask you,' he said, 'what this is; you Europeans know all things. Hath the sky such lights?'

'No, it is a siege,' said Herbert, 'and the lights are shells and cannon. Is the Sultaun at war?'

'I know not, but will ask.' And Herbert heard the word Feringhee in the answer. He was sure that his countrymen were near, and his heart yearned to them.

'There have been rumours of war,' said Ahmed, 'and we heard that the English were in the Barah Mahal; but they cannot have got so far, for the Sultaun had marched in person with the whole of the army.'

Herbert thought otherwise. He could imagine nothing but victory for the arms he had once borne, and for the cause in which he would gladly have died. After watching long they withdrew from the spot chilled and wearied, and all lay down to rest. But Herbert could not sleep; his thoughts were too engrossing for sleep. Escape was now possible, and long he deliberated whether it was not practicable alone. On the south, east, and north sides of the Droog were huge precipices, as we have already mentioned; the only access to it was from the west, by which he had come. Even were he to escape from the fort, could he venture to descend any of the passes to the plain? Narrow paths, which at the bottom branched out into endless ramification, led he knew not whither through dense forests that extended for miles and miles, the abode of pestilence and of wild beasts innumerable. The thought was appalling; and the more he weighed the risk in his mind, the less chance did there appear of success. Could it be that Ahmed would assist him? the obstacle of language had been broken through; and no sooner did his busy thoughts suggest the idea, than his mind clung to it. Ahmed was poor, he could not refuse money, and he would offer him anything he chose to demand—thousands, for liberty! He waited till his watch came, and when all were asleep and breathing heavily, he called him by name in a loud whisper.

'Ahmed! Ahmed!'

He was dozing even on his watch, and did not hear at first. Herbert was in agony lest the others should awake.

Ahmed answered at last. 'What dost thou require?' he said.

'Come here, I would speak to thee secretly.' He arose and crossed the hut; it was a good sign. He seated himself close to Herbert; perhaps he had too been thinking of the escape.

'Ahmed,' said the young man, 'thou hast been kind to me: I love thee, for thou hast spoken to me: thou art my friend. Wilt thou then aid me?'

'They say you English are deceitful and faithless,' replied the man.

'They wrong us—by thy head, they wrong us. Our enemies alone say so; we are faithful even to death. Wilt thou trust one, and that one me?'

The man moved, but spoke not.

'Wilt thou aid me?' continued Herbert, for he perceived he was listened to. 'Behold, I trust thee in thus speaking to thee, and am utterly in thy power; if it is thy will, thou canst denounce me to thine associates even now. See how I trust thee—thou wilt not betray me. For years I have languished in captivity. I have a father, mother, brethren, sisters—one other, too, even dearer than they. They think me dead, and the old have long mourned with bitter grief, even the grief of parents for a first-born and beloved. Hast thou no heart for this to plead for me within thee?'

Again the man writhed, but spoke not.

'Hast thou no tenderness, that I may appeal to it? Hast thou no father—mother—wife—who, if thou wert dead, would mourn for thee, but who, living, rejoice for thee?'

'I have all,' was the reply.

'I have not the last,' said Herbert sadly, 'that was a pang spared me. Yet there is one who in blighted hope, and crushed and withered affection, mourns me as long since numbered with the dead. Thou canst restore peace where there is sorrow, hope where there is despair.'

'I cannot aid thee, Sahib.'

'Thou canst! thou canst! My countrymen are yonder; I feel that they are,—they must be victorious, else they had not penetrated so far. Guide me to them, and thou wilt earn my gratitude, and with it a competence for life. Thou knowest the passes; to me the attempt unaided would be death.'

'It would indeed: alone I would not attempt them for a kingdom, even with my knowledge; but I feel for thee, Feringhee; thy looks are gentle, thy speech is soft; thou art not as I have been told the English are: I will believe thou art to be trusted.'

'Oh believe it, believe it, Ahmed! my life will be in thy hands; thou canst guide me to liberty or to death; I am ready to trust thee. Can I say more?'

'Enough, Sahib; I rely upon thee. I swear by Alla and the Prophet to guide thee safely to Coimbatoor—if it be true that thy countrymen are there: further than that, if they are not there, I should but lead thee into death and fall a sacrifice myself. But listen, I risk much; my parents live—they love me: I have too a wife and a child—they are dependent upon me. If we are detected, the vengeance of the Sultaun will fall on them, and that is fearful. Thou seest I have an equal risk with thyself;—now wilt thou trust *me?*'

'Thou hast, brave fellow! and I estimate thy generosity as that of a brother; but we have spoken of no reward.'

'Nor will I,' said the man; 'you are noble; your words—your appearance, even in those rags, is noble. I trust to you.'

'Gallant fellow! thy confidence shall be well repaid. If I live, thou shalt know no poverty, but wealth to the end of thy life, and honourable service, if thou choosest it. But enough—when shall we make the attempt?'

'The relief is expected to-morrow, or the day after; the men will bring us news, and upon that we will arrange all.'

By evening the next day the expected relief came. The news was true: the English besieged Coimbatoor, but with indifferent success; it was said that the Sultaun was out, and victorious even to the gates of Madras; the men were exulting over the discomfiture of the English.

'Darest thou now attempt it?' asked Ahmed that evening; 'the news of thy people is bad.'

'I will, should I perish in the attempt.'

'Then I will lead thee out to-morrow, on pretence of taking thee with me to hunt. I have already said thou shouldst have recreation, and they have agreed to allow it. Enough now; but gird up thy loins tightly and be ready, for we shall have far to go, and to tarry by the way is death.'

The morrow dawned,—a cloudy and damp day; the mighty mists lay still in the hollows and ravines, obscuring everything. Ahmed was in despair. 'Through those clouds,' he said, 'we can never penetrate, but should be lost among the precipices.' Long before noon, however, the wind arose, and stirring the vast volumes of cloud from their repose, caused them to boil up from the abysses around them, and gradually to melt into air.

'Come!' said Ahmed to Herbert, whose heart bounded, and his eye sparkled, as he heard the summons,—'Come, the men are about to return; we will see them a little way, and then turn off ourselves. Come! they are departing.'

He obeyed eagerly, and soon the Fort was left behind; and the narrow neck which connects the place to the main body of the chain—an awful precipice on each hand—was passed in safety. Soon they plunged deeper and deeper into the woods by a narrow path, descending till they reached one branch of the Baraudee, which, foaming and dashing amidst rocks, brawled on its way to the plain. Here they divided; the party ascending the green slope before them, and Herbert and his companion turning up the stream, apparently in search of game.

'Lie down! lie down!' cried Ahmed; 'Shookur Alla! they are gone, and there is yet day enough for us. Ere evening we must be on the edge of the range, and the morrow will see us far below it. Canst thou bear fatigue?'

'Any: look at me—I am stronger than thou art.'

The man regarded him earnestly, and read full well in the clear eye and open brow, ruddy cheek, and firmly knit frame, a defiance of danger. 'I fear not for thee,' he said; 'Alla Akbar! the victory will be ours.'

A while they lay concealed among the long fern, and then rising up, Ahmed looked carefully around him; the party was long out of sight, and they proceeded with light hearts and buoyant steps.

Ahmed had not overrated his knowledge of the mountains; he led Herbert along the edge of the stream for a while, and as they went along Herbert pulled wild flowers,—the flowers of his own England. Woodbine and wild rose, archis and wild hyacinth, and the graceful cyclamen, and fern and violets; and the more familiar buttercup and wild anemone. 'They know not that such a paradise exists in this land,' he said, 'and these shall be my tokens; even as the spies brought grapes and figs to the children of Israel in the desert.'

Hardly now he heeded the lovely scenery that was around him everywhere, among which the round top of his old prison occupied a conspicuous place, clothed with wood to its very summit; and its precipitous sides rising out of the huge chasm that now lay between him and it, at the bottom of which roared the Baraudee, leaping from ledge to ledge in foam, in an endless succession of cataracts. Now and then they would catch glimpses of the blue plain beyond which melted into the horizon; and the deep and gloomy ravine on their right hand presented an endless variety of views, of such exquisite beauty, that Herbert would often stop breathless to contemplate in admiration of their loveliness, for which his companion appeared to have no eyes.

They had now travelled for some hours, and the road had been a toilsome one, owing to the constantly recurring deep valleys which broke into the ravine we have mentioned.

It was now evening; the sun was sinking into the west amidst clouds of glory, and the huge shadows of the mountains were fast creeping over the plain. The precipices of Hulleekul-droog shone like gold under the red light, which, resting upon the vast forests and hanging woods, caused them to glow with a thousand rich tints; and wherever a small oozing of water spread itself down a naked rock, it glittered so that the eye could hardly behold it.

'Art thou fatigued, Sahib?' asked Ahmed; 'thou hast borne this well, and like a man. By Alla! I had thought thy race were as soft as women.'

'No! I can endure yet a good hour,' said Herbert gaily.

''Tis well! then we will push on. Why hast thou burthened thyself with those flowers? fling them away—thou wilt be the lighter.'

'Not so, my friend; these are the flowers of my own land, and I take them to my comrades; thou dost not know—thou canst not feel how dearly such things are prized in a distant land—bringing with them, as they do, remembrances of past time, and of those who shared it. On with thee! behold I follow.'

Hardly a mile further, on the very summit of the mountain, ere it declined into the plain, they reached a rock, beside which was a tiny footpath, hardly perceptible. 'This is our resting place for the night,' said Ahmed; 'many a time have I slept here, with a load of tobacco on my shoulders for the mountaineers, who are a curious people.'

'Ay, indeed!'

'Yes, I will tell thee all about them: but lay thyself down beneath this rock, and it will shelter thee from the cold wind. I will get some sticks, and we will have a fire; I should like a smoke, too, after this travel.' And so saying, he disencumbered himself of his arms, and turned off to a short distance.

Herbert lay for a while looking out on the glorious prospect, in a sense of the most delicious security and enjoyment. What exquisite visions were floating before his eyes, as, shutting them, he allowed the ideas to crowd into his soul!—visions of home, of love, of Amy, of his parents! Suddenly, however, there was a loud roar, the crash of which seemed to paralyse his heart: it was followed by a scream so shrill and piercing, that he never forgot it to his dying day. Hastily snatching up the sword which lay before him, he drew it, and hurried to the spot from whence it had proceeded—but his brave guide was gone for ever!

CHAPTER XXXIX.

THERE are few on earth, who in the chequered track of their earthly pilgrimage—often cheered by the glowing beams of a sunny mind, often obscured by despondency, often hurried on by impatience and querulousness, and yearning with vain desire to penetrate the veil of the hidden future—who do not recall to memory some crisis when the happiness they sought has been apparently within their reach—when the hand, stretched forth to grasp the cup, has been dashed down by a rude but irresistible force, which taught them in that moment how vain was their power, how little their strivings to attain their end, when compared with the Providence which held it in disposal. Providence, fate, destiny, chance—call it what we will—there is an overruling power, visible in the meanest events of our lives, which, if we follow it up to its source in our own hearts, cannot fail to impress us with awe—with a feeling of littleness, often mortifying, and hard for proud minds to bear,—a feeling that there is a power guiding, and often suddenly and rudely checking us, in the midst of a career which we have marked out for good—certainly for gratification—but which may not be accordant with the purposes of our being. Happy is the possessor of that temperament who, even in the midst of disappointment—when a murmur at misfortune, blighted hope, prolonged sickness, or blasted ambition rises to his lips—can say, 'It is for my good—it is the hand of Providence—I bow to its correction in humility.'

But it was difficult for Herbert Compton to be reasonable under so bitter a disappointment; wild with excitement, he roamed hither and thither without fear, for in that moment he had no thought of danger. The poor fellow who had perilled his all for him—the safety of his parents, of his wife—who had so trusted him as to commit without hesitation his future destiny into his hands—whose last act was one of careful kindness and solicitude —was gone for ever! The happiness, the exquisite enjoyment of a meeting with his countrymen, which he had tasted in anticipation, had been dashed from his hand in one moment!

How often, while there was light, did he awake the echoes of the mountains with the name of Ahmed! He roamed everywhere, tried to track the animal who had carried off his poor friend by the trail of his body through the fern, and succeeded for a short distance, but lost it again irretrievably. He returned to the spot where they had first stopped; the whole was a hideous dream, which in vain he tried to shut out from his thoughts. Vain indeed was the effort! the tiger's roar and Ahmed's piercing scream rang in his ears, and often he would start, as he thought they were repeated, during the fearful hours which ensued. As the night closed, the wind arose, and with it clouds came up out of the west, filled with cold driving rain; the ledge he was under afforded but slight protection, and yet it sheltered him enough to allow of a smouldering fire, which after many efforts he kindled.

The storm increased; dark masses of clouds hurried past, apparently close to his head, and the blast groaned and whistled through the ravines and around the peaks and precipices. Of the mountains he could see nothing, for the same black darkness which had surrounded Hulleekul-droog the night before, now enveloped him; there was only the little light of the fire, as the leaves and dead fern blazed up at times under the effect of an eddy of wind, and then utter darkness fell again. Hour after hour passed in deliberation as to his future conduct. Dare he attempt the passage of those fearful jungles alone? Encounter wild beasts, thread trackless forests, where there was no path, and which were filled with rank grass and reeds, thorny rattans, matted creepers, dank and noisome swamps, the abode of deadly pestilence? For the time he was free; but even if he gained the plain, did not a more terrible captivity await him perhaps in a hot and parching dungeon, where the fresh air and the beauteous face of nature would never be felt or seen? But he was not to be daunted; he thought he knew the direction,—his countrymen were before him, and the path was distinct enough, he supposed, for him to track it: this idea consoled him, and he fell asleep for a while, till the morning broke.

He awakened only to endure fresh disappointment; he was surrounded by dense mists, which, though sometimes they would partially clear away, filled the space before him so completely that he could see nought but a thick boiling mass, fearfully agitated by the wind, now rising up as though to overwhelm him, now sinking and displaying for an instant the bluff top of Hulleekul-droog or a part of its precipitous sides, or at an immeasurable and giddy depth the bottom of the chasm, with the Baraudee roaring and flashing among the darkness.

He was in despair, but he was calmer; even the utter hopelessness of attempting to proceed down a precipitous mountain-side into a trackless forest, enveloped in cloud, caused a revulsion of feeling, and a sense that there was an unseen but sensibly-felt protection afforded him—that the very obstacles in his path probably preserved him from following it on to destruction.

There was no other course left but to return—perhaps to captivity, for suspicion might be aroused against him,—to a life of wearisome endurance, but still with beautiful nature for a companion, in whose ever-varying and glorious features there was ever something new to contemplate and to adore.

Ahmed's sword, shield, and matchlock lay on the ground: he took them with him, vowing they should never part from him; the latter was useless for defence, for the charge was wet, and the powder-horn and bullet-pouches had been around the waist of the dead. The flowers he had gathered too lay beside them: they were faded now—fitting types of his withered hope; that day he was to have rejoiced over them with his countrymen! Alas! when would such an event now come; the future was a dreary blank before him, where so lately all had been bright and sunny; and with a sad heart, but with feelings subdued from the excitement of the past evening, he began to retrace his steps. This was no easy task, for the rain, which had cleared away for an hour or so after daylight, now began again to pour in torrents, and he was chilled to the heart. But the very difficulties before him caused him to summon all his energies to meet them, and he strove manfully and conquered. His worst suffering was faintness for want of food; for the cakes they had brought with them Ahmed had tied in a handkerchief about his back, which he had not removed.

As the night set in gloomily and dark, Herbert Compton, well nigh exhausted by hunger, fatigue, and cold, toiled up the steep and rugged path which led to the Fort from the stream below;

and though often missing the way, which in the darkness caused by the thick wood over his head was almost undiscernible, he at last crossed the narrow neck already mentioned, and soon after saw the welcome lights of the garrison huts twinkling among the trees above him. This lent him fresh energy, and in a few minutes he arrived before them. Hungry, wet and cold, he did not consider for a moment the probable issue of his reception, and entered that habitation where he had used to reside.

There was a group sitting smoking around a blazing fire, who started to their feet suddenly, as he thus unceremoniously presented himself; and after gazing earnestly at him for a moment, all simultaneously dashed towards him and seized him. Herbert did not struggle in their hands, nor could he answer the rapid and almost unintelligible inquiries for their missing companion which were poured forth in a torrent. In a few moments too they saw Ahmed's sword and shield, and their dark frowns and menacing looks were bent upon him, and the hand of more than one stole to the weapon by his side as if to inflict summary revenge on him who they might well suppose had destroyed their absent friend. Gradually, however, Herbert's calm and sorrowful manner impressed them with a sense of his innocence; and as they became more reasonable in their behaviour, he described as well as he was able, and mostly by signs, the event which had happened, and pointed in the direction of the place.

Sorrow was on all their faces, and many wept, for Ahmed had been a favourite among them; and while one of them set refreshment before the weary Herbert, the rest conversed in groups upon the subject. Although he could understand but little of what passed, he could see that it was their intention to put his innocence to the proof, by conducting them to the spot where the event had happened. He was right: they allowed him to rest that night without molestation, but by daylight he was awakened, and he found the majority of the little garrison, twelve or fourteen men, equipped for the expedition, each with his match lighted; after a hasty meal they proceeded.

The morning was clear and fine, and the air fresh and bracing: the errand upon which he was going was a sad one to Herbert, and yet there was a melancholy satisfaction in finding perhaps the body of the unfortunate Ahmed, and at any rate the cheering excitement of vigorous exercise, in a rapid walk over the beautiful hills. There were no traces of the storm of the day before, except an increased freshness and odour of the wild flowers: here and there vast masses of white vapour were hanging softly upon the precipices of the droog, or resting in the abysses at its foot. Herbert proceeded at a rapid pace before the rest.

There was evidently much surprise excited among them at the direction which he took, and many significant glances were exchanged from time to time; nor were these the less decided when they arrived at the rock and little footpath: several appeared at once to conclude that escape had been Ahmed's object, and they pointed significantly to the plain and to the path which led to it. Here was the place, however, and having explained as well as he could their arrival, and Ahmed's intention of lighting a fire, Herbert led them to the long fern whither he had gone for materials for the purpose.

They were all armed, and every man blew his match, and looked carefully as he proceeded; it was evident now that they believed him. The chief among them was in advance; he was a capital shot, and Herbert had often seen him hit the smallest marks when they practised for their amusement at the Fort. The trail of the body was quickly found, and these expert hunters at once traced it, where Herbert could see no mark, much further than he had any idea the tiger would have gone. Here and there, too, a bit of rag fluttered upon a thorny bush, which was a plain indication that they were right.

At last, as they proceeded more and more carefully, a crow suddenly arose from among some tall fern with a hoarse and startling croak, and, hovering over the spot, aroused many others; some vultures and kites, too, flew up and wheeled around, screaming discordantly; and a jackal skulked off into a near thicket, evidently disturbed from his repast.

'He is there!' said the leader of the party in a low tone; and a hasty colloquy took place among them for a moment: all seemed brave fellows, and again they advanced without hesitation.

They had scarcely gone many steps when some torn apparel met their eye, and a few steps further, lying amongst the fern, were the mangled remains of their poor comrade; his features were all gone, but the powder-horn and bullet-pouches were around his waist, and to his back was fastened the handkerchief, which still contained the cakes he had tied up in it. With a passionate burst of grief most of them darted to the spot, and looked on the sad spectacle—most sad to Herbert, who, overcome by bitter thoughts, gave full vent to emotions he did not seek to repress.

But they were not long inactive; a search for the tiger seemed determined on, and they proceeded in a body round and round the place. They had not gone far, however, when they heard a growl, a low harsh growl, which made the blood run cold in Herbert's veins; they stood for a moment, and it was repeated. It appeared close to them, and one fired in the direction. It was enough: with a roar which rent the air, the noble brute bounded forth from his lair of fern, his yellow-streaked sides shining in the bright sun: for an instant he regarded them with glaring eyes,—then turned and fled.

There was a precipice a little beyond: he stopped at the edge and looked over; it was evidently too high to leap, and as he hesitated on the brink one man fired;—the shot was well aimed. The tiger turned again, roared most fearfully, but immediately after staggered to the edge of the cliff; his hind quarters appeared paralysed and fell over, but he still held on by his claws, though they slipped every moment. The leader saw his opportunity, raised his gun and fired. Herbert heard the ball crash into the skull—saw the grim head quiver for a moment, the paws relax their hold, and the whole frame slip. All darted forward and looked over: it was a fearfully giddy place; the blue depth was filled with boiling mist—the tiger's body was descending rapidly, turning over and over; at last it hit a projection and bounded away, till the mist appeared to rise and hide it from their view.

'Enough!' cried the leader, 'let us depart.'

They returned to the dead; it was impossible to remove the remains, they were so mutilated; but they hastily dug a shallow place with their broad hunting-knives and laid them in it, covering the spot with thorns and large heavy stones. Then all lay down on the brow of the mountain and rested for a while; and Herbert was glad when they set out on their return homewards, for the spot was filled with too many bitter regrets for the dead, and for the untoward accident that once more had thrown him back into captivity, which now appeared endless; for as they passed the rock and pathway, they pointed to it and to the plain, and shook their heads—some laughing, others with frowns and threatening gestures, which told him plainly that to attempt to escape would be death. Henceforth his life became a blank.

. . . . . .

It was not long after Philip Dalton and his wife reached India with their companion young Hayward, that the aggressions of Tippoo Sultaun upon the Rajah of Travancore, and his known detention of prisoners since the peace of 1784, together with many insults upon the frontiers for which no satisfaction was ever obtained, determined Lord Cornwallis to declare war against him; and once this had been done in a formal manner, every nerve was strained by the Government of India to meet the exigency in a decisive and efficient manner.

It is foreign to our tale to describe every event of the war, which has already been so much more efficiently done in the histories of the period; besides we have a pleasant licence in such matters, without which it would be impossible for us to conduct our readers to any satisfactory conclusion of our history. We shall therefore only state that, availing himself of the undefended state of the passes, and while the Sultaun was occupied with his fruitless negotiations with the French, Lord Cornwallis ascended into Mysore, and, ere he could be opposed by any force, had advanced considerably towards the strong fort of Bangalore. There were partial engagements for some days between the Mysore cavalry, led often by the Sultaun in person, and the English; but they were attended by no decisive result, and did not operate in any way to check the invasion.

Bangalore fell: the siege and the heroic defence of its brave governor are themes which are still sung in the country, and will never pass from the memory of its inhabitants while there remains one of its itinerant bards, who, with two brass wires stretched between two gourds at each end of a stick, perambulate the towns and villages for a scanty and hard-earned subsistence.

The Sultaun retreated upon his capital, and to capture that was the object of the campaign; but ere the army could advance, it was thought necessary to reduce some small forts in the neighbourhood, and to throw into them garrisons of such Hindoo inhabitants of the country, who had welcomed the English invasion and already assisted it against the Sultaun, as would keep them from the occupation of the Sultaun's troops.

From his interest with the higher ranks of the army, and his talent and efficiency, Philip Dalton had, in the opening of the campaign, been appointed to the general staff of the army, while Charles Hayward remained with his regiment; they continued, however, together, both inhabiting the same tent, and as their history was known to many, they were objects of peculiar interest. Indeed poor Herbert's fate was one in which the sympathies of all were powerfully excited, and many were the sincere aspirations that the issue of the war might restore him and others, both English and native, to sorrowing and despairing relatives.

The reduction of the small forts we have alluded to was a service of no great difficulty; and when the army lay encamped near Balapoor—one of them—while arrangements were being made for its occupation, it was common for the officers to examine such places or objects of interest as the neighbourhood of their camp afforded. Pre-eminent among these was the famous rock whence prisoners used to be flung, and of which mention has already been made as connected with Herbert Compton.

No one, whether European or native, could approach this spot without feelings of horror; for the lonely rock stood alone in the plain; and the fearful use to which it had been devoted, both by Hyder and Tippoo, was fresh in the memory of all. A few in the force had seen and examined it, and Philip Dalton and Charles rode thither accompanied by a few mounted orderlies on the very first opportunity of leisure.

A silent feeling of sickening apprehension grew upon them as they approached it, and a thought would force itself upon Philip, despite of his hopes and prayers to the contrary, that Herbert's fate might have been the dreadful one experienced by the hundreds whose whitened bones and skulls lay around the foot of the rock; but he did not mention this to his companion, and they rode on in silence. At length they reached the rock, and, leaving their horses below, ascended to the top, where still stood, though somewhat dilapidated, the small hut or house we have once mentioned. But this did not attract their notice at first; the fatal brink, which had witnessed the frantic death-struggles of so many, was the spot to which they were led by the orderlies, who had a hundred marvellous tales to tell of events that happened there, and of the tremendous strength of those whose business it was to hurl the victims from the precipice. They looked over, too, and saw the bones and skulls scattered at the bottom, and shreds of white calico and red cloth fluttering among the bushes—the sad evidence of the fate of brave soldiers who had perished there. There was nothing there to induce them to remain, and Philip and his young friend turned away sickened from the spot.

'And this is the place where the unfortunate persons were confined,' said an orderly, who, pushing open a rude and half-broken door, ushered them into a mean and dilapidated apartment.

'Good God! it is covered with the names of poor fellows who have died here,' exclaimed Philip; 'what if *his* should be here? we must not leave an inch unexamined, Charles.'

'Why, do you think he was ever here?' asked the young man in an agitated tone.

'God forbid! but it is our duty to look; we may possibly gain a clue.'

And they fell to examining the walls with careful scrutiny. It was a painful task; there were many names; the hands which had written them were now dry bones bleaching without, or had long ago mouldered into dust; many were the humble prayers written there, and obscene words and curses mingled with them in strange combination. Many a direction, too, for parents and wives and children of those who were dead, in case others might visit the spot, and bear them to the far west.

'Heavens!' exclaimed young Hayward suddenly; 'Come here, Philip! quick!'

Dalton darted across the apartment, and Charles pointed to a small writing scratched in the plaster with a pin or nail; it was plain even to his swimming eyes and sickened heart.

'Herbert Compton.

'May 24, 17—. Many have been thrown from this abode of death; I have waited my turn; it will come to-morrow; it will deliver me from a life of misery and—'

There was no more—a stone flung against the wall had hit the rest and obliterated it.

Philip sank down and groaned aloud. That there should be such an end to his hopes, which this proved to have had foundation, was hard indeed to bear. Awhile Charles strove to comfort him, but both their hearts were sick, and they were poor comforters one to another.

'There may be further trace of him,' said Philip; 'let us look around.'

They did so. For a while they found nothing, but at length a joyful cry again broke forth from Charles. 'God be praised!' he said, 'come here and read, Philip.'

The writing on the wall was rough and misshapen, but they were characters of blessed hope to both; the words were these:—

'Captin Comtin was taking awey from this horible pleace verry ill, on the day of—

'John Simpson.'

'God be praised for this!' exclaimed Philip, as he fell on his knees and blessed Him aloud; 'there is yet hope, for assuredly he did not perish here, Charles.'

CHAPTER XL.

'THESE are too precious to remain here, Charles,' said Philip; we must remove them.' It was easily done: with their penknives they carefully cut round the plaster of each inscription, and then separated it from the wall without difficulty; they were precious relics, and the young men long gazed on them, with that depth of feeling which such memorials were well calculated to excite. 'Ah! Philip, if we could only trace him further,' said Charles.

'We thought not of this when we came hither,' he replied, 'and we should be thankful; it is just possible that some one in the town may have heard tidings of him if he were really ill, and we will go thither and inquire.'

They did not tarry on the rock for an instant; their horses awaited them at the bottom, and the distance between the rock and the small town being quickly traversed, they arrived in the bazaar. Philip directly made for the Chouree, where the former Kotwal and others sat engaged in their functions of superintending the market, and directing the issues of grain and forage to the followers of the British army.

They were received courteously by the functionary, who was all civility to his late conquerors: Philip at once opened the cause of his visit, and expressed his anxiety for intelligence, however vague, of his lost friend.

The Kotwal racked his brains, or appeared to do so; he could remember nothing about the rock or its victims, being fearful lest he should compromise himself by some unlucky remark or confession. 'So many had perished there,' he said; 'it was the Sultaun's order, and in Balapoor they never knew anything about them.'

'But was no one ever brought here?' asked Philip.

'Really he could not remember, so many went and came; how could he, the Kotwal, who saw a thousand new faces every day, retain a recollection of any? Prisoners too in hundreds passed by—sometimes remaining there for a day, but he never saw them; he had no curiosity, he had other business; he was in fact the Kotwal, upon whom rested all the affairs of the town.'

Philip was in despair. 'Can you get me no information?' he said; 'I do not speak the native language, and to me inquiry is useless.'

'Of course, if my lord wished it,' he would make every inquiry; and in truth he began in earnest with those about him; none, however, could remember anything but vague descriptions of prisoners passing and repassing; and Philip, after a long and patient investigation which led to no result, was about to depart, disappointed and vexed, when a man entered who had been absent on some message; he was one of the labourers, or scouts of the village, and the Kotwal immediately said to Philip, 'If any one can give you the information you seek, it is this man, for it was his business to attend upon the Sultaun's people who came hither with prisoners.'

He was immediately questioned, and gave ready answers; he perfectly remembered a Feringhee who was brought ill, and long remained at the Fakeer's Tukea,* beyond the town, lying upon the Chubootra;† they were told he was an officer, and an order came to him from the Sultaun himself, brought by Jaffar Sahib Jemadar.

'Surely, surely!' cried the Kotwal, whose memory appeared wonderfully refreshed; ''tis strange I should have forgotten him, seeing that he was often fed from my house; women you know, Sahib, have tender hearts, even for those of a different faith, and we knew nothing of the brave English then.'

'Canst thou guide me to this Fakeer?' said Philip to the man, who could speak indifferent Hindostanee.

'Certainly,' he replied; ''tis but a short distance.' And so saying he took up his long staff. Philip rose to depart.

'I will accompany you, sir,' said the Kotwal; 'the old Sein‡ is very curious in his behaviour to strangers, and may not be civil; besides he hath been ill of late.'

'I thank you,' returned Philip, 'but I would prefer going alone. I have no doubt the old man will be reasonable, even to a Feringhee. Salaam!'

Guided by the scout, who ran before their horses, they were quickly at the garden we have before mentioned. It had been respected by all; the little mosque was as purely clean, the space around it as neatly swept as ever: the flowers bloomed around the tiny fountain, and the noble trees overshadowed all as closely as when, sick and exhausted, Herbert Compton lay beneath their shade, and blessed God that he had found such a refuge and such a friend as the old Fakeer.

The venerable old man sat in his usual spot under the tamarind-tree; before him was his Koran, which he read in a mono-

* *Lit.* Pillow, the abode of a Fakeer. † Elevated seat or terrace.

‡ Respectful appellation of a Mahomedan Fakeer.

tonous tone; his face was very thin, and he looked weak and attenuated by sickness.

'Salaam, Baba!' said Philip advancing, 'we are English officers, who would speak to thee.'

'Salaam Aliekoom!' returned the old man benignantly, 'ye are welcome; the turn of destiny hath allowed us to say that to those whom we have called kafirs; but ye *are* welcome to the old Fakeer—all are welcome who come in peace and good will. What seek ye?'

'Father,' said Philip, much touched by the benevolence of his tone and appearance, 'thou art no bigot, and wilt aid us if thou canst. I seek a lost friend, as dear to me as a brother; I know not if it be the same, but I have heard that one of my race was tended by thee, and remained ill with thee for long; it may be he; didst thou know his name?'

'Holy Alla!' cried the old man eagerly, 'art thou aught to him who loved me as a son?'

'Alas! I know not his name, father.'

'His name! it was—' and he fell to musing, his forefinger between his teeth. 'I cannot remember it now,' he said, 'though it is daily on my lips. Ka— Ka—'

'Compton?' said Philip.

'The same! the same!' cried the old man; 'the same—Compton—Captain Compton; the name is music to me, Sahib; I loved that youth, for he was gentle, and often told me of your cool and beautiful land in the distant west, where the sun goes down in glory; and he taught me to love the race I heard reviled and persecuted.'

'Alla will reward thee!' said Philip; 'but canst thou tell me anything respecting his fate?'

'Alas! nothing; for a month he was with me, ill, very ill—we thought he would die; but the prayers of the old Fakeer were heard, and the medicines of his hand were blessed; and once more he spoke with reason and grew calm, and the fever left him; then, when his strength returned, an order from the Sultaun arrived, and it was a bold bad man that brought it, and he was taken away from me, and never since that have I gained any tidings of him. May his destiny have been good! my prayers have been night and day for him to that being who is your God and mine.'

Philip was much touched, and poured out his thanks to the old man most sincerely and with a full heart. 'Alas! I fear all trace of him is lost,' he said.

'Say not so, my son; I dread—but I hope. The Sultaun is

not always cruel—he is just; his death was never intended—his life was too valuable for that; he is most likely at Seringapatam, whither ye are proceeding they say—I would not despair. And now listen: Alla hath sent thee hither, thou who wast his friend; he gave me a letter, a packet which he wrote here in secret; I would ere this have delivered it in thy camp, but I am grown very feeble and infirm of late, the effect of illness, and I could not walk so far, wilt thou receive it? to me it has been a memorial of the young man, and I have looked on it often, and remembered his beautiful features, and his gratitude when I risked this my little possession, which to me is a paradise, in taking it from him.'

Eagerly, most eagerly Philip implored to see it, and the Fakeer rising attempted to walk to his humble residence, but with difficulty. Philip and Charles flew to his aid, and leaning on them, as he glanced from one to the other with evident pleasure, the old man reached the door. 'Remain here,' he said, 'the dwelling is low—ye are better here. I will return to you.' He did so in a few minutes, bearing the packet.

Philip took it with a delight he had no words to express, and was well nigh overpowered by his emotion as the familiar handwriting met his eye. 'There can be no doubt,' he said, 'that it was he—I would swear to his handwriting among a thousand.'

'Do not open it here,' said the Fakeer; 'but sit and speak to me of him and his parents, and his beloved, for I heard all,' continued the old man with a sigh, 'and pitied his sad fate.'

Philip told him all, and they talked for hours over the lost one; he told him how he had gone to England and married his sister; how the youth beside them was her brother of whom he had heard; and then the old man blessed the youth. 'Thou wilt not be the worse that I have done so,' he said; while a tear filled his eye—rested there for a while—then welling over, trickled down his furrowed cheek and was lost in his white beard.

Long, long they talked together, and the day was fast declining ere they left him, promising to return whenever they could; they took away the precious packet with them, to pore over its contents together in Philip's tent.

They opened it with eager anxiety; it was addressed 'To any English officer.' There were a few lines from Herbert, informing whomsoever should receive it that he was alive, and imploring him to forward it to the Government; and a few more descriptive of his captivity, of his escape from the rock, and his uncertainty for the future.

There were letters too to be forwarded, one to his father, one to Amy; another for Philip himself, which he opened impatiently. It was short—he said he dared not write much. He described his various trials and sufferings, and the kindness of the old Fakeer, without whose aid he must have perished: he besought him not to despair of finding him alive, even though years should intervene between that time and when the letter should reach him.

'Nor will I despair, dear Herbert,' cried Philip; 'never, never! The hand of Providence is clearly discernible through all this chain of events; it will lead us, Charles, to the close. Yet we must be secret: these letters must not be delivered, nor must our present success be known in England till we can confirm the glad tidings, or for ever despair.'

There was not a day while the army remained there that the friends did not visit the old Fakeer. They could not prevail on him to accept money; but there were articles which were of use to him—cloth, and blankets, and other trivial things, which he received gladly. They left him with sorrow, and with little hope that they should ever renew their intercourse with him. Yet they met again.

The progress of the army was slow; for the forage, except in a few places, had been destroyed, and the draught and carriage bullocks died by hundreds. The Nizam's force, too, had joined the British army, and it presented a most gorgeous Eastern display, far more imposing than any Philip had yet seen. Men of all nations of the East, and tribes of India, the courtly Persian, the reckless Afghan, the wild Beloche, the sturdy Pathan, the more slender and effeminate Dukhanee, the chivalrous Rajpoot and hardy Mahrattas, all were mingled in a wild confusion—men hardly belonging to any corps, and clustered round every leader's standard, apparently as fancy, or caprice, or hope of plunder dictated. The force was utterly inefficient, however, for the purposes of the war, for the leader had no control over it, nor could he supply it with food; and his fidelity to the English cause, if not the Nizam's also, was questionable.

At every day's march the distress of the army increased. Men were upon the lowest rations; the cavalry were almost inefficient from the starvation and weakness of their horses, and the active and irregular cloud of the Nizam's horse consumed what little forage was left in the country, long ere it could be collected by the English. The leaves of mango and other trees, where they could be procured, were even gladly devoured by the starved cattle in lieu of other food. Nevertheless, in spite of these discouraging prospects, the army advanced by slow marches; and as the heat was moderate—for the height of the table-land of Mysore, from three to four thousand feet, gives it a temperate climate at all seasons of the year—the troops, long accustomed only to the enervating climate of Coromandel, gained fresh vigour and health as they proceeded.

Meanwhile the advance of the English, though he often affected to despise it, was a source of the greatest alarm to the Sultaun. In vain had he consulted the stars, in vain tried magical arts. They still proceeded, and drew nearer to his capital daily. Nevertheless he heard accounts of the distress and famine prevalent in the English camp; and could he only gain time, even by negotiation or by retreat, he might protract the campaign so that the English would be obliged to retreat, and he would then pour upon them his whole force and annihilate them for ever. Night after night was occupied in discussions with his chief advisers, Meer Sadik, Kishun Rao and Purnea, but their counsel was hardly listened to in the wild schemes which were revolving in his mind.

'Our government is the gift of God!' he would cry. 'Are kafirs who heap abuse on the name of Mohamed his apostle to subdue it? Are we not blessed with holy dreams, with visions of conquest, and of possessing the five kingdoms of Hind? Are all these for naught? I tell ye nay, but true and holy revelations, even such as were made to Mohamed, whose shadow upon earth we are. Here we have daily written them—records of our thoughts—prophecies of our greatness, which as they become fulfilled we will read to ye. Ah, ye sceptics! Let the kafirs advance—they come into the snare. Ha, ha! their cattle are dying. How, Jaffar Sahib?'—he was present—'thou didst see them.'

'Peer-o-Moroshid! they are,' replied Jaffar Sahib; 'they can hardly drag the guns: even the men are harnessed, and work like beasts.'

'They will get tired of that, perhaps, soon. Let them come on, I say, even to the gates of the town. I fear not—why should I fear? my destiny is bright.'

'But why not give up the prisoners, Asylum of the Earth? May your generosity increase!' said Meer Sadik, whose dauntless spirit spoke out before the Sultaun. 'Dost thou not break faith in keeping them?'

'By Alla and the Prophet, thou art bold to say that, Meer Sadik. No! never shall they be wrested from me: rather would I kill them with my own hand. Have they not broken faith, to make war on us without a cause—to destroy our country, to enter into a league against us? We swear before ye, sirs, not one shall return alive.'

Tippoo retained Jaffar always about his person. He was spy, plotter, adviser, executioner, by turns. That night—shortly before the action which followed at Arikéra—they were alone in the Sultaun's tent. All had left him, and he was uneasy and fretful. No wonder, for his thoughts at night were terrible, and he could not bear to be alone. He had summoned one of his favourite ladies from the city, and sought in her society a respite from his thoughts. All was in vain: he could not shut out from himself his danger, though he scoffed at it openly.

'And thou hast seen him, Jaffar, and spoken with him?'

'I have: he is a conceited, arrogant Dukhanee—a man to be despised—a man whose rapacity is not to be satisfied.'

'And what said he?'

'He was haughty at first, and it was hard to hear how he spoke of thee, O Sultaun!'

The monarch gnashed his teeth. 'Ya Alla! grant me power to chastise those who mock thy favourite,' he cried, looking up devoutly. 'But thou gavest the letter?'

'I did.'

'And the bills for money?'

'Yes; he said he would forward that to the Prince at Hyderabad.'

'And will he fight against me? will he not come over at once and desert them?'

'He dare not; but he will be neutral, I think. But he is well where he is: his presence is a burthen to the kafir Feringhees; they wish him—anywhere. His men devour the forage, and they starve. Ha! ha! ha!'

'Good, Jaffar. Now listen; those prisoners, Jaffar—the boys—the cursed Feringhees know of them and the others.'

'Let them not trouble you, Light of the Earth! Your poor slave has, Inshalla! done some service.'

'How! wouldst thou return them?'

'Return them! no, by your head and eyes, no! What, eat so much abomination! Darest thou trust me? I am your slave, there can be no fear. I have eaten your salt, I am the child of your house; command me, and I will do thine orders.'

'What dost thou advise?'

'For the boys? they are young, they are but women—nay worse. Why shouldst thou hesitate?'

'Speak thy mind fully, Jaffar.'

'Death!' said the other in a hollow tone, as if he feared the very echo of the words.

'Good,' said the Sultaun, but his lip quivered as he spoke; 'thou wilt require a warrant. Write one, I will seal it.'

'I cannot write, O Sultaun.'

'Pah! why are men such fools? Give me the inkstand. There, go now—even now. Let it be done silently, the people must not know of it. One by one—thou knowest, and spill no blood. Enough, begone! thou must return to-morrow by this time, I have more work for thee.'

'On my head and eyes be it,' he said, and departed from the tent.

The Sultaun could not bear to be alone; he arose and entered the inner apartments. The lady was alone; she was very beautiful and very fair for her country. Her soft melting eye spoke of other love than that of the cold Sultaun's, and its expression was much heightened by the deep black tinge she had given to her eyelids. Her dress was the purest white muslin woven with silver flowers, which she had thrown over her gracefully, and which partially covered a petticoat of most gorgeous cloth-of-gold. The floor of the tent was covered with fine white calico, and on one side was a low couch, on the other a crimson satin mattress, which formed a dais, furnished with pillows of blue velvet. She arose and made a graceful salutation, but did not speak; for his brow was knit into a frown which she feared, and he was not safe when he looked so.

He threw himself upon the dais, and buried his face in his hands. He was long silent, but she dared not address him.

He spoke at last to himself, and she could hear every word in the still silence.

'It is my destiny,' he said gloomily—'the destiny of my house. The Brahmin who warned me—he who spoke out against me fearless of death, and now lives in the dungeon yonder, he told me of the Feringhees. Whence is their mighty power? They roll on, a fierce tide against me. Is there no hope? Ah, for one hour of his presence who was ever victorious over them—my father! but he is gone for ever, and I am alone—ay, alone.'

The girl was touched; she drew nearer to him.

'Men of Islam!' he resumed, after a pause, 'will ye not fight for me? Why should I fear? Alla Akbar! Assud Ali is false; he has taken the money and the letter. Pah! I have humbled myself to that proud Nizam Ali—to him who trampled on me and scorned my alliance. But no matter, we may be even with him yet. Assud Ali is false to his cause, and will aid mine. Ya

Alla kureem, that he may! Then the Mahrattas will follow: they are wily—they keep aloof—they will see how the game goes, and join the winners. Why should I fear? Zeman Shah in the north with the Afghans; then the men of Delhi and the Rohillas, the hill tribes. The French are now wary and cool, but they will rise: one action over, and all is safe. Then conquest comes, and these hateful sons of Satan are driven away for ever.'

At last he was silent. There were visions of gorgeous triumphs passing through his heart, which defied words to express them.

He looked up, and his eyes met those of the lady. 'Come hither,' he said, 'and sit by me. Thine eyes are full of love; they are not like those of men abroad. When I look into theirs, I read distrust, faithlessness; I doubt them all, Fureeda. They know of many things which, were they to tell the Feringhees—But no: they dare not. What thinkest thou, child—how goes the game?'

'I am your slave,' she said, 'but I will tell the truth. Men say thou dost not fight, and they are gloomy. Why are not the troops of the Sircar led on against the kafirs? Why are they kept in idleness, retreating day by day? Where are thy valiant cushoons—all thy artillery—all thy invincible and thundering cavalry? Arouse thee, O my lord! Let even a slave's voice aid that of thy mother—thy wife—those who would fain see the glory of the Faith exalted, and the tiger of Mysore rend to pieces the kafir English. Art thou a man and a soldier to bear this? By Alla! were I one, and in thy place,' she said, her eye flashing, 'I would mount my horse and cry Bismilla! as I led my warriors to victory. Art thou a coward?'

'Coward! sayest thou this to me?' cried the Sultaun, gnashing his teeth, as his small dagger flashed from its scabbard in his girdle, and was upraised to strike.

The lady trembled, but bowed low before him. 'Strike!' she said; 'I can die at thy feet. The lonely Fureeda will not be missed upon the earth; all who loved me are dead, thou well knowest, and my spirit yearns to be with theirs. Strike! I am ready.'

'And dost thou think me a coward, Fureeda?' he exclaimed, as his hand dropped.

'Alla and the Prophet forbid! I know thou art brave, but men complain. They tell thee not of it, but they complain that the old fire is quenched within thee. I, who fear not, tell thee this truth.'

'It is not, by Alla! I will show them it is not. We will see what the morrow brings. The night is gloomy and hot; there may be rain—in that they will be helpless; then we will set on them, and cry Alla Yar! Now get thee to thy bed. The night advances and we would be alone, for visions press on us which we would record for those destined to follow our steps.'

She left him, and lay down on the bed, but could not sleep. The night was oppressive, and she watched him. He wrote awhile; then she saw him put aside his paper and lie down—sleep had come to him. She arose, took a light shawl and threw it over him gently. Then she sat down and watched him. Presently the thunder muttered in the distance, and flash after flash of blue lightning penetrated through the tent, dimming the light of the lamp which burned beside him. The thunder came nearer and nearer, and the loud patter of heavy rain upon the canvas of the tent she thought would have awakened him; but he slept on. She was naturally terrified at thunder, but she did not relinquish her watch, for he was restless and disturbed in his sleep. Now and then he muttered names, and she could hear him when the roar of the thunder ceased for an instant or two. Soon his dreams were more distinct, and she shuddered as she listened.

'Jaffar!' he said, 'Jaffar! away with them to the rock—No, not yet!—do not kill them yet; there are two I love—spare them! do not spill blood—remember I told thee not. Kafirs, sons of defiled mothers, we will set on them to-morrow, Inshalla! Inshalla!—Coward! we are no coward.' Then after awhile his sleep was more uneasy, she saw his brows knit and his hands clench fast. 'Do not approach! Alla, Alla! they come. Aid me—holy Prophet, aid me, all ye saints!—Mathews! away, old man! I did not kill thee—it was not my orders. Away, or by Alla I will strike— Your faces are cold and blue; are the English so in death? Go, go, ye are devils from hell. Go! I will not come;—by Alla, I will not! Go! my destiny is yet bright and clear.'

Then he was quiet for a while, but big drops of sweat stood on his brow. She would have given worlds to wake him; she wondered the thunder did not, for peal after peal crashed overhead.

Once more he spoke: it was very hurried and low, and she could hear a word only now and then. 'Again, Mathews? kafir Feringhee! I tell thee it was not my order—the poison was not for thee. I will not come—there are devils with thee—hundreds! Why didst thou bring them from the rock? Why do ye look on me with your dead eyes? Away—I will strike!—old man, come no nearer! Ha! thy lips move, thou—'

There was a crash of thunder which seemed to rend the earth

—a flash of lightning which almost blinded her. Fureeda cowered to the ground as the Sultaun started up, his eyes glaring, and his hands clenched and thrust out before him, as he looked wildly around.

'They are gone,' he said. 'Holy Alla, what thunder! that is better than their voices. What! thou here, Fureeda? Did I speak, girl?'

'My lord was restless in his sleep, but I heard no words.' She dared not tell the truth.

'Enough—it is well. Alla aids us with this rain and storm; they will be in confusion, and we will set on them early. As the day dawns thou shalt see, girl, that we are no coward.'

CHAPTER XLI.

It was truly an awful night; the wind howled in fierce blasts over the plain, driving with it cold and piercing rain, which benumbed men who had only been accustomed to the heat of the Carnatic and the coast; the bullocks and horses of the cavalry, exhausted by dearth of food, could no longer struggle through the mud, and fell in great numbers to rise no more. Then men applied their shoulders to the wheels, and laid hold of the drag-ropes of the guns with wild energy, and urged them on with loud shouts and cries. Everywhere the most appalling confusion existed, for the enemy was in front, at a short distance, and, with their knowledge of the ground and of the country, what might not be effected during such a night?

But it was too wild even for the enemy to venture forth to an attack, which might after all be doubtful. The thunder roared and crashed overhead in stunning peals; men shouted, but were not heard; there was no road to be discovered, and infantry and cavalry, often mingled together, floundered on in the inky darkness.

Amongst the rest the commander vainly strove to track the road, but soon lost it, and with his staff wandered they knew not whither, while parties of the enemies' horse were everywhere abroad. It was a fearful risk for one on whom so much depended. They halted, at length, upon a rising ground, but could distinguish only wild groups of struggling figures, as the vivid lightning disclosed them for instants only at a time everywhere around them. Sometimes it appeared as if the enemy were surrounding them, for the deep booming sound of their kettle-drums and the wild shrill neighing of horses came clearly upon the blast at intervals; and in the distance they often thought they could see masses of troops marshalled in array, and the lightning flashing from the points of spears and bayonets.

Their situation was very precarious, and Philip and some others essayed to find the way back to the point from which they had set out, and after much difficulty they succeeded. Plunging through a ploughed field alone, he found a road beyond, and venturing slowly and cautiously, heard, through the din of thunder and roar of the wind, the welcome sound of English voices. It was enough, he retraced his steps to the place where he had left his general, by the glare of the lightning, and gave him the welcome news; he was eagerly followed, and once more the commander was placed in safety.

The wind and the rain ceased; gradually the storm passed onwards, and a few stars shone out here and there, gradually heralding the brilliant dawn. It broke at length to the expectant eyes of that wearied army, and in a short time the confusion of the night before was restored; men repaired to their proper standards, and discipline was once more restored.

With the earliest dawn the Sultaun had been astir, and, calling to him the leaders upon whom he most depended, he gave orders for an assault upon the exhausted English. 'They will be our prey,' he said; 'let them come on, let them fall into the trap which destiny has marked out for them. Shookr Alla! they have come so far that to retreat is impossible—they must advance into our hands. Go, in the name of the Most Mighty, go and conquer! your destiny is bright; this day will be a fair one for the honour of Islam, a day which men shall record in history, and the nations of the West tremble at when they hear it.'

The leaders wondered what had so suddenly changed his resolution of not giving battle, for the day before he had been obstinately bent upon retreat into the city; but they were glad, for the troops were loud in their murmurs, and retreat day after day before a weakened enemy was fast undermining any notions of discipline or subordination which still remained. They obeyed his various orders with alacrity; and as the light became broader and clearer, and the English army could be descried, a shower of rockets was directed against it, which, although annoying, was of little effect.

The Sultaun looked on from a rising ground; before him the two armies were spread out, his own cushoons in large masses, for the while inactive, with the long lines and columns of the English opposed to them, and the artillery vainly endeavouring to get the guns into position; the cattle were exhausted, and could hardly move. He saw the annoyance the rockets caused, and exulted.

'Shabash! Shabash! give them more; ride, Khan Sahib,' he said to an officer near him, 'and tell them not to spare the rockets and the shot. Mashalla! they fall into the midst of the kafirs and kill many; tell them they shall be rewarded well. Ha! they are about to charge. Holy Alla! look at the miserable horses, tottering as they move; *they* think to overwhelm the true believers—Ha! ha! ha! See, they advance—Dogs, kafirs, come on, ye defiled, to your destruction! Now, Rhyman Khan, upon them and annihilate them! Oh for Kasim Ali Patél! he would have led the charge. Ha! there is no need—they turn! they turn! the cowards—the less than men—the faint-hearted!'

But his exultation was soon checked, for when the lines of red-coats advanced he saw his own cushoons retire, and one fell into confusion. Assud Ali and his cloud of cavalry were close upon them—the Sultaun was in agony. 'If he is true to me he will not charge,' he cried. 'Alla! Alla! turn his heart; holy saints and martyrs, let him not destroy them! I vow coverings to your tombs and offerings. He will charge now—he moves; Alla Kereem, I cannot look at it.'

'He is steady,' exclaimed one near him; 'he stirs not.'

'Enough, enough! the bait has taken, and we are safe. Ha, ha, ha! Inshalla! there is no mind like ours, for, with the blessing of Alla, it is all-powerful over our enemies. Assud Ali will earn this day a hopeful reputation—may Alla give him a good digestion of it! And now, since the crisis is past, give orders to retire. We have checked the Feringhees, we have turned their boasted cavalry. Ye saw, sirs, they dared not attack; Alla Akbar! we will retire into the city; let them come on, we shall be ready to meet them.'

And he retreated that day to his fortified position under the guns of the fort; the English took up his late position upon the field, and advanced even beyond it; but the distress in the army was frightful, and there was no prospect of relief. Abercromby, who, it had been hoped, would have joined it, was not to be heard of, nor were the Mahrattas; there was no forage—every blade of grass, even the trees, had been destroyed; most of the wells and tanks were poisoned by branches of Euphorbium thrown into them; the cattle grew weaker and weaker, and died by hundreds. No man had hope that, before the efficient army of the Sultaun, and against a strong fort, there could be any possible hope of victory, and all looked anxiously for the decision of him who led them on.

It was on the evening of that day that Philip Dalton and Charles Hayward ascended a small hill near the camp, and looked forth over the glorious view which was spread out before them. A few miles distant was the city, the tall minarets of the mosque in the fort, and here and there a small dome, with clusters of white-terraced houses, sparkling among the thick groves which surrounded them; the long lines of the regular walls of the fort, and their tall cavaliers, could be seen; and in the plain before them redoubts were everywhere thrown up, between which the gay tents of the huge army glittered in the evening sun; for a flood of golden light poured upon the city and the camp from the declining sun; and as the light evening clouds sailed slowly on, the view was chequered by soft shadows, which added to the beauty of the scene. The broad Cavery glittered where waters stood deep in pools, and its broad and rocky bed could be seen around the fort and town, and stretching far away to the western hills; there was no bridge across the river, but with his telescope Philip could make out the ruins of that which had been destroyed. In all directions columns of white smoke were ascending, straight into the air, from the burning villages, which had been fired, lest they should afford protection or shelter to the enemy.

Both were long silent, as they sat looking upon the prospect, for their thoughts were sad; and the hope which had filled their hearts when they had left Bangalore victorious, trusting soon to be before Seringapatam and to see the Sultaun humbled, and the captives of years brought forth in triumph, had now given place to despair; for the delay even of a day was perilous to the whole army, and already the determination had been made of destroying the battering train, and retreating until a better system of supply for the army could be organised, and the strength of the exhausted cattle restored.

'Poor fellow!' said Philip—he was thinking of Herbert Compton as the city lay before him; 'if he be immured in a dungeon yonder, he will have heard our firing, he will have known of our advance, and we cannot conceive the state of anxiety and suspense he must be in, and how dreadful will be his disappointment.'

'Are we then to retreat, Philip?'

'I believe it is so determined,' he replied. 'For the public cause it is good, for we shall have gained experience; but we shall return soon, I trust, Charles. I hope and trust in a short time, when forage is more plentiful; and for you, proud Sultaun,' he said, looking towards the city, 'there is a severe reckoning in store. Oh, my poor Herbert! if thou art there, may God preserve you to a deliverance at our hands!'

But now the evening was fast closing in, and the fires of the Sultaun's army were sparkling in the dusky plain; gradually but quickly the city was fading before their sight, and the quiet pools of the Cavery, wherein the deep yellow and orange of the sky was reflected, shone more brightly amidst the gloom around them: there was no use in staying longer, and they arose and returned to the camp. In a few days, having destroyed the noble battering-train, the army retreated towards Bangalore.

The Sultaun sat on the high cavalier which stands at the south-east angle of the fort, surrounded by his officers; the busy camp of the English was within sight, in which it was plain that there was a movement; he was gloomy and dispirited, in spite of the force around him, which was ostentatiously displayed; there was a secret misgiving in his heart, a dread of private treachery, of the unfaithfulness of the army, though one and all had sworn to defend their trust; the men around him hardly spoke but in whispers.

'They will be upon us soon,' said the Khan to Kasim, who stood by him, 'and the thunder of the English cannon will be heard for the first time at Seringapatam. Ya Alla avert it! for their destiny is great.'

'Shame on thee, Khan!' cried the young man; 'let them come—I for one will welcome a stroke against the kafirs: I have not drawn a sword for months, and am tired of this inactivity.'

'Thou art not strong yet, Kasim.'

'As I ever was, Khan; feel my arm, its sinews are as firmly knit as ever; let them come, I say, and Alla defend the right! are we not the children of the faith, and they are infidels?'

'Kasim Ali! where is Kasim Ali?' cried the voice of the Sultaun. He answered and stepped forward.

'Look through this,' continued the monarch, handing his telescope to the young man; 'tell me what thou seest, for by Alla, I cannot believe mine own eyes.'

'Cowards!' cried the young man after a moment; 'they retreat; their backs are towards us.'

'Alla Hu Akbar! Ya Alla kureem!' cried the Sultaun; 'then our prayers have been listened to. Ha! ha! ha! they turn—the cowards—the kafir dogs! They are gone—away, after them, my friends—dog their steps to the very gates of Madras.

Inshalla! our hunt will be Cornwallis! A jaghire to him who brings us his head! Now are our dreams come true; our visions wherein we have trusted. Be not deceived, my friends; behold the proofs that I am the favoured of the Prophet, and that though sometimes the power of prophecy is withdrawn from us, yet the light which is within us burns still and will never be extinguished. Away, ye of the household cavalry! Kasim Ali, Rhyman Khan, away after them!—yet stay—go not too far; prudence and wariness have won us this victory; we must not abuse it. Ye must return in three days, when we will determine upon future operations. Begone!'

But as they prepared hastily for the service, the movement was countermanded, to the bitter disappointment of Kasim Ali; for the Sultaun feared risking his best horse against the combined forces of the English and the Nizam's cavalry, and ordered them to remain; nor was there for a considerable period any movement of interest. Strange it was that he made no attack upon the retiring English, nor any effort to retake Bangalore, his once favourite fortress; but the danger for the moment had passed away, and, though the thunder growled and the lightning flashed in the far distance, there appeared no immediate risk of the approach of the tempest.

The campaign had been an arduous one for poor Ameena, who had far overrated her strength; indeed the rapid marches made by the Sultaun, whose personal activity was wonderful, had sorely tried the Khan himself; and he had been selected for the duty of escorting the ladies of the harem from Bangalore to the capital. He had therefore had no part in the late movements of the campaign, but remained at his post without the city, accompanied by the young Patél, who was sufficiently recovered to bear once more his active share in the command of the body of horse to which he had been appointed.

But as soon as the immediate alarm of the British advance and siege of the fort was over, they returned to their old ways of life; the Khan to the enjoyment of the repose of his zenana, and to the society of Ameena, whose health, owing to fatigue and over-exertion, had been indifferent; and Kasim to his daily attendance at the Sultaun's Durbar, where he soon grew to be familiar with the strange and perplexing character he served.

So long as the hurry and bustle of the arriving and departing troops, the preparations for siege, and the constant alarms of the English continued, the minds of all were filled with speculations as to the issue of the war—some swayed by hope, some by fear. Kummoo was like the rest, and because the objects of her hate were absent, she was powerless; but when once more all was fairly tranquil, her thoughts returned rapidly into their old channels; and as the Khan never now visited her, but, contented with Ameena, merely sent cold inquiries as to the state of her health, she detested her sister-wife more than ever, and perhaps with better cause than at first, since the effect was more lasting.

From time to time she had urged her mother and her old servant to aid her in preparing the charms and spells which were to work Ameena's ruin; and after long delays, caused partly by the timidity of the old woman to begin, her deferred selection of lucky and unlucky days, and often by her scruples of conscience—for she believed firmly in her own power—a night was determined on when they were to attend and assist in the ceremony.

Meanwhile, and especially as the day drew near, the attention of the two wives was more and more turned upon Ameena. Gradually they had removed from her the thought that they were inimical to her, and at the time we speak of she could not have supposed that they, whose professions of friendship and acts of kindness were constant, harboured any thought of ill towards her. If the old woman herself had seen the innocent and beautiful being against whom she was plotting, it is probable her heart would have relented towards one whose thoughts were purity and innocence, and whose only sin was often an indulgence in thoughts of one—more tender than befitted her condition—whom she had loved from the first. And yet there was every excuse for her; the Khan was old, and weak in many points; and, though a brave soldier, so superstitious that the merest trifles affected him powerfully, and much of his time was spent in averting by ceremonies (for which he had to pay heavily) glances of the evil eye which he fancied had been cast on him when any pain or ache affected a frame already shaken by the wars of years.

Ameena could not love him, though he was kind and indulgent to her; she honoured, tended, respected him, as a child would do a father; but love, such as the young feel for each other in that clime, she felt not for him, and she had much ado to repress the feelings which her own heart, aided by her fond old nurse Meeran, constantly prompted for Kasim. Poor Ameena! she tried to be happy and cheerful; but she was like a fair bird in a gilded cage, which, though it often pours forth its songs in seeming joyousness still pines for liberty and the free company of its mates.

It was with mingled feelings of awe and superstitious terror that the Khan's two wives betook themselves to the house of Kummoo's mother, on the day assigned for the incantation. As their food had been cooked by their own women in their own private apartments, they had been able to practise the requisite abstinence from the various spices, condiments, and particular descriptions of food which had been interdicted by the old woman. They had bathed as often as had been directed, and observed all the injunctions to perfect purity of body that had been laid upon them. The night was dark and gloomy, and was well suited for their walk to and from the house unobserved. They hardly spoke, as, closely veiled, and under the guidance of Sozun, they entered the house and at once passed on to the inner apartments.

'Do not delay,' said Kummoo's mother; 'I am unclean; ye will be defiled if ye stay here; she is within, in the chamber.' They obeyed her, and entered it. It was a small square room; the floor was of beaten clay, and had been most carefully swept; the walls and roof were quite bare, and there was nothing whatever in the apartment. The old woman sat at the head of a square figure, divided into many compartments, traced on the floor, in which were written many Arabic characters and ciphers; the figure was a rude imitation of a man, in square lines and crosses; and the silence, the dim light of a miserable lamp, and the crouching figure of the old crone, who was mumbling some words as her beads passed rapidly through her fingers, inspired them with dread.

'Soh! ye are come at last, children,' she said, in answer to their benediction; 'are ye pure from all taint? In the name of Soleemān! of Pharoon! of Shudad! of Israeel! of Ulleekun and Mulleeckun! I conjure ye to say the truth. If ye are not, beware! for the evil of this will fall upon ye.'

'We are pure, O mother! we have eaten only what thou hast directed, and bathed as it was necessary.'

'Good! Now attend: here is a knife, and I have here a white fowl; one of you must behead it and scatter the blood over the charm.'

Both hesitated and trembled.

'Shame on ye, cowards!' cried the crone. 'Shame! without this the charm is vain—the offering is vain! Without this, do ye think they will attend to hear your commands?'

'Who, mother?'

'Who?—Muleeka, Hamoos, Mublut, Yoosuf, the deputies of the Shitan, Mullik Yeitshan, Shekh Suddoo, the Father of Mischief. Obey! I tell ye the time passes, and your livers will dry up instead of hers, if ye refuse to do this.'

Both again hesitated, but Kummoo was daring; she at last seized the knife and the fowl, and, in very desperation, at one stroke severed the head from the body.

'Hold it fast! hold it fast!' cried the crone, for its convulsive motions could hardly be restrained; 'it bleeds well—that is a good sign; so now hold it there: let the blood sprinkle over all. They are present now; I feel they drink the blood.' And she continued her incantation in a low tone, while her hearers were paralysed with fear.

At length she broke out aloud, and desired them to repeat the words, 'Ai Boodboo! Ai Shekh Suddoo! Ai Nursoo! Ai Numrood! Ai Murdood! and ye who are present, having drunk blood, enter into her—into Ameena—and possess her! Let her have no rest by night or by day! As in each of your names I pierce this lime with five needles, so may your sharp stings pierce her heart! as they rot by the acid, so may her liver consume within her! Ameen! Ameen! Ameen! Ameen! Ameen!' And as she pronounced each Ameen! she stuck a needle through the green lime she held in her hand. 'Enough!' she cried; 'it is done! Leave this at her door, or at her bedside, that she may see it when she rises in the morning. You will soon hear of her, Inshalla!'

They were glad to escape from the place, for guilt was in their hearts, and terror of the demons whom they believed to have been present. They did not even stay with the old lady, but hurried home as fast as was possible in the darkness. When all were asleep, Kummoo stole softly into the outer apartment of that where Ameena was, and deposited the charmed lime at the threshold of the door, surrounding it with a circle of red powder, as she had been directed: the door opened inwards, so there was no fear that it would be displaced.

CHAPTER XLII.

We fear we can hardly convey to our readers any adequate sense of the terror with which, as she arose in the morning, and opening the door, essayed to go forth to her ablutions for morning prayer, Ameena regarded the fatal sign which lay before her;

a faint cry which she had uttered roused the Khan, who darting to her side, beheld with equal or indeed greater dismay than hers, the dreadful sight.

A matter so trifling and absurd would even, to the most uneducated person in this enlightened land, only furnish matter for ridicule; but to Ameena and her husband, who with their countrymen generally were deeply imbued with the belief of jins, fairies, spirits of the air, and other supernatural agents and devils, supposed to be at the command of any who choose by study or penance to qualify themselves for the exercise of power over them, the sight was one of horror: the thought that their deaths were desired, the death of both, or certainly of one, first struck upon their hearts; a dull but a deadly blow it was to Ameena, to whom the first sight of the awful spectacle gave a terrible earnest that she was the person for whom it was intended.

The Khan could give her no comfort. She had no friend but her old nurse Meeran, who, even more superstitious than Ameena, and herself mistress as she thought of many potent charms, well knew the power which had directed such an one as that before them.

I would not assert that men of station, respectability, and education in India, among the Mahomedans, are not many of them free from the debasing belief in charms and witchcraft, even though their existence is allowed by the Koran; but no one will be hardy enough to deny that by far the greater part dare not disbelieve it; that many practise it in secret, if not themselves, at least by aid of Fakeers and old women; and that in their harems, among their ladies, to doubt the existence of it would be as sinful as to doubt that of the Prophet himself. But it must be remembered that the Khan was a man born in the lower grade of society, that he had been a reckless soldier of fortune, was ignorant, and, though he had risen to high rank and wealth, was far from having shaken off the superstitions with which he had begun life.

All that day dismay was in the household; all seemed equally struck with consternation; and the authors of the evil gave to Ameena their most hearty sympathy, while they exulted over the deed, and saw that the arrow drove home to her very heart. In the general consultation which ensued, they gave it as their opinion that it could have been intended for no other than Ameena, and that her evil destiny had led her to look upon it.

Kasim Ali was sent for by the Khan, and with better sense than the rest, tried to argue him out of a belief that there was any danger, to assure him that no one could have ill-will to one so pure, so innocent, and so unknown as his wife. But his heart misgave him as to the author of the evil; he dared not, however, mention this, and there was no cause for suspicion except in his own thoughts.

Devoted to the Khan, and more than ever anxious for Ameena, of whose declining health, under the horrible ideas that she was possessed by devils, which preyed on her, he constantly heard through the faithful Zoolfoo from Meeran, Kasim Ali spared no pains to give such ease as he could impart by the performance and directions of those ceremonies which were prescribed to be used in such cases. The most holy Fakeers were consulted; they made expeditions and offered Fateehas * at all the saints' and martyrs' tombs within reach, in her name. Puleetas or lamp-charms were burned in her name, and she was fumigated with the smoke. Charmed words were written by holy Fakeers and Moolas, which she sometimes ate among her food; at others they were washed off the paper into water which she drank.

Many of these ceremonies were so curious that we are almost tempted to describe them minutely; but as they would occupy much space (and, alas! we are restricted to pages and lines), we are compelled to abandon them to imagination; in truth they are so ridiculous and puerile, that perhaps they might only provoke risibility, especially in our fair readers, if we should relate them very gravely, and almost insist on their belief in their efficacy.

But all these efforts brought no relief to poor Ameena; sometimes she would rally awhile, and might be seen tending her few flowers, feeding her birds or her pigeons; and though with wasted and pallid features, and a hollow short cough, from which she could obtain no respite, she tried to throw off the dreadful weight at her heart, and would sometimes partially succeed, it would again return with redoubled force, and prostrating her strength reduce her, by the slow fever which came with it, to a state of weakness which prevented all motion. The poor girl would lie for hours in her open verandah, gazing up into the depths of the clear sky above her, in no pain, but with an intense yearning to be at rest for ever, to join the society of the angels and Peris, whom she fancied hovered there ready to receive her. How often she pined for home—to lie on her honoured mother's breast, and breathe away her life in happy repose; and often she implored the Khan to send her thither.

'It is impossible,' he said, 'to travel; the English hold the frontiers, the fierce marauding Mahrattas and the Nizam's forces

* Offerings for the remission of sins and favour of Heaven.

occupy the roads, and it would be madness to attempt so hazardous an undertaking.'

No! she was to hope; such illnesses were long, but, Inshalla! there was hope. Inshalla! the charms, the spells, the exorcisms would take effect, and she would rise again to be his own Ameena.

But, alas! we grieve to write it, that in one who possessed so many noble qualities, courage, frankness, honesty, sincerity, there should be one terrible failing—a vice rather—which, though not openly discernible, lurked at his heart, and ere long broke forth to the peril of poor Ameena.

Her wasted cheek, the hollow dull eye, though sometimes the large and expressive orbs flashed with a light almost painful to look on, and which to those around her was an earnest that the malignant spirits lurked still within her, caused gradually in the Khan an absence of affection, of solicitude—nay, of that love which he had once delighted to show. He was a sensualist; and in Ameena's faded beauty—for like a withered flower there were only the lineaments traceable of what existed in the full vigour of health; and in her wasted and enfeebled form, there was no enjoyment, no attraction. His change to her was gradual, very gradual, but it was perceptible. It would have been merciful, perhaps, had it come at once; it would have prevented days and nights of wretchedness which had no power of alleviation; and with the horrible thoughts and ideas which haunted her, the miserable one of being gradually deserted came upon her slowly, but too surely.

While she lay burned by consuming fever, pallid, exhausted, reduced almost to a skeleton, with parched lips and mouth, there moved around her bedside, ministering to her trifling wants with a mock gratification and assiduity, the work of a fiend glutting over the ruin she had caused, the noble form of Kummoo, her features full of beauty, her eyes flashing with love, her every motion one of grace and dignity. She always dressed with the most scrupulous care, generally in the purest white muslin, which, transparent as it was, when she wound it about the upper part of her perfect form, disclosed enough to attract notice, if not desire. She would study the times when the Khan was likely to arrive in his zenana, and, always contriving to be there before him, would rise to depart when he entered.

For a long time he permitted this, only returning the distant salutation she gave him; but gradually he spoke to her, asked after her health, then bade her remain, and so it continued from time to time, until they conversed gaily together.

And at first poor Ameena was glad that they were friends, and that there was a chance that the harmony of intercourse might be restored which once must have existed between them; but she never heard that he visited Kummoo in her own apartments, or that they met elsewhere than before her; she could not have objected had he done so, for Kummoo was his wife as well as she; but she often sighed for the past, and that her lot had not been cast with one, who with her and her alone would have gone through the pilgrimage allotted them upon earth, and in whose love she could have been blest.

Her trial came at last; she heard from Meeran, who had long discerned the approaching intimacy, and detected its gradual development, than the Khan had visited Kummoo in her apartments, that he had dined with her, and spent the evening in her company. She was glad at first, a feeling she had been trying to reason herself into by degrees; but Meeran in her zeal and love was indignant, and sought, but happily with no effect, to inflame her mistress's jealousy. Poor Ameena! jealousy she never felt—that pang was in mercy spared her; she smiled at her nurse's fears, told her that she looked to greater happiness from this—to sweeter intercourse with her sister-wife, and to a friendship which the Khan would share with both. Alas! these were dreams which cheated her pure and sunny mind, where no evil thought ever intruded—which was full of love and innocence.

But when neglect came—when a day passed and the Khan did not visit her—when she heard that he was constantly in Kummoo's society—when messages came from the lady to inquire after her health, and stated that because the Khan was with her she could not attend her; when day after day elapsed and she saw him not—and when he came his stay was short, his questions hurried and abrupt; and though in her meek and gentle nature she never complained, yet his demeanour would show that he was conscious of having wronged her, and he would be formal, and she fancied even cold—*then* the arrow which had been shot to her very heart of hearts rankled deeply, and, in the utter prostration of her intellect before the misery she suffered, she prayed earnestly for death, in the hope that ere many weeks or days she would be numbered with the dead, and her place among the children of earth become vacant for ever!

How Kummoo exulted in the success of her scheme! she heaped presents upon the old woman by whose aid she had effected it; she gave her jewels from her own stores, clothes of costly price, which the hag treasured up, though the grave was yawning to receive her, and which she vowed to expend in distributions to Fakeers and holy saints for the repose of Kummoo's soul, and her acceptation with Alla. Day after day brought confirmations of the evil work: the bolt had struck—the barb rankled, and could not be withdrawn: Ameena was ill—she wasted away—she burned with fever.

'Ha! ha!' cried the hag, 'did I not say, when your hand trembled at the sacrifice (it was well ye did it and the blood poured forth freely), that it was accepted—that they drank it? Ha! ye slaves to my will, Iblees and his legions, ye Musoo and Shekh Suddoo, and ye legions of Chooraeel! and ye nine sons of Satan! I thank ye all: abide within her; ye are not to come forth till the exorcism of a more powerful than I am is performed—and where will they find that one, my pearl and my ruby?'

And then by her counsel Kummoo had put herself in the way of the Khan; and as she bade her to wait patiently the working of the spell, so did she; not taking offence at fancied slights, but adorning herself with jewels, and disclosing her beauteous face to him from time to time. And when there was appearance that he relented, the old woman bade her prepare a feast for him, and gave her a powder to mingle with his food—a charm which should turn his heart, were it of stone, and cause it to become as wax in the hand of the moulder. A spell she had prepared in secret, the ingredients of which were only known to those students of her mystic art who had devoted years to its accomplishment.

She was successful: all went right. The Khan partook of her food; she sang and played to him, and displayed the witchery of her charms. He had never thought her so lovely; she was his wife, his own Kummoo, once more such as she had been when he took her from her home to his; and a bright field of enjoyment was spread out before them, wherein were flowers blooming, and no shadow to dim their brilliancy. Then came new clothes and jewels, and money and rich gifts, and the old woman partook of all, and laughed in her heart that she, and she alone, knew the depths of the human mind, whose own passions and not her demons were working the issue which she contemplated.

When is it, however, that guilt is satisfied by one step to gain an end desired? The very progress, the watching the slow process of the machinery of the plot, only causes insatiate desires to accelerate its motion, endless yearnings after the end; fears and doubts of success alternate with guilty terrors, which turn back again and meet the desires for completion. Now that Kummoo had gained her purpose, that the Khan was her daily companion, that Ameena, sick to death, neglected and thrown aside, mourned over her lost happiness, and was regarded as one in whom even devils abode, one whose fate it was to linger for a while, and then to pass away from the memories of men, even now Kummoo longed for her death, and looked to it impatiently. Once the devil within her had suggested poison, but she put that back with a strenuous effort. 'It cannot last long,' she thought; but it did, for Ameena lingered.

The thought constantly arose that Ameena would recover, that again she would see her in her hated beauty: the power she had gained over the Khan would then melt away, and her former state of degradation would be renewed. She held long conversations with Sozun, who, bad as she was, dared not even follow her mistress's thoughts of crime. Hoormut had gained nothing by the spell, for she was still neglected, and the wretched state of Ameena stung her conscience bitterly: often she longed to disclose all; but the dread of the shame and punishment which would have followed, and the vengeance of the reckless woman who had led her on, deterred her. It was enough for her that the mischief which was fast progressing had been done; she would aid its fulfilment no further.

Kasim Ali had been unavoidably absent for some time; the Sultaun's possessions in the Barah Mahal had gradually fallen before the forces of the English under Maxwell and Floyd, and one by one the strongholds had been reduced. Kistna Gherry still held out, and had earnestly applied for succours of money and men. The young and daring Kasim was the man on whom the Sultaun's eye rested for the performance of this feat—for it was one—to conduct a large force through the ground occupied by a powerful enemy. Kasim burned for distinction, and he fulfilled his trust manfully; for though pursued hard both by Maxwell and Floyd, at the head of the English cavalry, he eluded them, and, having attained his object, returned into Mysore with but little loss.

It was during his absence that the Khan's change towards Ameena had become visible; and on his return, in reply to his anxious queries as to whether she lived, he was told of her still precarious state, and her fresh cause for misery. Alas! Kasim Ali could not aid her, except by constant messages of kindness through Zoolficar, and proffers of service, even to death, should she require or command them. How often did he long to remonstrate with the Khan upon his behaviour, to implore him to allow her to depart to her own home, but he dared not; that would have been impossible.

. . . .

Months had passed: the English army, recruited and invigorated by the fine climate and the luxurious forage of Mysore, and, joined by the Nizam's troops under a new and more honest commander, and also by the Mahrattas, once more advanced upon the capital, in a far different condition to that in which they had before essayed its capture, and fought a battle within sight of their destination. As they proceeded, fort after fort fell before them. The impregnable Nundidroog, commanded by as brave an officer as the Sultaun possessed, Lutf Ali Beg, fell, and few of the garrison escaped. It would have taken the Sultaun months to reduce it with his whole army—which a single detachment of the English effected. Savundroog—'the abode of death'—where the Sultaun exulted that the English went, for he knew its impregnable strength and the deadly jungles by which it was surrounded,—that too fell by a *coup de main*. He could not credit it; he raved like a wild beast when the news was brought; but that did not alter the loss, and it was followed by other reverses day after day. It was true that the success of his son Futteh Hyder against Gurrumcoondah, which had been taken by the Nizam's troops, and which contained the family of his relation, Meer Sahib, revived him for a while; but the resolute and rapid approach of the English army upon his capital was not to be disguised, and their unvaried success smote hard at his heart, and daunted his army. But there were other causes for dismay on both sides.

Men had begun to ask among themselves, soon after the battle of Arikhéra, as day after day they attended the Durbar, and the band of beautiful English boys, upon whose dancing their eyes had rested in admiration, and to whose delicious voices they had used to listen, did not appear—what had become of them? The many others, too, who had long languished in confinement, and whom they had used to mock and deride—where were they? And then speculation and conjecture arose, and would not be still, for there went suspicion abroad that they had been destroyed, and it was right. Despite of the Sultaun's care, there were those who told openly in their drunkenness that they had strangled them, and that Jaffar Sahib Jemadar had looked on, and while he mocked their cries, had encouraged their destroyers: many others too had been secretly murdered in the lonely hill-forts, where they were confined, and even in the secret prisons and apartments of the palace.

Men openly talked of the butchery; and though they hated the English, yet they were men and soldiers, and abhorred the secret murders and the concealment; and all pitied and mourned over the fate of the poor boys, dreading the vengeance of the

English when the reckoning should come, and there should be few to meet it. Discontent openly showed itself everywhere: there was a feverish excitement among the troops, a restless desire that the English should arrive, and their suspense be dispelled either by victory or defeat.

The twenty-fifth day of January 1792 was one long remembered by those who witnessed it. The English army, led by its noble commander, now more like a triumphal procession than a slow invasion, had arrived on the distant heights, and were rapidly pouring from them upon the plain which led to the city; and the Sultaun, dreading an immediate attack, had ordered out the whole of his force, which in glittering array lined the fort-walls, the esplanade before it, the banks of the river, and the redoubts and batteries beyond. It was a gorgeous spectacle: that English host in long narrow and compact columns, their bayonets glancing in the sun, as they moved with measured tread to the sound of their martial music. Everywhere around in wild disorder were crowds of the Nizam's and the Mahratta horse, accompanied by numbers of elephants, many of the men in bright armour, with gay scarfs wound round their steel caps; others in coats-of-mail, or thickly-quilted satin tunics; many in gorgeous cloth of gold or silver, their horses' trappings of velvet or fine cloth; most in white, with gay scarfs and turbans—the whole everywhere restless, clamorous — thousands careering about, firing matchlocks as they advanced; now dashing out to the front and brandishing their spears, without any order, discipline or command, and crying shouts of abuse, or the various war cries of their respective faiths.

Under the walls was the Sultaun's army—a vast concourse, arrayed in their regiments, and in fair order at their various posts. Everywhere among them moved richly caparisoned elephants and horses, whose riders were as gaily dressed as those of the advancing army. The walls of the fort, the minarets of the mosque, the terraced houses, the trees, every rising ground, were covered with the inhabitants of the fort and the city, looking at the advancing stream of their enemies, which appeared to flow on without resistance. Above all glowed a sun dazzlingly bright, but now declining fast, whose slanting beams lighted up the scene, catching the various objects, and causing them to glitter even more than if they had come from above. The waters of the river—the plain covered with burning villages—whereon one army was in motion, the other waiting to receive them—the fort, the batteries, the mosque and temples, glowed with a brilliance and exciting effect, which the circumstances of the thousands present were not likely to efface from their remembrance.

CHAPTER XLIII.

After witnessing the gradual wasting and feverish excitement of her young mistress for some weeks, the faithful Meeran could no longer bear to see her wretched condition. She knew how devotedly Kasim Ali loved her, and she determined, as her last resource, to make an appeal to his generosity, if not to his love, to implore him to rescue her from the condition she was in, and to assist her to escape, or at once take her under his roof.

It was late in the evening before that on which the English arrived before the fort, that she betook herself to Kasim's abode. She had openly declared her intention to Ameena; indeed she had spoken to her of it for days before, and endeavoured gradually to prepare her to abandon the Khan and fly to her home—distant though it was—or to seek at once the protection of the Patél. His mother too, whose village, though many days' journey distant, she thought it possible she might be able to reach, and she felt assured would receive her, after resting there for a while, she could pursue her journey to Hyderabad; and Ameena timidly, distrustfully, and yet anxiously, had at last given permission to her to go and ascertain if it were possible.

Meeran had placed Zoolficar upon the watch to note the return of the young Patél from his tour of duty to rest for the night; and when she was apprised of that, she bade her young mistress farewell for the while, and telling her to be of good cheer, that she would soon return with joyful news, she departed.

Zoolfoo awaited her without, and in a few minutes they had arrived at the Patél's abode. Anxiously they looked around, lest any one should observe them, but there was only one woman at some distance, whom they hardly heeded; they opened the door of the court-yard, which they found unfastened, and leaving it in the same state (for they knew not why it was opened), they passed on to the Patél. He was wearied with his day's attendance on the Sultaun, and lay reclining on his carpet, reading as usual, which was a solace to him, after the empty compliment, the lies, the inflated vanity of the Sultaun's words, and more frequently of late his querulous remarks and violent bursts of passion. They hesitated for a minute; but he had heard the noise in the verandah, and, supposing it to be his servants, desired them to enter.

'It is I, Khodawund,' said Zoolfoo, 'and I have brought my sister—she would speak with thee.'

'Holy Prophet! what hath happened?' cried the young man, starting up in great agitation; 'she is not worse?'

'No, my lord; she is, praise be to Alla! better,' answered Meeran; 'I think her more cheerful than she hath been for many days. She arose to the evening prayer and walked about the court-yard; the wind was cool, and refreshed her. But ah! Patél, she is not what she was;' and Meeran burst into tears.

'I know, nurse; I know she is not; thy brother here hath daily brought me word of her—news which Alla, who sees my heart, knows that I think on day and night; in my dreams she is before me, in my waking thoughts I see her, sometimes lovely as when I first beheld her, and now dim-eyed and wasted. Alas! that such should be her destiny; alas! that so fair a flower should wither under the blighting chill of neglect. Would to Alla I could aid her! my life, my heart's blood should be hers if she—'

'I knew it! I knew it!' cried the nurse, in an ecstasy of delight, as she had listened to the young man, and now suddenly interrupted him; 'I knew it! Thou canst aid her, Patél Sahib—thou canst save her, O Jemadar, and thou wilt! thou wilt!' And she cast herself at his feet and sobbed aloud.

'Rise, Meeran, this is unseemly,' said Kasim gently; 'again I swear to thee, if I can aid her, even by peril of my life, I will do it.'

'Listen then, Meer Sahib,' she continued, rising and wiping her eyes; 'I have gained her consent—I have spoken to her already—I have told her thou art willing, that thou wilt aid her in flight—and assist her beyond the city, from whence she can escape to thy mother's, and wait there till thou canst be freed from hence, or that she can rest there till she has strength to go on. Wilt thou not aid her? By the head of thy mother, by thy hopes of paradise, I conjure thee to do it, O Patél!'

'But the Khan,' said Kasim, 'will he not let her go?—the enemy is in the path, but were it Satan I would face him for her.'

'The Khan?' cried the nurse,—'thooh! I spit on him for a man; his days are wasted in dalliance with her who, as sure as Alla rules above us, is the author of this calamity. Speak to him? No, by the Prophet!—she hath asked him a thousand times, and I have too. "The enemy is out," saith he, "the English kafirs, who would make a captive of her; it would be madness." Bah! they do not war against women as he does. No! there is no hope from him?'

'But will he not relent towards her?'

'Alla is my witness, no! for a week he hath not seen her, and the poor soul is cut to the heart by the neglcct; she is an angel or a peri, Meer Sahib, or she could not bear this indignity.'

Kasim sighed. 'Has she strength?' he said after a while.

'Ay, enough for that; her body is weak but her spirit is stout; if once she was bent on escape, it would turn her mind from the thought of the curse, and she would recover as soon as she had escaped from these accursed walls.'

'Alas!' sighed Kasim, 'how dare I leave my post at such a moment, when the English are upon us, and every man must be true to his salt? Why was not this said a week sooner?'

'Thou wert long absent, Meer Sahib, and since thou hast returned there has not been a day, hardly an hour, when I have not spoken to her of this.'

'Stay!' he cried, a sudden thought seeming to strike him; 'her father lives, does he not?'

'Inshalla! Meer Sahib, who does not know Roostum Ali Beg at Hyderabad—the bravest amongst its warriors?'

'Then he will be among the advancing army, surely,' cried the young man; 'and what matter if he is not? they will receive his daughter, and I will conduct her to them.'

'To whom, Meer Sahib, to whom?' she asked eagerly.

'To the troops of Nizam Ali Khan, who attend the English,—they will be before the city to-morrow.'

'Shookr Alla!' cried the woman, lifting up her hands and eyes in ecstasy, 'Shookr Alla! Oh, how I bless thee, Meer Sahib, for the news; that will lend her courage, that will make her beauteous eye flash again and her cheek glow; even should her father not be there, there will be a hundred others to whom the daughter of Roostum Ali Beg will be as a daughter. Ya Alla kureem! there is hope, there is hope at last; the day hath long been gloomy, but the evening is bright.'

'Rather say the night, sister,' said the cook; 'let this pass as a hideous dream which hath occupied our senses; let us awake to a bright morning, to share days of happiness with the Khanum, and to pray Alla that his devout Syud may soon be joined to her.'

'Ameen!' said the nurse: but Kasim could not speak, his thoughts were too busy.

'I will prepare all,' he said, after a while, 'a dooly and bearers shall he ready here; she must go at night. Dare she come here? will she, nurse?—will she speak one word to me ere she leaves us? wilt thou conduct her hither?'

'On my head and eyes be it!' said Meeran; 'on my head and eyes!'

'Then remember when I send to thee, come quickly; all will be prepared, and I will myself give her over to the leader of the Dakhan troops; if she will go to my mother's, she will become a daughter to her; and I— but no matter, let that be as it is written in our destiny. Go now, ye have tarried long.'

Ere they arose to depart, a female figure, which had been seated at the door, drinking in every word of their discourse with greedy ears, arose rapidly, and gliding away to the edge of the verandah, stepped from it into the court-yard, and squatted behind a thick bush of Méhndee which grew there. The joyful pair passed on, and, after allowing a few moments to elapse, she arose and followed them. That woman was Sozun.

. . . .

A few nights after, in a small chamber in the house of Kummoo's mother, adjoining the one which we have before mentioned, sat Kummoo and the wretched old woman her accomplice; they spoke in low tones and whispers, and in dread, for the cannon of the English roared without, and was answered in loud peals from the walls of the Fort. The siege had begun now two days; the issue of the night-attack of the 6th of February, and its effect upon the Sultaun's army, causing nearly one-half of its number to desert and fly from a service they had long detested, is well known. On the following morning twenty-three thousand were missing, and among them hundreds of the Europeans, upon whom he had placed such reliance; they preferred surrendering themselves into the hands of a generous enemy, to the service of a blood-stained and capricious monster. The rest of the army had retired within the walls, and, faithful to their cause, had determined to defend them to the last.

There was an awful din without; the roar of cannon, the incessant rattle of musketry, the hissing sound of shells as they descended and burst, came full on the ears of the guilty pair, and the old woman cowered to the ground in fright.

'Knoweth Hoormut-bee of this? why is she not here?' she asked, after a long silence.

'She knoweth it, mother,' said Kummoo, 'but she is a coward, a pitiful coward, and dared not venture forth when shot is flying; but it is late—come—why dost thou delay? thou saidst all was ready.'

'But the cannon, daughter—the noise—my heart is appalled.'

'Ay, who is the coward now? once thou didst call *me* a coward, Kureena; behold I am now ready. What are the cannon to us? arise and come, I say; I see thou hast prepared the figure—come, time passes, and the Khan expects me; he will be returned ere this from the Durbar.'

'She will die without it, daughter. Munoo and Shekh Suddoo came to me in my dreams last night,' said the hag, 'and they told me she would die; this new ceremony is useless.'

'I will not believe it. By Alla! thou liest, nurse; she was better, and I—I hate her. Come, here is gold for thee—thou lovest it—come!' And she disengaged a gold ring from her wrist, and forced it upon the other's, while she seized her arm and dragged her along.

'My blessings on thee, Khanum—the blessings of the old woman who is nigh death!' she said; 'this will feed a hundred Fakeers, this will purchase a hundred readings of the Koran for me when I am dead; my blessings on thee, daughter!'

'Come quickly!' cried Kummoo, 'come quickly! why tarriest thou—the materials have been ready these many days. Enter now—I follow thee.'

She did so, and closed the door.

The room was the one we have before mentioned; a magic figure, of a different form to the first, was drawn on the clay floor—a square, divided into compartments, with figures in each, or marks intended to represent them. The old hag as she entered made three low obeisances to each side of the figure, and, placing herself at the head, began a low monotonous chant, which was intended to be a chapter of the Koran read backwards, rocking the while to and fro; it was, in truth, mere unintelligible gibberish. After awhile she untied some earth and ashes from the corner of her doputta, and pouring water upon them, gradually increased her tone, kneading the mixture into a stiff clay. Soon she changed the incantation into the names of the many demons she had invoked before, and her tones became wilder and wilder as she formed the clay into the rude image of a human being. This done, she rested awhile, mumbling to herself with her eyes shut; and at length, taking from her cloth a number of small pegs of wood, she drove them into the head, the arms, the body, the legs and feet of the image, accompanying each with curses at which even Kummoo shuddered.

'Hast thou the shroud, daughter?' she said as she finished; 'behold the image is ready; a bonny image it is—the ashes of a kafir Hindoo, burned at the full moon, the earth of the grave of a woman who died in child-birth—I had much ado to find one—kneaded together. Hast thou the shroud?'

'Here it is, mother.'

'Ay, that will do, 'tis like a pretty corpse now. Take it away with thee, fair one, to thy home, to the embraces of thy lord. Mark! in three days there will be a young corpse in thy house, and remember to call me to the washing—'tis an old woman's business, and I love to look on such. Ha! ha! away! delay not—place it at her door, its head to the east, that she may see it in the morning ere the sun rises—away!'

Kummoo's brain was in a whirl, and she obeyed almost without speaking in reply; she hurried home through the thronged streets, little heeding any one—not even the shot which whistled above—and she reached her abode undiscovered.

For many nights Ameena had not slept so soundly or so refreshingly as on that when the plot intended to cause her death was proceeding to its completion. What if the cannon thundered without—she heard it not, she was secure in Kasim's faith; a day more—nay, the next night—she was to leave that roof, she hoped for ever! Meeran had been busily occupied in removing her mistress's jewels to Kasim's house, where a comfortable dooly was already prepared for her, and two stout ponies for herself and her brother; a few articles of clothing too, and some of the rich garments which the Khan had presented to Ameena in the days of their pleasant intercourse; there were many that she abandoned with a sigh, but it was impossible to take all.

The dreams of the sleeper were fresh and balmy visions; now she thought she wandered through groves, where the rich scent of tube-roses perfumed the air, and the song of birds was sweet to the charmed ear—by fountains, whose murmuring plash mingled with the sighs of the soft wind among the trees above them. Kasim Ali was beside her, pouring forth a tale of love, of devotion, to which she listened with delight and rapture. Again she was with her mother, her dear mother; and as she lay in her arms and wept tears of joy after their long separation, which were kissed from her cheeks as fast as they trickled over them—she felt a joy, a sense of security in her soul, which was delicious beyond expression. She fancied her mother spoke to her, and she awoke.

'Alla and the twelve holy Imaums keep thee this day! my rose of beauty!' said old Meeran, advancing; and kissing her forehead, she passed her hands over Ameena's head to take the evil from it; 'my blessing, and the blessing of holy angels and saints be on thee! how brightly thou didst smile in thy sleep! Alla bless thee, and the lady Muriam, the mother of Jesus! there is no sadness in thy face now.'

'None, dear nurse, none. I had such happy dreams, even when you awoke me. I thought, but no matter—' And she hid her face in the pillow.

'Ay, thou wert smiling in thy sleep, fairest, and my heart was glad; art thou strong to-day? remember it is to-night we go.'

Ameena blushed deeply. 'I remember,' she said; 'I am strong, I will meet him.'

'Bless thee, my daughter, he is noble, and worthy of thee; now listen and lie here for a while, it will rest thee; thou shalt rise towards afternoon. I have prepared all yonder, I and my good Zoolfoo. Ya Alla kureem! Ya Moula Ali! Ya Boorhanee Sahib! grant that the issue of this be favourable; now turn thee, fairest, and sleep again: may sweet visions be present to thee, for there is no longer aught to fear.'

Meeran left her: she had arisen early, and as she approached the door of her mistress's room, her eye caught the fatally intended image, which had been laid there; for a moment she was staggered, and her heart failed her, as she remembered its fearful import, but instantly she rallied. 'I bless thee, O gracious Alla! that she hath not seen this, she said; 'to me it will do no hurt, nor to her, for I will remove it.' But at first she hesitated to touch so foul a thing as that which in its corpse-clothes lay before her. 'Bismilla hir-ruh man-ir-ruhcem! in the name of the most clement and merciful!' she cried, in very desperation, as seizing the figure at last, and hiding it under her doputta, she hurried forth into the open air. 'It would be well to lay it at her own door,' she thought, as she passed near that of Kummoo-bee; 'but no, better to destroy it.'

She passed out into the street, the fresh grey dawn was breaking, and only an occasional firing disturbed the silence, except the howling of the dogs, which was dreadful. She looked for a dunghill; there was one not far off, occupied by a dozen dogs snarling at each other, and quarrelling for soft places amoug the ashes. With a volley of abuse and a few stones they fled, and Meeran proceeded to do her errand. 'May all the curses which were said over this image,' she cried aloud, 'descend upon the authors of it! may they dwell in their bones, their livers, their blood, and their flesh, Ameen! Ameen! Ameen!' She then spat on the face of the image, and throwing it on the ground with volleys of abuse, not of the most decent character, she trampled it to atoms under her feet, and pounded them with a stone till not a fragment remained entire; then taking up the dust, she threw it to the four quarters of the heavens; and then, and then only, felt satisfied that the spell was broken. Her return to her happy smiling mistress was the dearest proof she could have obtained that she was right.

. . . .

'Art thou sure, Sozun?—this is no lie of thine?—thou dost not dream?'

'As I told thee, Jaffar, I heard it with my own ears; as I passed along they entered his house. I had before suspected, and followed them, for I knew the place, and that he would be at home, and then he said as I have told thee.'

'And they have arranged for to-night?'

'Ay! at eight she will be there in his embrace.'

'Oh rare! rare!' cried Jaffar, 'the virtuous Kasim! the virtuous Syud! on whom the dancers cast their glances in vain. Oh rare! rare!' and he laughed heartily, and with a triumphant sound. 'What fortune!' he continued, 'both at once! both! who have wronged me of money, of credit, of rank. Ya Alla Mousoof! I shall be even with them. At eight, Sozun?'

'At eight. I heard it from Meeran, whom I have dogged these three days. I heard her say it to her brother.'

'Good! I will prevent it; now go, fair one, for to me thou art ever fair, Sozun, and beloved—come hither at ten, I shall be alone till morning; there will be confusion in the house, and thou wilt not be missed.' And thus saying, he took up his sword and passed forth on his errand.

The Khan was at his post, in a cavalier near the rampart; Jaffar ascended it: the men were working two heavy guns, and some French officers directed them from time to time; as he mounted the steps a shot was fired.

'Shabash Monseer!' cried the Khan, 'well aimed, by Alla! it hit a man yonder—I saw him go down. Ha, Jaffar Sahib, welcome; come and see the sport; stand here; so now, they are preparing another.'

'I would speak to thee privately, Khan; descend a few steps, there, we shall be unheard.'

'Ha! a message from the Sultaun. Well, I attend thee,' and he descended. 'Now speak; what is it?'

Jaffar regarded him for an instant, and chuckled; it was the laugh of the devil within him. 'Pardon the question,' he said, 'I would ask after thy house; thy wife is sick, I have heard?'

'Ay, truly; but by my beard I understand thee not, Jaffar; dost thou mock me?'

'No, by Alla! Hath she been really ill? At the point of death?'

He laughed again—but slightly. 'They say Kasim Ali Patél saved her life once, Khan Sahib.'

'Why dost thou ask? away with thy ribald jokes, Jaffar—I like it not. Thou knowest I will not brook insnlt, least of all from thee.'

'Pah!' said the other, 'I mean no insult; I mean well to thee.'

'Well?'

'Ay, well! Art thou sure thy wife was ill? was there no pretence? no deception of thee, to gain her own ends?'

'Pretence! deception!'

'Ay—why dost thou repeat my words? Did Kasim Ali ever perform ceremonies for her—for her, thy wife, Ameena?'

'Kasim Ali—for Ameena? Dog! how darest thou name *her* before me?'

'Dog in thy teeth!' cried the other fiercely; 'I tell thee, old man, I am thy friend, else I would have blood for that word. Khan Sahib, listen: thou art old—thou hast untarnished fame—men love thee—I, whom thou hast sneered at and reviled, love thee—I would not see thee wronged.'

'Wronged!'

'Ay, wronged! cannot such things be?—Old men have young wives—what is the consequence? Old man, I say, look to thine house to-night, for one will leave it to return no more.'

The Khan gasped for breath, and tottered to the wall of the cavalier, which prevented his falling; he rallied after an instant, and with his sword uplifted rushed upon Jaffar.

'Strike!' said the latter, as he drew himself up proudly, 'if thou canst strike one who speaks only for thy good!'

'For my good—O Alla!' groaned the Khan, dropping the point of his sword; 'messenger of evil! say that thou hast lied, and I will forgive thee—I will bless thee!'

'I cannot; by the holy Kaaba of Mecca, I swear it is too true.'

'True! blessed Prophet! give me patience; what! of Kasim Ali?—of my son?'

'Ay, and Ameena; thou hast been a dupe, Khan Sahib, as many another. Ha! ha!'

'Do not laugh,' said the miserable Khan, 'do not laugh—it is mockery to laugh; how didst thou hear this? tell me—I am calm, I can listen.'

'No matter how; wilt thou abide the proof? I will accompany thee at the hour.'

'Whither?'

'To the Patél's house; darest thou come?'

'Now! now!' shouted the Khan in frenzy, 'let me have immediate proof.'

'No, no! there has been no harm done yet—there may not be any meant. Wilt thou come with me at night?'

'I will.'

'Till then be calm. I may be wrong—I pray Alla I may be, for I honour the Patél; if we are wrong, we will say it is a visit; dost thou agree?'

The Khan was stupefied. 'What didst thou say?' he asked, 'I did not hear thee.'

Jaffar repeated his question.

'I will come; thou wilt find me here, Jaffar—here, at my post, like a soldier; if indeed by that time I am— But no matter—if I am alive I will accompany thee.'

'Farewell then, Alla keep thee!'

The Khan remained leaning against the cavalier; the shot was whistling around him, but he heard it not; there was no sound in his ears but one, the low but distinct 'Ay, and Ameena!' which Jaffar had uttered; he would have given worlds could they have been recalled.

CHAPTER XLIV.

'Come, my child! my sweet one, my rose! Now, come! What fear is there? Thou art closely veiled: all are in consternation, and men and women run hither and thither abroad, making vows and vain prayers that this firing may cease. Come! no one sees us. Zoolfoo waits without to protect thee; he is armed, in case of insult by the way—but of that there is no fear. Come! he expects thee. Even now his heart is burning for thee! why dost thou fear? thou art now strong.'

So spoke Meeran, as, when the evening fell, with passionate entreaty she implored her mistress at once to summon courage and accompany her. But the poor girl was greatly agitated; she had several times essayed to move, but had sunk down again upon the low bed on which she sat, closely muffled in a long white sheet.

'Alla help me! I cannot, nurse—it is impossible. Go—say to him I shall die here—I am content to die!' and she pressed her hand on her heart, in a vain attempt to still its throbbings. 'I have no strength to walk; my knees tremble; my heart fails me; there is no hope.' And she burst into tears.

'They will do her good,' thought Meeran; 'her heart is too full.' Awhile she waited; then recollecting that there was cool sherbet without, she ran for it. 'Drink!' she said, 'drink!—no, that is not enough.' For Ameena had but moistened her lips with it—she could not swallow. 'Drink! and thou wilt be better. Drink all, and thy heart will cool. So, now, Shabash! art thou not better, fairest?'

'I am, dear nurse,' said Ameena—'more composed perhaps than before; but it is useless—I cannot go. Hark! the din without is terrible.'

'This is folly, my child—folly. Where is thy courage? Art thou not a Moghul? Many a woman among them has wielded weapons ere now. What would thy father say if he saw thee? Come—fie on this coward heart of thine! Dost thou not remember when the Mahrattas were upon ye? thou hast often told me thou hadst no fear.'

Ameena was much agitated: it was not with fear—she was brave and fearless—but it was shame, an overwhelming sense of modesty, which she imagined she was about to outrage. What if he loved her?—he was a stranger to her, or should have been so; his home was not hers: her fair and precious fame was blasted for ever, should she be seen with him, or be known to have gone to his abode. But Meeran's taunts had roused her a little, for, with all her meekness and gentleness, there was as proud a spirit within her as ever roused to trumpet-call. She arose and made a step: the action was nothing—the effort of her mind was immense.

'Shookr Khoda! Bismilla—ir-ruhman—ir-ruheem!' said Meeran, seizing her arm, and supporting her tottering frame; 'come on—quick! quick!—so now lean on me. Holy Alla! how thou tremblest! Remember the curse!—Away from this spot, and thou art free. Think of that in thy heart, and be firm. 'Tis well—see, the moon even is propitious—she hath veiled her light for an instant. Bismilla! thy destiny has opened brightly; *now* dost thou fear?'

'Not so much—my heart is stiller; but, O nurse, what will he say?'

'He will adore thee, he will love thee, he will pity thee! Come, canst thou not think he burns to meet thee?—that his spirit is with thine now—even now?' As she spoke they passed out through one little court after another which belonged to the zenana. They went on to a small door which led into the street. Meeran coughed slightly—the signal was answered. They opened the door and went out. Zoolfoo was there, armed with sword and buckler; only that he was rather too stout, he would have looked quite martial.

'Keep close behind us!' said Meeran; 'close—we will lead. When we have entered the Patél's door, go thou round to the other, where the ponies are. All is prepared—is it not?'

'They are there even now,' said Zoolfoo, 'and the Patél waits. Bismilla! walk fast—I pray for ye as I go.'

They hurried on: the open fresh cool air had revived Ameena, and though she still trembled exceedingly, and her heart was in a tumult of conflicting feelings, she suffered herself to be led rather than walked, at as rapid a pace as Meeran thought it possible for one so weak to maintain. Ameena knew the house was near, but moments seemed like hours as they proceeded. There were many people in the streets, hurrying about confusedly, and many forms of shrouded women, like her own, some alone, others in company, walking very fast—soldiers, horsemen and artillery, proceeding to their destinations on and near the walls. Cries, oaths, the rattle and creaking of the artillery-wheels, and, above all, the roar of the cannon, resounded in Ameena's ears, and the din and confusion almost stunned her; but Meeran cheered her on, and she felt stronger as she proceeded.

Two persons were watching for her whom she little thought of; they were her husband and Jaffar.

'There!—dost thou see, Khan? dost thou see? They come, by Alla!' the latter whispered.

'Where, Jaffar? where? I see them not.'

'No, I was cheated! they turned off; they cannot be yonder—they would go to the door at once.'

The Khan breathed again. He was standing with Jaffar at the corner of a street, nearly opposite Kasim's abode; they were in the deep shadow of a high wall, and could not well be observed. The poor Khan panted and gasped for breath; his soul was on fire; revenge burned there, and suspicion of wrong. Sometimes during the day he thought he would fly to Ameena and implore her forgiveness—implore her to remain—throw himself at her feet and kiss them. Then again his passion arose at the thought that she should have been false—so false to have used so long a deception, as to have estranged him from her—driven him to another. Above all his revenge burned against Kasim Ali; his son he had fondly called him—his adopted—who would have inherited his wealth—he for whom he had been ever anxious. It was a base return to make, to seduce from him the tender being whom he had so long loved. But his thoughts were incoherent—a chaos of wild passion; he could not reason—he did not attempt it. Proof of their guilt was all he looked for, and often he prayed to Alla that it might not come. There was one spot on which his gaze was steadfast—the angle of the street which led into that where was Kasim's abode. He looked neither right nor left, nor up to the glorious planet that sailed on in her sea of deep azure, but straight on, sometimes clearly, sometimes dimly; and then he would fiercely dash away the tears which arose unconsciously to his eyes.

'Look! look! Khan,' said Jaffar in a hoarse whisper; 'again two figures! and now a man! see! he's fat— 'tis her brother! And one leads the other on. Oh the vile one, thus to pander to a man—her nose should be cut off! She hesitates, by Alla! the other drags her in—no—she stops—the cook passes on—shall I cut him down?'

'Ameena!' gasped the Khan in a low husky voice, stretching his arms out to her; 'Ameena, enter not!—away, home!—pass on!—anything—'tis his door—'tis the Patél's—thou hast no business there! thou hast— She hears not—Ya Alla kureem; she hath gone in of her own accord, and firmly.'

He had only spoken in a hoarse whisper, but he thought he had shouted those broken sentences.

'Art thou satisfied, Khan? am I thy friend now?' said Jaffar in a tone of triumph. 'Wilt thou see more?—follow, the door is open; softly, thou shalt see all; thou knowest the place; they will be in the inner room. Come, come! thou mayest yet prevent it.'

'Prevent what?' said the Khan abstractedly. He was bewildered; he could hardly speak, his mouth was so parched.

'Come and see! come! we may be late.' And Jaffar seized his arm and dragged him across the road; the door was ajar; they entered.

How slowly had sped the dull hours to Kasim Ali that evening! he had prepared all for the reception of Ameena, and had secured one of the posterns which led towards the river, by some of the men of his own risala, who he knew were faithful; they awaited his coming; there was personal danger, but it was nothing in comparison with her safety. There was no firing on that side, for there was no attack; but few men were there, and he would not be noticed in the confusion. His heart yearned to the poor invalid. Ameena his—under his roof—driven from the Khan by unkindness! he dared not think of what bliss might be hidden from them behind the veil of the future, but which could not follow now. Yet he should see her, should welcome her—speak to her. Oh! it was more than he had ever dared to hope. He was restless and impatient! now he paced his small chamber,—examined a hundred times the dooly which was there, arranged the pillows, and smoothed the soft bedding.

Again he tried to read—absurd! his ear was alive to every sound. At last the door of the court opened gently; he hardly breathed; something white entered—another form—and it was closed carefully. Both advanced towards him; he dared not show himself, lest they should retreat; the figures swam before his eyes. One lingered, but the other urged her on, and spoke cheerily. Still nearer they came—nearer—the foot of one was on the step; she appeared to totter—the woman behind caught her, and called his name; he darted to her, and, raising the slight form she supported in his nervous grasp, bore it into the inner apartment, and laid it upon his own soft cushions.

'Ameena! Ameena! speak to me,' he murmured in her ear; 'mine own, now and for ever! Ameena! look on me. Holy Alla! how thou art changed!'

Her veil had fallen from her face, and her pallid features and hollow eyes met his view; they were shut, and she dared not open them; but his voice was music in her ears, and she sought by no word or gesture to restrain his speech.

'Holy Alla! how thou art changed!—so sunken, so pale! but never heed, thou art safe now,—safe for ever. Now thou wilt know no pain or care, for I am to thee even as the tree of the forest to the creeper. Art thou well, fairest? strong enough to proceed? if not, rest here; thou wilt not be missed. I will tend thee—love thee: my whole soul is in thine, fairest! Oh, thou knowest not, Ameena, how I love thee, and have loved thee for years! Alla bless thee! thou art mine own confiding one, and I pray Alla bless thee for having trusted me!'

'Dost thou hear that, Khan?' whispered Jaffar; for they had stolen into the apartment. 'Dost thou see?'

The Khan panted hard and quick—so quick that his breath hardly came at times: it was marvellous they heard him not. His hand grasped his sword; he looked through a chink in the door with eyes that glared like a tiger's and were starting from their sockets.

'Dost thou believe now?' said Jaffar again, in a low devilish whisper. 'Ha! was I true? Look! he takes her hand—he fondles her! canst thou bear that? art thou a man? The woman is present too—Toba! toba *!'

'This is no time for dalliance,' said Meeran. 'Arise, Beebee! the dooly is ready. Come, we lose time; thou wilt follow, Patél Sahib?'

'I will. Arise, beloved!' and he raised her to her feet. 'Behold I attend thee; yet ere thou goest, one look, I implore thee—one kiss—the first—the last, perhaps, Kasim Ali will ever press on thy beauteous lips; one kind look, to say this presumption is forgiven.'

It was granted: the gentle being, as he supported her to the conveyance with his arm around her, turned on him a look so full of love from those glorious eyes glistening in lustrous beauty—a look of joy, of love, of gratitude, of passion, blended—that a delicious thrill shot through his frame; he clasped her to his heart; his lips were fastened to hers in a kiss which for the time gave them but one breath, one being; their souls mingled together in that sweet communion.

'Dost thou hear him, Khan?' whispered Jaffar, 'Ya Alla! that look of love! and now—'

The demon had done his work. In a frenzy, like a maddened beast, the Khan dashed through the door, which opened inwards. His sword was naked, and flashed as it was high upraised in his nervous and passionate grasp. A wild shriek burst from Meeran, and she fled.

'Devils!' he shouted in a voice of fury, 'Devils! Dog of a Patél! Rhyman Khan hath seen ye!'

The sword was quivering above his head, and it descended blindly, to annihilate, he thought, both at a blow. Kasim Ali stretched forth his arm to stay it; he was too late: the blood of Ameena, who was senseless, gushed forth over him, and her head fell back upon his bosom. Kasim tried to get at his sword, while he held the lifeless form on his arm; he tore it desperately down from the nail on which it hung above him, expecting another blow momentarily; it came not. His sword was tied to the scabbard, and the knot of the cord would not open; all

* Shame! shame!

was the work of an instant; he turned, ready to ward off another blow, and beheld a sight in which horror and pity struggled with revenge for mastery.

The Khan's sword was on the ground, his hands were clasped, his eyes staring and fixed upon Ameena; the sight of blood had calmed his fury.

'Miserable man, what hast thou done?' said Kasim hurriedly.

The Khan could not reply. He rolled his blood-shoot eyes upon Kasim, and waving his hand turned and fled.

'Ha! ha! ha!' laughed a voice he knew to be Jaffar's. He laid Ameena down, and looked at her with dim eyes—she seemed dead.

'I will revenge thee!' he cried, and darted after them.

He saw them pass the small door, close it violently; and when he had opened it, and dashed on into the open street, he saw them not, but taking the way opposite to theirs, he fled down it at his utmost speed.

A moment after him a woman with breathless haste entered by the same door. 'O Alla! grant,' she exclaimed, 'thou who didst soften my heart, grant I may not be too late. I vow offerings to thee, O holy saint of Sérah! O Mullik Rhyan! if I be in time. Something hath happened; Jaffar and the Khan fled past me. Alla, Alla! how he looked!'

She hurried through the courts, traversed the little verandah, and darted into the room; her sight for an instant failed her; there was a pool of blood on the white musnud, and the lady lay there—her white sheet and long hair dabbled in it. For an instant her heart was sick, but she rallied herself. 'If there is only life! Meeran, Meeran, where art thou? Holy Prophet! *if* there be only life, I vow to be her slave for ever! Lady, dear lady, dost thou hear? Meeran, Meeran, where art thou?'

'Who calls?' said Meeran, advancing terror-stricken from the other door in the court before them.

'It is I, Sozun; haste hither! we may yet save her. Quick! is thy heart so cowardly?'

'How camest thou here, Sozun?'

'No matter, I will tell thee—so raise her up.'

'Ya Mousoof Alla! Ya Beebee Muriam! what a gash!' exclaimed both, turning their heads away from the horrid sight for an instant. 'But she is warm,' said Meeran. 'Apostle of Alla! there may be life. Hold her, while I run for my brother—he is without.'

He came quickly; for a long time they doubted if she would revive, and her first breath was hailed with a burst of joy.

'I know a secure place,' said Sozun; 'she is not safe here. She will be discovered by the Khan, and he will kill her.'

'Art thou to be trusted, Sozun?' said Meeran; 'it was thou who didst cause this murder, and I mistrust thee.'

'Alla who sees my heart knows how true it is,' said the woman, 'and how bitter is my repentance. Ye may leave this poor flower if ye will; but never while Sozun hath life will she depart from her, come weal, come woe.' And as she said it she looked up fervently; and when Meeran saw that her eyes glistened with tears which fell over on her cheeks—that her features were quivering, and her lips moved in silent prayer, then she believed her, and yielded to the necessity of the moment.

Zoolficar, with their assistance, bound up the wound, which had cut deeply into the shoulder and neck, and had bled much, and they now laid the lady in the dooly. Only that she sighed now and then, she would have been thought to be dead; but there was life, and while life was in the nostrils there was hope. The bearers, who had been ready without from the first, were now called; and preceded by Sozun, they went on till they stopped at an obscure house behind the principal bazaar, in an unfrequented part of the Fort. The lady still lived, when they lifted her out of the dooly and laid here upon as soft and easy a bed as the house afforded.

. . . .

Kasim Ali passed a wild and restless night—in comparison of which, that upon the battle-field, when the jackal and hyena had howled around him, was remembered with pleasure. He searched every corner of the Fort, every ravelin, every bastion, the most miserable purlieus of the bazaar, which rung with wild shouts of revelry, of drunkenness and debauchery. He went into the thickest and hottest of the fire, where shot and shells and the deadly grape whistled around him. He examined every group of men, but saw neither the Khan nor Jaffar. Twice he returned to his house—once ere he had been long absent, dreading to behold again that beauteous form lying in its blood and disfigured by the gaping wound. It was not there—that misery, he thought, was spared him by the kind Meeran and her brother. 'They have taken it away to bury,' he thought; but where he knew not—the morning would reveal. Her blood lay there, clotted upon the white muslin, a horrible evidence of the crime that had been committed. He sought not to remove it; but it reminded him of the state of his own garments, which were saturated. He changed them, and again sallied out.

He returned towards morning, and wrote a few lines to the only other friend he possessed, a Moolah of the mosque in the Fort, to whom he had willed that his little property should be given, in case of his death and the Khan's, in trust for his mother; they were a few lines only, to tell of his fate; and for the second time he went forth, to seek death in the hot battle.

He found it not, however, all that night; and sick at heart, as the morning broke over the beleaguered city, he entered the court of the mosque, from the tall minarets of which the Muezzin was proclaiming the morning prayer. 'It will calm me,' he said, 'to join in it.'

As he entered he met his friend the Moolah. He could not resist the impulse, his spirit was oppressed, and he again requested the Moolah's kind administration of his property in case of his death, and the remission of its proceeds to his mother. Such requests were not uncommon at that period, and death was too busy in the Fort for every man not to prepare for his own end. The Sultaun arrived soon after from his early circuit of the walls, attended by his chief officers, and the morning prayer commenced.

It was finished, and men arose and were preparing to depart. 'Stay!' cried the Sultaun, 'we would speak to all.' And as he cast his eye around, 'Ye all here love me,' he said, in so melancholy a tone that most were touched by it. 'Ye, Kummur-ud-deen, Syud Sahib, Syud Ghuffoor, Bakir Sahib, and thou Kasim Ali, who once saved me, ye are all here. Alas! there are but few remaining like you. How many have been faithless, who have eaten my salt for years! Listen—our glory is gone—the light of the earth, the star of Islam is quenched. No more triumphs to the Faith—all is dark before us. Hear ye what we have come to; we asked for peace at the hands of the infidels—we asked the cause of this unjustifiable attack—why we were insulted and bearded in our very capital; but no answer is returned. The insatiate thirst of power and conquest is apparent in the reply of the kafir Cornwallis. Listen.'

There was perfect silence: every man felt that the Sultaun's spirit was broken, and melancholy was upon every face, as he unfolded a letter, and, mounting a step of the pulpit, began to read. It was short, and there were few ceremonious expressions: to resign half his territories, to pay the cost of the war, and to surrender his sons as hostages, were the humiliating terms proposed; and as they heard it, a burst of indignation arose from the assembly, which rung through the lofty arches and fretted roof of the mosque.

'I thank you, friends and brothers,' he said; 'ye feel for me—I bless ye, that ye have hearts for the unfortunate. But will you bear this? Will ye, whose victorious arms have ere now vanquished the kafirs, will ye submit to these insults?'

'If all in this fort were as true as we are,' cried Syud Ghuffoor, 'there would be no fear; but, alas! the faint-hearted tremble for their lives, as every English shot strikes the wall, and there are thousands such.'

'Alla be merciful to me!' said the Sultaun, bowing his head; 'are they so faithless? What say ye, sirs?'

Many replied, but only a few could answer for the men, and then many wept passionately. The grief of those strong warriors was moving to look on.

'And are we to die here—to die like dogs, like wild beasts in a cage?' broke out the Sultaun frantically, and throwing his turban on the ground; 'to have our children torn from us, our wives defiled before our eyes? to be plundered of our kingdom—torn from our throne—humbled in the dust? Are we to bear this from kafirs, from hogs too? Holy Alla, and Mahomed the Apostle, are we to suffer this indignity? are we to be so beaten down? Sirs, have ye no hearts? Where is your vaunted bravery? Ye have eaten my salt, ye have grown rich where ye were poor—have ye no gratitude? have ye no faith?'

'We have! we have!' cried one and all of that assembly. 'We will die at your feet; our lives are in your hand.'

'The infidels are before ye—they for whose presence ye have often longed, to prove your prowess. Will ye swear before Alla, and here in his house, to be faithful to me his servant, to your Sultaun?'

Then arose the oaths of all, in hoarse tones, as they waved their arms on high, and swore to be faithful till death.

''Tis well!' he said, 'else ye had been kafirs, fit only to herd with the vile. I bless ye, O my friends. Alla, who sees my aching heart, knows that I believe you true—true to the last—true in prosperity, true now in adversity; while I—I have often deceived ye, often been capricious. Will ye forgive me? I am no Sultaun now, but a poor worm before Alla, meaner than yourselves. Will ye forgive me?'

Then the passionate gestures and exclamations of devotion to him by the enthusiasts knew no bounds; and their wild and frantic cries and expressions of service unto death—to the shedding of their hearts' blood—broke forth without control. Those without, and the soldiery, caught up the wild excitement, thronged into the mosque, and filled the steps and the court, uttering violent exclamations.

'Blessed be Alla! your old fire is still within you,' cried Tippoo; 'and were I but rid of Cornwallis, that host yonder would disperse like smoke before the sun: we might pursue them to annihilation. Will no one rid me of him? Will no one lead a sortie from the fort, and dashing at his tent, ere he be suspected, bear him or his head hither? I vow a reward, such as it hath not entered into any one's thoughts to conceive, to him who doeth this: and those who fall ye well know are martyrs, and when they taste of death are translated into paradise, to the seventy virgins and undying youth.'

Unknown to each other, and from opposite sides, two men dashed forward eagerly to claim that service of danger. The one was Kasim Ali, the other a man from whose blood-shot eyes and haggard features—upon which anguish and despair were fearfully written—all shrank back as he passed them: it was Rhyman Khan.

CHAPTER XLV.

'KASIM! Kasim Ali! thou art not fit for this service; thou art weak—thy cheek is pale. Go, youth!' cried the Sultaun, 'there are a hundred others ready.'

'Not so, Light of Islam!' replied the young man. 'I was the first—it is my destiny—I claim the service; if it be written that I am to fall this day, the shot would reach me even in thy palace. I am not weak, but strong as ever I was; behold my arm.' And he bared it to the elbow; the muscles stood out in bold projections as he clenched his hand. 'Behold I am strong—I am full of power, therefore let it be so; Inshalla! your slave will be fortunate; there is no fear.'

'It is *my* right,' cried Rhyman Khan. The hollow tone of his voice as it fell on the Sultaun's ear caused even him to start. 'I was before him, bid me go instead; he is young and should be spared; the old soldier is ripe for death.'

'Prophet of Alla! what ails thee?' said the Sultaun to him. 'Why dost thou stare so, and roll thine eyes, Rhyman Khan? art thou ill?'

'I am well,' he answered, 'quite well. Ha! ha! quite well; but as I am thy slave, and have eaten thy salt for years, could I hear thy words unmoved? By Alla, no! therefore let me go, it is *my* right, for I am his elder.'

'Go, both of ye,' continued Tippoo; 'you have been friends, nay more, father and son; take whom ye will with ye. Go—may Alla shield ye both from danger! Go—if ye fall, your places will be indeed vacant, but your memories will dwell in the hearts of those who love brave deeds, and ye will die as martyrs in the cause of the faith; and this is a death that all covet; but we will pray for your success. Inshalla! victory awaits you, and honour and my gratitude when ye return. Go! ye have my prayers, and those of every true believer who will behold ye.'

Both saluted him profoundly, and then turning, their eyes met. 'Come!' said the Khan, 'we delay.' There was a burst of admiration from the assembly—a shout which rose and spread abroad to those without. 'Who will follow Rhyman Khan?' he cried aloud; 'whoever will, let him meet me at the southern gate in half-an-hour;' and so saying, he hurried rapidly in the direction of his home.

All was confusion there, for the lady Ameena, with Sozun and Meeran, were missing; he ordered his best horse to be prepared for action, and, without speaking, he passed into the apartments of Ameena and fastened the door.

They were as she had left them—nothing had been disturbed: her larks were singing cheerily; her looree, which knew him well, fluttered its bright wings, and screaming tried to fly to him; her gazelle ran up with a merry frisk, and rubbed its nose against his hand, and butted gently with its forehead, gazing at him with its large soft eyes. Her flowers were fresh and bright, and their odour was sweet in the cool morning air. His eye wandered around: every well-remembered object was there; but she whose joyous smile and sweet tones had made a heaven of the place, where was she? dead and cold he thought, disfigured in death by his own hand. He cast himself frantically on the bed, which remained in disorder even as she had left it, and groaned aloud.

How long he lay there he knew not: he had no thought of present time, only of the past, the blissful past, which floated before his mental vision, a bitter mockery. Some one knocked; it recalled him to his senses.

'They wait,' said Daood, 'the Patél and a hundred others: he has sent for thee.'

'I come,' cried the Khan, 'I come: it was well he remembered me; he seeks death as I do,' he added mentally.

'The lady Kummoo would speak to thee,' said a slave, as he passed out.

'Tell her I go to death!' he replied sternly; 'tell her I follow Ameena—away!' The girl stared at him as though the words had stunned her, gazed after him as he passed on, saw him spring quickly into his saddle, and dashing his heels into his noble charger, bound onwards at a desperate speed.

''Tis well thou art come, Khan,' said Kasim Ali, 'we have waited for thee.'

'Hush! why seekest thou death? thou art not fitted to die, Kasim.'

'More fit than thou, old man,' was his reply. 'Come, they wait—they remark thee; when we are before the judgment thou wilt know all. Come!'

The Khan laughed scornfully, for he remembered the kiss. 'Come, my friends,' he cried; 'follow Rhyman Khan for the faith and for Islam: Bismilla! open the gate.'

'For the faith! for Islam!' cried the devoted band as the heavy door opened, and emerging from the shadow of the gate and wall, the sunlight glanced upon their naked weapons, gay apparel, and excited horses, and they dashed in a fearful race toward the camp.

'Show us the tent of the great commander!' cried Kasim to a sentinel who stared at them as they passed, evidently taking them to be a body of the Nizam's horse.

'Yonder!' said the man, pointing to one at some distance.

'Follow Kasim Ali! Follow Rhyman Khan!' were the cries of the leaders, both urging their horses to full speed in reckless emulation. They had been observed, however: a staff-officer had watched them from the first, and suspected their intention; now he could not be mistaken; he flew to a picquet of native soldiers, and drew them up across the very path of the rapidly-advancing horsemen. Kasim marked the action, as the muskets obeyed the word of command; he saw the bright sun glance on a line of levelled barrels, and heard the sharp rattle which followed: his horse stumbled; as it fell, he saw the Khan toss his arms wildly into the air and reel in his seat, and the next moment his affrighted charger was flying riderless through the camp! He saw no more, he felt stunned for an instant, and his dead horse lay on his leg—causing exquisite pain; he extricated himself and tried to rise—his leg failed him, and he fell again to the ground—it was broken. Again he looked around, a number of men and horses lay confusedly together. Some writhing in pain and crying out for mercy, while the rest of the band were flying confusedly to the Fort.

The Sepoys who had fired ran up, headed by an English

officer. Kasim had lost his sword; it lay at a little distance, and he could not recover it. One of the men, seeing that he lived, raised his bayonet as he approached to kill him. He shut his eyes, and repeated the Kulma.

'Hold!' cried a voice, 'do not kill him—he is an officer; raise him up and disarm him.'

'Thou art a prisoner,' said the officer to Kasim; 'do not resist—art thou wounded?'

'My leg is broken,' said Kasim; 'kill me, I am not fit to live, I have no desire for life.'

'Poor fellow!' said the officer, 'he is in great pain. Lift him up, some of ye, and take him to my tent; he is evidently an officer, by his dress, and the rich caparisons of his horse.'

'Yonder lies my leader!' said Kasim, pointing to the Khan; 'raise me, and let me look upon him once more. We were friends in life until yesterday—in death we should not have been divided.'

They were touched by his words, and obeyed him. The Khan lay on his face, quite dead. They turned the body: Kasim looked upon the familiar features—they were already sharp and livid; there was a small hole in the forehead, from which a few drops of black blood had oozed; his death had been instant as thought. Kasim heeded not the pain he suffered, he felt as though his heart were bursting; and throwing himself beside the body, wept passionately.

After a while he tried to rise, and they assisted him. 'That was a gallant soldier!' he said to the officer; 'let him be buried as one, by men of my faith.'

'I will answer for it,' said a native officer, stepping forward; 'thou shalt hear this evening that the rites of our faith have been performed over him. If he was an enemy, yet he was a brother in the faith of Islam.'

'Enough! I thank thee, friend,' replied Kasim. 'Now lead on—I care not whether I live or die, since those I lived for are gone from the earth.'

But the officer's curiosity had been excited by his words and his appearance, which was eminently prepossessing. He was removed gently to his tent, and a bedding laid on the ground. A surgeon, a friend of the officer, was sent for, ; Kasim's leg was examined; the thigh was badly fractured above the knee, but the operation was skilfully performed, and in a manner which surprised Kasim. It was bound up, and he was soon in comparative ease. How little he had expected such kindness! And when he contrasted it with what would have been an Englishman's fate within the Fort, his heart was softened from the bigotry it had previously entertained.

The officer was Philip Dalton. He had long thought on the possibility of saving some captive, that he might gain information of the English prisoners, and he tended Kasim kindly. In a few days they were better friends; the cold reserve of Kasim had worn off before the frank manner of the Englishman, and they now conversed freely of the war, of their own vicissitudes and adventures, and of the present chances of success. Kasim soon perceived that all hope for the Sultaun was at an end, from the vigour of the attack and the efficiency of the army, and he knew that within the Fort existed dread and discontent. After a while Philip asked him of the prisoners—at first warily, and only hinting at their existence. But Kasim was faithful to his Sultaun, though he could have told him of the fearful murders which had been openly mentioned among the army, to avenge which they supposed the English thirsted. Yet he did not reveal them, even though he knew from Philip's own lips that the English had been informed of them by the hundreds who had deserted on the night of the first attack. Often Philip would ask him whether he had ever known any of the prisoners; whether he had ever spoken with them when on guard over them, or perchance escorting them from station to station: for he knew that the captives were frequently removed, lest they should attack those who attended them.

And when Kasim related to him his interference in behalf of an English prisoner at Bangalore, and his attempt to protect him in the Sultaun's Durbar, risking his life for him ere yet he was himself in service, Philip's cheek glowed, and his heart throbbed, in a silent conviction that it was Herbert himself.

'Was he tall, and brown-haired? and had he very large blue eyes?' he asked anxiously.

Kasim recollected himself: it was a long time ago, and his memory appeared to have been impaired by the late events; he had only seen him in times of great excitement. But after a long reflection, he thought it was the same; however, the prisoner's features had made little impression upon him.

'Poor youth!' added Kasim, 'I saw him no more.'

'How! what became of him?'

'He was doomed to die. While I was held back by men—for I was excited—I saw him dragged away. I heard the Sultaun give the fatal mandate to Jaffar,—a man whose heart is blacker than that of Satan.'

'He of whom thou hast told me so much of late?'

'Ay, the same. I heard mention made of the fatal rock, and the young Englishman was dragged forth, spat upon and insulted. Yet even then he spoke to me, and said that my action would be remembered in the judgment. Alas! I had no power to rescue him, and he must have died.'

'Gallant fellow!' cried Philip, 'the pain of that thought I can save thee; he died not there.'

'How dost thou know? what was he to thee, Sahib?'

'He was dear as a brother to me—he was my friend. I married his sister, after years of absence from my native land. When we took Balapoor, I went to the rock thou knowest of—it was in curiosity only. His name was written there, and that renewed the hope which had never been dead within our hearts: for one of the miserable victims had written that he had been taken away ill; and by a chance, sent by Providence, we traced him to a worthy Fakeer's Tukea,—thou mayest remember it?'

'I do; a cool shady place, where the wearied wayfarer is ever welcomed.'

'The kind old man tended him, administered medicine to him. He recovered, and we heard that he was taken away by that same Jaffar whom thou hast mentioned—whither, he could not tell.'

'Alas! then I fear there is no hope of his life. Jaffar is a devil, yet in such a matter he dare not act without the Sultaun's order. I remember,' he added after a pause, 'a conversation between them about an Englishman—it was before the siege; there was no one else present. Tippoo spoke of one who was skilled in fortification, in the arts of war and of gunnery, far above the French adventurers in his service, who after all are but pretenders to science. Could this be thy brother?

'It is! it is!' cried Philip, catching at the idea in desperation; 'it must be, he was eminently skilled in all. Your last words determine the idea that it was he. By your soul, tell me if you know aught of him.'

'Alas! no,' said the young man. 'Yet they concealed nothing: Jaffar said it was useless; that he had sent trusty messengers to him to the fort, through the jungles, at the peril of their lives, with offers of mercy, pardon, wealth, if he would take service in the army. He had spurned all; and then the Sultaun grew furious, and swore he might die there.'

'Did he mention the fort, the place where it was, in what direction?' asked Philip eagerly.

'No, and I know not, Sahib; it is not in this district. If he be still alive, he is in one of those lonely posts away to the west—in Coorg, or on the frontiers of Malabar, a little spot on the top of some lonely peak, piercing the sky, which is ever wrapped in clouds and mists, with its base surrounded by jungles, to traverse which days and weeks are required—garrisoned by the rude and barbarous infidels of the mountains, whose speech and appearance are hardly human. It is a horrible fate to think on, Sahib,' he said, shuddering; 'better that he should have died long ago. But, after all, it may not be your friend.

'Perhaps not,' said Philip, sighing; 'and yet I have hope; and when the Fort is stormed, and yon proud Sultaun brought to the reckoning he deserves, it will be hard if we gain not news of him we seek.'

'May Alla grant it, Sahib! Thou hast bound me to thee by the kindness thou hast shown a stranger and an enemy, and I will rejoice, even as thou dost, that thy friend and brother should be saved. But, alas! I have little hope. Yet when I recover, and this war is over, if I live I will search for thee and rescue him.'

'God bless thee!' cried Philip; 'I believe thee. Thou hast now known that we are not the miscreants which the bigots of the faith would represent us to be; and if thou canst bring me even news of his death, it will be a melancholy satisfaction, and will still the restless hopes which have so long gnawed at our hearts and excited us, only to be cast down into utter despair.'

. . . .

Days passed of constant success on the part of the English: their cannon played night and day upon the breaches, till they were almost practicable. Those in the Fort looked on in sullen despair, and abandoned themselves to a blind reliance on their destiny. It was in vain that Tippoo made the most passionate appeals to them to sally out and cut the English army to pieces; it was in vain he read to them the humiliating demands of the allies; in vain he raved, as he saw the groves of his favourite and beautiful gardens levelled with the earth, and transported to construct fascines and gabions for new parallels and trenches. The sorties were weak, and driven back with loss, and with the remembrance of the fatal issue of that led by Rhyman Khan and Kasim Ali, no one dared to hazard a similar attempt, though rewards beyond thought were offered by the frantic monarch. The murmurs within gradually increased, as the breaches widened daily, and men looked to the issue of the storm in fearful dread. Women shrieked in the streets, and men were everywhere seen offering vain sacrifices of sheep and fowls to the senseless idols of the temple, that the firing might cease.

At length it did; the Sultaun in despair yielding to terms of which he could not then estimate the leniency. The firing ceased, and though the maddened English could hardly be restrained from rushing into the Fort and searching its most secret apartments and hiding-places for their unhappy countrymen, they were kept back, and the negotiations proceeded.

The event is already matter of history, and we are not historians. Although even his children had gone from him as hostages into the British camp, in a paroxysm of passion the Sultaun desperately refused the cession of Coorg to its rightful owner, whom he had dispossessed—one of the terms of the treaty, but which he well knew, if yielded, would open a road into the heart of his dominions at any time. The stern resolution of the English commander—the presence of his victorious army, the threats of which were openly stated to him by his officers—the general discontent and dread which pervaded all, in spite of his appeals to their pride, their bigotry, and their courage—the repair of the breach while the English cannon ceased—all conspired to check their spirit. He sullenly yielded to a destiny he could not avert, and accepting the conditions, he delivered up those captives who were known to be in the Fort and province.

With what agonising apprehension did Philip Dalton and Charles Hayward fly from body to body of these men—some grown aged and careworn from misery and long confinement, while others, having been forcibly converted to the faith of Islam, now openly abjured its tenets, and flung away their turbans and other emblems of their degraded condition. Alas! Herbert Compton was not among them, nor could any one tell of his fate, though his name was remembered vividly; and it was known among them from Bolton, who was dead, that he had not perished at the rock of Hyder.

Now therefore, for the Sultaun again and again protested that he had given up all, and that Herbert had died soon after his escape from the rock, Philip and young Hayward abandoned all hope. True, for a while they thought that one of the strongholds of Coorg might contain their poor friend; but there too they were disappointed; and there was no longer a straw floating upon the waters of expectation at which they could catch in desperation; and hope, which had been for years buoyant, sank within them for ever.

The news of the victory reached England; the nation rejoiced at the triumph, that their bitterest enemy in the East had been humbled and despoiled of his fair provinces, and that the political horizon of their already increasing possessions was once more clear. But there were two families among the many who mourned for those who had met a soldier's death, which, though the bereavement was not a present one, yet felt it as acutely as if it had been recent; nay more so, since their hopes had been so long excited. They knew not that Amy had ever thought there was hope of Herbert's life; but long ere letters came, when it was known that the army was in Mysore, they saw her look for every succeeding dispatch with more and more impatience, and a feverish anxiety she could not conceal. And when the end came, they knew, from her agonised burst of bitter grief, that she too had lingered in hope even as they had.

But Amy's was a strong mind, and one which her affliction, though deep and heavy to bear, had never driven into repining. She looked with earnest hope to the future; and in reliance on the Divine power and wisdom, which she had early practised, and which never failed her in her need, she drew from that pure source consolation, which those who loved her most dearly could not impart; she had lived on a life of meek and cheerful piety, almost adored by the neighbourhood, and in sweet intercourse with those around her, whose constant care for her was amply repaid by her devoted affection.

CHAPTER XLVI.

THE Sultaun was not humbled by the issue of the campaign, though for a time his resources were straitened. On the contrary, he burned with revenge for the indignity which he had suffered, superadded to the fierce hate for the English which he had ever retained, and which rose now to a degree of ferocity he could hardly restrain. The demand of three millions and a half sterling made for the expenses of the war—for which, and the relinquishment of the territory he had agreed to resign, his children were held as hostages—he met partly by a payment from his own treasury, partly by a demand upon his army and his civil officers, and the residue was directed to be raised in the provinces, where means were employed for the purpose at which humanity shudders. Mild as had been his civil administration previously, and flourishing as was the cultivation of his whole country under the admirable administration of Purneah, his finance minister—often in marked contrast to the desolation of the English provinces, where the rule of Englishmen was not understood, nor their information as yet equal to the complexity of revenue affairs—there now ensued a remarkable contrast. As the oppression and forced contribution proceeded with horrible rigour, thousands fled into the English possessions, where they were received and protected; and this, while it did not check the infatuated persecution of many of his people, in whose welfare lay his own safety, added fresh cause for his hatred of those from whose protecting sway he could not withdraw them.

Meanwhile his restless mind embraced every subject which came, or which he fancied could come, within his grasp; astrology and magic, with all their absurd and debasing rites, were studied with greater avidity and attention than ever under the guidance of some who had pretensions to those sciences, both Brahmins and Mahomedans. From them he drew the most magnificent auguries of his future brilliant destiny; the past, he said, was but a cloud which, as he had ascertained from the stars, had hung over him from his birth; it was now dissipated, melted into thin air before the bright beams of the rising sun of his destiny. Physic, too, absorbed his attention; to perfection in which he made vast pretensions by aid of a thermometer, the true use of which he declared he had discovered by a revelation from the angel Gabriel, with whom he seemed to have established in his dreams a perfect confidence. It is only necessary, he would say, for a sick man to hold the bulb in his hand, and then, as the mercury rose or fell, so was the disease hot or cold; and according to its scale of progression, so should the remedies, differing in potency, be applied. Often he would, in his caprice, remark upon the altered look of any one present in his court; and in spite of their protestations of perfect health, apply the test, and administer a remedy upon the spot, which it would have been death almost to refuse.

The news of the revolutionary movement of 1789-90 in France, also, for which he had been gradually prepared by the adventurers in his service, infected him with a restless desire of imitation, which ran into the most ludicrous and often mischievous channels. As the French names of years and months were altered, so were his. A new era was instituted; and this being in direct opposition to the precepts of the Koran, which direct an implicit observance of them, he had recourse to his dreams and visions once more, by which it was for the while established.

In all departments of finance, of the army, of agriculture, of justice, there were perpetual alterations, sometimes undoubtedly with good effect, at others the most puerile and absurd. Words of command, invented from the Persian language, were given to his army, and new orders for their regulation and discipline constantly promulgated. He contemplated a fleet to exterminate the English one; which, having before defeated the French, had prevented them from sending such succour to his aid as he had expected. One hundred ships of immense force was to be the complement; of these, forty were directed to be commenced at Tellicherry, Mangalore, and his other ports on the western coast; and officers were appointed to them, commanders and admirals, who had never even seen the sea, had no conception what a ship was, save from the descriptions of others. Some of these men were sent to superintend their completion, others retained at court for instruction in the science of navigation and naval warfare; in which, as in his military pretensions, his dreams, visions, and assumed revelations, alone assisted him.

He was merchant and money-lender by turns; and huge warehouses, which still exist in the Fort of Seringapatam, long open rooms in the palace, capable of containing vast quantities of merchandise, were filled with every description of goods, which in time he forgot entirely, and so they remained till his death. By his system of banking, and of regulating, as he imagined, in his own person the exchanges of his dominions, he put a stop to the operations of the bankers of his capital, by whose assistance alone he was able to administer his affairs; nor would they resume their business until he agreed to abandon this one of the thousand schemes which were on foot for fame and aggrandisement.

New and perplexing laws were for ever being coined in the fertile mint of his own brain; new interpretations of the Koran, which he pretended to receive by inspiration, when in reality he understood not a word of its language, and very indifferently Persian, in which the commentaries upon it were written. The penal enactments against the lower classes of his Hindoo subjects were horrible; the meanest offences, the wearing of any scrap of green, the sacred colour of Mahomed, about their persons, or the transgression of any one of his arbitrary rules, was punished with death, or obscene mutilations, to which death would have been far preferable. These were often done in his own presence; and with Jaffar Sahib, Madar (who had once been his servant, but who had risen in rank), and many others, he was at no loss for instruments to carry them into execution. He would call himself the Tiger of the Faith—the beloved friend of Mahomed; and while he arrogated to himself the last title, the impiety of which shocked the religious among his officers, he acted up to the first not only in words, but in deeds, such as we have alluded to cursorily, by dressing his infantry in cotton jackets printed in tiger's stripes,—by sitting on the effigy of one for a throne, and by having two large ones chained in the court-yard of his palace, who were often made the executioners of his terrible will.

Many are the tales, too, even now very current in the country, of the ludicrous effects of his inspirations regarding particular people, whom, for some fancied lucky termination or commencement of their name, or some meaning he chose to attach to it, a fortunate horoscope, or even from lucky personal marks, he would select from the meanest ranks, to fill offices for which they were alike unfitted by education, talents, or acquirements, and who, when their incapacity was detected, were mercilessly disgraced. It has been said of him by an eminent historian,* whose account of the period is a vivid romance from first to last, that 'his were the pranks of a monkey, with the abominations of a monster'; and indeed it is impossible to give an idea of his character in juster terms.

Kasim Ali was again with him, and, rewarded, for his exertions on the day we have mentioned, had risen to a high rank among his officers. Unable to walk when the army broke up from before Seringapatam, Philip Dalton had persuaded him to travel by the easy stages at which the army proceeded, as well for the change which his weakened condition required, as for the continued attendance of the English surgeon under whose care he was placed. To this he had agreed, for in truth the representations of the noble-hearted Englishman had set many matters before him in a new light, and he now looked upon acts of the Sultaun with abhorrence which he had before considered as justifiable, nay, meritorious, when exercised upon infidels, whether Hindoos or English; and having accompanied Philip to Bangalore, he parted from him there with regret, and with a strong sense of his kind and generous behaviour, promising that should he ever discover any clue to the fate of poor Herbert, he would write; for the nations being now on good terms, the communications were open, and he could do so with safety.

For a long while, however, he was unfit to move; he made a report of his escape to the Sultaun, and receiving in return an honorary dress for his gallant behaviour, he was assured that his rank remained to him—nay, was increased; and having solicited leave of absence, he returned to his village to regain, in its quiet

* Wilks.

seclusion, the strength and peace of mind he had lost. Of Ameena he never thought but as one dead; for though he had written to his friend the Moola to endeavour to trace her fate, and to discover where she had been buried, in order that he might have the melancholy satisfaction of erecting a tomb over her remains, yet she could not be traced, nor her attendants, who were supposed to have escaped to the Nizam's army in the confusion which ensued after the siege, and her body to have been buried in some obscure place during the night on which she had been cut down. The Moola wrote word that the matter was not known, except perhaps to a few of the Khan's servants, who had not divulged it.

Kasim found, too, that he had been declared heir to most of the Khan's wealth, which was large; there was a handsome provision made for his two wives, besides their dower upon marriage, and it was said their families were satisfied with the will, which, regularly drawn up, had been deposited long before his death with responsible executors. In it a large sum was assigned to Ameena; but as she did not appear, it was kept in trust for her should it ever be claimed. Hoormut, the elder wife, had gone to her relations, at some distance from the city; and it was said that Kummoo, whose beauty was much spoken of, had been transferred to the Sultaun's zenana, the laxity of the morality of which would, Kasim thought, exactly suit her.

Kasim was thus raised to a handsome independence of station, and he spared no pains to make his mother's declining years as happy as was possible. A new and handsome abode was erected for her; his village walls were rebuilt, and strengthened against perhaps troublous times to come. A new mosque was built; and a neat serai, near the soldiers' tomb, marked the spot in which he had rescued Ameena. This was his favourite resort, where of an evening, spreading a carpet beneath the trees, he would remain, in conversation with those he loved and respected, the elders of his village, both Hindoo and Mahomedan, or else in silent and sad thought on the past,—on the happiness which had been so rudely dashed from his lips. His health continued very indifferent, and from time to time his leave of absence was renewed; however, at length he could delay no longer, and he once more resumed his attendance at the court of the Sultaun.

It was not, however, with the same feelings of indifference that he now regarded the monstrous acts of the Sultaun; his mind had been purged from the dross of bigotry by his residence in the English camp, where, besides Philip Dalton's society, there were many others who, either out of curiosity or to while away a tedious hour of ennui, would come to the pallet-side of the Jemadar, and listen to his conversation; relating in turn tales of their own green land, which to Kasim's senses appeared a paradise. Jaffar Sahib was an offence in his sight; and his increased favour with the Sultaun, his constant attendance on his person and at the Durbar, his now fearful reputation, and the memory of the past (for Kasim felt sure he was connected with that fatal night and Ameena's death), as well as the fate of the young Englishmen,—all caused a total revulsion of feeling towards the monarch, and he felt his situation becoming daily more distasteful to him, in spite of the splendid prospects which were undoubtedly in the distance. Kasim, too, was a good Mussulman; he was regular in his prayers, and hated innovations; and the endless capricious changes, the blasphemous conduct of the Sultaun, and his pretensions to supernatural power—his devotion to unholy and magical rites, which were openly mentioned, and, above all, his acts of cruelty and tyranny—determined him, and some others of his own character, to abandon a service in which their high notions of justice, decency, and piety were daily outraged.

By the partition treaty, also, the territory in which were situated the villages of Kasim Ali had been transferred to the Nizam, and he at last found it impossible to serve two masters. As long as he remained at home, the authorities dreaded him, and were quiet; but after a time a system of annoyance commenced, of which he had such frequent accounts, that he was soon left no resource between selling his patrimony and cleaving for ever to the ruler of Mysore, or abandoning his service and retiring into seclusion. Had the Sultaun's conduct not shocked him by its levity and brutality, he might have sold his villages, and withdrawn his family into Mysore; but he shrank from that, and, having converted his property into bills on Hyderabad, Adoni, or other towns which were readily negotiable in the district he belonged to, he prepared himself for a journey, and formally tendered his resignation to the Sultaun in open Durbar.

There were many of his friends who had advised him to ask for leave, and write his intention of not returning from his own home; but he thought this a cowardly manner of proceeding, and determined that his memory should not be reproached with cowardice, and that it should remain as it stood, high among those who were honoured in the army. At an evening Durbar, therefore, when all were present, and many eyes fixed on him (for his resolution was known), he arose, stepped forward, and having made the tusleemat, said to the Sultaun,—

'Your slave would make a petition, if he is permitted?'

'Surely,' said the Sultaun; 'what did Kasim Ali ever say that was not welcome?'

'My lord,' he began, 'it is hard for one who hath received benefits at thy hands, and who in a bright prospect before him—the glorious career of the lion of the faith—seeth no end but advancement, to shut it out from his sight, and to deny himself the pleasure of seeing day by day the Light of Islam—the Lion of the Faith. O Sultaun! be merciful to thy servant, and forgive the request he makes, that he may retire from thy service into the obscurity and quiet he has long coveted. It is well known to all this assembly, that thy slave is one to whom the stirring events of life have no charm—the intrigues, the factions, the wavering politics of a court, no attraction. If I have hitherto preserved my place here, it has been by kindness and forbearance, not by merit. Another far more fitted than I am will succeed me, and I shall be content in the administration of my property, which, distant as it is, requires my constant attention and care.'

Tippoo stared at him, and Kasim felt uncomfortable; he could not remember that any one had ever made such a request before, and he could not foresee the result. Yet the Sultaun had been in good humour all the day, and he hoped for the best.

'What do I hear, Kasim Ali—that thou wouldst leave my service?'

'Even so, Huzrut! When thou wast in peril of thy life, mine was risked freely, though others hung back. I, and he that is gone—may his memory live in honour!—led those into the English camp who might have ended the war, had Alla so willed it. In adversity I stood by thee, and I have not quitted thee since, for these six years. Thou art now prosperous: the French are thy friends; thou art courted by the nations of Hind; thou art at peace with the English—long may this continue—thou art prosperous everywhere; and now when all is fair and bright around thee, I would in the season of joy take my leave, grateful for a thousand benefactions from the liberal hand of him who has not ceased to uphold me since I was a youth.'

'Thou art joking, Kasim Ali,' said Tippoo; 'and yet thou hast a serious face. By your soul, say this is not meant!'

'It is in very truth, O Prince! I have long meditated it. I waited only till my lord's mind was happy and free from care to announce it, for I would not have my memory linked with painful recollections, but with pleasant thoughts.'

The Sultaun's brow darkened. 'Thou art considerate, young

man!' he said bitterly. 'When I was happy and merry in my heart, thou must needs mar all by this news. By Alla! I would rather thou hadst told it when the storm within me was at the highest; but no matter; thou hast served us well and faithfully—we shall long remember it; nor would we detain any one against his will. We have (blessed be the Prophet!) hundreds in our valiant army to fill vacant places. Therefore go—thou hast thy leave. Yet thou shalt not have it to say I was churlish in this; thou art dismissed with honour. Bring hither two shawls, a turban, and an ornament for the head—also a noble horse from my stables, and a sword and shield from the private armoury,' he cried to an attendant. 'Ye shall see, sirs,' how Tippoo estimates greatness, and how he rewards it.'

Kasim was much moved: he had expected a stormy scene, an absolute refusal; he had prepared himself for it, and for flight if necessary; now he could have cried like a child; all the Sultaun's caprice, cruelty, and impiety were forgotten. There sate before him the benefactor and the steady friend of years. He continued gazing on him, and often he felt the tears rush to his eyes, as though they would have had vent. The attendant entered with a tray; upon it were a pair of magnificent shawls of Cashmere, a superb mundeel, and a jewel of great value for the forehead. The Sultaun examined them with the air of a merchant. 'They are a handsome pair, and worthy of him,' he said; 'and this too is rich, and the diamonds of good water. Approach, Kasim Ali!'

He obeyed: the Sultaun arose, cast over his shoulders the rich shawls, took the turban and jewel from the tray, and presented him with them. 'Embrace me,' he said,—'I love thee: I shall ever remember thee gratefully, Kasim Ali; and thou wilt not forget the poor servant of Alla, Tippoo Sultaun: should his enemies revile him, there will be one whose tongue will speak his praise. Shouldst thou ever feel disposed to return, thy place is open to thee; or if as a guest, thou art ever welcome. Go—may Alla keep thee!'

'Never will I forget thee, O benefactor!' cried Kasim, completely overcome; 'never will I allow a word to be said against thee; and in my home—in the wide world—wherever I go, men shall know of the generosity of the lion of Mysore. I go—my prayers are for thee and thy prosperity night and day.'

Kasim made low obeisances as he passed out of the audience-hall; he cast a last look round the well-known place; what scenes he had witnessed there, of joy and misery, frantic enthusiasm and fierce bigotry, torture, and even death! Dreams, visions, lewd and vile torrents of abuse against the English; poems, letters of war, of intrigue, of policy, of every conceivable kind. Enough! they were gone for ever, and he was glad that the feverish existence was at an end; henceforth before him was the peaceful and quiet existence he had so long coveted.

The horse, richly caparisoned, stood at the palace-gate, and men bearing the sword and shield. Kasim bounded into the saddle, and before the admiring spectators, many of them his kind friends, caused him to curvet and bound to show how perfectly the animal was trained; and then saluting them he rode on. Next morning he was on his way beyond the Fort.

That night Jaffar was alone with the Sultaun; they had conversed long on various matters. At last Jaffar exclaimed, 'May I be your sacrifice! it was wrong to let Kasim Ali go.'

'Why?' said Tippoo.

'He knows too much,' was the reply.

'But he is faithful, Jaffar?'

The fellow laughed. 'He is a good friend to the English.'

'To the English?'

'Ay! remember how often he has spoken in their favour, how often he has bearded others who reviled them. May I be your sacrifice! he is unfaithful, or why should he leave thee?'

The Sultaun was struck by the remark. 'If I thought so,' he said quickly.

'Why should he for months have been collecting his money?' continued Jaffar; 'every rupee he could collect has gone to Hyderabad, bills, hoondees, gold, all except what he has with him; he has ground the uttermost couree from those who owed him anything.'

'Is this true?'

'Ay, by your head! shall I bring the Sahoukars who gave them?'

'Ya Alla!' cried the Sultaun, 'what a serpent have I been nourishing! Thou saidst to Hyderabad?'

'Ay, he will go to Sikundur Jah, and fill his ears with tales of thee for the English, and give them a plan of this fort. Was he not always with the engineers?'

'Enough, good fellow,' said the Sultaun sternly; 'he must not reach the city—dost thou understand?'

'I will not lose a moment; the men will have to travel fast, but they can overtake him.'

'Will they dare attack him? methinks there are few who would attempt that, even among thy devils.'

'There are some of them who would attack hell itself and its king Satan,' said the man with a grin, 'when they have had bhang enough; trust me, it shall be done. He escaped me once,' said Jaffar, as he went out; 'he will be lucky if he does so again; we shall be even at last.'

. . . .

Kasim Ali rode on gaily; with him were a number of men who had previously obtained leave of absence, and had stayed for the advantage of his society and safe conduct, for he was respected by all. They were proceeding, some on horseback, others on ponies, to various parts of the north of Mysore; some to his own district, some to Hyderabad. The road was light under their horses' feet, and coss after coss passed almost without their knowledge, as they conversed freely and merrily together. At the point where the river Madoor crosses the road to Bangalore there is a good deal of thick jungle, but they heeded not the pass, though it was noted for robbers; they were too formidable a party to be attacked. As they proceeded carelessly, a shot whistled from among some bushes to the left—it went harmless; another, and Kasim felt a sting in his left arm, and he saw a man fall.

'Upon them!' he cried, drawing his sword; 'upon the sons of defiled mothers!' and he dashed into the jungle, followed by the best mounted; ten or twelve men were flying at their utmost speed—but they had a poor chance before those determined horsemen. Kasim cut at two as he passed them; they were not killed but badly wounded; three others were despatched.

'I know that rascal's face,' said one of his companions, as the prisoners were brought up; 'it is one of Jaffar's devils.'

'Ay, and this is another,' said Kasim; 'he was in the Durbar yesterday morning.'

'Tell us why thou hast done this?' he said; 'why didst thou attack me? what have I ever done to harm thee?'

'Nothing,' said one sullenly; 'it was the Sultaun's order.'

'Thou liest!' cried Kasim, striking him.

'Do not beat me,' he replied; 'but behold, here is the order to give us horses to overtake thee, shouldst thou have gone on. We knew not that thou hadst tarried in the city last night; we arose and came on to the last village; they told us there thou hadst not passed, and we waited for thee. Behold! this is the Sultaun's seal.'

It was truly so—his private seal: Kasim well knew it; he shuddered as he looked on it. 'Why should there have been such black treachery?'

'Go!' said he to the man, recollecting himself, 'thou are but the instrument of others; go—may Alla give thee a better heart! Tell thy master I recognise his work; and bid him say to the Sultaun, or say it thyself—the love that was between us is broken for ever. Go!'

'Let us press on, my friends,' said Kasim, 'not by the road, but by bye-paths. Though I know not what vengeance I have provoked, ye see I am not safe.'

They did so, and it was well that they travelled fast, for the baffled tiger raved at the loss of his prey, and many men pursued Kasim and his companions, but in vain.

CHAPTER XLVII.

THE morning of the twenty-sixth of April 1798 was a scene of universal excitement in the fort of Seringapatam. As the day advanced, crowds of men collected in the great square before the palace; soldiers in their gayest costumes, horsemen, and caparisoned elephants, which always waited upon the Sultaun and his officers. The roofs of the houses around, those of the palace particularly, the old temples, and the flat terraces of its courts and dhurrumsalas, even the trees were crowded with human beings, on the gay colours of whose dresses a brighter sun had never shone. There arose from the mighty mass of garrulous beings a vast hubbub of sounds, increased by the Sultaun's loud kettle-drums, the martial music of the band of a French regiment, the shrill blasts of the collery horns, neighings of horses and trumpetings of elephants, as they were urged hither and thither.

No one in this soberly-dressed land can have an idea of the gorgeous appearance of these spectacles; for an eastern crowd, from the endless variety of its bright colours, and the picturesqueness and grace of its costumes,—its gaily caparisoned horses, elephants, and camels,—is of all others in the world the most beautiful and impressive.

In the centre of the square was an open space, kept by French soldiers; in the middle of this stood a small tree, which had been uprooted and planted there; but already its leaves had faded and drooped. It was covered with gay ribbons of all colours and of gold and silver tissue, which fluttered in the fresh breeze and glittered in the sun: this was surmounted by a spear, on which was the red cap of liberty, the fearful emblem of the French revolution.

Around it were many French officers, some dressed fantastically and crowned with wreaths of green leaves, others in brilliant uniforms, their plumes and feathers waving. Many of them spoke with excited gestures from time to time, and swore round oaths at the Sultaun's delay; for the sun had climbed high into the heaven, and no shade was there to save them from its now scorching beams.

The amicable issue of the embassy to Paris, sent by Tippoo in 1788, had been exaggerated by the envoys to enhance their consequence; and the French officers in his service had by every possible means in their power kept this feeling alive. When the revolution broke out, the roar of which faintly reached the Sultaun of Mysore, it was represented to him by those of the French nation who were there, in such terms of extravagant eulogium, while its bloody cruelties were concealed, or, if mentioned, declared to be acts of retributive justice, that the Sultaun's mind, itself a restless chaos of crude ideas of perpetual changes and progression, eagerly caught at the frenzied notions of liberty which the Frenchmen preached. At the same time it is almost impossible to conceive how an Asiatic monarch born to despotism could have endured such an anomaly as his position presents—one who with the most petty jealousy and suspicion resisted any restriction of, or interference with, his absolute will and direction of all affairs, even to the most minute and unimportant of his government, whether civil or military.

From time to time, allured by the certainty of good pay in his army, many needy adventurers came to him from the Isle of France, who were entertained at once, and assumed, if they did not possess it, a knowledge of military affairs. These kept up a constant correspondence with their parent country; and willing to humour the Sultaun, while indulging their own spleen, they poured into his ready ear the most virulent abuse of the English, and constant false statements of their losses by sea and land; while the accounts of French superiority and French victory were related in tones of exaggerated triumph.

Ripaud, an adventurer with more pretension and address than others, having arived at Mangalore, and discerning the bent of the court from Tippoo's authorities there, represented himself to be an envoy from the French republic, and was invited at once to the capital. It may well be supposed that he did not underrate his own assumed influence, nor the immense advantages of an embassy in return; and one was sent by Tippoo, which, meeting with various adventures by the way, returned at last, not with the mighty force he had been led to expect, but with a few needy officers, the chief of whom was Chapuis, men who determined to raise for themselves at his court a power equal to that of Perron at the court of Sindia, and of Raymond at that of the Nizam.

This was a feverish period for India, when those two mighty nations, England and France, were striving for supremacy. True, the power of the English was immeasurably more concentrated and effective, and their resolute and steady valour more highly appreciated than the brilliant but eccentric character of the French. Still, however, the latter power had increased extraordinarily since the last war with Tippoo; and 45,000 men at Sindia's court, over whom Perron held absolute sway, and 14,000 under Raymond at Hyderabad, were pledged by their leaders to aggrandize the power of their nation, and to disseminate the principles of the revolution.

Chapuis had laboured hard to effect his object; a man of talent and quick-witted, he had at once assumed a mental superiority over the Sultaun, which he maintained. He had flattered, cajoled, and threatened by turns; he had written to the French Government in his behalf—he had promised unlimited supplies of men and ammunition—he had bewildered the Sultaun's mind with the sophistries of the revolution, with vague notions of liberty, equality, and the happiness which was to follow upon the earth from the adoption of these principles by all ranks—he had told him of the rapid rise of Buonaparte, of his magnificent victories, and inflamed him with visions of conquest even more vast than those of the French general.

The French expedition to Egypt became known, their successes and their subjugation of the country. That seemed but the stepping-stone to greater achievements. Alexander with a few Greeks had penetrated into India and had subdued all in his path. Buonaparte, with his victorious armies, far outnumbering the Greeks, was at a point from whence he could make an immediate descent upon Bombay; then would Perron lead Sindia into his alliance—Raymond, the Nizam. The Mahrattas, a wavering power, would side with the strongest. Zeman Shah and his hardy Afghans had already promised co-operation, so had the Rajpoots, and the men of Delhi and those of Nipal; last of all Tippoo himself, who had single-handed already met and defeated the English in the field. All were to join in one crusade against the infidel, the detested English, and expel them for ever from India. It is no wonder that the wild and restless ambition of the Sultaun was excited, his intrigues more and more frequent, and, as success seemingly lay within his grasp, that he himself was more open and unguarded.

'Join but our society,' Chapuis would say to him, 'you league yourself with us,—you identify yourself with the French republic, —its interests become yours,—your welfare its most anxious care. You become the friend, the brother of Buonaparte, and at once attach him to you by a bond which no vicissitudes can dissever.'

And he yielded, though with dread, for he knew not the meaning of the wild ceremony they proposed, of destroying the symbols of royalty, and reducing himself to a level with the meanest of his subjects; it was a thing abhorrent to his nature, one which he dared not disclose even to his intimates, but to which he yielded, drawn on by the blindest ambition that ever urged a human being to destruction.

The Frenchmen had long waited; at length there arose a shout, and the kettle-drums and loud nagaras from the palace proclaimed that the Sultaun was advancing. He approached slowly, dressed in the plainest clothes; no jewel was in his turban, only his rosary around his neck, a string of pearls without a price, for each bead had been exchanged for another when one more valuable could be purchased. A lane was formed through the crowd, and his slaves, headed by Jaffar, his confidential officer, preceded him, forcing the people back by rude blows of their sheathed sabres, and shouting his titles in extravagant terms.

All hailed the spectacle as one to exult in, though they could not understand it; but to the Sultaun it was one of bitter humiliation, his feelings at which he could hardly repress. He passed on, the crowd making reverence to him as he moved; he did not return their salutation, his eyes were downcast, and he bit his lips almost till the blood came. Before him was the place where he was going to a moral death—to abjure his power over men—to allow himself to be on equality with the meanest, to hold authority over them, not of inherent right, but by their sufferance. Had any one known his intention, and spoken one word to him in remonstrance, he would have turned; but the men were before him to whom he had sworn obedience, and he proceeded. Chapuis advanced, he saw his agitation, and in a few hurried words implored him to be firm, reminding him of the issue at stake, and this rallied him.

He led him to the tree; there was an altar beneath, as if for sacrifice; a small fire burned on it, and its thin blue smoke rose among the branches, and melted away into air; a perfume was thrown from time to time into the flame, which spread itself abroad as the smoke was dissipated.

Chapuis and some others officiated as priests of the mysteries, and they knelt before the altar, while one made a passionate invocation to liberty, which another tried in vain to explain to the Sultaun. It was finished: they arose, and Chapuis advanced toward him. 'Hast thou the emblems?' he said.

The Sultaun took them from an attendant, the feather of gold tinsel he always wore in his turban, and an ornament of trifling value for the head.

'These are all,' he said; 'be quick.'

'They will be nothing without your Highness's own turban,' replied Chapuis; 'placed in that, your people will understand the ceremony; otherwise it is vain. Your Highness remembers your promise and mine. I have performed mine; see that thou, O Sultaun, dost not fail!'

The others echoed his words, and urged the Sultaun to obey.

Hesitating and almost trembling, he did so.

'They will not understand,' he said to himself, 'they cannot comprehend this mummery; they cannot hear what the Frenchmen say, much less understand their broken language.'

He took the turban from his brows, and gave it into Chapuis' hand. The officer placed in it the tinsel feather, and threw it contemptuously into the fire. An attendant raised and unfurled a scarlet chuttree, or umbrella, over the monarch's head: that too was remarked.

'It must follow,' said Chapuis to him; 'that is a regal emblem,—there must be none left of the abomination.' He caught it from the attendant and flung it on the fire.

There arose a deep murmur of indignation from the multitude to see their monarch's turban taken from his head and burned; to see his chuttree forcibly taken and destroyed was more than they could bear without an expression of excitement, and cries of indignation rent the air.

'To hell with the Feringhees!—cut them down!—what impiety is this? What insult to the Sultaun?' And many drew their swords and raised them on high to strike. The Frenchmen were in imminent peril, but they were firm.

It was a grand and striking scene—that excited crowd—those fierce gestures—gleaming weapons—and those hoarse shouts and threats. In the centre, the group on which all eyes were fixed, the bare-headed Sultaun, and those few needy adventurers, reckless and unprincipled, who had gained a mastery over one whose smallest gesture would have caused their instant annihilation.

'Peace!' he cried, raising his arm; 'it is our will—it is decreed.' The multitude was hushed, but many a muttered threat was spoken, many a prayer for the dire omen to be averted, many an expression of pity for the position of one whom all feared and many even venerated.

And truly, to see that degradation done to one who knew not its meaning, who, bareheaded before his people, and under a fierce sun, stood and looked on at the destruction of the emblems of his power—might have caused pity for his condition; but it did not in those who stood around him; the act sealed their own power—they had no thought of pity.

As the last fragments burned to ashes in the blaze of the fire, Chapuis lowered the spear on which was the cap, and presented it to the monarch. 'Wear it!' he said, 'consecrated as it is in the smoke of those emblems which are destroyed for ever; wear it—an earnest of the victories thou wilt gain.'

The Sultaun put it on. Chapuis seized a tri-coloured flag which an officer bore near him, and waved it above his head. It was the signal agreed on: the artillerymen were at their posts on the ramparts, and the roar of two thousand and three hundred cannon proclaimed that Tippoo, the Light of the Faith, the Lion of Islam, the Sultaun of Mysore, was now citizen Tippoo of the French Republic, one and indivisible.

Then followed the coarse salutations of the French soldiery, who, excited by liquor and by the event, rushed around the Sultaun, and seized his hand, shaking it in rude familiarity; his cup of humiliation was full, and he returned to his palace in bitter mortification and anger. There were many of his officers who, deeply touched by the mockery of the exhibition, remonstrated with him, and advised him to revoke the act by a solemn scene in the mosque, attended by all his army and the high religious functionaries. But it was impossible to arouse him to the act—to shake off the domination to which he had subjected himself; and while it was whispered abroad that the Sultaun had become a Feringhee, those who wished well to his cause saw that he had with his own hands struck a vital blow at its interests.

It was happy for the British cause in India that a nobleman was appointed to the responsible station of Governor-General, who, from the moment he undertook the office, and during his passage out to India, bent his whole mind to the complete investigation of the politics of the country he came to govern. He was happy in having those with him who could afford him an insight into the designs and wishes of the native princes, and there is no doubt that Lord Mornington resolved to act upon many suggestions he received even before he arrived. To the intrigues of the Sultaun his notice had been particularly attracted, and the designs of the French were too obvious to be unnoticed for a moment. By a chain of events, which are points of history, the Sultaun's intrigues with the French Government of the Mauritius became known; the proclamations of its governor were received at Calcutta, and though doubted at first, from the continued expressions of friendship made by the Sultaun, yet their authenticity was established beyond a doubt by subsequent inquiries.

After the scene in the fort which we have mentioned, Tippoo abandoned himself to the councils of his French officers. He was admitted by them, as a proof of brotherhood, to a participation in the secrets of the correspondence held between Chapuis, Raymond, and Perron. Buonaparte was successful in Egypt, and it was debated only when the time should be fixed for the army of Tippoo to be set in motion and to overwhelm Madras. The army itself was full of confidence, and great attention had been paid to its discipline by the French; all branches were more perfectly efficient than they had ever been. The Sultaun had now no apprehension about the fort, for he had been surrounding it with another wall and ditch, and the gates had been strengthened by outworks. There never was a time when all his prospects were so bright, when the political condition of India suggested movement—when all the native princes, by one exertion on his part, might be incited to make common cause against the English, and when, by the proposed expedition against Manilla, the British forces would be much reduced, both at Madras and in Bengal. It was at this hazardous moment that the genius of Lord Mornington, guided by the sound views of the political agents at the various courts, decided upon the line of action to be pursued. The French interest in India was to be annihilated at all hazards; therefore, after a preparatory treaty with the Nizam, an English force, by rapid marches, arrived at Hyderabad, and joining the subsidiary force there, surrounded the French camp, which was found to be in a state of previous mutiny against its officers. The whole submitted; and a blow, moral as well as physical, was struck against the French influence, from which it never recovered.

The effect of this news at Seringaptam may be imagined; and when it was followed up by that of the glorious victory of Nelson at the mouth of the Nile, the Sultaun's spirit fell. It was in vain that he wrote apparently sincere letters to the Governor-General, and at the same moment dispatched camel-loads of treasure to Sindia to urge him to move southwards; the one estimated the true worth of the correspondence, and the wily Mahratta, though he took the money, yet stirred not a foot; he had too much at stake to be led into a quarrel of which he could not see any probable termination. Tippoo's ambassadors at the courts of Sindia and Holkar, of the Peshwa, of the Rajah of Berar, all wrote word that these potentates would join the cause; but their letters were cold and wary, and the Sultaun discovered too late that he must abide the brunt of the blow himself.

His dread of the English was vented daily in his Durbar, in compositions the most abominable that his fertile brain could invent. Besides his pretended supernatural revelations, letters were read, purporting to be from Delhi, from Calcutta, from Lucknow, describing the atrocious conduct of the English, the forced conversion of Mahòmmedans to Christianity, the violation of females of rank by the soldiery, the plunder and sack of towns given up to rapine; and after reading them, Tippoo would give vent to frantic prayers that judgment might come upon them. In this, however, as in many other instances, he overreached the mark he aimed at. A few of the flatterers around him, at every succeeding story, swore to spread it abroad; and while they applauded, pretended to feel excitement; but they ridiculed them in secret, and they were soon listened to, except by the most bigoted, with contempt.

Thus passed the whole of 1798, a year of anxious suspense to the British in India, when their power rested in a balance which a hair might have turned. During this period the mind of Tippoo presents a humiliating spectacle; now raving for conquest, now sunk in despair and dread at the slow but certain preparations of the English—at times prosecuting, with all the bigotry and savageness of his nature, conversions of the Hindoos in various parts of his dominions, and at others bowing down in slavish obedience to the dictates of the Brahmins, and offering up in the temples of the fort sacrifices in secret for the discomfiture of his enemies; while in the retired apartments of the palace magical rites were held—abominable orgies, at which he himself assisted, to relate which as we have heard them told, would be to defile our pages with obscenities too gross to be repeated.

In the midst of this mental darkness there would break out gleams of kindly feeling towards his sons, his officers, oftentimes to a sick servant; and upon the lady Fureeda he lavished such love as his heart, cold by nature, possessed, and whom his secret sufferings, absolute prostration of intellect at times when fresh disastrous news reached him, would inspire with a compasion she would fain have expressed in words, in those consolings which to a fond and wounded spirit are acceptable and bearable only from a woman.

There was another on whom his memory rested, and whom he besought, now by threats, now by immense rewards, to join his cause—it was Herbert Compton. His existence was known only to Jaffar and the Sultaun; the latter had, during the lapse of years and while the repairs of his fort proceeded, offered him rank, power, women, all that his imagination could suggest to dazzle a young man, but in vain; he had threatened him with death, but this was equally vain. Herbert had looked on death too long to fear it; and despite of the climate, the weary life he led had grown almost insupportable, and he saw no relief from it; death would have been welcome to him, but he was suffered to live on. Even the visits of Jaffar were events which, however trying to him at the time, and exciting to one so secluded, were yet looked back upon with pleasure from the very thought they created. Sometimes the Sultaun would relent towards him, and seem on the point of releasing him and others; but the shame of the act, the indignant remonstrance that he dreaded from the British, and the advice of Jaffar himself, deterred him. Thus the poor fellow lingered on almost without hope or fear, and in the end, amidst other more stirring and anxious matters, his existence was almost forgotten.

How often too would Tippoo's thoughts revert to Kasim Ali, his conduct to whom, in spite of the treachery denounced by Jaffar, would sometimes rise up in judgment against his conscience. To do him justice, however, it should be mentioned that, when the emissaries of Jaffar returned foiled and with Kasim's message, he did make inquiries in the bazaars relative to the money which Jaffar had told him Kasim Ali had remitted to Hyderabad; and he found all his statements so completely established, that they confirmed in his mind at the time the conviction that Kasim had been false to him, and that his falsehood had been long meditated, and at last successfully executed. But this wore off at length; and for one so esteemed, nay loved, there remained a painful impression that injustice had been done; to say the truth, when all around him were suspected, the flatterers and courtiers from their habitual subserviency, and his elder and more trusted officers from their blunt advice and open condemnation of many of his schemes and proceedings, he often longed for the presence of the young Patél, who would in his own person have united the qualities he most needed—sincere affection, joined to a mild demeanour and an honest heart.

Early in 1799 it was impossible to disguise from himself that the time had come when he should either make resistance against the English invasion—for his attack upon Madras had long been abandoned as impracticable even by the French—or he should march forth at the head of his army and oppose them. He determined on the latter course; and leaving his trusty commanders, Syud Sahib and Poornea, in charge of the Fort, he marched, on a day when his astrologers and his own calculations of lucky and unlucky days promised an uninterrupted career of prosperity and victory, to meet the Bombay army, which was approaching through Coorg, at the head of fifty thousand men, the flower of his troops. Once in the field, his ancient vigour and courage revived; his army was in the highest efficiency; the Bombay force he knew could not be a fifth of his own; and by selecting his own ground, which he should be enabled to do, he might practise the same manœuvre as he had done at Perambaukum with Baillie, and, by drawing them into an ambuscade, destroy them. His low estimation, however, of the English, was fated to be corrected; and though at Sedaseer, where he met the Bombay army, he led in person several desperate charges upon the British, and though under his eye his troops fought well, and were driven back with loss, only to advance again and again in a series of desperate onsets for five hours, yet he was defeated. Losing all presence of mind and confidence in his army, although there was every chance of success had he persevered in his attacks on Lieut.-General Stuart's corps, he retreated from the scene of action upon the capital, to draw from thence fresh troops with which he might oppose the march of the grand army from the East.

And now began that gloomy thought for the future, that utter despair of his life which continued to the last, chequered only by fits of the wildest excitement, by blind reliance at times upon vain rites and ceremonies, and forced hilarity, which, the effect of despair, was even more fearful to behold. The great drama of his fate was rapidly drawing to a close—a gorgeous spectacle, with mighty men and armies for actors, and the people of India for spectators.

CHAPTER XLVIII.

THE morning of the twenty-seventh of March broke with unclouded splendour; the army of the Sultaun were expecting their enemies with impatience, and the result was looked to with confidence. Tippoo had been urged by Chapuis to take up a position upon the Madoor, in the same pass as that where Kasim Ali had been attacked; but the Frenchmen had lost very considerably the influence they possessed since the news of their defeat in Egypt, and the discomfiture of Raymond at Hyderabad, and he determined to pursue the bent of his own inclination, both as to the ground he should select and the disposition of his troops. Since daylight he had been on horseback, indefatigable in marshalling his army. The ground he had selected was commanding, and covered the road. Malvilly, he knew, was the destination of the English on that day; and as it was one marked by a particularly auspicious conjunction of the planets, he determined on trying the result of a general action. When a few attempted to dissuade him that morning from opposing the English, lest by a defeat he should dispirit his troops and unfit them for the siege which all felt sure must follow, he flew into a violent passion.

'Are we cowards,' he said, 'that we should retire before the kafirs and cowardly English? No! let them come on—the base-born rascals! let them come on and taste of death! if our father—may his name be ever honoured!—could overwhelm the English in the field, should we not follow so exalted an example? No, by the Prophet! we will not retire; the day is fortunate—the planets are in good conjunction. If ye are cowards, and like not the English shot—go! your absence is better than your presence.'

But all swore to fight to the last drop of blood, and the Sultaun's disposition was made. Soon after sunrise all were at their posts—the heavy guns in the centre, the infantry behind. Two corps, one of them the favourite Kureem Cushoon, were pushed forward upon the flanks, and hundreds of rocket-men were interspersed with the line. It was a gallant and inspiring sight to see that huge force drawn up in steady array, determined upon retrieving their fame that day, and fighting for Islam and for their Sultaun.

They had waited long: the Sultaun had heard from scouts that the English had left their camp long before dawn, and their coming was looked for with eagerness. 'They will fly,' he cried, 'when they see the array; the sons of dogs and swine will not dare to face the true believers.'

'Yes,' said Nedeem Khan and Nusrut Ali, favourites who were always near him, 'it will be as my lord says, we shall have no fighting. Will they dare to advance against these cannon, and the various divisions which are drawn up in such wonderful order that not even a rat could get between?'

'Infatuation!' said Meer Ghuffoor to Abdool Wahab; 'for all the boastings of those young coxcombs, thou wilt see them turn and fly. I have served the English, and know them well. Ere an hour elapses after the first shot, we shall be in full retreat.'

'I trust not, Meer Sahib,' said the other; 'but what is that yonder?'

''Tis they! 'tis they!' cried the Sultaun. 'Now upon them, my sons! upon them, and let us see ye do brave deeds. Your Sultaun is beholding you!'

It was indeed a beautiful sight to behold. The Sultaun was on a high ground, and could see all. A few English red-coats were first seen—then more; the sun glanced from their bright bayonets and musket-barrels as they proceeded. Gradually column after column came on; though they were still at some distance, there was a halt perceived, and considerable bustle.

'They retreat! they retreat!' cried the Sultaun, in an ecstasy of joy, clapping his hands and laughing in his excitement. It was changed in an instant, when, after a short disposition of the troops, the English army advanced; but it appeared such a mere handful of men, when compared with his own force, that his derision grew even louder. 'Ha! ha!' he cried, 'they have left half their army to keep their baggage. They hold me cheap indeed to attempt to attack me with the few that are yonder! But it is well: Inshalla! ye will see, sirs, ye will see! What troops are those on the left?' he asked after a while, as he examined them with a telescope; 'what green standard is that? Dare the infidels to use the sacred colour?'

Just then the breeze unfurled the standard to its full width, and, as all descried the white crescent and ball beneath it, a cry of exultation burst from the Sultaun.

''Tis the standard of Sikundur Jah! 'Tis they—the effeminate Dekhanees!—men who are no better than eunuchs. Advancing upon my own Cutcherie too—upon the Kureem Cushoon! Inshalla! Inshalla! let them come. The renegades from the faith, advancing against the favoured of the Prophet! Holy Mohamed confound them!'

The English army halted: its long columns deployed into lines steadily and gracefully; it was a beautiful sight in that bright sun. There was a large opening in the line, and Tippoo rode forward, urging his cavalry to break through and attack the general, who with his staff was beyond. 'Ah! had I Kasim Ali and my brave old Rhyman Khan now, they would shame ye!' he cried to those who he fancied were tardy in movement; but they did their duty—they charged.

'Steady, men!' cried the officer at the head of the regiment nearest the point of danger—it was Philip Dalton; 'let them come near.'

The cavalry thundered on—a grand picturesque mass—shouting their cries of 'Deen! deen!' and 'Alla Yar!' The English were not to be daunted; they were steady as rocks, and awaited the word, 'Present—fire!' The effect was deadly. As the smoke cleared away, the flying mass was seen in wild confusion, and before the line a heap of men and horses struggling. A few daring fellows had, however, dashed through the interval, and fell gallantly fighting in the rear.

Meanwhile the Sultaun's infantry advanced steadily and firmly; he cheered them on, putting himself at their head even within shot, and then he turned to watch his favourite division. It was composed of picked men: their arms, dress, discipline, were all superior to the rest of the army; they were advancing against the Nizam's troops, and were confident of victory. The Sultaun was in an ecstasy of delight. Little imagined he then to whom he was opposed; that one led the troops, which he expected would fly like dust before the whirlwind, to whom fear was unknown—who bore within him the germ of that renown which has raised him to the proudest, the most glorious pinnacle of heroic fame—Wellesley! Wellington! What heart so callous that does not bound at those illustrious names, recalling with them victories upon victories to his remembrance—not the result of fortuitous circumstances, but of devoted bravery, of admirable foresight, of consummate skill, of patience and fortitude under every privation through a long series of years—the most splendid array of triumph that ever the world beheld, which, already so glorious, will yet increase in after times to a renown more brilliant than we can at present estimate.

'Now ye will see them run!—now they will fly! Forward, my brave fellows! forward to victory! I vow every man a month's pay, and a jaghire to their commander. Look! they halt—not a man wavering! it is a gallant sight. They will fire! —then upon them with the steel. Shookr Alla! how many have fallen!' he exclaimed, as the division fired, and many of those opposed to it fell. 'Now charge!—charge, for the love of Alla! —why do ye wait? ye lose time. Alla! Alla! the enemy fire in turn! Merciful Prophet! how many have tasted of death! Never heed, however—now is the time!—while they are loading, upon them!—upon them! Ya Kubeer! Ya Hyder!'

It was fearful to look on him: his hands were clasped together, his eyes strained, his features quivering with excitement and anxiety. On the issue of a moment was victory or ruin.

'Curse them!' he cried; 'curse them! they waver. Holy Prophet! why dost thou not turn them? Alla! Alla! why dost thou not blast the infidels? They waver! the Feringhees are upon them!—they fly!—now there is no hope—Prophet of Alla, spare them!'

It was a sight which curdled his blood: his favourite corps turned—they dared not abide the charge of the British and Nizam's division, led by the gallant Wellesley; and the cavalry, headed by his old enemy Floyd, dashed out upon them. Hundreds went down before that terrible charge: the Cushoon, which had so lately inspired confidence, turned as one man, and in an instant became a confused rabble, flying for their lives; in the midst of whom were the English cavalry, riding down the fugitives, while they cut at them with their long swords.

The Sultaun gazed breathless and stupefied for a few moments: no one dared to speak. At last he turned, his face wore a ghastly expression of horror, at which his attendants shuddered. For an instant he looked back; the cavalry thundered on—other portions of his troops were giving way before them. He could look no more, but dashing his heels into the flanks of his charger, fled from the field.

'Shabash! Shabash! well done, gallant fellow!' cried many English officers, surrounding a richly-dressed native, apparently of rank, who, clad in a magnificent suit of chain-armour over a cloth-of-gold vest, with a bright steel cap on his head, and upon a noble chesnut horse, now rode up at full gallop, accompanied by many of his risala, as martial in appearance as himself, and equally well mounted. Their swords were red with blood, and their faces flushed and excited with conquest. 'Well done! well done! ye have earned the good-will of the General, and ye will be rewarded.'

'I thank you,' he said; 'you are kind, and flatter our poor services; but can you tell me where Colonel Dalton is?'

'He is yonder,' said an officer; 'come, I will lead you to him.'

The action was now over. Philip had borne an honourable part, and was attending to his wounded men when Kasim rode up to him.

'Behold!' he said, showing his sword, 'I have fulfilled my promise; I am faithful to the salt I eat; thou wilt testify to that?'

'Noble fellow! I will indeed; thou hast distinguished thyself before the army. Come, I will lead thee to the General,—he will love to look on one so brave and devoted.'

'They were my old companions,' said Kasim, 'but I knew them not; my heart was steeled against them; had I wavered, I was disgraced for ever. Ye suspected me, but now I am free of taint.'

'Thou art indeed, and thou wilt see how grateful an English commander can be. Come!'

That night Kasim, Philip Dalton, and many others were in the General's tent; they had been asking him about the road. He seemed to think a while.

'Will ye take my advice?' he asked, 'the advice of one who is not worthy to give it?'

'Say on,' replied the General.

'Abandon this road, then,' said Kasim; 'there is a ford at Sosillay, two easy marches from hence; it is deep, but the water is now low and it will be practicable. I will guide you to it, if you will trust me. You will cross the river there—forage is plentiful, the other bank is clear of troops, and ye can hurry on and surprise the city.'

'Is this true?' said the General.

'By your head and eyes—by your salt, it is!'

'Will any one answer for you? it is a fearful risk.'

Kasim looked round; his eyes met Philip's. 'Come,' he said, 'if thou art for a ride, come this night and I will show it thee: I and my men will escort thee: Wilt *thou* trust me?'

'To the death!' said Philip.

'I believe him,' said the General; 'and he will see that this great service shall be rewarded. Nevertheless I should like to know more about the ford, and if it can be reconnoitered. Will you make the report, colonel? you can take an escort of cavalry.'

'With pleasure; you shall know early to-morrow.'

'And I will accompany you,' said another officer; 'it will be a pleasant ride.'

'Come, gentlemen,' said Kasim, 'we lose time, and we have a long ride before us.'

. . . .

The Sultaun, plunged into despair, had retired westward. The army had collected, but thousands were missing, killed, or had deserted from his standard. Still there was hope: his officers were yet faithful; the forage of the north bank of the Cavery was utterly destroyed; and the active Poornea, at the head of the irregular cavalry, was out burning villages and setting fire to the grass of the wide plains. If the English should advance, they would be drawn on to defeat as before. There was still hope: his plans of defence were being matured: troops poured into the Fort from all sides, and provisions for a year. He had treasure too, and there was no fear. What could the English, with their small amount of artillery, effect against the hundreds of cannon in the Fort and the new fortifications? 'Let them come on!' he would say; 'with that fort before, and a bare country behind them, let us see how long they will stay!' And his words were echoed by his sycophants; but it was easy to see, for all that, how dread gnawed at his heart.

On the evening of the fourth day after the action, he was in his tent of audience. He was confident, for no news had been heard of the English army, and it had not advanced upon the road as he had expected. He hoped it had retreated, or was stationary for want of forage; and he was even asserting broadly that it had.

Suddenly a messenger entered with dismay upon his face. Tippoo knew not what to think. All his officers were present, and every one trembled, though they knew not what to expect.

'Speak, Madur-bukhta!' cried Tippoo fiercely; 'what hast thou to say?'

'May I be your sacrifice! May I be pardoned,' stammered the man; 'the English—the kafirs—have crossed the river!'

'Crossed the river?' echoed all; 'how? where?'

'Dog!' cried the Sultaun, 'if thou liest, I will have thee torn asunder. Where did they cross?'

'At Sosillay.'

'At Sosillay! Who has been the traitor? Is any one missing?'

'May I be your sacrifice!' said an officer, 'it must be Kasim Ali Patél. He was seen hewing down the true believers at Malvilly.'

'Kasim Ali!' gasped the Sultaun; 'Alla help me! then all is lost.' And he sank down on his musnud in stupor.

Long he remained so, only at times repeating 'Kasim Ali' and 'Sosillay!'

Hardly any one spoke except in whispers. After some delay,

sherbet was brought to him, and he seemed to revive. He sat up, passed his hand across his forehead, as though his brain was bewildered ; then he arose, and looked around him ; his face was wan and careworn ; those few minutes appeared to have done the work of years. Many burst into tears.

'Ye weep,' he said, 'ye weep ; why should ye weep for one abandoned of Alla ? I have no hope now. Why stay ye with a man who is doomed ? why link your fate to a drowning wretch, who hath not even a straw upon the whirlpool of his fate to clutch at ? Go ! ye have served me well--ye have fought for me, bled for me. Go—may Alla keep ye ! Ye have been my friends, my companions. I have been harsh, often cruel. Will ye pardon me ? will ye pardon a poor slave of Alla ? Go ! I—I—have ever loved ye, and now—'

He was interrupted : an officer, with streaming eyes, rushed from a side of the tent, and throwing himself at the Sultaun's feet, clasped his knees and sobbed passionately aloud.

Tippoo could endure no more. He who had been by turns bitter in sarcasm, brutal in mirth, cruel, proud, exacting, unfeeling, tyrannical, overbearing among his subjects, was now humbled. He appeared to struggle for a moment ; but, unable to quell the wild tumult within him, he burst into tears—the first he had ever been seen to shed.

Then ensued a scene which words cannot paint—a scene of passionate raving, of tears, of oaths, of fidelity to death. Men embraced one another, and swore to die side by side. Those who had cherished animosities for years, cast themselves on each other's breasts, and forgot enmity in the bond of general affliction. All swore before Alla and the Prophet, by the Sultaun's head and the salt they ate, that they would die as martyrs ; they determined to retreat upon the city, and to fight under its walls to death.

The army retired, and awaited the onset, but they were disappointed ; the English army passed three miles to the left, in glittering array, and encamped at the opposite side of the Fort to that on which the former attack had been made, and for the time the Sultaun exulted in his safety.

Days passed : the thunder of cannon ceased not night or day, and the hearts of all were appalled. No mercy was expected from the British. Death would have been welcome at first ; but its gradual approach, and the stern progression of the English to victory, could not be shut out from men's eyes. All the redoubts beyond the Fort had been carried long ago ; even the French, upon whom the eye of the Sultaun rested in hope, were beaten back by the native troops of his enemies, though they fought bravely. Then he felt how he had been cajoled, deceived, betrayed into destruction. To all his letters to the English commander there was but one reply—send the money and the hostages, and the cannon shall cease, but not before. At this his proud heart rebelled; there were those around him who still ridiculed the idea of danger, but he well knew its reality. Day by day the mosque resounded with his frantic prayers; the Moolas to this day tell how impious they were—how he raved, prayed, cursed by turns, till those who heard believed that a judgment would follow them.

He held no communication with his family, for his presence in the zenana was ever a signal for an outburst of grief. He lived in his hall of audience, or in a small room off it, where most part of the day and night was passed in vain astrological calculations, or those horrible magical rites we have before alluded to; at other times he was upon the walls, directing cannon, and firing with his own hand.

The breach became practicable; the guns on both sides of it had long been silenced, and men looked on at the work of destruction, and heard the storm of shot, shells, and grape which poured through it, in sullen despair. The brave Meer Ghuffoor, who was devoted to the Sultaun, saw that it could not be defended much longer; when the day dawned he went to the monarch, to try to rouse him to a sense of his danger: it was vain.

'There is nothing between thee and thine enemies, O my Sultaun!' said the Syud; 'nothing to prevent the storm. Their men are ready in the trenches, and have been there since it was light; I have watched them. The walls are gone. If your slave is permitted, he will commence a wall and a ditch across the inside that cannot be breached, and it will stop them.'

'Go, Syud, we fear not,' said the Sultaun; we have hope in other things; events will happen which thou knowest not of. The English will be blasted this day—withered from the face of the earth. Already we have ordered Fateehas for to-morrow. Go, old man! we feel for thy zeal, but there is no fear; Mars is yet in the circle of planets.'

'Thou wilt never see to-morrow,' said the Syud prophetically, 'unless what I advise is done. I will do it; I have sought death these many days, but it comes not—I may find it there.'

'Go then, in the name of the Shitan, go!' cried the Sultaun hastily; 'trouble me no more. Do as thou wilt, but trouble me not.—So, Runga Swamee! what news? hast thou prepared all?'

'Alas!' said the Syud as he went out, 'I shudder at his communion with those Brahmin infidels. I would to Alla I were with my old brethren in arms; but that is now impossible, and death alone will be honourable to the old soldier.'

'All is prepared, O Sultaun,' replied the Brahmin; 'we wait for the men—thou hast them ready?'

'Ay, there are twelve dogs, sons of unchaste mothers, swine!—take them.'

'The goddess will be pleased, O Sultaun—she will drink their blood. To-night, to-night she will put fear into their hearts; she will send rain—the river will fill—they will be cut off.'

'Ha! ha! ha!' laughed the Sultaun, 'and twelve base-born Feringhees will go to hell. Who is without—Jaffar?'

'Refuge of the world! I am here.'

'Hast thou obeyed the orders I gave thee yesterday?'

'Protector of the poor! I have; not one lives now—Feringhee, Moslim, or Hindoo; the prisoners died in the night. It was hard work, there were so many, but it was done,' and he chuckled. 'There were twelve spared—the last twelve.'

'Good: if the Fort is taken, the kafirs will look in vain for their brethren. Now go thou to the prison, take the twelve sons of perdition who were captured in the sortie, bind them hand and foot, and convey them to the temple. Thou art ready, Runga Swamee? As the sun rises, their blood must flow, one by one. The men are ready, the priests wait, the swords are sharp—what more? Enough—go! thou understandest, Jaffar?'

'Ay, my lord.'

'Hast thou sent for him—for Compton?'

'The men go to-morrow.'

'Good: when he comes he shall be the next offering, if thou wantest more, Pundit.'

'I am thankful,' replied the man: 'thou wilt gain much favour for this and thy gifts to Brahmins—thirty thousand years of protection for every offering.'

'Inshalla!' said the Sultaun; 'go! time flies.'

It was noon, the day was bright and hot, and a strong mirage flickered upon the white tents of the English camp, the parched ground around them, and the black and rocky bed of the river. In the camp many men were moving about, and marching to and fro. The Sultaun was looking at them with his telescope, but saw nothing to excite alarm. He was gayer than usual, for he had seen his face in a jar of oil, and the reflection had been fortunate.

'Rain will fall to-night in the hills,' he said to a favourite near him, Rajah Khan, as he observed some heavy masses of white fleecy clouds in the west, which hung over the nearer hills and shrouded the distant peaks. 'The Brahmins are right, the sacrifice has done good; after all, only a few Feringhees have gone to hell before their time—ha! ha!'

'May your prosperity increase!' said the officer; 'they have deserved their death.'

As he spoke a man rushed up the steps of the cavalier. Tears were in his eyes, and his manner was wild.

'What has happened, O fool?' said the Sultaun; 'hast thou seen the devil?'

'Khodawund!' said the soldier, speaking with difficulty, 'the Syud, the holy Meer Ghuffoor is dead.'

'Merciful Alla!' cried Tippoo, 'art thou sure of this?'

'Alas! quite sure, Light of the World! I carried him away: behold his blood.'

'It was his destiny,' said the Sultaun gloomily; 'it was once said his fate was linked with mine,—let it come. His death was that of a soldier, may mine be the same! Go! let him be buried with honour. We will dine here,' he added to an attendant; 'we feel hot within, and this air from the water is cool.'

His light repast was soon finished, and again he sat looking towards the trenches. He thought there were many men in them; as if by mutual consent, the firing had ceased on both sides, and no sound arose except the busy hum of the city: in the English camp all was still as death. He speculated for a while idly upon the unusual quietness, and looked again. On a sudden a man climbed upon the mound of the trench; he was tall and noble in appearance; his height was exaggerated by his position—he looked a giant. The Sultaun's heart sank within him; he could not be mistaken in those features—it was Baird, whom he had so often reviled. 'He comes to revenge the old man,' he muttered—'to revenge Mathews!'

It was a noble sight to see that one man stand thus alone in front of both armies: he appeared to look at the Fort for an instant, then drew his sword from its scabbard, and as it came forth it flashed in the sunlight. He waved it high in the air. Another leaped to his side: he was a native, and wore a steel cap and glittering chain-armour; a shield hung on his arm, and he waved a broad sabre. They leaped together from the mound, followed by hundreds, who with loud cheers dashed on in regular order.

'Prophet of Alla!' cried the Sultaun, 'they come—Baird and

Kasim Ali! Look to the breach! every man to the breach! defend it with your lives!'

He was hurrying away, when a thought appeared to strike him. 'Stay! he cried, 'bring water; we have eaten, and are unclean; we would not die like a kafir, but one for whom the Apostle waits ere he enters Paradise. I come, O Mohamed! I come quickly now.'

CHAPTER XLIX.

'To the breach! to the breach!' was now the cry far and wide; those who loved the Sultaun hurried there to die, to stop with their bodies the ascent of the devoted English—a living wall in place of that which had been torn down.

It was a sight on which men looked with throbbing hearts and aching eyes from both sides—those in the English camp, and those in the Fort. There were but few cannon to stop the English; all upon the breach had been dismounted, and no one dared show himself upon the dismantled defences to plant others. But as the British advanced, a storm of shot and rockets met them, which was enough to have turned more daring men. Many went down before it, many writhed and struggled; the column was like a march of ants where a human foot has just trodden, some hurrying on, a few turning to carry away a wounded and disabled comrade.

'They are drunk!' cried the Sultaun; 'the hogs—the kafirs—they have been plied with wine. Be firm, brothers, and fear not, though they are desperate. Be firm, ye with the long spears, and do ye of the Kureem Kutcheree regain your lost fame! Remember, we are present,—a hundred rupees for every Feringhee! Look to your aim—they cannot pass the ditch.'

Such broken sentences escaped him from time to time, as he fired upon the enemy with his own hand, often with deadly aim; but though the resistance made was desperate, what was able to withstand the hot ardour of this assault? Man after man went down before the strong arm of Baird, who toiled like a knight of old in the breach, cheering on his men with loud cries of revenge for the murdered. Kasim fought beside him, and equalled the deeds of the British leader.

'They bear charmed lives!' cried the Sultaun, dashing to the ground the gun he had just fired; 'twice have I struck down the men close to them, but the balls harmed them not.'

'Retire, I beseech you, O Prince!' cried Rajah Khan and a hundred others around him; 'this is no place for you; on our lives be it we drive them back.'

'No; I will die here,' said Tippoo doggedly; 'they shall pass into the Fort over my body; but the ditch is yet before them—they cannot pass it unless it is filled as it was at— Bah! why should I have thought of that scene?'

This passed in a moment: the struggle on the breach was over—the defenders and their enemies lay there in heaps; still there was the ditch to cross, which was wide and deep; for an instant even Baird was staggered, and his men ran right and left seeking for a passage. Kasim Ali and he were close together; there was a scaffolding, and a plank over it leading to the rampart on the other side: it was enough, the way was found, and hundreds poured over it quicker than thought.

It was the last sight the Sultaun saw—everything else swam before his eyes; he looked stupefied, and said, hurriedly and gloomily, 'It is finished—where are my bearers? take me to the palace—the women must die—every one: we would not have them defiled by the kafirs. Come! haste! or we are too late.'

They led him to his palankeen, mingling with the fugitives, who in the passage between the two walls were rushing on to the small postern where it had been left; men had been sent for it, but what bearers could struggle against that frantic crowd? As they hurried on, Rajah Khan vainly endeavoured to persuade him to fly by the river-gate; Poornea and his son were out, he said, and they might yet escape to the fastnesses of the west.

'Peace!' cried the Sultaun; 'the women are sacred—they must die first; then we will throw ourselves upon the kafirs, cry Alla Yar, and die. May hell be their portion!' he exclaimed suddenly, as he stumbled and fell. They raised him—a shot had struck him; he was sick to death, but they were strong men, and they urged him on, supporting him. Another cry he uttered—they saw blood pour from his back—he was wounded once more; but the gate was close at hand, and they strained every nerve to reach it. Hundreds were struggling there: the fierce English were behind, advancing with loud oaths and cheers, maddened by excited revenge, slaughter, lust, and hope of plunder. A fearful thing is a strife like that, when men become monsters, thirsting for blood.

They reached the palankeen, and laid the Sultaun in it.

'Water! water!' he gasped; 'air! I am choking! take me out, take me out, I shall die here! Water! for the love of Alla, water! one drop! one drop!'

'Remember the murdered, give no quarter,' cried many whose bayonets were already reeking with blood. 'Here is a gate, we shall be inside directly—hurrah!'

'They come, Huzrut,' said Rajah Khan, trying to rouse the dying man; 'they come, they are near, let us tell them who thou art, they will spare thee.'

'Spare me!' he cried, rousing himself at the last words. 'No! they burn for revenge, and I should be hung like a dog; no! I will die here.' He was very faint, and spoke feebly.

'Here is a prince—I'll be the first!' cried a soldier, dashing into the gateway and snatching rudely at the rosary which was around the Sultaun's neck.

It rallied the expiring lamp of life. 'Dog of a kafir! son of an unchaste mother!' cried the Sultaun, gnashing his teeth as he seized a sword which lay by him, 'get thee to hell!' and he struck at him with all his might; it was the last effort of life, but it was not fatal.

'Damnation!' muttered the man, setting his teeth with the pain of the wound, as he raised his musket.

He fired, the ball pierced the skull, the Sultaun's eyes glared for an instant, quivered in their sockets, then his head fell, and he was dead. The lion of the faith, the refuge of the world, had gone to his account!

'Well met, noble Kasim,' cried Philip Dalton, as heading his party he dashed down the cavalier which had first been gained, and was now in the body of the place; 'keep with me; thou knowest the prisons?'

'Every one, colonel; but haste! they may even now be destroying them.'

Philip shuddered, there was no time for thought. Many men were around him, and they rushed on, led by Kasim Ali, whose reddened sword, and armour sprinkled with blood, showed how he had been employed.

Eagerly, and with excitement which hardly admitted thought, so engrossing was it, did those two and Charles Hayward search every part of the Fort, and every place where it was possible that prisoners could have been concealed: they found none. And when the palace was opened they rushed into its most secret prisons and burst them open; they found traces of recent habitation by Englishmen; and while their fears were horribly confirmed, their last hopes for Herbert Compton departed.

'Ah! could I but meet the villain Jaffar!' cried Kasim, as they gave up further search, for it was now dark; 'if indeed he be alive, then would we wring from him the fate of your poor friend. Inshalla! he may be found: I know his haunts, and will watch them all night; I will come to thee in the morning.'

'I shall be here with my regiment,' Dalton said sadly; 'but I have no hope, for that cowardly villain will have fled long ere now with his ill-gotten wealth.'

The morning broke gloomily after that fearful day and night; for during the latter there had been appalling alarms, shots, screams from terrified, plundered, and often violated women; there were many dreadful excesses, but they were checked. As the day advanced, order was restored once more, and the moderation of the English in their victory, their justice, and protection of all, is yet sung and said through the country by wandering minstrels.

The Sultaun's body had been discovered where he had fallen; his faithful attendant lay beside him, with others who had fought with him to the last. They were brought into the palace, and recognised by the women with unfeigned and bitter grief. Of all that host of secluded women, two only truly mourned his fate. The one was his mother, the other Fureeda, who could with difficulty be torn from his body, as they took it away for burial. Her love had grown with misfortune; for in her society he had found rest from care and from his own restless mind; of late he had visited no other, and, despite of his vices, she had felt security with him, whom no one else looked on without fear; and as his fate approached, she foresaw it, pitied, and loved him.

The last rites of the faith had been performed upon the body. The grave clothes, which, brought from Mekha, had been for years in his possession, were put on with the requisite ceremonies, ablutions, and fumigations; the sheet, filled with flowers, was laid over the body; the attendant Moolas chanted thrice those parts of the Koran, the 'Soora e fateeha,' and the 'Qool hoo Alla!' They were about to raise it, to place it in the coffin, when two women again rushed in; the one was old, wrinkled, and grey—it was his nurse; she beat her bare and withered breasts, and, kneeling beside the corpse, showed them to it with passionate exclamations. 'Thou hast sucked them,' she cried, 'when I was young, and they were full of milk! Alas! alas! that I should have lived to say I bestow it on thee.'

The other was Fureeda; she spoke not, but sobbed bitterly, as she looked on the pinched and sharpened features, and livid face of him who had till the last clung to her with affection.

They were removed with difficulty, and the procession passed out slowly, the Moolas chanting the funeral service with slow and melancholy cadences. The conquerers of the dead awaited his coming, and, in silent homage to their illustrious enemy, lifted their plumed hats from their brows, as the body passed on to its last resting-place beside the noble Hyder. The troops, which had the day before been arrayed in arms against him, now paid the last honours to his death; and through a street of British soldiers, resting upon their firearms reversed, while their bands played the dead march in Saul, the procession wound its way. Without in the street were thousands of men, who, frantic in their grief, cried aloud to Alla; and women, who beat their breasts, and wailed, or else uttered piercing shrieks of woe, flung dust into the air, and, casting loose their hair, strove to prostrate themselves before the body of the dead. The solemn chant proceeded; each verse sung by the Moolas, who in their flowing robes preceded the coffin, was repeated by all around. The body was surrounded by all the officers of Tippoo's late army who had survived, and those of the Nizam's force, on foot; and there was one of his sons on horseback, who sat in a kind of stupor at the overwhelming affliction.

The day had been gloomy, and was close and hot; not a breath of wind stirred the trees, and heavy lurid masses of clouds hung over the city, from whence at times a low muttering growl of thunder would break, and seemingly rattle all over the heavens. Men felt heavily the weight of the atmosphere, and every now and then looked up at the threatening mass which hung above them.

Through the plain, which extends to the mausoleum of Hyder, the multitude poured; and as the procession gradually approached its goal, the frantic cries of the people increased, almost drowning the melancholy dead march and the chant which arose, now one, now the other, and sometimes both blended into a wild harmony upon the still air. Then there was a momentary silence, only to be succeeded by bursts of grief even more violent than before. The thunder appeared to increase in loudness every moment, while flashes of lightning darted across the heavens from side to side.

The procession reached the burial-place; the grenadiers formed a street, rested upon their firearms reversed, and the body passed on. The band now ceased, and the bier being laid down, the body was taken from it, preparatory to being laid in the grave. The Moola (for one alone now officiated) raised his voice in the chant of the first creed; it was a powerful one, but now sounded thin and small among that vast assembly; he had said only a few words, when a flash of lightning burst from above, nearly blinding them, and a peal of thunder followed, so crashing, so stunning, that the stoutest hearts quailed under it. It died away, and as it receded far into the east, the melancholy tone of the Moola's voice, which had been drowned in it, again arose clear and distinct, like the distant wail of a trumpet.

The heavens were still for a while; but as the body was laid in its last narrow resting-place, its face to the west, and as the Moolas chanted out 'Salāam wo Aliekoom wo Ruhmut Ullāāh!' * again a crashing peal burst forth, and their words were lost in the deafening roar. Now peal after peal rolled from the clouds. As yet there was no rain nor wind, and the black mass appeared almost to descend upon the tall palm-trees which waved above, and flashes of lightning so vivid that the heavens blazed under the light, darted from it, and played fearfully around. Men looked at each other in awe and wonder, and felt their own littleness, when the mighty lay cold in death before them, and the thunder of his Creator roared, seemingly as in deprecation of the deeds of his life.

The companies formed on each side of the grave to pay their last tribute of respect to a soldier's memory, and the word was given—'Fire!' The rattle which followed seemed to be taken up by the sky; away rolled the awful echoes into the far west, and, lost for a moment among the huge crags and mountains of the Ghâts, seemed to return with double force to meet the peals of artillery and volleys of musketry which broke from the Fort and the British army. The bands struck up again, but they were dimly heard; and, as all returned to the sound of their merry music, it seemed a mockery amidst the din and turmoil of that tempest.

. . . .

But we must carry our readers back to Herbert Compton, over whom years had passed, chequered by no events save the visits of Jaffar Sahib, to urge upon him compliance with the Sultaun's demands for assistance, plans of fortifications, or military instructions. The Sultaun had from the first taken it into his head that Herbert was a man of education and skill beyond his fellows; and as every idea was esteemed a revelation from Providence, he had clung to this one with all the obstinacy of his nature, for he had a necessity for the aid Herbert might have given. Often he would forget him for months. Once or twice, provoked by his

* Peace and the grace of God be with you.

obstinate refusals, he had issued orders for his death, and revoked as fast as he had written them. Herbert had lingered on upon those mountains, the cold and mists of which, exaggerated to the Sultaun, made him suppose that the place was the one where hardship would be the greatest, and life the most difficult to bear. But he knew not of that glorious climate, of its cool, fresh, elastic, invigorating breezes; of its exquisite scenery; of the thousands of wild flowers, and green hills and hanging woods; deep wooded glens, in which brawled clear and sparkling rivers, now chafing over a pebbly bed, now creeping still under some golden mossy bank, covered with wild thyme and violets, from among which peered the modest primrose, the graceful cyclamen and tall fern, which nodded over the sparkling water. He knew not what ecstasy it was to Herbert to lie at length upon the soft sward, and to listen to the melody of the blackbird, which in the joy of its heart trilled its liquid song, and was answered joyously by its mate—or to see the lark, high in air, wheeling around in wide circles, till it was lost to sight, the same as he had used to listen to with Amy in the groves of Beechwood. Herbert's thoughts were often carried back to the past, remembering with the minutest exactitude every tone, every word of their sweet converse.

It was an unreal life, with none of the world's occurrences before him; from his high prison he looked forth over a wide country, but he could only speculate idly upon what was passing in the world. He had no hope of deliverance,—for ever since the first siege of the city, of which he heard after the English had departed, he had ceased to think of liberty except in death. He had no hope that his life, his intellect, which he felt to be strong and vigorous, would ever be called into the action they were fitted for;—nor his kind heart, his affectionate sympathies find again objects on which to fix. He had no companion but nature, upon whose varying face he could always look with delight, while he listened to the brawling streams, the murmurs of the waving woods—those sweet voices with which she peoples her solitudes.

Yet latterly he had found a companion. One of the guards brought a dog; Herbert attached it to himself, and the man gave it him when he went away. He could speak to it—he could speak English to it; and as they would sit upon a sunny bank together, he listening idly to the murmuring plash of waters, the hum of bees, watching the bright flies, as they sported in the sunbeams, or the butterflies flying from flower to flower—drinking in the loveliness of the prospects, whether over the vast blue plains and endless ranges of mountains, or inwards, among the quiet peaceful valleys and swelling hills—he would, after musing a while, speak to his favourite of her he loved, of his home, of his mother; and often, when tears started to his eyes, and his voice faltered, the dog would look at him wistfully, and whine gently as he scratched him with his paw; he seemed to know there was something wrong, and he thus expressed his sympathy; and when Herbert arose to go, he would run in wide circles upon the mountain-side, chasing the larks from their nests, tearing the grass with his teeth, and barking so joyfully that Herbert's spirit would be gladdened too.

But who can tell his yearnings for home—for the sight of a face beside those of his guards—for one word from a countryman? If ever he should escape, what tidings might be in store for him —of the changes, the events of years? Escape! alas that was impossible. Everywhere the same rugged sides presented themselves, everywhere the same vast forests below, to enter which was death, and beyond them the territory of the Sultaun. He often longed to make a second attempt to be free, but his better thoughts proved its utter impracticability.

One day a few showers had fallen, and the air was soft and balmy; the dry winds of May had already abated, and the summer was beginning to burst forth. Herbert was lying upon the spot which we have once mentioned in Hulleekul Droog; his little garden was freshened by the late rain, and the odour of the flowers came to him gratefully, as he looked over the wide prospect, now so familiar, yet, for all that, presenting in colour, in effect, perpetually new features.

The Naik of his guard came to him. 'Arise!' he said, 'I have news for thee.'

'Speak!' said Herbert—'what news? is Jaffar coming again? is he arrived?'

'Not so,' said the man, 'thou art to travel.'

Herbert's heart sank within him.

'To travel!' he said anxiously; 'has the Sultaun sent for me?'

'No,' said the man, '*he* has not—he is dead. The English have taken the city, and the Sultaun is no more.'

'Merciful Providence!' cried Herbert aloud in his own tongue; 'is this true, or is it a dream? *killed*, didst thou say?'

'Ay, Sahib,' said the man, dashing a tear from his eye; 'he was a great man, and has died like a soldier! Wilt thou come? thy countrymen will look for thee now, and perhaps the act of taking thee to them will give me favour in their eyes. As to this post, it will be abandoned—no one will need it; and if we remain here, no one will remember us. What dost thou think?'

But he spoke to one who heeded not his words—they hardly

fell upon his ear. Herbert had knelt down, and on the spot where his first vision of escape had come to him, where he now heard he was free, he poured forth thoughts that were too big for words—incoherently, perhaps—what matter? they rose out of a grateful, glowing heart, and ascended to the throne of Him who looked into it and saw the feelings there, while the words that expressed them passed away upon the sighing wind unheeded.

Herbert arose. 'Art thou ready?' he said.

'To-morrow morning, Sahib; ere the dawn breaks—there is a moon—we will set out. In four days, if we travel fast, we shall be at the city.'

. . . .

'Have you seen the poor fellow who has been just brought into camp upon a cot, Dalton?' said an officer of the staff, who lounged into Philip's tent, about noon, some days after the above. 'It seems he was confined in a hill-fort, and the garrison have brought him in. Poor fellow! he is in a high fever; for they rested by the way in the jungles, and there he took it. But —— is looking after him; they have taken him into the hospital.'

'Some native, I suppose,' said Philip, looking up; he was writing to his wife.

'No—an Englishman; it was supposed there were none left, but—'

'Good heavens!' cried Philip, seizing his cap, and rushing precipitately from the tent. 'If it should be he!—merciful Providence!—*if*—'

He flew across the camp; the officer looked after him in wonder. 'What can he mean?' he said aloud. He saw Philip run at full speed to the hospital tent, and he followed him there more leisurely and looked in. Philip was kneeling beside the bed of the sufferer, whose hands were clasped in his; the tears were streaming down his cheeks, and he was striving to speak. The other's eyes were upraised, while his lips moved as if in prayer, and a look of silent thankfulness, of joy, of perfect peace and happiness was upon his handsome features, which he could hardly have conceived expressible by any emotions. He looked for a few minutes, and then hurried away to hide his own. 'It must be Captain Compton,' he said, 'so long missing; I will not disturb them.'

It was indeed. In that silent grasp of the hand,—in the long, earnest, loving embrace which had preceded it,—in the recognition at once of the friend, and even brother, of his early years, Herbert had already forgotten all his sufferings. He had caught a branch upon the shore he had so long floated past, and leaped upon it; and now secure, could even in that moment follow the frail raft which had so long borne his sad fortunes, and gradually lose sight of it in the visions which opened before him.

Not long did he remain on that humble pallet; removed to Philip's tent, and in his company and that of Charles Hayward, he felt, as they told him of the events of the past, that it was like one of those blissful fancies which had cheated him so often. He fell asleep, and dreamed of joy and peace, vaguely and indefinitely, and awoke refreshed by rest, and the prescriptions of the surgeon who attended him; he gazed around, and his eyes met the happy faces and joyful looks of his friends,—then, then only, did he feel it all to be true.

CONCLUSION.

DAY by day Herbert made progress towards recovery, and with peace of mind returned strength and vigour. He had been ill for nearly a fortnight before the time we speak of, and had been tended with that constant and unremitting solicitude by his dear friends and brothers, which can easily be imagined, but not easily described. There was another too, the brave Kasim Ali, who had been quickly summoned to Philip's tent after the arrival of the lost one, and who had rejoiced in his recovery with joy as genuine as the others.

'How often I told you to hope, Sahib,' he would exclaim, as he looked on the joy of the friends, and their love for each other. 'How often I said he was not dead; that the Sultaun (may his sepulchre be honoured!) would not destroy him.'

And then they would shake their heads, and think that if the Sultaun had been alive, how little would have been the chance of their ever meeting again upon earth.

'You appear to cling to his memory with fondness,' said Dalton, in reply to a burst of praise which Kasim had uttered; 'yet he used you ill, and would have killed you.'

'I do,' he replied; 'he was a great man—such an one as Hind will never see again. He had great ambition, wonderful ability, perseverance, and the art of leading men's hearts more than they were aware of, or cared to acknowledge; he had patient application, and nothing was done without his sanction, even to the meanest affairs, and the business of his dominions was vast. You will allow he was brave, and died like a soldier. He was kind and considerate to his servants, and a steady friend to those he loved. Mashalla! he was a great man.'

'Yet he was treacherous to you, Meer Sahib,' said Philip.

'Ay, and had he not been so, ye might now have been far from hence. Ye see, sirs, the power of destiny, which, working even by such mean instruments as myself and Jaffar, has wrought great ends.'

'What treachery?' said Herbert. 'I have wondered to see thee here in the English camp, but thought thou mightest have been admitted to protection like the rest of the Sultaun's officers.'

'It is a long tale,' said Kasim, 'but your brother, the colonel, knows much of it already, and he will tell it to you.'

'Not so,' said Philip, 'tell it yourself, I should only blunder in the narration;' and he added, 'since we have been together, I have never asked after the lady you loved, Meer Sahib; it is a painful question, perhaps, and may awaken thoughts and feelings long since dead. You smile—I rejoice to see it.'

'You know, Sahib, we Moslems are not given to speaking of our wives or families,' said Kasim, 'and therefore I have never mentioned her; but she lives, I rejoice to say, and is as beautiful to my eyes as ever.'

'Come!' said Herbert, 'if it be a tale of love, let me hear it; I have talked long enough, and can listen patiently.'

Kasim then related his adventures, from the time he had appeared a youth in Tippoo's Durbar, to that in which, wearied by his cruelties and uneven temper, he had left him, and had so narrowly escaped assassination.

'I reached my village,' he continued, 'and long remained in secrecy, enjoying the quiet of my own home. I read my favourite poets, wrote verses, and a history of my own adventures, to pass the time; but in truth, after so much excitement, I at length grew tired of the dull life, and looked around me for employment. The administration of the affairs and collection of the revenue of my district happened then to be vacated by the person who had held the offices, and, as I understood the duties perfectly, I solicited and obtained the situation by help of a douceur to the minister: in its duties, and in the suppression of the disorders of the country, I found ample employment. Still I had never visited the city of Hyderabad, and as I had need to go there to arrange some matters with the minister regarding the revenue collections, I determined upon a short visit, and was courteously received both by him and by the Prince, who spoke much to me of the Sultaun's character, and the wild schemes of conquest which he meditated.

'I was delighted with the city, and the polite and courtly character of its nobles, and I remained longer than I had intended. One day I was riding towards the minister's house, in order to take my leave of him, previously to my departure, when a woman, rather old, but decently dressed as a servant, whose features at first sight appeared familiar to me, ran towards me in the open street, and catching hold of the rein of my horse uttered a loud cry of joy. The horse was a spirited one, and began to curvet and bound, and she dared not approach me. I saw her speak to my groom; and when she had learned where I lived, she told him she would come in the evening, waved her hand to me, and darted down a narrow street. All that day I wondered much who she could be; I could not by any effort recall her name to my memory, and though I had an engagement with a friend, I waited at home till late.

'About dark a woman came, closely veiled, leading another. Both, as they entered, threw themselves at my feet, and kissed them repeatedly, uttering expressions of joy; they could not speak intelligibly for some time, nor would they unveil, though I could hear from their voices that they were aged. At length one playfully pulled the veil from the other's head, and to my joy and surprise I beheld Meeran. I recognised her instantly, and, raising her up, embraced her cordially. Sahib, the other was Sozun.

'I was, as you may suppose, breathless to know Ameena's fate. Was she alive? or did that hated place I remembered hold her mortal remains? "Speak, I conjure you," I cried, "for I burn with impatience."

'"She lives, Meer Sahib," said Meeran; "she lives, blessed be Alla and Moula Ali, and the Apostle and the Lady Muriam! to whom we have offered up Fateehas for her recovery on every anniversary of that event. Ah, Meer Sahib, it is before me now!"

'"Alive!" I cried; "but perhaps she is another's; some nobleman hath heard of her beauty, and hath sought her in second marriage?"

'"No, by your soul!" cried Sozun; "she lives, and thinks but of you. She is as beautiful as a houri; the years that have passed now seem but as hours; her skin is as fair, her eye as bright, her form as round and perfect as ever."

'"And the wound?" I asked.

'"Ah! it was a horrible gash," said Meeran, shuddering, 'and it was long before it healed; she will show you the place if—if—"

'"Come," said I, "come! I burn to see her. I am not married; I never should have married, perhaps. Come! it is my destiny. Ya Alla kureem, how it hath been worked out!"

'They led the way joyfully: her mother had been advised of my presence in the city by Meeran in the morning, and, closely veiled, she sat in her private apartment, awaiting me. Her husband was absent on some military duty, so I had to arrange all with her.

'How my heart beat as I entered the house! To be once more under the same roof with her who had loved me so long and so truly—to be there in the hope that ere many hours should elapse she would be mine—mine for ever! Sahib, I had fought and bled on a battle-field, yet I never felt so agitated as I did at that moment.

'A cry of joy from the old lady welcomed me. "Blessed be Alla!" she said, as she embraced me like a son; "blessed be his name, that thou art here! Oh that my lord were here, to welcome thee, and greet thee as a son!"

'"And Ameena," I said, "tell me, by your soul, how is she? Doth she still remember Kasim Ali? I am rich, I am high in rank; I have left the Sultaun's service, and am now in that of your own Government. What delay need there be? Let me, I beseech you, speak to her, and send for the Moola to read the Nika."

'"Fie!" said the old lady, "that would be indecent haste."

'"What, after years of absence, mother? nay, say not so, but tell her I am here."

'"Wait," she said; "I will return immediately."

'I arose and walked about, burning with love, with hope, with joy. The passion which for years had been smothered within me broke out as freshly, as strongly as when I had first seen her. The memory of that kiss was as if it still lingered on my lips. I heard a movement, a sort of hesitation at the door; I thought the old lady would come in. A figure entered, veiled from head to foot; it was a useless precaution—my heart told me that it was

Ameena. I rushed towards her, caught her tottering form in my arms, removed the veil from her lovely features, and in a moment more strained her to my heart in an embrace which she did not resist; and in a kiss which united our souls once more, I pledged to her my faith and love for ever.

'Yes, she was as fair as ever; even more beautiful in the mature charms of womanhood, than had been the girl I bore from the dreadful waters, or preserved from the maddened elephant. There was more fulness in her form, more fire in the large and soft eye, which, filled with tears, rested on me. She clung to me as though I should never part from her again, and her hand trembled in mine.

'I understood her. "I will not go from thee, fairest! most beloved!" I cried; "more even than the bulbul to the rose! more than Mejnoon to Leila will I be to thee!"

'Her mother entered soon after; she saw Ameena unveiled and in my arms. She gently chid her, but she did so no longer when the fair and gentle creature bent on her an imploring look, and nestled closer to my bosom.

'The next evening the Moola came: all had been prepared in the meanwhile, and such a marriage as mine wanted no long ceremony—it was that only of the Koran. Some friends were sent for: in their presence I wrote a settlement upon Ameena, and received an assignment of all her property; it was little needed, for henceforth our lot was to be together for good or for evil. There was a screen put up in the apartment; the ladies came behind it; I heard the rustle of their garments, and the tinkling of their anklets—it was like delicious music. The few prayers were quickly read, the witnesses signed and sealed the papers, and they left me. I heard the old lady bless her daughter, and the servants join in a fervent Ameen! In a few moments the screen was withdrawn, and I was alone with Ameena. Sirs, the true believer when he enters Paradise, and is welcomed by the beauteous houris that await his coming, is not more blessed than I was then. Hours flew, and still we talked over the past, and the miseries and sufferings of that dreadful time.

'"Tell me," I said, "how you escaped, and show me the place—the wound."

'She bared her beauteous neck, modestly and shrinkingly. I looked on the wound and kissed it; it was on her shoulder, and had reached the back of her neck. A heavy gold necklace and chain, she said, had saved her life; but for that she must have been killed.

'" But," she continued, "I knew nothing until I found myself in a small hut; Sozun was there, and Meeran. I shrank from Sozun, for I knew her to have been an evil woman; but she was vehement in her protestations of affection, and I believed her. I knew not till long after how nearly she had been connected with my fate; but she has been faithful, and that is long since forgiven and forgotten in her constancy. The house belonged to her daughter, and her husband was a foot-soldier in the army; they were kind and good to me, and the faithful Zoolfoo bound up my wound; indeed he sewed it up, which gave me great pain; but I was soon strong again, and I inquired for the Khan and for you; they said you had both fallen, and I mourned you as dead. Afterwards when the Sultaun capitulated, and there was peace, I followed my protector as a humble woman, and attended by Meeran and Sozun, under pretence of making offerings at a shrine, we escaped from the Fort, and entered that of the troops of the Dekhan: although my father had not accompanied them, yet I found his intimate friend Sikundur Beg, with whose daughters I had been a playmate. He was a father to me, gave me his palankeen to travel hither, and in my own home I speedily recovered."

'I should weary you, sirs,' continued Kasim after a pause, 'were I to tell you of her daily increasing love, and the joy I felt in her society. I wrote word to my mother that I had met her and was married; and the old lady, transported with joy, actually travelled up to the city to greet her daughter. I was fortunate in meeting with a good deputy in the person of my excellent uncle, and I remained at the city with Ameena's family. Her father arrived in due time from his post, and there never was a happier circle united on this earth than ours. I became known in the city: there was talk of a war with the Sultaun, and I was offered the command of a risala of horse, and received a title from the Government; they are common, but I was honoured. "Distinguish thyself," said the minister, "thou shalt have a jaghire* for life." Sirs, ye know the rest. He has given me two villages near my own, the revenue of which, with my patrimony, and the command of five hundred horse, most of which are my own, makes me easy for life. My mother (she has old-fashioned notions) sometimes hints that the marriage was not regular, that I should even now ask the young daughter of a nobleman of high rank, and go through all the forms with her; but I am content, sirs, with one wife, and I wish to Alla that all my countrymen were so too; for I am well as-

* Estate.

sured that to one alone can a man give all his love, and that where more than one is, there ensue those jealousies, envies, wild passions, evil, and sin, which were well-nigh fatal to my Ameena.'

'Thou art a noble fellow!' exclaimed both; and Charles Hayward too—for he also had been a listener—added his praise; 'and believe me,' added Dalton, 'thou wilt often be remembered, and thy wife too, when we are far away in our own land. If it be not beyond the bounds of politeness, carry her our affections and warmest wishes for years of happiness with thee. I would that my wife could have known her! she must have loved one so sorely tried, yet so pure in heart. Thou wilt see her at Bangalore, Meer Sahib, and will tell thy wife of her.'

The tears started to Kasim Ali's eyes: he brushed them away hastily. 'I am a fool,' said he; 'but if any one, when I served him who ruled yonder, had told me that I should have loved Englishmen, I would have quarrelled with him even to bloodshed; and now I should be unhappy indeed if I carried not away your esteem. I thank you for your interest in Ameena. I will tell her much of you and your fortunes; and when you are in your own green and beautiful land, and you wander beneath cool shady groves and beside murmuring rivers, or when you are in the peaceful society of your own homes, something will whisper in your hearts that Kasim Ali and Ameena speak of you with love. I pray you then remember us kindly, and now bid me depart to-day,' he said—but his voice trembled. 'I have spoken long, and the Captain is weary.'

Dalton's regiment moved soon after, and Kasim and his risala accompanied it; they marched by easy stages, and soon the invalid was able once more to mount a horse, and to enjoy a gallop with the dashing Risaldar, whose horsemanship was beyond all praise. At Bangalore they halted some time, it was to be a station for the Mysore field-force, and Dalton's regiment was to belong to it. His wife had arrived from Madras, and the deeply attached brother and sister were once more united after so long and painful an absence. Kasim saw her there; and though he thought it profanation to gaze on one so fair, yet he often paid his respectful homage to her while he stayed, and told the wondering Ameena, and in after days his children, of the fair skin, golden hair, and deep blue eyes of the English lady; and as he would dwell in rapture upon the theme, they thought that the angels of Paradise could not be fairer.

When Kasim Ali could stay no longer, he came to take his

leave. 'I shall pass the old Fakeer,' he said; 'have you any message for him? the old man still lives, and prays for you.'

'We will go to him,' said Philip; ''tis but a day's ride.' Herbert agreed readily, and they set out that day.

The old man's joy at seeing them cannot be told; the certainty that his poor efforts were estimated with gratitude, were to him more than gold or precious stones; but his declining years were made happy by an annuity, which was regularly paid, and he wanted no more the casual charity of passing travellers.

And there, beneath those beauteous trees, which even now remain, and which no one can pass without admiration, the friends parted, with sincere regret, and a regard which never diminished, though they never met again. The martial and picturesque companions of the Risaldar awaited him; Philip and Herbert watched him as he bounded into his saddle, and soon the gay and glittering group was lost behind the trees at a little distance.

About three weeks after the Fort had fallen, two men, one driving a heavily-laden pony, passed out of the gate of the Fort, and took their way towards the river; the rain had fallen much during that and the previous day, but there was as yet no more water than usual in the river.

'Come on, Madar!' said one whom our readers will easily recognise; 'that beast goes as slow as if he had an elephant's load; come on! we are lucky to get across, for there is no water in the river.'

'I tell thee the brute will never travel, Jaffar; the load is too heavy. Why wouldst thou not buy the other?'

'I could not afford it,' he said; 'one is enough; come on!'

The pony was laden with gold and silver bars and heavy stuffs, cloth of gold and silver, the plunder of years, and more especially of that night when the Sultaun was killed, for Jaffar knew the places where the silver and gold utensils were kept, and he had laden himself with the spoil.

'He! he! he!' said he chuckling, 'we will go to Madras and live with the kafir Feringhees; no one will know us there, and we can trade with this money.'

'Good!' said Madar, 'it is a wise thought; may your prosperity increase!'

They were now on the edge of the river. Opposite the Fort it is broad, and the bed, one sheet of rock, has been worn into thousands of deep holes and gulleys by the impetuous stream. It was no easy matter to get the over-laden beast across these, and he often stumbled and fell against the sharp rocks.

'The curses of the Shitan light on thee!' cried Jaffar to the animal, as it lay down at last, groaning heavily, and he screwed its tail desperately to urge it on. 'Wilt thou not get up? Help me, Madar, to raise it.'

They did so by their united strength, but ere it had gone a few paces it fell again. Jaffar was in despair. There was no resource but to unload it, and carry the burden piece by piece to the bank. They were doing this when a loud roaring was heard.

'What was that?' said Madar.

'Nothing, fool,' said the other; 'the wind, I dare say.'

It was not—it was the roaring of the mighty river, as it poured down beyond the sharp turn above the Fort—a wall of water three feet high—foaming, boiling, roaring, dashing high into the air—a vast brown, thick, muddy mass, overwhelming everything in its course. Madar fled at once to the bank.

Jaffar cursed aloud; the bundles had been tied up with scrupulous care, lest the money should fall out, and it was hard to lose all after years of toil. He tugged desperately at the knots—they would not come untied; he drew his sword and cut fiercely at them, bars of gold fell out; he seized as much as he could hold in his hands, and turned to fly. Some men were on the shore with Madar hallooing to him; he could not hear their words, but he thought they pointed to a rock higher than the rest; he got upon it, or in another instant the roaring flood would have overwhelmed him. He was safe for a minute; the waters were rising gradually but fearfully fast; he clutched the rock, he screamed, he prayed wildly; the rush of the boiling waters appeared to increase; his brain grew dizzy; then he tried to scramble up higher—to stand upright. In attempting this his foot slipped; those on the bank saw him toss his arms wildly into the air, and the next instant he was gone! The fearful tide rolled on in its majesty, but there was no sign of a living thing upon its turbid waters.

Herbert did not long wait at Bangalore. Letters to England had now preceded him more than a month; they had gone in a ship of war, which was some guarantee for their safe arrival. There was danger on the seas, but he thought not of that. Home—Amy was before him, more vividly than it is possible for us to paint; the days seemed to pass as weeks, as the gallant fleet sailed along, for home bounded their prospect; ere five months had passed they anchored at the Nore. Philip Dalton and Charles were soon to follow.

It was on a bright warm day, early in December, that a travelling carriage, with four horses, was seen driving at desperate speed into the town of ——; it stopped at the inn.

'Horses on to my father's—to Alston,' cried a gentleman within; 'quick, quick!' The landlord looked at him for a moment; it was not Mr. Compton's son, the clergyman; no, this was a darker, taller, handsomer person than him; he looked again, and then exclaimed, 'It cannot be!—surely it cannot be Captain Compton?'

'Yes, I am he,' was the reply; 'but pray be quick!'

'Hurrah!' cried the jolly landlord, throwing up his cap into the air; 'hurrah for the Captain! three cheers for Captain Compton, and God bless him! You shall have a barrel of ale, my lads, to-day, for this joy. I little thought to have ever seen you alive again, sir.'

'Thank you, thank you,' said Herbert; 'I will come soon and see you; now drive on, boys, at full speed;' and away they dashed.

An anxious party was assembled that day at the old Rectory; in trembling expectation of the sound of wheels, all felt nervous and agitated, and some laughed and cried by turns.

Poor Amy! it is difficult to describe her feelings of joy, of silent thankfulness. Her beauty was more radiant than ever; the purity of her complexion, with the exquisite expression of her eyes, was more striking, far more, than that of the lively and joyous girl of six years ago.

There was one who heard the sound of wheels long before the rest—it was Amy; the others watched her; her face, which had been flushed and deadly pale by turns, was lighted up on a sudden with a joy so intense that they almost feared for the consequences. On a sudden she appeared to listen more earnestly, then she arose, but no one followed her; she went to the door, passed into the hall, seemed to gaze vacantly around, returned, sank into a chair, and pressing her hand to her heart, panted for breath. Soon after a carriage at full speed dashed past the house; a man opened the door—jumped out almost ere it had stopped—hurried with breathless haste into the hall—passed a crowd of servants who were sobbing with joy, and in another instant he was in the room. Amy sprang to meet him with outstretched arms, and uttering a low cry of joy threw herself into his embrace, and was strained to his heart in silent rapture. Others hung round him, sobbing too, but their tears were those of joy and gratitude; the past was even then forgotten, for they beheld their long-lost Herbert safe, and knew, as he pressed to his the faithful heart which had so long loved him, that their past sorrow would soon be turned into rejoicing.

THE END.

COLSTON AND SON, PRINTERS, EDINBURGH.

STANDARD WORKS OF FICTION—*continued.*

X.

RALPH DARNELL. By the late Colonel MEADOWS TAYLOR. New and Cheaper Edition.

XI.

THE CONFESSIONS of a THUG. By the late Colonel MEADOWS TAYLOR. New and Cheaper Edition.

'A story so powerfully and graphically told does not soon lose its hold on the imagination.'—*Daily News.*

XII.

TARA. A Mahratta Tale. By the late Colonel MEADOWS TAYLOR. New and Cheaper Edition.

'We recommend it to all who care to know something of native life in India on its nobler side, as a book of very high calibre.'—*Spectator.*

XIII.

ISRAEL MORT, OVERMAN. By JOHN SAUNDERS. New Edition.

'Conceived with no little power and originality.'—*Times.*

XIV.

KITTY. By Miss BETHAM EDWARDS.

'Lively and clever. . . . There is a certain dash in every description; the dialogue is bright and sparkling.'—*Athenæum.*

XV.

PANDURANG HARI; or, Memoirs of a Hindoo. With a Preface by Sir H. BARTLE L. FRERE, G.C.S.I., C.B.

'We advise our readers to read it absolutely through. If they do this they cannot fail to be both amused and interested.'—*Times.*

XVI.

GIDEON'S ROCK. By KATHERINE SAUNDERS.

'Especially worthy of commendation.'—*Queen.*

XVII.

JOAN MERRYWEATHER. By KATHERINE SAUNDERS.

'Of rare interest and power.'—*Edinburgh Daily Review.*

XVIII.

MARGARET and ELIZABETH. By KATHERINE SAUNDERS.

'A very beautiful story.'—*Pall Mall Gazette.*

XIX.

BY STILL WATERS. By EDWARD GARRETT.

'It has more than pleased, it has charmed us.'—*Nonconformist.*

XX.

BEATRICE AYLMER. By MARY HOWARD.

'These tales possess considerable merit.'—*Court Journal.*

A LIST OF

C. KEGAN PAUL AND CO.'S

PUBLICATIONS.

4.80.

A LIST OF C. KEGAN PAUL AND CO.'S PUBLICATIONS.

ADAMS (F. O.), F.R.G.S.

The History of Japan. From the Earliest Period to the Present Time. New Edition, revised. 2 volumes. With Maps and Plans. Demy 8vo. Cloth, price 21*s.* each.

ADAMS (W. D.).

Lyrics of Love, from Shakespeare to Tennyson. Selected and arranged by. Fcap. 8vo. Cloth extra, gilt edges, price 3*s.* 6*d.*

Also, a Cheap Edition. Fcap. 8vo. Cloth, price 2*s.* 6*d.*

ADAMS (John), M.A.

St. Malo's Quest, and other Poems. Fcap. 8vo. Cloth, 5*s.*

ADAMSON (H. T.), B.D.

The Truth as it is in Jesus. Crown 8vo. Cloth, price 8*s.* 6*d.*

ADON.

Through Storm & Sunshine. Illustrated by M. E. Edwards, A. T. H. Paterson, and the Author. Crown 8vo. Cloth, price 7*s.* 6*d.*

A. J. R.

Told at Twilight; Stories in Verse, Songs, &c. Fcap. 8vo. Cloth, price 3*s.* 6*d.*

A. K. H. B.

A Scotch Communion Sunday, to which are added Certain Discourses from a University City. By the Author of "The Recreations of a Country Parson." Second Edition. Crown 8vo. Cloth, price 5*s.*

From a Quiet Place. A New Volume of Sermons. Crown 8vo. Cloth, price 5*s.*

ALBERT (Mary).

Holland and her Heroes to the year 1585. An Adaptation from Motley's "Rise of the Dutch Republic." Small crown 8vo. Cloth, price, 4*s.* 6*d.*

ALLEN (Rev. R.), M.A.

Abraham; his Life, Times, and Travels, 3,800 years ago. Second Edition. With Map. Post 8vo. Cloth, price 6*s.*

ALLEN (Grant), B.A.

Physiological Æsthetics. Large post 8vo. 9*s.*

ALLIES (T. W.), M.A.

Per Crucem ad Lucem. The Result of a Life. 2 vols. Demy 8vo. Cloth, price 25*s.*

AMATEUR.

A Few Lyrics. Small crown 8vo. Cloth, price 2*s.*

AMOS (Prof. Sheldon).

Science of Law. Third Edition. Crown 8vo. Cloth, price 5*s.*

Volume X. of The International Scientific Series.

ANDERSON (Rev. C.), M.A.

New Readings of Old Parables. Demy 8vo. Cloth, price 4*s.* 6*d.*

Church Thought and Church Work. Edited by. Second Edition. Demy 8vo. Cloth, price 7*s.* 6*d.*

The Curate of Shyre. Second Edition. 8vo. Cloth, price 7*s.* 6*d.*

ANDERSON (Col. R. P.).

Victories and Defeats. An Attempt to explain the Causes which have led to them. An Officer's Manual. Demy 8vo. Cloth, price 14*s.*

ANDERSON (R. C.), C.E.

Tables for Facilitating the Calculation of every Detail in connection with Earthen and Masonry Dams. Royal 8vo. Cloth, price £2 2*s.*

ARCHER (Thomas).

About my Father's Business. Work amidst the Sick, the Sad, and the Sorrowing. Crown 8vo. Cloth, price 2*s*. 6*d*.

Army of the North German Confederation.

A Brief Description of its Organization, of the Different Branches of the Service and their *rôle* in War, of its Mode of Fighting, &c. &c. Translated from the Corrected Edition, by permission of the Author, by Colonel Edward Newdigate. Demy 8vo. Cloth, price 5*s*.

ARNOLD (Arthur).

Social Politics. Demy 8vo. Cloth, price 14*s*.

Free Land. Crown 8vo. Cloth, price 6*s*.

AUBERTIN (J. J.).

Camoens' Lusiads. Portuguese Text, with Translation by. With Map and Portraits. 2 vols. Demy 8vo. Price 30*s*.

Aunt Mary's Bran Pie.

By the author of "St. Olave's." Illustrated. Cloth, price 3*s*. 6*d*.

Aurora.

A Volume of Verse. Fcap. 8vo. Cloth, price 5*s*.

AVIA.

The Odyssey of Homer Done into English Verse. Fcap. 4to. Cloth, price 15*s*.

BAGEHOT (Walter).

Physics and Politics; or, Thoughts on the Application of the Principles of "Natural Selection" and "Inheritance" to Political Society. Fourth Edition. Crown 8vo. Cloth, price 4*s*.

Volume II. of The International Scientific Series.

Some Articles on the Depreciation of Silver, and Topics connected with it. Demy 8vo. Price 5*s*.

The English Constitution. A New Edition, Revised and Corrected, with an Introductory Dissertation on Recent Changes and Events. Crown 8vo. Cloth, price 7*s*. 6*d*.

BAGEHOT (Walter)—*continued.*

Lombard Street. A Description of the Money Market. Seventh Edition. Crown 8vo. Cloth, price 7*s*. 6*d*.

BAGOT (Alan).

Accidents in Mines: their Causes and Prevention. Crown 8vo. Cloth, price 6*s*.

BAIN (Alexander), LL.D.

Mind and Body: the Theories of their relation. Sixth Edition. Crown 8vo. Cloth, price 4*s*.

Volume IV. of The International Scientific Series.

Education as a Science. Crown 8vo. Second Edition. Cloth, price 5*s*.

Volume XXV. of The International Scientific Series.

BAKER (Sir Sherston, Bart.).

Halleck's International Law; or Rules Regulating the Intercourse of States in Peace and War. A New Edition, Revised, with Notes and Cases. 2 vols. Demy 8vo. Cloth, price 38*s*.

The Laws relating to Quarantine. Crown 8vo. Cloth, price 12*s*. 6*d*.

BALDWIN (Capt. J. H.), F.Z.S.

The Large and Small Game of Bengal and the North-Western Provinces of India. 4to. With numerous Illustrations. Second Edition. Cloth, price 21*s*.

BANKS (Mrs. G. L.).

God's Providence House. New Edition. Crown 8vo. Cloth, price 3*s*. 6*d*.

Ripples and Breakers. Poems. Square 8vo. Cloth, price 5*s*.

BARING (T. C.), M.A., M.P.

Pindar in English Rhyme. Being an Attempt to render the Epinikian Odes with the principal remaining Fragments of Pindar into English Rhymed Verse. Small Quarto. Cloth, price 7*s*.

BARLEE (Ellen).

Locked Out: a Tale of the Strike. With a Frontispiece. Royal 16mo. Cloth, price 1*s*. 6*d*.

BARNES (William).

An Outline of English Speechcraft. Crown 8vo. Cloth, price 4*s.*

Poems of Rural Life, in the Dorset Dialect. New Edition, complete in 1 vol. Crown 8vo. Cloth, price 8*s.* 6*d.*

Outlines of Redecraft (Logic). With English Wording. Crown 8vo. Cloth, price 3*s.*

BARTLEY (George C. T.).

Domestic Economy: Thrift in Every Day Life. Taught in Dialogues suitable for Children of all ages. Small crown 8vo. Cloth, limp, 2*s.*

BAUR (Ferdinand), Dr. Ph.

A Philological Introduction to Greek and Latin for Students. Translated and adapted from the German of. By C. KEGAN PAUL, M.A. Oxon., and the Rev. E. D. STONE, M.A., late Fellow of King's College, Cambridge, and Assistant Master at Eton. Second and revised edition. Crown 8vo. Cloth, price 6*s.*

BAYNES (Rev. Canon R. H.)

At the Communion Time. A Manual for Holy Communion. With a preface by the Right Rev. the Lord Bishop of Derry and Raphoe. Cloth, price 1*s.* 6*d.*

*** Can also be had bound in French morocco, price 2*s.* 6*d.*; Persian morocco, price 3*s.*; Calf, or Turkey morocco, price 3*s.* 6*d.*

Home Songs for Quiet Hours. Fourth and cheaper Edition. Fcap. 8vo. Cloth, price 2*s.* 6*d.*

This may also be had handsomely bound in morocco with gilt edges.

BECKER (Bernard H.).

The Scientific Societies of London. Crown 8vo. Cloth, price 5*s.*

BELLINGHAM (Henry), Barrister-at-Law.

Social Aspects of Catholicism and Protestantism in their Civil Bearing upon Nations. Translated and adapted from the French of M. le Baron de Haulleville. With a Preface by His Eminence Cardinal Manning. Crown 8vo. Cloth, price 6*s.*

BENNETT (Dr. W. C.).

Narrative Poems & Ballads. Fcap. 8vo. Sewed in Coloured Wrapper, price 1*s.*

Songs for Sailors. Dedicated by Special Request to H. R. H. the Duke of Edinburgh. With Steel Portrait and Illustrations. Crown 8vo. Cloth, price 3*s.* 6*d.*

An Edition in Illustrated Paper Covers, price 1*s.*

Songs of a Song Writer. Crown 8vo. Cloth, price 6*s.*

BERNSTEIN (Prof.).

The Five Senses of Man. With 91 Illustrations. Second Edition. Crown 8vo. Cloth, price 5*s.*

Volume XXI. of The International Scientific Series.

BETHAM - EDWARDS (Miss M.).

Kitty. With a Frontispiece. Crown 8vo. Cloth, price 6*s.*

BEVINGTON (L. S.).

Key Notes. Small crown 8vo. Cloth, price 5*s.*

BISSET (A.)

History of the Struggle for Parliamentary Government in England. 2 vols. Demy 8vo. Cloth, price 24*s.*

BLASERNA (Prof. Pietro).

The Theory of Sound in its Relation to Music. With numerous Illustrations. Second Edition. Crown 8vo. Cloth, price 5*s.*

Volume XXII. of The International Scientific Series.

Blue Roses; or, Helen Malinofska's Marriage. By the Author of "Véra." 2 vols. Fifth Edition. Cloth, gilt tops, 12*s.*

*** Also a Cheaper Edition in 1 vol. With Frontispiece. Crown 8vo. Cloth, price 6*s.*

BLUME (Major W.).

The Operations of the German Armies in France, from Sedan to the end of the war of 1870-71. With Map. From the Journals of the Head-quarters Staff. Translated by the late E. M. Jones, Maj. 20th Foot, Prof. of Mil. Hist., Sandhurst. Demy 8vo. Cloth, price 9*s.*

BOGUSLAWSKI (Capt. A. von).

Tactical Deductions from the War of 1870-71. Translated by Colonel Sir Lumley Graham, Bart., late 18th (Royal Irish) Regiment. Third Edition, Revised and Corrected. Demy 8vo. Cloth, price 7*s.*

BONWICK (J.), F.R.G.S.

Egyptian Belief and Modern Thought. Large post 8vo. Cloth, price 10*s.* 6*d.*

Pyramid Facts and Fancies. Crown 8vo. Cloth, price 5*s.*

The Tasmanian Lily. With Frontispiece. Crown 8vo. Cloth, price 5*s.*

Mike Howe, the Bushranger of Van Diemen's Land. With Frontispiece. Crown 8vo. Cloth, price 5*s.*

BOSWELL (R. B.), M.A., Oxon.

Metrical Translations from the Greek and Latin Poets, and other Poems. Crown 8vo. Cloth, price 5*s.*

BOWEN (H. C.), M.A.

English Grammar for Beginners. Fcap. 8vo. Cloth, price 1*s.*

Studies in English, for the use of Modern Schools. Small crown 8vo. Cloth, price 1*s.* 6*d.*

Simple English Poems. English Literature for Junior Classes. In Four Parts. Parts I. and II., price 6*d.* each, now ready.

BOWRING (L.), C.S.I.

Eastern Experiences. Illustrated with Maps and Diagrams. Demy 8vo. Cloth, price 16*s.*

BOWRING (Sir John).

Autobiographical Recollections. With Memoir by Lewin B. Bowring. Demy 8vo. Price 14*s.*

Brave Men's Footsteps.

By the Editor of "Men who have Risen." A Book of Example and Anecdote for Young People. With Four Illustrations by C. Doyle. Sixth Edition. Crown 8vo. Cloth, price 3*s.* 6*d.*

BRIALMONT (Col. A.).

Hasty Intrenchments. Translated by Lieut. Charles A. Empson, R.A. With Nine Plates. Demy 8vo. Cloth, price 6*s.*

BRODRICK (The Hon. G. C.).

Political Studies. Demy 8vo. Cloth, price 14*s.*

BROOKE (Rev. S. A.), M.A.

The Late Rev. F. W. Robertson, M.A., Life and Letters of. Edited by.

I. Uniform with the Sermons. 2 vols. With Steel Portrait. Price 7*s.* 6*d.*

II. Library Edition. 8vo. With Two Steel Portraits. Price 12*s.*

III. A Popular Edition, in 1 vol. 8vo. Price 6*s.*

Theology in the English Poets.—COWPER, COLERIDGE, WORDSWORTH, and BURNS. Third Edition. Post 8vo. Cloth, price 9*s.*

Christ in Modern Life. Thirteenth Edition. Crown 8vo. Cloth, price 7*s.* 6*d.*

Sermons. First Series. Eleventh Edition. Crown 8vo. Cloth, price 6*s.*

Sermons. Second Series. Third Edition. Crown 8vo. Cloth, price 7*s.*

The Fight of Faith. Sermons preached on various occasions. Third Edition. Crown 8vo. Cloth, price 7*s.* 6*d.*

Frederick Denison Maurice: The Life and Work of. A Memorial Sermon. Crown 8vo. Sewed, price 1*s.*

BROOKE (W. G.), M.A.

The Public Worship Regulation Act. With a Classified Statement of its Provisions, Notes, and Index. Third Edition, Revised and Corrected. Crown 8vo. Cloth, price 3*s.* 6*d.*

Six Privy Council Judgments—1850-1872. Annotated by. Third Edition. Crown 8vo. Cloth, price 9*s.*

BROUN (J. A.).

Magnetic Observations at Trevandrum and Augustia Malley. Vol. I. 4to. Cloth, price 63*s*.

The Report from above, separately sewed, price 21*s*.

BROWN (Rev. J. Baldwin), B.A.

The Higher Life. Its Reality, Experience, and Destiny. Fifth and Cheaper Edition. Crown 8vo. Cloth, price 5*s*.

Doctrine of Annihilation in the Light of the Gospel of Love. Five Discourses. Third Edition. Crown 8vo. Cloth, price 2*s*. 6*d*.

BROWN (J. Croumbie), LL.D.

Reboisement in France; or, Records of the Replanting of the Alps, the Cevennes, and the Pyrenees with Trees, Herbage, and Bush. Demy 8vo. Cloth, price 12*s*. 6*d*.

The Hydrology of Southern Africa. Demy 8vo. Cloth, price 10*s*. 6*d*.

BRYANT (W. C.)

Poems. Red-line Edition. With 24 Illustrations and Portrait of the Author. Crown 8vo. Cloth extra, price 7*s*. 6*d*.

A Cheaper Edition, with Frontispiece. Small crown 8vo. Cloth, price 3*s*. 6*d*.

BULKELEY (Rev. H. J.).

Walled in, and other Poems. Crown 8vo. Cloth, price 5*s*.

BURCKHARDT (Jacob).

The Civilization of the Period of the Renaissance in Italy. Authorized translation, by S. G. C. Middlemore. 2 vols. Demy 8vo. Cloth, price 24*s*.

BURTON (Mrs. Richard).

The Inner Life of Syria, Palestine, and the Holy Land. With Maps, Photographs, and Coloured Plates. 2 vols. Second Edition. Demy 8vo. Cloth, price 24*s*.

*** Also a Cheaper Edition in one volume. Large post 8vo. Cloth, price 10*s*. 6*d*.

BURTON (Capt. Richard F.).

The Gold Mines of Midian and the Ruined Midianite Cities. A Fortnight's Tour in North Western Arabia. With numerous Illustrations. Second Edition. Demy 8vo. Cloth, price 18*s*.

The Land of Midian Revisited. With numerous illustrations on wood and by Chromolithography. 2 vols. Demy 8vo. Cloth, price 32*s*.

CALDERON.

Calderon's Dramas: The Wonder-Working Magician—Life is a Dream—The Purgatory of St. Patrick. Translated by Denis Florence MacCarthy. Post 8vo. Cloth, price 10*s*.

CANDLER (H.).

The Groundwork of Belief. Crown 8vo. Cloth, price 7*s*.

CARLISLE (A. D.), B. A.

Round the World in 1870. A Volume of Travels, with Maps. New and Cheaper Edition. Demy 8vo. Cloth, price 6*s*.

CARPENTER (E.).

Narcissus and other Poems. Fcap. 8vo. Cloth, price 5*s*.

CARPENTER (W. B.), M.D.

The Principles of Mental Physiology. With their Applications to the Training and Discipline of the Mind, and the Study of its Morbid Conditions. Illustrated. Fifth Edition. 8vo. Cloth, price 12*s*.

CAVALRY OFFICER.

Notes on Cavalry Tactics, Organization, &c. With Diagrams. Demy 8vo. Cloth, price 12*s*.

CHAPMAN (Hon. Mrs. E. W.).

A Constant Heart. A Story. 2 vols. Cloth, gilt tops, price 12*s*.

CHEYNE (Rev. T. K.).

The Prophecies of Isaiah. Translated, with Critical Notes and Dissertations by. Two vols., demy 8vo. Cloth. Vol. I., price 12*s*. 6*d*.

Children's Toys, and some Elementary Lessons in General Knowledge which they teach. Illustrated. Crown 8vo. Cloth, price 5*s*.

CHRISTOPHERSON (The late Rev. Henry), M.A.

Sermons. With an Introduction by John Rae, LL.D., F.S.A. Second Series. Crown 8vo. Cloth, price 6*s*.

CLAYDEN (P. W.).

England under Lord Beaconsfield. The Political History of the Last Six Years, from the end of 1873 to the beginning of 1880. Second Edition. With Index, and Continuation to March, 1880. Demy 8vo. Cloth, price 16*s*.

CLERK (Mrs. Godfrey).

'Ilâm en Nâs. Historical Tales and Anecdotes of the Times of the Early Khalifahs. Translated from the Arabic Originals. Illustrated with Historical and Explanatory Notes. Crown 8vo. Cloth, price 7*s*.

CLERY (C.), Major.

Minor Tactics. With 26 Maps and Plans. Fourth and Revised Edition. Demy 8vo. Cloth, price 16*s*.

CLODD (Edward), F.R.A.S.

The Childhood of the World: a Simple Account of Man in Early Times. Sixth Edition. Crown 8vo. Cloth, price 3*s*.

A Special Edition for Schools. Price 1*s*.

The Childhood of Religions. Including a Simple Account of the Birth and Growth of Myths and Legends. Third Thousand. Crown 8vo. Cloth, price 5*s*.

A Special Edition for Schools. Price 1*s*. 6*d*.

Jesus of Nazareth. With a brief Sketch of Jewish History to the Time of His Birth. Small crown 8vo. Cloth, price 6*s*.

COLERIDGE (Sara).

Pretty Lessons in Verse for Good Children, with some Lessons in Latin, in Easy Rhyme. A New Edition. Illustrated. Fcap. 8vo. Cloth, price 3*s*. 6*d*.

Phantasmion. A Fairy Tale. With an Introductory Preface by the Right Hon. Lord Coleridge, of Ottery St. Mary. A New Edition. Illustrated. Crown 8vo. Cloth, price 7*s*. 6*d*.

COLERIDGE (Sara)—*continued*.

Memoir and Letters of Sara Coleridge. Edited by her Daughter. With Index. 2 vols. With Two Portraits. Third Edition, Revised and Corrected. Crown 8vo. Cloth, price 24*s*.

Cheap Edition. With one Portrait. Cloth, price 7*s*. 6*d*.

COLLINS (Mortimer).

The Secret of Long Life. Small crown 8vo. Cloth, price 3*s*. 6*d*.

Inn of Strange Meetings, and other Poems. Crown 8vo. Cloth, price 5*s*.

COLLINS (Rev. R.), M.A.

Missionary Enterprise in the East. With special reference to the Syrian Christians of Malabar, and the results of modern Missions. With Four Illustrations. Crown 8vo. Cloth, price 6*s*.

CONWAY (Hugh).

A Life's Idylls. Small crown 8vo. Cloth, price 3*s*. 6*d*.

COOKE (M. C.), M.A., LL.D.

Fungi; their Nature, Influences, Uses, &c. Edited by the Rev. M. J. Berkeley, M.A., F.L.S. With Illustrations. Second Edition. Crown 8vo. Cloth, price 5*s*.

Volume XIV. of The International Scientific Series.

COOKE (Prof. J. P.)

The New Chemistry. With 31 Illustrations. Fourth Edition. Crown 8vo. Cloth, price 5*s*.

Volume IX. of The International Scientific Series.

Scientific Culture. Crown 8vo. Cloth, price 1*s*.

COOPER (T. T.), F.R.G.S.

The Mishmee Hills: an Account of a Journey made in an Attempt to Penetrate Thibet from Assam, to open New Routes for Commerce. Second Edition. With Four Illustrations and Map. Post 8vo. Cloth, price 10*s*. 6*d*.

COOPER (H. J.).

The Art of Furnishing on Rational and Æsthetic Principles. New and Cheaper Edition. Fcap. 8vo. Cloth, price 1*s*. 6*d*.

COPPÉE (François).
L'Exilée. Done into English Verse with the sanction of the Author by I. O. L. Crown 8vo. Vellum, price 5*s*.

CORY (Lieut. Col. Arthur).
The Eastern Menace; or, Shadows of Coming Events. Crown 8vo. Cloth, price 5*s*.

Ione. A Poem in Four Parts. Fcap. 8vo. Cloth, price 5*s*.

CORY (William).
A Guide to Modern English History. Part I. MDCCCXV.—MDCCCXXX. Demy 8vo. Cloth, price 9*s*.

Cosmos.
A Poem. Fcap. 8vo. Cloth, price 3*s*. 6*d*.

COURTNEY (W. L.).
The Metaphysics of John Stuart Mill. Crown 8vo. Cloth, price 5*s*. 6*d*.

COWAN (Rev. William).
Poems: Chiefly Sacred, including Translations from some Ancient Latin Hymns. Fcap. 8vo. Cloth, price 5*s*.

COX (Rev. Sir G. W.), Bart.
A History of Greece from the Earliest Period to the end of the Persian War. New Edition. 2 vols. Demy 8vo. Cloth, price 36*s*.

The Mythology of the Aryan Nations. New Edition. 2 vols. Demy 8vo. Cloth, price 28*s*.

A General History of Greece from the Earliest Period to the Death of Alexander the Great, with a sketch of the subsequent History to the present time. New Edition. Crown 8vo. Cloth, price 7*s*. 6*d*.

Tales of Ancient Greece. New Edition. Small crown 8vo. Cloth, price 6*s*.

School History of Greece. With Maps. New Edition. Fcap. 8vo. Cloth, price 3*s*. 6*d*.

The Great Persian War from the Histories of Herodotus. New Edition. Fcap. 8vo. Cloth, price 3*s*. 6*d*.

COX (Rev. Sir G. W.), Bart.—*continued.*
A Manual of Mythology in the form of Question and Answer. New Edition. Fcap. 8vo. Cloth, price 3*s*.

COX (Rev. Sir G. W.), Bart., M.A., and EUSTACE HINTON JONES.
Popular Romances of the Middle Ages. Second Edition in one volume. Crown 8vo. Cloth, price 6*s*.

COX (Rev. Samuel).
Salvator Mundi; or, Is Christ the Saviour of all Men? Sixth Edition. Crown 8vo. Cloth, price 5*s*.

The Genesis of Evil, and other Sermons, mainly Expository. Crown 8vo. Cloth, price 6*s*.

CRAUFURD (A. H.).
Seeking for Light: Sermons. Crown 8vo. Cloth, price 5*s*.

CRESSWELL (Mrs. G.).
The King's Banner. Drama in Four Acts. Five Illustrations. 4to. Cloth, price 10*s*. 6*d*.

CROMPTON (Henry).
Industrial Conciliation. Fcap. 8vo. Cloth, price 2*s*. 6*d*.

DANVERS (N. R.).
The Suez Canal: Letters and Documents descriptive of its Rise and Progress in 1854-56. By Ferdinand de Lesseps. Translated by. Demy 8vo. Cloth, price 10*s*. 6*d*.

Parted. A Tale of Clouds and Sunshine. With 4 Illustrations. Extra Fcap. 8vo. Cloth, price 3*s*. 6*d*.

Little Minnie's Troubles. An Every-day Chronicle. With Four Illustrations by W. H. Hughes. Fcap. Cloth, price 3*s*. 6*d*.

Pixie's Adventures; or, the Tale of a Terrier. With 21 Illustrations. 16mo. Cloth, price 4*s*. 6*d*.

Nanny's Adventures; or, the Tale of a Goat. With 12 Illustrations. 16mo. Cloth, price 4*s*. 6*d*.

DAVIDSON (Rev. Samuel), D.D., LL.D.
The New Testament, translated from the Latest Greek Text of Tischendorf. A New and thoroughly Revised Edition. Post 8vo. Cloth, price 10*s*. 6*d*.

DAVIDSON (Rev. Samuel), D.D., LL.D.—*continued.*

Canon of the Bible: Its Formation, History, and Fluctuations. Second Edition. Small crown 8vo. Cloth, price 5*s.*

DAVIES (G. Christopher).

Mountain, Meadow, and Mere: a Series of Outdoor Sketches of Sport, Scenery, Adventures, and Natural History. With Sixteen Illustrations by Bosworth W. Harcourt. Crown 8vo. Cloth, price 6*s.*

Rambles and Adventures of Our School Field Club. With Four Illustrations. Crown 8vo. Cloth, price 5*s.*

DAVIES (Rev. J. L.), M.A.

Theology and Morality. Essays on Questions of Belief and Practice. Crown 8vo. Cloth, price 7*s.* 6*d.*

DAVIES (T. Hart.).

Catullus. Translated into English Verse. Crown 8vo. Cloth, price 6*s.*

DAWSON (George), M.A.

Prayers, with a Discourse on Prayer. Edited by his Wife. Fifth Edition. Crown 8vo. Price 6*s.*

Sermons on Disputed Points and Special Occasions. Edited by his Wife. Third Edition. Crown 8vo. Cloth, price 6*s.*

Sermons on Daily Life and Duty. Edited by his Wife. Second Edition. Crown 8vo. Cloth, price 6*s.*

DE L'HOSTE (Col. E. P.).

The Desert Pastor, Jean Jarousseau. Translated from the French of Eugène Pelletan. With a Frontispiece. New Edition. Fcap. 8vo. Cloth, price 3*s.* 6*d.*

DENNIS (J.).

English Sonnets. Collected and Arranged. Elegantly bound. Fcap. 8vo. Cloth, price 3*s.* 6*d.*

DE REDCLIFFE (Viscount Stratford), P.C., K.G., G.C.B.

Why am I a Christian? Fifth Edition. Crown 8vo. Cloth, price 3*s.*

DESPREZ (Philip S.).

Daniel and John; or, the Apocalypse of the Old and that of the New Testament. Demy 8vo. Cloth, price 12*s.*

DE TOCQUEVILLE (A.).

Correspondence and Conversations of, with Nassau William Senior, from 1834 to 1859. Edited by M. C. M. Simpson. 2 vols. Post 8vo. Cloth, price 21*s.*

DE VERE (Aubrey).

Legends of the Saxon Saints. Small crown 8vo. Cloth, price 6*s.*

Alexander the Great. A Dramatic Poem. Small crown 8vo. Cloth, price 5*s.*

The Infant Bridal, and other Poems. A New and Enlarged Edition. Fcap. 8vo. Cloth, price 7*s.* 6*d.*

The Legends of St. Patrick, and other Poems. Small crown 8vo. Cloth, price 5*s.*

St. Thomas of Canterbury. A Dramatic Poem. Large fcap. 8vo. Cloth, price 5*s.*

Antar and Zara: an Eastern Romance. INISFAIL, and other Poems, Meditative and Lyrical. Fcap. 8vo. Price 6*s.*

The Fall of Rora, the Search after Proserpine, and other Poems, Meditative and Lyrical. Fcap. 8vo. Price 6*s.*

DOBSON (Austin).

Vignettes in Rhyme and Vers de Société. Third Edition. Fcap. 8vo. Cloth, price 5*s.*

Proverbs in Porcelain. By the Author of "Vignettes in Rhyme." Second Edition. Crown 8vo. 6*s.*

DOWDEN (Edward), LL.D.

Shakspere: a Critical Study of his Mind and Art. Fourth Edition. Large post 8vo. Cloth, price 12*s.*

Studies in Literature, 1789-1877. Large post 8vo. Cloth, price 12*s.*

Poems. Second Edition. Fcap. 8vo. Cloth, price 5*s.*

DOWNTON (Rev. H.), M.A.

Hymns and Verses. Original and Translated. Small crown 8vo. Cloth, price 3*s.* 6*d.*

DRAPER (J. W.), M.D., LL.D.

History of the Conflict between Religion and Science. Eleventh Edition. Crown 8vo. Cloth, price 5*s.*

Volume XIII. of The International Scientific Series.

DREW (Rev. G. S.), M.A.

Scripture Lands in connection with their History. Second Edition. 8vo. Cloth, price 10s. 6*d*.

Nazareth: Its Life and Lessons. Third Edition. Crown 8vo. Cloth, price 5*s*.

The Divine Kingdom on Earth as it is in Heaven. 8vo. Cloth, price 10s. 6*d*.

The Son of Man: His Life and Ministry. Crown 8vo. Cloth, price 7*s*. 6*d*.

DREWRY (G. O.), M.D.

The Common-Sense Management of the Stomach. Fifth Edition. Fcap. 8vo. Cloth, price 2*s*. 6*d*.

DREWRY (G. O.), M.D., and BARTLETT (H. C.), Ph.D., F.C.S.

Cup and Platter: or, Notes on Food and its Effects. New and cheaper Edition. Small 8vo. Cloth, price 1*s*. 6*d*.

DRUMMOND (Miss).

Tripps Buildings. A Study from Life, with Frontispiece. Small crown 8vo. Cloth, price 3*s*. 6*d*.

DU MONCEL (Count).

The Telephone, the Microphone, and the Phonograph. With 74 Illustrations. Small crown 8vo. Cloth, price 5*s*.

DURAND (Lady).

Imitations from the German of Spitta and Terstegen. Fcap. 8vo. Cloth, price 4*s*.

DU VERNOIS (Col. von Verdy).

Studies in leading Troops. An authorized and accurate Translation by Lieutenant H. J. T. Hildyard, 71st Foot. Parts I. and II. Demy 8vo. Cloth, price 7*s*.

EDEN (Frederick).

The Nile without a Dragoman. Second Edition. Crown 8vo. Cloth, price 7*s*. 6*d*.

EDMONDS (Herbert).

Well Spent Lives: a Series of Modern Biographies. Crown 8vo. Price 5*s*.

Educational Code of the Prussian Nation, in its Present Form. In accordance with the Decisions of the Common Provincial Law, and with those of Recent Legislation. Crown 8vo. Cloth, price 2*s*. 6*d*.

EDWARDS (Rev. Basil).

Minor Chords; or, Songs for the Suffering: a Volume of Verse. Fcap. 8vo. Cloth, price 3*s*. 6*d*.; paper, price 2*s*. 6*d*.

ELLIOT (Lady Charlotte).

Medusa and other Poems. Crown 8vo. Cloth, price 6*s*.

ELLIOTT (Ebenezer), The Corn-Law Rhymer.

Poems. Edited by his Son, the Rev. Edwin Elliott, of St. John's, Antigua. 2 vols. Crown 8vo. Cloth, price 18*s*.

ELSDALE (Henry).

Studies in Tennyson's Idylls. Crown 8vo. Cloth, price 5*s*.

Epic of Hades (The). By the author of "Songs of Two Worlds." Ninth and finally revised Edition. Fcap. 8vo. Cloth, price 7*s*. 6*d*.

*** Also an Illustrated Edition with seventeen full-page designs in photomezzotint by GEORGE R. CHAPMAN. 4to. Cloth, extra gilt leaves, price 25*s*.

Eros Agonistes. Poems. By E. B. D. Fcap. 8vo. Cloth, price 3*s*. 6*d*.

Essays on the Endowment of Research. By Various Writers.
Square crown 8vo. Cloth, price 10*s*. 6*d*.

EVANS (Mark).

The Gospel of Home Life. Crown 8vo. Cloth, price 4*s*. 6*d*.

The Story of our Father's Love, told to Children. Fourth and Cheaper Edition. With Four Illustrations. Fcap. 8vo. Cloth, price 1*s*. 6*d*.

A Book of Common Prayer and Worship for Household Use, compiled exclusively from the Holy Scriptures. Fcap. 8vo. Cloth, price 2*s*. 6*d*.

The King's Story Book. In three parts. Fcap. 8vo. Cloth, price 1*s*. 6*d*. each.

*** Part I., with four illustrations and Picture Map, now ready.

EX-CIVILIAN.

Life in the Mofussil; or, Civilian Life in Lower Bengal. 2 vols. Large post 8vo. Price 14*s.*

EYRE (Maj.-Gen. Sir V.), C.B., K.C.S.I., &c.

Lays of a Knight-Errant in many Lands. Square crown 8vo. With Six Illustrations. Cloth, price 7*s.* 6*d.*

FARQUHARSON (M.).

I. Elsie Dinsmore. Crown 8vo. Cloth, price 3*s.* 6*d.*

II. Elsie's Girlhood. Crown 8vo. Cloth, price 3*s.* 6*d.*

III. Elsie's Holidays at Roselands. Crown 8vo. Cloth, price 3*s.* 6*d.*

FERRIS (Henry Weybridge).

Poems. Fcap. 8vo. Cloth, price 5*s.*

FIELD (Horace), B.A. Lond.

The Ultimate Triumph of Christianity. Small crown 8vo. Cloth, price 3*s.* 6*d.*

FINN (the late James), M.R.A.S.

Stirring Times; or, Records from Jerusalem Consular Chronicles of 1853 to 1856. Edited and Compiled by his Widow. With a Preface by the Viscountess STRANGFORD. 2 vols. Demy 8vo. Price 30*s.*

FLEMING (James), D.D.

Early Christian Witnesses; or, Testimonies of the First Centuries to the Truth of Christianity. Small crown 8vo. Cloth, price 3*s.* 6*d.*

Folkestone Ritual Case (The). The Argument, Proceedings, Judgment, and Report, revised by the several Counsel engaged. Demy 8vo. Cloth, price 25*s.*

FOOTMAN (Rev. H.), M.A.

From Home and Back; or, Some Aspects of Sin as seen in the Light of the Parable of the Prodigal. Crown 8vo. Cloth, price 5*s.*

FOWLE (Rev. Edmund).

Latin Primer Rules made Easy. Crown 8vo. Cloth, price 3*s.*

FOWLE (Rev. T. W.), M.A.

The Reconciliation of Religion and Science. Being Essays on Immortality, Inspiration, Miracles, and the Being of Christ. Demy 8vo. Cloth, price 10*s.* 6*d.*

The Divine Legation of Christ. Crown 8vo. Cloth, price 7*s.*

FOX-BOURNE (H. R.).

The Life of John Locke, 1632—1704. 2 vols. Demy 8vo. Cloth, price 28*s.*

FRASER (Donald).

Exchange Tables of Sterling and Indian Rupee Currency, upon a new and extended system, embracing Values from One Farthing to One Hundred Thousand Pounds, and at Rates progressing, in Sixteenths of a Penny, from 1*s.* 9*d.* to 2*s.* 3*d.* per Rupee. Royal 8vo. Cloth, price 10*s.* 6*d.*

FRISWELL (J. Hain).

The Better Self. Essays for Home Life. Crown 8vo. Cloth, price 6*s.*

One of Two; or, A Left-Handed Bride. With a Frontispiece. Crown 8vo. Cloth, price 3*s.* 6*d.*

FYTCHE (Lieut.-Gen. Albert), C.S.I., late Chief Commissioner of British Burma.

Burma Past and Present, with Personal Reminiscences of the Country. With Steel Portraits, Chromolithographs, Engravings on Wood, and Map. 2 vols. Demy 8vo. Cloth, price 30*s.*

GAMBIER (Capt. J. W.), R.N.

Servia. Crown 8vo. Cloth, price 5*s.*

GARDNER (H.).

Sunflowers. A Book of Verses. Fcap. 8vo. Cloth, price 5*s.*

GARDNER (J.), M.D.

Longevity: The Means of Prolonging Life after Middle Age. Fourth Edition, Revised and Enlarged. Small crown 8vo. Cloth, price 4*s.*

GARRETT (E.).

By Still Waters. A Story for Quiet Hours. With Seven Illustrations. Crown 8vo. Cloth, price 6*s.*

GEBLER (Karl Von).

Galileo Galilei and the Roman Curia, from Authentic Sources. Translated with the sanction of the Author, by Mrs. George Sturge. Demy 8vo. Cloth, price 12*s*.

GEDDES (James).

History of the Administration of John de Witt, Grand Pensionary of Holland. Vol. I. 1623—1654. Demy 8vo., with Portrait. Cloth, price 15*s*.

G. H. T.

Verses, mostly written in India. Crown 8vo. Cloth, price 6*s*.

GILBERT (Mrs.).

Autobiography and other Memorials. Edited by Josiah Gilbert. Third Edition. With Portrait and several Wood Engravings. Crown 8vo. Cloth, price 7*s*. 6*d*.

GILL (Rev. W. W.), B.A.

Myths and Songs from the South Pacific. With a Preface by F. Max Müller, M.A., Professor of Comparative Philology at Oxford. Post 8vo. Cloth, price 9*s*.

GLOVER (F.), M.A.

Exempla Latina. A First Construing Book with Short Notes, Lexicon, and an Introduction to the Analysis of Sentences. Fcap. 8vo. Cloth, price 2*s*.

GODWIN (William).

William Godwin: His Friends and Contemporaries. With Portraits and Facsimiles of the handwriting of Godwin and his Wife. By C. Kegan Paul. 2 vols. Demy 8vo. Cloth, price 28*s*.

The Genius of Christianity Unveiled. Being Essays never before published. Edited, with a Preface, by C. Kegan Paul. Crown 8vo. Cloth, price 7*s*. 6*d*.

GOETZE (Capt. A. von).

Operations of the German Engineers during the War of 1870-1871. Published by Authority, and in accordance with Official Documents. Translated from the German by Colonel G. Graham, V.C., C.B., R.E. With 6 large Maps. Demy 8 o. Cloth, price 21*s*.

GOLDIE (Lieut. M. H. G.)

Hebe: a Tale. Fcap. 8vo. Cloth, price 5*s*.

GOLDSMID (Sir Francis Henry).

Memoir of. With Portrait. Crown 8vo. Cloth, price 5*s*.

GOODENOUGH (Commodore J. G.), R.N., C.B., C.M.G.

Memoir of, with Extracts from his Letters and Journals. Edited by his Widow. With Steel Engraved Portrait. Square 8vo. Cloth, 5*s*.

*** Also a Library Edition with Maps, Woodcuts, and Steel Engraved Portrait. Square post 8vo. Cloth, price 14*s*.

GOSSE (Edmund W.).

Studies in the Literature of Northern Europe. With a Frontispiece designed and etched by Alma Tadema. Large post 8vo. Cloth, price 12*s*.

New Poems. Crown 8vo. Cloth, price 7*s*. 6*d*.

GOULD (Rev. S. Baring), M.A.

Germany, Present and Past. 2 Vols. Demy 8vo. Cloth, price 21*s*.

The Vicar of Morwenstow: a Memoir of the Rev. R. S. Hawker. With Portrait. Third Edition, revised. Square post 8vo. Cloth, 10*s*. 6*d*.

GRANVILLE (A. B.), M.D., F.R.S., &c.

Autobiography of A. B. Granville, F. R. S., &c. Edited, with a brief Account of the concluding Years of his Life, by his youngest Daughter, Paulina B. Granville. 2 vols. With a Portrait. Second Edition. Demy 8vo. Cloth, price 32*s*.

GREY (John), of Dilston.

John Grey (of Dilston): Memoirs. By Josephine E. Butler. New and Revised Edition. Crown 8vo. Cloth, price 3*s*. 6*d*.

GRIFFITH (Rev. T.), A.M.

Studies of the Divine Master. Demy 8vo. Cloth, price 12*s*.

GRIFFITHS (Capt. Arthur).

Memorials of Millbank, and Chapters in Prison History. With Illustrations by R. Goff and the Author. 2 vols. Post 8vo. Cloth, price 21*s*.

GRIMLEY (Rev. H. N.), M.A.
Tremadoc Sermons, chiefly on the SPIRITUAL BODY, the UNSEEN WORLD, and the DIVINE HUMANITY. Second Edition. Crown 8vo. Cloth, price 6*s*.

GRÜNER (M. L.).
Studies of Blast Furnace Phenomena. Translated by L. D. B. Gordon, F.R.S.E., F.G.S. Demy 8vo. Cloth, price 7*s*. 6*d*.

GURNEY (Rev. Archer).
Words of Faith and Cheer. A Mission of Instruction and Suggestion. Crown 8vo. Cloth, price 6*s*.

Gwen: A Drama in Monologue. By the Author of the "Epic of Hades." Second Edition. Fcap. 8vo. Cloth, price 5*s*.

HAECKEL (Prof. Ernst).
The History of Creation. Translation revised by Professor E. Ray Lankester, M.A., F.R.S. With Coloured Plates and Genealogical Trees of the various groups of both plants and animals. 2 vols. Second Edition. Post 8vo. Cloth, price 32*s*.

The History of the Evolution of Man. With numerous Illustrations. 2 vols. Large post 8vo. Cloth, price 32*s*.

Freedom in Science and Teaching. From the German of Ernst Haeckel, with a Prefatory Note by T. H. Huxley, F.R.S. Crown 8vo. Cloth, price 5*s*.

HAKE (A. Egmont).
Paris Originals, with twenty etchings, by Léon Richeton. Large post 8vo. Cloth, price 14*s*.

Halleck's International Law; or, Rules Regulating the Intercourse of States in Peace and War. A New Edition, revised, with Notes and Cases. By Sir Sherston Baker, Bart. 2 vols. Demy 8vo. Cloth, price 38*s*.

HARCOURT (Capt. A. F. P.).
The Shakespeare Argosy. Containing much of the wealth of Shakespeare's Wisdom and Wit, alphabetically arranged and classified. Crown 8vo. Cloth, price 6*s*.

HARDY (Thomas).
A Pair of Blue Eyes. New Edition. With Frontispiece. Crown 8vo. Cloth, price 6*s*.

HARDY (Thomas)—*continued*.
The Return of the Native. New Edition. With Frontispiece. Crown 8vo. Cloth, price 6*s*.

HARRISON (Lieut.-Col. R.).
The Officer's Memorandum Book for Peace and War. Second Edition. Oblong 32mo. roan, elastic band and pencil, price 3*s*. 6*d*.; russia, 5*s*.

HAWEIS (Rev. H. R.), M.A.
Arrows in the Air. Crown 8vo. Second Edition. Cloth, price 6*s*.

Current Coin. Materialism—The Devil—Crime—Drunkenness—Pauperism—Emotion—Recreation—The Sabbath. Third Edition. Crown 8vo. Cloth, price 6*s*.

Speech in Season. Fourth Edition. Crown 8vo. Cloth, price 9*s*.

Thoughts for the Times. Eleventh Edition. Crown 8vo. Cloth, price 7*s*. 6*d*.

Unsectarian Family Prayers. New and Cheaper Edition. Fcap. 8vo. Cloth, price 1*s*. 6*d*.

HAWKER (Robert Stephen).
The Poetical Works of. Now first collected and arranged with a prefatory notice by J. G. Godwin. With Portrait. Crown 8vo. Cloth, price 12*s*.

HELLWALD (Baron F. von).
The Russians in Central Asia. A Critical Examination, down to the present time, of the Geography and History of Central Asia. Translated by Lieut.-Col. Theodore Wirgman, LL.B. Large post 8vo. With Map. Cloth, price 12*s*.

HELVIG (Major H.).
The Operations of the Bavarian Army Corps. Translated by Captain G. S. Schwabe. With Five large Maps. In 2 vols. Demy 8vo. Cloth, price 24*s*.

Tactical Examples: Vol. I. The Battalion, price 15*s*. Vol. II. The Regiment and Brigade, price 10*s*. 6*d*. Translated from the German by Col. Sir Lumley Graham. With numerous Diagrams. Demy 8vo. Cloth.

HERFORD (Brooke).

The Story of Religion in England. A Book for Young Folk. Crown 8vo. Cloth, price 5*s*.

HEWLETT (Henry G.).

A Sheaf of Verse. Fcap. 8vo. Cloth, price 3*s*. 6*d*.

HINTON (James).

Life and Letters of. Edited by Ellice Hopkins, with an Introduction by Sir W. W. Gull, Bart., and Portrait engraved on Steel by C. H. Jeens. Second Edition. Crown 8vo. Cloth, 8*s*. 6*d*.

Chapters on the Art of Thinking, and other Essays. With an Introduction by Shadworth Hodgson. Edited by C. H. Hinton. Crown 8vo. Cloth, price 8*s*. 6*d*.

The Place of the Physician. To which is added Essays on the Law of Human Life, and on the Relation between Organic and Inorganic Worlds. Second Edition. Crown 8vo. Cloth, price 3*s*. 6*d*.

Physiology for Practical Use. By various Writers. With 50 Illustrations. 2 vols. Second Edition. Crown 8vo. Cloth, price 12*s*. 6*d*.

An Atlas of Diseases of the Membrana Tympani. With Descriptive Text. Post 8vo. Price £6 6*s*.

The Questions of Aural Surgery. With Illustrations. 2 vols. Post 8vo. Cloth, price 12*s*. 6*d*.

The Mystery of Pain. New Edition Fcap. 8vo Cloth limp, 1*s*.

HOCKLEY (W. B.).

Tales of the Zenana; or, A Nuwab's Leisure Hours. By the Author of "Pandurang Hari." With a Preface by Lord Stanley of Alderley. 2 vols. Crown 8vo. Cloth, price 21*s*.

Pandurang Hari; or, Memoirs of a Hindoo. A Tale of Mahratta Life sixty years ago. With a Preface by Sir H. Bartle E. Frere, G. C. S. I., &c. New and Cheaper Edition. Crown 8vo. Cloth, price 6*s*.

HOFFBAUER (Capt.).

The German Artillery in the Battles near Metz. Based on the official reports of the German Artillery. Translated by Capt. E. O. Hollist. With Map and Plans. Demy 8vo. Cloth, price 21*s*.

HOLMES (E. G. A.).

Poems. First and Second Series. Fcap. 8vo. Cloth, price 5*s*. each.

HOLROYD (Major W. R. M.).

Tas-hil ul Kālām; or, Hindustani made Easy. Crown 8vo. Cloth, price 5*s*.

HOOPER (Mary).

Little Dinners: How to Serve them with Elegance and Economy. Thirteenth Edition. Crown 8vo. Cloth, price 5*s*.

Cookery for Invalids, Persons of Delicate Digestion, and Children. Crown 8vo. Cloth, price 3*s*. 6*d*.

Every-Day Meals. Being Economical and Wholesome Recipes for Breakfast, Luncheon, and Supper. Second Edition. Crown 8vo. Cloth, price 5*s*.

HOOPER (Mrs. G.).

The House of Raby. With a Frontispiece. Crown 8vo. Cloth, price 3*s*. 6*d*.

HOPKINS (Ellice).

Life and Letters of James Hinton, with an Introduction by Sir W. W. Gull, Bart., and Portrait engraved on Steel by C. H. Jeens. Second Edition. Crown 8vo. Cloth price 8*s*. 6*d*.

HOPKINS (M.).

The Port of Refuge; or, Counsel and Aid to Shipmasters in Difficulty, Doubt, or Distress. Crown 8vo. Second and Revised Edition. Cloth, price 6*s*.

HORNE (William), M.A.

Reason and Revelation: an Examination into the Nature and Contents of Scripture Revelation, as compared with other Forms of Truth. Demy 8vo. Cloth, price 12*s*.

HORNER (The Misses).

Walks in Florence. A New and thoroughly Revised Edition. 2 vols. Crown 8vo. Cloth limp. With Illustrations.

Vol. I.—Churches, Streets, and Palaces. 10*s.* 6*d.* Vol. II.—Public Galleries and Museums. 5*s.*

HOWELL (James).

A Tale of the Sea, Sonnets, and other Poems. Fcap. 8vo. Cloth, price 5*s.*

HUGHES (Allison).

Penelope and other Poems. Fcap. 8vo. Cloth, price 4*s.* 6*d.*

HULL (Edmund C. P.).

The European in India. With a MEDICAL GUIDE FOR ANGLO-INDIANS. By R. R. S. Mair, M.D., F.R.C.S.E. Third Edition, Revised and Corrected. Post 8vo. Cloth, price 6*s.*

HUTCHISON (Lieut.-Col. F. J.), and Capt. G. H. **MACGREGOR.**

Military Sketching and Reconnaissance. With Fifteen Plates. Small 8vo. Cloth, price 6*s.*

The first Volume of Military Handbooks for Regimental Officers. Edited by Lieut.-Col. C. B. BRACKENBURY, R.A., A.A.G.

HUTTON (Arthur), M.A.

The Anglican Ministry. Its Nature and Value in relation to the Catholic Priesthood. With a Preface by his Eminence Cardinal Newman. Demy 8vo. Cloth, price 14*s.*

HUXLEY (Prof.)

The Crayfish: An Introduction to the Study of Zoology. With Eighty-two Illustrations. Crown 8vo. Cloth, price 6*s.*

Volume XXVIII. of the International Scientific Scientific Series.

INCHBOLD (J. W.).

Annus Amoris. Sonnets. Fcap. 8vo. Cloth, price 4*s.* 6*d.*

INGELOW (Jean).

Off the Skelligs. A Novel. With Frontispiece. Second Edition. Crown 8vo. Cloth, price 6*s.*

The Little Wonder-horn. A Second Series of "Stories Told to a Child." With Fifteen Illustrations. Small 8vo. Cloth, price 2*s.* 6*d.*

Indian Bishoprics. By an Indian Churchman. Demy 8vo. 6*d.*

International Scientific Series (The).

I. **Forms of Water: A Familiar Exposition of the Origin and Phenomena of Glaciers.** By J. Tyndall, LL.D., F.R.S. With 25 Illustrations. Seventh Edition. Crown 8vo. Cloth, price 5*s.*

II. **Physics and Politics;** or, Thoughts on the Application of the Principles of "Natural Selection" and "Inheritance" to Political Society. By Walter Bagehot. Fourth Edition. Crown 8vo. Cloth, price 4*s.*

III. **Foods.** By Edward Smith, M.D., &c. With numerous Illustrations. Fifth Edition. Crown 8vo. Cloth, price 5*s.*

IV. **Mind and Body: The Theories** of their Relation. By Alexander Bain, LL.D. With Four Illustrations. Sixth Edition. Crown 8vo. Cloth, price 4*s.*

V. **The Study of Sociology.** By Herbert Spencer. Seventh Edition. Crown 8vo. Cloth, price 5*s.*

VI. **On the Conservation of Energy.** By Balfour Stewart, LL.D., &c. With 14 Illustrations. Fifth Edition. Crown 8vo. Cloth, price 5*s.*

VII. **Animal Locomotion;** or, Walking, Swimming, and Flying. By J. B. Pettigrew, M.D., &c. With 130 Illustrations. Second Edition. Crown 8vo. Cloth, price 5*s.*

VIII. **Responsibility in Mental Disease.** By Henry Maudsley, M.D. Third Edition. Crown 8vo. Cloth, price 5*s.*

IX. **The New Chemistry.** By Professor J. P. Cooke. With 31 Illustrations. Fourth Edition. Crown 8vo. Cloth, price 5*s.*

X. **The Science of Law.** By Prof. Sheldon Amos. Third Edition. Crown 8vo. Cloth, price 5*s.*

XI. **Animal Mechanism.** A Treatise on Terrestrial and Aerial Locomotion. By Prof. E. J. Marey. With 117 Illustrations. Second Edition. Crown 8vo. Cloth, price 5*s.*

XII. **The Doctrine of Descent and Darwinism.** By Prof. Oscar Schmidt. With 26 Illustrations. Third Edition. Crown 8vo. Cloth, price 5*s.*

International Scientific Series (The)—*continued.*

XIII. The History of the Conflict between Religion and Science. By J. W. Draper, M.D., LL.D. Eleventh Edition. Crown 8vo. Cloth, price 5*s*

XIV. Fungi; their Nature, Influences, Uses, &c. By M. C. Cooke, LL.D. Edited by the Rev. M. J. Berkeley, F.L.S. With numerous Illustrations. Second Edition. Crown 8vo. Cloth, price 5*s*.

XV. The Chemical Effects of Light and Photography. By Dr. Hermann Vogel. With 100 Illustrations. Third and Revised Edition. Crown 8vo. Cloth, price 5*s*.

XVI. The Life and Growth of Language. By Prof. William Dwight Whitney. Second Edition. Crown 8vo. Cloth, price 5*s*.

XVII. Money and the Mechanism of Exchange. By W. Stanley Jevons, F.R.S. Fourth Edition. Crown 8vo. Cloth, price 5*s*.

XVIII. The Nature of Light: With a General Account of Physical Optics. By Dr. Eugene Lommel. With 188 Illustrations and a table of Spectra in Chromo-lithography. Second Edition. Crown 8vo. Cloth, price 5*s*.

XIX. Animal Parasites and Messmates. By M. Van Beneden. With 83 Illustrations. Second Edition. Crown 8vo. Cloth, price 5*s*.

XX. Fermentation. By Prof. Schützenberger. With 28 Illustrations. Second Edition. Crown 8vo. Cloth, price 5*s*.

XXI. The Five Senses of Man. By Prof. Bernstein. With 91 Illustrations. Second Edition. Crown 8vo. Cloth, price 5*s*.

XXII. The Theory of Sound in its Relation to Music. By Prof. Pietro Blaserna. With numerous Illustrations. Second Edition. Crown 8vo. Cloth, price 5*s*.

XXIII. Studies in Spectrum Analysis. By J. Norman Lockyer. F.R.S. With six photographic Illustrations of Spectra, and numerous engravings on wood. Crown 8vo. Second Edition. Cloth, price 6*s*. 6*d*.

XXIV. A History of the Growth of the Steam Engine. By Prof. R. H. Thurston. With numerous Illustrations. Second Edition. Crown 8vo. Cloth, price 6*s*. 6*d*.

International Scientific Series (The)—*continued.*

XXV. Education as a Science. By Alexander Bain, LL.D. Third Edition. Crown 8vo. Cloth, price 5*s*.

XXVI. The Human Species. By Prof. A. de Quatrefages. Second Edition. Crown 8vo. Cloth, price 5*s*.

XXVII. Modern Chromatics. With Applications to Art and Industry, by Ogden N. Rood. With 130 original Illustrations. Crown 8vo. Cloth, price 5*s*.

XXVIII. The Crayfish: an Introduction to the Study of Zoology. By Prof. T. H. Huxley. With eighty-two Illustrations. Crown 8vo. Cloth, price 6*s*.

Forthcoming Volumes.

Prof. W. KINGDON CLIFFORD, M.A. The First Principles of the Exact Sciences explained to the Non-mathematical.

W. B. CARPENTER, LL.D., F.R.S. The Physical Geography of the Sea.

Sir JOHN LUBBOCK, Bart., F.R.S. On Ants and Bees.

Prof. W. T. THISELTON DYER, B.A., B.Sc. Form and Habit in Flowering Plants.

Prof. MICHAEL FOSTER, M.D. Protoplasm and the Cell Theory.

H. CHARLTON BASTIAN, M.D., F.R.S. The Brain as an Organ of Mind.

Prof. A. C. RAMSAY, LL.D., F.R.S. Earth Sculpture: Hills, Valleys, Mountains, Plains, Rivers, Lakes; how they were Produced, and how they have been Destroyed.

P. BERT (Professor of Physiology, Paris). Forms of Life and other Cosmical Conditions.

The Rev. A SECCHI, D.J., late Director of the Observatory at Rome. The Stars.

Prof. J. ROSENTHAL, of the University of Erlangen. General Physiology of Muscles and Nerves.

FRANCIS GALTON, F.R.S. Psychometry.

J. W. JUDD, F.R.S. The Laws of Volcanic Action.

Prof. F. N. BALFOUR. The Embryonic Phases of Animal Life.

International Scientific Series (The)—*continued.*

J. Luys, Physician to the Hospice de la Salpêtrière. The Brain and its Functions. With Illustrations.

Dr. Carl Semper. Animals and their Conditions of Existence.

Prof. Wurtz. Atoms and the Atomic Theory.

George J. Romanes, F.L.S. Animal Intelligence.

Alfred W. Bennett. A Handbook of Cryptogamic Botany.

JACKSON (T. G.).
Modern Gothic Architecture. Crown 8vo. Cloth, price 5*s*.

JACOB (Maj.-Gen. Sir G. Le Grand), K.C.S.I., C.B.
Western India before and during the Mutinies. Pictures drawn from life. Second Edition. Crown 8vo. Cloth, price 7*s*. 6*d*.

JENKINS (Rev. Canon).
The Girdle Legend of Prato. Small crown 8vo. Cloth, price 2*s*.

JENKINS (E.) and RAYMOND (J.), Esqs.
A Legal Handbook for Architects, Builders, and Building Owners. Second Edition Revised. Crown 8vo. Cloth, price 6*s*.

JENKINS (Rev. R. C.), M.A.
The Privilege of Peter and the Claims of the Roman Church confronted with the Scriptures, the Councils, and the Testimony of the Popes themselves. Fcap. 8vo. Cloth, price 3*s*. 6*d*.

JENNINGS (Mrs. Vaughan).
Rahel: Her Life and Letters. With a Portrait from the Painting by Daffinger. Square post 8vo. Cloth, price 7*s*. 6*d*.

Jeroveam's Wife and other Poems. Fcap. 8vo. Cloth, price 3*s*. 6*d*.

JEVONS (W. Stanley), M.A., F.R.S.
Money and the Mechanism of Exchange. Fourth Edition. Crown 8vo. Cloth, price 5*s*.
Volume XVII. of The International Scientific Series.

JOEL (L.).
A Consul's Manual and Shipowner's and Shipmaster's Practical Guide in their Transactions Abroad. With Definitions of Nautical, Mercantile, and Legal Terms; a Glossary of Mercantile Terms in English, French, German, Italian, and Spanish. Tables of the Money, Weights, and Measures of the Principal Commercial Nations and their Equivalents in British Standards: and Forms of Consular and Notarial Acts. Demy 8vo. Cloth, price 12*s*.

JOHNSTONE (C. F.), M.A.
Historical Abstracts. Being Outlines of the History of some of the less-known States of Europe. Crown 8vo. Cloth, price 7*s*. 6*d*.

JONES (Lucy).
Puddings and Sweets. Being Three Hundred and Sixty-Five Receipts approved by Experience. Crown 8vo., price 2*s*. 6*d*.

JOYCE (P. W.), LL.D., &c.
Old Celtic Romances. Translated from the Gaelic by. Crown 8vo. Cloth, price 7*s*. 6*d*.

KAUFMANN (Rev. M.), B.A.
Utopias; or, Schemes of Social Improvement, from Sir Thomas More to Karl Marx. Crown 8vo. Cloth, price 5*s*.

Socialism: Its Nature, its Dangers, and its Remedies considered. Crown 8vo. Cloth, price 7*s*. 6*d*.

KAY (Joseph), M.A., Q.C.
Free Trade in Land. Edited by his Widow. With Preface by the Right Hon. John Bright, M.P. Third Edition. Crown 8vo. Cloth, price 5*s*.

KER (David).
The Boy Slave in Bokhara. A Tale of Central Asia. With Illustrations. Crown 8vo. Cloth, price 3*s*. 6*d*.

The Wild Horseman of the Pampas. Illustrated. Crown 8vo. Cloth, price 3*s*. 6*d*.

KERNER (Dr. A.), Professor of Botany in the University of Innsbruck.
Flowers and their Unbidden Guests. Translation edited by W. Ogle, M.A., M.D., and a prefatory letter by C. Darwin, F.R.S. With Illustrations. Sq. 8vo. Cloth, price 9*s*.

KIDD (Joseph), M.D.
The Laws of Therapeutics, or, the Science and Art of Medicine. Crown 8vo. Cloth, price 6*s*.

KINAHAN (G. Henry), M.R.I.A., &c., of her Majesty's Geological Survey.
Manual of the Geology of Ireland. With 8 Plates, 26 Woodcuts, and a Map of Ireland, geologically coloured. Square 8vo. Cloth, price 15*s*.

KING (Alice).
A Cluster of Lives. Crown 8vo. Cloth, price 7*s*. 6*d*.

KING (Mrs. Hamilton).
The Disciples. A Poem. Third Edition, with some Notes. Crown 8vo. Cloth, price 7*s*. 6*d*.
Aspromonte, and other Poems. Second Edition. Fcap. 8vo. Cloth, price 4*s*. 6*d*.

KINGSLEY (Charles), M.A.
Letters and Memories of his Life. Edited by his WIFE. With 2 Steel engraved Portraits and numerous Illustrations on Wood, and a Facsimile of his Handwriting. Thirteenth Edition. 2 vols. Demy 8vo. Cloth, price 36*s*.
*** Also a Cabinet Edition in 2 vols. Crown 8vo. Cloth, price 12*s*.
All Saints' Day and other Sermons. Second Edition. Crown 8vo. Cloth, 7*s*. 6*d*.
True Words for Brave Men: a Book for Soldiers' and Sailors' Libraries. Fifth Edition. Crown 8vo. Cloth, price 2*s*. 6*d*.

KNIGHT (A. F. C.).
Poems. Fcap. 8vo. Cloth, price 5*s*.

KNIGHT (Professor W.).
Studies in Philosophy and Literature. Large post 8vo. Cloth, price 7*s*. 6*d*.

LACORDAIRE (Rev. Père).
Life: Conferences delivered at Toulouse. A New and Cheaper Edition. Crown 8vo. Cloth, price 3*s*. 6*d*.

Lady of Lipari (The).
A Poem in Three Cantos. Fcap. 8vo. Cloth, price 5*s*.

LAIRD-CLOWES (W.).
Love's Rebellion: a Poem. Fcap. 8vo. Cloth, price 3*s*. 6*d*.

LAMONT (Martha MacDonald).
The Gladiator: A Life under the Roman Empire in the beginning of the Third Century. With four Illustrations by H. M. Paget. Extra fcap. 8vo. Cloth, price 3*s*. 6*d*.

LAYMANN (Capt.).
The Frontal Attack of Infantry. Translated by Colonel Edward Newdigate. Crown 8vo. Cloth, price 2*s*. 6*d*.

LEANDER (Richard).
Fantastic Stories. Translated from the German by Paulina B. Granville. With Eight full-page Illustrations by M. E. Fraser-Tytler. Crown 8vo. Cloth, price 5*s*.

LEE (Rev. F. G.), D.C.L.
The Other World; or, Glimpses of the Supernatural. 2 vols. A New Edition. Crown 8vo. Cloth, price 15*s*.

LEE (Holme).
Her Title of Honour. A Book for Girls. New Edition. With a Frontispiece. Crown 8vo. Cloth, price 5*s*.

LENOIR (J.).
Fayoum; or, Artists in Egypt. A Tour with M. Gérome and others. With 13 Illustrations. A New and Cheaper Edition. Crown 8vo. Cloth, price 3*s*. 6*d*.

LEWIS (Edward Dillon).
A Draft Code of Criminal Law and Procedure. Demy 8vo. Cloth, price 21*s*.

LEWIS (Mary A.).
A Rat with Three Tales. With Four Illustrations by Catherine F. Frere. Crown 8vo. Cloth, price 5*s*.

LINDSAY (W. Lauder), M.D., &c.
Mind in the Lower Animals in Health and Disease. 2 vols. Demy 8vo. Cloth, price 32*s*.

LOCKER (F.).
London Lyrics. A New and Revised Edition, with Additions and a Portrait of the Author. Crown 8vo. Cloth, elegant, price 6*s*.
Also, a Cheaper Edition. Fcap. 8vo. Cloth, price 2*s*. 6*d*.

LOCKYER (J. Norman), F.R.S.

Studies in Spectrum Analysis; with six photographic illustrations of Spectra, and numerous engravings on wood. Second Edition. Crown 8vo. Cloth, price 6*s*. 6*d*.

Vol. XXIII. of The International Scientific Series.

LOMMEL (Dr. E.).

The Nature of Light: With a General Account of Physical Optics. Second Edition. With 188 Illustrations and a Table of Spectra in Chromo-lithography. Second Edition. Crown 8vo. Cloth, price 5*s*.

Volume XVIII. of The International Scientific Series.

LONSDALE (Margaret).

Sister Dora. A Biography, with Portrait engraved on steel by C. H. Jeens, and one illustration. Twelfth edition. Crown 8vo. Cloth, price 6*s*.

LORIMER (Peter), D.D.

John Knox and the Church of England: His Work in her Pulpit, and his Influence upon her Liturgy, Articles, and Parties. Demy 8vo. Cloth, price 12*s*.

John Wiclif and his English Precursors, by Gerhard Victor Lechler. Translated from the German, with additional Notes. 2 vols. Demy 8vo. Cloth, price 21*s*.

LOTHIAN (Roxburghe).

Dante and Beatrice from 1282 to 1290. A Romance. 2 vols. Post 8vo. Cloth, price 24*s*.

LOWNDES (Henry).

Poems and Translations. Crown 8vo. Cloth, price 6*s*.

LUCAS (Alice).

Translations from the Works of German Poets of the 18th and 19th Centuries. Fcap. 8vo. Cloth, price 5*s*.

MAC CLINTOCK (L.).

Sir Spangle and the Dingy Hen. Illustrated. Square crown 8vo., price 2*s*. 6*d*.

MACDONALD (G.).

Malcolm. With Portrait of the Author engraved on Steel. Fourth Edition. Crown 8vo. Price 6*s*.

The Marquis of Lossie. Second Edition. Crown 8vo. Cloth, price 6*s*.

MACDONALD (G.)—*continued*.

St. George and St. Michael. Second Edition. Crown 8vo. Cloth, 6*s*.

MACKENNA (S. J.).

Plucky Fellows. A Book for Boys. With Six Illustrations. Second Edition. Crown 8vo. Cloth, price 3*s*. 6*d*.

At School with an Old Dragoon. With Six Illustrations. Second Edition. Crown 8vo. Cloth, price 5*s*.

MACLACHLAN (A. N. C.), M.A.

William Augustus, Duke of Cumberland: being a Sketch of his Military Life and Character, chiefly as exhibited in the General Orders of His Royal Highness, 1745—1747. With Illustrations. Post 8vo. Cloth, price 15*s*.

MACLACHLAN (Mrs.).

Notes and Extracts on Everlasting Punishment and Eternal Life, according to Literal Interpretation. Small crown 8vo. Cloth, price 3*s*. 6*d*.

MACNAUGHT (Rev. John).

Cœna Domini: An Essay on the Lord's Supper, its Primitive Institution, Apostolic Uses, and Subsequent History. Demy 8vo. Cloth, price 14*s*.

MAGNUSSON (Eirikr), M.A., and PALMER (E.H.), M.A.

Johan Ludvig Runeberg's Lyrical Songs, Idylls and Epigrams. Fcap. 8vo. Cloth, price 5*s*.

MAIR (R. S.), M.D., F.R.C.S.E.

The Medical Guide for Anglo-Indians. Being a Compendium of Advice to Europeans in India, relating to the Preservation and Regulation of Health. With a Supplement on the Management of Children in India. Second Edition. Crown 8vo. Limp cloth, price 3*s*. 6*d*.

MALDEN (H. E. and E. E.)

Princes and Princesses. Illustrated. Small crown 8vo. Cloth, price 2*s*. 6*d*.

MANNING (His Eminence Cardinal).

Essays on Religion and Literature. By various Writers. Third Series. Demy 8vo. Cloth, price 10*s*. 6*d*.

MANNING (His Eminence Cardinal)—*continued.*

The Independence of the Holy Sec, with an Appendix containing the Papal Allocution and a translation. Cr. 8vo. Cloth, price 5*s*.

The True Story of the Vatican Council. Crown 8vo. Cloth, price 5*s*.

MAREY (E. J.).

Animal Mechanics. A Treatise on Terrestrial and Aerial Locomotion. With 117 Illustrations. Second Edition. Crown 8vo. Cloth, price 5*s*.

Volume XI. of The International Scientific Series.

MARKHAM (Capt. Albert Hastings), R.N.

The Great Frozen Sea. A Personal Narrative of the Voyage of the "Alert" during the Arctic Expedition of 1875-6. With six full-page Illustrations, two Maps, and twenty-seven Woodcuts. Fourth and cheaper edition. Crown 8vo. Cloth, price 6*s*.

MARRIOTT (Maj.-Gen. W. F.), C.S.I.

A Grammar of Political Economy. Crown 8vo. Cloth, price 6*s*.

Master Bobby: a Tale. By the Author of "Christina North." With Illustrations by E. H. Bell. Extra fcap. 8vo. Cloth, price 3*s*. 6*d*.

MASTERMAN (J.).

Half-a-dozen Daughters. With a Frontispiece. Crown 8vo. Cloth, price 3*s*. 6*d*.

MAUDSLEY (Dr. H.).

Responsibility in Mental Disease. Third Edition. Crown 8vo. Cloth, price 5*s*.

Volume VIII. of The International Scientific Series.

MAUGHAN (W. C.).

The Alps of Arabia; or, Travels through Egypt, Sinai, Arabia, and the Holy Land. With Map. Second Edition. Demy 8vo. Cloth, price 5*s*.

MEREDITH (George).

The Egoist. A Comedy in Narrative. 3 vols. Crown 8vo. Cloth.

The Ordeal of Richard Feverel. A History of Father and Son. In one vol. with Frontispiece. Crown 8vo. Cloth, price 6*s*.

MERRITT (Henry).

Art-Criticism and Romance. With Recollections, and Twenty-three Illustrations in *eau-forte*, by Anna Lea Merritt. Two vols. Large post 8vo. Cloth, 25*s*.

MICKLETHWAITE (J. T.), F.S.A.

Modern Parish Churches: Their Plan, Design, and Furniture. Crown 8vo. Cloth, price 7*s*. 6*d*.

MIDDLETON (The Lady).

Ballads. Square 16mo. Cloth, price 3*s*. 6*d*.

MILLER (Edward).

The History and Doctrines of Irvingism; or, the so-called Catholic and Apostolic Church. 2 vols. Large post 8vo. Cloth, price 25*s*.

The Church in Relation to the State. Crown 8vo. Cloth, price 7*s*. 6*d*.

MILLER (Robert).

The Romance of Love. Fcap. 8vo. Cloth, price 5s.

MILNE (James).

Tables of Exchange for the Conversion of Sterling Money into Indian and Ceylon Currency, at Rates from 1*s*. 8*d*. to 2*s*. 3*d*. per Rupee. Second Edition. Demy 8vo. Cloth, price £2 2*s*.

MIVART (St. George), F.R.S.

Contemporary Evolution: An Essay on some recent Social Changes. Post 8vo. Cloth, price 7*s*. 6*d*.

MOCKLER (E.).

A Grammar of the Baloochee Language, as it is spoken in Makran (Ancient Gedrosia), in the Persia-Arabic and Roman characters. Fcap. 8vo. Cloth, price 5*s*.

MOFFAT (Robert Scott).

The Economy of Consumption; an Omitted Chapter in Political Economy, with special reference to the Questions of Commercial Crises and the Policy of Trades Unions; and with Reviews of the Theories of Adam Smith, Ricardo, J. S. Mill, Fawcett, &c. Demy 8vo. Cloth, price 18*s*.

The Principles of a Time Policy: being an Exposition of a Method of Settling Disputes between Employers and Employed in regard to Time and Wages, by a simple Process of Mercantile Barter, without recourse to Strikes or Locks-out.

MOFFAT (Robert Scott)—*continued.*
Reprinted from "The Economy of Consumption," with a Preface and Appendix containing Observations on some Reviews of that book, and a Re-criticism of the Theories of Ricardo and J. S. Mill on Rent, Value, and Cost of Production. Demy 8vo. Cloth, price 3*s.* 6*d.*

MOLTKE (Field-Marshal Von).
Letters from Russia. Translated by Robina Napier. Crown 8vo. Cloth, price 6*s.*

Notes of Travel. Being Extracts from the Journals of. Crown 8vo. Cloth, price 6*s.*

Monmouth: A Drama, of which the Outline is Historical. Dedicated by permission to Mr. Henry Irving. Small crown 8vo. Cloth, price 5*s.*

MORE (R. Jasper).
Under the Balkans. Notes of a Visit to the District of Philippopolis in 1876. With a Map and Illustrations from Photographs. Crown 8vo. Cloth, price 6*s.*

MORELL (J. R.).
Euclid Simplified in Method and Language. Being a Manual of Geometry. Compiled from the most important French Works, approved by the University of Paris and the Minister of Public Instruction. Fcap. 8vo. Cloth, price 2*s.* 6*d.*

MORICE (Rev. F. D.), M.A.
The Olympian and Pythian Odes of Pindar. A New Translation in English Verse. Crown 8vo. Cloth, price 7*s.* 6*d.*

MORSE (E. S.), Ph.D.
First Book of Zoology. With numerous Illustrations. Crown 8vo. Cloth, price 5*s.*

MORSHEAD (E. D. A.)
The Agamemnon of Æschylus. Translated into English verse. With an Introductory Essay. Crown 8vo. Cloth, price 5*s.*

MORTERRA (Felix).
The Legend of Allandale, and other Poems. Small crown 8vo. Cloth, price 6*s.*

MUSGRAVE (Anthony).
Studies in Political Economy. Crown 8vo. Cloth, price 6*s.*

NAAKE (J. T.).
Slavonic Fairy Tales. From Russian, Servian, Polish, and Bohemian Sources. With Four Illustrations. Crown 8vo. Cloth, price 5*s.*

NEWMAN (J. H.), D.D.
Characteristics from the Writings of. Being Selections from his various Works. Arranged with the Author's personal approval. Third Edition. With Portrait. Crown 8vo. Cloth, price 6*s.*

*** A Portrait of the Rev. Dr. J. H. Newman, mounted for framing, can be had, price 2*s.* 6*d.*

NICHOLAS (Thomas), Ph.D., F.G.S.
The Pedigree of the English People: an Argument, Historical and Scientific, on the Formation and Growth of the Nation, tracing Race-admixture in Britain from the earliest times, with especial reference to the incorporation of the Celtic Aborigines. Fifth Edition. Demy 8vo. Cloth, price 16*s.*

NICHOLSON (Edward Byron).
The Christ Child, and other Poems. Crown 8vo. Cloth, price 4*s.* 6*d.*

The Rights of an Animal. Crown 8vo. Cloth, price 3*s.* 6*d.*

The Gospel according to the Hebrews. Its Fragments translated and annotated, with a critical Analysis of the External and Internal Evidence relating to it. Demy 8vo. Cloth, price 9*s.* 6*d.*

NICOLS (Arthur), F.G.S., F.R.G.S.
Chapters from the Physical History of the Earth. An Introduction to Geology and Palæontology, with numerous illustrations. Crown 8vo. Cloth, price 5*s.*

NOAKE (Major R. Compton).
The Bivouac; or, Martial Lyrist, with an Appendix—Advice to the Soldier. Fcap. 8vo. Price 5*s.* 6*d.*

NORMAN PEOPLE (The).
The Norman People, and their Existing Descendants in the British Dominions and the United States of America. Demy 8vo. Cloth, price 21*s.*

NORRIS (Rev. Alfred).
The Inner and Outer Life Poems. Fcap. 8vo. Cloth, price 6*s.*

Notes on Cavalry Tactics, Organization, &c. By a Cavalry Officer. With Diagrams. Demy 8vo. Cloth, price 12*s*.

Nuces: Exercises on the Syntax of the Public School Latin Primer. New Edition in Three Parts. Crown 8vo. Each 1*s*.

*** The Three Parts can also be had bound together in cloth, price 3*s*.

O'BRIEN (Charlotte G.).

Light and Shade. 2 vols. Crown 8vo. Cloth, gilt tops, price 12*s*.

O'MEARA (Kathleen).

Frederic Ozanam, Professor of the Sorbonne; His Life and Works. Second Edition. Crown 8vo. Cloth, price 7*s*. 6*d*.

Oriental Sporting Magazine (The).

A Reprint of the first 5 Volumes, in 2 Volumes. Demy 8vo. Cloth, price 28*s*.

OWEN (F. M.).

John Keats. A Study. Crown 8vo. Cloth, price 6*s*.

OWEN (Rev. Robert), B.D.

Sanctorale Catholicum; or Book of Saints. With Notes, Critical, Exegetical, and Historical. Demy 8vo. Cloth, price 18*s*.

PALGRAVE (W. Gifford).

Hermann Agha; An Eastern Narrative. Third and Cheaper Edition. Crown 8vo. Cloth, price 6*s*.

PALMER (Charles Walter).

The Weed: a Poem. Small crown 8vo. Cloth, price 3*s*.

PANDURANG HARI;

Or, Memoirs of a Hindoo. With an Introductory Preface by Sir H. Bartle E. Frere, G.C.S.I., C.B. Crown 8vo. Price 6*s*.

PARKER (Joseph), D.D.

The Paraclete: An Essay on the Personality and Ministry of the Holy Ghost, with some reference to current discussions. Second Edition. Demy 8vo. Cloth, price 12*s*.

PARSLOE (Joseph).

Our Railways: Sketches, Historical and Descriptive. With Practical Information as to Fares, Rates, &c., and a Chapter on Railway Reform. Crown 8vo. Cloth, price 6*s*.

PATTISON (Mrs. Mark).

The Renaissance of Art in France. With Nineteen Steel Engravings. 2 vols. Demy 8vo. Cloth, price 32*s*.

PAUL (C. Kegan).

Mary Wollstonecraft. Letters to Imlay. With Prefatory Memoir by, and Two Portraits in *eau forte*, by Anna Lea Merritt. Crown 8vo. Cloth, price 6*s*.

Goethe's Faust. A New Translation in Rime. Crown 8vo. Cloth, price 6*s*.

William Godwin: His Friends and Contemporaries. With Portraits and Facsimiles of the Handwriting of Godwin and his Wife. 2 vols. Square post 8vo. Cloth, price 28*s*.

The Genius of Christianity Unveiled. Being Essays by William Godwin never before published. Edited, with a Preface, by C. Kegan Paul. Crown 8vo. Cloth, price 7*s*. 6*d*.

PAUL (Margaret Agnes).

Gentle and Simple: A Story. 2 vols. Crown 8vo. Cloth, gilt tops, price 12*s*.

*** Also a Cheaper Edition in one vol. with Frontispiece. Crown 8vo. Cloth, price 6*s*.

PAYNE (John).

Songs of Life and Death. Crown 8vo. Cloth, price 5*s*.

PAYNE (Prof. J. F.).

Lectures on Education. Price 6*d*.

II. Fröbel and the Kindergarten system. Second Edition.

A Visit to German Schools: Elementary Schools in Germany. Notes of a Professional Tour to inspect some of the Kindergartens, Primary Schools, Public Girls' Schools, and Schools for Technical Instruction in Hamburgh, Berlin, Dresden, Weimar, Gotha, Eisenach, in the autumn of 1874. With Critical Discussions of the General Principles and Practice of Kindergartens and other Schemes of Elementary Education. Crown 8vo. Cloth, price 4*s*. 6*d*.

PEACOCKE (Georgiana).

Rays from the Southern Cross: Poems. Crown 8vo. With Sixteen Full-page Illustrations by the Rev. P. Walsh. Cloth elegant, price 10*s*. 6*d*.

PELLETAN (E.).

The Desert Pastor, Jean Jarousseau. Translated from the French. By Colonel E. P. De L'Hoste. With a Frontispiece. New Edition. Fcap. 8vo. Cloth, price 3*s*. 6*d*.

PENNELL (H. Cholmondeley).

Pegasus Resaddled. By the Author of "Puck on Pegasus," &c. &c. With Ten Full-page Illustrations by George Du Maurier. Second Edition. Fcap. 4to. Cloth elegant, price 12*s*. 6*d*.

PENRICE (Maj. J.), B.A.

A Dictionary and Glossary of the Ko-ran. With copious Grammatical References and Explanations of the Text. 4to. Cloth, price 21*s*.

PERCIVAL (Rev. P.).

Tamil Proverbs, with their English Translation. Containing upwards of Six Thousand Proverbs. Third Edition. Demy 8vo. Sewed, price 9*s*.

PESCHEL (Dr. Oscar).

The Races of Man and their Geographical Distribution. Large crown 8vo. Cloth, price 9*s*.

PETTIGREW (J. Bell), M.D., F.R.S.

Animal Locomotion; or, Walking, Swimming, and Flying. With 130 Illustrations. Second Edition. Crown 8vo. Cloth, price 5*s*.

Volume VII. of The International Scientific Series.

PFEIFFER (Emily).

Quarterman's Grace, and other Poems. Crown 8vo. Cloth, price 5*s*.

Glan Alarch: His Silence and Song. A Poem. Second Edition. Crown 8vo. price 6*s*.

Gerard's Monument, and other Poems. Second Edition. Crown 8vo. Cloth, price 6*s*.

Poems. Second Edition. Crown 8vo. Cloth, price 6*s*.

Sonnets and Songs. New Edition. 16mo, handsomely printed and bound in cloth, gilt edges, price 4*s*.

PINCHES (Thomas), M.A.

Samuel Wilberforce: Faith—Service—Recompense. Three Sermons. With a Portrait of Bishop Wilberforce (after a Photograph by Charles Watkins). Crown 8vo. Cloth, price 4*s*. 6*d*.

PLAYFAIR (Lieut.-Col.), Her Britannic Majesty's Consul-General in Algiers.

Travels in the Footsteps of Bruce in Algeria and Tunis. Illustrated by facsimiles of Bruce's original Drawings, Photographs, Maps, &c. Royal 4to. Cloth, bevelled boards, gilt leaves, price £3 3*s*.

POLLOCK (W. H.).

Lectures on French Poets. Delivered at the Royal Institution. Small crown 8vo. Cloth, price 5*s*.

POUSHKIN (A. S.).

Russian Romance. Translated from the Tales of Belkin, &c. By Mrs. J. Buchan Telfer (*née* Mouravieff). Crown 8vo. Cloth, price 3*s*. 6*d*.

POWER (H.).

Our Invalids: How shall we Employ and Amuse Them? Fcap. 8vo. Cloth, price 2*s*. 6*d*.

POWLETT (Lieut. N.), R.A.

Eastern Legends and Stories in English Verse. Crown 8vo. Cloth, price 5*s*.

PRESBYTER.

Unfoldings of Christian Hope. An Essay showing that the Doctrine contained in the Damnatory Clauses of the Creed commonly called Athanasian is unscriptural. Small crown 8vo. Cloth, price 4*s*. 6*d*.

PRICE (Prof. Bonamy).

Currency and Banking. Crown 8vo. Cloth, price 6*s*.

Chapters on Practical Political Economy. Being the Substance of Lectures delivered before the University of Oxford. Large post 8vo. Cloth, price 12*s*.

Proteus and Amadeus. A Correspondence. Edited by Aubrey De Vere. Crown 8vo. Cloth, price 5*s*.

PUBLIC SCHOOLBOY.

The Volunteer, the Militiaman, and the Regular Soldier. Crown 8vo. Cloth, price 5s.

Punjaub (The) and North Western Frontier of India. By an old Punjaubee. Crown 8vo. Cloth, price 5s.

QUATREFAGES (Prof. A. de).

The Human Species. Second Edition. Crown 8vo. Cloth, price 5s.

Vol. XXVI. of The International Scientific Series.

RAVENSHAW (John Henry), B.C.S.

Gaur: Its Ruins and Inscriptions. Edited with considerable additions and alterations by his Widow. With forty-four photographic illustrations and twenty-five fac-similes of Inscriptions. Super royal 4to. Cloth, 3*l.* 13*s.* 6*d.*

READ (Carveth).

On the Theory of Logic: An Essay. Crown 8vo. Cloth, price 6s.

REANEY (Mrs. G. S.).

Blessing and Blessed; a Sketch of Girl Life. With a frontispiece. Crown 8vo. Cloth, price 5s.

Waking and Working; or, from Girlhood to Womanhood. With a Frontispiece. Crown 8vo. Cloth, price 5s.

English Girls: their Place and Power. With a Preface by R. W. Dale, M.A., of Birmingham. Second Edition. Fcap. 8vo. Cloth, price 2*s.* 6*d.*

Just Anyone, and other Stories. Three Illustrations. Royal 16mo. Cloth, price 1*s.* 6*d.*

Sunshine Jenny and other Stories. Three Illustrations. Royal 16mo. Cloth, price 1*s.* 6*d.*

Sunbeam Willie, and other Stories. Three Illustrations. Royal 16mo. Cloth, price 1*s.* 6*d.*

REYNOLDS (Rev. J. W.).

The Supernatural in Nature. A Verification by Free Use of Science. Second Edition, revised and enlarged. Demy 8vo. Cloth, price 14*s.*

Mystery of Miracles, The. By the Author of "The Supernatural in Nature." Crown 8vo. Cloth, price 6*s.*

RHOADES (James).

Timoleon. A Dramatic Poem. Fcap. 8vo. Cloth, price 5*s.*

RIBOT (Prof. Th.).

English Psychology. Second Edition. A Revised and Corrected Translation from the latest French Edition. Large post 8vo. Cloth, price 9*s.*

Heredity: A Psychological Study on its Phenomena, its Laws, its Causes, and its Consequences. Large crown 8vo. Cloth, price 9*s.*

RINK (Chevalier Dr. Henry).

Greenland: Its People and its Products. By the Chevalier Dr. HENRY RINK, President of the Greenland Board of Trade. With sixteen Illustrations, drawn by the Eskimo, and a Map. Edited by Dr. ROBERT BROWN. Crown 8vo. Price 10*s.* 6*d.*

ROBERTSON (The Late Rev. F. W.), M.A., of Brighton.

Notes on Genesis. New and cheaper Edition. Crown 8vo., price 3*s.* 6*d.*

Sermons. Four Series. Small crown 8vo. Cloth, price 3*s.* 6*d.* each.

Expository Lectures on St. Paul's Epistles to the Corinthians. A New Edition. Small crown 8vo. Cloth, price 5*s.*

Lectures and Addresses, with other literary remains. A New Edition. Crown 8vo. Cloth, price 5*s.*

An Analysis of Mr. Tennyson's "In Memoriam." (Dedicated by Permission to the Poet-Laureate.) Fcap. 8vo. Cloth, price 2*s.*

The Education of the Human Race. Translated from the German of Gotthold Ephraim Lessing. Fcap. 8vo. Cloth, price 2*s.* 6*d.*

Life and Letters. Edited by the Rev. Stopford Brooke, M.A., Chaplain in Ordinary to the Queen.

I. 2 vols., uniform with the Sermons. With Steel Portrait. Crown 8vo. Cloth, price 7*s.* 6*d.*

II. Library Edition, in Demy 8vo., with Two Steel Portraits. Cloth, price 12*s.*

ROBERTSON (The Late Rev. F. W.), M.A., of Brighton—*continued.*

III. A Popular Edition, in one vol. Crown 8vo. Cloth, price 6s.

The above Works can also be had half-bound in morocco.

*** A Portrait of the late Rev. F. W. Robertson, mounted for framing, can be had, price 2s. 6d.

ROBINSON (A. Mary F.).

A Handful of Honey-suckle. Fcap. 8vo. Cloth, price 3s. 6d.

RODWELL (G. F.), F.R.A.S., F.C.S.

Etna: a History of the Mountain and its Eruptions. With Maps and Illustrations. Square 8vo. Cloth, price 9s.

ROOD (Ogden N.).

Modern Chromatics, with Applications to Art and Industry. With 130 Original Illustrations. Crown 8vo. Cloth, price 5s.

Vol. XXVII. of The International Scientific Series.

ROSS (Mrs. E.), ("Nelsie Brook").

Daddy's Pet. A Sketch from Humble Life. With Six Illustrations. Royal 16mo. Cloth, price 1s.

ROSS (Alexander), D.D.

Memoir of Alexander Ewing, Bishop of Argyll and the Isles. Second and Cheaper Edition. Demy 8vo. Cloth, price 10s. 6d.

RUSSELL (Major Frank S.).

Russian Wars with Turkey, Past and Present. With Two Maps. Second Edition. Crown 8vo., price 6s.

SADLER (S. W.), R.N.

The African Cruiser. A Midshipman's Adventures on the West Coast. With Three Illustrations. Second Edition. Crown 8vo. Cloth, price 3s. 6d.

SALTS (Rev. Alfred), LL.D.

Godparents at Confirmation. With a Preface by the Bishop of Manchester. Small crown 8vo. Cloth, limp, price 2s.

SAMAROW (G.).

For Sceptre and Crown. A Romance of the Present Time. Translated by Fanny Wormald. 2 vols. Crown 8vo. Cloth, price 15s.

SAUNDERS (Katherine).

Gideon's Rock, and other Stories. Crown 8vo. Cloth, price 6s.

Joan Merryweather, and other Stories. Crown 8vo. Cloth, price 6s.

Margaret and Elizabeth. A Story of the Sea. Crown 8vo. Cloth, price 6s.

SAUNDERS (John).

Israel Mort, Overman: A Story of the Mine. Cr. 8vo. Price 6s.

Hirell. With Frontispiece. Crown 8vo. Cloth, price 3s. 6d.

Abel Drake's Wife. With Frontispiece. Crown 8vo. Cloth, price 3s. 6d.

SAYCE (Rev. Archibald Henry).

Introduction to the Science of Language. Two vols., large post 8vo. Cloth, price 25s.

SCHELL (Maj. von).

The Operations of the First Army under Gen. von Goeben. Translated by Col. C. H. von Wright. Four Maps. Demy 8vo. Cloth, price 9s.

The Operations of the First Army under Gen. von Steinmetz. Translated by Captain E. O. Hollist. Demy 8vo. Cloth, price 10s. 6d.

SCHELLENDORF (Maj.-Gen. B. von).

The Duties of the General Staff. Translated from the German by Lieutenant Hare. Vol. I. Demy 8vo. Cloth, 10s. 6d.

SCHERFF (Maj. W. von).

Studies in the New Infantry Tactics. Parts I. and II. Translated from the German by Colonel Lumley Graham. Demy 8vo. Cloth, price 7s. 6d.

SCHMIDT (Prof. Oscar).

The Doctrine of Descent and Darwinism. With 26 Illustrations. Third Edition. Crown 8vo. Cloth, price 5s.

Volume XII. of The International Scientific Series.

SCHÜTZENBERGER (Prof. F.).

Fermentation. With Numerous Illustrations. Second Edition. Crown 8vo. Cloth, price 5s.

Volume XX. of The International Scientific Series.

SCOTT (Leader).

A Nook in the Apennines: A Summer beneath the Chestnuts. With Frontispiece, and 27 Illustrations in the Text, chiefly from Original Sketches. Crown 8vo. Cloth, price 7*s*. 6*d*.

SCOTT (Patrick).

The Dream and the Deed, and other Poems. Fcap. 8vo. Cloth, price 5*s*.

SCOTT (W. T.).

Antiquities of an Essex Parish; or, Pages from the History of Great Dunmow. Crown 8vo. Cloth, price 5*s*. Sewed, 4*s*.

SCOTT (Robert H.).

Weather Charts and Storm Warnings. Illustrated. Second Edition. Crown 8vo. Cloth, price 3*s*. 6*d*.

Seeking his Fortune, and other Stories. With Four Illustrations. Crown 8vo. Cloth, price 3*s*. 6*d*.

SENIOR (N. W.).

Alexis De Tocqueville. Correspondence and Conversations with Nassau W. Senior, from 1833 to 1859. Edited by M. C. M. Simpson. 2 vols. Large post 8vo. Cloth, price 21*s*.

Journals Kept in France and Italy. From 1848 to 1852. With a Sketch of the Revolution of 1848. Edited by his Daughter, M. C. M. Simpson. 2 vols. Post 8vo. Cloth, price 24*s*.

Sermons to Naval Cadets. Preached on board H.M.S. "Britannia." Small crown 8vo. Cloth, price 3*s*. 6*d*.

Seven Autumn Leaves from Fairyland. Illustrated with Nine Etchings. Square crown 8vo. Cloth, price 3*s*. 6*d*.

SHADWELL (Maj.-Gen.), C.B.

Mountain Warfare. Illustrated by the Campaign of 1799 in Switzerland. Being a Translation of the Swiss Narrative compiled from the Works of the Archduke Charles, Jomini, and others. Also of Notes by General H. Dufour on the Campaign of the Valtelline in 1635. With Appendix, Maps, and Introductory Remarks. Demy 8vo. Cloth, price 16*s*.

SHAKSPEARE (Charles).

Saint Paul at Athens: Spiritual Christianity in Relation to some Aspects of Modern Thought. Nine Sermons preached at St. Stephen's Church, Westbourne Park. With Preface by the Rev. Canon FARRAR. Crown 8vo. Cloth, price 5*s*.

SHAW (Major Wilkinson).

The Elements of Modern Tactics. Practically applied to English Formations. With Twenty-five Plates and Maps. Small crown 8vo. Cloth, price 12*s*.

*** The Second Volume of "Military Handbooks for Officers and Non-commissioned Officers." Edited by Lieut.-Col. C. B. Brackenbury, R.A., A.A.G.

SHAW (Flora L.).

Castle Blair: a Story of Youthful Lives. 2 vols. Crown 8vo. Cloth, gilt tops, price 12*s*. Also, an edition in one vol. Crown 8vo. 6*s*.

SHELLEY (Lady).

Shelley Memorials from Authentic Sources. With (now first printed) an Essay on Christianity by Percy Bysshe Shelley. With Portrait. Third Edition. Crown 8vo. Cloth, price 5*s*.

SHELLEY (Percy Bysshe).

Poems selected from. Dedicated to Lady Shelley. With Preface by Richard Garnett. Printed on hand-made paper. With miniature frontispiece. Elzevir. 8vo., limp parchment antique. Price 6*s*., vellum 7*s*. 6*d*.

SHERMAN (Gen. W. T.).

Memoirs of General W. T. Sherman, Commander of the Federal Forces in the American Civil War. By Himself. 2 vols. With Map. Demy 8vo Cloth, price 24*s*. *Copyright English Edition.*

SHILLITO (Rev. Joseph).

Womanhood: its Duties, Temptations, and Privileges. A Book for Young Women. Second Edition. Crown 8vo. Price 3*s*. 6*d*.

SHIPLEY (Rev. Orby), M.A.

Principles of the Faith in Relation to Sin. Topics for Thought in Times of Retreat. Eleven Addresses. With an Introduction on the neglect of Dogmatic Theology in the Church of England, and a Postscript on his leaving the Church of England. Demy 8vo. Cloth, price 12*s*.

SHIPLEY (Rev. Orby, M.A.) —*continued.*

Church Tracts, or Studies in Modern Problems. By various Writers. 2 vols. Crown 8vo. Cloth, price 5*s.* each.

SHUTE (Richard), M.A.

A Discourse on Truth. Large Post 8vo. Cloth, price 9*s.*

SMEDLEY (M. B.).

Boarding-out and Pauper Schools for Girls. Crown 8vo. Cloth, price 3*s.* 6*d.*

SMITH (Edward), M.D., LL.B., F.R.S.

Health and Disease, as Influenced by the Daily, Seasonal, and other Cyclical Changes in the Human System. A New Edition. Post 8vo. Cloth, price 7*s.* 6*d.*

Foods. Profusely Illustrated. Fifth Edition. Crown 8vo. Cloth, price 5*s.*

Volume III. of The International Scientific Series.

Practical Dietary for Families, Schools, and the Labouring Classes. A New Edition. Post 8vo. Cloth, price 3*s.* 6*d.*

Tubercular Consumption in its Early and Remediable Stages. Second Edition. Crown 8vo. Cloth, price 6*s.*

SMITH (Hubert).

Tent Life with English Gipsies in Norway. With Five full-page Engravings and Thirty-one smaller Illustrations by Whymper and others, and Map of the Country showing Routes. Third Edition. Revised and Corrected. Post 8vo. Cloth, price 21*s.*

Songs of Two Worlds. By the Author of "The Epic of Hades." Fifth Edition. Complete in one Volume, with Portrait. Fcap. 8vo. Cloth, price 7*s.* 6*d.*

Songs for Music.

By Four Friends. Square crown 8vo. Cloth, price 5*s.*
Containing songs by Reginald A. Gatty, Stephen H. Gatty, Greville J. Chester, and Juliana Ewing.

SPEDDING (James).

Reviews and Discussions, Literary, Political, and Historical, not relating to Bacon. Demy 8vo. Cloth, price 12*s.* 6*d.*

SPENCER (Herbert).

The Study of Sociology. Seventh Edition. Crown 8vo. Cloth, price 5*s.*

Volume V. of The International Scientific Series.

SPICER (H.).

Otho's Death Wager. A Dark Page of History Illustrated. In Five Acts. Fcap. 8vo. Cloth, price 5*s.*

STAPLETON (John).

The Thames: A Poem. Crown 8vo. Cloth, price 6*s.*

STEDMAN (Edmund Clarence).

Lyrics and Idylls. With other Poems. Crown 8vo. Cloth, price 7*s.* 6*d.*

STEPHENS (Archibald John), LL.D.

The Folkestone Ritual Case. The Substance of the Argument delivered before the Judicial Committee of the Privy Council. On behalf of the Respondents. Demy 8vo. Cloth, price 6*s.*

STEVENS (William).

The Truce of God, and other Poems. Small crown 8vo. Cloth, price 3*s.* 6*d.*

STEVENSON (Robert Louis).

An Inland Voyage. With Frontispiece by Walter Crane. Crown 8vo. Cloth, price 7*s.* 6*d.*

Travels with a Donkey in the Cevennes. With Frontispiece by Walter Crane. Crown 8vo. Cloth, price 7*s.* 6*d.*

STEVENSON (Rev. W. F.).

Hymns for the Church and Home. Selected and Edited by the Rev. W. Fleming Stevenson.

The most complete Hymn Book published.

The Hymn Book consists of Three Parts: I. For Public Worship.—II. For Family and Private Worship.—III. For Children.

*** *Published in various forms and prices, the latter ranging from 8d. to 6s. Lists and full particulars will be furnished on application to the Publishers.*

STEWART (Prof. Balfour), M.A., LL.D., F.R.S.

On the Conservation of Energy. Fifth Edition. With Fourteen Engravings. Crown 8vo. Cloth, price 5*s*.

Volume VI. of The International Scientific Series.

STORR (Francis), and TURNER Hawes).

Canterbury Chimes; or, Chaucer Tales retold to Children. With Illustrations from the Ellesmere MS. Extra Fcap. 8vo. Cloth, price 3*s*. 6*d*.

STRETTON (Hesba).

David Lloyd's Last Will. With Four Illustrations. Royal 16mo., price 2*s*. 6*d*.

The Wonderful Life. Thirteenth Thousand. Fcap. 8vo. Cloth, price 2*s*. 6*d*.

Through a Needle's Eye: a Story. 2 vols. Crown 8vo. Cloth, gilt top, price 12*s*.

STUBBS (Lieut.-Colonel F. W.)

The Regiment of Bengal Artillery. The History of its Organization, Equipment, and War Services. Compiled from Published Works, Official Records, and various Private Sources. With numerous Maps and Illustrations. 2 vols. Demy 8vo. Cloth, price 32*s*.

STUMM (Lieut. Hugo), German Military Attaché to the Khivan Expedition.

Russia's advance Eastward. Based on the Official Reports of. Translated by Capt. C. E. H. Vincent. With Map. Crown 8vo. Cloth, price 6*s*.

SULLY (James), M.A.

Sensation and Intuition. Demy 8vo. Cloth, price 10*s*. 6*d*.

Pessimism: a History and a Criticism. Demy 8vo. Price 14*s*.

Sunnyland Stories.

By the Author of "Aunt Mary's Bran Pie." Illustrated. Small 8vo. Cloth, price 3*s*. 6*d*.

Sweet Silvery Sayings of Shakespeare. Crown 8vo. Cloth gilt, price 7*s*. 6*d*.

SYME (David).

Outlines of an Industrial Science. Second Edition. Crown 8vo. Cloth, price 6*s*.

Tales from Ariosto. Retold for Children, by a Lady. With three illustrations. Crown 8vo. Cloth, price 4*s*. 6*d*.

TAYLOR (Algernon).

Guienne. Notes of an Autumn Tour. Crown 8vo. Cloth, price 4*s*. 6*d*.

TAYLOR (Sir H.).

Works Complete. Author's Edition, in 5 vols. Crown 8vo. Cloth, price 6*s*. each.

Vols. I. to III. containing the Poetical Works, Vols. IV. and V. the Prose Works.

TAYLOR (Col. Meadows), C.S.I., M.R.I.A.

A Noble Queen: a Romance of Indian History. Crown 8vo. Cloth. Price 6*s*.

Seeta. 3 vols. Crown 8vo. Cloth.

Tippoo Sultaun: a Tale of the Mysore War. New Edition with Frontispiece. Crown 8vo. Cloth, price 6*s*.

Ralph Darnell. New and Cheaper Edition. With Frontispiece. Crown 8vo. Cloth, price 6*s*.

The Confessions of a Thug. New Edition. Crown 8vo. Cloth, price 6*s*.

Tara: a Mahratta Tale. New Edition. Crown 8vo. Cloth, price 6*s*.

TELFER (J. Buchan), F.R.G.S., Commander, R.N.

The Crimea and Trans-Caucasia. With numerous Illustrations and Maps. 2 vols. Medium 8vo. Second Edition. Cloth, price 36*s*.

TENNYSON (Alfred).

The Imperial Library Edition. Complete in 7 vols. Demy 8vo. Cloth, price £3 13*s*. 6*d*.; in Roxburgh binding, £4 7*s*. 6*d*.

Author's Edition. Complete in 6 Volumes. Post 8vo. Cloth gilt; or half-morocco, Roxburgh style:—

Vol. I. Early Poems, and English Idylls. Price 6*s*.; Roxburgh, 7*s*. 6*d*.

TENNYSON (Alfred)—*continued.*

VOL. II. Locksley Hall, Lucretius, and other Poems. Price 6*s.*; Roxburgh, 7*s.* 6*d.*

VOL. III. The Idylls of the King (*Complete*). Price 7*s.* 6*d.*; Roxburgh, 9*s.*

VOL. IV. The Princess, and Maud. Price 6*s.*; Roxburgh, 7*s.* 6*d.*

VOL. V. Enoch Arden, and In Memoriam. Price 6*s.*; Roxburgh, 7*s.* 6*d.*

VOL. VI. Dramas. Price 7*s.*; Roxburgh, 8*s.* 6*d.*

Cabinet Edition. 12 vols. Each with Frontispiece. Fcap. 8vo. Cloth, price 2*s.* 6*d.* each.

CABINET EDITION. 12 vols. Complete in handsome Ornamental Case. 32*s.*

Pocket Volume Edition. 13 vols. In neat case, 36*s.* Ditto, ditto. Extra cloth gilt, in case, 42*s.*

The Royal Edition. Complete in one vol. Cloth, 16*s.* Cloth extra, 18*s.* Roxburgh, half morocco, price 20*s.*

The Guinea Edition. Complete in 12 vols., neatly bound and enclosed in box. Cloth, price 21*s.* French morocco, price 31*s.* 6*d.*

The Shilling Edition of the Poetical and Dramatic Works, in 12 vols., pocket size. Price 1*s.* each.

The Crown Edition. Complete in one vol., strongly bound in cloth, price 6*s.* Cloth, extra gilt leaves, price 7*s.* 6*d.* Roxburgh, half morocco, price 8*s.* 6*d.*

*** Can also be had in a variety of other bindings.

Original Editions:

The Lover's Tale. (Now for the first time published.) Fcap. 8vo. Cloth, 3*s.* 6*d.*

Poems. Small 8vo. Cloth, price 6*s.*

Maud, and other Poems. Small 8vo. Cloth, price 3*s.* 6*d.*

The Princess. Small 8vo. Cloth, price 3*s.* 6*d.*

Idylls of the King. Small 8vo. Cloth, price 5*s.*

Idylls of the King. Complete. Small 8vo. Cloth, price 6*s.*

TENNYSON (Alfred)—*continued.*

The Holy Grail, and other Poems. Small 8vo. Cloth, price 4*s.* 6*d.*

Gareth and Lynette. Small 8vo. Cloth, price 3*s.*

Enoch Arden, &c. Small 8vo. Cloth, price 3*s.* 6*d.*

In Memoriam. Small 8vo. Cloth, price 4*s.*

Queen Mary. A Drama. New Edition. Crown 8vo. Cloth, price 6*s.*

Harold. A Drama. Crown 8vo. Cloth, price 6*s.*

Selections from Tennyson's Works. Super royal 16mo. Cloth, price 3*s.* 6*d.* Cloth gilt extra, price 4*s.*

Songs from Tennyson's Works. Super royal 16mo. Cloth extra, price 3*s.* 6*d.*

Also a cheap edition. 16mo. Cloth, price 2*s.* 6*d.*

Idylls of the King, and other Poems. Illustrated by Julia Margaret Cameron. 2 vols. Folio. Half-bound morocco, cloth sides, price £6 6*s.* each.

Tennyson for the Young and for Recitation. Specially arranged. Fcap. 8vo. Price 1*s.* 6*d.*

Tennyson Birthday Book. Edited by Emily Shakespear. 32mo. Cloth limp, 2*s.*; cloth extra, 3*s.*

*** A superior edition, printed in red and black, on antique paper, specially prepared. Small crown 8vo. Cloth, extra gilt leaves, price 5*s.*; and in various calf and morocco bindings.

In Memoriam. A new Edition, choicely printed on handmade paper, with a Miniature Portrait in *eau forte* by Le Rat, after a photograph by the late Mrs. Cameron. Bound in limp parchment, antique, price 6*s.*, vellum 7*s.* 6*d.*

Songs Set to Music, by various Composers. Edited by W. G. Cusins. Dedicated by express permission to Her Majesty the Queen. Royal 4to. Cloth extra, gilt leaves, price 21*s.*, or in half-morocco, price 25*s.*

THOMAS (Moy).
A Fight for Life. With Frontispiece. Crown 8vo. Cloth, price 3*s*. 6*d*.

THOMPSON (Alice C.).
Preludes. A Volume of Poems. Illustrated by Elizabeth Thompson (Painter of "The Roll Call"). 8vo. Cloth, price 7*s*. 6*d*.

THOMSON (J. Turnbull).
Social Problems; or, an Inquiry into the Law of Influences. With Diagrams. Demy 8vo. Cloth, price 10*s*. 6*d*.

Thoughts in Verse.
Small Crown 8vo. Cloth, price 1*s*. 6*d*.

THRING (Rev. Godfrey), B.A.
Hymns and Sacred Lyrics. Fcap. 8vo. Cloth, price 5*s*.

THURSTON (Prof. R. H.).
A History of the Growth of the Steam Engine. With numerous Illustrations. Second Edition. Crown 8vo. Cloth, price 6*s*. 6*d*.

TODHUNTER (Dr. J.)
Alcestis: A Dramatic Poem. Extra fcap. 8vo. Cloth, price 5*s*.
Laurella; and other Poems. Crown 8vo. Cloth, price 6*s*. 6*d*.

TOLINGSBY (Frere).
Elnora. An Indian Mythological Poem. Fcap. 8vo. Cloth, price 6*s*.

TRAHERNE (Mrs. A.).
The Romantic Annals of a Naval Family. A New and Cheaper Edition. Crown 8vo. Cloth, price 5*s*.

Translations from Dante, Petrarch, Michael Angelo, and Vittoria Colonna. Fcap. 8vo. Cloth, price 7*s*. 6*d*.

TURNER (Rev. C. Tennyson).
Sonnets, Lyrics, and Translations. Crown 8vo. Cloth, price 4*s*. 6*d*.

TYNDALL (John), LL.D., F.R.S
Forms of Water. A Familiar Exposition of the Origin and Phenomena of Glaciers. With Twenty-five Illustrations. Seventh Edition. Crown 8vo. Cloth, price 5*s*.
Volume I. of The International Scientific Series.

VAN BENEDEN (Mons.).
Animal Parasites and Messmates. With 83 Illustrations. Second Edition. Cloth, price 5*s*.
Volume XIX. of The International Scientific Series.

VAUGHAN (H. Halford), sometime Regius Professor of Modern History in Oxford University.
New Readings and Renderings of Shakespeare's Tragedies. Vol. I. Demy 8vo. Cloth, price 15*s*.

VILLARI (Prof.).
Niccolo Machiavelli and His Times. Translated by Linda Villari. 2 vols. Large post 8vo. Cloth, price 24*s*.

VINCENT (Capt. C. E. H.).
Elementary Military Geography, Reconnoitring, and Sketching. Compiled for Non-Commissioned Officers and Soldiers of all Arms. Square crown 8vo. Cloth, price 2*s*. 6*d*.

VOGEL (Dr. Hermann).
The Chemical Effects of Light and Photography, in their application to Art, Science, and Industry. The translation thoroughly revised. With 100 Illustrations, including some beautiful specimens of Photography. Third Edition. Crown 8vo. Cloth, price 5*s*.
Volume XV. of The International Scientific Series.

VYNER (Lady Mary).
Every day a Portion. Adapted from the Bible and the Prayer Book, for the Private Devotions of those living in Widowhood. Collected and edited by Lady Mary Vyner. Square crown 8vo. Cloth extra, price 5*s*.

WALDSTEIN (Charles), Ph. D.
The Balance of Emotion and Intellect: An Essay Introductory to the Study of Philosophy. Crown 8vo. Cloth, price 6*s*.

WALLER (Rev. C. B.)
The Apocalypse, Reviewed under the Light of the Doctrine of the Unfolding Ages and the Restitution of all Things. Demy 8vo. Cloth, price 12*s*.

WALTERS (Sophia Lydia).

The Brook: A Poem. Small crown 8vo. Cloth, price 3*s*. 6*d*.

A Dreamer's Sketch Book. With Twenty-one Illustrations by Percival Skelton, R. P. Leitch, W. H. J. Boot, and T. R. Pritchett. Engraved by J. D. Cooper. Fcap. 4to. Cloth, price 12*s*. 6*d*.

WARTENSLEBEN (Count H. von).

The Operations of the South Army in January and February, 1871. Compiled from the Official War Documents of the Head-quarters of the Southern Army. Translated by Colonel C. H. von Wright. With Maps. Demy 8vo. Cloth, price 6*s*.

The Operations of the First Army under Gen. von Manteuffel. Translated by Colonel C. H. von Wright. Uniform with the above. Demy 8vo. Cloth, price 9*s*.

WATERFIELD, W.

Hymns for Holy Days and Seasons. 32mo. Cloth, price 1*s*. 6*d*.

WATSON (Sir Thomas), Bart., M.D.

The Abolition of Zymotic Diseases, and of other similar enemies of Mankind. Small crown 8vo. Cloth, price 3*s*. 6*d*.

WAY (A.), M.A.

The Odes of Horace Literally Translated in Metre. Fcap. 8vo. Cloth, price 2*s*.

WEBSTER (Augusta).

Disguises. A Drama. Small crown 8vo. Cloth, price 5*s*.

WEDMORE (Frederick).

The Masters of Genre Painting. With sixteen illustrations. Crown 8vo. Cloth, price 7*s*. 6*d*

WELLS (Capt. John C.), R.N.

Spitzbergen—The Gateway to the Polynia; or, A Voyage to Spitzbergen. With numerous Illustrations by Whymper and others, and Map. New and Cheaper Edition. Demy 8vo. Cloth, price 6*s*.

Wet Days, by a Farmer. Small crown 8vo. Cloth, price 6*s*.

WETMORE (W. S.).

Commercial Telegraphic Code. Second Edition. Post 4to. Boards, price 42*s*.

WHITAKER (Florence).

Christy's Inheritance. A London Story. Illustrated. Royal 16mo. Cloth, price 1*s*. 6*d*.

WHITE (A. D.), LL.D.

Warfare of Science. With Prefatory Note by Professor Tyndall. Second Edition. Crown 8vo. Cloth, price 3*s*. 6*d*.

WHITNEY (Prof. W. D.)

The Life and Growth of Language. Second Edition. Crown 8vo. Cloth, price 5*s*. *Copyright Edition.*

Volume XVI. of The International Scientific Series.

Essentials of English Grammar for the Use of Schools. Crown 8vo. Cloth, price 3*s*. 6*d*.

WICKHAM (Capt. E. H., R.A.)

Influence of Firearms upon Tactics: Historical and Critical Investigations. By an Officer of Superior Rank (in the German Army). Translated by Captain E. H. Wickham, R.A. Demy 8vo. Cloth, price 7*s*. 6*d*.

WICKSTEED (P. H.).

Dante: Six Sermons. Crown 8vo. Cloth, price 5*s*.

WILLIAMS (A. Lukyn).

Famines in India; their Causes and Possible Prevention. The Essay for the Le Bas Prize, 1875. Demy 8vo. Cloth, price 5*s*.

WILLIAMS (Charles), one of the Special Correspondents attached to the Staff of Ghazi Ahmed Mouktar Pasha.

The Armenian Campaign: Diary of the Campaign of 1877 in Armenia and Koordistan. With Two Special Maps. Large post 8vo. Cloth, price 10*s*. 6*d*.

WILLIAMS (Rowland), D.D.

Life and Letters of, with Extracts from his Note-Books. Edited by Mrs. Rowland Williams. With a Photographic Portrait. 2 vols. Large post 8vo. Cloth, price 24*s*.

Stray Thoughts from the Note-Books of the Late Rowland Williams, D.D. Edited by his Widow. Crown 8vo. Cloth, price 3*s*. 6*d*.

WILLIAMS (Rowland), D.D.—*continued.*

Psalms, Litanies, Counsels and Collects for Devout Persons. Edited by his Widow. New and Popular Edition. Crown 8vo. Cloth, price 3*s.* 6*d.*

WILLIS (R.), M.D.

Servetus and Calvin: a Study of an Important Epoch in the Early History of the Reformation. 8vo. Cloth, price 16*s.*

William Harvey. A History of the Discovery of the Circulation of the Blood. With a Portrait of Harvey, after Faithorne. Demy 8vo. Cloth, price 14*s.*

WILLOUGHBY (The Hon. Mrs.).

On the North Wind—Thistledown. A Volume of Poems. Elegantly bound. Small crown 8vo. Cloth, price 7*s.* 6*d.*

WILSON (H. Schütz).

Studies and Romances. Crown 8vo. Cloth, price 7*s.* 6*d.*

The Tower and Scaffold. A Miniature Monograph. Large fcap. 8vo. Price 1*s.*

WILSON (Lieut.-Col. C. T.).

James the Second and the Duke of Berwick. Demy 8vo. Cloth, price 12*s.* 6*d.*

WINTERBOTHAM (Rev. R.), M.A., B.Sc.

Sermons and Expositions. Crown 8vo. Cloth, price 7*s.* 6*d.*

Within Sound of the Sea. By the Author of "Blue Roses," "Vera," &c. Third Edition. 2 vols. Crown 8vo. Cloth, gilt tops, price 12*s.*

*** Also a cheaper edition in one Vol. with frontispiece. Crown 8vo. Cloth, price 6*s.*

WOINOVITS (Capt. I.).

Austrian Cavalry Exercise. Translated by Captain W. S. Cooke. Crown 8vo. Cloth, price 7*s.*

WOLLSTONECRAFT (Mary).

Letters to Imlay. With a Preparatory Memoir by C. Kegan Paul, and two Portraits in *eau forte* by Anna Lea Merritt. Crown 8vo. Cloth, price 6*s.*

WOOD (Major-General J. Creighton).

Doubling the Consonant. Small crown 8vo. Cloth, price 1*s.* 6*d.*

WOODS (James Chapman).

A Child of the People, and other poems. Small crown 8vo. Cloth, price 5*s.*

WRIGHT (Rev. David), M.A.

Waiting for the Light, and other Sermons. Crown 8vo. Cloth, price 6*s.*

WYLD (R. S.), F.R.S.E.

The Physics and the Philosophy of the Senses; or, The Mental and the Physical in their Mutual Relation. Illustrated by several Plates. Demy 8vo. Cloth, price 16*s.*

YOUMANS (Eliza A.).

An Essay on the Culture of the Observing Powers of Children, especially in connection with the Study of Botany. Edited, with Notes and a Supplement, by Joseph Payne, F.C.P., Author of "Lectures on the Science and Art of Education," &c. Crown 8vo. Cloth, price 2*s.* 6*d.*

First Book of Botany. Designed to Cultivate the Observing Powers of Children. With 300 Engravings. New and Cheaper Edition. Crown 8vo. Cloth, price 2*s.* 6*d.*

YOUMANS (Edward L.), M.D.

A Class Book of Chemistry, on the Basis of the New System. With 200 Illustrations. Crown 8vo. Cloth, price 5*s.*

YOUNG (William).

Gottlob, etcetera. Small crown 8vo. Cloth, price 3*s.* 6*d.*

ZIMMERN (H.).

Stories in Precious Stones. With Six Illustrations. Third Edition. Crown 8vo. Cloth, price 5*s.*